Handbook of Research on Innovations in Systems and Software Engineering

Vicente García Díaz
University of Oviedo, Spain

Juan Manuel Cueva Lovelle
University of Oviedo, Spain

B. Cristina Pelayo García-Bustelo
University of Oviedo, Spain

Volume I

A volume in the Advances in Systems Analysis, Software Engineering, and High Performance Computing (ASASEHPC) Book Series

Managing Director: Lindsay Johnston
Acquisitions Editor: Kayla Wolfe
Production Editor: Christina Henning
Development Editor: Austin DeMarco
Typesetter: Kaitlyn Kulp
Cover Design: Jason Mull

Published in the United States of America by
Information Science Reference (an imprint of IGI Global)
701 E. Chocolate Avenue
Hershey PA, USA 17033
Tel: 717-533-8845
Fax: 717-533-8661
E-mail: cust@igi-global.com
Web site: http://www.igi-global.com

Library of Congress Cataloging-in-Publication Data

Handbook of research on innovations in systems and software engineering / Vicente Garcia Diaz, Juan Manuel Cueva Lovelle, and B. Cristina Pelayo Garcia-Bustelo, editors.
pages cm
Includes bibliographical references and index.
ISBN 978-1-4666-6359-6 (hardcover) -- ISBN 978-1-4666-6360-2 (ebook) -- ISBN 978-1-4666-6362-6 (print & perpetual access) 1. Systems engineering. 2. Software engineering. I. Garcia Diaz, Vicente, 1981- editor of compilation. II. Cueva Lovelle, Juan Manuel, editor of compilation. III. Pelayo Garcia-Bustelo, Begona Cristina, 1971- editor of compilation.
TA168.H327 2014
620'.00420285--dc23

2014021056

This book is published in the IGI Global book series Advances in Systems Analysis, Software Engineering, and High Performance Computing (ASASEHPC) (ISSN: 2327-3453; eISSN: 2327-3461)

British Cataloguing in Publication Data
A Cataloguing in Publication record for this book is available from the British Library.

All work contributed to this book is new, previously-unpublished material. The views expressed in this book are those of the authors, but not necessarily of the publisher.

For electronic access to this publication, please contact: eresources@igi-global.com.

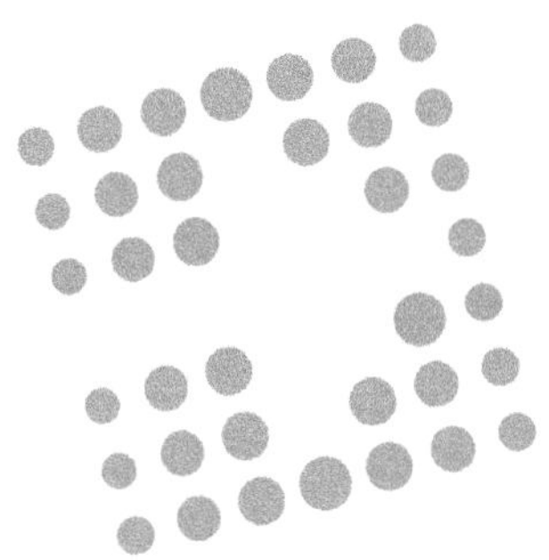

Advances in Systems Analysis, Software Engineering, and High Performance Computing (ASASEHPC) Book Series

Vijayan Sugumaran
Oakland University, USA

ISSN: 2327-3453
EISSN: 2327-3461

Mission

The theory and practice of computing applications and distributed systems has emerged as one of the key areas of research driving innovations in business, engineering, and science. The fields of software engineering, systems analysis, and high performance computing offer a wide range of applications and solutions in solving computational problems for any modern organization.

The **Advances in Systems Analysis, Software Engineering, and High Performance Computing (ASASEHPC) Book Series** brings together research in the areas of distributed computing, systems and software engineering, high performance computing, and service science. This collection of publications is useful for academics, researchers, and practitioners seeking the latest practices and knowledge in this field.

Coverage

- Computer Graphics
- Software Engineering
- Enterprise Information Systems
- Virtual Data Systems
- Computer Networking
- Computer System Analysis
- Network Management
- Parallel Architectures
- Performance Modelling
- Engineering Environments

IGI Global is currently accepting manuscripts for publication within this series. To submit a proposal for a volume in this series, please contact our Acquisition Editors at Acquisitions@igi-global.com or visit: http://www.igi-global.com/publish/.

The Advances in Systems Analysis, Software Engineering, and High Performance Computing (ASASEHPC) Book Series (ISSN 2327-3453) is published by IGI Global, 701 E. Chocolate Avenue, Hershey, PA 17033-1240, USA, www.igi-global.com. This series is composed of titles available for purchase individually; each title is edited to be contextually exclusive from any other title within the series. For pricing and ordering information please visit http://www.igi-global.com/book-series/advances-systems-analysis-software-engineering/73689. Postmaster: Send all address changes to above address.

Titles in this Series

For a list of additional titles in this series, please visit: www.igi-global.com

Handbook of Research on Architectural Trends in Service-Driven Computing
Raja Ramanathan (Independent Researcher, USA) and Kirtana Raja (IBM, USA)
Information Science Reference • copyright 2014 • 759pp • H/C (ISBN: 9781466661783) • US $515.00 (our price)

Handbook of Research on Embedded Systems Design
Alessandra Bagnato (Softeam R&D, France) Leandro Soares Indrusiak (University of York, UK) Imran Rafiq Quadri (Softeam R&D, France) and Matteo Rossi (Politecnico di Milano, Italy)
Information Science Reference • copyright 2014 • 520pp • H/C (ISBN: 9781466661943) • US $345.00 (our price)

Contemporary Advancements in Information Technology Development in Dynamic Environments
Mehdi Khosrow-Pour (Information Resources Management Association, USA)
Information Science Reference • copyright 2014 • 410pp • H/C (ISBN: 9781466662520) • US $205.00 (our price)

Systems and Software Development, Modeling, and Analysis New Perspectives and Methodologies
Mehdi Khosrow-Pour (Information Resources Management Association, USA)
Information Science Reference • copyright 2014 • 365pp • H/C (ISBN: 9781466660984) • US $215.00 (our price)

Handbook of Research on Emerging Advancements and Technologies in Software Engineering
Imran Ghani (Universiti Teknologi Malaysia, Malaysia) Wan Mohd Nasir Wan Kadir (Universiti Teknologi Malaysia, Malaysia) and Mohammad Nazir Ahmad (Universiti Teknologi Malaysia, Malaysia)
Engineering Science Reference • copyright 2014 • 686pp • H/C (ISBN: 9781466660267) • US $395.00 (our price)

Advancing Embedded Systems and Real-Time Communications with Emerging Technologies
Seppo Virtanen (University of Turku, Finland)
Information Science Reference • copyright 2014 • 502pp • H/C (ISBN: 9781466660342) • US $235.00 (our price)

Handbook of Research on High Performance and Cloud Computing in Scientific Research and Education
Marijana Despotović-Zrakić (University of Belgrade, Serbia) Veljko Milutinović (University of Belgrade, Serbia) and Aleksandar Belić (University of Belgrade, Serbia)
Information Science Reference • copyright 2014 • 476pp • H/C (ISBN: 9781466657847) • US $325.00 (our price)

Agile Estimation Techniques and Innovative Approaches to Software Process Improvement
Ricardo Colomo-Palacios (Østfold University College, Norway) Jose Antonio Calvo-Manzano Villalón (Universidad Politécnica De Madrid, Spain) Antonio de Amescua Seco (Universidad Carlos III de Madrid, Spain) and Tomás San Feliu Gilabert (Universidad Politécnica De Madrid, Spain)
Information Science Reference • copyright 2014 • 399pp • H/C (ISBN: 9781466651821) • US $215.00 (our price)

www.igi-global.com

701 E. Chocolate Ave., Hershey, PA 17033
Order online at www.igi-global.com or call 717-533-8845 x100
To place a standing order for titles released in this series, contact: cust@igi-global.com
Mon-Fri 8:00 am - 5:00 pm (est) or fax 24 hours a day 717-533-8661

List of Contributors

Table of Contents

Foreword xxv

Preface xxvii

Acknowledgment xxxiii

Volume I

Section 1
Software Development Process

Chapter 1
Graphical Modeling of Security Goals and Software Vulnerabilities 1
David Byers, Linköping University, Sweden
Nahid Shahmehri, Linköping University, Sweden

Chapter 2
Developing Secure Software Using UML Patterns 32
Holger Schmidt, TÜV Informationstechnik GmbH, Germany
Denis Hatebur, University Duisburg-Essen, Germany, & ITESYS Institut für Technische Systeme GmbH, Germany
Maritta Heisel, University Duisburg-Essen, Germany

Chapter 3
A Framework of Statistical and Visualization Techniques for Missing Data Analysis in Software Cost Estimation 71
Lefteris Angelis, Aristotle University of Thessaloniki, Greece
Nikolaos Mittas, Aristotle University of Thessaloniki, Greece
Panagiota Chatzipetrou, Aristotle University of Thessaloniki, Greece

Chapter 4
Using Business Value Models to Elicit Services Conducting Business Transactions 98
Tharaka Ilayperuma, University of Ruhuna, Sri Lanka
Jelena Zdravkovic, Stockholm University, Sweden

Chapter 5
Cloud Computing Economics 125
Stamatia Bibi, Aristotle University of Thessaloniki, Greece
Dimitrios Katsaros, University of Thessaly, Greece
Panayiotis Bozanis, University of Thessaly, Greece

Chapter 6
Object-Oriented Cognitive Complexity Measures: An Analysis 150
Sanjay Misra, Covenant University, Nigeria
Adewole Adewumi, Covenant University, Nigeria

Chapter 7
QSE: Service Elicitation with Qualitative Research Procedures 171
Ville Alkkiomäki, Lappeenranta University of Technology, Finland
Kari Smolander, Lappeenranta University of Technology, Finland

Chapter 8
A Proposed Pragmatic Software Development Process Model 186
Sanjay Misra, Covenant University, Nigeria
M. Omorodion, Federal University of Technology – Minna, Nigeria
Amit Mishra, Federal University of Technology – Minna, Nigeria
Luis Fernandez, University of Alcala de Henares, Spain

Section 2
Model-Driven Engineering

Chapter 9
Modelling, Simulation, and Analysis for Enterprise Architecture 202
Tony Clark, Middlesex University, UK
Balbir Barn, Middlesex University, UK
Vinay Kulkarni, Tata Consultancy Services, India

Chapter 10
Quality-Driven Database System Development within MDA Approach 237
Iwona Dubielewicz, Wrocław University of Technology, Poland
Bogumila Hnatkowska, Wrocław University of Technology, Poland
Zbigniew Huzar, Wrocław University of Technology, Poland
Lech Tuzinkiewicz, Wrocław University of Technology, Poland

Chapter 11
Rule-Based Domain-Specific Modeling for E-Government Service Transactions 269
Guillermo Infante Hernández, Universidad de Oviedo, Spain
Aquilino A. Juan Fuente, Universidad de Oviedo, Spain
Benjamín López Pérez, Universidad de Oviedo, Spain
Edward Rolando Núñez-Valdéz, Universidad de Oviedo, Spain

Volume II

Detailed Table of Contents

Security has become recognized as a critical aspect of software development, leading to the development of various security-enhancing techniques, many of which use some kind of custom modeling language. Models in different languages cannot readily be related to each other, which is an obstacle to using several techniques together. The sheer number of languages is, in itself, also an obstacle to adoption by developers. The authors have developed a modeling language that can be used in place of four existing modeling languages: attack trees, vulnerability cause graphs, security activity graphs, and security goal indicator trees. Models in the new language can be transformed to and from the earlier language, and a precise definition of model semantics enables an even wider range of applications, such as testing and static analysis. This chapter explores this new language.

Chapter 2
Developing Secure Software Using UML Patterns 32
Holger Schmidt, TÜV Informationstechnik GmbH, Germany
Denis Hatebur, University Duisburg-Essen, Germany, & ITESYS Institut für Technische Systeme GmbH, Germany
Maritta Heisel, University Duisburg-Essen, Germany

This chapter presents a security engineering process based on UML security problem frames and concretized UML security problem frames. Both kinds of frames constitute patterns for analyzing security problems and associated solution approaches. They are arranged in a pattern system that makes dependencies between them explicit. The authors describe step-by-step how the pattern system can be used to analyze a given security problem and how solution approaches can be found. Then, solution approaches are specified by generic security components and generic security architectures, which constitute architectural patterns. Finally, the generic security components and the generic security architecture that composes them are refined, and the result is a secure software product built from existing and/or tailor-made security components.

Chapter 3
A Framework of Statistical and Visualization Techniques for Missing Data Analysis in Software Cost Estimation 71
Lefteris Angelis, Aristotle University of Thessaloniki, Greece
Nikolaos Mittas, Aristotle University of Thessaloniki, Greece
Panagiota Chatzipetrou, Aristotle University of Thessaloniki, Greece

Software Cost Estimation (SCE) is a critical phase in software development projects. However, due to the growing complexity of the software itself, a common problem in building software cost models is that the available datasets contain lots of missing categorical data. The purpose of this chapter is to show how a framework of statistical, computational, and visualization techniques can be used to evaluate and compare the effect of missing data techniques on the accuracy of cost estimation models. Hence, the authors use five missing data techniques: Multinomial Logistic Regression, Listwise Deletion, Mean Imputation, Expectation Maximization, and Regression Imputation. The evaluation and the comparisons are conducted using Regression Error Characteristic curves, which provide visual comparison of different prediction models, and Regression Error Operating Curves, which examine predictive power of models with respect to under- or over-estimation.

Chapter 4
Using Business Value Models to Elicit Services Conducting Business Transactions..........................98
Tharaka Ilayperuma, University of Ruhuna, Sri Lanka
Jelena Zdravkovic, Stockholm University, Sweden

Traditional organizational structures evolve towards online business using modern IT – such as cloud computing, semantic standards, and process- and service-oriented architectures. On the technology level, Web services are dominantly used for modeling the interaction points of complex Web applications. So far, development of Web services has matured on the technical perspective considering for example the development of standards for message exchanges and service coordination. However, business concepts, such as economic assets exchanged in transactions between cooperating actors, cannot be easily traced

in final Web service specifications. As a consequence, business and IT models become difficult to keep aligned. To address this issue, the authors propose an MDD approach to elicit business services and further software services using REA business model as the starting point. The proposal focuses on a value-explorative elicitation of business services at the top level and model transformations using UML 2 to the system level by utilizing well-defined mappings.

Cloud services and technologies are currently receiving increased attention from the industry mostly due to business-driven promises and expectations. Significant innovations in virtualization and distributed computing, as well as improved access to high-speed Internet and a weak economy, have accelerated interest in cloud computing. However, is the migration to the Cloud the most profitable option for every business? Enterprise adoption of cloud computing often requires a significant transformation of existing Information Technology (IT) systems and processes. To justify such a change, a viable business case must be made based on the economics of transformation. This chapter presents a study of the basic parameters for estimating the potential infrastructure and software costs deriving from building and deploying applications on cloud and on-premise assets. Estimated user demand and desired quality attributes related to an application are also addressed in this chapter as they are aspects of the decision problem that also influence the choice between cloud and in-house solutions.

This chapter presents the analysis of ten recently proposed object-oriented metrics based on cognitive informatics. The metrics based on cognitive informatics use cognitive weight. Cognitive weight is the representation of the understandability of the piece of software that evaluates the difficulty experienced in comprehending and/or performing the piece of software. Development of metrics based on Cognitive Informatics (CI) is a new area of research, and from this point of view, for the analysis of these metrics, it is important to know their acceptability from other existing evaluation and validation criteria. This chapter presents a critical review on existing object-oriented cognitive complexity measures. In addition, a comparative study based on some selected attributes is presented.

The chapter introduces QSE, the Qualitative Service Elicitation method. It applies qualitative research procedures in service elicitation. Service engineering practice lacks lightweight methods to identify service candidates in projects with tight schedules. The QSE provides a systematic method to analyze requirement material in service-oriented systems development with feasible effort by utilizing the procedures of the grounded theory research method to elicit service candidates from business process descriptions and business use case descriptions. The chapter describes the method with examples and a case study.

The rapid growth in technology and the dynamism in our society today poses a lot of problems for Software Engineering practitioners. The result is a series of software development process methods that can be used to combat or meet up with the problems. What we can do is evolve, grow, and adapt to the changes that come along with development. This is the dynamism inherent in man—to adapt to change and improve ourselves and our existing systems—since the world is a far cry from what it was a few decades ago. On this basis lay the need to develop the model proposed in this chapter to meet the variations that exist as a result of technological development.

Modern organizations need to address increasingly complex challenges including how to represent and maintain their business goals using technologies and IT platforms that change on a regular basis. This has led to the development of modelling notations for expressing various aspects of an organization with a view to reducing complexity, increasing technology independence, and supporting analysis. Many of these Enterprise Architecture (EA) modelling notations provide a large number of concepts that support the business analysis but lack precise definitions necessary to perform computer-supported organizational analysis. This chapter reviews the current EA modelling landscape and proposes a simple language for the practical support of EA simulation including business alignment in terms of executing a collection of goals against prototype execution.

Chapter 10
Quality-Driven Database System Development within MDA Approach 237
Iwona Dubielewicz, Wrocław University of Technology, Poland
Bogumila Hnatkowska, Wrocław University of Technology, Poland
Zbigniew Huzar, Wrocław University of Technology, Poland
Lech Tuzinkiewicz, Wrocław University of Technology, Poland

The chapter presents an extended version of a quality-driven, MDA-based approach for database system development. The extension considers the relationship between successive models in the MDA approach. In particular, it gives rise to the introduction of domain ontology as a model preceding the CIM model as well as allows assessment of the extent to which the successive model is conformant with the preceding model. The chapter consists of four parts. The first part gives a short presentation of quality models and basic MDA concepts. The second one discusses the specific relationships between software development and quality assessment processes. The third part presents the Q-MDA framework and the proposal of a new quality characteristic (model conformance) with some measures for assessing the quality of a specific model in the context of other models. The last part contains an example of the framework application limited to the proposed quality model extension.

Chapter 11
Rule-Based Domain-Specific Modeling for E-Government Service Transactions............................ 269
Guillermo Infante Hernández, Universidad de Oviedo, Spain
Aquilino A. Juan Fuente, Universidad de Oviedo, Spain
Benjamín López Pérez, Universidad de Oviedo, Spain
Edward Rolando Núñez-Valdéz, Universidad de Oviedo, Spain

There is an explosion of different software platforms and protocols used to achieve systems interoperation. Among those platforms are the e-government transactions systems used mainly by public sector organizations to deliver demanded services to citizens. This scenario brings the appearance of communications gap among public organizations that share common processes, services, and regulations. Therefore, to find a solution to integrate these platforms becomes a relevant issue to be treated. This chapter proposes a rule-based domain-specific modeling environment for public services and process integration formed by common public service elements and a set of process integration rules. This approach provides a mechanism to integrate the conforming pieces of public transactions among different platforms. In addition, a service and a process meta-model is proposed in order to formalize the information structures. A set of process integration rules is also presented to complete the proposed model.

Chapter 12
Developing Software with Domain-Driven Model Reuse 283
Audris Kalnins, University of Latvia, Latvia
Tomasz Straszak, Warsaw University of Technology, Poland
Michał Śmiałek, Warsaw University of Technology, Poland
Elina Kalnina, University of Latvia, Latvia
Edgars Celms, University of Latvia, Latvia
Wiktor Nowakowski, Warsaw University of Technology, Poland

This chapter presents an approach to software development where model-driven development and software reuse facilities are combined in a natural way. It shows how model transformations building a Platform Independent Model (PIM) can be applied directly to the requirements specified in RSL by domain experts. Further development of the software case (PSM, code) is also supported by transformations, which in addition ensure a rich traceability within the software case. Alternatively, the PSM model and code can also be generated directly from requirements in RSL, thus providing fast development of the final code of at least a system prototype in many situations. The reuse support relies on a similarity-based comparison of requirements for software cases. If a similar part is found in an existing software case, a traceability link-based slice of the solution can be merged into the new case. The implementation of the approach is briefly sketched.

Chapter 13
Quantitative Productivity Analysis of a Domain-Specific Modeling Language 313
Joe Hoffert, Indiana Wesleyan University, USA
Douglas C. Schmidt, Vanderbilt University, USA
Aniruddha Gokhale, Vanderbilt University, USA

Model-Driven Engineering (MDE), in general, and Domain-Specific Modeling Languages (DSMLs), in particular, are increasingly used to manage the complexity of developing applications in various domains. Although many DSML benefits are qualitative (e.g., ease of use, familiarity of domain concepts), there is a need to quantitatively demonstrate the benefits of DSMLs (e.g., quantify when DSMLs provide savings in development time) to simplify comparison and evaluation. This chapter describes how the authors conducted quantitative productivity analysis for a DSML (i.e., the Distributed Quality-of-Service [QoS] Modeling Language [DQML]). The analysis shows (1) the significant quantitative productivity gain achieved when using a DSML to develop configuration models compared with not using a DSML, (2) the significant quantitative productivity gain achieved when using a DSML interpreter to automatically generate implementation artifacts as compared to alternative methods when configuring application entities, and (3) the viability of quantitative productivity metrics for DSMLs.

Chapter 14
Developing Executable UML Components Based on fUML and Alf 345
S. Motogna, Babeş-Bolyai University, Romania
I. Lazăr, Babeş-Bolyai University, Romania
B. Pârv, Babeş-Bolyai University, Romania

Model-driven architecture frameworks provide an approach for specifying systems independently of a particular platform and for transforming such system models for a particular platform, but development processes based on MDA are not widely used today because they are in general heavy-weight processes: in most situations they cannot deliver (incrementally) partial implementations to be executed immediately.

Executable UML means an execution semantics for a subset of actions sufficient for computational completeness. This chapter uses Alf as the fUML-based action language to describe the operations for iComponent: the proposed solution for a platform-independent component model for dynamic execution environments. Moreover, a UML profile for modeling components is defined and applied, following agile principles, to the development of service-oriented components for dynamic execution environments. The intended use of the proposed approach is enterprise systems.

Volume II

Internet of Things (IoT) is a paradigm that promotes a world in which smart objects and electronic devices communicate and coordinate autonomously to perform a wide range of tasks. From a technical point of view, the development of IoT systems is not an easy task; due to the great heterogeneity among smart objects and the large number of technologies applied, the developers of these systems must have strong technical knowledge. In this chapter, the authors use the eclipse modelling framework to define a domain-specific language that allows specifying the coordination and communication between different types of smart objects, regardless of the smart object technical characteristics. The proposed domain specific language has been designed to be used in an intuitive and easy way for people without technical knowledge. This solution aims to be useful in many areas and to achieve constant adaptation and evolution of IoT systems.

Software modernization is a new research area in the software industry that is intended to provide support for transforming an existing software system to a new one that satisfies new demands. Software modernization requires technical frameworks for information integration and tool interoperability that allow managing new platform technologies, design techniques, and processes. To meet these demands, Architecture-Driven Modernization (ADM) has emerged as the new OMG (Object Management Group) initiative for modernization. Reverse engineering techniques play a crucial role in system modernization. This chapter describes the state of the art in the model-driven modernization area, reverse engineering in particular. A framework to reverse engineering models from object-oriented code that distinguishes three different abstraction levels linked to models, metamodels, and formal specification is described. The chapter includes an analysis of technologies that support ADM standards and provides a summary of the principles that can be used to govern current modernization efforts.

Chapter 17
Is Modeling a Treatment for the Weakness of Software Engineering? 411
Janis Osis, Riga Technical University, Latvia
Erika Asnina, Riga Technical University, Latvia

Experts' opinions exist that the way software is built is primitive. The role of modeling as a treatment for Software Engineering (SE) became more important after the appearance of Model-Driven Architecture (MDA). The main advantage of MDA is architectural separation of concerns that showed the necessity of modeling and opened the way for Software Development (SD) to become engineering. However, this principle does not demonstrate its whole potential power in practice, because of a lack of mathematical accuracy in the initial steps of SD. The question about the sufficiency of modeling in SD is still open. The authors believe that SD, in general, and modeling, in particular, based on mathematical formalism in all its stages together with the implemented principle of architectural separation of concerns can become an important part of SE in its real sense. They introduce such mathematical formalism by means of topological modeling of system functioning.

Chapter 18
Optimized and Distributed Variant Logic for Model-Driven Applications.......................................428
Jon Davis, Curtin University, Australia
Elizabeth Chang, University of New South Wales, Australia & Australian Defence Force Academy, Australia

The customization of Enterprise Information Systems (EIS) is expensive throughout its lifecycle, especially across an enterprise-wide distributed application environment. The authors' ongoing development of a temporal meta-data framework for EIS applications seeks to minimize these issues with the application model supporting the capability for end users to define their own supplemental or alternate application logic as what they term Variant Logic (VL). VL can be applied to any existing model object, defined by any authorized user, through modeling rather than coding, then executed by any user as an alternative to the original application logic. VL is also preserved during automated application updates and can also interoperate directly between similar model-based execution instances within a distributed execution environment, readily sharing the alternate logic segments. The authors also present an enhanced pre-processing architecture that optimizes the execution of Logic Variants to the same execution order of single path model logic.

Chapter 19
High-Integrity Model-Based Development 479
K. Lano, King's College London, UK
S. Kolahdouz-Rahimi, King's College London, UK

Model-Based Development (MBD) has become increasingly used for critical systems, and it is the subject of the MBDV supplement to the DO-178C standard. In this chapter, the authors review the requirements of DO-178C for model-based development, and they identify ways in which MBD can be combined with formal verification to achieve DO-178C requirements for traceability and verifiability of models. In particular, the authors consider the implications for model transformations, which are a central part of MBD approaches, and they identify how transformations can be verified using formal methods tools.

Chapter 20
DSL TUNNOS Commerce: Model-Driven Architecture Applied to E-Commerce Platforms...........500
Giovanny Mauricio Tarazona Bermúdez, Francisco José de Caldas District University, Colombia
Ana Belén Rodríguez Arias, University of Oviedo, Spain
Luz Andrea Rodríguez Rojas, University of Oviedo, Spain

In the last decade, e-commerce has achieved rapid evolution from simple and static systems on the Web that provided information and promoted products to complex systems and dynamic applications that support business processes. Reuse and interoperability are strategies to face the challenge in software development in a dynamic context and rapid technological changes. To achieve these strategies, it is necessary to work with conceptual models that faithfully collect business semantics and, through of automatic tools (or semiautomatic) model transformation, get the model to be implemented in the appropriate platform. In this chapter, to successfully perform such a task, the authors work on a methodological framework with model-driven technologies that are considered the most appropriate approach, both technically and economically, so that organizations can easily adapt to the technological changes that arise at any time.

Section 3
Mobile Software Engineering

Chapter 21
Mobile Interaction in Real Augmented Environments: Principles, Platforms, Models, Formalisms, Development Processes, and Applications 511
Bertrand David, Ecole Centrale de Lyon, France
René Chalon, Ecole Centrale de Lyon, France

In this chapter, the authors describe a real augmented environment and its associated mobile interactions based on wearable computers with appropriate interaction devices that can be either classical computer interaction devices or real objects augmented with computer interfaces called tangible objects. After presenting the main principles, they describe a concrete platform, related models, formalisms, and MDA development processes, as well as several applications. These examples are contextual collaborative maintenance of industrial appliances and associated just-in-time mobile learning, a nutritional coaching system supporting practice and learning of management of nutritional decisions in relation to specific requirements in health or high-level sport, and a serious game helping to master lean manufacturing.

Chapter 22
Application Security for Mobile Devices 562
Gabriele Costa, Università degli Studi di Genova, Italy
Aliaksandr Lazouski, Consiglio Nazionale delle Ricerche, Italy
Fabio Martinelli, Consiglio Nazionale delle Ricerche, Italy
Paolo Mori, Consiglio Nazionale delle Ricerche, Italy

In these last years, mobile devices, such as mobile phones and tablets, have become very popular. Moreover, mobile devices have become very powerful and commonly run fairly complex applications such as 3D games, Internet browsers, e-mail clients, social network clients, and many others. Hence, an adequate

security support is required on these devices to avoid malicious application damage or unauthorized accesses to personal data (such as personal contacts or business email). This chapter describes the security support of the current commercial mobile devices along with a set of approaches that have been proposed in the scientific literature to enhance the security of mobile applications.

System architectures that deliver real-time services to customers must be flexible, scalable, and support a wide range of communication channels. This chapter presents an architecture that was designed to support multiple delivery channels and was successfully used to implement mobile banking services. The considerations behind the design and the approach used to deliver SMS-based mobile services using service-oriented architecture principles are reviewed and some of the practical challenges that were encountered with the implementation are explored. The ability for this solution architecture to support other real-time service channels is also examined.

The authors present a user-centric design flow for ease of use for specifying Wireless Sensor Network applications even for heterogeneous hardware. The design flow provides very high abstraction and user guidance to refrain the user from implementation, deployment, and hardware details including heterogeneity of the available sensor nodes. Automatic event configuration is accomplished by using a flexible Event Specification Language (ESL) and Event Decision Trees (EDTs) for distributed detection and determination of real world phenomena. EDTs autonomously adapt to heterogeneous availability of sensing capabilities by pruning and subscription to other nodes for missing information. The authors analyze the approaches in theory and praxis. They present two of numerous simulated scenarios proving the robustness and energy efficiency of the approach while having learnt appropriate configuration properties that are required for correct sensing. They can deal with failing sensors despite performing pretty well in terms of accuracy and number of messages exchanged.

Mobile devices such as smartphones and tablets have become very popular and together with the enhancements on mobile networks have changed the way the users interact. New applications and paradigms (such as social and collaborative networks) have appeared, and their development is now more important than ever. In this scenario, the technology of mobile software agents is an adequate option, since mobile agents can be used to overcome the difficulties and limitations of such an environment. Mobile software agents need a middleware (the agent execution platform) that allows them to exist and provides them the means to develop their potential. There exist a number of such platforms with different features but also some limitations. In this chapter, the authors discuss in detail all these questions and survey the most popular agent platforms from the point of view of their potential use in mobile environments.

Chapter 26
A Generic Architectural Model Approach for Efficient Utilization of Patterns: Application in the Mobile Domain 682
Jouni Markkula, University of Oulu, Finland
Oleksiy Mazhelis, University of Jyväskylä, Finland

A software pattern describes the core of the solution to a problem that tends to (re-)occur in a particular environment. Such patterns are commonly used as a means to facilitate the creation of an architectural design satisfying the desired quality goals. In this chapter, the practical challenges of efficient usage of patterns in domain-specific software development are presented. The specific domain considered here is the mobile domain, for which is given a sample collection of potentially useful patterns. After that, a novel generic architectural model approach for organizing patterns is presented. In this approach, the identification of relevant patterns is considered as the process of reducing the set of candidate patterns by domain-implied constraints. These constraints can be incorporated in a domain-specific generic architectural model that reflects the commonalities in the solutions of the particular domain. This approach has been validated with a real company application development case.

Chapter 27
Putting Personal Smart Spaces into Context 710
Ioanna Roussaki, National Technical University of Athens, Greece
Nikos Kalatzis, National Technical University of Athens, Greece
Nicolas Liampotis, National Technical University of Athens, Greece
Pavlos Kosmides, National Technical University of Athens, Greece
Miltiades Anagnostou, National Technical University of Athens, Greece
Efstathios Sykas, National Technical University of Athens, Greece

The convergence between mobile telecommunications and the Future Internet opened the way for the development of innovative pervasive computing services. The self-improving Personal Smart Spaces (PSSs) are coupling next generation mobile communications facilities with the features provided by the static smart spaces to support a more ubiquitous, mobile, context-aware, and personalised smart space. Addressing the advanced requirements of PSSs regarding the establishment of a robust distributed context management framework is a challenging task. Evaluating such a system is not a straightforward process, especially when it is also based on comparative assessments of its performance, as various existing systems demonstrate different unique characteristics making the quantitative comparisons quite complex and difficult to accomplish. This chapter elaborates on a context modelling and management approach that is suitable for addressing the PSS requirements and provides experimental evaluation evidence regarding its performance.

Chapter 28
Reasoning Qualitatively about Handheld Multimedia Framework Quality Attributes........................731
Daniel Hein, Garmin International, USA
Hossein Saiedian, The University of Kansas, USA

Today's mobile handheld devices, such as smartphones and action cameras, are well equipped for a wide range of multimedia and context-aware tasks. Such tasks can leverage traditional services like streaming audio and video as well as newer services like sensor fusion. Ubiquitous network access, coupled with an increasingly sophisticated mixture of device-based hardware and software, is enabling context-aware applications at an unprecedented rate. The objective of this chapter is to discuss specific quality attributes with respect to device-side software architectures providing these multimedia and sensor capabilities. This chapter focuses specifically on device-side client architectures rather than network or server architectures. Specific domain requirements and quality attributes are first derived through a synthesis of current research and industry trends, and subsequently analyzed. The analysis reveals some qualitative results that seem unintuitive at first glance but that become more understandable when provided with rationale relative to the handheld domain context.

Compilation of References xxxiv

About the Contributors lxxxvi

Index civ

Foreword

While traditionally taught as two separate subjects, Systems Engineering (SYE) and Software Engineering (SE) have become increasingly intertwined, with SYE methods widely adapted to SE and SE methods to SYE (Fairly & Willshire, 2011), as Table 1 shows. This complementarity between SYE and SE has naturally given rise to an interdisciplinary approach called "Systems and Software Engineering (SSE)," which integrates successful methods and best practices in both SYE and SE and offers a holistic approach to systems development.

The question thus arises: Why do we need such an approach? There are at least two answers.

First, today's systems comprise not only hardware, but also software. The division between the physical and digital worlds has become blurring (Feiler, et al., 2006). Therefore, traditional SE approaches or SYE approaches are no longer adequate to today's complex systems development.

Second, from the software development perspective, there are unprecedented demands on high quality software and low failure rates in software and software projects (Standish Group, 2003). The inability of current SE practices to meet these demands calls for new approaches. SSE is a promising approach as it combines best practices of both SE and SYE.

Yet, as a new approach, we have a limited understanding as to how it will make a difference in future systems development and what tools and techniques it affords. The *Handbook of Research on Innovations in Systems and Software Engineering* provides this knowledge. The Handbook offers an excellent sampling of current research and development in SSE and presents advanced SSE tools and techniques for building successful software. Specifically, the book contains 28 solid chapters that cover three critical

Table 1. Cross-fertilisation between systems engineering and software engineering (Fairly & Willshire, 2011)

Systems Engineering Methods Adapted to Software Engineering	Software Engineering Methods Adapted to Systems Engineering
• Stakeholder Analysis. • Requirements Engineering. • Functional Decomposition. • Design Constraints. • Architectural Design. • Design Criteria. • Design Trade-offs. • Interface Specification. • Traceability. • Configuration Management. • Systematic Verification and Validation.	• Model-Driven Development. • Software Modelling. • Use Cases. • Object-Oriented Design. • Iterative Development. • Agile Methods. • Continuous Integration. • Process Modelling. • Process Improvement. • Incremental Verification and Validation.

areas of SSE, concerning software development processes, methods and applications. The chapters on software development processes addresses issues related to software qualities, such as security, costs, and performance metrics. The chapters on software development methods focus on Model-Driven Engineering (MDE), an important approach for both SYS and SE, as Table 1 shows. Finally, the chapters on software applications are related to Mobile Software Engineering. These applications range from developing mobile environments to novel architectures to quality of services. They serve as perfect examples to elucidate why we need SSE to solve emerging software development problems. The handbook is a timely reference for researchers, practitioners and students who are interested in SSE.

Liping Zhao
University of Manchester, UK

Liping Zhao *is a senior lecturer in the School of Computer Science at the University of Manchester. She works in the area of software engineering, with a particular focus on discovering and developing reusable software patterns and finding technologies to bridge the gap between natural language specifications of software requirements and initial software models. She published the first papers on domain-specific patterns for software analysis and design and was the first to use the scientific concepts of symmetry and symmetry breaking to explain the meaning of software patterns and why they are important. Most recently, she led the research and development of an innovative software system that applies advanced natural language processing and modeling techniques to automatically transforming natural language specifications of software requirements into initial software models. She received three IBM Faculty Awards for her outstanding contributions to software patterns and service sciences.*

REFERENCES

Fairley, R., & Willshire, M. J. (2011). Teaching software engineering to undergraduate system engineering students. In *Proceedings of the 24th IEEE-CS Conference on Software Engineering Education and Training* (CSEE&T 2011) (pp. 219-226). Honolulu, HI: IEEE.

Feiler, P. H., Sullivan, K., Wallnau, K. C., Gabriel, R. P., Goodenough, J. B., Linger, R. C., & Schmidt, D. (2006). *Ultra-large-scale systems: The software challenge of future*. Pittsburgh, PA: Software Engineering Institute, Carnegie Mellon University.

Standish Group. (2003). *The chaos report*. Author.

Preface

A common problem in recent years is the growth of software development complexity due to customer demand for more features and fewer errors. Furthermore, due to recent advancements in technology, it has become necessary to utilize software in multiple domains and professional areas. This leads to problems such as development teams becoming experts in one particular area, necessitating an adjustment period when the team starts new projects in other professional areas.

However, software engineering continually offers new tools that, when properly used, can help in the difficult task of developing software complying with the triple constraint of project management (scope, time, and cost) that is cited in numerous sources.

This book focuses primarily on improvements for software development, supported by two of its main pillars, Model-Driven Engineering (MDE), based on the use of models as a fundamental support in software development, and the specific development of software for mobile devices, one of the areas with the biggest and most exciting changes in recent years.

The mission of this book is to bring researchers, practitioners, and students to some of the most promising fields in computer science, helping all to understand the current state of the art and know what the future will bring. The objectives include:

- Bringing together the most relevant research on systems and software engineering.
- Updating the scientific literature on systems and software engineering.
- Identifying and addressing the complexities encountered in the application of new software engineering technologies.
- Understanding the most important issues to be addressed by scientists in the coming years.

The target audience of this book will be composed of professionals and researchers working in any field of systems and software engineering. Moreover, the book will also be a reference for researchers, professionals, and students in computer science and related fields. The book will provide a much needed reference on the state of the art of advanced tools and techniques that are either available or under development to support the maximization of the efficacy and efficiency of software development. It will also provide foundations to professionals, researchers, and academics on the underlying theory and current applications for use in the future advancement of the existing body of knowledge. This combination of theory, applications, and success stories will provide the reader with an important and detailed view of recent developments in the field and lay the foundation for future research.

Regarding the distribution of sections and chapters, they are distributed as follows:

Section 1 is related to the software development process or software development life-cycle in general. There are several models for such process, each describing approaches to a variety of tasks or activities that take place during it. The eight chapters, though different, are primarily concerned with close aspects to the use of models as a means to facilitate the development of software. Topics covered include security, software vulnerabilities, cost estimation, business services elicitation, metrics, and software process methods.

- Chapter 1 focuses on security goals and software vulnerabilities by the development of a modeling language that can be used in place of four existing languages: attack trees, vulnerability cause graphs, security activity graphs, and security goal indicator trees. Artifacts in the new language can be transformed to and from earlier languages, and a precise definition of model semantics enables an even wider range of applications, such as testing and static analysis.
- Chapter 2 focuses on a security engineering process based on UML security problem frames and concretized UML security problem frames. Both kinds of frames constitute patterns for analyzing security problems and associated solution approaches. The authors describe step-by-step how the pattern system can be used to analyze a given security problem and how solution approaches can be found.
- Chapter 3 focuses on how a framework of modern statistical, computational, and visualization techniques can be used to evaluate and compare the effect of missing data techniques on the accuracy of cost estimation models. For the illustration of the framework, the authors use five missing data techniques: Multinomial Logistic Regression, Listwise Deletion, Mean Imputation, Expectation Maximization, and Regression Imputation.
- Chapter 4 focuses on an approach to elicit business services, and further software services, using the Resources, Events, Agents (REA) business model as the starting point. The proposal aims to perform a value-explorative analysis and modeling of business services at the top level, and model transformations using UML 2 to the system level, by utilizing well-defined mappings.
- Chapter 5 focuses on presenting a study of the basic parameters for estimating the potential infrastructure and software costs deriving from building and deploying applications on cloud and on-premise assets. Estimated user demand and desired quality attributes related to an application are also addressed in this chapter as they are aspects of the decision problem that also influence the choice between cloud and in-house solutions.
- Chapter 6 focuses on presenting the analysis of 10 recently proposed object-oriented metrics based on cognitive weights. Cognitive weight is the representation of the understandability of the piece of software that evaluates the difficulty experienced in comprehending and/or performing the piece of software. This chapter presents a critical review of existing object-oriented cognitive complexity measures. In addition, a comparative study based on some selected attributes is presented.
- Chapter 7 focuses on introducing the Qualitative Service Elicitation (QSE) method. It applies qualitative research procedures in service elicitation. Service engineering practice lacks lightweight methods to identify service candidates in projects with tight schedules. The QSE provides a systematic method to analyze requirement material in service-oriented systems development with feasible effort by utilizing the procedures of the grounded theory research method to elicit service candidates from business process and use case descriptions.

- Chapter 8 focuses on discussing the rapid growth in technology and the dynamism it presents in our society today, which poses a lot of problems for the software engineering practitioners. The result is a series of software development process methods that can be used to combat or meet up with the problems it creates for developers. On this basis lays the need to develop the model proposed in this chapter to meet up with variations that exist as a result of technological advancement.

Section 2 is related to Model-Driven Engineering, which is an important and emerging approach in software engineering to increase the level of abstraction of the development tasks. In recent years, Model-Driven Engineering has become a critical area of study, as companies and research institutions have started to emphasize the importance of using models as first-class artifacts in the software development process of complex systems. The 11 chapters include topics such as simulation, quality, tools, rule-based environments, requirements, productivity analysis, semantics, legacy systems, domain-specific languages, formalisms, customizations, and transformations.

- Chapter 9 focuses on modern organizations, which need to address increasingly complex challenges including how to represent and maintain their business goals using technologies and IT platforms that change on a regular basis. This chapter reviews the current Enterprise Architecture (EA) modelling landscape and proposes a simple language for the practical support of EA simulation including business alignment in terms of executing a collection of goals against prototype execution.
- Chapter 10 focuses on presenting an extended version of a quality-driven, model-driven approach for database system development. The extension consists of considering the relationship between successive models. In particular, it gives rise to the introduction of a domain ontology as a model preceding the computer-independent model as well as allows one to assess to what extent the successive model is conformant with the preceding model.
- Chapter 11 focuses on proposing a rule-based domain-specific modeling environment for public services and process integration formed by common public service elements and a set of process integration rules. This approach provides a mechanism to integrate the conforming pieces of public transactions among different platforms. In addition, a service and a process meta-model is proposed in order to formalize the information structures needed for their integration.
- Chapter 12 focuses on presenting an approach to software development where model-driven development and software reuse facilities are combined in a natural way. The proposed solution is based on requirements written in semiformal requirements language. This model-based language lets one capture the essence of any software system in the form of domain knowledge and its usage in use case scenarios by wiki-like hyperlinks.
- Chapter 13 focuses on describing how the authors conducted quantitative productivity analysis for a domain-specific modeling language. The analysis shows (1) the significant quantitative productivity gain achieved, (2) the improvement achieved when using an interpreter to automatically generate implementation artifacts as compared to alternative methods when configuring application entities, and (3) the viability of quantitative productivity metrics.

- Chapter 14 focuses on Executable UML, which provides semantics for a subset of actions sufficient for computational completeness. This chapter uses Alf, as the fUML-based action language to describe the operations for iCOMPONENT: the proposed solution for a platform-independent component model for dynamic execution environments. Moreover, a UML profile for modeling components is defined and applied to the development of service-oriented components for dynamic execution environments.
- Chapter 15 focuses on Internet of Things (IoT) as a paradigm that promotes a world in which smart objects and electronic devices are coordinated autonomously to perform a wide range of tasks. The authors define a domain-specific language that allows specifying the coordination and communication between different types of smart objects, regardless of the smart object technical characteristics. The proposed language has been designed to be used in an intuitive and easy way for people without technical knowledge.
- Chapter 16 focuses on modernization of legacy systems. For many years, traditional reengineering has been a solution to software modernization. However, reengineering often fails because it involves ad hoc and non-standardized processes. Software modernization requires technical frameworks for information integration and tool interoperability that allow managing new platform technologies, design techniques, and processes. To meet these demands, Architecture-Driven Modernization (ADM) has emerged.
- Chapter 17 focuses on discussing the role of modeling as a treatment for software engineering since the question about the sufficiency of modeling in software development is still open. The authors believe that software development, in general, and modeling, in particular, based on mathematical formalism in all its stages together with the implemented principle of architectural separation of concerns can become an important part of software engineering in its real sense.
- Chapter 18 focuses on the customization of Enterprise Information Systems (EIS) scale applications, which can be very expensive, incurring substantial additional lifecycle costs to produce and maintain customizations. The development of a temporal meta-data framework for EIS applications seeks to greatly minimize these issues, with the application logic model supporting the capability for end users to define their own supplemental or alternate application logic meta-data.
- Chapter 19 focuses on a review of requirements of the DO-178C standard for Model-Based Development (MBD) and the identification of ways in which MBD can be combined with formal verification to achieve DO-178C requirements for traceability and verifiability of models. In particular, the authors consider the implications for model transformations, which are a central part of MBD approaches, and identify how transformations can be verified using formal methods tools.
- Chapter 20 focuses on e-commerce, which has achieved rapid evolution from simple and static systems on the Web, which provided information and promoted products, to complex systems and dynamic applications that support business processes. The reuse and interoperability are strategies to face the challenge in a dynamic context with rapid technological changes. To achieve these strategies, the authors work with conceptual models that faithfully collect business semantics.

Section 3 is related to Mobile Software Engineering, one of the trendiest areas related to software development. The eight chapters deal with different aspects of mobile software engineering. Topics include augmented environments, malicious applications, real-time services, intelligent environments, usability, mobile software agents, patterns, distributed context management, and quality attributes.

- Chapter 21 focuses on a real augmented environment and its associated mobile interactions based on wearable computers with appropriate interaction devices that can be either classical computer-interaction devices or real objects augmented with computer interfaces called tangible objects. After presenting the main principles, the authors describe a concrete platform, related models, formalisms, and the development processes, as well as several applications.
- Chapter 22 focuses on an adequate security support on mobile devices to avoid malicious applications that damage the device or perform unauthorized accesses to personal data (such as personal contacts or business mails). This chapter describes the security support of the current commercial mobile devices along with a set of approaches that have been proposed in the scientific literature to enhance the security of mobile applications.
- Chapter 23 focuses on system architectures delivering real-time services to customers, which must be flexible, scalable, and support a wide range of communication channels. This chapter presents an architecture that was designed to support multiple delivery channels and was successfully used to implement mobile banking services. The considerations behind the design and the approach used to deliver SMS-based mobile services using service-oriented architecture principles are reviewed.
- Chapter 24 focuses on pervasive intelligent environments, where Wireless Sensor Networks (WSNs) surround and serve people at any place and any time. A proper usability is considered essential for WSNs supporting real life applications. With this chapter, the authors aim at ease of use for specifying new applications that have to autonomously cope with expected and unexpected heterogeneity, sudden failures, and energy efficiency.
- Chapter 25 focuses on mobile software agents, which need the presence of a middleware to allow them to exist and provide them the means to develop their potential. There exist a number of such platforms with different features, but also some limitations that must be taken into account if they are going to be used in the development of mobile applications. In this chapter, the authors discuss in detail related questions and survey the most popular agent platforms to find out how they can be used in mobile environments.
- Chapter 26 focuses on a novel generic architectural model approach for organizing patterns as a solution for efficient utilization of patterns in a specific domain. In this approach, the identification of relevant patterns is considered as the process of reducing the set of candidate patterns by domain-implied constraints, such as functionality, platform, and problems. These constraints can be incorporated in a domain-specific generic architectural model that reflects the commonalities in the solutions of the particular domain.
- Chapter 27 focuses on the convergence between mobile telecommunications and the Future Internet. Addressing the advanced requirements of self-improving Personal Smart Spaces (PSSs) regarding the establishment of a robust distributed context management framework is a challenging task. This chapter elaborates on a context modelling and management approach that is suitable for addressing the PSS requirements and provides experimental evaluation evidence regarding its performance.

- Chapter 28 focuses on discussing specific quality attributes with respect to device-side software architectures providing multimedia and sensor capabilities. This chapter focuses specifically on device-side client architectures, rather than network or server architectures. Specific domain requirements and quality attributes are first derived through a synthesis of current research and industry trends, and subsequently analyzed.

As a conclusion, we think that the book can be used to understand new research on innovations in systems and software engineering, which will be an exciting area of work in the coming years in the software development industry.

Vicente García Díaz
University of Oviedo, Spain

Juan Manuel Cueva Lovelle
University of Oviedo, Spain

B. Cristina Pelayo García-Bustelo
University of Oviedo, Spain

Acknowledgment

We would like to thank all the people who have contributed to this book. A special thanks to Dr. Liping Zhao, who has kindly written the prologue and Austin DeMarco, Managing Editor for IGI Global, who had helped us at any moment. Similarly, we would like to thank all the other people who have participated in this project but have not been mentioned in this text.

Vicente García Díaz
University of Oviedo, Spain

Juan Manuel Cueva Lovelle
University of Oviedo, Spain

B. Cristina Pelayo García-Bustelo
University of Oviedo, Spain

Section 1

Software Development Process

Chapter 1
Graphical Modeling of Security Goals and Software Vulnerabilities

David Byers
Linköping University, Sweden

Nahid Shahmehri
Linköping University, Sweden

ABSTRACT

Security has become recognized as a critical aspect of software development, leading to the development of various security-enhancing techniques, many of which use some kind of custom modeling language. Models in different languages cannot readily be related to each other, which is an obstacle to using several techniques together. The sheer number of languages is, in itself, also an obstacle to adoption by developers. The authors have developed a modeling language that can be used in place of four existing modeling languages: attack trees, vulnerability cause graphs, security activity graphs, and security goal indicator trees. Models in the new language can be transformed to and from the earlier language, and a precise definition of model semantics enables an even wider range of applications, such as testing and static analysis. This chapter explores this new language.

INTRODUCTION

Modern society has rapidly become dependent on computers, and by extension dependent on computer software. As a result, the impact of software failure can be tremendous. Over the years we have seen software failures with consequences ranging from the amusingly absurd (Grisogono, 1999)[1], to the terrifyingly lethal (Schmitt, 1991)[2].

While most software failures are caused by flaws in the software being triggered unintentionally, some failures are the result of vulnerabilities being intentionally exploited. Over the last several decades the economic impact of the most publicized IT security incidents has been estimated to be tens of billions of dollars, worldwide (Hoy et al., 1989; Rhodes, 2001; Computer Economics, 2002, 2003). This does not include costs incurred

DOI: 10.4018/978-1-4666-6359-6.ch001

by individuals or institutions due to e.g. identity theft or lost business. The total cost of cybercrime and cyber espionage was recently estimated at $100 *billion* per year (Center for Strategic and International Studies, 2013). Security problems are not limited to mainstream computing. Serious vulnerabilities have been reported in industrial control systems, healthcare systems, automotive systems, and other kinds of embedded systems. The impact of vulnerabilities coupled with their prevalence in all kinds of software, clearly demonstrates that software security is a critical issue.

Our work concentrates on improving the ability of developers using conventional methods to address typical software security issues. Typical software security issues include the prevention of known vulnerabilities and the identification and fulfillment of common security goals. Known vulnerabilities account for nearly all publicly reported vulnerabilities, and failure to implement common security goals for nearly all design flaws we have observed.

We have developed a process improvement methodology, called S3P, that is based on detailed analysis of vulnerability causes (Byers, Ardi, Shahmehri, & Duma, 2006; Ardi, Byers, & Shahmehri 2006; Byers & Shahmehri, 2007, 2008, 2009; Byers, 2013). The S3P uses models to describe both vulnerability causes and mitigating activities. This work is complemented by the SHIELDS EU project (SHIELDS, n.d.), which developed a shared repository for security models, and tied together multiple model-based activities for secure software development.

In this chapter we present a graphical modeling language, the security goal model (SGM) language, that can be used in place of attack trees, security activity graphs (SAG), vulnerability cause graphs (VCG), and security goal indicator trees (SGIT). Table 1 summarizes these languages. An SGM shows how a given security goal can be fulfilled, and can be used for purposes as diverse as process improvement, automatic testing, static analysis, and manual inspection. Models in the traditional languages can be transformed to SGMs, and SGMs can be viewed using any of the traditional notations. This means that developers familiar with the older notations need not learn the SGM language unless they need the improvements the new language provides (Byers & Shahmehri, 2010).

The SGM language offers several benefits over using the older languages. A minor benefit is that a single language is easier to learn, use, and build tool support for than it is for multiple languages. More importantly, models in the four languages we cover are often closely related and may contain similar or identical elements. When using conventional languages, information cannot be shared or reused between models of different types. Using SGMs, models that would previously have used different languages can share elements,

Table 1. Graphical modeling languages covered by SGMs

Name	Purpose
Attack trees	Attack trees are used to model how to perform attacks. In an attack tree, the root is a successful attack, and other vertices are sub-attacks. Sub-attacks may be combined with *and* and *or*. Attack trees are used in risk analysis.
Vulnerability cause graphs	Vulnerability cause graphs (VCGs) model how vulnerabilities are caused. The original purpose of VCGs was software process improvement. The SGM language is a direct successor of the VCG language.
Security activity graphs	Security activity graphs (SAGs) model how to perform security-related activities. SAGs were designed to be used in conjunction with VCGs to help developers find the best way to prevent vulnerabilities.
Security goal indicator trees	Security goal indicator trees (SGITs) model how to perform goal-directed manual inspection of software development artifacts.

thereby exposing the relationships between different models and the security goals they represent and creating opportunities for reuse of model elements and partial models.

For example, a VCG may contain a cause use of unsafe API. The same concept could occur as a negative goal in an SGIT for secure coding practices. Using conventional languages, there would be no connection between vulnerability and goal, but with SGMs, the two models would share use of unsafe API as a common subgoal. Furthermore, once the subgoal use of unsafe API is modeled using a SGM, that benefits all models in which the subgoal is used, whereas previously one would have to model the corresponding VCG cause and SGIT subgoal separately.

SGMs can be used in many stages of software development. Figure 1 illustrates the relationship of SGM-using and SGM-producing activities to a typical iteration in the software lifecycle. Examples include threat/attack modeling, in which SGMs model how attacks are performed, and yield potential vulnerabilities as well as mitigating actions; vulnerability cause analysis, in which the causes behind problems detected late in the software lifecycle are modeled, in order to identify preventative actions; and realization of requirements, in which SGMs are used to identify how to realize security-related requirements, guiding primarily architecture, design and implementation tasks. Several of these applications can be formulated in terms of model semantics. This is discussed in *applications*, below.

Our approach is not a formal method for software security. Formal methods are usually based on formally specifying system requirements or design, including security aspects, then either generating the system or verifying that the system (or a model of the system) conforms to the specification. Notable examples of this approach include Event-B (Jean-Raymond-Abrial, Butler, Hallerstede, & Voisin, 2006) (in which systems are generated from Event-B specifications); ASLan, a language for specifying security and trust properties, which are verified with the AVANTSSAR validation platform (AVANTSSAR Consortium, 2009); Secure Tropos (Mouratidis & Giorgini, 2007), which extends the Tropos (Bresciani,

Figure 1. SGM-supported activities in relation to software development

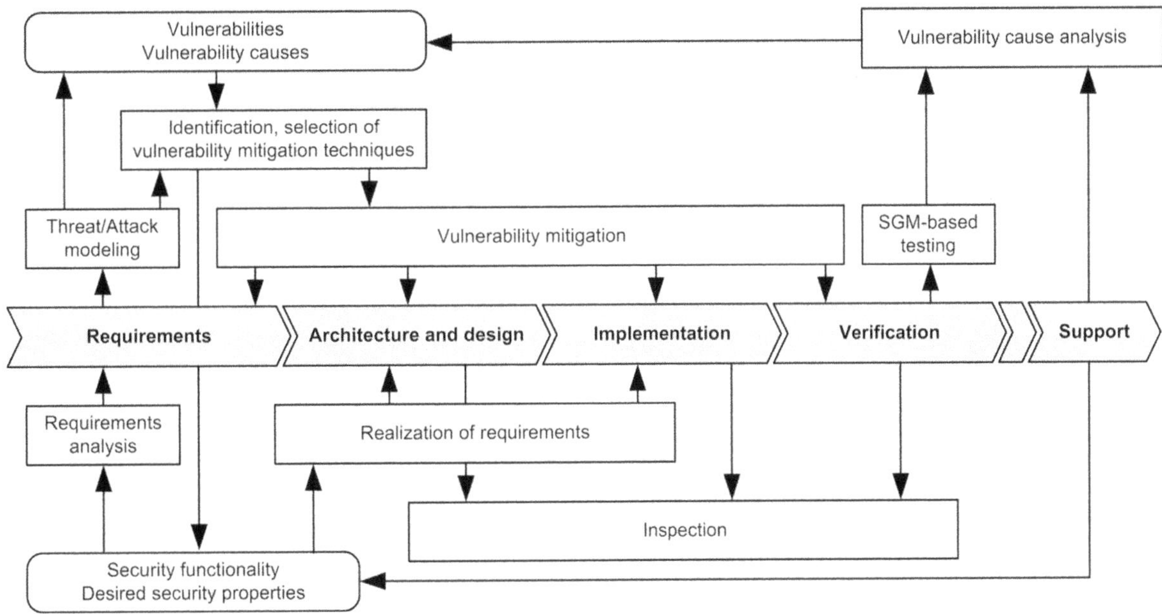

Perini, Giorgini, Giunchiglia, & Mylopoulos, 2004) agent-oriented software development method with security-related models and activities; UMLSec (Jürjens, 2005); various approaches for specifying and analyzing security protocols, access control policies and other system properties (Basin, Mödersheim, & Viganò, 2005; Armando & Compagna, 2008; Viganò, 2006; Lodderstedt, Basin, & Doser, 2002; Fisler, Krishnamurthi, Meyerovich, & Tschantz, 2005; Zhang, Ryan, & Guelev, 2005).

Formal methods can be very powerful, but are often perceived as prohibitively difficult, time-consuming, and expensive. Although the adoption of formal methods will probably increase, conventional software development methods will remain dominant for a very long time to come. Our goal is to improve the ability developers using conventional software development methods, including modeling languages like UML (Object Management Group, 2007), to address software security issues.

SECURITY GOAL MODELS

Core Concepts

Practical use of the security goal model (SGM) language is enhanced by the ability to re-use and interconnect fragments of security knowledge and related models. Our definition of the SGM language is based on the assumption that a data model with the properties of the one described here is used.

A *core element* represents some kind of security-related knowledge, such as a security goal, a vulnerability, a security-related activity, a vulnerability cause, or a threat. Two core elements may not represent the same thing.

A *model* is a formal description of some aspect of a core element. For example, a model can describe how to perform an attack, what causes a vulnerability, how a goal can be fulfilled, or a how to test for a security property. Models consist of model elements, such as vertices and edges, which in turn may be connected to core elements.

Core elements and models are associated with each other through *model associations*. Each model association connects one core element to one model and indicates the nature of the relationship through a *role* attribute.

Core elements can be related to each other through *core element associations*. Each core element association connects two core elements and indicates the nature of the relationship through a *role* attribute. For example, an attack could be related to a security goal with the role threatens to indicate that the attack *threatens* the fulfillment of the goal.

In practice, all these basic elements should be stored in a database so that the structure formed by the various relationships (model associations, core element associations and links between model elements and core elements) can be traversed and queried. Figure 2 shows a UML model of these concepts, as they are implemented in the SHIELDS project (SHIELDS, n.d.).

Relations between core elements, models and model elements can create a rich net of interconnections that allow developers to relate different fragments of security knowledge to each other in a useful and meaningful way. Figure 3 visualizes how several items could be related to each other. Consider the situation where threat modeling (e.g. using abuse case diagrams) has identified that *unauthorized access* is a relevant threat, and a developer needs to determine how to mitigate the threat. By following the links in the data model, the developer can rapidly see how the threat can be realized, how relevant attacks are performed, what kind of best practices mitigate the attacks, and what kind of vulnerabilities are commonly associated with the threat. The developer can also determine that *encrypting passwords* and *using stored procedures* are two suitable mitigating techniques. Furthermore, the relationships provide traceability, which is particularly important in

Figure 2. UML model of the core concepts used in SGMs

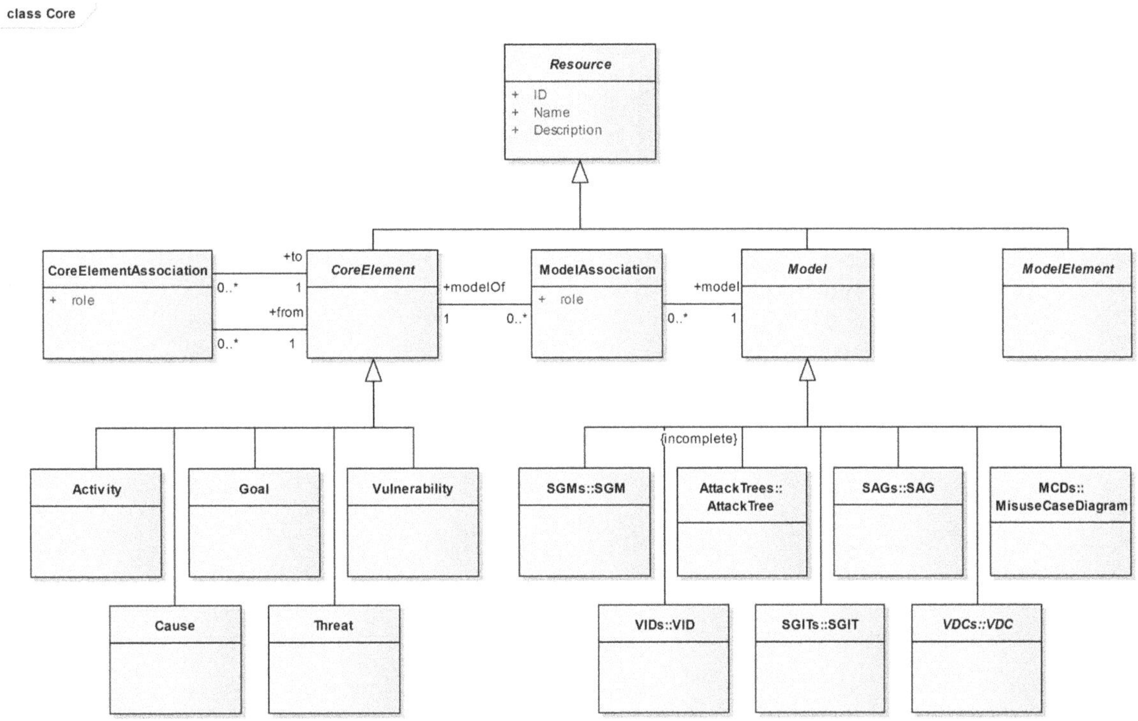

maintenance, by connecting specific practices or requirements to the threats that motivated them.

The models themselves also contain relations between the elements. These are not shown in Figure 3.

Introduction to Security Goal Models

There are many kinds of modeling languages for expressing various aspects of security. In this section we describe security goal models (SGMs), a graphical language that is general enough to cover and improve on several existing languages, including attack trees (Schneier, 1999), VCGs (Byers et al., 2006), SAGs (Byers & Shahmehri, 2008) and SGITs (Peine, Jawurek, & Mandel, 2008). These languages are all used to express how specific kinds of security goals can be achieved. Attack trees describe how attacks can be performed; VCGs describe how vulnerabilities are caused; SAGs enumerate options for preventing vulnerabilities; and SGITs describe how to perform manual inspection for evidence of security goals. The SGM language is used to describe arbitrary security goals, thereby enabling re-use of work (models and core elements) for multiple purposes and making it easy to relate models of different kinds of goals to each other.

In the context of SGMs, the term *security goal* is understood to mean anything that can affect the security of a system, or that contributes to or counteracts the fulfillment of some other security goal. In particular, all the core elements discussed in "Core Concepts," above, can be seen as security goals.

A security goal model shows how a particular security goal can be fulfilled by breaking it down into simpler subgoals. Each subgoal is in turn a security goal, and can be modeled using a security goal model.

Figure 3. Example of relations between core concepts

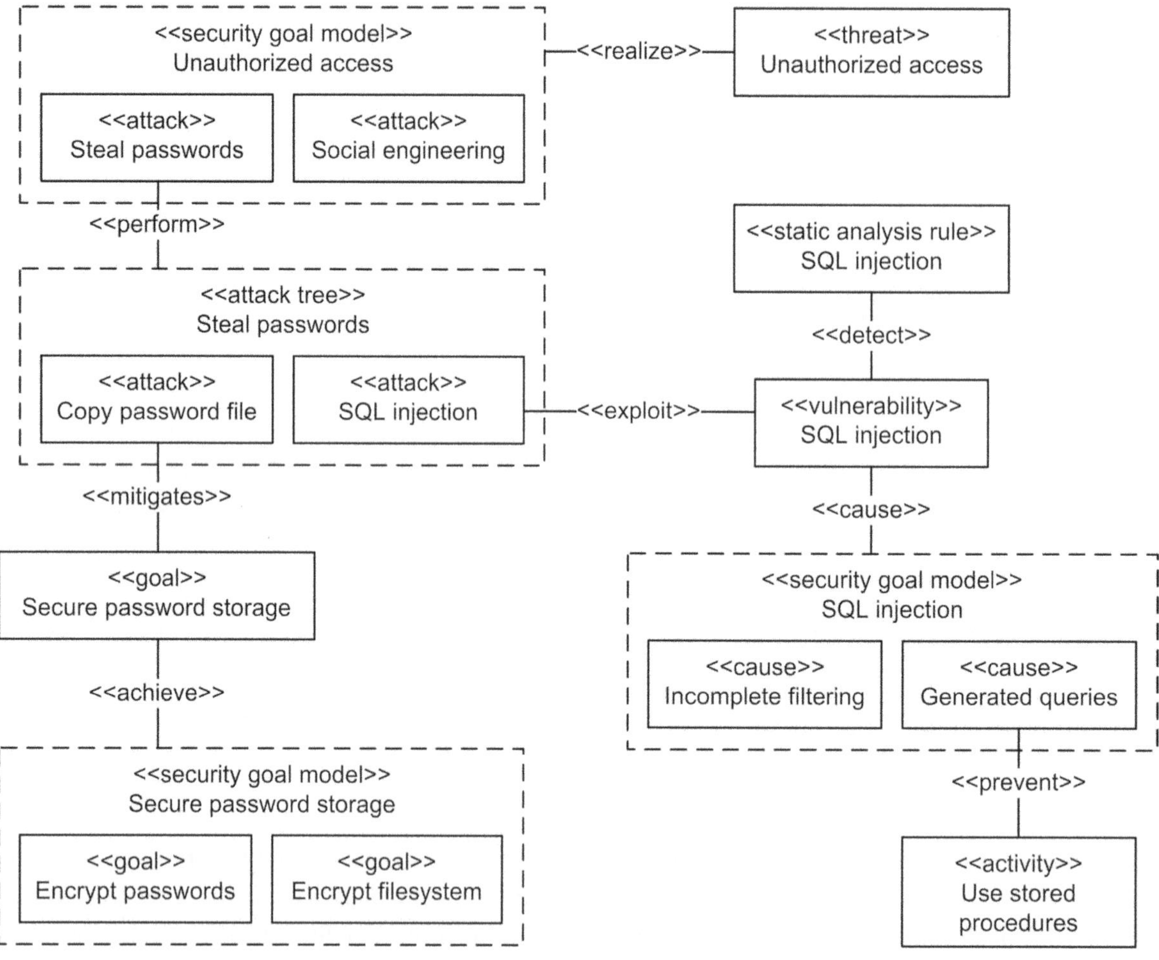

Since a security goal model may contain the same subgoal more than once, we maintain a clear separation between the subgoals themselves and their appearance in a model. The goals themselves are core elements, and their appearances in models are model elements. Each model element may reference a single core element and each core element may be referenced by several distinct model elements. Figure 2 shows how core elements, models and model elements are related to each other. Model-specific properties, such as size and position, are associated with model elements, not core elements.

An SGM is a directed acyclic graph. Vertices refer to core elements and represent subgoals; solid edges represent dependencies between subgoals; and dashed edges can be thought of as modeling information flow (and only appear in extended SGMs). The modeling language is fully defined in the next two sections.

Figure 4 shows a VCG and a corresponding extended SGM for a buffer overflow vulnerability. The model as a whole shows how the vulnerability can be caused. Subgoals drawn in black are *counteracting* subgoals, things that counteract the vulnerability (e.g., the use of adaptive buffers

Figure 4. VCG and corresponding SGM for the causes of CVE-2009-1274

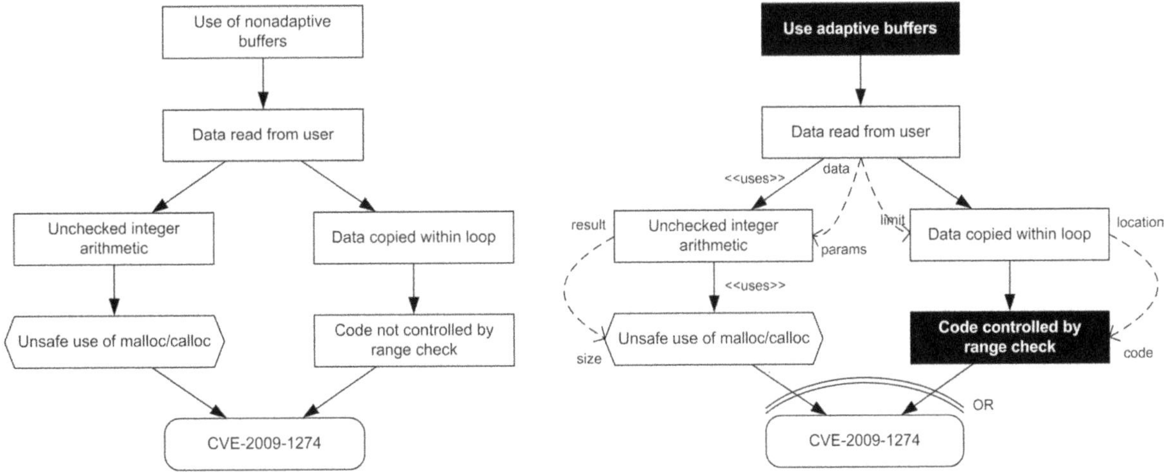

counteracts this type of buffer overflow). The corresponding VCG looks very similar but does not include the information flow that clarifies the precise relationships between elements of the model; this information would have to be inferred by the user of the model.

Figures 5 and 6 show an attack tree and a corresponding SGM for an attack on an on-line software distribution service. The root of the SGM, at the bottom of the graph, is the security goal (a successful attack), and the remaining elements are subgoals. Subgoals drawn with angled sides are also modeled using SGMs. The attack tree is larger than the SGM and includes several duplications (in particular the *influence person* subgoal is repeated three times, with two variations).

Figure 7 shows part of an SGM for the security property *secure password management* and subgoal *password quality is checked.* Traditionally, the process of inspecting for these goals could have been modeled using an SGIT. Again, the black subgoal represents something that counteracts the overall goal (in this case, allowing username and password to be the same indicates that password quality is not checked). The corresponding SGIT would be larger, since some elements would be duplicated, and would not include information flow.

These three examples illustrate how SGMs can model attacks, vulnerabilities and security properties. In all cases the SGM is more precise (through the use of information flow), more compact than, and at least as readable as the corresponding attack tree, VCG, or SGIT.

The Security Goal Modeling Language

When defining the modeling formalism, we use the concepts syntax, semantic domain and semantic transformation. For a complete treatment of these terms as applied to modeling, see 'Meaningful Modeling: What's the Semantics of "Semantics"' (Harel & Rumpe, 2004).

The syntax describes the expressions that can be formed in the modeling language. In the case of security goal models, the primitive elements of the language are graph elements, such as vertices and edges, and expressions are graphs that satisfy specific constraints.

The semantic domain specifies the concepts of discourse, and is related to how models are to be used. Thus, a given modeling language can be associated with a variety of semantic domains, each specifying the concepts necessary for a particular

Figure 5. Attack tree for the attack replace software

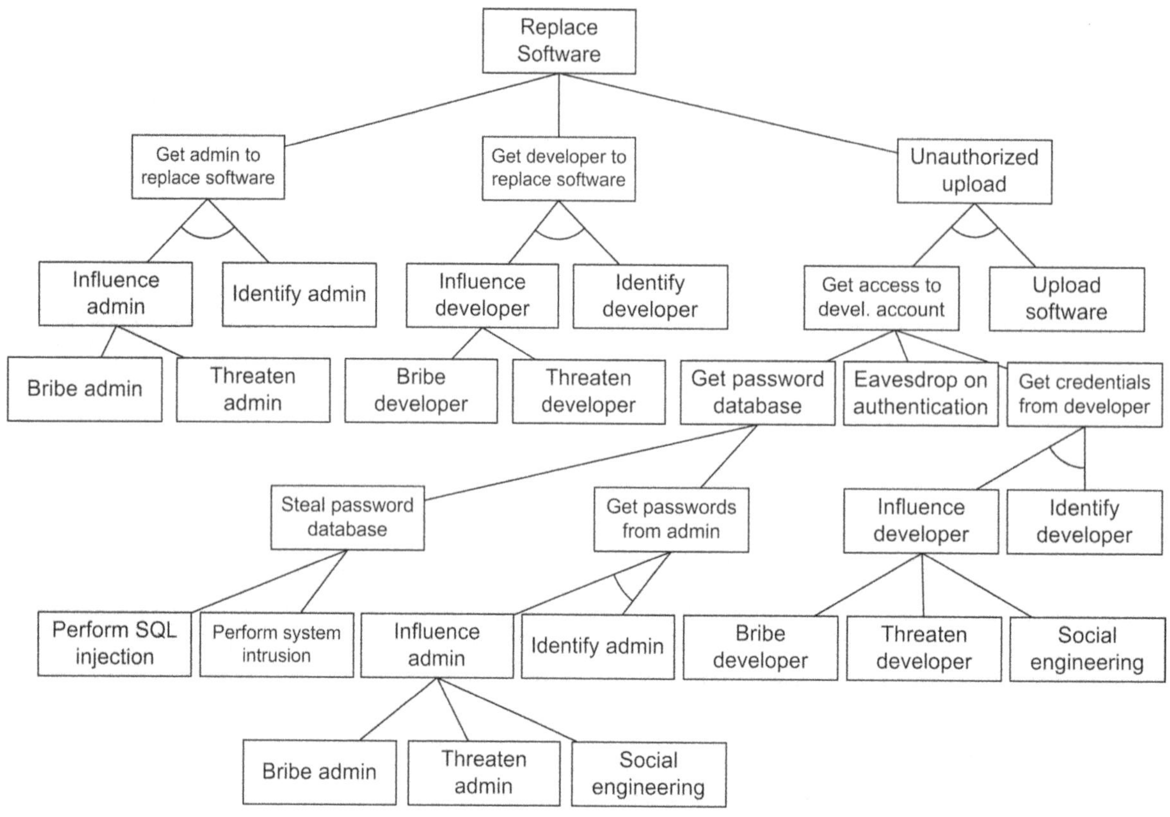

use of the language. The semantic transformation is a mapping from syntactic expression to elements in the semantic domain.

Syntax

Figure 8 shows the abstract syntax of the SGM language in a UML class diagram. Elements with italicized names are abstract and cannot appear directly in models. All generalizations are disjoint (members of a general class can be members of only one of its specializations) and complete (no specializations other than those shown exist) unless otherwise specified. Only required attributes are included in the figure.

The *Root* is a vertex that is reachable through dependence edges from all subgoal elements. The root cannot have any successors through dependence edges.

A *Subgoal* represents a goal that contributes to (*contributing subgoal*) or counteracts (*counteracting subgoal*) the overall goal that the SGM models. Every subgoal must be associated with exactly one core element and has at most one predecessor and at least one successor through dependence edges. A single model can contain several subgoals, both contributing and counteracting, that reference the same core element.

Operators represent logical combinations of dependencies, either *And* or *Or*. Every operator

Figure 6. Security goal model for the attack replace software

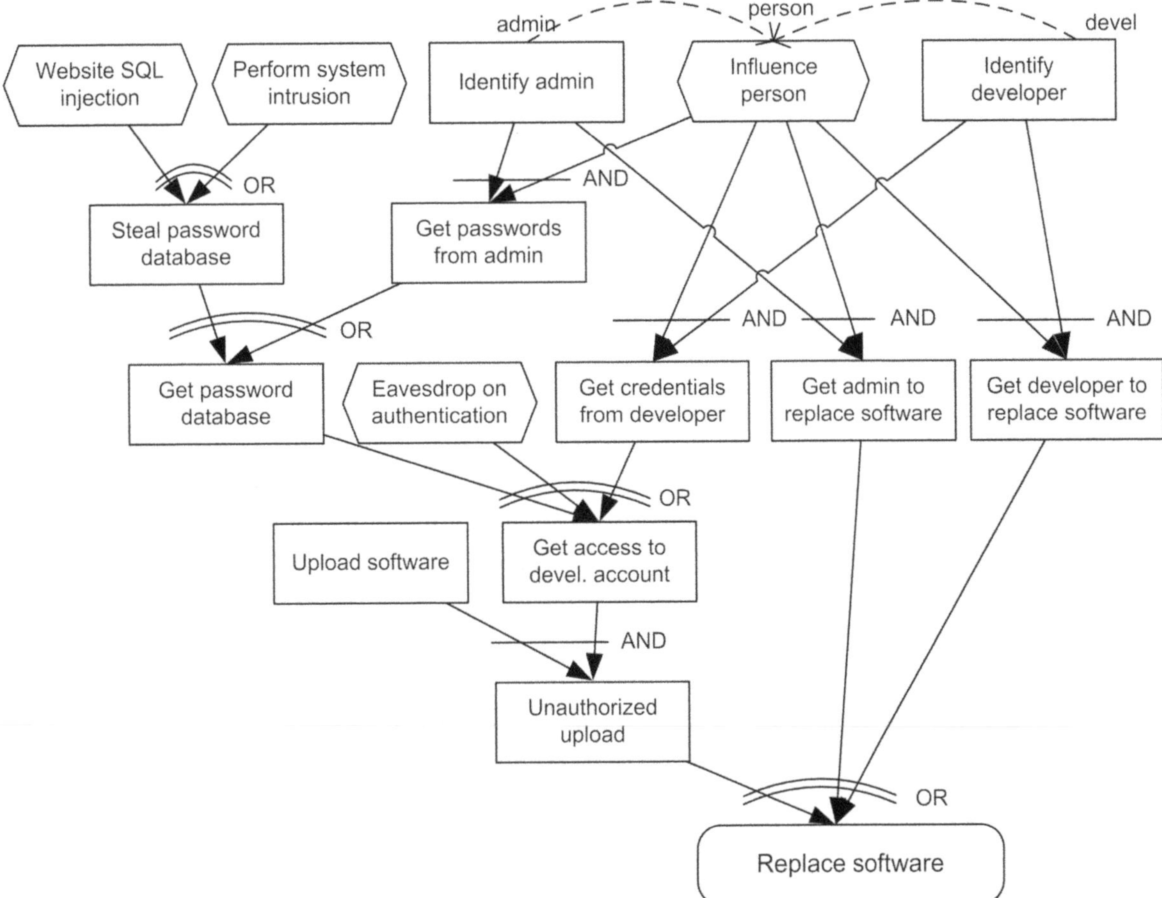

must have at least one predecessor through a dependence edge and exactly one successor through a dependence edge.

A *DependenceEdge* is a directed edge that represents any kind of dependence between subgoals and/or operators. An edge from *A* to *B* indicates that in order to fulfill the overall goal, both *A* and *B* must be fulfilled (assuming they are not counteracting). The reason for a dependence edge can be specified using stereotypes.

Subgoals can have one or more *InformationPorts*. Each port is either an *InputPort,* which represents some information used in the subgoal, or an *OutputPort*, which represents information produced by the subgoal. The unchecked integer arithmetic subgoal in Figure 6 shows how information ports can be used: the subgoal has an input port representing operands and an output port representing the result.

Information ports can be connected using *InformationEdges*, which are used to add constraints to individual subgoals. For example, the edge from secure creation of passwords to password quality is checked in Figure 7 signifies that it is the securely created password's quality that is to be checked, not some other password. An information edge is directed and may originate at any port, but must terminate at an input port. An edge from *A* to *B*

Figure 7. Security goal model for goals secure password management and password quality is checked

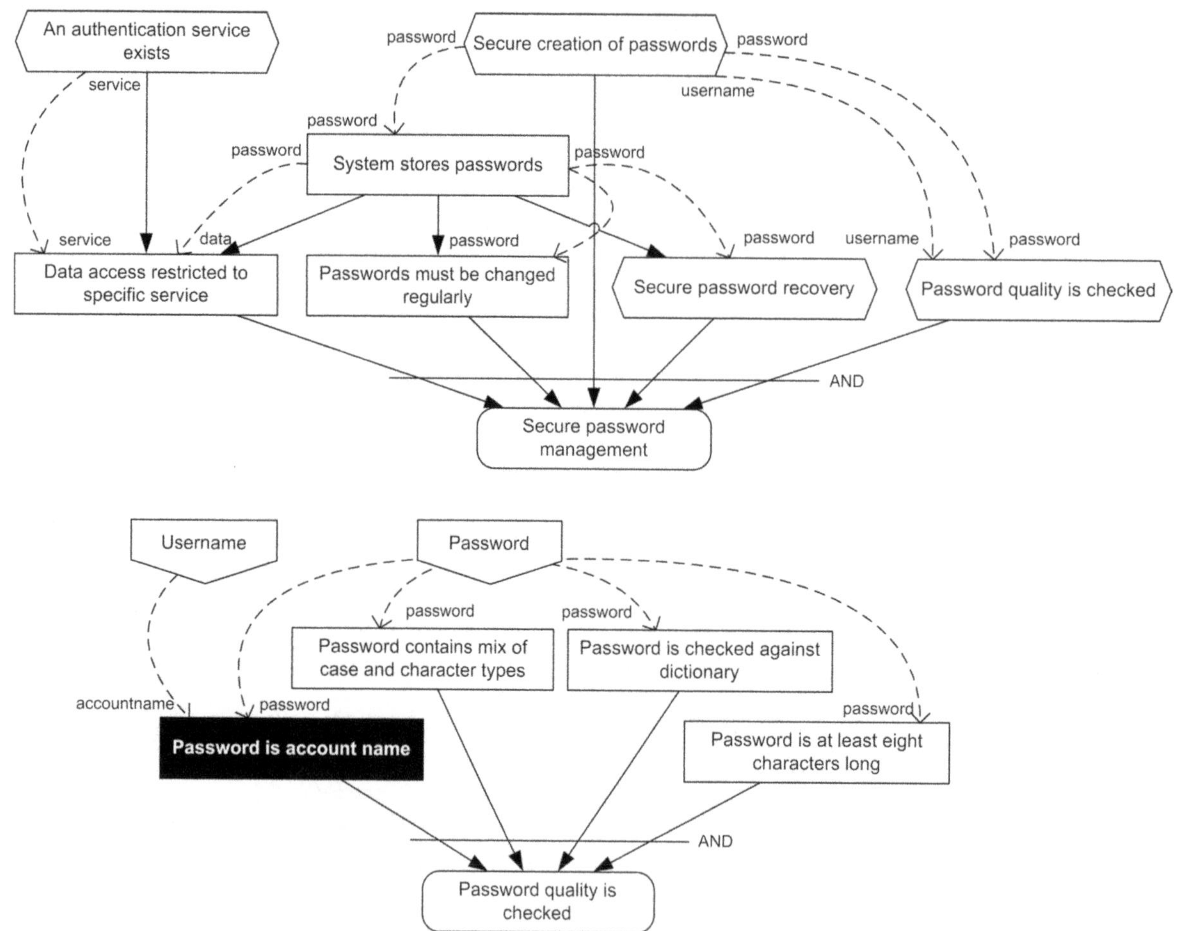

signifies that the information at port *B* is the same as the information at port *A*, provided that *A* and its dependencies are fulfilled.

Input and *Output* vertices link the ports of core elements to their models. If a subgoal *E* is modeled by SGM *G*, then *G* contains one input vertex for each input port of *E*, and one output vertex for each output port of *E*. Every input vertex has one output port and every output vertex has one input port.

An *Annotation* is an arbitrary comment. Annotations may be associated with other model elements through *AnnotationEdges*. A *Stereotype* is an annotation on an edge, usually a dependence edge, used to explain why the edge exists. While the reason for including an edge does not affect whether the overall goal is fulfilled or not, it can make the graph easier to understand. In models created to date, we have identified the stereotypes listed in Table 2, all suitable for dependence edges.

The *Model*, *CoreElement*, and *ModelElement* elements are discussed in "Core Concepts," above. Elements *SGMElement*, *Vertex*, and *Edge* are abstract, and thus never instantiated directly. The *SGM* element represents an entire SGM.

Visual Representation

Elements in the syntactic domain are visually represented as shown in Table 3. The symbols have been chosen to be similar to those used in VCGs and SGITs, but there are some differences:

Figure 8. Abstract syntax for security goal models

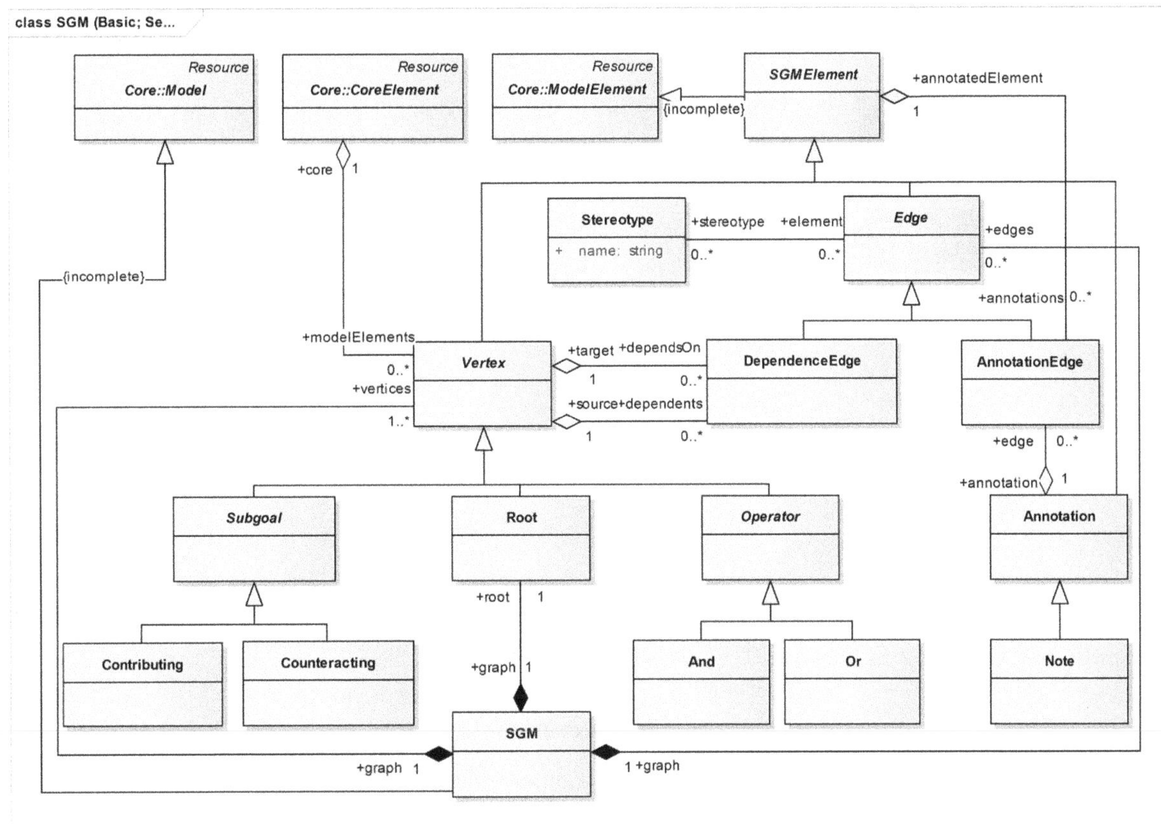

Table 2. Stereotypes identified in SGMs to date

Name	Explanation
causes	A subgoal is the direct consequence of another. Typically the subgoals will be vulnerability causes.
prerequisite	A subgoal cannot be fulfilled unless another has also been fulfilled. For example, the existence of a logging component is a prerequisite to messages being sent to the logging component.
uses	An operation uses the result of another. For example, a memory allocation may use the result of an unchecked multiplication.

- The shape of subgoals differs from those used in SGITs since SGITs only use one shape for all indicators. SGMs use the simpler shape for simpler subgoals, and the more complex shape for more complex (i.e. modeled) subgoals.
- SGITs use color to show if an indicator is positive or negative. SGMs do not use color since red/green color blindness is fairly common. The indication for counteracting subgoals in SGMs (black element background) is also visible even if most of the element is obscured.
- SGITs use explicit vertices for operators; VCGs use a special vertex types for the *and* operator and have no explicit indication of the *or* operator. The design used in SGMs is intended to reduce clutter in the

Table 3. Visual representation of security goal model elements

Symbol	Element
Name / Name	Vertex representing an unmodeled subgoal (i.e. one that is not associated with a security goal model). Black text on which indicates contributing; white text on black indicates counteracting.
Name / Name	Vertex representing subgoals associated with security goal models. Black text on which indicates contributing; white text on black indicates counteracting.
Root	Root.
A <<stereo>> B	Dependence edge; B depends on A. The edge has stereotype "stereo".
OR / AND	Operation *or* and operation *and*, with three operands each. Text labels are optional.
A src dst B	Information edge. There is an information edge connecting information port *src* of vertex *A* to information port *dst* of vertex *B*.
src > > dst	Port type indications: *src* is an output port and *dst* is an input port. These indications are optional.
Input / Output	Input vertex (named "input") and output vertex (named "output").
Note	Annotation.
A B	Annotation edge; A is an annotation for B.

graph. Furthermore, it is a common representation in attack trees, which are closely related to security goal models.

The design of the information edge is chosen so it is visually distinct from dependence edges (bent, not straight, dashed, not solid). The dashed line reflects that information edges are less crucial to the model than dependence edges.

Note that the port type is typically only important when constructing the model, so indication of port type is optional, in order to reduce the clutter in complex graphs. Information edges may have stereotypes.

The design of inputs and outputs are inspired by notation used in the Taverna workflow system (Hull et al., 2006).

A large model with fully connected information ports can appear quite cluttered. Since information edges are not always important (for example, information edges can be ignored when using the model to determine how to prevent a vulnerability), security goal models can be displayed with only dependence edges.

Semantics

The semantics of the SGM language is defined as two separate transformations: The first is a syntactic transformation that translates an object graph adhering to the abstract syntax into a 6-tuple, replacing the operators, input and output vertices with more general relations. The second is the semantic transformation that translates the 6-tuple into a set of scenarios, each of which describes a valid way to fulfill the modeled security goal (similar to Mauw and Oostdijk's formalization of attack trees (Mauw & Oostdijk, 2006). The scenarios can then be interpreted in a manner appropriate to each individual application. Interpretations have been developed for testing (Mammar et al., 2009) and Datalog (Ceri, Gotlob & Tanca, 1989) for use in static analysis (SHIELDS project consortium, 2010).

Definitions

First we introduce some common notation. $\mathcal{P}(V)$ denotes the powerset of *V*; $\mathcal{P}^+(V)$ denotes the set of non-empty subsets of *V*. $\mathcal{M}^+(V)$ is the set of sub-multisets of multiset *V* and $\mathcal{M}^+(V)$ is the set of non-empty sub-multisets of multiset *V*. Multisets are written as $\langle ... \rangle$. The distributed product of sets of multisets is defined as

$$V \otimes W = \{v \uplus w \quad v \in V, w \in W\}.$$

The operator $\otimes_{i \in I}$ is the generalization of $\otimes$.

Given a relation

$$R \subseteq N \times \mathcal{M}^+(N'),$$

where $N' \subseteq N$, we say that n_2 is *reachable through R* from n_1 iff there exists an element (n_1, X) in R such that $n_2 \in X$ or n_2 is reachable through R from any element in X. We say that R is *acyclic* if there is no element *n* such that *n* is reachable through *R* from itself.

The following basic domains and functions are used in the definition of the translations, as well as in the Datalog interpretation.

- SGM: The universe of all security goal models.
- $Node$: The universe of all SGM subgoals.
- $Port$: The universe of all SGM ports.
- $Type$: The universe of all type names.
- $IE = Port \times Port$: The universe of all information edges.
- $Scenario = \mathcal{M}^+(Node) \times \mathcal{P}(IE)$: The universe of all *scenarios*.
- $Suite = \mathcal{P}(Scenario)$: The universe of all *scenario suites*.
- $Types : Node \rightarrow \mathcal{P}^+(Type)$: The types of a node.

We use a definition of security goal models that eliminates operators, input vertices and output vertices. Operators are replaced by the $\rightarrow_d$ relation, which maps a vertex *n* to a set whose elements are multisets of vertices that *n* depends on. The ports of all input and output vertices are associated with the SGM root instead.

Definition: Security Goal Model

A security goal model *T* is a 6-tuple

$$(N,P,\text{node},\rightarrow_i,\rightarrow_d,n_0),$$

where N is a finite subset *Node* such that $n_0 \in N$; P is a finite subset of *Port*; node is a function $\text{node}: P \rightarrow N$ denoting the node that a given port belongs to; $\rightarrow_i$ is a finite acyclic relation $\rightarrow_i \subseteq P \times P$ denoting the information edges in the SGM; $\rightarrow_d$ is a finite acyclic relation

$$\rightarrow_d \subseteq N \times \mathcal{M}^+(N \setminus \{n_0\})$$

denoting the dependencies in the SGM. The set of end nodes of the SGM T is defined as

$$E(T) = \{n \in N \mid \nexists x : n \rightarrow_d x\}.$$

All $n_i \in N \setminus \{n_0\}$ must be reachable through $\rightarrow_d$ from n_0.

Translation from Graphical Notation

Let G be an SGM in graphical notation. We define the helper sets V,W,X and helper function

$$D : \textbf{Node} \rightarrow \mathcal{P}(\mathcal{M}^+(\textbf{Node}))$$

in Box 1.

The set V is the set of input and output vertices. These are not included in the 6-tuple, but their ports will be associated with the root. The set W is the set of all subgoals and the set X is the set of all information edges. Finally, the function D encodes the effects of operations, which are not included in the 6-tuple. We can now derive the SGM

$$T = \{N,P,\text{node},\rightarrow_i,\rightarrow_d,n_0\}$$

shown in Box 2.

The set N is the set containing all subgoals and the root. The set P is constructed by collecting all ports from both input and output vertices, and from subgoals. The node function is constructed by mapping each port to the subgoal it was associated with, and ports associated with input and output vertices to the root. The $\rightarrow_i$ relation is essentially a copy of all information edges, with edges moved from input and output vertices to

Box 1.

$$V = \{n \in G.\text{vertices} \mid \text{Types}(n) \cap \{\text{Input},\text{Output}\} \neq \varnothing\}$$
$$W = \{n \in G.\text{vertices} \mid \text{Subgoal} \in \text{Types}(n)\}$$
$$X = \{e \in G.\text{edges} \mid e \in \textbf{IE}\}$$
$$D(n) = \begin{cases} \{n\} & \text{if } n \in W \\ \bigcup_{p \in n.\text{dependsOn}} D(p) & \text{if Or} \in \text{Types}(n) \\ \bigotimes_{p \in n.\text{dependsOn}} D(p) & \text{if And} \in \text{Types}(n) \end{cases}$$

Box 2.

$$N = W \cup \{G.\text{root}\}$$
$$P = \{n.\text{port} \mid n \in V\} \cup (\bigcup_{n \in W} n.\text{ports})$$
$$\text{node} = \{p \mapsto n \mid n \in W : p \in n.\text{ports}\} \cup \{p \mapsto n_o \mid \exists n \in V : p = n.\text{port}\}$$
$$\rightarrow_i = \{(s,d) \mid \exists e \in X : s = e.\text{source}, d = e.\text{target}\}$$
$$\rightarrow_d = \{(n,s) \mid n \in N, n.\text{dependsOn} \neq \varnothing, s \in D(n.\text{dependsOn})\}$$
$$N_0 = G.\text{root}$$

the root. The construction of $\rightarrow_d$ maps non-end nodes to their predecessors in the graph, with the effects of operations accounted for.

Transformation to Scenario Suites

The semantics of a security goal model is defined in terms of *scenarios* and *scenario suites*. A scenario is a set of subgoals together with the information edges that connect them. A scenario suite is a set of scenarios. The semantics of an SGM is the scenario suite that contains all scenarios that represent ways to fulfill the SGM.

Let *T* be an SGM

$$\{N, P, \text{node}, \rightarrow_i, \rightarrow_d, n_0\}.$$

The semantic transformation of *T*,

$$\mathcal{S}[\![\_]\!] : \textbf{SGM} \rightarrow \textbf{Suite}$$

is defined by:

$$\mathcal{S}[\![T]\!] = \{(b,e) \mid b \in \mathcal{N}[\![n_0]\!], e = I(b)\}$$

$$\mathcal{N}[\![n]\!] = \begin{cases} \{\langle n \rangle\} & \text{if } n \in E(T) \\ \{\langle n \rangle\} \otimes (\bigcup_{n \rightarrow_d X} \bigotimes_{m \in X} \mathcal{N}[\![m]\!] & \text{if } n \notin E(T) \end{cases}$$

$$I(b) = \{(x,y) \in \rightarrow_i \mid \text{node}(x) \in b, \text{node}(y) \in b\}$$

The semantic transformation ST is valid if, and only if, $\bigcup_{(b,e) \in \mathcal{S}[\![T]\!]} e = \rightarrow_i$ (i.e. every information edge is included in some scenario).

Example of Semantic Transformation

Consider the SGM in Figure 9, which is the model from Figure 4 with all subgoals and ports renamed. The semantic transformation for this model takes place in two steps: from the graphical notation to a tuple, and from a tuple to a scenario suite.

Translation from the graphical notation yields the SGM

$$T = (N, P, \text{node}, \rightarrow_i, \rightarrow_d, n_0),$$

where (Box 3).

Figure 9. Security goal model for CVE-2009-1274 (simplified)

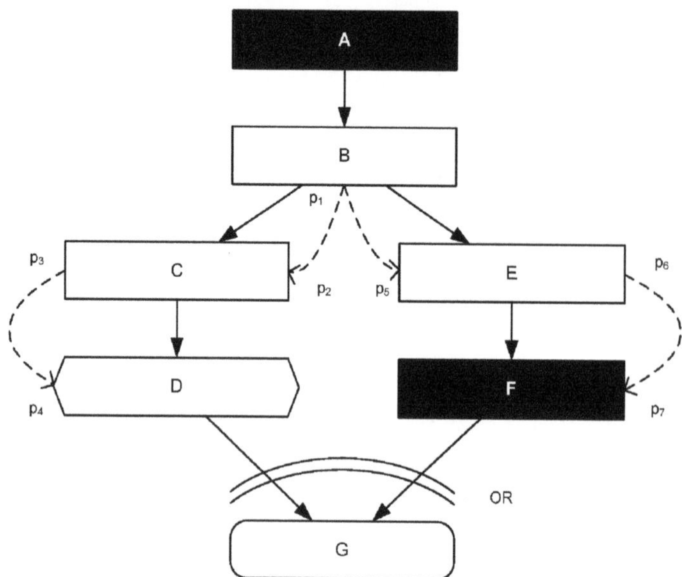

Box 3.

$$N = \{A,B,C,D,E,F,G\}$$
$$P = \{p_1, p_2, p_3, p_4, p_5, p_6, p_7\}$$
$$\text{node} = \{p_1 \to B,\ p_2 \to C,\ p_3 \to C, p_4 \to D, p_5 \to E, p_6 \to E, p_7 \to F\}$$
$$\to_i = \{(p_1, p_2),(p_3, p_4),(p_1, p_5),(p_6, p_7)\}$$
$$\to_d = \{(B,\langle A\rangle),(C,\langle B\rangle),(D,\langle C\rangle),(E,\langle B\rangle),(F,\langle E\rangle),(G,\langle D\rangle),(G,\langle F\rangle)\}$$
$$n_0 = G$$

In this 6-tuple N contains the subgoals and the root, P is the set of all ports, node maps ports to the vertices they belong to, $\to_i$ is the set of information edges, and $\to_d$ the set of dependencies. Note the values of $G \to_d n$: the *or* operation has resulted in two tuples involving G; had there been an *and* operation instead, there would have been a single tuple, (G,D,F).

The next step transforms the 6-tuple T into a scenario suite. The fact that there are two tuples involving G in $\to_d$ will cause the scenario suite to contain two distinct scenarios shown in Box 4.

In other words, the goal modeled can be achieved in two different ways; in this case that means there are two ways to cause the modeled vulnerability.

This example does not require the use of multisets. Multisets allow a given subgoal to appear more than once in a scenario, but models where this occurs are atypical. For example, if the *or* in Figure 9 had been an *and*, then subgoals A and B

Box 4.

$$\mathcal{S}[\![T]\!] = \{(\langle A,B,C,D,G\rangle,\{(p_1,p_2),(p_3,p_4)\}),(\langle A,B,E,F,G\rangle,\{(p_1,p_5),(p_6,p_7)\})\}$$

would have appeared twice in the single scenario that would have resulted. For some applications (e.g. testing), a normal set may be adequate, but for others (e.g. when detecting redundancies in models), multisets are necessary.

Creating Security Goal Models

The first step in creating an SGM is developing a thorough understanding of the security goal in question. Depending on the type of goal, this activity may take a variety of forms. For vulnerabilities, it may involve detailed code review, static analysis or even exploit development. For other goals, reviews of development practices or techniques may be required.

After completing the initial analysis, a base SGM is created consisting of only a root. The SGM is then built through a process of iterative refinement.

- **Process:** Security goal modeling.
- **Inputs:** Analysis of a security goal G.
- **Outputs:** An SGM for G.

1. **Create SGM:** Create a new SGM containing only a root.
2. **Analyze Next Vertex:** Pick any vertex N in the SGM that has not yet been completely analyzed and complete the following steps:
    a. **Determine if N needs to be modeled.** If N is not already associated with an SGM, but represents a combination or sequence of subgoals (e.g. causes or sub-activities), then N is complex.
    b. **Determine if N Overlaps Others:** If N is not complex, then ensure that the subgoal it represents does not partially overlap any other subgoal. If it does, then both the subgoal that N represents and the subgoal it overlaps with are complex.
    c. **Determine if There Are Several Ways to Realize N:** If N is a subgoal that can be realized in multiple ways, then it is complex.
    d. **Determine if the Success of N Must Be Verified:** If N is an action or event, then determine whether it is necessary to verify the success of the activity or outcome of the event. If so, then N is complex, consisting of an implementation and a verification. The verification should be modeled using an SGM.
    e. **Convert Complex Vertices:** If any vertices have been determined to be complex, then consider splitting them (and the subgoals they represent) into multiple simpler vertices or modeling them using SGMs. Continue from step 2 if N was converted.
    f. **Identify Predecessor Candidates:** Identify subgoals that may be predecessors of N by answering the questions such as "under what circumstances is N a concern?" and "what could have caused this". Additionally, if the subgoal that N represents is present in other SGMs, consider its predecessors in those models as potential candidates. This step is discussed in greater detail below.
    g. **Organize Predecessor Candidates:** Add the predecessor candidates identi-

fied in the previous step to the SGM using appropriate relationships. This step is discussed in greater detail below.

3. **Iterate:** Repeat from step 2 until there are no more vertices in the SGM that have not been completely analyzed.
4. **Optimize and Validate:** When the SGM is complete, it should be optimized for reuse and clarity. Following optimization, it should be checked and improved on by a second analyst or team of analysts. This step is discussed in greater detail below.

Identifying and Organizing Predecessors

The predecessors of a vertex *N* in a SGM should represent conditions and events that, when present, lead to the subgoal that *N* represents being present or being able to contribute to the overall goal being modeled. For example, if *N* represents the subgoal error values are in the same range as data values, and the overall goal being modeled is a vulnerability, then a reasonable predecessor would be a single variable is used to store error and data – if error values and data are always separated, then the fact that their ranges overlap will not contribute to the overall goal.

Identifying potential predecessors of a vertex starts with answering the following questions:

1. If *N* Represents a Condition:
   a. Which other conditions will cause this condition to arise?
   b. Under which other conditions is this condition a cause for concern?
   c. Which events will result in this condition?
2. If *N* Represents an Event:
   a. Which events will cause this event to occur?
   b. Under which conditions is this event a cause for concern?
   c. Which conditions will cause this event to occur?
3. If *N* Represents an Activity:
   a. Which events must occur for this activity to take place?
   b. Which conditions must hold for this activity to be effective?
   c. Which activities must be performed together with this activity?
   d. Which activities must be performed before this activity?

Answering these questions usually results in a combination of subgoals that can be expressed as a propositional logic formula. For example, assume we determine that for vertex *N* to be a concern, condition *A* and at least one of conditions *B*, *C* and *D* must hold true, this can be expressed as *A and (B or C or D)*.

If identified using the questions above, each potential predecessor identified should initially be a contributing subgoal. Some of these should then be negated and converted to counteracting subgoals. The following guidelines can be used in this process:

1. Is the subgoal already present in the database? Then it should not be converted.
2. Is the negation of the subgoal present in the database? Then it should be replaced by its negation, used as a counteracting subgoal.
3. Does the subgoal express a negative condition, non-occurrence of an event, a failure of some sort, or the non-execution of an action? Then it should be negated, the negation entered into the database, and used as a counteracting subgoal. For example use of nonadaptive buffers should be replaced with use of adaptive buffers, as a counteracting subgoal.

In order to promote a flat and easy-to-understand model, expressions should be converted to disjunctive normal form. After conversion, each term of the expression can be used as a predecessor of the current vertex. For example, *A and (B or C or D)* should be converted to *(A and B) or (A and C) or (A and D)*, yielding an *or* operation with three operands as the predecessor of N. Each operand will be a sequence, or *and* operation.

In actual use the expressions arrived at in this step are simpler than the example shown here. Complex expressions are an indication that modeling is progressing in too large steps.

When the subgoal for which predecessors are being identified is already present in some other SGM, then the predecessors in that SGM are possible predecessor candidates in the SGM being built. Conversely, any new predecessors identified are candidates for inclusion in pre-existing SGMs containing the same subgoal.

Information Ports and Edges

The process described above results in an SGM without information edges. If information edges are desired, then the following steps must also be followed.

Information Ports

Whenever a new subgoal is created determine which input ports and which output ports it should have by answering the following questions:

1. If the Subgoal is an Event:
    a. What does this event affect?
    b. Where does this event occur?
    c. What or who is involved in this event?
    d. When does this event occur?
2. If the Subgoal is a Condition:
    a. What determines the presence or absence of this condition?
    b. When can this condition occur?
    c. What affects or is affected by this condition?
3. If the Subgoal is an Action:
    a. Who or what performs this action?
    b. What is used to perform this action?
    c. What is produced by performing this action?
    d. When is this action performed?

Information Edges

If the SGM models a subgoal that has information ports, add the corresponding input and output elements to the SGM. For every input port *I* of every subgoal *N* in the SGM, identify the source of the information, and create an information edge from the source to *I* on subgoal *N*. If no source can be found in the SGM, then the model may be incomplete.

Correspondence to Other Languages

The SGM language was developed in part to reduce the number of modeling languages used in software security. Although SGMs have a clear advantage in expressive power, the existing languages have the advantage of familiarity.

We have defined transformations to and from attack trees, VCGs, SAGs, and SGITs so that developers can use familiar notation to create and use SGMs. Any model expressed using one of the earlier languages can be transformed to an SGM without loss of fidelity. SGMs can be transformed to earlier notation provided that certain reasonable constraints are met (e.g. an attack tree cannot be used to model how to perform software inspection). Information, such as information edges, that cannot be represented in the target language is lost.

SGMs can be used to model arbitrary security goals, but conventional languages are targeted at specific kinds of security aspects. Therefore it does not always make sense to convert an SGM to earlier notations. For example, there is little point in converting an SGM representing an attack into an SGIT. The sections below describe the conditions for conversion to each of the earlier notations.

The ability of an SGM to accurately represent models created in other languages means that the SGM language can also be used as a way to store models in e.g. a shared repository, such as that developed in the SHIELDS project.

VCG View

VCGs are used to model the potential causes of vulnerabilities. They consist of causes and vulnerabilities and edges. Logic is expressed using implicit or and explicit conjunctions.

Anything that can be expressed with a VCG can be expressed with an SGM. Causes correspond to contributing subgoals (VCGs cannot express counteracting subgoals); implicit or and conjunctions correspond to SGM operations; and the VCG exit node corresponds to the SGM root.

An SGM that expresses how a vulnerability is caused (i.e. the SGM models a vulnerability) can be converted to a VCG. However, due to the differences in how logic is expressed (SGMs are more general than VCGs) a conversion procedure has only been defined for the subset of SGMs that can be converted without altering the semantics of the model. Figure 10 shows an SGM and the VCG that can be (nearly) automatically derived from it. Here, there is loss of fidelity due to the weaker expressive power of the VCG language: the information edges and ports are lost, and the dependency between *data is not safely filtered for SQL* and *dynamic SQL query construction* is altered. If the resulting VCG were to be converted back to an SGM, the result would be like the original SGM but without information edges or ports, with a contributing subgoal instead of the counteracting one, and with a dependence edge from *data is not safely filtered for SQL* to *SQL table names are available.*

Conversion from VCGs

The following points outline an algorithm that converts a VCG to an SGM. It is initialized by processing the exit node of the VCG. Listing 1 shows pseudocode for the algorithm.

To convert a VCG, process its exit node. To process a single VCG node *V*, yielding a single SGM node as the result (updating the SGM as a side effect):

Figure 10. SGM and the result of automatic conversion to VCG

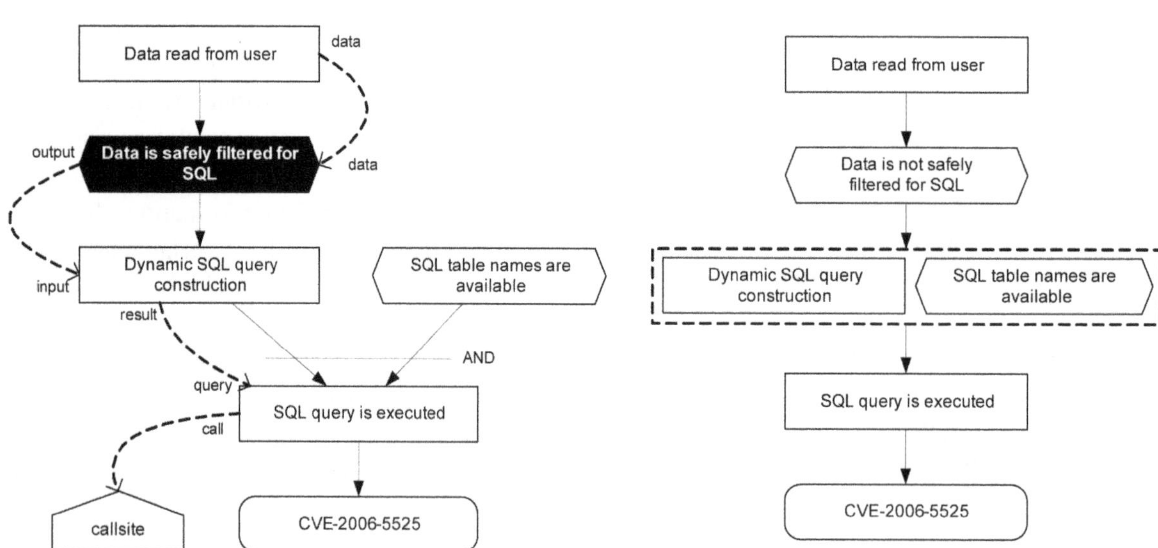

Listing 1. Conversion from VCG to SGM

```
def vcg_to_sgm(vcg):
  done = dict()
  def predecessors(v,t):
    if len(v.predecessors()) > 1:
      n = Or()
      Edge(n,t)
      t = n
    for p in v.predecessors():
      x = process(p)
      Edge(x,t)
    return t
  def process(v):
    if v in done:
      return done[v]
    if isinstance(v,Exit):
      n = Root()
      predecessors(v,n)
    elif isinstance(v,Conjunction):
      n = And()
      x = None
      for c in v.clauses:
        t = Contributing(c.relatedCoreElement)
        Edge(t,n)
        if x is None:
          x = predecessors(v,t)
        else:
          Edge(x,t)
    elif isinstance(v,Cause):
      n = Contributing(v.relatedCoreElement)
      predecessors(v,n)
    done[v] = n
    return n
  return process(vcg.exit)
```

- If *V* has already been processed, then perform no other processing and yield the same result as the previous time.
- If *V* is the exit node, then create a root *R* and add it to the SGM. Process the predecessors of *V*, using *R* as the target node. Yield *R* as the result.
- If *V* is a conjunction, create a new and operation and process each of its clauses. Yield the new and node as the result.

- If V is a cause node linked to cause C and a clause of a conjunction J, then create a contributing subgoal N linked to cause C and add it to the SGM. Process the predecessors of J, using N as the target node. Yield N as the result.
- If V is a cause node linked to cause C, but is not a clause of a conjunction, then create a contributing subgoal N linked to cause C and add it to the SGM. Process the predecessors of V, using N as the target node. Yield N as the result.

To process the predecessors of V with SGM node T as the target (updating the SGM as a side effect):

- For each predecessor P_i of V, process P_i yielding N and add an edge from N to T to the SGM.

This conversion does not lose any information: everything that can be expressed in a VCG can also be expressed in an SGM.

Conversion to VCG

An SGM that models the causes of a vulnerability (i.e. models a vulnerability and has only causes as subgoals), and that uses and operations in a limited way can be converted to a VCG without losing any information other than that conveyed by information edges and ports.

Listing 2 shows pseudocode for a procedure that converts from an SGM to a VCG. It traverses the SGM from the root in a depth-first manner. To avoid duplication of elements in the resulting VCG, partial results are memoed. In this pseudocode, a VCG is represented as a set of vertices and edges. The subset of SGMs supported includes those created by applying the VCG-to-SGM conversion in listing 1.

Note that since VCGs can only represent contributing causes, any counteracting subgoals in the SGM must be rephrased as contributing causes. This must usually be done by a human.

- If V has already been processed, then yield the same result as last time.

- If V is the Root, then create a new VCG exit node E and add it to the VCG. Process the predecessor of V with E as the target. Yield E as the result.
- If V is a contributing subgoal associated with cause C then create VCG cause node N associated with C. Process the predecessor of V with N as the target. Yield N as the result. Counteracting subgoals are handled the same way, with the exception that the "inverse" of the cause is associated with the cause node.
- If V is an and operation whose predecessors are all subgoals with identical predecessors, then create a new conjunction C. For each predecessor of V, create the corresponding cause node and make it a clause of C. Process the predecessor of any of the predecessors of V with C as the target. Yield C as the result.

To process the predecessor P of V with target T, create a worklist that initially contains P. Perform the following steps until the worklist is empty:

- Let P be the first item on the worklist, and remove it from the worklist.
- If P is an or operation, then add its predecessors to the worklist. This flattens the structure of nested or operations.
- If P is not an or operation, process P yielding N and add an edge from N to T.

Listing 2. Conversion from SGM to VCG

```
def sgm_to_vcg(r):
  done = dict()
  def predecessors(v,t):
    worklist = list(v.dependeOn())
    while len(worklist) > 0:
      (p,worklist) = (worklist[0],worklist[1:])
      if isinstance(p,Or):
        worklist.extend(p.dependsOn())
      else:
        n = process(p)
        Edge(n,t)
  def process(v):
    if v in done:
      return done[v]
    if isinstance(v,Root):
      n = Exit()
      predecessors(v,n)
    elif isinstance(v,Contributing):
      n = Cause(v.relatedCoreElement)
      predecessors(v,n)
    elif isinstance(v,And):
      p = v.dependsOn()[0].dependsOn()
      for c in v.dependsOn():
        if not (isinstance(c,Subgoal) and
                p == c.dependsOn()):
          raise "Can't convert"
      n = Conjunction()
      for c in v.dependsOn():
        t = Cause(c.relatedCoreElement)
      predecessors(v.dependsOn()[0],n)

    done[v] = n
    return n
  return process(r)
```

SAG View

SAGs are used to model how to prevent vulnerability causes (and by extension, vulnerabilities), and to model how to perform or verify security-related activities. They are trees whose leaves are activities and whose internal nodes are and and or gates.

Anything that can be expressed with a SAG can be expressed with an SGM. Activities correspond to subgoals and gates to operations. The SAG root corresponds to the SGM root.

Conversion from SAG

An SGM can be created from a SAG by simply replacing all SAG gates with the corresponding SGM operations, and all SAG activities with equivalent SGM subgoals.

Conversion to SAG

An SGM that models how to perform an activity (i.e. models an activity) can be converted to a SAG, losing only the information conveyed by information edges and ports. Listing 3 shows pseudocode for a procedure that converts from an SGM to a SAG.

Attack Tree View

Attack trees are used to model how to perform an attack. They consist of attacks, and gates and or gates.

Anything that can be expressed with an attack tree can be expressed with an SGM. Attacks correspond to subgoals and gates to operations. The attack tree root corresponds to the SGM root.

Conversion from Attack Tree

An SGM can be created from an attack tree by simply replacing all attack tree gates with the corresponding SGM operations, and all attacks with the equivalent SGM subgoals.

Conversion to Attack Tree

An SGM that expresses how to perform an attack (i.e. models an attack) can be converted to an attack tree, losing only the information conveyed by information edges and ports. To create the attack tree, simply replace all subgoals with attacks and SGM operations with the corresponding attack tree gates.

SGIT View

An SGIT shows how to perform inspection for some desired security property (or security functionality). An SGIT consists of indicators, gates, dependencies and specialization trees.

Anything that can be expressed by an SGIT can also be expressed with an SGM. Indicators in the SGIT correspond to subgoals in the SGM (positive indicators are contributing subgoals; negative indicators are counteracting subgoals); SGIT gates correspond to SGM operations; indicator specialization trees can be emulated by attaching SGMs to subgoals; and dependencies can be expressed as subgoals. The edges within an SGIT express concepts similar to the dependence edges in SGMs.

Conversion from SGIT

Conversion from an SGIT to an SGM is done by simply replacing all indicators with the corresponding subgoals (counteracting for negative indicators, contributing for positive indicators) and replacing SGIT gates with the corresponding SGM operations.

Dependencies of the SGIT root on other SGITs can be expressed as dependencies on the SGM root. Indicator specialization trees can be expressed as subgoals modeled with SGMs.

Conversion to SGIT

An SGM that models the implementation of a security feature or fulfillment of a security property can be converted to an SGIT with the loss of information conveyed by information edges and ports. Furthermore, since SGITs do not support indicators being modeled by SGITs, the structure of the SGM has to be flattened: any subgoals that are modeled using SGMs must be replaced by the

Listing 3. Conversion from SGM to SAG

```
def sgm_to_sag(sag):
    def process(v,prev):
        if isinstance(v,Root):
            n = Root()
            process(v.dependsOn()[0],n)
            return n

        elif isinstance(v,And):
            if not isinstance(prev,And):
                t = And()
                Edge(t,prev)
                prev = t
            for p in v.dependsOn():
                process(p,prev)

        elif isinstance (v,Or):
            if not isinstance(prev,Or):
                t = Or()
                Edge(t,prev)
                prev = t
            for p in v.dependsOn():
                process(p,prev)

        elif isinstance (v,Subgoal):
            n = Activity(v.relatedCoreElement)
            if v.dependsOn():
                if not isinstance(prev,And):
                    t = And()
                    Edge(t,prev)
                    prev = t
                for p in v.dependsOn():
                    process(p,prev)
            Edge(n,prev)
    return process(sag.root,None)
```

SGMs themselves, until no modeled subgoals remain. Additionally, the SGM structure must be converted to a tree, which may result in duplication of nodes.

This conversion does not yield any indicator specialization trees. To the extent that such information is available in the SGM it will become part of the SGIT itself.

Applications

Security goal models have many potential applications that can be defined in terms of the semantic transformation of the SGM. These definitions are shown in Table 4. The applications that have been implemented (either for SGMs or for one of the earlier formalisms) are discussed in the following sections.

Software Process Improvement

The Sustainable Software Security Process (S3P) uses VCGs for modeling vulnerability causes and SAGs to model mitigating activities in the software lifecycle (Byers & Shahmehri, 2007). This method uses models to guide developers in determining how to prevent vulnerabilities.

Using SGMs in place of both VCGs and SAGs improves ease-of-use, as there is then only one kind of model to deal with. For this application, basic SGMs are sufficient, but the improvements to the language and notation make the models easier to create and easier to use.

Static Analysis

We have developed a static analysis tool that associates predicates with vertices in an SGM that models a vulnerability (SHIELDS project consortium, 2010). The tool uses the structure of the SGM to compose a Datalog program that is interpreted to detect vulnerabilities in a subset of Java. Use of SGMs in this application makes it easy to compose new detection rules (expressed as SGMs) from existing components (i.e. subgoals), and makes explicit what the tool detects.

Passive Testing

Institut Telecom together with Montimage SARL have developed a method for passive testing (i.e. analysis of execution traces) that can detect the presence of vulnerability causes (Mammar et al., 2009). Predicates are associated with the causes in a VCG. Full analysis rules are derived based on the semantic transformation of the vulnerability model. A testing tool for C programs has been developed that uses this method. One of the difficulties in this application is that VCGs do not express detailed relationships between causes that are necessary for accurate detection, resulting in a significant number of false positives. The use of information edges in the SGM reduces the number of false positives to suitable levels.

Manual Inspection

Fraunhofer IESE has developed an inspection method that uses SGITs to support manual inspec-

Table 4. Applications of SGMs in terms of the semantic transformation

Application	Use of fundamental semantics
Determine how to implement goal modeled by *g*	Determine an appropriate set of conditions or actions that would cause the goal to be fulfilled.
Determine how to prevent vulnerability modeled by *g*	Determine an appropriate set of conditions or actions that would cause the goal *not* to be fulfilled.
Detect the vulnerability modeled by *g*	Observe of real-world phenomena (e.g. through testing or inspection) and use the model to determine if the observed phenomena would result in the goal being fulfilled.
Determine if the goal modeled by *g* is fulfilled	Observe of real-world phenomena (e.g. through testing or inspection) and use the model to determine if the observed phenomena would result in the goal being fulfilled.
Eliminate the vulnerability modeled by *g*	Observe the real-world phenomena related to a goal that is fulfilled, and determine an appropriate set of actions or conditions that when changed would result in the goal *not* being fulfilled.

tion of software development artifacts (Peine et al., 2008). SGMs can replace SGITs in this inspection method, either directly or after conversion to SGITs. If used directly, SGMs enable more precise inspection through the use of information edges. For the most part, information edges will express constraints that inspectors would automatically assume. However, if inspection is supported by a tool, information edges could improve the accuracy of the inspection process.

Security Assurance

The Common Criteria (ISO/IEC 15408) is a standard for information technology security evaluation. Version 2 of the Common Criteria concerned itself only with security functionality, not vulnerability prevention. Vulnerability cause graphs and security activity graphs can be used to add vulnerability awareness to the Common Criteria, particularly at higher evaluation assurance levels (Ardi, September 2009; Ardi & Shahmehri, 2009). Version 3.1 addresses the oversight in previous versions by adding requirements on security architecture and TSF internals, but concrete methods similar to those developed for version 2 are still needed to meet the requirements and demonstrate that they have been met. SGMs are more suited for this application than VCGs and SAGs: counteracting subgoals are very common, and they are handled more naturally in SGMs than in VCGs and SAGs; the added precision provided by information edges is important in evaluation; and the improved expressiveness provided by stereotypes and port names makes the models easier to understand.

Risk Analysis and Mitigation

SGMs and the connections between core elements are a powerful tool in risk analysis for software. Using e.g. misuse cases as a starting point it is easy to identify relevant vulnerabilities and attacks. When these are modeled using SGMs, it is possible to follow the links further, e.g. from vulnerabilities to other potential attacks, and to activities and other security goals that can mitigate the identified risks. When multiple modeling languages are used, these relationships are difficult to express and analyze.

CONCLUSION

Security goal models (SGMs) are a way to describe how arbitrary security goals can be achieved. In this context a security goal is anything that affects security, including security functionality, security properties, attacks, mitigating activities, and even vulnerabilities. SGMs can be used for a number of purposes. To date the applications include threat analysis, software process improvement, inspection, and with the addition of application-specific data, automatic testing and static analysis.

The modeling language is designed to cover and improve on four older modeling languages: vulnerability cause graphs, security activity graphs, attack trees and security goal indicator trees. It improves on these models mainly by permitting more precise dependencies between model elements and by allowing specification of dependency type. Furthermore, unlike attack trees and SGITs, the semantics of SGMs is fully defined.

Since there are already applications that use these older languages, we have also presented procedures for converting to and from SGMs, although the conversion from an SGM to a different language will usually result in some loss of information or precision.

A unified language makes it possible to relate models created for different purposes to each other, thereby providing developers with a more complete and cohesive view of security issues. Furthermore, the data model that underpins the SGM language supports associating models of other types, e.g. misuse case diagrams, access control models, and formal specifications with each other and with SGMs.

REFERENCES

Abrial, J.R., Butler, M., Hallerstede, S., & Voisin, L. (2006, June). An open extensible tool environment for Event-B. In Proceedings of ICFEM 2006 (Vol. 4260, pp. 588-605). Berlin: Springer-Verlag.

Ardi, S., Byers, D., & Shahmehri, N. (2006). Towards a structured unified process for software security. In *Proceedings of the 2nd international workshop on software engineering for secure systems (SESS06)* (p. 3-9). Shanghai, China: IEEE Computer Society. doi:10.1145/1137627.1137630

Ardi, S., & Shahmehri, N. (2009, September) *Secure software development for higher common criteria evaluation assurance levels.* Paper presented at the 10th International Common Criteria Conference & Exhibition. Tromsø, Norway.

Ardi, S., & Shahmehri, N. (2009) Introducing vulnerability awareness to common criteria's security targets. In *Proceedings of the fourth international conference on software engineering advances* (ICSEA 2009) (pp. 419-424). Porto, Portugal: IEEE Computer Society. doi:10.1109/ICSEA.2009.67

Armando, A., & Compagna, L. (2008). Sat-based model-checking for security protocols analysis. *International Journal of Information Security, 7*(1), 3–32. doi:10.1007/s10207-007-0041-y

AVANTSSAR Consortium. (2009, July). *ASLan v.2 with static service and policy composition.* Deliverable D2.2.

Basin, D., Mödersheim, S., & Viganò, L. (2005). OFMC: A symbolic model checker for security protocols. *International Journal of Information Security, 4*(3), 181–208. doi:10.1007/s10207-004-0055-7

Bresciani, P., Perini, A., Giorgini, P., Giunchiglia, F., & Mylopoulos, J. (2004). Tropos: An agent-oriented software development methodology. *Autonomous Agents and Multi-Agent Systems, 8*(3), 203–236. doi:10.1023/B:AGNT.0000018806.20944.ef

Byers, D. (2013). *Improving software security by preventing known vulnerabilities.* (Doctoral dissertation). Linköping Studies in Science and Technology, Linköping University, Sweden.

Byers, D., Ardi, S., Shahmehri, N., & Duma, C. (2006). Modeling software vulnerabilities with vulnerability cause graphs. In *Proceedings of the International Conference on Software Maintenance* (ICSM06) (p. 411-422). Washington, DC: IEEE Computer Society.

Byers, D., & Shahmehri, N. (2007). Design of a process for software security. In *Proceedings of the Second International Conference on Availability, Reliability and Security* (ARES07). Washington, DC: IEEE Computer Society.

Byers, D., & Shahmehri, N. (2008). A cause-based approach to preventing software vulnerabilities. In S. T. Stefan Jakoubi & E. R. Weippl (Eds.), *Proceedings of the the third international conference on availability, reliability and security* (ARES08) (pp. 276-283). Washington, DC: IEEE Computer Society.

Byers, D., & Shahmehri, N. (2009). Prioritisation and selection of software security activities. In *Proceedings of the fourth international conference on availability, reliability and security* (ARES09) (pp. 201-207). Washington, DC: IEEE Computer Society.

Byers, D., & Shahmehri, N. (2010). Unified modeling of attacks, vulnerabilities and security activities. In *Proceedings of the 6th international workshop on software engineering for secure systems (SESS10)*. Cape Town, South Africa: IEEE Computer Society. doi:10.1145/1809100.1809106

Byers, D., & Shahmehri, N. (2011). Modeling security goals and software vulnerabilities. In L. Petre, K. Sere, & E. Troubitsyna (Eds.), *Dependability and computer engineering: Concepts for software-intensive systems* (pp. 171–198). IGI Global. doi:10.4018/978-1-60960-747-0.ch009

Center for Strategic and International Studies. (2013, July). *The economic impact of cypercrime and cyber espionage*. Retrieved from http://www.mcafee.com/us/resources/reports/rp-economic-impact-cybercrime.pdf

Ceri, S., Gottlob, G., & Tanca, L. (1989). What you always wanted to know about datalog (and never dared to ask. *IEEE Transactions on Knowledge and Data Engineering*, *1*(1), 146–166. doi:10.1109/69.43410

Conficker Working Group. (n.d.). *Conficker infection tracking*. Retrieved from http://www.confickerworkinggroup.org/wiki/pmwiki.php/ANY/InfectionTracking

Economics, C. (2003, August). *August 2003 – worst virus season ever?* Retrieved from http://www.computereconomics.com/article.cfm?id=867

Economics, C. (2002, September). *Malicious code attacks had $13.2 billion economic impact in 2001*. Retrieved from http://www.computereconomics.com/article.cfm?id=133

Fisler, K., Krishnamurthi, S., Meyerovich, L. A., & Tschantz, M. C. (2005). Verification and change-impact analysis of access-control policies. In *Proceedings of the 27th international conference on software engineering* (pp. 196-205). New York: ACM.

Grisogono, A.-M. (1999). *What those killer kangaroos really fired*. Defense Systems Daily.

Harel, D., & Rumpe, B. (2004). Meaningful modeling: What's the semantics of "semantics"? *Computer*, *37*(10), 64–72. doi:10.1109/MC.2004.172

Hoy, J., Brewer, M., Peterson, B., Dittmer, G., Braskett, D., & Porteus, D. (1989). *Virus highlights need for improved internet management*. United States General Accounting Office report GAO/IMTEC-89-57.

Hull, D., Wolstencroft, K., Stevens, R., Goble, C., Pocock, M. R., Li, P., & Oinn, T. (2006, July). Taverna: A tool for building and running workflows of services. *Nucleic Acids Research*, *34*(suppl. 2), w729–32. doi:10.1093/nar/gkl320 PMID:16845108

Jürjens, J. (2005). *Secure systems development with UML*. Berlin: Springer.

Lodderstedt, T., Basin, D. A., & Doser, J. (2002). SecureUML: A UML-based modeling language for model-driven security. In *Proceedings of the 5th international conference on the unified modeling language* (p. 426-441). London, UK: Springer-Verlag.

Mammar, A., Cavalli, A., de Oca, E. M., Ardi, S., Byers, D., & Shahmehri, N. (2009, June). Modélisation et détection formelles de vulnérabilités logicielles par le test passif. In *Proceedings of 4ème conférence sur la sécurité des architectures réseaux et des systèmes d'information*. Academic Press.

Mauw, S., & Oostdijk, M. (2006). Foundations of attack trees. In Proceedings of Information security and cryptology, (pp. 186–198). Berlin: Springer.

Mouratidis, H., & Giorgini, P. (2007). Secure tropos: A security-oriented extension of the tropos methodology. *International Journal of Software Engineering and Knowledge Engineering*, *17*(2), 285–309. doi:10.1142/S0218194007003240

Peine, H., Jawurek, M., & Mandel, S. (2008). Security goal indicator trees: A model of software features that supports efficient security inspection. In *Proceedings of the 2008 11th IEEE high assurance systems engineering symposium* (p. 9-18). Washington, DC: IEEE Computer Society.

Porras, P., Saidi, H., & Yegneswaran, V. (2009, March). *An analysis of Conficker's logic and redezvous points* (Technical Report). Menlo Park, CA: SRI International. Retrieved from http://mtc.sri.com/Conficker/

Rhodes, K. A. (2001, August). *Code red, code red II, and SirCam attacks highlight need for proactive measures.* GAO Testimony Before the Subcommittee on Government Efficiency, Financial Management and Intergovrenmental Relations, Commitee on Government Reform, House of Representatives. (Report number GAO-01-1073T)

Schmitt, E. (1991, June 6). U.S. details flaw in patriot missile. *The New York Times*.

Schneier, B. (1999, December). Attack trees. *Dr. Dobbs Journal*.

SHIELDS. (n.d.). *Detecting known vulnerabilities from with design and development tools*. Retrieved from http://www.shields-project.eu/

SHIELDS Project Consortium. (2010). *Final report on inspection methods and prototype vulnerability recognition tools.* SHIELDS project deliverable D4.3. Retrieved from http://www.shields-project.eu/

Spafford, E. H. (1988, November). *The internet worm program: An analysis* (Tech. Rep. No. CSD-TR-823). West Lafayette, IN: Department of Computer Sciences, Purdue University.

UML 2.1.1 superstructure and infrastructure. (2007). *Specification*. Author.

US-CERT/NIST. (2008). *Vulnerability summary CVE-2008-4250*. Retrieved from http://nvd.nist.gov/nvd.cfm?cvename=CVE-2008-4250

Viganò, L. (2006). Automated security protocol analysis with the AVISPA tool. *Electronic Notes in Theoretical Computer Science*, *155*, 61–86. doi:10.1016/j.entcs.2005.11.052

Zhang, N., Ryan, M., & Guelev, D. P. (2005, September). Evaluating access control policies through model checking. In *Proceedings of the 8th international conference on information security, ISC 2005* (Vol. 3650, pp. 446-460). Berlin: Springer.

KEY TERMS AND DEFINITIONS

Attack(n): Any interaction with a system with the purpose of causing a violation of the system's security policy.

Cause(n): A condition or events that occurs during the software lifecycle and may contribute to a vulnerability in a software product.

Security Activity(n): An activity or combination of activities applied during the system lifecycle that contributes towards fulfilling, or that fulfils, one or more security goals.

Security Goal(n): A goal that, when met, contributes to meeting some other security goal or ensures that one or more security properties desired by some stakeholder holds. Security goals are not always good things: a vulnerability can be considered a security goal since it contributes to meeting an attacker's goal of a successful attack.

Security Model(n): A description of a phenomenon or behavior related to security, often simplified by abstracting certain details.

Security Policy(n): A specification of what states of a given system are allowed, and which are not.

Vulnerability(n): A feature of a system that may be used in a way that results in a violation of a security policy. A vulnerability can be a specific instance, e.g. a specific flaw in a specific version of a product, or a class of vulnerabilities (e.g. *buffer overflow* or *injection flaw*).

ENDNOTES

1. Kangaroos armed with multicolored beach balls appear during testing of military training software.
2. Flaws in the Patriot missile battery cause it to fail to intercept incoming missiles, resulting in multiple deaths in the Gulf war.

Chapter 2
Developing Secure Software Using UML Patterns

Holger Schmidt
TÜV Informationstechnik GmbH, Germany

Denis Hatebur
University Duisburg-Essen, Germany, & ITESYS Institut für Technische Systeme GmbH, Germany

Maritta Heisel
University Duisburg-Essen, Germany

ABSTRACT

This chapter presents a security engineering process based on UML security problem frames and concretized UML security problem frames. Both kinds of frames constitute patterns for analyzing security problems and associated solution approaches. They are arranged in a pattern system that makes dependencies between them explicit. The authors describe step-by-step how the pattern system can be used to analyze a given security problem and how solution approaches can be found. Then, solution approaches are specified by generic security components and generic security architectures, which constitute architectural patterns. Finally, the generic security components and the generic security architecture that composes them are refined, and the result is a secure software product built from existing and/or tailor-made security components.

INTRODUCTION

It is acknowledged that a thorough requirements engineering phase is essential to develop a software product that matches the specified requirements. This is especially true for *security requirements*.

We propose a security engineering process that focuses on the early phases of software development covering security requirements and security architectures. The basic idea is to make use of special *patterns* for security requirements analysis and development of security architectures.

Security requirements analysis makes use of patterns for structuring, characterizing, and analyzing *problems* that frequently occur in security engineering. Similar patterns for functional requirements have been proposed by Jackson (2001). They are called *problem frames*. Accordingly, our

DOI: 10.4018/978-1-4666-6359-6.ch002

patterns are named *security problem frames*. Furthermore, for each of these frames, we have defined a set of *concretized security problem frames* that take into account generic security mechanisms to prepare the ground for solving a given security problem. Both kinds of patterns are arranged in a pattern system that makes dependencies between them explicit. We describe how the pattern system can be used to analyze a given security problem, how solution approaches can be found, and how dependent security requirements can be identified.

Afterwards, we develop a corresponding security architecture based on platform-independent *generic security components* and *generic security architectures*. Each concretized security problem frame is equipped with a set of generic security architectures that represent the internal structure of the software to be built by means of a set of generic security components. After a generic security architecture and generic security components are selected, the latter must be refined to platform-specific security components. For example, existing component frameworks can be used to construct a platform-specific security architecture that realizes the initial security requirements.

The rest of the chapter is organized as follows: First, we introduce problem frames and present a literature review. Second, we give an overview of our security engineering process. Then we present the different development phases of the process in detail. Each phase of our process is demonstrated using the example of a secure text editor application. Finally, we outline future research directions and give a summary and a discussion of our work.

BACKGROUND

In the following, we first present problem frames and second, we discuss our work in the context of other approaches to security engineering.

Problem Frames

Patterns are a means to reuse software development knowledge on different levels of abstraction. They classify sets of software development problems or solutions that share the same structure. Patterns are defined for different activities at different stages of the software life-cycle. *Problem frames* by Jackson (2001) are a means to analyze and classify software development problems. *Architectural styles* are patterns that characterize software architectures (for details see (Bass & Clements & Kazman, 1998) and (Shaw & Garlan (1996)). *Design patterns* by Gamma, Helm, Johnson, and Vlissides (1995) are used for finer-grained software design, while *idioms* by Coplien (1992) are low-level patterns related to specific programming languages.

Using patterns, we can hope to construct software in a systematic way, making use of a body of accumulated knowledge, instead of starting from scratch each time. The problem frames defined by Jackson (2001) cover a large number of software development problems, because they are quite general in nature. Their support is of great value in the area of software engineering. Jackson (2001) describes them as follows: „A problem frame is a kind of pattern. It defines an intuitively identifiable problem class in terms of its context and the characteristics of its domains, interfaces, and requirement." (p. 76). Jackson introduces five basic problem frames named *required behaviour*, *commanded behaviour*, *information display*, *simple workpieces*, and *transformation*.

Problem frames are described by frame diagrams, which basically consist of rectangles and links between these. As an example, Figure 2 shows the frame diagram of the problem frame *simple workpieces* in UML (Unified Modeling Language) notation (UML Revision Task Force 2007).We describe problem frames using class diagrams extended by stereotypes (see Figure 1). All elements of a problem frame diagram act as

Figure 1. Stereotypes

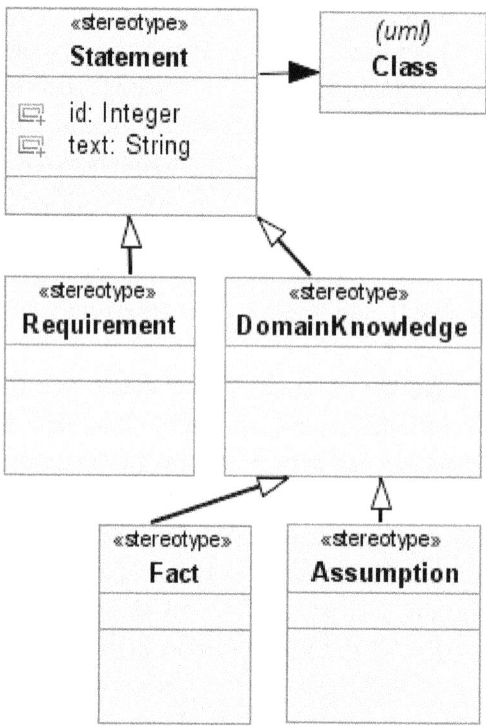

placeholders, which must be instantiated to represent concrete problems. Doing so, one obtains a problem description that belongs to a specific problem class.

The task is to construct a *machine* that improves the behavior of the environment it is integrated in. The class with the stereotype <<machine>> represents the software to be developed (possibly complemented by some hardware). The classes with domain stereotypes (e.g., <<CausalDomain>> or <<BiddableDomain>>) represent problem domains that already exist in the application environment. The domain stereotypes are defined in the UML profile depicted in Figure 3.

In frame diagrams, interfaces connect domains, and they contain shared phenomena. Shared phenomena may be events, operation calls, messages, and the like. They are observable by at least two domains, but controlled by only one domain. For example, if a user types a password to log into an IT-system, this is a phenomenon shared by the user and the IT-system. It is controlled by the user. For example, in Figure 2 the notation U!E3 means that the phenomena in the set E3 are controlled by the domain User. These interfaces are represented as associations, and the name of the associations contain the phenomena and the domain controlling the phenomena.

The associations can be replaced by interface classes, whose operations correspond to phenomena. The interface classes are either controlled or observed by the connected domains, represented by dependencies with the stereotypes <<controls>> or <<observes>>. Each interface can be controlled by at most one domain. A controlled interface must be observed by at least one domain, and an observed interface must be controlled by exactly one domain.

Problem frames substantially support developers in analyzing problems to be solved. They show what domains have to be considered, and what knowledge must be described and reasoned

Figure 2. Simple workpieces problem frame

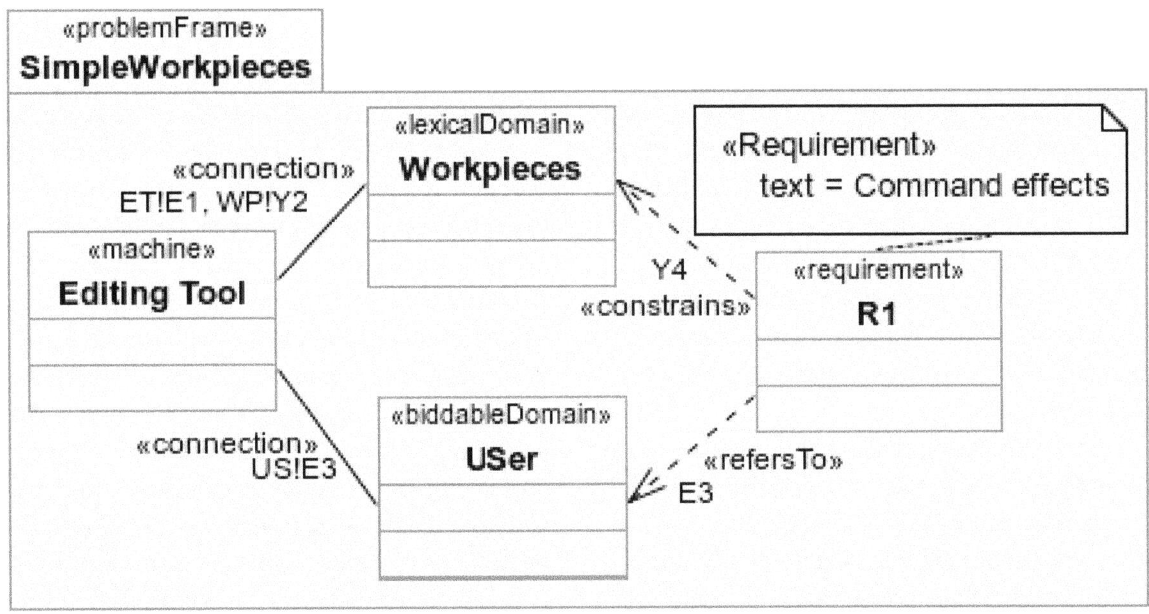

Figure 3. Domain hierarchy

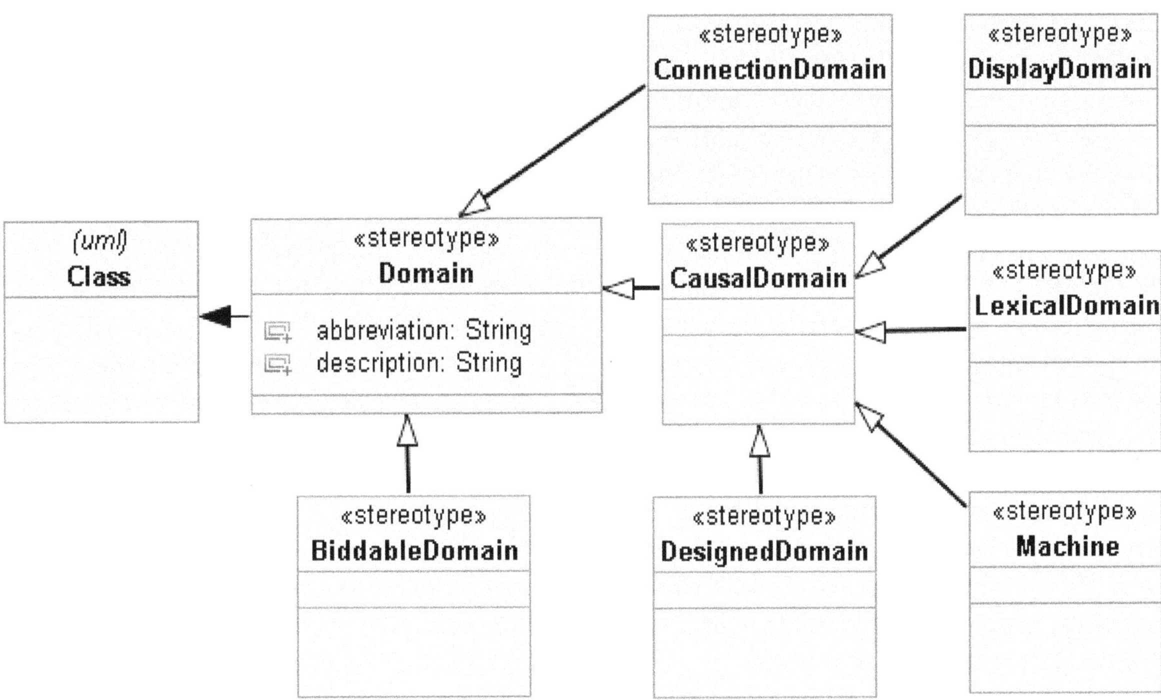

about when analyzing the problem in depth. Developers must elicit, examine, and describe the relevant properties of each domain. These descriptions form the domain knowledge. The domain knowledge consists of assumptions and facts. Assumptions are conditions that are needed, so that the requirements are accomplishable. Usually, they describe required user behavior. For example, it must be assumed that a user ensures not to be observed by a malicious user when entering a password. Facts describe fixed properties of the problem environment, regardless of how the machine is built.

Domain knowledge and requirements are special statements. A statement is modeled similarly to a SysML requirement [25] as a class with a stereotype. In this stereotype a unique identifier and the statement text are contained as stereotype attributes. Figure 1 shows the stereotype <<Statement>> that extends the metaclass Class of the UML metamodel.

When we state a requirement we want to change something in the world with the machine to be developed. Therefore, each requirement constrains at least one domain. This is expressed by a dependency from the requirement to a domain with the stereotype <<constrains>>. Such a constrained domain is the core of any problem description, because it has to be controlled according to the requirements. Hence, a constrained domain triggers the need for developing a new software (the machine), which provides the desired control.

A requirement may refer to several domains in the environment of the machine. This is expressed by a dependency from the requirement to a domain with the stereotype <<refersTo>>. The referred domains are also given in the requirements description. In Figure 2, the Workpieces domain is constrained, because the Editing Tool has the role to change it on behalf of user commands for achieving the commanded effects.

Furthermore, Jackson distinguishes causal domains that comply with some physical laws, lexical domains that are data representations, and biddable domains that are usually people. The domain types are modeled by the stereotypes <<BiddableDomain>> and <<CausalDomain>> being subclasses of the stereotype <<Domain>>. A lexical domain (<<LexicalDomain>>) is modeled as a special case of a causal domain. To describe the problem context, a connection domain between two other domains may be necessary. Connection domains establish a connection between other domains, usually by means of technical devices. They are modeled as classes with the stereotype <<ConnectionDomain>>. Connection domains are, e.g., video cameras, sensors, or networks. This kind of modeling allows one to add further domain types, such as <<DisplayDomain>> (introduced by Côté & Hatebur & Heisel & Schmidt & Wentzlaff (2008)) being a special case of a causal domain. Figure 3 depicts the domain stereotypes defined in our UML Profile.

Software development with problem frames proceeds as follows: first, the environment in which the machine will operate is represented by a context diagram. Like a frame diagram, a context diagram consists of domains and interfaces. However, a context diagram contains no requirements (see Figure 8 for an example). Then, the problem is decomposed into subproblems. If ever possible, the decomposition is done in such a way that the subproblems fit to given problem frames. To fit a subproblem to a problem frame, one must instantiate its frame diagram, i.e., provide instances for its domains, phenomena, and interfaces. The instantiated frame diagram is called a *problem diagram*. Furthermore, relevant domain knowledge about the domains contained in the frame diagram must be elicited, examined, and documented.

Successfully fitting a problem to a given problem frame means that the concrete problem indeed exhibits the properties that are characteristic for the problem class defined by the problem frame. A problem can only be fitted to a problem frame if the involved problem domains belong to the domain types specified in the frame diagram. For example, the "User" domain of Figure 2 can only be instantiated by persons, but not for example by some physical equipment like an elevator.

Since the requirements refer to the environment in which the machine must operate, the next step consists in deriving a specification for the machine (see Jackson & Zave (1995) for details). The specification describes the machine and is the starting point for its construction.

Related Work

In this section, we discuss our work in connection with a selection of other approaches to engineering security requirements and security architectures.

Security Requirements Engineering

To elicit security requirements, the threats to be considered must be analyzed. Lin & Nuseibeh & Ince & Jackson (2004) use the ideas underlying problem frames to define so-called anti-requirements and the corresponding abuse frames. The purpose of anti-requirements and abuse frames is to analyze security threats and derive security requirements. Hence, abuse frames and security problem frames complement each other.

Gürses & Jahnke & Obry & Onabajo & Santen & Price (2005) present the MSRA (formerly known as CREE) method for multilateral security requirements analysis. Their method concentrates on confidentiality requirements elicitation and employs use cases to represent functional requirements. The MSRA method can be useful to be applied in a phase of the security requirements engineering process that mainly precedes the application of security problem frames.

SREF - Security Requirements Engineering Framework by Haley & Laney & Moffett & Nuseibeh (2008) is a framework that defines the notion of security requirements, considers security requirements in an application context, and helps answering the question whether the system can satisfy the security requirements. Their definitions and ideas overlap our approach, but they do not use patterns and they do not give concrete guidance to identify and elicit dependent security requirements.

Moreover, there exist other promising approaches to security requirements engineering, such as the agent-oriented Secure Tropos methodology by Mouratidis & Giorgini (2007) and the goal-driven KAOS - Keep All Objectives Satisfied approach by van Lamsweerde (2004).

A comprehensive comparison of security requirements engineering approaches (including the one presented in this chapter) can be found in (Fabian, B. & Gürses, S. & Heisel, M. & Santen, T. & Schmidt, H., 2010).

Security Architectures

Architectural patterns – named architectural styles – are introduced by Bass & Clements & Kazman (1998) and Shaw & Garlan (1996). These patterns do not consider security requirements, and they are not integrated in a security engineering process.

Similarly, the AFrames by Rapanotti & Hall & Jackson & Nuseibeh (2004) do not consider security requirements. These patterns correspond to the popular architectural styles Pipe-and-Filter and Model-View-Controller (MVC), which the authors apply to Jackson's problem frames for transformation and control problems.

Hall & Jackson & Laney & Nuseibeh & Rapanotti (2002) extend machine domains of problem diagrams by architectural considerations. They do not deal with security requirements, and they do not derive software architectures explicitly. Instead, their extension of the problem frames approach allows one to gather architectural structures and services from the problem environment.

There exist several techniques to evaluate the security properties of architectures, e.g., formal proving of security properties (Moriconi & Qian & Riemenschneider & Gong, 1997), analysis by means of Petri nets and temporal logics (Deng & Wang & Tsai & Beznosov, 2003), or evaluation of used security patterns (Halkidis & Tsantalis & Chatzigeorgiou & Stephanides, 2008).

Choppy & Hatebur & Heisel (2005, 2006) present architectural patterns for Jackson's basic problem frames. The patterns constitute layered architectures described by UML composite structure diagrams (UML Revision Task Force 2007). The authors also describe how these patterns can be applied in a pattern-based software development process. Hatebur & Heisel (2005) describe similar patterns for security frames. These frames are comparable to security problem frames, which are enhancements of the original security frames presented in (Hatebur & Heisel, 2005). Compared to the architectural patterns presented in this chapter, the mentioned papers do not consider behavioral interface descriptions and operation semantics. Furthermore, only a vague general procedure to derive components for a specific frame diagram is given. Architectural patterns especially for the problem class of confidential data storage using encryption are not described. And as a last difference, a refinement to implementable architectures is not considered. Nevertheless, the papers by Choppy & Hatebur & Heisel (2005, 2006) and Hatebur & Heisel (2005) as well as the idea to systematically preserve quality requirements from early requirements engineering to software design presented by Schmidt & Wentzlaff (2006) constitute the basis for the enhancements presented in this chapter.

Patterns for Security Engineering

Patterns for security engineering are mainly used during the phase that follows the phases presented in this chapter, i.e., they are applied in the fine-grained design of secure software. Many authors advanced the field of security design patterns for years, e.g., (Schumacher & Fernandez-Buglioni & Hybertson & Buschmann & Sommerlad, 2005) and (Steel & Nagappan & Lai, 2005). A comprehensive overview and a comparison of the different existing security design patterns is given by Scandariato & Yskout & Heyman & Joosen (2008). Fernandez & Larrondo-Petrie & Sorgente & Vanhilst (2007) propose a methodology to systematically use security design patterns during software development. The authors use UML activity diagrams (UML Revision Task Force, 2007) to identify threats to the system, and they use security design patterns during fine-grained design to treat these threats. Mouratidis & Weiss & Giorgini (2006) present an approach to make use of security design patterns that connects these patterns to the results generated by the Secure Tropos methodology by Mouratidis & Giorgini (2007).

The relation between our concretized security problem frames, which still express problems, and security design patterns is much the same as the relation between problem frames and design patterns: the frames describe problems, whereas the design/security patterns describe solutions on a fairly detailed level of abstraction. Furthermore, since security design patterns are more detailed than our generic security components and architectures, they can be applied after a composed generic security architecture is developed.

Furthermore, the security standard Common Criteria (International Organization for Standardization (ISO) and International Electrotechnical Commission (IEC), 2009) and KAOS make use of patterns for security engineering. The Common Criteria introduces security functional requirements, which are textual patterns to express security mechanisms on an abstract level. They are comparable to concretized security problem frames. KAOS provides formal patterns to describe security goals specified using a linear real-time temporal logic.

OVERVIEW OF A SECURITY ENGINEERING PROCESS USING PATTERNS

We present in this chapter a *security engineering process using patterns* (SEPP). SEPP is an iterative and incremental process that consists of two phases. It follows a top-down and platform-independent approach until a generic security architecture is selected in phase two. Then, it takes a bottom-up and platform-specific approach to search for given security components that realize the generic security architecture.

Phase 1: Security Requirements Analysis: This phase starts with an initial set of security requirements, which is analyzed in detail by incrementally and iteratively processing six analysis steps. The result of this phase is a consolidated set of security requirements including solution approaches.

Step 1: Describe Environment: The environment in which the software development problem is located is described in detail, developing a context diagram and expressing domain knowledge about the domains that occur in the context diagram. The domain knowledge describes the environment of the machine. This concerns especially potential attackers. The distinction of facts and assumptions is particularly important for security requirements. A machine usually cannot satisfy security requirements unconditionally. It can provide security mechanisms that contribute to system security, but cannot enforce system security on their own.

Step 2: Select and Instantiate Security Problem Frames: The software development problem is decomposed into smaller subproblems. The security-relevant subproblems are analyzed and documented based on security problem frames (SPF).

Step 3: Select and Instantiate Concretized Security Problem Frames: Generic solution approaches are selected for the previously documented security problems. The generic solution mechanisms are documented based on concretized security problem frames (CSPF).

Step 4: Check for Related SPFs: Based on a pattern system of SPFs and CSPFs, SPFs that are commonly used in combination with an already used CSPF can be found.

Step 5: Analyze Dependencies: Based on the pattern system, dependent security problems are identified, which can be either assumed to be already solved or they have to be considered as new security requirements to be solved by generic security mechanisms.

Step 6: Analyze Possible Conflicts: The pattern system shows possible conflicts between security requirements and generic solution mechanisms. If a conflict is relevant, it must be resolved.

The process is described as an *agenda* (Heisel, 1998) that summarizes the input development artifacts, the output development artifacts, and validation conditions for each step. Furthermore, each step is complemented by a method describing how to develop the output artifacts from the input artifacts.

Phase 2: Security Architecture: Generic security architectures are selected and realized using existing security components from APIs or component frameworks. The result of this phase is a platform-specific and implementable security architecture that realizes the machines of the instantiated CSPFs.

Step 1: Create Generic Security Architecture using Generic Components: A generic security architecture that consists of a set of generic security components is selected for each CSPF instance, based on domain knowledge and constraints of the application domain.

Step 2: Refine Generic Security Architecture: The combined generic security architecture is refined to a platform-specific security architecture based on, e.g., existing security components. Glue code is written to connect the components according to the chosen generic security architecture.

USING PROBLEM FRAMES FOR SECURITY REQUIREMENTS ENGINEERING

We present security problem frames, concretized security problem frames, the pattern system, and the process steps for security requirements engineering. The described techniques are then applied to the secure text editor case study.

Security Problem Frames

Jackson (2001) states that his five basic problem frames are "... far from a complete or definitive set" (p. 76). To meet the special demands of software development problems occurring in the area of security engineering, we introduced *security problem frames* (Hatebur & Heisel & Schmidt, 2006). SPFs are a special kind of problem frames, which consider *security requirements.* Similarly to problem frames, SPFs are *patterns.* The SPFs we have developed strictly refer to the *problems* concerning security. They do not anticipate a solution. For example, we may require the confidential storage of data without being obliged to mention encryption, which is a means to achieve confidentiality. The benefit of considering security requirements without reference to potential solutions is the clear separation of problems from their solutions, which leads to a better understanding of the problems and enhances the re-usability of the problem descriptions, since they are completely independent of solution technologies.

Each SPF consists of a name, an intent, a frame diagram with a set of predefined interfaces, an informal description, a security requirement template, and an effect. The latter is a formal representation of the security requirement template. Effects are expressed as formulas in Z notation (Spivey, 1992), based on a metamodel for problem frames developed by Hatebur & Heisel & Schmidt (2008a). The metamodel formally specifies problem frames and problem frame constituents such as domains and interfaces by means of a UML class diagram (UML Revision Task Force 2007) and OCL (Object Constraint Language) constraints (UML Revision Task Force 2012). We use the instances of the classes of the metamodel as types for the formulas representing effects.

Confidentiality is the absence of unauthorized disclosure of information (Pfitzmann & Hansen, 2006). A typical confidentiality statement is to "Preserve confidentiality of domain constrained in the functional statement representing an asset for stakeholders and prevent disclosure by attackers."

A statement about confidentiality is modeled as a class with the stereotype <<Confidentiality>> in our profile. This stereotype is a specialization of the stereotype <<Dependability>> as shown in Figure 4. For confidentiality requirements, the constrained domain, the stakeholder, and the attacker have to be specified:

The *constrained domain* is a causal domain representing a stored, shown, or transmitted asset. This domain has to be constrained using a dependency with the stereotype <<constrains>>. Even if assets usually are lexical domains, we may model the asset with the stereotype <<CausalDomain>>, because in some cases the storage device, the display or the connection and not the asset itself is modeled. The confidentiality requirement complements a functional requirement. The

Figure 4. UML dependability problem frames profile – confidentiality

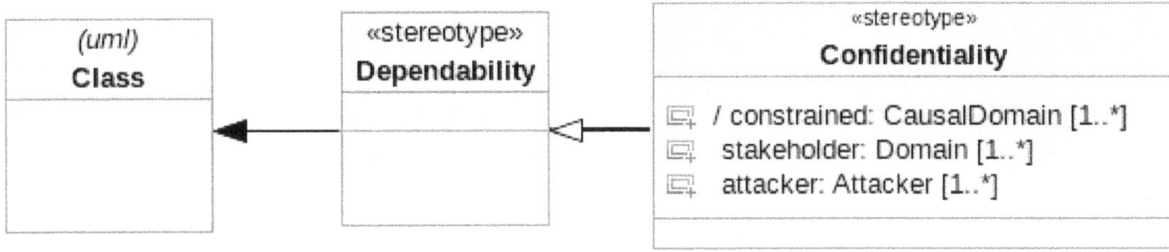

confidentiality requirement constrains the same domain as the complemented functional requirement. For example, if a display is constrained by the functional requirement, confidentiality is achieved by not showing the asset; if a storage or a connection are constrained by the functional requirement, confidentiality is achieved by not storing or sending the asset in readable form (e.g., by encryption). The attribute constrained is modeled as a derived attribute and it is derived from the dependencies with the stereotype constrains.

For confidentiality, we also need to consider the data's *stakeholder*. The stakeholder is referred to, because we want to allow the access only to stakeholders with legitimate interest (Gürses et al., 2005). The instances of stakeholder and attacker must be disjoint.

For confidentiality, we need to consider an *attacker*. This attacker must be described in detail. We suggest describing at least the objective of the attackers, their skills, equipment, knowledge, and the time the attackers have to prepare and to perform the attack (see Figure 5). A similar kind of description is suggested in the Common Methodology for Information Technology Security Evaluation (CEM) (International Organization for Standardization (ISO) and International Electrotechnical Commission (IEC), 2009b). As shown in Figure 5, the stereotype Attacker is a specialized BiddableDomain. The reference to an Attacker is necessary, because we can only ensure confidentiality with respect to an Attacker with given properties. The reference from the stereotype Confidentiality to the attacker is given by an attribute of the stereotype. The multiplicity of [1..*] ensures that at least one attacker is referenced.

As an example, we present in detail the *SPF confidential data storage,* which describes the problem class of confidentially storing data:

Name

SPF confidential data storage.

Figure 5. Attacker in UML dependability problem frames profile

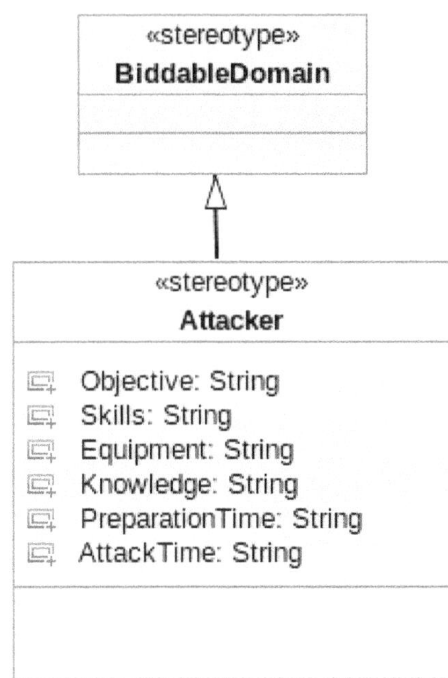

Intent

Conceal data (e.g., files, folders, metadata, etc.) stored on some storage device (e.g., hard disks, memory cards, smartcard, etc.).

Frame Diagram

Figure 6 shows the frame diagram of the SPF confidential data storage. Note that it also shows the CSPF if detailed phenomena are defined.

Predefined Interfaces

The interfaces of the SPF confidential data storage (e.g. E1, Y2 in Figure 6) are defined as follows and explained in the informal description:

- E1 = {OperationsOnStoredData_HS}
- Y2 = {ContentOfStoredData}
- E3 = {OperationsOnStoredData_MS}
- Y4 = {Obervations_SM}
- Y5 = {Obervations_CSM}
- Y6 = {ContentOfStoredData, Observations}
- E7 = {SpyOperations}
- Y8 = {OperationsOnStoredData}

Informal Description

The malicious environment is represented by the domains *Malicious subject, Spy machine, and Malicious subject display.* The domain *Stored data* represents the data to be protected against the malicious environment. The *Malicious subject* domain uses the interface MS!E7 (between *Malicious subject* and *Spy machine*) to spy (*SpyOperations*) on the *Stored data* domain. The interface SM!Y4 (between *Malicious subject* and *Spy machine*) is used by the *Malicious subject* domain to receive some observations (*Obervations_SM*), e.g., meta-information about *Stored data* such as its length or type, from the *Spy machine* domain. The *Spy machine* domain is connected directly to the *Stored data* domain via interfaces SD!Y4 and SM!E7 to represent that the *Malicious subject*

Figure 6. (C)SPF confidential data storage (using password-based encryption)

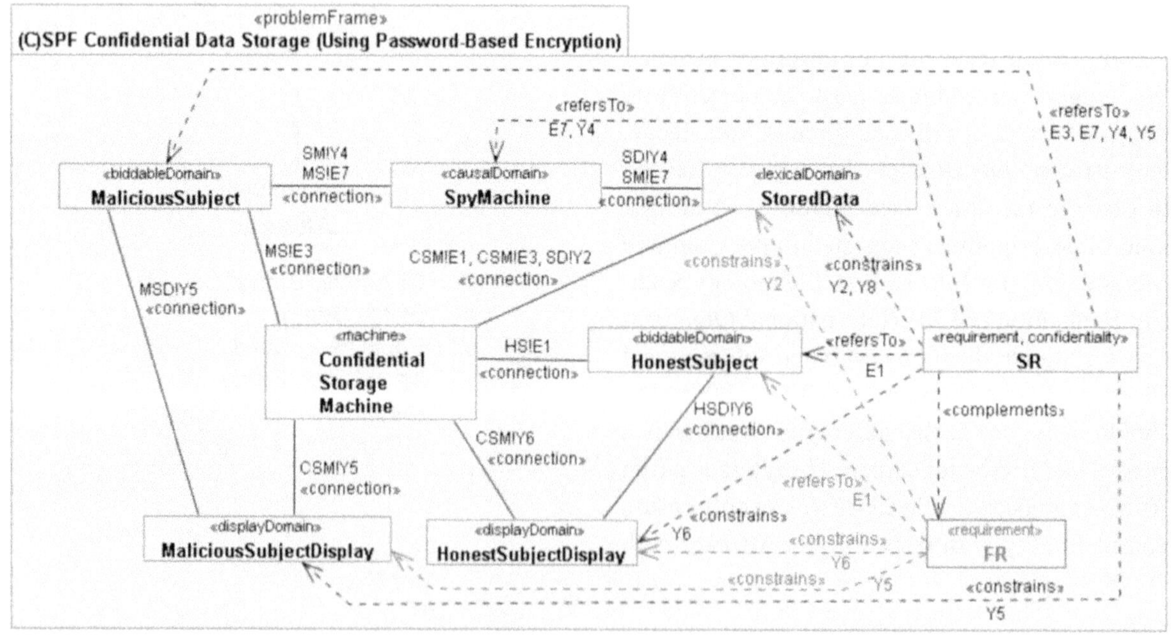

domain is not restricted to only access the *Stored data* domain through the machine domain *Confidential storage machine*. For example, access to the *Stored data* domain can also be possible via the operating system.

The *Malicious subject* domain can execute some operations (*OperationsOnStoredData_MS*) on the *Stored data* domain using the machine domain via interface MS!E3 (between *Malicious subject* and *Confidential storage machine*). Similarly, the honest environment represented by the domains *Honest subject* and *Honest subject display* can execute some operations (*OperationsOnStoredData_HS*) on the *Stored data* domain using the machine domain via interface HS!E1 (between *Honest subject* and *Confidential storage machine*).

According to the commands from the (malicious or honest) environment, the machine accesses the domain *Stored data* via interfaces CSM!E1 and CSM!E3. The content of *Stored data* (*ContentOfStoredData*) is received by the machine domain using the interface SD!Y2. Afterwards, the content of *Stored data* and some observations are shown to the domain *Honest subject* using the *Honest subject display* domain (via interface CSM!Y6 between *Confidential storage machine* and *Honest subject display* and via interface HSD!Y6 between *Honest subject display* and *Honest subject*).

The domain *Malicious subject* can possibly make some observations (*Obervations_CSM*), e.g., meta-information about *Stored data* such as its length or type, using the *Malicious subject display* (via interface CSM!Y5 between *Confidential storage machine* and *Malicious subject display* and via interface MSD!Y5 between *Malicious subject display* and *Malicious subject*).

Security Requirement Template

The security requirement (SR) complements the functional requirement (FR) about data storage and constrains the same domains. To specify security requirements, templates can be used. The security requirement template is described as follows: Preserve confidentiality of *Stored data* for honest environment (consisting of *Honest subject* and *Honest subject display*) and prevent disclosure to malicious environment (consisting of *Malicious subject, Spy machine,* and *Malicious subject display*).

Effect

An honest environment consists of an honest subject and an honest subject display, whereas a malicious environment consists of a malicious subject, a spy machine, and a malicious subject display. The set of all honest environments *HonestEnvironment* is a set of pairs consisting of elements of the domains *Honest subject* and *Honest subject display*, as indicated by the powerset operator ℙ. Similarly, the set of all malicious environments *MaliciousEnvironment* is a set of triples consisting of elements of the domains *Malicious subject, Spy machine,* and *Malicious subject display* (see Box 1).

Box 1.

HonestEnvironment: ℙ(*HonestSubject* × *HonestSubjectDisplay*)

MaliciousEnvironment: ℙ(*MaliciousSubject* × *SpyMachine* × *MaliciousSubjectDisplay*)

∀ *cosd*: *ContentOfStoredData*; *he*: *HonestEnvironment*; *me*: *MaliciousEnvironment* ·
$conf_P$(*cosd*, *he*, *me*)

∀ *sd*: *StoredData*; *he*: *HonestEnvironment*; *me*: *MaliciousEnvironment* ·
$conf_D$(*sd*, *he*, *me*)

Informally speaking, the effect expresses that the confidentiality of the phenomenon *ContentOfStoredData* (see interfaces SD!Y2 between *Confidential storage machine* and *Stored data*, HSD!Y6 between *Honest subject display* and *Honest subject*, and CSM!Y6 between *Confidential storage machine* and *Honest subject display*) and of the domain *StoredData* is preserved for the *HonestEnvironment* and that disclosure by the *MaliciousEnvironment* is prevented.

To formally express this effect, we specify two versions of a relation *conf*. The version of $conf_P$ deals with the confidentiality of a phenomenon, the version $conf_D$ deals with the confidentiality of a lexical domain. We define *conf* as a set of triples of a phenomenon (or a lexical domain), an honest environment, and a malicious environment. Each triple describes that the confidentiality of the phenomenon (or of the lexical domain) is preserved for the honest environment and that disclosure by the malicious environment is prevented.

The universally quantified formulas that express the effect make use of the relation *conf*: the first formula expresses that the confidentiality of each possible instance *cosd* of the phenomenon *ContentOfStoredData* is preserved for each possible instance *he* of the *HonestEnvironment* and that disclosure by each possible instance *me* of the *MaliciousEnvironment* is prevented. The second formula expresses a similar condition for each possible instance *sd* of the lexical domain *StoredData*.

Further SPFs exist, e.g., the *SPF distributing secrets* that represents the problem to deliver secrets such as passwords and encryption keys to the correct recipients, the *SPF authentication* that represents the problem to authenticate users or systems, the *SPF integrity-preserving data transmission* that represents the problem to transmit data over an insecure channel in an integrity-preserving way, and several others. Hatebur & Heisel & Schmidt (2008b) present an overview of the available SPFs.

Concretized Security Problem Frames

Solving a security problem is achieved by choosing generic security mechanisms (e.g., encryption to keep data confidential). The generic security mechanisms are represented by *concretized security problem frames* (CSPF).

Each CSPF consists of a name, an intent, a frame diagram with a set of predefined interfaces, an informal description, a concretized security requirement template, necessary conditions, and a list of related SPFs. The necessary conditions must be met by the environment for the generic security mechanism that the CSPF represents to be applicable. If the necessary conditions do not hold, the effect described in the according SPF cannot be established. The necessary conditions are expressed in Z notation. A *concretized security requirements template* refers to the effect described in the according SPF and the necessary conditions. More precisely, it is expressed as an implication: if the necessary conditions hold, then the effect is established. The effects of the SPFs and the necessary conditions of the CSPFs serve to represent dependencies between SPFs and CSPFs explicitly. The list of related SPFs serves to exhibit security problems that often occur when the security mechanism represented by the CSPF at hand is applied.

As an example, we present in detail the *CSPF confidential data storage using password-based encryption*. This CSPF represents the generic security mechanism password-based encryption according to the password-based cryptography standard PKCS #5 v2.0 (RSA Laboratories, 1999), which can be used to solve problems that fit to the SPF confidential data storage problem class. Another CSPF that solves such a security problem is the *CSPF confidential data storage using key-based encryption*.

Name

CSPF confidential data storage using password-based encryption.

Intent

Conceal data (e.g., files, folders, metadata, etc.) stored on some storage device (e.g., hard disks, memory cards, smartcard, etc.) using a password-based encryption mechanism.

Frame Diagram

The frame diagram of the CSPF confidential data storage using password-based encryption is similar to the frame diagram of the SPF confidential data storage shown in Figure 6. For this reason, we do not explicitly show it here. Instead, we briefly describe the differences between the two frame diagrams: The domain *Stored data* is replaced by the domain *Encrypted stored data.* Furthermore, the usage of a password-based encryption mechanism leads to modifications of the interfaces (see informal description for details).

Predefined Interfaces

The interfaces of the CSPF confidential data storage using password-based encryption are defined as follows:

- E1 = {OperationsOnEncryptedStoredData_HS, Password}
- Y2 = {EncryptedContentOfStoredData}
- E3 = {OperationsOnEncryptedStoredData$_{MS}$, WrongPassword}
- Y4 = {EncryptedContentOfStoredData, Obervation_SSM}
- Y5 = {Obervations_CSM}
- Y6 = {ContentOfStoredData, Observations}
- E7 = {SpyOperations}
- Y8 = {OperationsOnEncryptedStoredData}

Informal Description

Since the domain *Stored data* is replaced by the domain *Encrypted stored data*, the interface SD!Y4 is replaced by the interface ESD!Y4. Compared to the SPF confidential data storage, the phenomenon *ContentOfStoredData* of the interfaces SD!Y2 (between *Confidential storage machine* and *Encrypted stored data*), ESD!Y4 (between *Encrypted stored data* and *Spy machine*), and SM!Y4 (between *Spy machine* and *Malicious subject*) is replaced by the phenomenon *EncryptedContentOfStoredData.* Accordingly, the phenomenon *OperationsOnStoredData_HS* of the interfaces HS!E1 (between *Honest subject* and *Confidential storage machine*) and CSM!E1 (between *Confidential storage machine* and *Honest subject*) is replaced by the phenomenon *OperationsOnEncryptedStoredData_HS.* These interfaces additionally contain the phenomenon *Password* that represents a password used by the honest environment for encryption and decryption. Furthermore, the phenomenon *OperationsOnStoredData_MS* of the interfaces MS!E3 (between *Malicious subject* domain and *Confidential storage machine*) and CSM!E3 (between *Confidential storage machine* and *Malicious subject*) is replaced by the phenomenon *OperationsOnEncryptedStoredData_MS.* These interfaces additionally contain the phenomenon *WrongPassword* that represents a password used by the malicious environment for encryption and decryption.

Finally, the phenomenon *OperationsOnStoredData* of the phenomena set Y8 (at the requirement reference connected to *Encrypted stored data*) is replaced by the phenomenon *OperationsOnEncryptedStoredData.*

Concretized Security Requirement Template

The concretized security requirement template (CSR) is described as follows: If *Password* is unknown to malicious environment, then confidentiality of *Stored data* is preserved for honest environment and disclosure to malicious environment is prevented.

Necessary Conditions

Shown in Box 2. Passwords used by the honest environment must be different from the ones used by the malicious environment. Otherwise, a password-based encryption mechanism is not applicable. In practice, this necessary condition has to be assumed. That is, we have to assume that the malicious environment does not guess the right password. It cannot be fulfilled by a security mechanism. This necessary condition is formally expressed based on a set *RightPasswords* that represents the valid passwords chosen by the honest environment, and a set *WrongPasswords* that represents the invalid passwords chosen by the malicious environment. Thus, we formally express the necessary conditions by stating that these two sets are disjoint.

Furthermore, passwords used by the honest environment must not be known by the malicious environment. This necessary condition is formally described by the first universally quantified formula which expresses that the confidentiality of each possible instance *pwd* of the phenomenon *Password* is preserved for each possible instance *he* of the *HonestEnvironment* and that disclosure by each possible instance *me* of the *MaliciousEnvironment* is prevented.

Moreover, passwords used by the honest environment must be transmitted to the machine domain in an integrity-preserving way. To formally express this necessary condition, we specify a relation *int* as a set of triples of a phenomenon (or a lexical domain), an honest environment, and a malicious environment. Each triple describes that the integrity of the phenomenon (or of the lexical domain) is preserved for the honest environment and that modification by the malicious environment is prevented. Consequently, the second universally quantified formula expresses the mentioned necessary condition using the relation int_p: the integrity of each possible instance *pwd* of the phenomenon *Password* is preserved for each possible instance *he* of the *HonestEnvironment* and modification by each possible instance *me* of the *MaliciousEnvironment* is prevented.

Box 2.

```
HonestEnvironment: P(HonestSubject × HonestSubjectDisplay)
MaliciousEnvironment: P(MaliciousSubject × SpyMachine × MaliciousSubjectDis-
play)
RightPasswords: P Password
WrongPasswords: P Password
RightPasswords ∩ WrongPasswords = ∅
∀ pwd: Password; he: HonestEnvironment; me: MaliciousEnvironment ·
                         Conf_p(pwd, he, me)
      ∀ pwd: Password; he: HonestEnvironment; me: MaliciousEnvironment ·
                         Int_p(pwd, he, me)
```

Related SPFs

- SPF integrity-preserving data storage.

Further CSPFs exist, e.g., the *CSPF distributing secrets using negotiation* that represents the generic security mechanism to deliver secrets using a negotiation mechanism, the *CSPF authentication using passwords* that represents the generic security mechanism to authenticate users by passwords, the *CSPF integrity-preserving data transmission using symmetric encryption* that represents the generic security mechanism to transmit data over an insecure channel in an integrity-preserving way using a symmetric mechanism, and several others. Hatebur & Heisel & Schmidt (2008b) present an overview of the available CSPFs.

Pattern System

We developed a catalog of SPFs and CSPFs. Both kinds of frames are arranged in a *pattern system* (Hatebur & Heisel & Schmidt, 2007), which indicates dependent, conflicting, and related frames. The pattern system is represented as a table and is partly shown in Table 1. The complete pattern system can be found in (Hatebur & Heisel & Schmidt, 2008b).

The pattern system is constructed by analyzing the necessary conditions of the different CSPFs and the effects of the different SPFs. We check the necessary conditions of a CSPF and syntactically match them with the effects of all SPFs. For example, the necessary conditions of the CSPF confidential data storage using password-based encryption and the CSPF confidential data storage using key-based encryption require integrity-preserving and confidential paths for the passwords and the encryption keys, respectively. The effect of the SPF integrity-preserving data transmission provides an integrity-preserving path, and the effect of the SPF confidential data transmission provides a confidential path. For this reason, the mentioned CSPFs depend on the SPF integrity-preserving data transmission and the SPF confidential data transmission. Consequently, the rows that belong to these CSPFs in Table 1 are marked at the positions of the columns that belong to the SPF integrity-preserving data transmission and the SPF confidential data transmission with the letter "D". Furthermore, the necessary conditions of the CSPF confidential data storage using key-based encryption require that encryption keys must be distributed and that these encryption keys are confidentially stored. Thus, this CSPF depends on the SPF confidential data storage and on the SPF distributing secrets. The row that belongs to this CSPF in Table 1 is marked at the positions of the columns that belong to the SPF confidential data storage and SPF distributing secrets with the letter "D".

Table 1. (C)SPF pattern system

	...	SPF confidential data storage	SPF confidential data transmission	SPF integrity-preserving data storage	SPF integrity-preserving data transmission	SPF Distributing Secrets	...
...							
CSPF confidential data storage using password-based encryption		C	D	R	D		
CSPF confidential data storage using encryption key-based encryption		C, D	D	R	D	D	
...							

The fact that a CSPF concretizes an SPF is represented in Table 1 by the letter "C". For example, in the row of the CSPF confidential data storage using password-based encryption is a letter "C" at the position of the column of the SPF confidential data storage.

Furthermore, the "Related" sections of the CSPFs are represented in Table 1 by the letter "R". The rows of the CSPFs confidential data storage using password-based encryption and using encryption-key based encryption are marked with the letter "R" at the positions of the column of the SPF integrity-preserving data storage. The "Related" sections are helpful, since they indicate at an early stage of software development possible security problems that commonly occur in combination with the generic solution mechanism at hand and the security problem it solves.

Additionally, possible interactions between generic security mechanisms represented as CSPFs and security requirements represented as SPFs are indicated by the pattern system. We do not discuss this part of the pattern system here. Hatebur & Heisel & Schmidt (2008b) describe this part of the pattern system in detail based on a case study of a software to handle legal cases.

The (C)SPFs we developed form a self-contained pattern system: for any necessary condition of a CSPF covered by the pattern system, there exists at least one SPF contained in the pattern system that provides a matching effect. Therefore, the (C)SPFs contained in the pattern system can be used to *completely* analyze a given security problem, whose initial security requirement is covered by one of the frames.

The explicit knowledge of the dependencies between the SPFs and their concretized counterparts increases the value of our approach. The guidance provided by the dependency relations of the pattern system helps to structure the security requirements engineering process, to avoid confusion, and to analyze security problems and their solution approaches in depth. Hence, the security requirements engineering process will result in a consolidated set of security requirements and solution approaches, which is complete with respect to the initial set of security requirements. Compared to the initial set of security requirements, the final set of security requirements additionally contains dependent and related security requirements that may not have been known initially.

Security Requirements Analysis Method

Figure 7 shows an overview of SEPP's security requirements analysis lifecycle. The arrows are annotated with inputs or with conditions (in square brackets). The latter must be true to proceed with the step the arrow under consideration is pointing at. The arrow pointing at the "End" state is annotated with SEPP's overall output of the first phase. Each of the steps is described according to the following template:

- **Input:** Artifacts necessary to accomplish the step.
- **Output:** Artifacts that are created or modified during the execution of the step.
- **Validation Conditions:** Necessary semantic conditions that an output artifact must fulfill in order to serve its purpose properly (Heisel, 1998).

Before we explain SEPP step-by-step, we note that some activities to be executed for a comprehensive security requirements analysis are not explicitly mentioned in the descriptions of SEPP's security requirements analysis steps. These activities concern the maintenance of the following development artifacts:

- **Attacker Model:** Describes assumptions about potential attackers. For example, the Common Evaluation Methodology (CEM) (International Organization for

Figure 7. SEPP's security requirements analysis lifecycle

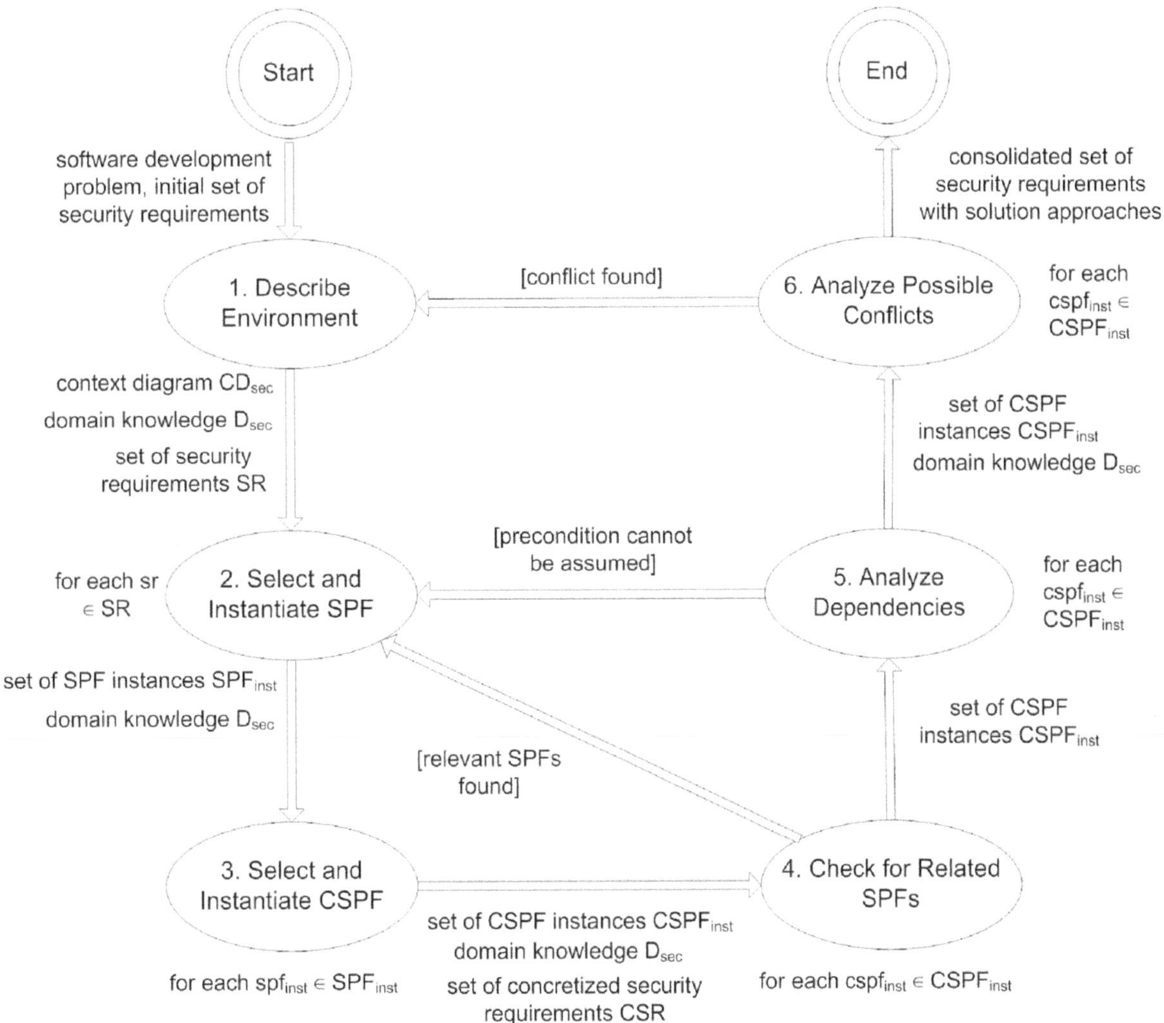

Standardization (ISO) and International Electrotechnical Commission (IEC), 2006) defines the attack potential of a potential attacker as a function of time, expertise, knowledge, and equipment. It also identifies two numeric values for each of these factors. The first value is for identifying and the second one is for exploiting a vulnerability. By assuming values for the input variables of the function, we can calculate the attack potential.

- **Results from Threat Analysis:** Represent potential threats. For example, attack trees by Schneier (1999) can be applied.
- **Results from Risk Analysis:** Represent the risk of an attack and the resulting loss. For example, a risk analysis method such as CORAS by Lund & Solhaug & Stølen (2011) can be applied.
- **Glossary:** Contains all used names, type information (if applicable), and references to artifacts that contain the names.

These artifacts are initially constructed in SEPP's first step. After every refinement step, i.e., the steps from requirements analysis and specification to architectural and fine-grained design and finally implementation, new threats can arise. For example, the decision for a particular security mechanism, the definition of a certain length for cryptographic keys, and the usage of a specific security component of a component framework enlarge the attack surface of the system to be developed. Hence, the attacker model as well as the results from threat and risk analysis must be kept up-to-date in all phases of the software development life-cycle. Note that SEPP covers the early phases of software development. Consequently, it does not cover the analysis of security problems arising during fine-grained design and implementation. Nevertheless, the threats identified in the late phases of software development can result in new security requirements to which SEPP can be applied.

Moreover, in each step results from functional requirements analysis may be used to support the construction of the security-relevant artifacts. For example, a context diagram that emerged from functional requirements analysis can be used as a starting point for the construction of a context diagram that contains security-relevant entities and relations.

SEPP starts given a textually described software development problem with an initial set of security requirements *SR*. For example, the initial security requirements can be obtained by using the methods proposed by Gürses & Jahnke & Obry & Onabajo & Santen & Price (2005) and by Fernandez & Red & Forneron & Uribe & Rodriguez G. (2007).

Step 1: Describe Environment

All security-relevant entities contained in the environment and relations between them are modeled. Given a context diagram that emerged from functional requirements analysis, it is extended by security-relevant entities and relations. The result is a context diagram CD_{sec}. An example is shown in Figure 8. The area named "Malicious environment" represents the extension by security-relevant entities and relations.

Domain knowledge, i.e., facts and assumptions, about the environment in which the software development problem is located is collected and documented. Especially, domain knowledge about the malicious environment is considered. An example for domain knowledge about a malicious environment is the assumed strength of a potential attacker. The result is a set of security-relevant domain knowledge D_{sec} that consists of a set of security-relevant facts F_{sec} and a set of security-relevant assumptions A_{sec}. Collecting the domain knowledge D_{sec} involves the construction of an attacker model, a threat model, and the application of a risk analysis method.

Input

- Textual description of software development problem.
- Set of initial security requirements *SR*.

Output

- Context diagram CD_{sec} including security-relevant domains and phenomena.
- Security-relevant domain knowledge $D_{sec} \equiv F_{sec} \wedge A_{sec}$.
- Attacker model.
- Results from threat analysis.
- Results from risk analysis.

Validation Conditions

- Domains and phenomena of context diagram CD_{sec} must be consistent with *SR* and D_{sec}.
- Context diagram CD_{sec} must contain malicious environment.

Figure 8. Context diagram "Secure Text Editor"

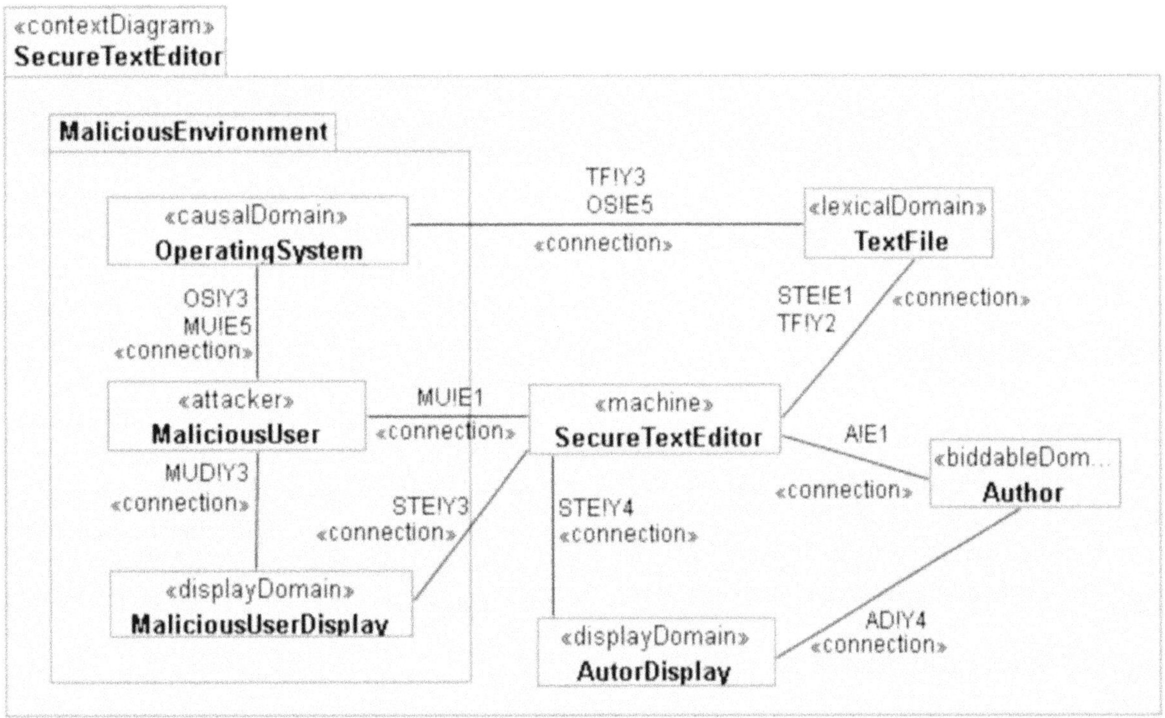

Step 2: Select and Instantiate SPF

This step must be executed for each security requirement $sr \in SR$. To determine an SPF that is appropriate for the given environment and the security requirement $sr \in SR$, the latter is compared with the informal descriptions of the security requirement templates of the SPFs contained in our pattern system. The result is a set of SPFs candidates from which the SPF to be instantiated is selected by considering the security-relevant environment represented by CD_{sec} and the security-relevant domain knowledge D_{sec}.

More precisely, the context diagram CD_{sec} represents the environment of a complex problem, which is decomposed into subproblems that fit to SPFs using decomposition operators such as "leave out domain" or "combine several domains into one domain". Thus, an SPF candidate that fits to the decomposed environment of the corresponding subproblem is selected.

Afterwards, the SPF is instantiated by assigning concrete values to the domains, phenomena, interfaces, effect, and the security requirement template. The instantiation of an SPF may result in additional security-relevant domain knowledge, which is added to the set of security-relevant domain knowledge D_{sec}. For example, if in the course of the problem decomposition a domain is split into several domains, domain knowledge about these new domains is collected and documented.

After this step is executed for each security requirement $sr \in SR$, the result of this step is a set of security problems SPF_{inst} represented as instantiated SPFs. Furthermore, the set of security-relevant domain knowledge D_{sec} may be updated.

Input

- All results of Step 1.

Output

- Set of SPF instance SPF_{inst}.
- Security-relevant domain knowledge added to D_{sec}.

Validation Conditions

- Each security requirement $sr \in SR$ is covered by some SPF instance $spf_{inst} \in SPF_{inst}$.
- Each SPF instance $spf_{inst} \in SPF_{inst}$ can be derived from the context diagram CD_{sec} by means of certain decomposition operators.

Step 3: Select and Instantiate CSPF

This step must be executed for each SPF instance $spf_{inst} \in SPF_{inst}$. To solve a security problem characterized by an instance of an SPF, a generic security mechanism based on the CSPFs linked to the applied SPF is chosen. The pattern system indicates the CSPFs linked to an SPF by positions marked with "C" in the SPF's column. From the different generic security mechanisms that are represented by CSPFs, an appropriate CSPF is selected. To decide if a CSPF is appropriate, the security-relevant environment represented by CD_{sec} and the security-relevant domain knowledge D_{sec} is considered. For example, if users should select secrets for an encryption mechanism, a password-based encryption mechanism should take precedence over an encryption-key based mechanism. Furthermore, the selection can be accomplished according to other quality requirements such as usability or performance requirements or according to the presumed development costs of the realizations of the generic security mechanisms represented by the different CSPFs.

After a CSPF is selected, it is instantiated by assigning concrete values to the domains, phenomena, interfaces, necessary conditions, and the concretized security requirement template. Normally, domains and phenomena contained in the SPF instance are re-used for the instantiation of the corresponding CSPF. The instantiation of a CSPF may result in additional security-relevant domain knowledge, which must be added to the set of security-relevant domain knowledge D_{sec}, e.g., domain knowledge about passwords or encryption keys.

After this step is executed for each SPF instance $spf_{inst} \in SPF_{inst}$, the result is a set of CSPF instances $CSPF_{inst}$ and a corresponding set of concretized security requirements *CSR*. Furthermore, the security-relevant domain knowledge D_{sec} may be updated.

Input

- All results of Step 2.

Output

- Set of CSPF instances $CSPF_{inst}$.
- Set of concretized security requirements *CSR*.
- Security-relevant domain knowledge added to D_{sec}.

Validation Conditions

- For each security requirement $sr \in SR$ there exists a concretized security requirement $csr \in CSR$, and vice versa.
- Each concretized security requirement $csr \in CSR$ is covered by some CSPF instance $cspf_{inst} \in CSPF_{inst}$.
- Domains and phenomena of each CSPF instance $cspf_{inst} \in CSPF_{inst}$ are re-used from the corresponding SPF instance.

Step 4: Check for Related SPFs

This step must be executed for each CSPF instance $cspf_{inst} \in CSPF_{inst}$. SPFs that are commonly used in combination with the described CSPF are indicated in the pattern system by positions marked with "R" in the CSPF's row. This information helps to find missing security requirements right in the beginning of the security requirements engineering process.

After this step is executed for each CSPF instance $cspf_{inst} \in CSPF_{inst}$, the result of this step is a set of related security requirements and a corresponding set of SPFs. The related security requirements are added to the set of security requirements *SR* and the SPFs are instantiated by returning to step 2.

Input

- All results of Step 3.

Output

- Related security requirements added to the set of security requirements *SR,*
- Set of SPFs that correspond to the related security requirements,

Validation Conditions

- The new security requirements are relevant for the given software development problem.

Step 5: Analyze Dependencies

This step must be executed for each CSPF instance $cspf_{inst} \in CSPF_{inst}$. The necessary conditions of a CSPF instance are inspected to discover dependent security problems. Two alternatives are possible to guarantee that these necessary conditions hold: either, they can be *assumed* to hold, or they have to be established by instantiating a further SPF, whose effect matches the necessary conditions to be established. Such an SPF can easily be determined using the pattern system: the corresponding positions in the row of the instantiated CSPF are marked with "D".

Only in the case that the necessary conditions *cannot* be assumed to hold, one must instantiate further appropriate SPFs. Then, steps 2 - 4 must be applied to the dependent SPFs.

The security-relevant domain knowledge D_{sec} helps to decide whether the necessary conditions can be assumed to hold or not. For example, assumptions on the strength of passwords chosen by honest users can lead to the assumption that malicious users cannot guess the honest user passwords. In contrast, if encryption keys must be delivered to the correct recipients over an insecure network, additional security mechanisms to authenticate the recipients and to transmit the encryption keys in a confidential and integrity-preserving way must be taken into consideration.

This step is executed for each CSPF instance $cspf_{inst} \in CSPF_{inst}$ until all necessary conditions of all CSPF instances can be proved or assumed to hold. The result of this step is a set of dependent security requirements and a corresponding set of SPFs.

Input

- All results of Step 4.

Output

- Dependent security requirements added to the set of security requirements *SR.*
- Set of SPFs that correspond to the dependent security requirements.

Validation Conditions

- Each necessary condition of each $cspf_{inst} \in CSPF_{inst}$ is either assumed to hold or treated by some SPF.
- If a necessary condition is assumed, a justification is stated.

Step 6: Analyze Possible Conflicts

This step must be executed for each CSPF instance $cspf_{inst} \in CSPF_{inst}$. The pattern system indicates possible conflicts between the SPF instances and the CSPF instances by rows marked with "I" (for "interaction"). If a possible conflict is discovered, it must be decided if the conflict is relevant for the application domain using D_{sec}. In the case that it is relevant, the conflict must be resolved by modifying or prioritizing the requirements. An example of relaxing security requirements for the benefit of usability requirements can be found in Schmidt & Wentzlaff (2006). This step can result in modified sets of security requirements and concretized security requirements. In such a case, all previous steps must be re-applied to the modified security requirements.

This step is executed for each CSPF instance $cspf_{inst} \in CSPF_{inst}$ until all possible conflicts are analyzed and all relevant conflicts are resolved. Finally, we obtain a set of CSPF instances $CSPF_{inst}$ that can solve the security problems represented by the SPF instances as well as modified sets of security requirements *SR* and concretized security requirements *CSR* with all conflicts resolved.

Input

- All results of Step 5.

Output

- Consolidated set of security requirements *SR*.
- Consolidated set of concretized security requirements *CSR*.
- Security-relevant domain knowledge added to D_{sec}.

Validation Conditions

- The set of security requirements *SR* contains no more conflicts and is complete with respect to the initial set of security requirements.
- The set of concretized security requirements *CSR* contains no more conflicts and is complete with respect to the initial set of security requirements.

All in all, the security requirements analysis method results in a consolidated set of security problems and solution approaches that additionally cover all dependent and related security problems and corresponding solution approaches, some of which may not have been known initially.

Basic Constraints for All Steps

For all steps, our UML profile can be used for modelling. When working with the profile, the developer has to follow a set of rules, e.g.:

- Not all combinations of stereotypes are permitted. For example, the stereotypes <<CausalDomain>> (or subtypes) and <<BiddableDomain>> are not allowed to be applied together on one class. All diagram types rely on the same basic notational elements. However, not all existing notational elements are allowed to be used in the different diagram types. In a context diagram, allowed elements are classes with the stereotype <<domain>> or a subtype of <<domain>>, <<interfaces>>, dependencies with the stereotypes <<observes>>, <<controls>>, associations with the stereotype <<connection>> or a subtype of <<connection>>, and comments.

- In one project we only have one context diagram.
- If we do not have to build anything, the context need not be described. Therefore, the context diagram has at least one machine domain.
- Since connection domains are used for domains forwarding information, connection domains (in the context diagram) have at least one observed and one controlled interface.
- If a machine should change something in its environment (and otherwise it would not be built), a machine has to control at least one interface.
- Since problem diagrams and the corresponding patterns are used to describe requirements, packages with the stereotype ProblemDiagram and ProblemFrame must contain at least one requirement.
- Requirements should be stated in terms of the environment, and therefore they should not constrain the machine itself.
- Since a machine cannot force a user to do something, a requirement does not constrain a biddable domain.
- As for the context diagram, connection domains in a problem diagram or problem frame have at least one observed and one controlled interface.
- Names of domains, interfaces and statements must be unique. Otherwise, referencing these model elements is quite difficult and it is hard to distinguish if the repeated model elements are the same or different.
- The abbreviation of the stereotype <<Domain>> must be set and identical for all domain stereotypes applied to one class. This is necessary for defining which domain controls a phenomenon annotated at a connector.
- A controlled interface must be observed by at least one domain. If an interface is controlled and not observed, it is useless within a model.
- An observed interface must be controlled by exactly one domain. If several domains control the same interface, priorities need to be defined. Priorities can only be defined by a domain which takes the role of a voter, not by an interface itself. An interface not controlled by a domain is useless within a model.

The first constraint can be checked with the OCL expression shown in Listing 1.

The OCL expression in Listing 1 checks that no class has the stereotypes <<CausalDomain>> (or subtypes) and <<BiddableDomain>> (or subtypes) applied together: in line 1 and 2, we select the owned elements of the package with the stereotype <<ContextDiagram>>. Line 3 selects the elements being classes. In line 4, all the classes of the model are selected that satisfy the condition stated within the select-statement. In line 5, we gather the set of stereotypes for each class cl. Only those classes should be selected that have the stereotype <<BiddableDomain>> or a direct subtype of <<BiddableDomain>> and the stereotype <<CausalDomain>> or a subtype of <<CausalDomain>>. Since it is difficult to iterate through the different inheritance hierarchies of stereotypes with EMF, we explicitly move to each level of inheritance (keyword general). As we currently have three hierarchy levels, we limit our constraints to this number (lines 5-10). Note that if new domain types are to be introduced, this limit may need to be adapted. In line 11, we finally check that no class with both stereotypes exist, by comparing the size of the set to 0.

Listing 1. Constraint "Not all combinations of stereotypes are permitted"

```
Package.allInstances() ->select(p |  p.oclAsType(Package).getAppliedStereo-
types() .name
        ->includes('ContextDiagram')).clientDependency.target
->select(oclIsTypeOf(Class)).oclAsType(Class)
->select(oe | (
  oe.oclAsType(Class).getAppliedStereotypes().name ->includes('BiddableDomain')
or
  oe.oclAsType(Class).getAppliedStereotypes().general.name
->includes('BiddableDomain')
) and (
  oe.oclAsType(Class).getAppliedStereotypes().name ->includes('CausalDomain')
or
  oe.oclAsType(Class).getAppliedStereotypes().general.name
->includes('CausalDomain') or
  oe.oclAsType(Class).getAppliedStereotypes().general.general.name
->includes('CausalDomain')
)) ->size()=0
```

Constraints for Modeling Security Aspects

When working with the profile, the developer has to follow a set of rules, e.g. for confidentiality:

- A security requirement always complements (stereotype <<complements>>) a functional requirement.
- Each confidentiality statement constrains a causal domain.
- The attribute 'constrained' contains the constrained domains.
- A confidentiality stereotype refers to at least one attacker.
- A confidentiality stereotype refers to at least one biddable domain (stakeholder - not the attacker).

The second constraint can be checked with the OCL expression shown in Listing 2.

The OCL expression in Listing 2 checks that each confidentiality statement constrains a causal domain. All classes in the model with the stereotypes <<Confidentiality>> and also <<Statement>> or <<Requirement>> are selected, and for all confidentiality statements the following condition is checked (lines 1-3). The dependencies starting at this class (clientDependency) with the stereotype <<constrains>> (line 4) are considered. The targets of the 'constrains' are checked to have the stereotype <<CausalDomain>> or a subtype, and the boolean results are collected (lines 5-8). It is checked by counting the positive results if there is at least one causal domain (or a subtype) constrained (line 9).

Tool Support

To support the application of SEPP, we created the tool UML4PF. Basis is the Eclipse platform[1] together with its plug-ins EMF[2] and OCL[3]. Our

Listing 2. Constraint "Each confidentiality statement constrains a causal domain"

```
Class.allInstances()->select(getAppliedStereotypes().name ->
includes('Confidentiality'))
->select(getAppliedStereotypes().name -> includes('Statement') or
  getAppliedStereotypes().name -> includes('Requirement'))->forAll(
  clientDependency -> select(r | r.oclAsType(Dependency).getAppliedStereo-
types().name -> includes('constrains'))
.oclAsType(Dependency).target.getAppliedStereotypes() -> collect(
  name->includes('CausalDomain') or
  general.name->includes('CausalDomain') or
  general.general.name->includes('CausalDomain')
)->count(true)>=1)
```

UML profile is conceived as an eclipse plug-in, extending the EMF meta-model. The Eclipse profiles and the OCL constraints are stored in XMI-format. With these constraints, we check the validity and consistency of the current model. The functionality of our tool UML4PF comprises the following:

- It checks if the model is valid and consistent by using our OCL constraints.
- It returns the location of invalid parts of the model.
- It automatically generates model elements, e.g., it generates observed and controlled interfaces from association names.

The graphical representation of the different diagram types can be manipulated by using any EMF-based editor. We selected Papyrus[4] as it is available as an Eclipse plug-in, open-source, and EMF-based.

Case Study: Secure Text Editor

We now apply the techniques introduced in the previous sections to the following software development problem:

A secure text editor should be developed. The text editor should enable a user to create, edit, open, and save text files. The text files should be stored confidentially.

The informal security requirement (*SR*) can be described as follows:

Preserve confidentiality of Text file except for its file length for honest environment and prevent disclosure to malicious environment.

Note: We decide to focus on confidentially storing text files. The given software development problem can also be interpreted such that the security requirement also covers confidential editing operations, e.g., confidential clipboard copies. For reasons of simplification, this is not covered in the security requirements analysis. For the same reason, the create and edit functionality of the secure text editor is not covered in our case study. Practically, it is very difficult to develop 100% confidential systems. Hence, as an example, we discuss a security requirement that allows the secure text editor to leak the file length.

According to the first step of our security requirements analysis method, the context diagram shown in Figure 8 is developed. Note: we do not show the interfaces of the context diagram explicitly, since they are similar to the interfaces of the instantiated SPF confidential data storage shown in Figure 9. Furthermore, the attacker model and the results of the threat and risk analysis are not shown explicitly. For example, the attacker model comprises assumptions on the strength and the abilities of potential attackers, and an analyzed threat covers the usage of the domain *Operating system* to access the domain *Text file.*

In the second step, we instantiate the SPF confidential data storage as shown in Figure 9 to capture the *SR*. The interfaces of the SPF confidential data storage are instantiated as follows:

- E1 = {Save, Open}
- Y2 = {TextFile}
- Y3 = {LengthOfTextFile}
- Y4 = {TextFile, LengthOfTextFile}
- E5 = {Spy}
- Y6 = {Saving, Opening}

According to the commands from the (malicious and honest) environment, the machine accesses the domain *Textfile*, and opens a file or saves one. An opened file is shown to the domain *Author* using the *Author display* domain. We assume that the domain *Malicious user* can observe the length of the opened file via the domains *Malicious user display* and *Operating system.*

In the third step, we decide to use a password-based encryption mechanism to conceal text files. For such an encryption mechanism, passwords are necessary. The passwords should be generated and memorized by the users. Since the users must memorize the passwords, a symmetric encryption mechanism is to be preferred over an asymmetric one. This is a trade-off between the usability and the security of the password-based encryption mechanism: asymmetric encryption keys must be much larger compared to symmetric keys to

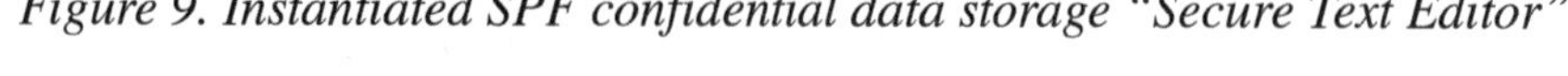
Figure 9. Instantiated SPF confidential data storage "Secure Text Editor"

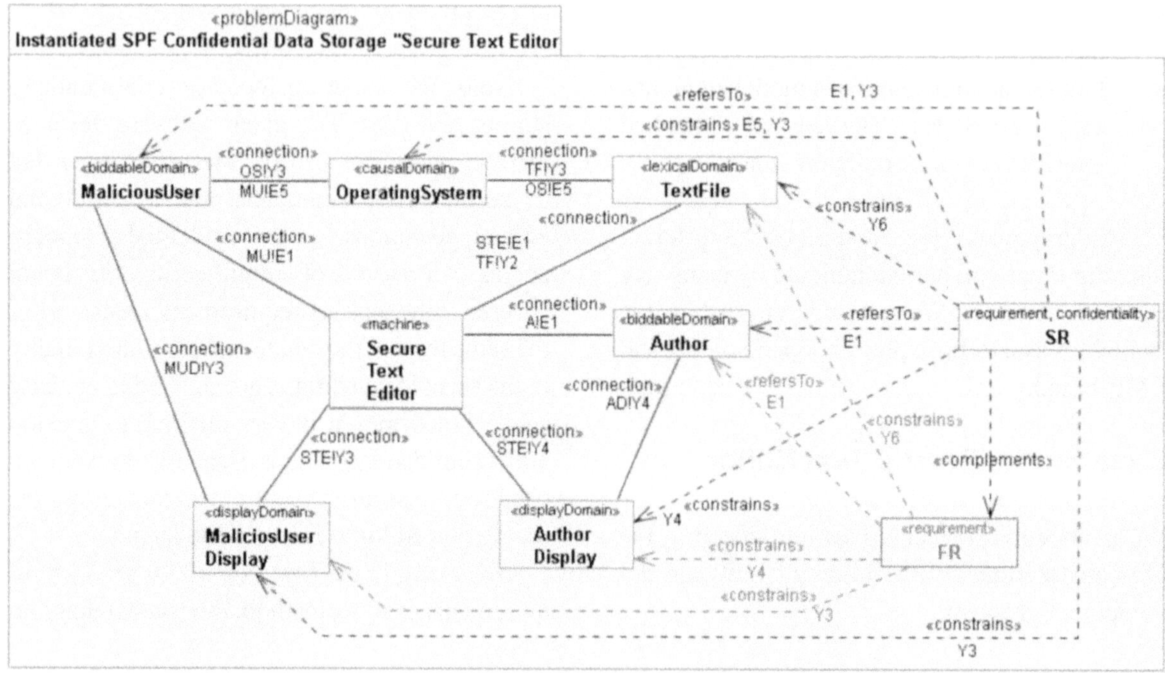

achieve a similar level of encryption strength. Because of the encryption key lengths, it is more difficult for users to memorize asymmetric keys than symmetric ones.

Using passwords for encryption leads to the assumptions that the users do not reveal their passwords and that they choose passwords that guarantee a certain level of security.

Note that the latter assumption can be transformed into a requirement: the users should not be able choose trivial passwords. Such a requirement can be realized by password checking mechanisms to prevent users from choosing trivial passwords, e.g., words from dictionaries, proper names, and so on.

According to the pattern system, we decide to select the CSPF confidential data storage using password-based encryption. The structure of the CSPF instance shown in Figure 10 is similar to the instantiated SPF confidential data storage shown in Figure 9 with the difference that the domain *Text file* is replaced by the domain *Encrypted text file*. The differences between the SPF instance and the CSPF instance are located in the interfaces. The interfaces of the CSPF instance are instantiated as follows:

- E1 = {Save, Open, Password}
- Y2 = {EncryptedContentOfTextFile}
- E3 = {Save, Open, WrongPassword}
- Y4 = {EncryptedContentOfTextFile, LengthOfTextFile}
- Y5 = {WrongContentOfTextFile, LengthOfTextFile}
- Y6 = {TextFile, LengthOfTextFile}
- E7 = {Spy, WrongPassword}
- E8 = {Spy}
- Y9 = {Saving, Opening}

Since the text files are encrypted by the encryption mechanism, the interfaces TF!Y2 (between *Confidential storage machine* and *Text file*) and

Figure 10. Instantiated CSPF confidential data storage using password-based encryption "Secure Text Editor"

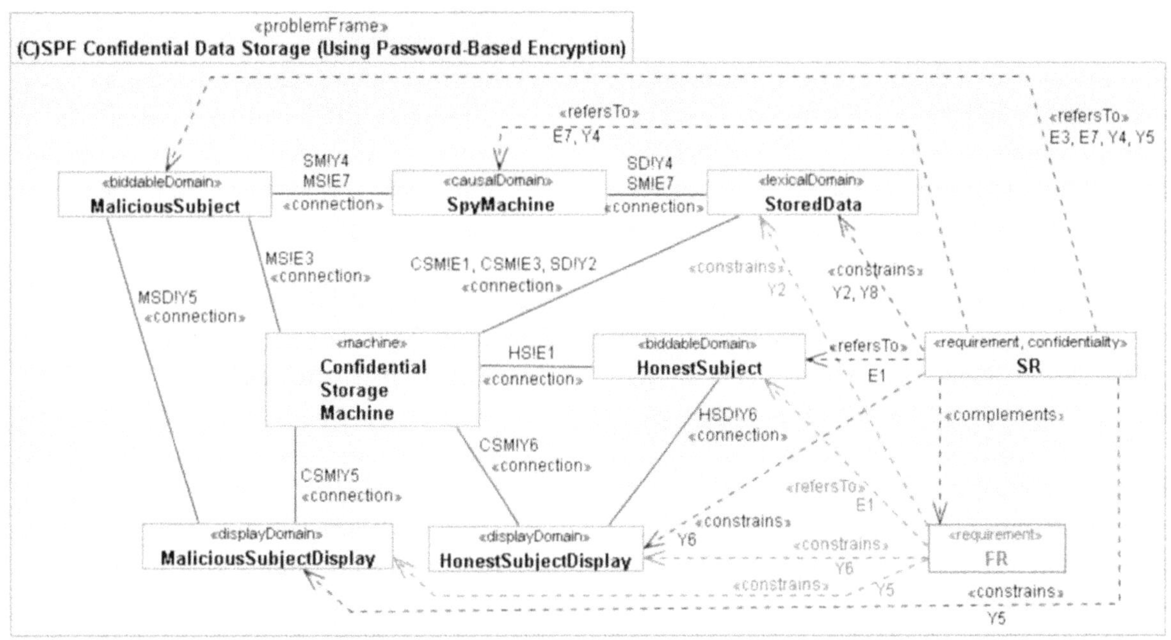

TF!Y4 (between *Text file* and *Operating system*) contain the phenomenon *EncryptedContentOfTextFile*. The authors can enter passwords for encrypting and decrypting text files. Therefore, the interfaces A!E1 (between *Author* and *Confidential storage machine*) and STE!E1 (between *Confidential storage machine* and *Textfile*) contain the phenomenon *Password*. The malicious users can also enter passwords under the assumption that they cannot guess passwords of authors. Therefore, the interfaces MU!E3 (between *Malicious user* and *Confidential storage machine*), STE!E3 (between *Confidential storage machine* and the *Text file*), and MU!E7 (between *Malicious user* and *Operating system*) contain the phenomenon *WrongPassword*. The concretized security requirement (*CSR*) derived from the *SR* is phrased as follows:

If *Password* is unknown to malicious environment, then confidentiality of *Textfile* except for its file length for honest environment is preserved and disclosure to malicious environment is prevented.

In step four, the pattern system is inspected to check for related security problems. According to the pattern system, the SPF integrity-preserving data storage is related to the CSPF confidential data storage using password-based encryption. This SPF is indeed relevant in the given application context: the integrity of text files stored by authors should be preserved and modification by malicious environment should be prevented. However, for reasons of simplification, this related SPF is not considered here.

In step five, the instantiated necessary conditions (not shown, since they are similar to the necessary conditions of the CSPF except for the types) of the instantiated CSPF are inspected. The first necessary condition is assumed to hold, because we assume that a malicious user cannot guess passwords of an author. The second necessary condition is assumed to hold, because we assume that an author does not reveal passwords to a malicious user. The third necessary condition is assumed to hold, because we assume that there is no malicious user able to intercept and modify passwords of an author.

In step six, our security requirements engineering method proceeds with an analysis of potential conflicts between security requirements. Since only one SPF (and one CSPF) is instantiated, it is not necessary to analyze any potential conflicts between security requirements.

No further SPFs must be instantiated, because each necessary condition is covered by an assumption.

DEVELOPMENT OF A SECURITY ARCHITECTURE

In the following, we move on to the design phase of software development, i.e., the two-step construction of a software architecture:

1. Development of a generic architecture using generic components to construct a *platform-independent* secure software architecture that realizes the specified security requirements and
2. Construction of a *platform-specific* secure software architecture based on the previously developed platform-independent secure software architecture and a component framework or an application programming interface (API).

Step 1: Create Generic Security Architecture using Generic Components

Software components are reusable software parts. We represent software components by means of UML composite structure diagrams (UML Revision Task Force 2007) and *interface specifications*. The latter consist of several parts: structural and syntactic descriptions are expressed as UML class diagrams (interface classes). Semantic descriptions of the operations provided and used by the components' interfaces are expressed as OCL pre- and postconditions. Behavioral descriptions are expressed as UML sequence diagrams.

The generic security components discussed in this section constitute special software components that realize concretized security requirement templates. We call them "generic", because they are a kind of conceptual pattern for software components. They are platform-independent. An example for a generic security component is an encryption component defined referring neither to a specific encryption mechanism such as AES or DES nor to specific encryption keys, such as encryption keys with a certain length.

We use generic security components to structure the machine domain of a CSPF. They describe the machine's interfaces to its environment and the machine-internal interfaces of its components. Each CSPF is linked to a set of generic security components.

A machine domain of a CSPF can be structured by means of generic security components according to the following principles:

- Each interface of the machine with the environment must coincide with an interface of some component.
- Components of the same purpose can be combined, e.g., several storage management components can be combined to one such component.
- For each interface between the machine and a biddable or display domain a user interface component must be introduced. Interfaces to another display or machine domain can result in an additional user interface component (especially if such an interface is security-critical, e.g., an interface to enter a password).
- For each interface from the machine to a lexical domain, a storage management component must be introduced. Symbolic phenomena correspond to return values of operations or to getter/setter operations.
- For each interface of the machine domain with a causal domain, a driver component must be introduced. Causal phenomena correspond to operations provided by driver components.
- For password or encryption key handling, key management components or key negotiation components must be introduced.
- For encryption key generation, random number generator and encryption key generator components must be introduced.
- For symmetric / asymmetric encryption / decryption, corresponding encryptor / decryptor components must be introduced.
- For integrity mechanisms, hash and MAC calculation components must be introduced.

Following the described principles, we developed a catalog of generic security components for each available CSPF. These components can be combined to obtain a set of generic security architectures that realize the concretized security requirement template of a CSPF.

The generic security components constructed for a CSPF can be combined to obtain generic security architectures according to the following principles:

- An adequate basic software architecture to connect the generic security components has to be selected, e.g., a layered architecture.
- If components can be connected directly, one connects these components.
- If components cannot be connected directly (e.g., because a component provides incompatible input for another component), additional components to interconnect them must be introduced.

- Interfaces between the machine and its environment must be introduced in the generic security architecture according to the generic security components that provide or use these interfaces.

As examples, we present generic security components and architectures for the CSPF confidential data storage using password-based encryption.

Generic Security Components for CSPF Confidential Data Storage Using Password-Based Encryption

Figure 11 shows on the left-hand side a generic security component for handling passwords expressed as a UML composite structure diagram and a class diagram.

The component *PasswordReader* provides an interface *PwdRIf*. It consists of the operations *readPassword()* and *destroyPassword()*.

The behavior of the *PasswordReader* component is described using the UML sequence diagram (UML Revision Task Force, 2007) in Figure 12. After the operation *readPassword()* is called via the interface *PwdRIf*, the component calls the operation *showPasswordDialog()* via the used interface *EnvIf* that shows a dialog to the user and requests a password from her/him. Then, the user can submit a password *pwd* to the component, which returns this password to the caller of the operation *readPassword()*. Afterwards, this password must be wiped out from memory using the operation *destroyPassword()*.

OCL pre- and postconditions can be used to enrich the generic security component *PasswordReader* with security-relevant operation semantics. For example, constraints on the quality of the password captured by the operation *readPassword()*: e.g., a minimal password length, occurrence of special characters, etc. can be expressed.

The generic security component Encryptor/Decryptor shown on the right-hand side of Figure 11 provides an operation *encrypt(pt: Plaintext; pwd: Password)* that encrypts a plaintext *pt* using a password *pwd* to a ciphertext *ct*. Additionally, it provides an inverse operation *decrypt(ct: Ciphertext; pwd: Password)* that calculates the plaintext *pt* given the ciphertext *ct* and the password *pwd*.

The generic security components described previously must be combined to obtain generic

Figure 11. Generic security components "PasswordReader" and "SecretManagement" with interfaces classes

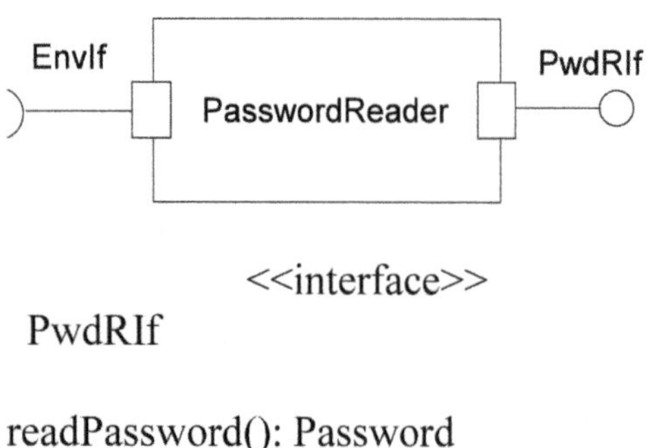

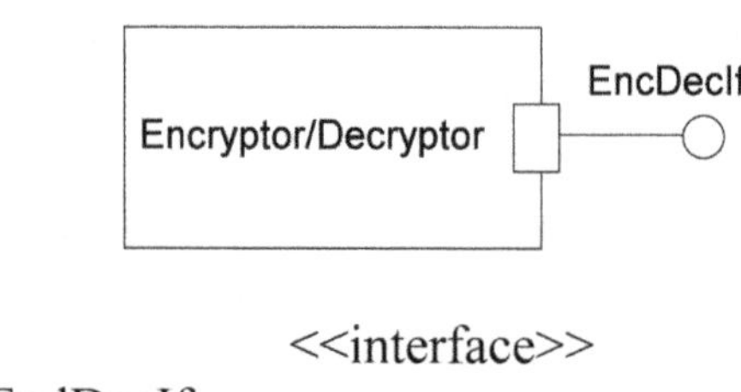

encrypt(pt: Plaintext; pwd: Password): Ciphertext
decrypt(ct: Ciphertext; pwd: Password): Plaintext

Figure 12. Behavior of the generic security component "PasswordReader"

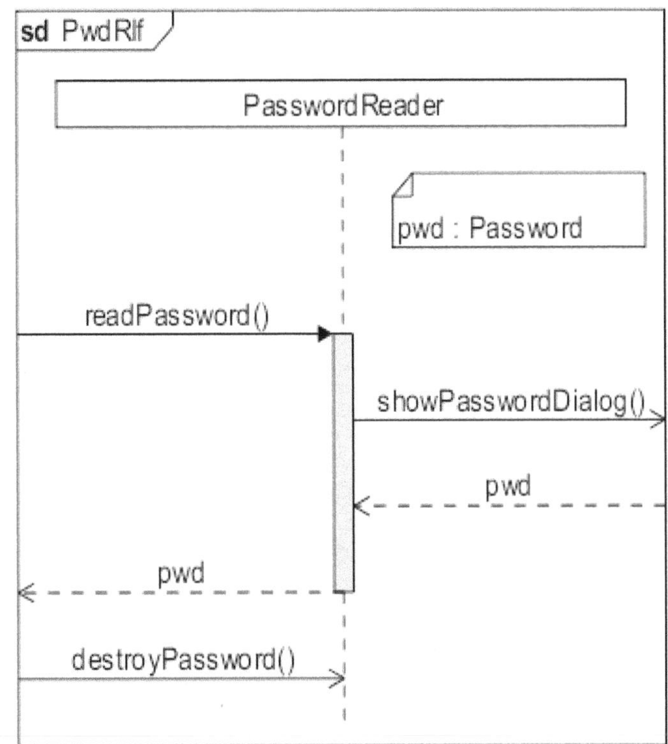

security architectures. Since generic security components are platform-independent, so are generic security architectures. Each CSPF is linked to a set of generic security architectures that realize the concretized security requirement template.

As an example, we present a generic security architecture for the CSPF confidential data storage using password-based encryption in Figure 13.

According to the previously presented general procedure to set up a generic security architecture of a CSPF's machine domain, we introduce *UserInterface* and *StorageManager* components to let a user interact with the software and to access a storage device, respectively. To realize the concretized security requirement template of the CSPF, we use the generic security components *PasswordReader* and *Decryptor/Encryptor*. These components are arranged in a *layered architecture* using an *Application* layer component.

Generic security architectures can also be applied to software development problems of higher complexity, i.e., problems that are divided into several subproblems, by composing the according sub-architectures. While Choppy & Hatebur & Heisel (2006) present an approach based on different kind of subproblem dependencies, we present the following principles for combining generic security architectures, thereby generating a platform-independent global generic secure software architecture:

The Application layer components can be combined into one Application layer component realizing the collaboration of the different generic security components.

If the same generic security component is selected for different subproblems (i.e. they are part of different generic security architectures), two cases must be distinguished:

Figure 13. Generic security architecture "CSPF Confidential Data Storage Using Password-Based Encryption"

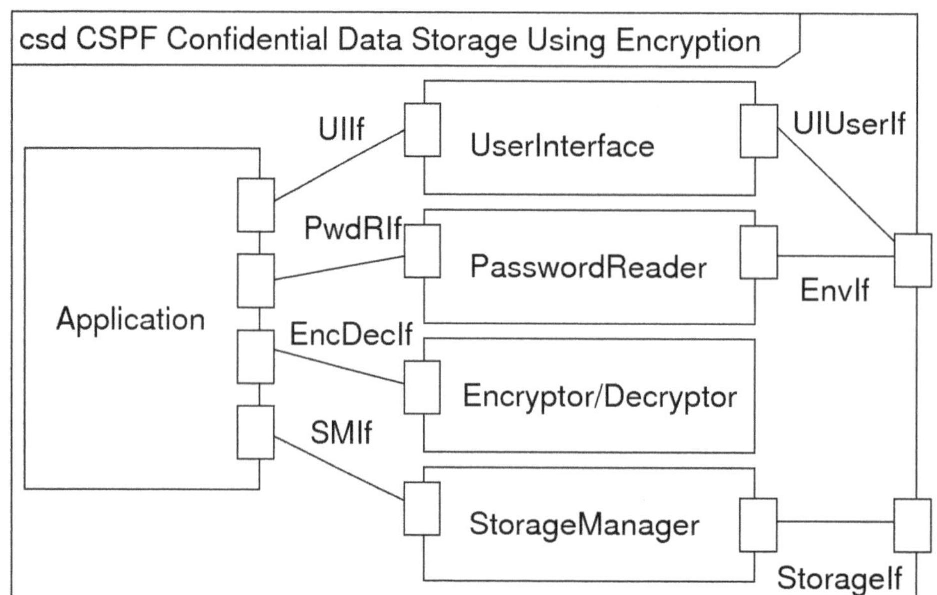

Details on the implementation of the security requirements are not yet known at this stage of the development process, e.g. is DES or AES used to realize symmetric encryption. In this case, the decision to combine the generic security component must be postponed until enough information is available. Practically, this information is given once an API or component framework has been selected.

If enough detail is already available at this stage of the development process, the question is whether the same security requirements are addressed. If the security requirements are equal, the global security architecture only contains one generic security component of this kind. Otherwise two generic security component of this kind are introduced.

Step 2: Refine Generic Security Architecture

In the following, we consider the refinement of the platform-independent generic security architecture to a platform-specific and implementable security architecture. It consists of several substeps:

1. Select an adequate component framework or API, e.g., the security APIs BouncyCastle or Sun's javax.crypto.*.
2. Select given components from the chosen component framework or API:
   a. Compare the interfaces, the operation semantics, and the behavioral description of the generic security components with the documentation of the component framework or API to find adequate existing components.
   b. Normally, several existing components must be used to realize one generic security component; in this case glue code must be written to connect the existing components in such a way that the specification of the generic security component is fulfilled.
   c. In the rare case that the specification of an existing component matches

the specification of a generic security component, the existing component can be used without customization.

d. Those generic security components that cannot be treated by the selected component framework or API must be implemented from scratch, based on the specification of the generic security component.

Finally, glue code is written to connect the components according to the refined generic security architecture.

Case Study: Secure Text Editor

First, we select a generic security architecture for each applied CSPF. For the secure text editor case study, the generic security architecture shown in Figure 13 is adequate, since it comprises a component for password-based encryption/decryption and a component to obtain a password from a user.

We refine this generic architecture using the Java Standard Edition 6 API provided by Sun. As examples, we present the refined *PasswordReader* component in Figure 14 and the refined *Encryptor/Decryptor* component in Figure 15. The refined *PasswordReader* component consists of a Wrapper component that represents the glue code necessary to combine the components pwdField, *pbeKeySpec*, *secretKeyFactory*, and *secretKey* provided by Sun's Java Standard Edition 6 API. The *pwdField* component provides a graphical text field to retrieve a password from a user. It makes the user input unreadable, while the password is entered into text field.

The other components are used to construct a symmetric encryption key compliant to a specific password-based cryptography specification (e.g., PKCS #5) from the user password.

The refined *Encryptor/Decryptor* component is constructed similarly. It also consists of a *Wrapper* component that connects the components *cipher* and *pbeParamSpec* from Sun's Java Standard Edition 6 API. The *cipher c*omponent provides the functionality of a cryptographic cipher for encryption and decryption. The *pbeParamSpec* component is necessary to construct a parameter set for password-based encryption as defined in the PKCS #5 standard.

Figure 14. Refined "PasswordReader" component

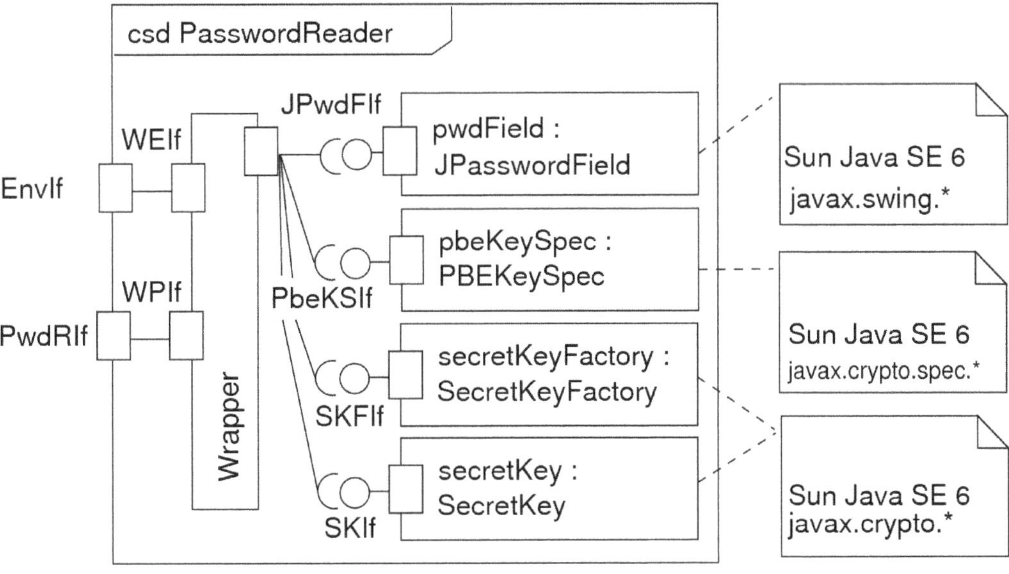

Figure 15. Refined encryptor/decryptor component

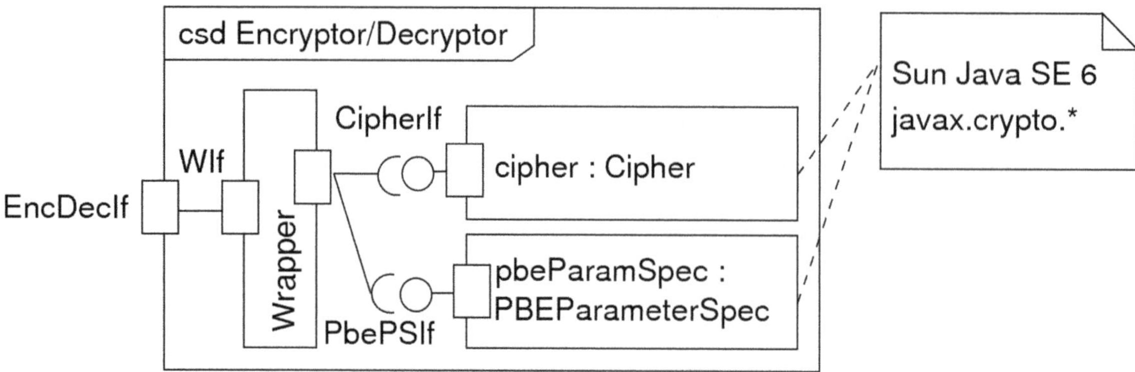

Due to space limitations, we do not describe the component-internal interfaces in detail and we do not show the other refined security components. The result of SEPP's last phase applied to the secure text editor case study is a security architecture that makes use of given components provided by Sun's Java Standard Edition 6 API. The next last step of phase two is programming the *Wrapper* components and the glue code to connect the refined generic security components. Finally, testing and deployment have to be performed.

We implemented two versions of the case study, one based on the BouncyCastle API and another one based on Sun's javax.crypto.* API. Both versions re-use existing modules of the APIs according to the refined security components shown in Figure 14 and Figure 15.

The amount of glue code to implement the wrapper components ranges between 20 to 50 lines of code per component.

FUTURE RESEARCH DIRECTIONS

In the future, we intend to find new patterns to extend the catalogue of SPFs and CSPFs.

We would like to consider probabilistic confidentiality properties and the compositionality of confidentiality-preserving refinement. Moreover, we plan to elaborate more on composition principles to combine generic security architectures to a combined generic security architecture that preserves the security requirements of the different generic security subarchitectures.

Furthermore, we intend to describe the generic security components and the generic security architectures using formal methods. We would like to formally show refinements between the CSPFs and the generic security components/architectures.

CONCLUSION

We presented SEPP, a security engineering process that makes use of different kinds of patterns. It covers security requirements engineering and the construction of security architectures.

SEPP starts with an extensive security requirements engineering phase, which is based on SPFs and CSPFs. These special kinds of problem frames are arranged in a pattern system. They serve to structure, characterize, analyze, and finally solve software development problems in the area of software and system security. SEPP supports to obtain a complete set of security requirements by analyzing the necessary conditions of the used CSPFs and deciding if they can be assumed or must be established by applying more frames.

SEPP's second phase covers the development of security architectures, which are constructed based on generic security architectures and generic security components. The generic security architectures are refined using existing or tailor-made security components. The results are platform-specific and implementable software architectures that realize the specified security requirements.

REFERENCES

Bass, L., Clements, P., & Kazman, R. (1998). *Software architecture in practice*. Reading, MA: Addison-Wesley.

BouncyCastle API. (n.d.). Retrieved June 24, 2009, from http://www.bouncycastle.org/

Choppy, C., Hatebur, D., & Heisel, M. (2005). Architectural patterns for problem frames. In *Proceedings - Software,* (pp. 198-208). Washington, DC: IEEE Computer Society.

Choppy, C., Hatebur, D., & Heisel, M. (2006). Component composition through architectural patterns for problem frames. In *Proceedings of the Asia Pacific Software Engineering Conference (APSEC)* (pp. 27-36). Washington, DC: IEEE Computer Society. doi:10.1109/APSEC.2006.27

Coplien, J. O. (1992). *Advanced C++ programming styles and idioms*. Reading, MA: Addison-Wesley.

Côté, I., Hatebur, D., Heisel, M., Schmidt, H., & Wentzlaff, I. (2008). A systematic account of problem frames. In *Proceedings of the European Conference on Pattern Languages of Programs* (EuroPLoP) (pp. 749-767). Universitätsverlag Konstanz.

Deng, Y. & Wang, J. & Tsai, J. J. P. & Beznosov, K. (2003). An approach for modeling and analysis of security system architectures. *IEEE Transactions on Knowledge and Data Engineering, 15*(5).

Fabian, B., Gürses, S., Heisel, M., Santen, T., & Schmidt, H. (2010). A comparison of security requirements engineering methods. *Requirements Engineering, 15*(1), 7–40. doi:10.1007/s00766-009-0092-x

Fernandez, E. B., la Red, M. D. L., Forneron, J. Uribe, V. E., & Rodriguez, G. G. (2007). A secure analysis pattern for handling legal cases. In *Proceedings of Latin America Conference on Pattern Languages of Programming*. Retrieved June 24, 2009, from http://sugarloafplop.dsc.upe.br/wwD.zip

Gamma, E., Helm, R., Johnson, R. E., & Vlissides, J. (1995). *Design patterns - elements of reusable object-oriented software*. Reading, MA: Addison Wesley.

Gürses, S., Jahnke, J. H., Obry, C., Onabajo, A., Santen, T., & Price, M. (2005). Eliciting confidentiality requirements in practice. *In Proceedings of the Conference of the Centre for Advanced Studies on Collaborative Research (CASCON)*, (pp. 101-116). New York: IBM Press.

Haley, C. B., Laney, R., Moffett, J., & Nuseibeh, B. (2004). Picking battles: The impact of trust assumptions on the elaboration of security requirements. In C. D. Jensen & S. Poslad & T. Dimitrakos (Eds.), *Proceedings of the International Conference on Trust Management* (iTrust) (LNCS) (vol. 2995, pp. 347-354). Berlin: Springer.

Haley, C. B., Laney, R., Moffett, J., & Nuseibeh, B. (2008). Security requirements engineering: A framework for representation and analysis. IEEE Transactions on Software Engineering, 34(1).

Halkidis, S. T., Tsantalis, N., Chatzigeorgiou, A., & Stephanides, G. (2008). Architectural risk analysis of software systems based on security patterns. IEEE Transactions on Dependable and Secure Computing, 5(3).

Hall, J. G., Jackson, M., Laney, R. C., Nuseibeh, B., & Rapanotti, L. (2002). Relating software requirements and architectures using problem frames. In *Proceedings of IEEE International Requirements Engineering Conference (RE)*, (pp. 137-144). Washington, DC: IEEE Computer Society. doi:10.1109/ICRE.2002.1048516

Hatebur, D., & Heisel, M. (2005). Problem frames and architectures for security problems. In B. A. Gran & R. Winter & G. Dahll (Ed.), *Proceedings of the International Conference on Computer Safety, Reliability and Security (SAFECOMP)* (LNCS) (vol. 3688, pp. 390-404). Berlin: Springer. doi:10.1007/11563228_30

Hatebur, D., Heisel, M., & Schmidt, H. (2006). Security engineering using problem frames. In G. Müller (Ed.), *Proceedings of the International Conference on Emerging Trends in Information and Communication Security (ETRICS)* (LNCS) (vol. 3995, pp. 238-253). Berlin: Springer. doi:10.1007/11766155_17

Hatebur, D., Heisel, M., & Schmidt, H. (2007). A pattern system for security requirements engineering. In *Proceedings of the International Conference on Availability, Reliability and Security (AReS)* (pp. 356-365). Washington, DC: IEEE Computer Society.

Hatebur, D., Heisel, M., & Schmidt, H. (2008a). A formal metamodel for problem frames. In *Proceedings of the International Conference on Model Driven Engineering Languages and Systems (MODELS)* (LNCS) (vol. 5301, pp. 68–82). Berlin: Springer. doi:10.1007/978-3-540-87875-9_5

Hatebur, D., Heisel, M., & Schmidt, H. (2008b). Analysis and component-based realization of security requirements. In *Proceedings of the International Conference on Availability, Reliability and Security (AReS)* (pp. 195–203). IEEE Computer Society.

Heisel, M. (1998). Agendas - A concept to guide software development activities. In *Proceedings of the IFIP TC2 WG2.4 working Conference on Systems Implementation: Languages, Methods and Tools* (pp. 19-32). London: Chapman & Hall.

International Organization for Standardization (ISO) and International Electrotechnical Commission (IEC). (2006). *Common evaluation methodology 3.1, ISO/IEC 18405*. Retrieved June 24, 2009, from http://www.commoncriteriaportal.org

Jackson, M. (2001). *Problem frames: Analyzing and structuring software development problems*. Reading, MA: Addison-Wesley.

Jackson, M., & Zave, P. (1995). Deriving specifications from requirements: An example. In *Proceedings of the Internation Conference on Software Engineering (SE)* (pp. 15-24). New York: ACM Press.

Java Standard Edition, SUN 6 API. (n.d.). Retrieved June 24, 2009, from http://java.sun.com/javase/6/docs/api/overview-summary.html

Laboratories, R. S. A. (1999). *Password-based cryptography standard PKCS #5 v2.0*. Retrieved June 24, 2009, from ftp://ftp.rsasecurity.com/pub/pkcs/pkcs-5v2/pkcs5v2-0.pdf

Lin, L., Nuseibeh, B., Ince, D., & Jackson, M. (2004). Using abuse frames to bound the scope of security problems. In *Proceedings of IEEE International Requirements Engineering Conference (RE)* (pp. 354-355). Washington, DC: IEEE Computer Society.

Lund, M. S., Solhaug, B., & Stølen, K. (2011). *Model-driven risk analysis - The CORAS approach*. Berlin: Springer. doi:10.1007/978-3-642-12323-8

Moriconi, M., Qian, X., Riemenschneider, R. A., & Gong, L. (1997). Secure software architectures. In *Proceedings of the IEEE Symposium on Security and Privacy* (pp. 84 – 93). Washington, DC: IEEE Computer Society.

Mouratidis, H., & Giorgini, P. (2007). Secure tropos: A security-oriented extension of the tropos methodology. *International Journal of Software Engineering and Knowledge Engineering*, *17*(2), 285–309. doi:10.1142/S0218194007003240

Mouratidis, H., Weiss, M., & Giorgini, P. (2006). Modelling secure systems using an agent oriented approach and security patterns. *International Journal of Software Engineering and Knowledge Engineering*, *16*(3), 471–498. doi:10.1142/S0218194006002823

Rapanotti, L., Hall, J. G., Jackson, M., & Nuseibeh, B. (2004). Architecture Driven Problem Decomposition. In *Proceedings of IEEE International Requirements Engineering Conference (RE)*, (73-82). Washington, DC: IEEE Computer Society.

Scandariato, R., Yskout, K., Heyman, T., & Joosen, W. (2008). *Architecting software with security patterns* (Report No. CW515). Katholieke Universiteit Leuven - Department of Computer Science.

Schmidt, H., & Wentzlaff, I. (2006). Preserving software quality characteristics from requirements analysis to architectural design. In *Proceedings of the European Workshop on Software Architectures (EWSA)*, (LNCS) (vol. 4344, pp. 189-203). Berlin: Springer. doi:10.1007/11966104_14

Schneier, B. (1999). Attack trees. *Dr. Dobb's Journal*. Retrieved June 24, 2009, from http://www.schneier.com/paper-attacktrees-ddj-ft.html

Schumacher, M., Fernandez-Buglioni, E., Hybertson, D., Buschmann, F., & Sommerlad, P. (2005). *Security patterns: Integrating security and systems engineering*. Washington, DC: Wiley & Sons.

Shaw, M., & Garlan, D. (1996). *Software architecture - Perspectives on an emerging discipline*. Upper Saddle River, NJ: Prentice-Hall.

Spivey, M. (1992). *The Z notation - A reference manual*. Upper Saddle River, NJ: Prentice Hall. Retrieved June 24, 2009, from http://spivey.oriel.ox.ac.uk/mike/zrm

Steel, C. & Nagappan, R., & Lai, R. (2005). *Core security patterns: Best practices and strategies for J2EE, web services, and identity management*. Academic Press.

SUN javax.crypto. API*. (n.d.). Retrieved June 24, 2009, from http://java.sun.com/javase/6/docs/api/javax/crypto/package-summary.html

UML Revision Task Force, Object Management Group (OMG). (2007). *OMG Unified Modeling Language: Superstructure*. Retrieved June 24, 2009, from http://www.omg.org/spec/UML/2.1.2/

UML Revision Task Force, Object Management Group (OMG). (2012). *Object Constraint Language Specification*. Retrieved June 2, 2014, from http://www.omg.org/spec/OCL/2.3.1

van Lamsweerde, A. (2004). Elaborating security requirements by construction of intentional anti-models. In *Proceedings of the International Conference on Software Engineering (ICSE)*, (pp. 148-157). Washington, DC: IEEE Computer Society. doi:10.1109/ICSE.2004.1317437

Weiss, M., & Mouratidis, H. (2008). Selecting security patterns that fulfill security requirements. In *Proceedings of the 16th IEEE International Conference on Requirements Engineering (RE'08)*, Washington, DC: IEEE Computer Society. doi:10.1109/RE.2008.32

KEY TERMS AND DEFINITIONS

Concretized Security Problem Frames: Problem frames describing security problems with a generic solution mechanism.

OCL: Object constraint language, defined by the Object Management Group, used to specify constraints on UML diagrams.

Problem Frames: Patterns for the software engineering analysis phase.

Security Architecture: Architecture of a software considering the security requirements.

Security Components: Parts of a software, their purpose is to solve security problems.

Security Problem Frames: Problem frames describing security problems without anticipating a solution.

Security Requirements Engineering: Activity of a software engineer in the software engineering analysis phase.

UML: Unified modeling language, defined by the Object Management Group, defines diagrams to specify structure and behavior of software systems.

ENDNOTES

1 http://www.eclipse.org/

2 https://www.eclipse.org/modeling/emf/

3 http://projects.eclipse.org/projects/modeling.mdt.ocl

4 http://www.eclipse.org/papyrus/

Chapter 3
A Framework of Statistical and Visualization Techniques for Missing Data Analysis in Software Cost Estimation

Lefteris Angelis
Aristotle University of Thessaloniki, Greece

Nikolaos Mittas
Aristotle University of Thessaloniki, Greece

Panagiota Chatzipetrou
Aristotle University of Thessaloniki, Greece

ABSTRACT

Software Cost Estimation (SCE) is a critical phase in software development projects. However, due to the growing complexity of the software itself, a common problem in building software cost models is that the available datasets contain lots of missing categorical data. The purpose of this chapter is to show how a framework of statistical, computational, and visualization techniques can be used to evaluate and compare the effect of missing data techniques on the accuracy of cost estimation models. Hence, the authors use five missing data techniques: Multinomial Logistic Regression, Listwise Deletion, Mean Imputation, Expectation Maximization, and Regression Imputation. The evaluation and the comparisons are conducted using Regression Error Characteristic curves, which provide visual comparison of different prediction models, and Regression Error Operating Curves, which examine predictive power of models with respect to under- or over-estimation.

INTRODUCTION

Software has become the key element of any computer-based system and product. The complicated structure of software and the continuously increasing demand for quality products justify the high importance of software engineering in today's world as it offers a systematic framework for development and maintenance of software. One of the most important activities in the initial project phases is Software Cost Estimation (SCE). During this stage a software project manager at-

DOI: 10.4018/978-1-4666-6359-6.ch003

tempts to estimate the effort and time required for the development of a software product. The importance of software engineering and the role of cost estimation in software project planning has been discussed widely in literature. (Jorgensen & Shepperd 2007). Cost estimations may be performed before, during or even after the development of software.

The complicated nature of a software project and therefore the difficult problems involved in the SCE procedures emerged a whole area of research within the wider field of software engineering. A substantial part of the research on SCE concerns the construction of software cost estimation models. These models are built by applying statistical methodologies to historical datasets which contain attributes of finished software projects. The scope of cost estimation models is twofold: first, they can provide a theoretical framework for describing and interpreting the dependencies of cost with the characteristics of the project and second they can be utilized to produce efficient cost predictions. Although the second utility is the most important for practical purposes, the first utility is equally significant, since it provides a basis for thorough studies of how the various project attributes interact and affect the cost. Therefore, the cost models are valuable not only to practitioners but also to researchers whose work is to analyse and interpret.

In the process of constructing cost models, a major problem arises from the fact that missing values are often encountered in some historical datasets. Very often missing data are responsible for the misleading results regarding the accuracy of the cost models and may reduce their explanatory and prediction ability. The aforementioned problem is very important in the area of software project management because most of the software databases suffer from missing values and this can happen for several reasons.

A common reason is the cost and the difficulties that some companies face in the collection of the data. In some cases, the cost of money and time needed to collect certain information is forbidding for a company or an organization. In other cases, the collection of data is very difficult because it demands consistence, experience, time and methodology for a company. An additional source of incomplete values is the fact that data are often collected with a different purpose in mind, or that the measurement categories are generic and thus not applicable to all projects. This seems especially likely when data are collected from a number of companies. So, for researchers whose purpose is to study projects from different companies and build cost models on them, the handling of missing data is an essential preliminary step (Chen, Boehm, Menzies & Port 2005).

Many techniques deal with missing data. The most common and straightforward one is *Listwise Deletion* (LD), which simply ignores the projects with missing values. The major advantage of the method is its simplicity and the ability to do statistical calculations on a common sample base of cases. The disadvantages of the method are the dramatic loss of information in cases with high percentages of missing values and possible bias in the data. These problems can occur when there is some type of pattern in the missing data, i.e. when the distribution of missing values in some variables is depended on certain valid observations of other variables in the data.

Other techniques estimate or "impute" the missing values. The resulting complete data can then be analyzed and modelled by standard methods (for example regression analysis). These methods are called *imputation methods*. The problem is that most of the imputation methods produce continuous estimates, which are not realistic replacements of the missing values when the variables are categorical. Since the majority of the variables in the software datasets are categorical with many missing values, it is reasonable to use an imputation method producing categorical values in order to fill the incomplete dataset and then to use it for constructing a prediction model.

From the above discussion we can identify the components of the complex problem, which we address in this chapter. In general, we assume that there is an available dataset with cost data from historical projects. Each project is characterized by several categorical variables (attributes or features), while a number of values of these variables are missing. The purpose is to build a cost model (usually by least squares regression) using this incomplete dataset. The question is therefore how to handle the missing data in order to build a model with as much accuracy as possible. It is clear that this is a decision-making problem in the sense that we need to compare and decide on which is the "most accurate" (or equivalently the "least inaccurate") method among a number of alternatives.

The goal of this chapter is to present a combination of advanced statistical, computational and visualization approaches which can be used in the aforementioned decision-making procedure. The methodologies described are generic, in the sense that can be applied to: (a) any incomplete dataset, (b) any cost estimation model and (c) the comparison of any missing data techniques.

In order to illustrate the overall methodology framework, we chose to present the work with: (a) a specific dataset, i.e. a subset of the ISBSG software project repository (http://www.isbsg.org/) (b) a least squares regression cost model and (c) five specific missing data techniques: multinomial logistic regression (which was introduced in the context of SCE) and four more traditional and generic methods, namely listwise deletion, mean imputation, expectation maximization and regression imputation. The reason for these choices was our familiarity with the imputation methods and the dataset, resulting from our previous research experience. The combination of methods we apply for the comparisons is also based on our previous research. Specifically, we use different error measures, nonparametric statistical tests, resampling techniques and graphical methods, some of them recently introduced in cost estimation.

The structure of the chapter is the following: First we outline related work in the area and then we describe the different mechanisms creating missing data along with the most common techniques for handling them. In the following section, we present the dataset used in the analysis and the statistical methods. Then, we give the results of the statistical analysis and finally we conclude by discussing the findings along with possible future research directions.

BACKGROUND

Although the problem of handling missing data has been treated adequately in the statistical literature and in various real-world datasets, there are relatively sparse published works concerning software cost missing data.

Emam & Birk (2000) used multiple imputation in order to induce missing values in their analysis of software process data performance.

Strike, Emam, & Madhavji (2001) compared LD, MI and eight different types of hot-deck imputation for dealing with missing data in the context of software cost modeling. Three missing data mechanisms were evaluated (MCAR, MAR and NI) and two patterns of missing data were simulated (univariate and monotone) in order to induce missing values on a complete large software engineering dataset. The results showed that all the missing data techniques performed well and therefore the simplest technique, LD, is a reasonable choice. However, best performance was obtained by using hot-deck imputation with Euclidean distance and a z-score standardization.

Myrtveit, Stensrud & Olsson (2001) analyzed datasets with missing data and LD, MI, similar response pattern imputation (SRPI) and full information maximum likelihood (FIML) were evaluated on an enterprise resource planning (ERP) dataset with real missing values. The results indicated that FIML is appropriate when data are not missing completely at random. LD, MI and SRPI resulted in biased prediction models unless the data is MCAR. Also, MI and SRPI, compared to LD, were suitable only if the dataset after applying LD was very small in order to construct a meaningful prediction model.

Cartwright, Shepperd, & Song (2003) examined sample mean imputation (SMI) and k-NN on two industrial datasets with real missing data. They found that both methods improved the model fit but k-NN gave better results than SMI.

Song, Shepperd & Cartwright (2005) used two imputation methods in their research. Class mean imputation (CMI) and k-nearest neighbors (k-NN) were considered with respect to two mechanisms of creating missing data: missing completely at random (MCAR) and missing at random (MAR).

In a previous work (Sentas & Angelis, 2005), a statistical methodology known as "Multinomial Logistic Regression" (MLR) was suggested for the estimation and the imputation of categorical missing values. Specifically, MLR was applied on a complete (i.e. with no missing values) dataset from the International Software Benchmarking Standards Group (ISBSG) data base. The missing values were created artificially by simulating three different mechanisms: *missing completely at random* (MCAR), *missing at random* (MAR) and *non-ignorable missingness* (NI). The study was designed to involve three percentages of incomplete data (10%, 20% and 30%) and MLR method was compared with four other missing data techniques: *listwise deletion* (LD), *mean imputation* (MI), *expectation maximization* (EM) and *regression imputation* (RI). The experimentation was designed to explore the effects of imputation on the prediction error produced by a regression model and showed the efficiency of MLR as an imputation method.

Twala, Cartwright & Shepperd (2006) compared seven missing data techniques (listwise deletion (LD), expectation maximization single imputation (EMSI), k-nearest neighbour single imputation (kNNSI), mean or mode single imputation (MMSI), expectation maximization multiple imputation (EMMI), fractional cases (FC) and surrogate variable splitting (SVS) using eight industrial datasets. The results reveal that listwise deletion (LD) is the least effective technique for handling incomplete data while multiple imputation achieves the highest accuracy rates. Furthermore, they proposed and showed how a combination of MDTs by randomizing a decision tree building algorithm leads to a significant improvement in prediction performance for missing values up to 50%.

Wong, Zhao, Chan & Victor (2006) applied a statistical methodology in order to optimize and simplify software metric models with missing data. In order to deal with missing data, they used a modified k-nearest neighbors (k-NN) imputation method. The results indicate that their methodology can be useful in trimming redundant predictor metrics and identifying unnecessary categories assumed for a categorical predictor metric in the model.

Van Hulse & Khoshgoftaar (2008) presented a comprehensive experimental analysis of five commonly used imputation techniques (mean imputation (MI), regression imputation (RI), Bayesian multiple imputation (BMI), REPTree imputation (RTI) and instance-based learning imputation (IBLI). The authors concluded that Bayesian multiple imputation and regression imputation are the most effective techniques, while mean imputation performs extremely poorly. Also, the authors took under consideration three different mechanisms (MCAR, MAR and NI) governing the distribution of missing values in a dataset, and examined the impact of noise on the imputation process.

Zhang Yang, & Wang (2011) adapted a naive Bayes and EM (Expectation Maximization) for software effort prediction, and develop two embedded strategies: missing data toleration and missing data imputation, to handle the missing data in software effort datasets. Experiments performed on ISBSG and CSBSG (Chinese Software Benchmarking Standard Group) datasets showed that the proposed strategies cannot be generalized to be applied in all the other software effort datasets.

The same authors (2012) attempted to clarify the root cause of missingness of software effort data. When missingness was regarded as absent features, they developed Max-margin regression to predict real effort of software projects. On the other hand, when missingness was regarded as unobserved values, they used existing imputation techniques to impute missing values. Experiments on ISBSG and CSBSG data sets demonstrate that, with the tasks of effort prediction, the treatment regarding missingness in software effort data set as unobserved values can produce more desirable performance than that of regarding missingness as absent features.

Regression analysis plays an important role in SCE. Although there are several forms of regression models, the ordinary least squares regression seems to be one of the most popular techniques. It is used for fitting a linear parametric model for the cost variable by minimizing the sum of squared residuals. This means that a linear equation is first assumed between the dependent variable and the predictors and next its parameters, the regression coefficients, are estimated by the least squares method. The role of regression in SCE is thoroughly discussed in the systematic reviews by Mair & Shepperd (2005) and Jorgensen & Shepperd (2007).

Although least squares regression is an easily implemented and straightforward method, there are certain assumptions to consider when fitting a model. The most important ones are: (a) the relationship between the predictor variables and the dependent variable is linear and (b) the residuals are normally distributed and uncorrelated with the predictors. These two assumptions are usually addressed in the case of software project data by using the logarithmic transformations of the cost (dependent) variable and the size (independent) variable (Kitchenham & Mendes 2004; Mendes & Lokan 2008). In our application, we followed the same practice.

The issue of data quality is critical in SCE. In the paper by Liebchen & Shepperd (2008), the researchers discuss the problem of data quality, reporting their concerns about the quality of some of the datasets that are used to learn, evaluate and compare prediction models. In our application which will be described later, we took into account the importance of data quality by removing from the ISBSG dataset the projects which are of low quality (rated with C and D) and from the remaining (rated with A and B) we used only those projects measured by the same sizing method.

Another issue related to the reliability of the specific ISBSG dataset, is whether a multi-organizational dataset can be used to build efficient models in comparison to models built on data from a single company. Several studies address this problem, often with contradictory results. See for example the papers by Jeffery, Ruhe & Wieczorek, (2000 and 2001) and by Mendes, Lokan, Harrison & Triggs (2005). Unfortunately, the lack of a widely acceptable and reliable dataset which can be used to test any statistical model and method does not allow us to draw general conclusions. However, our purpose is to present specific statistical methodologies which can be applied to any dataset, either multi-organizational or from a single company.

Regarding the comparison of different models, there is a large amount of papers suggesting various measures of prediction error (Kitchenham, Pickard, MacDonell & Shepperd 2001, Foss, Stensurd, Kitchenham, & Myrtveit 2003) and statistical procedures (Stensrud & Myrtveit, 1998, Kitchenham & Mendes, 2009). An extended review of comparison methods is presented in Mittas & Angelis 2013a. The most common tests for comparing error measures on the same data are the *parametric paired sample t-test* and the *non-parametric Wilcoxon signed rank test* (Kitchenham & Mendes 2004, Mittas & Angelis, 2008a, Mendes & Lokan 2008).

A common problem encountered in the comparisons with statistical tests is that the prediction error measures are skewed with outliers, so it is not easy to assume a theoretical distribution, especially the Gaussian. In a previous study (Mittas & Angelis, 2008a), we proposed a statistical simulation method, the *permutation tests,* in order to test the significance of differences between software cost estimation models. This method is based on resampling, i.e. on drawing a large number of samples from the original sample in order to "reconstruct" the underlying theoretical distribution and for this reason the hypothesis test is carried out without worrying about the distribution of the variables.

Although statistical procedures are critical for comparisons, there is always the need for a visual inspection and comparison of the whole distributions of error measures. In two related studies (Mittas & Angelis 2008b & 2010), we introduced the *Regression Error Characteristic* (REC) analysis as a class of visualization techniques for the evaluation of the predictive power and comparison of different models. REC analysis was recently introduced in software cost estimation to aid the decision of choosing the most appropriate cost estimation model during the management of a forthcoming project (Mittas & Angelis 2012). Finally, a new Graphical User Interface tool known as StatREC presented by Mittas, Mamalikidis & Angelis (2012), which facilitates the visualization and hypothesis testing of error distributions through their graphical representation as REC curves.

Another straightforward tool for comparing prediction methodologies in different operating conditions is Regression Receiver Operating Curves (RROC) (Mittas & Angelis 2013b). The authors aimed to evaluate the predictive power of alternative estimation techniques when underestimation and overestimation are not of equal importance since the various studies consider underestimations and overestimations of the actual cost to have equal importance which is hardly true in practice and extremely risky for an organization and the customers.

From the above summary, it is clear that in the present chapter we extend and combine our previous research results in the following directions: (a) by comparing the newer MLR imputation method with the four older missing data techniques (LD, MI, EM, RI) using a dataset with real (not simulated) missing values, (b) by evaluating the effect of the missing data techniques on the prediction error of a regression model, measuring three different aspects of prediction performance, namely *accuracy*, *bias* and *spread* and (c) by using for statistical comparisons of the imputation methods the permutation tests, the REC curves and RROCs.

MISSING DATA MECHANISMS AND MISSING DATA TECHNIQUES

Missing Data Mechanism

The methods of handling missing data are directly related to the mechanisms that caused the incompleteness. Generally, these mechanisms fall into three classes according to Little & Rubin (2002):

1. **Missing Completely at Random (MCAR):** The missing values in a variable are unrelated to the values of any other variables, whether missing or valid.
2. **Non-Ignorable Missingness (NI):** NI can be considered as the opposite of MCAR in the sense that the probability of having missing values in a variable depends on the variable itself (for example a question regarding skills may be not answered when the skills are in fact low).
3. **Missing at Random (MAR):** MAR can be considered as an intermediate situation between MCAR and NI. The probability of having missing values does not depend on the variable itself but on the values of some other variable.

Unfortunately, it is very difficult to recognize if the mechanism is MCAR, MAR or NI in a dataset with real missing values, which is the case of this chapter. Comparisons under the assumption of specific mechanisms have been considered in Sentas & Angelis (2005) where we used artificial missing data in order to simulate the distribution of missing values. In the present work, no such assumption is made, since the data contain real missing values and their underlying mechanism is unknown.

Missing Data Techniques (MDTs)

In order to handle the missing data, we used the following techniques according to Little & Rubin (2002):

1. **Listwise Deletion (LD):** It is a typical method that belongs to a broader class, namely the deletion methods. According to LD, cases with missing values for any of the variables are omitted from the analysis.
2. **Mean Imputation (MI):** This method replaces the missing observations of a certain variable with the mean of the observed values in that variable. It is a simple method that generally performs well, especially when valid data are normally distributed. In our study, the categorical variables with missing values have been preprocessed and transformed using ANOVA (ANOVA is analyzed in the next part of the chapter), with respect to their effect on the effort, so the resulting variables used in the cost model were finally ordinal. Since the ordinal values are essentially rankings, we decided to use the mean ranking as an imputed value for the missing values. This is consistent to the statistical theory which frequently uses the mean ranking in non-parametric statistical tests.
3. **Regression Imputation (RI):** The missing values are estimated through the application of multiple regression where the variable with missing data is considered as the dependent one and all other variables as predictors.
4. **Expectation Maximization (EM):** The EM algorithm is an iterative two step procedure obtaining the maximum likelihood estimates of a model starting from an initial guess. Each iteration consists of two steps: the Expectation (E) step that finds the distribution for the missing data based on the known values for the observed variables and the current estimate of the parameters and the Maximization (M) step that replaces the missing data with the expected value.
5. **Multinomial Logistic Regression (MLR):** Used to model the relationship between a polytomous (its values are more than two categories) dependent variable and a set of *k* predictor variables which are either categorical (factors) or numerical. MLR can be used for imputation by considering as dependent the categorical variable with the missing values and as predictors all the others. A similar method has already been used for prediction of productivity by Sentas, Angelis, Stamelos & Bleris (2004), while MLR has already been applied and proposed in Sentas & Angelis (2005), as we already mentioned. Hosmer & Lemeshow (1989) have proposed more detailed descriptions on models with categorical data.

The above techniques are chosen for reasons of consistency with our previous work in Sentas & Angelis (2005). As MLR is a method proposed in the context of SCE, it is reasonable to compare it with the other four methods which are well known, have been extensively used and they are implemented in statistical software. We must also emphasize the fact that there are other effective non-imputation techniques, such as the Full Information Maximum Likelihood (FIML) method analyzed by Myrtveit, Stensrud & Olsson (2001), which can fit a model without imputing the missing values. However, the basic assumption of this method is that the data are continuous and come from a multivariate normal distribution, which is not true in our case where the data contain categorical variables. Also, the chapter focuses mainly on the methods of comparisons which can be applied in any other imputation method.

RESEARCH METHODOLOGY

The method for comparing MLR with the other four MDTs was based on measuring the impact of each of the MDTs on the predictive accuracy of a cost estimation model. Below we describe the dataset we used, the accuracy measures employed for the comparisons and finally a general design of the study.

Selection of the Dataset

The dataset we used for our application contains 152 projects derived from the International Software Benchmarking Standards Group (ISBSG) project repository (http://www.isbsg.org/). The dataset was formed according to the recommendation of ISBSG, i.e. we chose only projects with quality rating A and B, their size was measured only by the IFPUG method while they all had as 'Recording Method', the staff hours (recorded). Finally, we decided to keep only the categories '1 only', '1+2' and 'TOTAL only' from 'Resource Level'. In Table 1 we can see the original variables of the dataset.

Variables of the Cost Model

The cost models built on the data under different MDTs were all linear least squares regression models, constructed by considering as dependent variable the logarithm of work effort (*lneffort*). Only two of the predictor variables are numerical, i.e. the year of implementation (*year*) and the logarithm of function points (*lnfpoints*). The logarithmic transformations for effort and function points were applied since they satisfy the normality assumptions of the linear regression model and improve their efficiency (Maxwell, 2002). Since the rest of the predictor variables are categorical with a large number of categories each, we conducted a preliminary study in order to merge the original categories into homogeneous groups and therefore to work with only a few categories for each factor.

This was achieved first by analysis of variance (ANOVA), in order to identify the most important factors and next by concatenation of the categories with similar mean effort values. The categories of each factor were represented by ordinal values according to their impact on the mean effort. The categorical variables resulted from this study are given in Table 2.

Two of the categorical predictor variables have real missing observations. These are: 'DBMS used' (*dbms*) and 'Business Area Type' (*bartype*), with 41 and 16 missing observations in each one respectively.

Table 1. Variables in the dataset of ISBSG with real missing values

Variable	Full Name
fpoints	Function Points
Develp	Development type
Platfr	Development platform
Lang	Language type
Primar	Primary Programming Language
implem (year)	Implementation Date
Orgtype	Organisation Type
Bartype	Business Area Type
Apltype	Application Type
Pacost	Package Costomaziation
Dbms	DBMS Used
Usdmet	Used Methodology

Table 2. The categorical predictor variables used for the cost models

Variable	Description and Levels
develp	Left out from the analysis
platfr	Development platform. Levels: 1=MainFrame or MF, 2=Mid Range or MR, 3=PC
lang	Language type. Levels: 1=3GL, 2=4GL, 3=Application Generator or ApG
primar_4	Primary Programming Language. Levels (after merging): 1={access, natural, pl/i}, 2={easytrieve, oracle, power builder, sql, telon, visual basic, ideal}, 3={ C, C++, cobol, other 4gl, other apg, }, 4={ C/VB, cobol II, coolgen}
orgtype_4	Organisation Type. Levels (after merging): 1={ computers, consultancy, energy, medical and health care, professional services}, 2={communication, community services, electricity/ gas/water, electronics, financial, property & business services, insurance, manufacturing, public administration}, 3={ aerospace/automotive, banking, construction, distribution, government, transport & storage}, 4 ={consumer goods, defense, occupational health and safety, wholesale & retail trade}
bartype_4	Business Area Type. Levels (after merging): 1={ accounting, activity tracking, claims processing-product pays claim, engineering, environment, fine enforcement, generate & distribute electricity, research & development, sales & marketing, telecommunications}, 2={banking, financial (excluding banking), inventory, architectural, project management & job control, provide computer services and IT consultation}, 3={insurance, legal, manufacturing, pension funds managements, personnel, procurement, public administration}, 4={ transport/shipping, blood bank, chartered flight operation, energy generation, logistics}
apltype	Left out from the analysis
pacost	Left out from the analysis
dbms_4	DBMS Used. Levels (after merging): 1={ACCESS, ADABAS, MS SQL Server, ORACLE, RDB, WATCOM}, 2={DB2/2, IMS, Other, SYBASE, WATCOM SQL}, 3={IDMS, DB2, DATA COM, ADABAS V5, RDB 6.0, RDMS}, 4={CA-IDMS, FOXPRO, GUPTA SQL BASIC, INTERACTIVE, RDB 4-2-1, ORACLE V7}
usdmet	Left out from the analysis

Validation Procedure and Accuracy Measures

The prediction accuracy for each of the comparative models was evaluated through the hold-out procedure. Primarily, we split the dataset into two subsets: a training set with 120 projects and a test set with 32 projects with no missing values. Using the five known MDTs, we replaced the missing observations with predictions, simultaneously to both categorical predictor variables '*dbms*' and '*bartype*' of the training set. So, five complete datasets resulted, one for each MDT. A cost regression model was built on each of the above datasets and its accuracy was evaluated on the test dataset.

Based on the actual value Y_A and the estimated value Y_E, various error functions for the evaluation of the predictive power of the models have been proposed in the SCE literature (Foss, Stensurd, Kitchenham, & Myrtveit, 2003) describing different aspects of their performances. Although the thorough debate concerning the appropriateness of the evaluation measures (Kitchenham, Pickard, MacDonell,& Shepperd, 2001), there has been noted a lack of convergence about which accuracy indicators are suitable for the comparison procedure. Having in mind the abovementioned disagreement, we decided to utilize three measures of local error in order to obtain a more representative view of the predictive performances of the comparative models:

1. The absolute error (AE),

$$AE_i = \left|Y_{A_i} - Y_{E_i}\right| \quad (1)$$

2. The error ratio (z),

$$z_i = \frac{Y_{Ei}}{Y_{Ai}} \quad (2)$$

3. The magnitude of relative error (MRE),

$$MRE_i = \frac{\left|Y_{Ai} - Y_{Ei}\right|}{Y_{Ai}} \quad (3)$$

As we have already mentioned, these error functions measure different aspects of the prediction performance. More precisely, *absolute errors* are used in order to measure the *accuracy* whereas Kitchenham, Pickard, MacDonell & Shepperd (2001), propose the utilization of the error ratio *z* which is clearly related to the distribution of the residuals, as a measure of *bias* for the predictions obtained by a model. Ideally, an optimum estimation is equal to the actual value (z=1), whereas z-values greater or less than 1 show overestimation or underestimation, respectively. On the other hand, the most commonly used measure is the magnitude of relative error (MMRE), but Foss, Stensurd, Kitchenham,& Myrtveit (2003) demonstrate that it does not always select the "best" model. On the other hand, Kitchenham, Pickard, MacDonell, & Shepperd (2001) suggest that *magnitude of relative error* measures the *spread* of the variable z.

These local measures can be the basis for the evaluation of the overall prediction performance of the comparative models by computing a statistic (usually the mean or median) for them. The most commonly used measures in SCE are shown in Box 1.

Formal Statistical Comparisons

Except from the overall prediction performance computed from the error functions ((1), (2) and (3)), these samples of errors can be used in order to draw conclusions concerning the differences of the comparative models. The statistical significance of the difference can be tested through traditional and simulation techniques (Mittas & Angelis 2008a).

Due to the fact that the AEs are usually non-normally distributed, we decided to use the traditional non-parametric Wilcoxon sign rank test for matched pairs (Kitchenham & Mendes 2004, Mittas & Angelis 2008a, Mendes & Lokan

Box 1.

$$MdAE = median\left\{AE_i\right\} \quad MAE = \frac{1}{n}\sum_{i=1}^{n} AE_i \quad (4)$$

$$Medianz = median\{z_i\} \quad Meanz = \frac{1}{n}\sum_{i=1}^{n} z_i \quad (5)$$

$$MdMRE = median\left\{MRE_i\right\} \quad MMRE = \frac{1}{n}\sum_{i=1}^{n} MRE_i \quad (6)$$

2008). The Wilcoxon method tests whether two related (paired) samples have the same median. In our case we considered as the first of the paired samples the AEs derived by MLR and as the second sample, the AE sample derived by each of the other methods (LD, RI, EM and MI). In all tests we consider as statistically significant a difference with p-value (significance) smaller than 0.05. All the tests conducted are one-tailed (directional) in the sense that the alternative hypothesis is that a certain statistic of the AEs derived from the MLR is smaller than that of a comparative model (LD, RI, EM and MI).

The problem with the software projects cost data is that the samples are quite small and skewed, so it is not easy to make assumptions regarding the distribution of the prediction errors resulting from a certain process or a model and from which the accuracy measures are calculated. For such small-sized type of data it is known from the statistical literature that a certain class of simulation methods may be proved quite beneficial (Mittas & Angelis 2008a)

More specifically, *permutation tests* are utilized in order to investigate the error reduction obtained by the MLR method. Permutation tests are resampling techniques which "reconstruct" the underlying theoretical distribution, based on rearrangements of the data. The method generates a large number of paired samples (for (1), (2) and (3)) where each pair is permuted randomly. The statistic under consideration is computed for each generated paired sample and its sampling distribution is used for testing any hypothesis (for further details see Mittas & Angelis 2008a)

As we have already mentioned, the accuracy of a prediction model can be evaluated through the AEs. For this reason we follow a similar approach presented above for the case of Wilcoxon test, whereas the statistic under consideration is the median of AEs. The algorithm for the evaluation of the permutation test can be described by the following steps:

1. The paired data are randomly permuted as we already described.
2. The difference of the statistic under consideration (median of AEs) is computed.
3. Steps 1 and 2 are repeated a large number of times.
4. The statistic from the original sample is computed and is located in the sampling distribution of all values obtained from Steps 1-3 in order to estimate the significance of the hypothesis (p - value).

Graphical Comparison through Regression Error Characteristic Curve

As we have already mentioned, despite the wide variety of accuracy measures appeared so far in SCE literature, the presentation of overall accuracy tables does not provide any information about the distributions of errors. Furthermore, the tests presented in the previous section make inference about a parameter of the comparative distributions of errors (mean or median) and do not provide any further information for the performances of the comparative models at any other point of their distributions. All of the issues discussed above led us to suggest a graphical tool (Mittas & Angelis, 2010) that can be utilized for comparison purposes in order to reinforce the results of accuracy measures and statistical hypothesis tests through an easily interpretable manner.

Regression Error Characteristic (REC) curve is a recently proposed visualization technique that can also be incorporated in the comparison procedure of alternative prediction models. REC curves, proposed by Bi and Bennett (2003), are a generalization of Receiver Operating Characteristic (ROC) curves that are often utilized in classification problems. A REC curve is a two-dimensional graph where the horizontal axis (or x-axis) represents the *error tolerance* (i.e. all possible values of error for a model) of a predefined accuracy measure and the vertical axis (or y-axis) represents the *accuracy* of a prediction model. Accuracy is defined as the percentage of projects that are predicted within the error tolerance e.

$$accuracy\ (e) = \frac{\#(\text{projects with error} \leq e)}{\#(\text{projects})} \tag{7}$$

REC curves have been introduced in the SCE area in Mittas & Angelis (2008b, 2010), where it was suggested that their utilization can be proved quite beneficial since they reinforce the knowledge of project managers obtained either by single accuracy indicators or by comparisons through formal statistical tests. They demonstrate that the most important feature is the ability to present easily accuracy results to non-experts and support the decision-making. In addition, REC curves are very informative since they take into account the whole error distribution and not just a single indicator of the errors providing a graphical tool that can guide the modelling process (identification of extreme points) by the inspection of their shapes. Further details of their advantages, interesting characteristics and also the algorithm for their construction can be found in Mittas & Angelis, (2008b, 2010).

In Figure 1, we present the REC curves of three hypothetical comparative models. Generally, a prediction model performs well if the REC curve climbs rapidly towards the upper left corner. It is obvious that Model A outperforms both Model B and Model C since its REC curve is always above the corresponding curves of the comparative models. Considering the curves of Model B and Model C, no conclusion can be derived for the overall prediction performances. On the other hand, valuable information for their performances on different ranges of errors can be derived by the

Figure 1. An example of REC curves

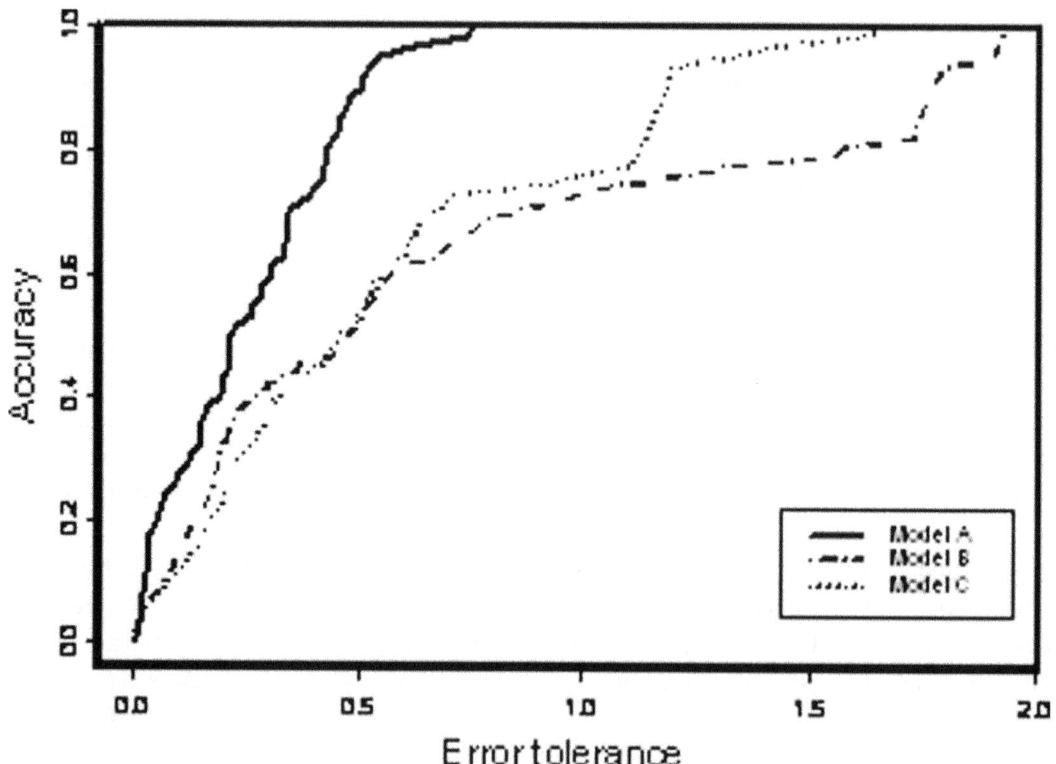

inspection of their relative positions. Their REC curves reveal that Model B seems to be the "best" choice for small values of errors but the opposite is the case as the error tolerance becomes higher (higher than 0.5).

Although the utilization of statistical comparisons should be always carried out in order to verify the differences between comparative prediction models, specific limitations (i.e. difficulties to the interpretation of the statistical results, heavily-skewed distributions etc) render this hardly applicable. REC curves give the opportunity to a practitioner to draw significant findings by an alternative visualization technique for the whole distribution of error functions. Moreover, there are cases in which a project manager requires further information for the prediction power of alternative models on very specific ranges of the actual cost variable (i.e. effort or productivity). This is due to the fact that the cost of a forthcoming project is not uniform and may have different impact for the earnings of an organization. More precisely, a project manager wishes to get a better insight for projects with high actual cost since an inaccurate prediction can lead to high overruns. On the other hand, a practitioner is also interested in projects with small actual cost in order to bid other contracts and increase the profits of the organization.

The abovementioned analysis can be carried out through partial REC curves proposed by Torgo (2005), whereas in our previous study (Mittas & Angelis, 2010) we present the application of partial REC curves in SCE in a more systematic fashion by detailing the basic principles, properties and the algorithm for constructing them. In general, a partial REC curve can be constructed in the same way as the REC curves by simply estimating the distribution of the prediction errors only for those cases falling within the range of particular interest (i.e. projects with small or high actual cost).

In Figure 2 (a) and (b), we present an illustrative example of the partial REC curves. The critical question we posed is which model presents the best prediction power for projects with small or high actual cost. So, after the estimation of errors obtained by the three hypothetical models, we have to partition our dataset into two subsets containing projects with small and high actual cost. The partial REC curves for small (Figure 2(a)) and high (Figure 2(b)) costs suggest that Model A outperforms both Model B and Model C everywhere, since its curves are always above the corresponding curves of Model B and Model C. On the other hand, Model B seems to outperform Model C for projects with low cost (Figure 2 (a)) but the opposite holds for the projects with high

Figure 2. An example of Partial REC curves (a) for small actual costs and (b) for high actual costs

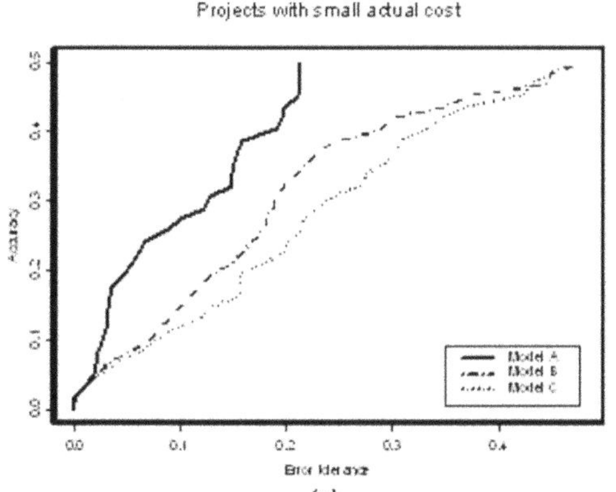

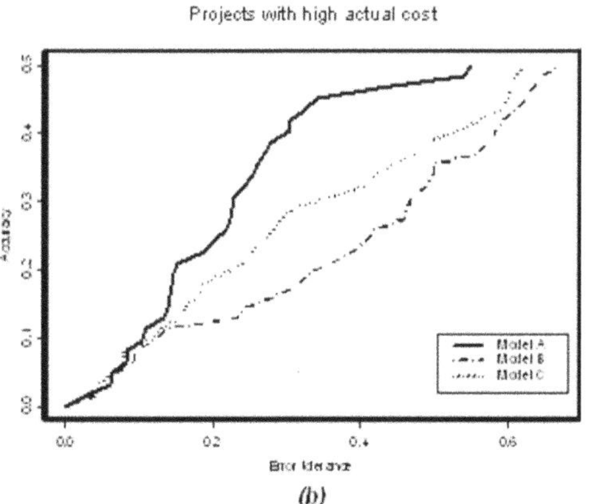

cost (Figure 2 (b)). Now, let us just ignore for the needs of the example Model A which is the best overall. After a rough estimation of the project's cost level (low or high) we would choose Model B for low cost forthcoming projects and Model C for high cost projects, combining in this way the predictions derived from the two comparative models.

Despite the fact that REC curves provide a straightforward manner to visualize and compare the predictive performance of competitive models, they do not take into account that the loss of under- or over-estimating of a forthcoming project is not always symmetric. Underestimations can cause serious effects on the project management and decision-making, since there is always the risk to erroneously allocate resources or staff on the development life-cycle (Kemerer, 1987). The wrong managerial decisions can lead to poor quality of the deliverables and thus bad reputation for the organization (Briand, Langley, & Wieczorek 2000). On the contrast, an overestimation can increase rapidly the chance to reject a new contract, since there is a general belief from the project manager that it would not be beneficial for the development firm to undertake a forthcoming project (Mukhopadhyay, Vicinanza & Prietula 1992).

Towards this direction, Mittas & Angelis (2013) proposed the adaptation of RROC analysis to the SCE area aiming to improve the comparison of prediction models through a more realistic approach taking into account the real business situations in which under- and over-estimations have a different impact on the organizations. RROC analysis is totally based on the RROC space (Hernandez-Orallo, 2013), which represents the *total error* (or *sum*) *of overestimation* (SOE) (Equation 8) on the *x*-axis and the *total error* (or *sum*) of *underestimation* (SUE) (Equation 9) on the *y*-axis for each candidate prediction model. Again, the *error* (e_i) is a loss function, which is defined as the difference between the estimated Y_{E_i} and actual Y_{A_i} values of each project i $\left(e_i = Y_{E_i} - Y_{A_i}\right)$.

$$SOE = \sum_{i=1}^{n} \left\{ e_i \mid e_i > 0 \right\} \tag{8}$$

$$SUE = \sum_{i=1}^{n} \left\{ e_i \mid e_i < 0 \right\} \tag{9}$$

Figure 3 illustrates the notion of RROC space through the examination of three hypothetical prediction models. In the best scenario, an ideal model will lie on the upper left corner with zero SOE and SUE values indicating no prediction error. In addition, models that present equal values for SOE and SUE will lie on the diagonal reference line indicating a balanced situation. The relative position of other points that do not lie on the reference line signifies systematic bias. More precisely, a point above the diagonal line corresponds to situations, in which the corresponding model tends to overestimate the actual cost. On the other hand, a model, which is prone to underestimations, will lie below the diagonal.

In our example, Model A lies more close to the upper left corner and can be considered as the best model compared with the alternative ones in terms of predictive power. Indeed, Hernandez-Orallo (2013) showed that a global measure of bias (mean error-ME) can be easily evaluated from SOE and SUE values through the following formula.

$$ME = \frac{1}{n} \sum_{i=1}^{n} e_i = \frac{SOE + SUE}{n} \tag{10}$$

Concerning the systematic bias of the models, we can observe that Model B is the closest one to the diagonal line and seems to produce the least biased predictions. On the contrary, Model C presents the highest vertical distance from the line indicating predictions with the highest bias.

Figure 3. An example of RROC space

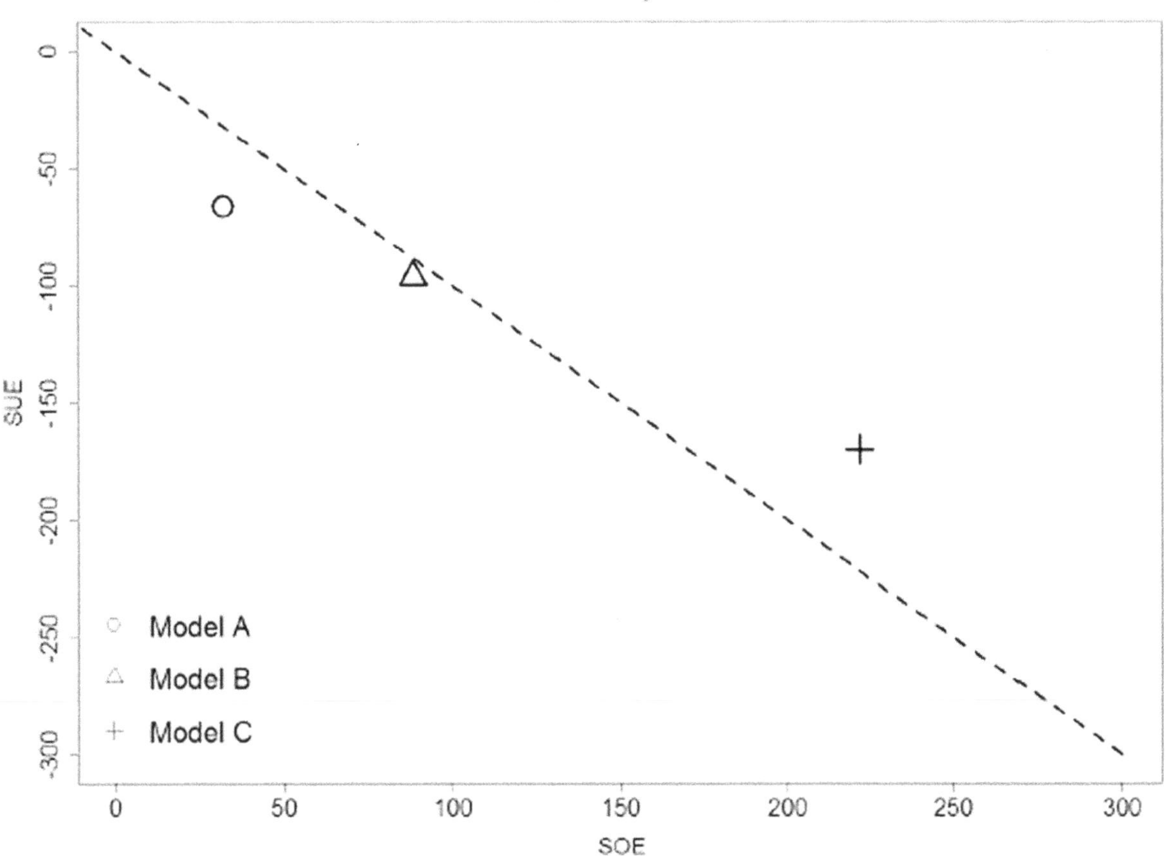

Finally, the relative positions of Model A and Model C with respect to the diagonal line indicate underestimation and overestimation, respectively.

Analogous to the classification task, the next step of RROC analysis is to construct a curve, which represents the predictive power of a candidate model over a different range of values of the dependent variable. For this reason, Hernandez-Orallo (2013) proposed the utilization of a constant term, namely the *shift*, which can be considered as a threshold value. Given a vector of predictions

$$\mathbf{Y}_E = (Y_{E_1}, Y_{E_2}, ..., Y_{E_n})$$

derived from a certain model, the objective is to obtain a modified set of estimates

$$\mathbf{Y}'_E = (Y_{E_1} + s, Y_{E_2} + s, ..., Y_{E_n} + s)$$

by adding a shift s. Finally, Hernandez-Orallo (2013) proposed an algorithm for the evaluation of different shift values, so as to construct the overall RROC of a candidate model.

Figure 4 shows the RROCs for the three hypothetical models, in which the initial performances without the usage of any shift value ($s = 0$) are portrayed with large symbols. The overall conclusion is that Model A dominates both Model B and Model C, since the corresponding RROC is always above the comparative models. On the other hand, we can infer that Model C is certainly the worst candidate. This practically means that this specific model is not able to pro-

Figure 4. An example of RROCs

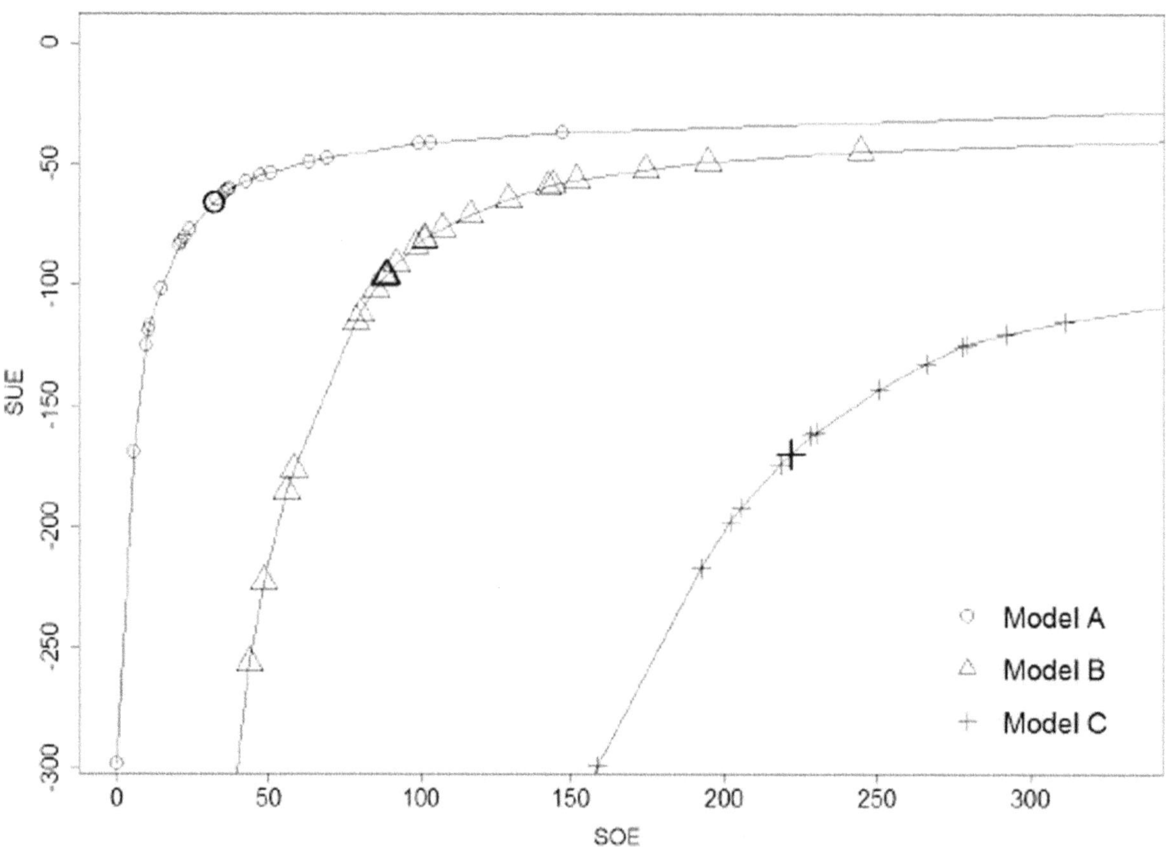

vide accurate estimates for any shift value, since there is no region on the RROC space, in which it is optimal.

EXPERIMENTATION RESULTS

In order to fit an effort prediction model in each of the above datasets, we used ordinary least squares (OLS) regression. For each of the five models, the independent variables were always the same. This was done on purpose, in order to preserve the balance of the experimental design and to have a common base for the comparisons. Indeed, removing or adding variables would cause additional sources of variation on accuracy measures and would therefore complicate the analysis and the interpretation of the results. As independent variables of the models we consider the numerical variable '*lnfpoints*' and the two categorical variables '*dbms_4*' and '*barthype_4*' which are the variables with real missing values.

In Table 3, we summarise the results of the comparison of the five missing data techniques in the dataset of ISBSG with real missing values. In general, the above results are in agreement with the results in Sentas & Angelis (2005), but the comparisons in this study extend the prior knowledge due to the evaluation of different error functions. The MLR method appears the best performance in terms of accuracy, bias and spread since the corresponding indicators have the lowest mean and median values. On the other hand, MI gives the worst performance in all the

Table 3. Overall prediction measures from the five MDT

MDT	MAE	MdAE	Meanz	Medianz	MMRE	MdMRE
MLR	**2153.04**	**890.44**	**1.16**	**0.91**	**62.45**	**42.86**
LD	2445.92	1240.74	1.17	1.14	65.76	55.62
RI	2538.96	1386.64	1.31	1.20	73.20	50.22
EM	2712.19	1550.29	1.32	1.11	73.78	56.25
MI	4293.78	1649.70	1.55	1.35	96.68	64.05

measures. A closer examination of the indicators reveals a large divergence between the mean and medians of the local measures of errors. This fact may be due to the existence of extreme outlying points and further investigation is needed through REC curves. Moreover, the presence of outliers justifies the utilization of more robust statistical comparisons such as the non-parametric Wilcoxon procedure and permutation tests.

The non-parametric Wilcoxon tests between the AEs of the MLR and the AEs derived by each of the other methods (LD, RI, EM and MI) are presented in Table 4. Since all the values are less than 0.05, there is a statistically significant difference between the performance of MLR and each of the other methods. As the samples of AEs are small-sized, permutation tests should also be carried out in order to have a more realistic aspect of the abovementioned results. As we can see in Table 4, the findings are also verified by the p-values of permutation tests and we can infer that MLR seems to be a good choice.

The graphical comparisons through REC curves also indicate the error reduction caused by MLR. More precisely, in Figure 5 (a) and (b) the AEs REC curves for all the comparative models are presented. In order to obtain a more clear inspection of the error distributions, we decided to compare MLR with LD and RI (Figure 5 (a)) and MLR with EM and MI (Figure 5 (b)), separately based on the rankings of their performances. The horizontal dashed reference line from 0.5 intersects each REC curve at a point which corresponds to the median value of the AEs. In this manner, we can geometrically evaluate the overall MdAE for each one of the comparative models. The AE REC curve for MLR is always above the corresponding curves of the rest models verifying the results derived from formal statistical comparisons and overall prediction measures. Moreover, LD seems to have a slightly better accuracy performance than RI whereas MI the worst in all the ranges of possible AE values. An interesting characteristic of all the REC curves is that they are flat for high values of AEs and they do not reach the value of 1 until the error tolerance becomes high. This fact signifies the presence of extreme outlying points which are also responsible for the large variability between the mean and median values of AE presented in Table 3.

Concerning the bias of the models, the mean values of the error z ratio indicate that all methods are prone to overestimation since all values are higher than 1. Due to the fact that the mean statistic is affected by the presence of extreme outliers and the data is highly skewed, we should examine the median as a more robust measure of central tendency for the z distributions. Using

Table 4. Significance of all paired samples tests

Comparison	Wilcoxon Test	Permutation Test
MLR-LD	0.018/Sig.	0.043/Sig.
MLR-RI	0.030/Sig.	0.021/Sig.
MLR-EM	0.037/Sig.	0.012/Sig.
MLR-MI	0.012/Sig.	0.018/Sig.

Figure 5. (a) AE REC curves for MLR, LD, RI, (b) AE REC curves for MLR, EM, MI, (c) z REC curves for MLR, LD, RI, (d) z REC curves for MLR, EM, MI, (e) MRE REC curves for MLR, LD, RI, (f) MRE REC curves for MLR, EM, MI

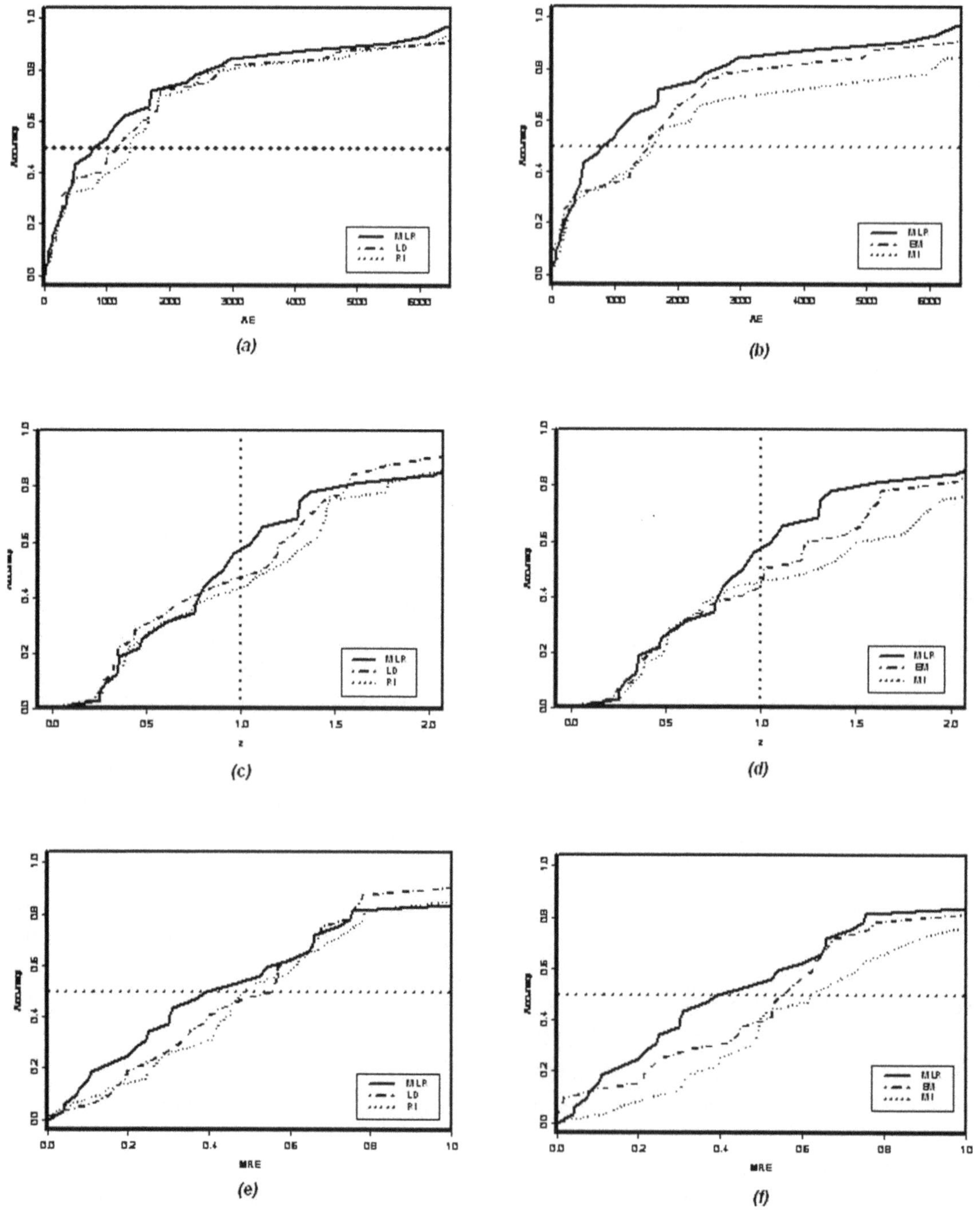

the medians, it is clear that only MLR favours underestimates, whereas the other models are susceptible to overestimates.

In Figures 5 (c) and (d) we constructed the REC curves representing the error ratio z for each comparative model. This graph has interesting characteristics since the curve of the better model has to be under the curve of the comparative one for values smaller than 1 (optimum value) and above the curve of the comparative one for values higher than 1. For better illustration, we present with a vertical dashed reference line the critical value of 1 that signifies the under- or overestimations. Furthermore, we can also assess whether a model favours under or over-estimation by the examination of error tolerance at accuracy 0.50 (that is the median). The medianz statistic of MLR is the closest to the optimum value of 1 and appears to be the least biased model whereas MI the most biased model (Figure 5 (d)). On the other hand, LD outperforms MLR for error tolerance higher than 1.6. So, there are a few high outlying points of z values produced by MLR which also affect the mean statistic of the error sample.

As far as the spread of z error ratio concerns, the distributions of MREs (Figures 5 (e) and (f)) show that MLR outperforms the other models and has the lowest median value. In addition, the comparison of MLR and LD models signifies that MLR has bad performance for high values of MREs (higher than 70%) indicating again the existence of outliers.

In our previous analysis, we presented in detail how REC curves can lead a project manager to select the "best" imputation technique. Although this is one of the most crucial issues that have to be addressed for the best management of a new software project, the aforementioned analysis concerns the overall prediction performances of comparative models. As we have already pointed out, partial REC curves offer a specialized analysis and valuable information about the performances of the comparative imputation techniques on specific ranges of interest.

Let us suppose that a practitioner has to investigate how the prediction models perform separately for small and for large values of the dependent variable (effort). In the first step of the partial REC analysis, we have to define the range of interest. For this reason, we calculated the median of the empirical distribution of the dependent variable and we constructed the partial REC curves for each one of the following subsets:

- Projects that have small actual effort that is

$$\text{actual effort} \leq Median\,.$$

- Projects that have high actual effort that is

$$\text{actual effort} > Median\,.$$

With this partition both the first subset (with small effort projects) and the second subset (with high effort projects) contains 16 (50%) cases.

The partial REC analysis concerning the accuracy (AE) of the prediction performance for the first subset is presented in Figure 6 (a) and (b). Regarding the accuracy of the imputation techniques, we can observe that MLR climbs more rapidly to the upper left corner compared with the other models. Another interesting issue coming up from the visual inspection of their performances is that the top of the curves is extremely flat for the cases of (LD, RI, EM and MI) and does not reach 0.5 until the error tolerance becomes high, indicating the presence of outliers. On the other hand, all models present similar performances for error tolerance smaller than 500. This practically means that there is no difference in the prediction power of the comparative models for small values of AE whereas MLR significantly outperforms for higher values of AE for the first subset.

The partial REC analysis is also conducted for the second subset of large effort projects (Figure 6 (c) and (d)). Contrary to the first subset, the partial REC curve of MLR reveals that this im-

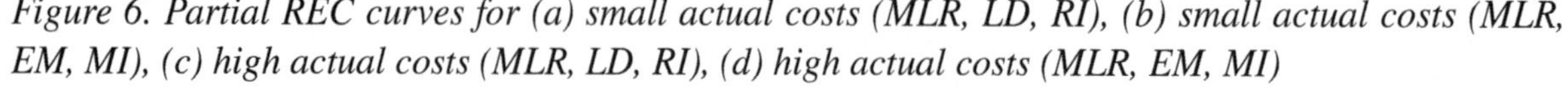

Figure 6. Partial REC curves for (a) small actual costs (MLR, LD, RI), (b) small actual costs (MLR, EM, MI), (c) high actual costs (MLR, LD, RI), (d) high actual costs (MLR, EM, MI)

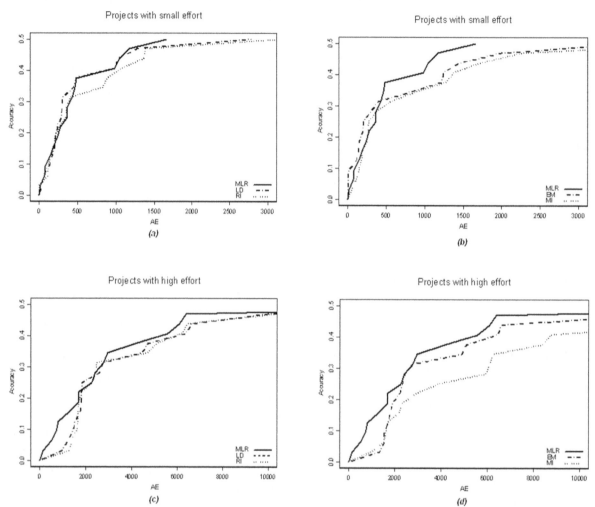

putation method appears the "best" performance for the whole range of error tolerance since its curve outperforms the corresponding curves of the comparative imputation techniques. Now, ignoring for the needs of the analysis MLR which is the best overall, we can point out that LD and RI present similar partial REC curves and for this reason they can be considered as the second "best" imputation techniques for projects with high actual costs.

In the next step of the graphical comparison, we perform the RROC analysis to derive conclusions about the predictive power of the five competitive models with respect to over- and under-estimations (Table 5). Figure 7 represents the RROC space for the models of the experimental study. It is clear that all models except from MI are prone to underestimations, since they lie below the diagonal reference line. In addition, the vertical distances of MI, RI and LD from the diagonal indicate that these models present the least biased predictions.

Although the RROC space provides certain information about the capabilities of the models to provide accurate estimates, a more interesting approach is to evaluate the prediction performances of models over a range of possible outcomes of

Table 5. SOE, SUE and ME measures from the five MDT

MDT	SOE	SUE	ME
MLR	9975.601	-58921.68	-1529.57
LD	31613.03	-46656.43	-470.1064
RI	36859.64	-44387.09	-235.23
EM	41959.08	-44830.97	-89.75
MI	98901.86	-38499.15	1887.59

Figure 7. RROC space for MLR, LD, RI, EM and MI

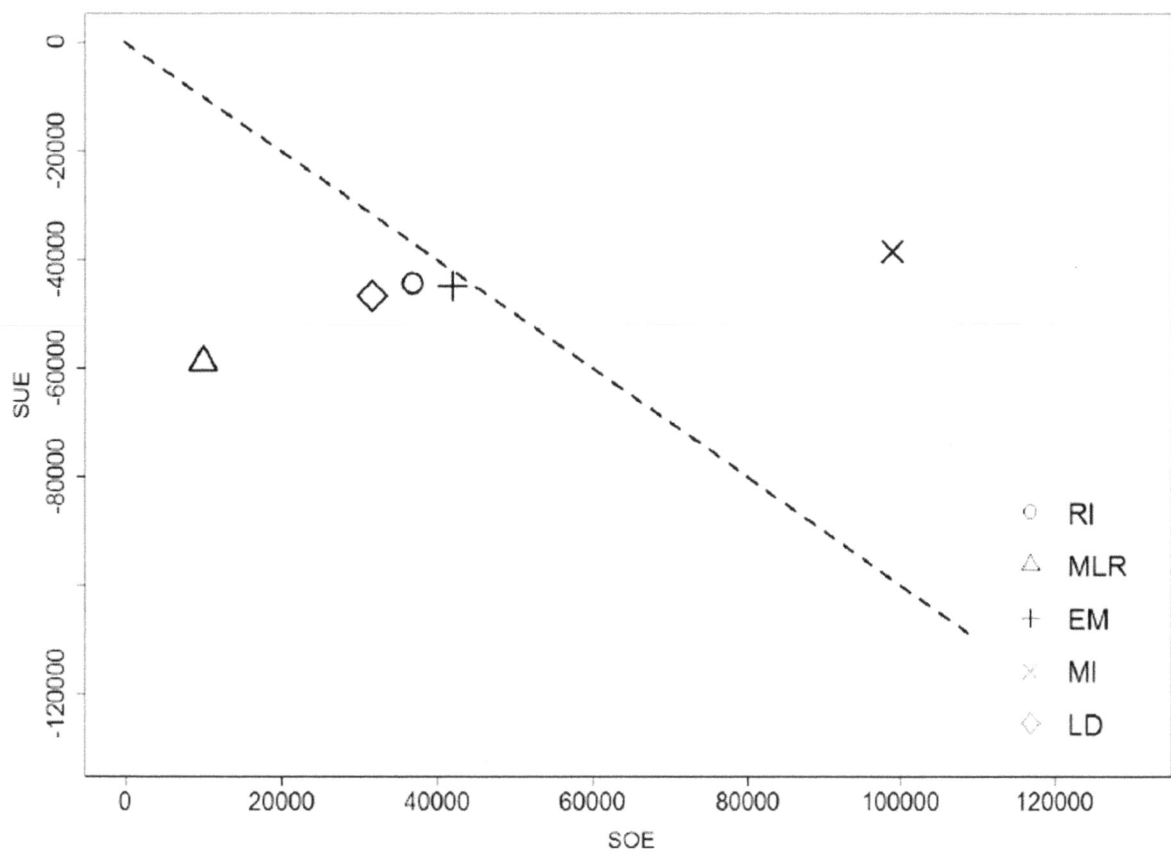

the dependent variable. Hence, in Figure 8, we demonstrate the RROCs derived from different shift values. The inspection of the graph shows that MLR dominates the competitive models over the whole region of RROC space. Furthermore, RI and LD can be considered as the second best choice with similar predictive power. Finally, MI should be not used in the estimation process, since there is no region on the RROC space, where it is optimal indicating poor performance.

In summary, the combination of the statistical and computational methods which we applied for the comparisons between MLR and the other missing data techniques managed to reveal the

Figure 8. RROCs for MLR, LD, RI, EM and MI

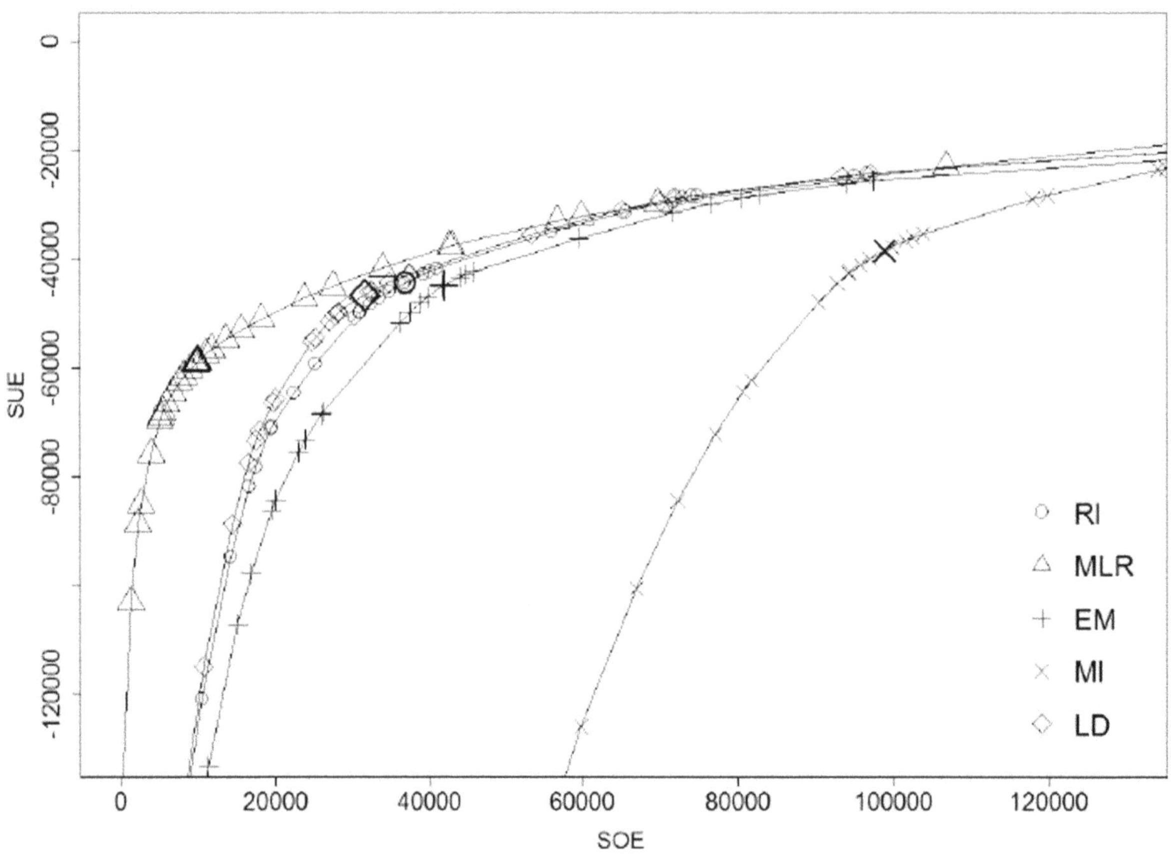

superiority of MLR not only for the whole distribution of errors but also over specific ranges of the actual effort, especially for projects with high actual effort. In addition, MLR seems to dominate the competitive models over a range of different prediction values.

CONCLUSION AND DIRECTIONS FOR FUTURE RESEARCH

This chapter presents a combination of statistical, computational and visualization methods for handling missing data and for the comparison of missing data techniques applied in software cost datasets for the construction of prediction models. These methods have been introduced in previous works of the authors (Sentas & Angelis (2005), Mittas & Angelis (2008a, 2008b and 2010)), and in the present work are presented as a comprehensive framework which can help a researcher or a practitioner to decide and choose the most suitable missing data technique. The proposed methodology is described as a case study using a dataset with real missing values and specific methods for: (a) building the prediction model, (b) handling the missing data and (c) comparing the missing data techniques by statistical and graphical methods.

More specifically: (a) we used a very popular cost prediction method in SCE, the least squares regression, (b) we applied five missing data techniques: multinomial logistic regression (MLR), Listwise Deletion (LD), Mean Imputation (MI), Expectation Maximization (EM) and Regression Imputation (RI) and (c) we used functions of the prediction error, non-parametric and resampling statistical tests and also two graphical tools, the Regression Error Characteristic (REC) curves and the Regression Receiver Operating Curves (RROC) in order to compare the performance of MLR with the other four well-known and older methods. The rationale for these comparisons was our previous experience, when we suggested the use of MLR as efficient method for imputing categorical data and compared it with the same missing data techniques. However, our previous work was based on simulated missing data and the comparisons were purely statistical. For the present case study we used a software project dataset with real missing observations and also a comprehensive framework for comparisons.

It is important to note that the missing data techniques were evaluated for their effect on the cost prediction model. That is why we used the results of regression under the application of different missing data approaches in order to make inferences. In general, the results confirmed our previous beliefs for the efficiency of MLR. The combination of the methods used in the present work, showed that MLR gives better results than the other methods in this specific dataset with real missing data.

A very important point of concern is whether an imputation technique produces a new dataset that can be further used for purposes other than cost estimation. In this regard, we have to emphasize that the methods discussed in this chapter, have a specific role: to provide a dataset as a basis for building a cost estimation model. Under this perspective it is clear that the imputation procedure is essentially a method producing artificial data which will be used for a specific reason. These data cannot be used in a straightforward manner for other inferential purposes. So, the result of a comparison between missing data techniques using a cost estimation criterion does not mean that the "best" method under this criterion is necessarily a representative dataset as a whole.

In summary, the conclusions derived from the case study were: First, the comparison of MLR with the compared MTD's revealed high efficiency of the method in terms of accuracy, bias and spread. More specifically, MLR gave significantly better results than the comparative techniques in terms of accuracy that was evaluated through the AE indicators. Second, MLR was the only method that produced the least biased estimates. Moreover, the central location statistics and the inspections of REC curves for MRE measuring the spread of the distributions reflected the very good performance of MLR, compared to the other methods. On the other hand, MI technique appeared to have the "worst" performance in all the aspects of error. The comparisons indicated also that LD showed quite good performance. The comparison of MLR and LD signified that the latter had better performance for high values of error tolerance in terms of bias and spread. The good performance of the LD method may be a consequence of the fact that possibly the missing values in both the categorical variables of our dataset are unrelated to the values of any other variables, whether missing or valid (MCAR mechanism). The aforementioned interpretation is based on our results in Sentas & Angelis (2005), where LD performed well in the case of low percentage of missing values (10%) and MCAR mechanism of missing data. Concerning the utilization of RROC analysis, the visualization tool shows generally that all methods except MI underestimated the cost of projects. On the other hand, the construction of RROCs with different shift values showed that MLR seems to dominate the comparative methods, whereas LD and RI form the second best group in terms of predictive performance. Finally, the curve of MI indicates again that it was the "worst" candidate.

It is obvious that the above results cannot be generalized for all datasets. The purpose of this study was not to show the superiority of MLR in any dataset and with respect to any other method, but rather to illustrate how the complex problem of missing data can be manipulated by a combination of different methods. The ideas discussed here can be applied to any dataset for the comparison of any other missing data techniques. A general conclusion from the experimentations is that the problems encountered in cost estimation require a variety of advanced methods for efficient decision making and modeling.

The research questions and therefore the directions for future research are several. There are many more MDTs in the literature which deserve thorough comparative studies on various datasets. It would be also interesting to study the effect of missing data techniques on other prediction models and methods, for example on estimation by analogy. Other measures, especially designed for missing data of software projects, could be used or invented so as to evaluate the imputation methods with the highest precision. Furthermore, it would be interesting to include in the analysis, multiple additional performance criteria based on project attributes other than the cost (e.g. bug count estimation). In this manner, although the model will be constructed and compared with respect to the cost attribute, the effectiveness of the imputed values can be tested towards other dimensions. Another issue is the combination of other advanced methods for the comparisons. Finally, the application of the proposed techniques can go beyond software cost estimation, for example in the estimation of other attributes (defects, quality, etc) of more general classes of products.

REFERENCES

Bi, J., & Bennet, K. P. (2003). Regression error characteristics curves. In *Proceedings of the 20th International Conference on Machine Learning (ICML-2003)* (pp. 43-50). ICML.

Briand, L. C., Langley, T., & Wieczorek, I. (2000, June). A replicated assessment and comparison of common software cost modeling techniques. In *Proceedings of the 22nd international conference on Software engineering* (pp. 377-386). ACM. doi:10.1145/337180.337223

Cartwright, M. H., Shepperd, M. J., & Song, Q. (2003). Dealing with missing software project data. *In Proceedings of the 9th IEEE International Metrics Symposium (METRICS'03)* (pp. 154-165). IEEE. doi:10.1109/METRIC.2003.1232464

El Emam, K., & Birk, A. (2000). Validating the ISO/IEC 15504 measure of software requirements analysis process capability. *IEEE Transactions on Software Engineering*, *26*(6), 541–566. doi:10.1109/32.852742

Foss, T., Stensrud, E., Kitchenham, B., & Myrtveit, I. (2003). A simulation study of the model evaluation criterion MMRE. *IEEE Transactions on Software Engineering*, *29*(11), 985–995. doi:10.1109/TSE.2003.1245300

Hernández-Orallo, J. (2013). ROC curves for regression. *Pattern Recognition*, *46*(12), 3395–3411. doi:10.1016/j.patcog.2013.06.014

Hosmer, D. W., & Lemeshow, S. (1989). *Applied logistic regression*. New York: John Willey & Sons.

Jeffery, R., Ruhe, M., & Wieczorek, I. (2000). A comparative study of two software development cost modelling techniques using multi-organizational and company-specific data. *Information and Software Technology*, *42*(14), 1009–1016. doi:10.1016/S0950-5849(00)00153-1

Jeffery, R., Ruhe, M., & Wieczorek, I. (2001). Using public domain metrics to estimate software development effort. In *Proceedings of the 7th IEEE International Metrics Symposium (METRICS'01)* (pp. 16-27). IEEE.

Jorgensen, M., & Shepperd, M. (2007). A systematic review of software development cost estimation studies. *IEEE Transactions on Software Engineering*, *33*(1), 33–53. doi:10.1109/TSE.2007.256943

Kemerer, C. (1987). An empirical validation of software cost estimation models. *Communications of the ACM*, *30*(5), 416–429. doi:10.1145/22899.22906

Kitchenham, B., & Mendes, E. (2004) A comparison of cross-company and within-company effort estimation models for web applications. In *Proceedings of the 8th International Conference on Empirical Assessment in Software Engineering (EASE 2004)* (pp. 47-55). EASE. doi:10.1049/ic:20040398

Kitchenham, B., & Mendes, E. (2009). Why comparative effort prediction studies may be invalid. In *Proceedings of the 5th ACM International Conference on Predictor Models in Software Engineering*. ACM. doi:10.1145/1540438.1540444

Kitchenham, B., Pickard, L., MacDonell, S., & Shepperd, M. (2001). What accuracy statistics really measure. *IEE Proceedings on Software*, *148*(3), 81–85. doi:10.1049/ip-sen:20010506

Liebchen, G., & Shepperd, M. (2008) Data sets and data quality in software engineering. In *Proceedings of the 4th ACM International Workshop on Predictor Models in Software Engineering* (pp. 39-44). ACM. doi:10.1145/1370788.1370799

Little, R. J. A., & Rubin, D. B. (2002). *Statistical analysis with missing data*. John Wiley & Sons.

Mair, C., & Shepperd, M. (2005). The consistency of empirical comparisons of regression and analogy-based software project cost prediction. In *Proceedings of the International Symposium on Empirical Software Engineering* (pp. 491-518). Academic Press. doi:10.1109/ISESE.2005.1541858

Maxwell, K. (2002). *Applied statistics for software managers*. Prentice-Hall.

Mendes, E., & Lokan, C. (2008). Replicating studies on cross- vs single-company effort models using the ISBSG database. *Empirical Software Engineering*, *13*(1), 3–37. doi:10.1007/s10664-007-9045-5

Mendes, E., Lokan, C., Harrison, R., & Triggs, C. (2005). A replicated comparison of cross-company and within-company effort estimation models using the ISBSG database. In *Proceedings of the 11th IEEE International Software Metrics Symposium (METRICS'05)* (pp.36-45). IEEE. doi:10.1109/METRICS.2005.4

Mittas, N., & Angelis, L. (2008a). Comparing cost prediction models by resampling techniques. *Journal of Systems and Software*, *81*(5), 616–632. doi:10.1016/j.jss.2007.07.039

Mittas, N., & Angelis, L. (2008b). Comparing software cost prediction models by a visualization tool. In *Proceedings of the 34th Euromicro Conference on Software Engineering and Advanced Applications (SEAA'08).* (pp. 433-440). SEAA. doi:10.1109/SEAA.2008.23

Mittas, N., & Angelis, L. (2010). Visual comparison of software cost estimation models by regression error characteristic analysis. *Journal of Systems and Software*, *83*(4), 621–637. doi:10.1016/j.jss.2009.10.044

Mittas, N. & Angelis L. (2012). A permutation test based on regression error characteristic curves for software cost estimation models. *Empirical Software Engineering, 17*(1-2), 34-61.

Mittas, N., & Angelis, L. (2013a). Ranking and clustering software cost estimation models through a multiple comparisons algorithm. *IEEE Transactions on* Software Engineering, *39*(4), 537–551.

Mittas, N., & Angelis, L. (2013b). Overestimation and underestimation of software cost models: Evaluation by visualization. In *Proceedings of Software Engineering and Advanced Applications (SEAA)*. IEEE.

Mittas, N., Mamalikidis, I., & Angelis, L. (2012). StatREC: A graphical user interface tool for visual hypothesis testing of cost prediction models. In *Proceedings of the 8th International Conference on Predictive Models in Software Engineering. ACM*. doi:10.1145/2365324.2365331

Mukhopadhyay, T., Vicinanza, S., & Prietula, M. (1992). Examining the feasibility of a case-based reasoning model for software effort estimation. *Management Information Systems Quarterly, 16*(2), 155–171. doi:10.2307/249573

Myrtveit, I., Stensrud, E., & Olsson, U. (2001). Analyzing data sets with missing data: An empirical evaluation of imputation methods and likelihood-based methods. *IEEE Transactions on Software Engineering, 27*(11), 999–1013. doi:10.1109/32.965340

Sentas, P., & Angelis, L. (2006). Categorical missing data imputation for software cost estimation by multinomial logistic regression. *Journal of Systems and Software, 79*(3), 404–414. doi:10.1016/j.jss.2005.02.026

Sentas, P., Angelis, L., Stamelos, I., & Bleris, G. (2005). software productivity and effort prediction with ordinal regression. *Information and Software Technology, 47*(1), 17–29. doi:10.1016/j.infsof.2004.05.001

Song, Q., Shepperd, M. J., & Cartwright, M. (2005). A Short Note on Safest Default Missingness Mechanism Assumptions. *Empirical Software Engineering, 10*(2), 235–243. doi:10.1007/s10664-004-6193-8

Stensrud, E., & Myrtveit, I. (1998). Human performance estimating with analogy and regression models: An empirical validation. In *Proceedings of the 5th IEEE International Software Metrics Symposium (METRICS'98)* (pp. 205–213). IEEE. doi:10.1109/METRIC.1998.731247

Strike, K., El Emam, K., & Madhavji, N. (2001). Software cost estimation with incomplete data. *IEEE Transactions on Software Engineering, 27*(10), 890–908. doi:10.1109/32.962560

Torgo, L. (2005). Regression error characteristic surfaces. In *Proceedings of the 11th ACM SIGKDD International Conference on Knowledge Discovery and Data Mining (KDD '05)*, (pp. 697-702). ACM.

Twala, B., Cartwright, M., & Shepperd, M. (2006). Ensemble of missing data techniques to improve software prediction accuracy. In *Proceedings of the 28th International Conference on Software Engineering*, (pp. 909 – 912). Academic Press. doi:10.1145/1134285.1134449

Van Hulse, J., & Khoshgoftaar, T. (2008). A comprehensive empirical evaluation of missing value imputation in noisy software measurement data. *Journal of Systems and Software, 81*(5), 691–708. doi:10.1016/j.jss.2007.07.043

Wong, W. E., & Zhao, J. & Chan, Victor K.Y. (2006). Applying statistical methodology to optimize and simplify software metric models with missing data. In *Proceedings of the 2006 ACM Symposium on Applied Computing* (pp. 1728-1733). ACM. doi:10.1145/1141277.1141687

Zhang, W., Yang, Y., & Wang, Q. (2011). Handling missing data in software effort prediction with naive Bayes and EM algorithm. In *Proceedings of the 7th International Conference on Predictive Models in Software Engineering* (p. 1). ACM. doi:10.1145/2020390.2020394

Zhang, W., Yang, Y., & Wang, Q. (2012). A comparative study of absent features and unobserved values in software effort data. *International Journal of Software Engineering and Knowledge Engineering*, *22*(2), 185–202. doi:10.1142/S0218194012400025

Zhihao Chen, , Boehm, B., Menzies, T., & Port, D. (2005). Finding the right data for cost modeling. *IEEE Software*, *22*(6), 38–46. doi:10.1109/MS.2005.151

KEY TERMS AND DEFINITIONS

Imputation: Imputation is the estimation of missing values by statistical techniques. The missing values are filled in and the resultant completed dataset can be analysed by standard methods.

Missing Data Techniques: These are statistical methods that have been developed in order to deal with the problem of missing data. These methods involve deletion of cases or variables and imputation methods.

Missing Values: A Missing value occurs when no data value is stored for the variable in the current observation.

Regression Error Characteristic (REC) Curves: A REC curve is a two-dimensional graph for visualization of the prediction error of a model. The horizontal axis represents the error tolerance and the vertical axis represents the accuracy. Accuracy is defined as the percentage of cases that are predicted within the error tolerance.

Regression Receiver Operating Curves (RROC): RROC's represent the predictive power of alternative models on a two-dimensional plot providing easily-interpretable information.

Resampling Methods: These are statistical methods based on drawing new samples from an original sample of data in order to reconstruct the distribution of the initial population where the sample came from. They are used for various procedures, for example for computing confidence intervals and for making statistical tests. Common resampling techniques include bootstrap, jackknife and permutation tests.

Software Cost Estimation: The process of predicting the cost, in terms of effort or time, required to develop or maintain a software product. Software cost estimation is usually based on incomplete and noisy data, requiring statistical analysis and modeling.

Statistical Tests: Methods for making decisions using empirical data. Statistical tests are based on probability theory and especially on probability distributions in order to make an inference on whether a specific result is significant, in the sense that it is unlikely to have occurred by chance.

Chapter 4
Using Business Value Models to Elicit Services Conducting Business Transactions

Tharaka Ilayperuma
University of Ruhuna, Sri Lanka

Jelena Zdravkovic
Stockholm University, Sweden

ABSTRACT

Traditional organizational structures evolve towards online business using modern IT – such as cloud computing, semantic standards, and process- and service-oriented architectures. On the technology level, Web services are dominantly used for modeling the interaction points of complex Web applications. So far, development of Web services has matured on the technical perspective considering for example the development of standards for message exchanges and service coordination. However, business concepts, such as economic assets exchanged in transactions between cooperating actors, cannot be easily traced in final Web service specifications. As a consequence, business and IT models become difficult to keep aligned. To address this issue, the authors propose an MDD approach to elicit business services and further software services using REA business model as the starting point. The proposal focuses on a value-explorative elicitation of business services at the top level and model transformations using UML 2 to the system level by utilizing well-defined mappings.

INTRODUCTION

Since the emergence of the Internet, enterprises have opened their core functions to customers, suppliers, business partners and financial institutions. The intensive growth of World Wide Web has created opportunities for all kinds of enterprises to make their value offerings available to consumers as software services (i.e. e-services). An example of this is the proliferation of bookstores on the Web that let Internet users browse their catalogues, place orders, and make payments.

A problem common to the actors participating in such collaborations is to identify what offerings they should make available as software services for others. Business collaborations between

DOI: 10.4018/978-1-4666-6359-6.ch004

stakeholders of business value constellations can be described using business models. A business model is made in order to make clear who the actors are in a business scenario and explain their relations, which are formulated in terms of *economic values* exchanged between the actors or more precisely, *business transactions* occur between actors. Thereby, business models capture the business transactions between actors, and the events that result in the creation and distribution of the values among the actors.

Model Driven Development (MDD) provides a basis for the alignment between business and IT by promoting the role of models and automatic creation of code by predefined model transformations. Current Web service solutions have succeed in aligning with business processes enabling thus loosely-integrated and reusable task automations – here, the business information is captured on a procedural, that is, tactical level.

From the technical perspective, Web services have become a common technology for modelling interactions of Web applications. So far, development of Web services has focused on structural and operational aspects. Designing applications directly to these perspectives is tedious, error prone, and business functionality remains invisible. Raising the level of abstraction to separate business specifications from implementation details is a well-established trend in system development and is one of the main goals of MDA, Model Driven Architecture which is a particular Model Driven systems development approach in MDD paradigm (Kleppe et al., 2003). One of the major issues in the MDA discipline is the choice of model types to be used on different levels of abstraction. According to (Loniewski et al., 2010), majority of existing proposals do not use business requirements as the starting point. They also argue that those who even consider business requirements do not use them exclusively to describe business requirements in Model Driven Development (MDD) contexts and thereby to serve as the inputs for model-driven transformation process.

In this chapter, we explore the capability of business value models to elicit a portfolio of business transactions at the computational independent, *i.e. business level.* Further exploring such business transactions across a whole collaboration lifecycle, i.e. starting from planning to post-actualization, enable us to elicit an entire enterprise-wide service portfolio within the business level. At the same level, process models are used to describe the service behavior. To enable mapping of the elicited business services further to software services at the system level, we rely on the use of UML profiles as a structured way to set a model's focus on a specific architectural style, such as in this case – service-oriented. Conceptualized in this way, the method that we propose is capable to support integration and alignment of economic value propositions of the collaborating business actors with the Information Systems (IS) created using Web services. The method has a practical relevance for exploring the enterprise models in more depth from the business perspective, in order to identify software services and design systems accordingly.

To facilitate the outlined business orientation in a model-driven Web service engineering, we have identified two important needs:

- *To use adequate service models and modelling frameworks.* Services exist in collaborative business environments, and as such they should be conceptualized accordingly.
- *To enable binding of business and software service-oriented system models more precisely and unambiguously.* Models can be of different abstraction levels, and thereby facilitating correct propagation of model information from higher to lower abstraction level is required.

Following the outlined concerns, in this paper, we propose a MDD method for elicitation and design of business-driven Web services. The method is based on the use of two models at, mainly, two abstraction levels – Business level and System level. The first we have defined by using the extended REA/Open-edi framework (Geerts et al. 2002), and the second by using the UML profile for software services (Johnston, 2005).

The chapter is structured as follows. Next section introduces business value models, and gives a brief overview of process modeling. In the section after, our MDD-based method for software service identification and description is explained ad exemplified. The two final sections conclude the study and point out possible research directions for the business-driven system development.

BUSINESS AND PROCESS MODELING

Enterprise models are used to describe actors, information, resources, relations and processes of an organisation (Marshall, 2000). Business models and process models are parts of enterprise models, having distinct purposes and describing different aspects of an enterprise. Business models give a high-level view of the processes taking place in and between organizations, by identifying actors, economic values and the business transactions (i.e. exchanges of values) between the actors. These models provide a declarative view, i.e. they explain *"what"* of a business. Process models define the tactics of a business (i.e. *"how"*), by dealing with operational and procedural aspects of business communications. These models are typically expressed through low-level concepts such as control flow, data flow and message passing. Such concepts are not easily understood by business experts and users, who instead prefer to understand processes through business oriented notions like value exchanges.

Thereby, an approach when modelling a business that will be further realised with IS, is to start with a business model to explain business transactions, and then complement it with process models to describe the ways those transactions are carried out by coordinations of business activities. In this way, it becomes possible to trace operational design decisions back to explanations and motivations expressed in terms of actual business transactions that occur in business value constellations. A more detailed argumentation on a complementary use of business models and business process models the reader may find in studies (Gordijn et al., 2000) and (Johannesson, 2007).

Business Value Models

The purpose of a business value model is to describe the transfer of economic values that take place among actors in business value constellations. These values may include goods, information, services, or money. Examples of actors are consumers, companies, and government authorities. Business models have a special characteristic in that they are formulated declaratively. There exist a number of efforts for business value modeling in the research community, such as the business ontologies (Fox, 1992), (Gordijn 2004), and (Osterwalder 2004). For our purpose we will make use of one long- and well-established business model ontology - REA (McCarthy, 1982).

The REA Framework

The Resource-Event-Agent (REA) framework was formulated originally by McCarthy (1982) and further developed in (Geerts & McCarthy, 1999). REA was first proposed as a knowledge basis for accounting information systems and focused on representing increases and decreases of value in an organization. It has been later extended to form a foundation for enterprise information systems architectures (Hruby, 2006), and also to define a conceptual foundation for modelling service systems (Poels, 2010), (Sicilia et al. 2010). It has also been applied to UN/CEFACT e-commerce frameworks (2006).

The core concepts in the REA ontology are *resource*, *event*, and *agent*. It is assumed that every

Figure 1. The core elements of the REA ontology: resources (economic values), events and agents

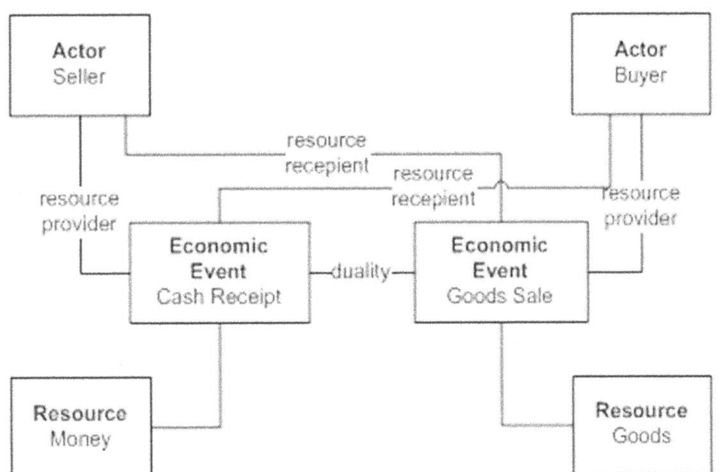

business operation can be described as an event where two agents exchange economic values, i.e. resources. Economic resources may be classified as *goods, rights or services*. To acquire a resource, an agent (i.e. actor) has to give up some other resource. For example, in a goods purchase, the buyer has to give up money in order to receive some goods. Conceptually, two events are taking place: one where the amount of money is given away and another where an amount of goods is obtained. This combination of events is called a *duality* and is an expression of economic reciprocity - an event receiving some resource is always accompanied by an event provisioning another resource. In business value modelling, combinations such reciprocal events are generally called: *business transactions*.

The concepts of the REA ontology are not supported with a specific graphic modeling notation. Here, we use an entity-relationship like notation to depict the elements and relations in a REA business model, as illustrated in Figure 1. The model is created from the seller's perspective, and the business transaction it depicts consists of two reciprocal economic events: Goods Sale and Cash Receipt, with accompanied resources - Goods and Money respectively.

In the study of Geerts and McCarthy in (Geerts et al. 2002), the REA framework has been extended to capture additional granularity levels of business activities of enterprises. The resulting framework has integrated three vertical layers: Value Chain, Business Process and Business Event: (Figure 2). Thus, it enables modeling of top business processes (business transactions) and their constituted reciprocal economic events with associated resources down to detailed business events (i.e. activities) explored across business transaction life-cycle proposed in ISO Open-edi initiative (2006), and thereby links low-level business activities with high-level processes in the value chain.

In our proposal, we use the REA framework in Figure 2 to describe the declarative part of the proposed business level model.

Business Transaction Life-Cycle

From the life-cycle perspective, a business transaction typically spans a number of phases. ISO Open-EDI initiative (2006) considers a transaction as consisting of five phases (activities): *planning, identification, negotiation, actualization* and *post-actualization*. These phases encompass the following activities:

Figure 2. Three-layered REA framework (Geerts et al., 2002), with Open-EDI collaboration phases

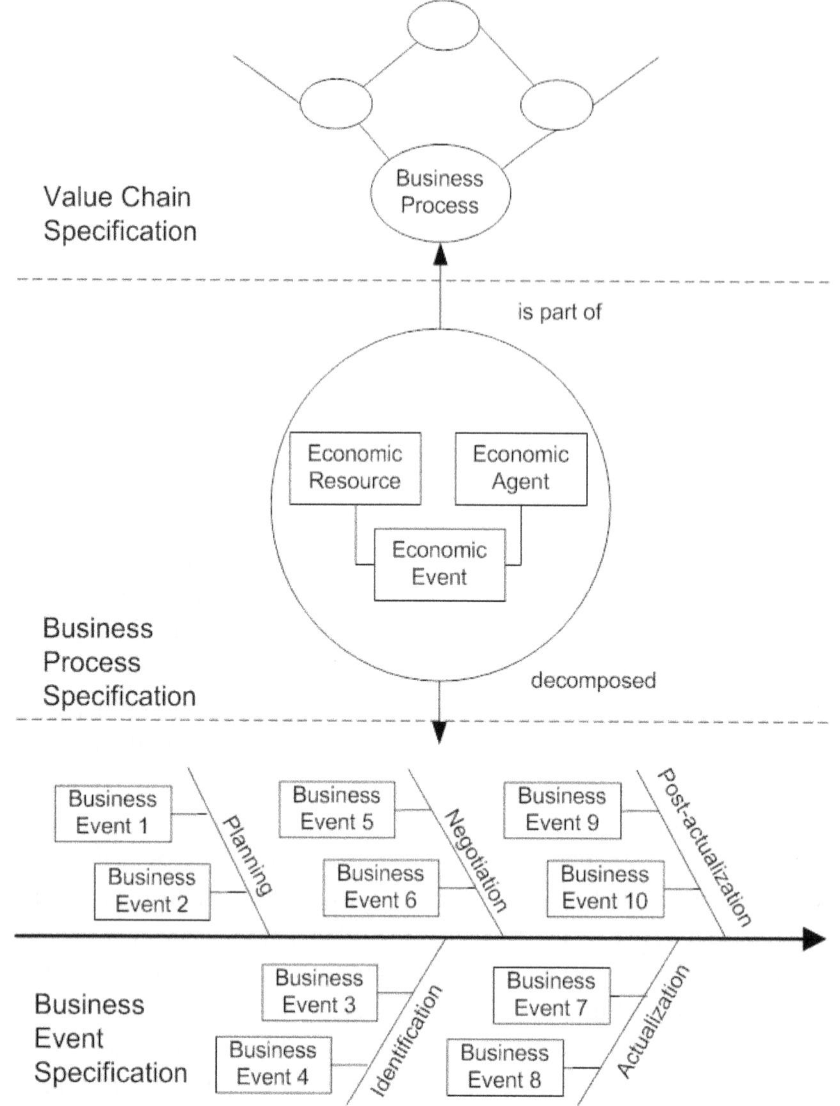

- In *the planning phase*, the customer and the provider are engaged in activities to identify the actions needed for selling or purchasing goods and services. As an example, a distributor sends catalogues to potential customers.
- *The identification phase* involves the activities needed to exchange information among providers and potential customers regarding selling or purchasing goods and services. For example, a provider sends a quotation to a customer.
- During *the negotiation phase*, contracts are proposed and completed. Detailed specifications of goods and services, quantity, price, terms, and conditions are determined in this phase. If required, the parties involved may make bids and put forward

counter offers. For example, a customer sends offer to a provider and the provider sends the counter offer to the customer.

- *The actualization phase* includes all the activities necessary for exchanging goods and services between involved actors as agreed during negotiations. For example, the provider sends advance shipping notice when goods are prepared for shipping.
- *The post-actualization phase* encompasses all the activities and associated exchanges of information between involved actors after the goods and services are provided. For example, the customer may send a warranty invocation to the provider.

In the chapter, the described Open-EDI framework is utilized to identify business services and business events in the business event specification layer (see Figure 2) that correspond to business transaction explored in the business process specification layer (see Figure 2) in the above framework. The objective is the obtainment of a *value-explorative business-oriented method* for identifying comprehensive set of business services accross life-cycles of business transactions.

Process Models

Process models are used to steer day-to-day business activities of enterprises. A well-known definition describes a business process "as a specific ordering of work activities across time and place, with a beginning, an end, and clearly defined inputs and outputs; a structure for action" (Davenport, 1992). The main idea behind is that a business process is a sequence of activities that achieves a goal by transforming an input into a valuable output.

There exist many languages and notations that can be used to design business process models. Some of them are widely accepted in both industrial and academic communities, such as Business Process Modelling Notation, BPMN (OMG, 2011), Event-Driven Process Chains, EPC (Scheer et al. 2005) and UML 2 Activity Diagrams (Amber, 2004). UML has been widely adopted for modelling concepts and their behaviour as it enables modelling at different levels of abstraction and relationships between model elements can be established across modelling perspectives. Being based on a common meta-language, the Meta Object Facility, MOF (OMG 2013), UML facilitates the need for interoperability between different A models in MDD-based system developments. For these reasons, we will express the process models at business and system levels using UML 2 Activity Diagrams.

When designing business processes, the consideration must be paid to different perspectives that together constitute a complete process model. Curtis et al. (1992) have proposed that a process design should include four perspectives: *organizational, functional, informational* and *behavioural*:

- **Organizational Perspective:** This perspective describes the distribution of the responsibility for executing process activities. The main focus here is on the notion of the actor. An actor can be an organization unit, or a software system. UML 2 uses the partition notion to depict this perspective.
- **Functional Perspective:** The perspective concerns how a process can be decomposed into activities that are to be executed. An activity can be either atomic, or composite. A composite activity can recursively refined to atomic activities; these notions correspond to activities and actions in UML 2 notation, respectively.
- **Informational Perspective:** Here the main concern is on the resources that are manipulated by a process. A resource can be either traditional or informational. Product and services are traditional resources, while data and artifacts are informational

resources. A resource is consumed or produced by a process activity. UML 2 offers the object node to depict the informational aspect.

- **Behavioural Perspective:** This perspective concerns the flow of activities within a process. The control flow expresses when an activity is to be executed in relation to others. In UML 2, a number of control-flow components are available: decision and merge nodes, fork-and-join node, start and end nodes, and so forth.

With the EPC modeling technique, in addition to the outlined design perspectives, it is also possible to depict and classify the "output" perspective of a process, as a material or as a service.

In the chapter, we utilize the described framework to elicit the components of process models that the business modeler should include when modeling the service behavior in business and system levels, to enable a complete elicitation of the service implementation at the implementation level.

DESIGNING BUSINESS AND SOFTWARE SERVICES ON THE mdD BASIS

Service Modeling

In the business science community it is accepted that a business service, or simply *service*, is a business activity offered by a service provider to its environment. Thereby, a *software service* is defined as the provisioning of a service over an electronic network, such as the Internet, where its functionality is commonly delivered via a Web service. A service, or a software service, can be composite, meaning that its realization requires several other services or basic activities ordered in a process.

Design of software services has so far mainly focused on operational aspects, such as the development of standards for message exchanges and service coordination. The terms service orchestration and service choreography have become broadly used to describe two modeling aspects of service processes (Peltz, 2003).

Orchestration is used when the objective is to obtain an executable process model, controlled from one party's perspective. The model includes business logic and a task execution order, where the tasks may be realized from both internal and external software services. Choreography is used to model a collaborative process specification, showing an ordering of interactions of services of all the involved parties. However, a much less concern is set on the business settings in which the services are used. At the same time, the actual use of software services has evolved from a point-wise use towards large-scale use across enterprise boundaries (Piccinelli et al. 2001). This increase of the usage scope has resulted in a need for explicitly analyzing the business values that services deliver to rationalize their economic viability.

In the long run, software services that do not support the business values cannot be justified. Lately, the research in both academic and industrial communities, implies that when designing service-oriented software solutions, constructive results are obtained by starting analyzing business models of enterprises (Baida et al. 2005), (Cherbakov et al. 2005), (Andersson et al. 2007), (Boerner et al. 2009), (Estrada et al. 2010). This fact, according to the referred studies, is shifting the focus of large scale software service design to the context of economic value transfers. Thereby, two classes of services have been recognized:

- Business services which are identified on the business model level.
- Software services that realize the business services, typically implemented using Web Services.

Using this relationship between business and software services as a guide for software service design, it becomes natural to identify and develop services in a top-down manner starting from the strategic and economic aims of an enterprise and deriving software services aligned to those services.

Following model-driven principles for IS development, a number of research studies have reported proposals for software service design, defined in the form of a Platform Independent Model (PIM) or more generally, system level model. Many of them utilize the UML profile concept to describe and scope a technology independent model, such as: a) a SOA-based model, proposed in (López-Sanz et al. 2008), b) a software service model proposed by IBM (Johnston, 2005) targeted for helping architects to map out an entire, enterprise-wide e-service portfolio, which is after detailed by developers, who provide final Web service specifications, or c) a process-oriented system model, capable of capturing e-service orchestrations (Amsden et al. 2003). Some other studies have augmented the starting abstraction level by considering the business process perspective as a basis for creating Computational Independent Model-CIM (business level model); the process activities are further mapped to software components or services at the system level (Rosen, 2003), (Vidales et al. 2008), (Kherraf et al. 2008). Being focused solely on business processes at the business level, that is, on an operational perspective, the aforementioned studies have not considered the business viability of software services and are rather set to capture the functional requirements to support their realization.

In contrast to the above outlined works, the research presented in (Cherbakov et al. 2005, Nayak et al. 2007, Arsanjani et al. 2008, Fritscher et al. 2011, Iacob et al. 2012) have elicited that when addressing business-IT alignment, more constructive results in service identification are obtained by starting to analyze high-level business architectures of enterprises. The research studies presented in (Jones 2005), (Hess et al. 2007) and (Sewing et al. 2008) have argued to consider entire enterprise architectures comprising both business and IT elements and their interrelations, as a comprehensive container for identifying business services and software services. In their works, they have proposed methodologies for developing service-oriented architectures starting from the top value-creating business- activities, actors and objects, which are then mapped to IT service assets.

Also, research activities in (Gordijn et al., 2008, (Derzsi et al., 2008, Wang et al., 2010, Zdravkovic et al. 2012) have proposed that when addressing business-to-IT service integration, the starting point should be the business models of enterprises that describe business transactions that are being carried out by involved actors along with the resources exchanged by these transactions. However, even being model-oriented, these proposals do not define models and model transformations as recommended in the MDD paradigm.

Our approach differs from the above referred studies in the way that we propose a MDD-based method for designing software services that are aligned with the business requirements specified in a firm's business model. In particular, we propose designing a service-centered Business level model relying on two model types. Firstly, a REA/Open-edi -based value-oriented service modelling framework spanning all the major phases of a business transaction, that is, planning, identification, negotiation, actualization and post-actualization for obtaining a business service modelling instrument easy understandable and apprehensible for business stakeholders. This provides a basis for describing business requirements. Secondly, every business service is described in further details using a process orchestration which captures functional aspects of the elicited business requirements. Following the argumentation given in the previous section on the need to use business and process models complementary, in this way we obtain a complete business service portfolio relevant for a multi-actor collaboration.

Transforming a given business level models to an software service based system level model containing both declarative and behavioral description for each elicited software service, using a set of transformation rules. In the next section, we describe our approach for defining the outlined models, and the transformations between them, and we illustrate it on the case of the on-line game provider business.

Method Description and Application

Case Study: MMOG

A Massively Multiplayer Online Games (MMOG) business involves several actors: the Game Provider, the Game Player and the Internet Service Provider. The Game Provider is the principal actor responsible for producing a game content, as well as for distributing it to the Game Players. To distribute the games, the Game Provider uses services from the Internet Service Provider (ISP) who in return receives a payment.

Business Level: An Explorative Business Model with Collaboration Process Models

The business level model describes the business context and requirements relevant for a system development computational independent way. As such, the model plays a vital role in bridging the gap between business and technology, i.e. establishing traceability between enterprise models and system models.

In what follows, we propose a business level model that relies on the use of the three-layered REA framework (see Figure 2). The aim here is to describe a high-level view of the activities taking place between organizations and people, by identifying the actors involved in a business constellation, as well as the values they offer to each other by conducting business transactions. One of the major issues in business modeling concerns the need for a systematic approach for designing business value models in order to identify the offerings of the involved actors, while spanning a whole business transaction life-cycle. Thereby, as the major business level model component, we propose an explorative business modelling instrument that encompasses the resource (i.e. value) assortment across a whole business transaction life-cycle, starting from the planning up to post-actualization (see Figure 2). Such a model forms a complete basis for identification of the business services that are to be provisioned by an actor within his business portfolio. Furthermore, there is a need to describe the behavior for the identified business services, where process models are commonly utilized. Following this, we describe the basis of our method for creating business level model, in two steps:

Step 1: *Where we design a three-layered business transaction-centric REA/Open-edi business value model to identify candidates for business services.* According to the REA/Open-edi framework (see Figure 2), the method for describing the business of an enterprise comprises the decomposition of business activities along three granularity layers: value chain layer, business processes layer and business events layer.

- **Value Chain Specification (Layer 1):** The focus of the value chain layer is to capture full entrepreneurial intent of business owner considering enterprise-wide value creation processes. In service industries, the traditional Porter's value chain (Porter 1998) has been found as non-fitting, as the resulting chain analysis based on production-driven business processes often blurs the focus off service-centric value creations. In (Stabell et al. 1998), it is argued that present enterprise value configurations conform to three generic types: the traditional *value chain*, *value shops* and *value networks*. While the former is related to traditional goods selling business environments, the latter two configurations are suitable to service environments – *value shops* model the activities and resources to resolve a particular customer problem, while *value networks* create values by organizing and facilitating exchanges between a set of customers. Each of the three configurations helps in eliciting a different set of value added business processes. The MMOG case taken as the example in this study conforms to the value network configuration assuming that the essence of its value creation lies in an indirect linkage of customers through an online multiplayer gaming environment. Following (Stabell et al. 1998), the value-added processes of the value network are:

- ◦ **Network Promotion and Contract Management:** Consisting of activities associated with inviting customers to join the network, the initialization, management, and termination of contracts governing service provisioning and charging.
- ◦ **Service Provisioning:** Consisting of activities associated with establishing, maintaining, and terminating links between customers and billing for the values received.
- ◦ **Network Infrastructure Operations:** Consisting of activities associated with maintaining a physical and information infrastructure. The activities keep the value network in an active status, ready to service customer requests.

Furthermore, it has been argued in (Gailly et al. 2009) that in a collaborative setting, the business transaction, defined as a set of activities, can be equalized with the concept of the top-level business process as defined in the first layer of the REA/Open-edi framework. Taking this into account, the first step for creating the business service model is to identify business (i.e. value-adding) processes (i.e. transactions) in the highest layer of the REA/Open-edi framework, using a suitable value configuration.

- **Business Process Specification (Layer 2):** Moving to the middle layer of the framework, every identified business transaction in the top layer is explored to define the Agents involved in it, as well as the reciprocal Economic Events that exchange Economic Resources.
- **Business Event Specification (Layer 3):** At the bottom layer of the framework, the economic exchanges from Layer 2 are expanded over the five ordered Open-edi transaction phases (planning, identification, negotiation, actualization and post-actualization). Here, we intend to define the candidate business services capable of provisioning business transactions that exchange resources specified in the middle layer. Depending on the economic resource type being offered to the consumer (i.e. goods, rights or services), business services in the actualization phase differ:
    - ◦ When the economic resource is a service, then it will directly correspond to one or more business services;
    - ◦ When the economic resource is a good, then a business service provisioning the custody of that good or evidence document for the good ownership will be added;

- In case the resource is a right, the business service will be created to provision the evidence document for that right.

Application of Step 1: Generating a CIM/business transaction-centric REA/Open-edi Business Value Model for the MMOG case:

- **Layer 1 Value Chain Specification:** The value creation of the MMOG case lies in linking multiple players in an online gaming environment and allowing them to interactively play games. As such, it resembles the value network configuration. Considering the primary activities of the value network configuration, we identify the following business processes (i.e. business transactions) for the value chain specification layer (Figure 6):
  - **Network Promotion and Contract Management:** "Player Profile Handling" for managing requests for information related to obtainment of access to online gaming contents.
  - **Service Provisioning:** The "Games Access Handling" process for Game Provider managing the requests from Game Players for obtaining access to the online gaming content.
  - **Network Infrastructure Operations:** The "Hosting Management" for handling activities related to the obtainment of hosting services from the Game Provider by the Internet Service Provider (ISP) in order to make gaming content accessible online.
- **Layer 2 Business Process Specification:** We further explore the "Games Access Handling" process to identify economic events and resource exchanges at the second layer. Here, we identify economic events "Provide Games Access" and "Obtain Payment Rights" from the Game Provider's perspective. The former economic event is responsible for provisioning the resource "Games Access" to the Game Players, whereas the latter for receiving the "Right to payment" resource from the Game Player. This duality of economic events gives rise to the aggregated service "Provisioning of Games Access".
- **Layer 3 Business Service/Event Specification:** The elicited aggregated service in Layer 2 is further explored along the 5 transaction phases to identify business services and contained business events.
  - **Planning:** Since the commitment for providing the games access is already established by the "Player Profile Handling" business transaction, a business service pertaining to the planning phase may not be elicited for the transaction "Provisioning of Games Access".
  - **Identification:** Considering provisioning of access to games, it is important that game players identify themselves by providing their use credentials. As such, the business service "Player Accreditation Handling" is elicited.
  - **Negotiation:** The collaboration between the game provider and a game player concerns obtaining invoicing rights for games access provisioning. Accordingly, the business service, "Games Access Contract handling" is identified.
  - **Actualization:** This phase concerns the provisioning access to games selection and collecting player characteristics (e.g. for upgrading games) and, obtaining a fee for the rendered games accessing. Thereby, "Games

Access Provisioning", and "Payment Handling" business services are elicited.

- **Post-Actualization:** The goal of the game provider in the post-actualization of this collaboration is to provide help to game players solve their issues related to accessing and playing of games as well as to collecting and sharing the information (e.g. with Player Profile Handling transaction) regarding payments related to the game player. Thereby the business services "Help Desk Service Provisioning" and "Payment Due Information Sharing" are elicited as shown in Figure 3.

Step 2: *Where we define processes to describe the behavior of the business services elicited in Step 1.* Designing process models from the REA business model involves business modeler deciding on how to model processes to describe the behavior of services, and also determining the activities that should be defined in those processes. Below, we outline the rules for designing process models from the REA business model.

Every process model should describe the behavior of a single business service elicited in the Business Service/Event Specification in Layer 3 of REA/OpenEdi business value model. Taking the key business events identified in layer 3 of the business model (see Figure 3), a process model is created to include the service choreography, i.e. the interactions of the service with others, as well as the service orchestration (belonging to the provider of the business service, namely "the principal actor").

The workflow of every business service should be modeled considering organizational, functional, informational and behavioral design aspects.

Application of Step 2: *Generating Business Level/Process Models for the MMOG case* - In Figure 3, we consider, for instance, the business service *Games Access Contract Provisioning*. Following Step 1, a process shall be created from the perspective of the MMOG provider.

The business modeller will first consider the organizational perspective; thereby, he will create two UML partitions: *Game Player* and *Game Provider*. Starting with the functional perspective, the modeler will explore the major business events in this service: a) obtaining a chosen selection of games from the player, b) providing contract terms, c) obtaining right to payment, and d) offering games contract and games access rights. By creating a composition of the outlined business events (behavioral aspect), refining them to the level of atomic business activities and including the internal rules, the modeler will create a process model as depicted in Figure 4. When drawing the activities, he will also consider the informational aspect, i.e. the messages/documents that have to be exchanged, and model those using UML objects (see Figure 4). As a result, the obtained service process will begin when the Game Provider receives a games selection from the Game Player; then the Game Provider checks an internal database to examine if the player has a subscription with a payment due or not. Based on this information, the provider will either offer a contract for the Game Player, or decide on a direct acceptance of the player.

Figure 3. A depiction of the REA/Open-EDI layered model for the MMOG case

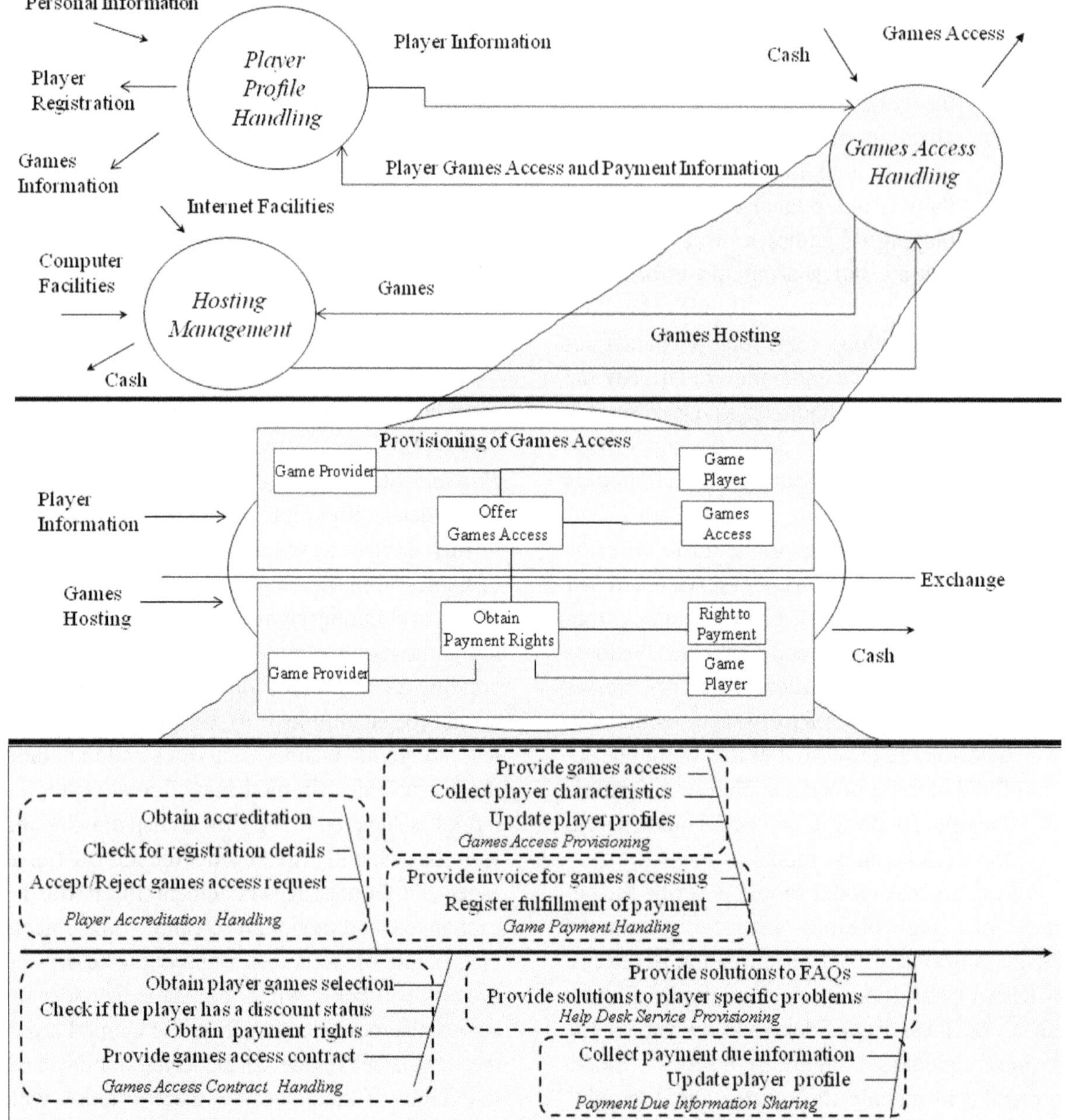

Step 2 Completes when the behaviors of all the services from the REA business model are well-described with the process models documented using UML 2 Activity Diagrams, and where all four process design perspectives are included. Regarding the contents of messages and documents, they may be provided using, for example, an informational model depicted with a

Figure 4. UML activity diagram exploring the details of the Games Access Contract Handling service

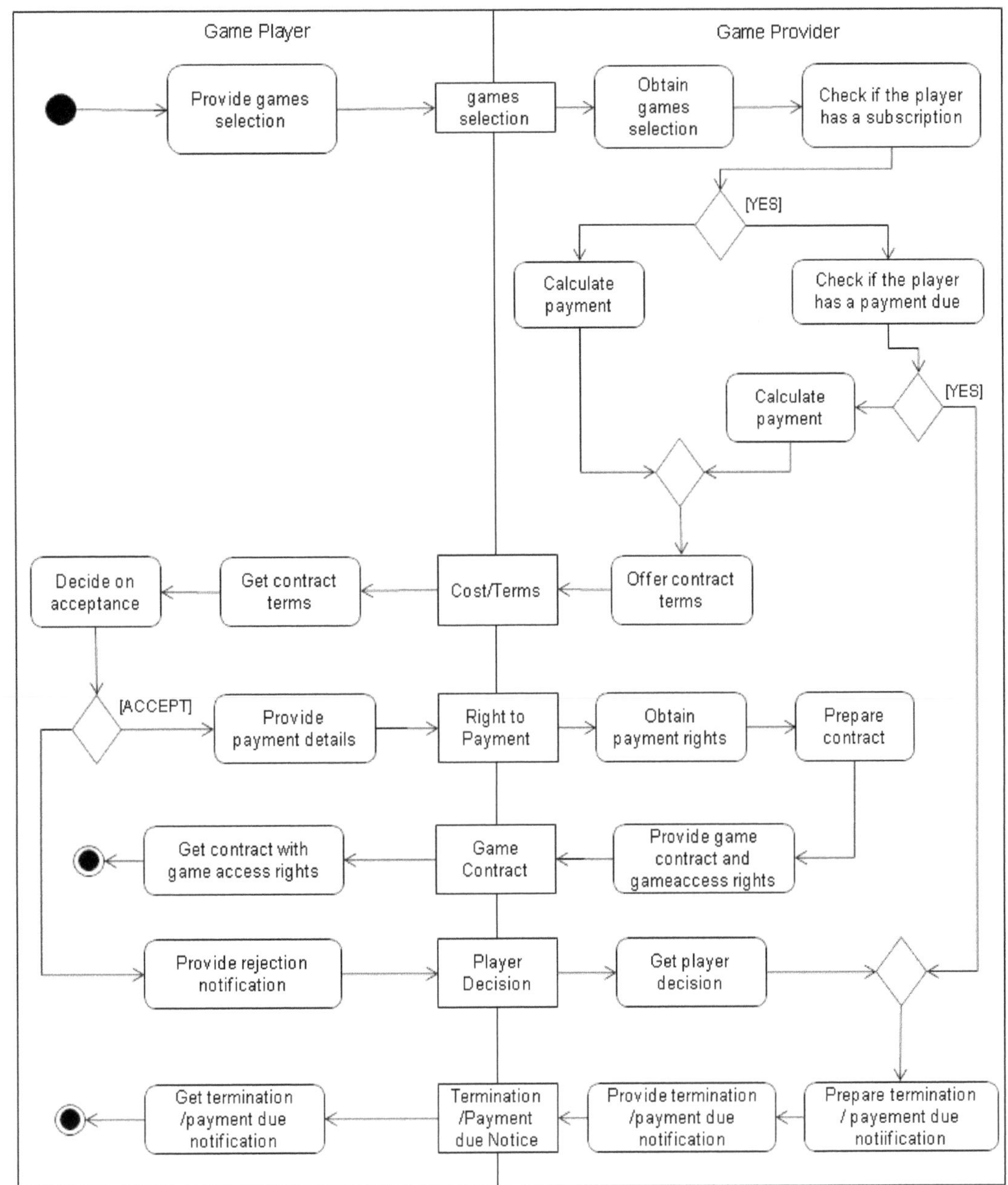

UML class diagram, or simply, by attaching the electronic forms of documents to the depicted information objects.

To summarize, the business level model proposed in this section consists of a business value model spanning a whole business transaction life-cycle, where the business services are mapped-out, and a number of process models depicting the behavior of each of the services.

System Level: A System Model Defining Software Service Structures and Behaviors

The business and process models, developed to define the proposed computation independent business level model, are used as the input for creating a UML-based system level model.

The process of creating a system level model from a business level model implies defining transformation rules between the two models. To create a mapping of the services elicited in the business level, to the system level, we rely on the use of the UML profile concept, which in the MDD context provides a common way to focus toward a specific architectural style, to enable the model to properly capture and express specific information. A profile enables bundling of specialized semantics through the notion of stereotypes, a common UML extension mechanism. Here, we utilize the UML 2 Profile for Software Services, as proposed by IBM (Johnston, 2005). This profile is relatively small and thereby, facilitates a reasonably straightforward modeling of software service structures using UML Class Diagrams. To explore the software service orchestration, i.e. service control- and data-flow, we utilize UML 2 Activity Diagrams. Thereby, the final system level model will reflect both service structure and service behavior aspects. In the next section we explain in detail the design of system level model components, as well as the rules for mapping out these components from the business level model. In the rest of the text we will denote those two complementing system level models as System level/Software Service Contract, and System level/ Software Service Behavior.

Figure 5 depicts the conceptual model of IBM UML 2 Profile for Software Services. Primarily, the model consists of stereotyped extensions of the elements of UML 2 meta-model, such as Classes, Classifiers, Collaborations, etc. In Table 1, we describe briefly the major elements.

In our approach, certain profile elements are not modelled explicitly in the system level model. *Service Collaboration* and *Service Channel* contain the details belonging to a platform specific level and therefore, we omit the use of these elements. As for the service *Protocol* element, we define it using the UML 2 activity diagram, to define a complete orchestration for every identified e-service. In this way, the final result will reflect a system model including both service structure (i.e. *service contract*) and service behaviour aspects.

Defining Business Level to System Level Transformations

When defining the transformation rules, the system modeler uses the Business level/Process Model and considers the functional, organizational, behavioral and informational aspects as a classification basis for transformations to System Level. The modeling focus is set on the provider of the business service, i.e. the principal actor, to obtain the service contracts and orchestrations on a software system level. The majority of transformations is set to the System Level/Service Profile (i.e. class diagram); the behavioral aspect is transformed directly to the System Level/Service Behaviour.

Organisational Aspect

The first rule concerns the distribution of responsibilities for executing services at a system level. The modelling focus is set on the provider of the business service, i.e. the principal actor, as explained earlier. The transformation rules for mapping business to system levels are presented below.

Rule 1a: Each non-principal actor partition in the Business level/Process Model is mapped to a Partition in the System level to host the interaction activities of the principal actor toward that actor.

Figure 5. IBM UML 2 Profile for software services (Johnston, 2005)

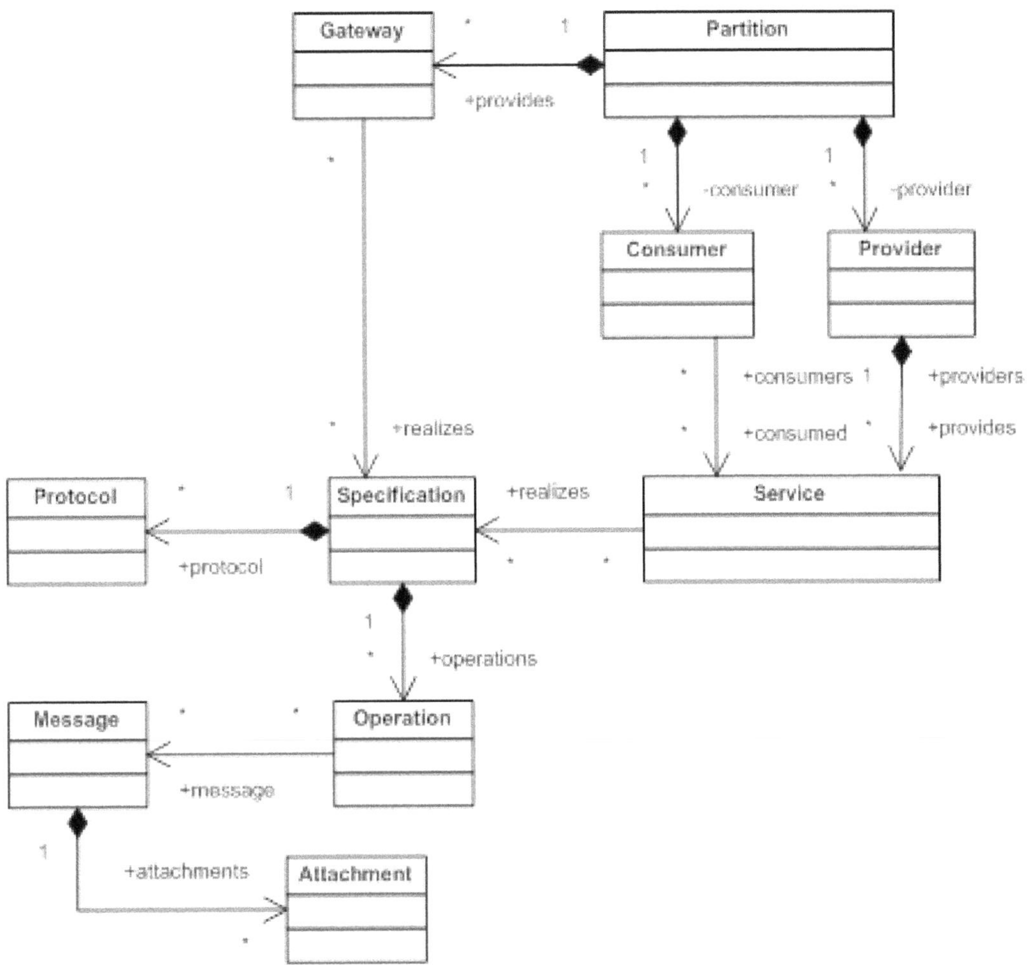

Table 1. Different elements of UML 2 profile for software services

Partition	*Partition* element defines responsibility or system boundaries for offering different services.
Service Provider	A *Service Provider* provides one or more *Services*.
Service Consumer	*Service Consumer* element is used as a classifier to identify consumers of a *Service*.
Service	The *Service* element acts as a name tag of a service offered by the *Service Provider*, where the actual definition of what it offers, is given with *Service Specification*.
Service Specification	The *Service Specification* element identifies both the service interface, that is, a set of operations. The element can also specify the order of invocation of the operations associated with it, using the protocol state machine (i.e. *Protocol*).
Operation	The *Operation* element defines the atomic functionalities of the *Service* element.
Message	The *Message* element represents the containers for the service input or output data.
Message Attachment	*Message Attachment* is associated to the *Message* element as a property. For example, a *Message* element may contain product details while the images of these products are delivered as *Message Attachment* elements.
Service Gateway	The *Service Gateway* considers the openness of the *Service*, by denoting the *Service Specification* elements available to access within a partition.

Rule 1b: The partition of the principal actor is refined to the partitions that will include information retrieval/storing activities, by determining the providers of these activities.

- **Design Considerations:** For every added Partition element type in System level /Service Profile by following Rule 1, the elements of type Service Provider, Service, Service Specification and Service Gateway (optionally) are automatically created.
- **Application to MMOG Case:**

Rule 1a: The partition *GamePlayer* in the Business level activity diagram is mapped to the *GamePlayerManagement* partition element in the System level class diagram. The *GamePlayerManagement* partition will include the interactions of the Game Provider to the Game Player. For this partition, a Service Provider, Service, Service Specification and Service Gateway elements are created and named *GamePlayerManager*, *GameContract*, *GameContractInterface* and *GamePlayerManagementGateway*. The Gateway element is added to define that the service specification is accessible outside its hosting partition. (see Figure 6).

Rule 1b: *SubscriptionManagement* partition is added to host the information retrieval activities of the Game Provider, such as *Check if the player has a subscription* in Business level activity diagram in Figure 5. As in the previous example, for the created partition, Service Provider, Service and Service Specification and Gateway elements are added, as depicted in Figure 6.

Functional Aspect

The second rule concerns the transformation of the activities from Business to System Level:

Rule 2a: Every activity in Business level /Process Model concerning the interactions between partitions is transformed to a send, receive, or send-receive service Operation element.

Figure 6. System level/service profile (UML 2 class diagram)

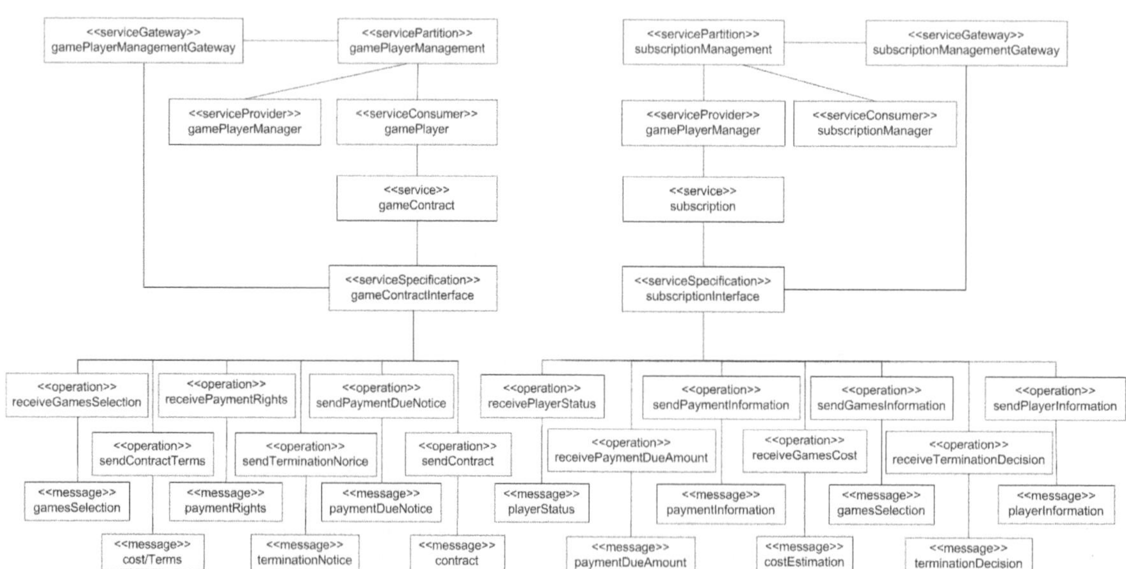

Rule 2b: Additional send, receive, send-receive operations are created for every new partition identified in *Rule1*, to model the interaction activities for that partitions.

Rule 2c: An activity modeled in Business level model is decomposed, or aggregated to conform to the functions of the existing systems (for example, "receive customer profile" in a Business level model may be decomposed to "receive customer contact" and "receive customer history" in a System Level Model, if those information are provided by different existing system services)

Activities that concern assignments (i.e. "delegations"), rules and calculations will be mapped only to the System level/Service Behavior; as such activities do not correspond to service operations. Those activities are the part of the internal process system logic of the principal actor.

- **Design Considerations:** Following *Rule 2*, Operation elements are added in System level/Service Profile.
- **Application to MMOG Case:**
  Rule 2a: The activity "Provide games selection" from the Business level/Process Model (see Figure 4) is mapped to the Operation *"receiveGamesSelection"* within the *GameContractInterface* (Figure 6).
  Rule 2b: The Operation element *receiveGamesCost* within *SubscriptionInterface* is added (Figure 6).
  Rule 2c: The activity element *Provide termination/payment due notification* in the Business level/Process Model is decomposed to Operation elements *"sendTerminationNotice"* and *"sendPaymentDueNotice"* within the *GameContractInterface* (Figure 6).

The *"Check if the player has a subscription"* and *"check if the player has a payment due"* in the Business level are the assignment-type of activities, and as such, are mapped to *"selectPlayerInformation"* and *"selectPaymentDueInformation"* in the System level/Service Behaviour (Figure 7). In the similar way, the rest of interaction activities in Business level /Process Model are transformed, and a final operation portfolio is obtained as depicted in Figure 6.

Informational Aspect

The third rule concerns the transformation of information resources from Business Level to System Level.

Rule 3a: Every information resource is transformed to a Message element.

Rule 3b: If an information resource (artifact) is supported differently due to changes in the functional aspect (*Rule 2*), then the resource granularity will be changed (decomposed, or aggregated).

- **Design Considerations:** Information objects in Business level/Process Model are mapped to Message, and optionally, to Message Attachment elements in System level/Service Profile, according to the described rule. The system modeller should derive information objects in parallel to the functional aspect discussed above.
- **Application to MMOG Case:**

Rule 3a: The information resource *"Games selection"* from the Business level/Process Model (see Figure 4) is mapped to the Message element *"gamesSelection"* (Figure 6).

Rule 3b: Considering the decomposition of the activity *Provide termination/payment due*

Figure 7. System level/service behavior (UML 2 activity diagram)

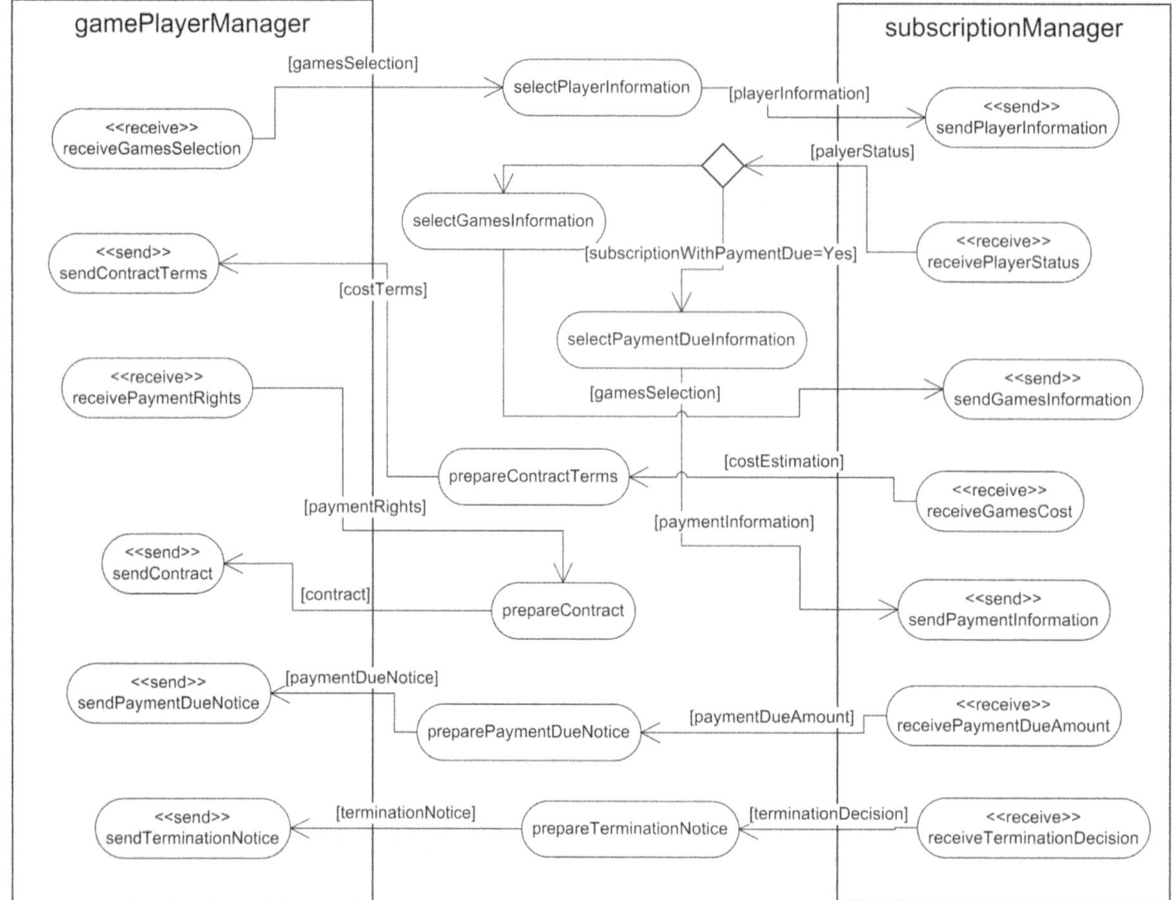

notification in the functional aspects in *Rules 2(c)*, the information resource *"Termination/payment due notice"* from the Business Level/Process Model (see Figure 4) is decomposed to the Message elements *"terminationNotice"* and *"paymentDueNotice"* in System level/Service Profile (Figure 6).

Behavioural Aspect

The fourth rule concerns the transformation of the service control-flow from business level model to system level model. Since the Service Profile model does not support modelling of control-flow, the transformation of this aspect is performed between the business level and system level activity diagrams. The flow in system level activity diagram will generally follow the flow defined in Business level/Process Model; however, the flow will be adjusted due to the identification of new activities, and messages.

Rule 4: The control flow as given in the Business level/Process Model is reused in System level/Service Behavior Model; the flow is refined to support the orderings of new elements, as added with *Rule 2* (functional aspect). The internal, flow-related activities, such as rules and assignments, are mapped from Business level model (rules), or created at this stage (assignments).

Figure 6 depicts the structure part of the system level service model obtained when applying the five transformation rules on the business service –*Games Access Contract Handling* (see Figure 3).

Figure 7 depicts the behavioral part of the System Level service model obtained when applying the transformation rules on the business service – *Games Access Contract Handling* at business level model (see Figure 3).

To summarize, in this section we have defined a method for obtaining a system level model from a business level model using a set of ordered transformation rules. The transformations start by mapping out the business services as tagged in the Business level/Business Model to software services in the system level model, where the System level/Service Profile model is created to define the service contract, and a System level/ Service Behaviour model to explore the service coordination.

From the System Level to Execution

Finally, the obtained platform independent system level model should be transformed into an executable implementation, The primary aim of this chapter was to give an approach for transforming a business-oriented business level model to a service-oriented system level model. For that reason, in this section we will give only brief guidelines for how an executable artefact can be obtained from the proposed system level model.

The system level model, as we have defined it in the previous sections, includes both the structural and behavioral aspects of software services. As such, the model supports creating executable service-oriented solutions including service static specification and coordination. For instance, in case the Web services are the target technology platform, then the given system level model will be automatically converted to: a) WSDL documents, from the System level/Service Profile, for specifying the Web service interfaces, operations and messages - i.e. the contracts, and b) to a workflow-like specification, such as WS-BPEL (OASIS, 2007), from the UML activity diagram, for getting the sequences of invocations of the obtained Web services and the operations.

In our running example, the UML class diagram in the system level model is used to create WSDL specifications for two identified software services: *gameContract* and *subscription* (see Figure 6). For instance, the Message and Service Specification profile elements associated with these services can be mapped to WSDL Message types and PortTypes respectively. An excerpt of WSDL specification for the software service *gameContract* as obtained from system level is shown in Box 1.

The BPEL specification for the execution can be obtained by mapping the system level models and their constituent components to different BPEL elements. For instance, the UML activity diagram is mapped to the BPEL control-flow, Operations in the class diagram to the BPEL activities, Partition elements to the BPEL partner declarations, etc. Below, we exemplify a BPEL specification that will be obtained for the previously explored top software service – *Games Access Contract Handling*. In particular, the UML class diagram in Figure 6 is converted to BPEL process declaration. The control flow and the activities in the UML activity diagram from Figure 7 define the BPEL activity flow (Box 2).

The automatic transformations from UML models to BPEL specifications are discussed and proposed in a number of papers; for more details the reader is referred to (White, 2005), (Amsden et al., 2003).

FUTURE RESEARCH DIRECTIONS

In MDD, models are so far mostly considered in the system development process, leaving thus business level models less explored (Vidales et al., 2008). In this chapter, we have set the focus on defining a business level model, which elicits value-based services in a business value model and

Box 1.

```
<wsdl:message name="gamesSelection">
        <wsdl:part name="gamesInfo" type="someType"/>
</wsdl:message>
<wsdl:message name="costTerms">
        <wsdl:part name="cost" type="xsd:string"/>
</wsdl:message>
…..
…..
<wsdl:portType name="gameContractInterface ">
        <wsdl:operation name=" receiveGamesSelection">
        <wsdl:input message=" gamesSelection"/>
        ……
        ……
        </wsdl:operation>
</wsdl:portType>
```

along different phases of a business transaction life-cycle. In this way obtained model, we have further transformed to a system level capturing software service structure and behaviour. From that perspective, a number of directions for future work appear as relevant:

- **Extending Business Level Model with Strategic Aspects:** In regard to business-to-IT alignment, identifying consumer needs across different phases of a business collaboration and mapping them to the activities required to fulfil these needs would be of a high importance. Incorporating the motivation behind the business transactions, that depicts value configuration, in the business model would improve the accuracy of the model specification and thereby the identification of services. This can be achieved by, for instance, considering a goal-supported business model at this top level, where the business transactions are elicited as the means for the achievement of the goals of consumers.
- **Augmenting the Automation of Business Level-to-System Level Transformations:** A way to achieve a smoother transformation between the two models is to clearly define and structure the Business level meta-data. For instance, a UML profile including declarative business aspects (i.e. value exchanges, actors, etc.), as well as procedural (i.e. process activities and execution rules), would be helpful in getting a comprehensive meta-data model at the Business level model. To facilitate semantic matching between different models, a possibility is to use ontologies for defining meta-data; this is already proposed in certain research studies. Having such defined Business level model would also facilitate a pattern-based mapping to more specific components at the system level.
- **Capturing Service Protocols:** When defining business services, in our approach, we have considered a whole business life-cycle, i.e. planning, identification, negotiation, actualization and post-actualization

Box 2.

```
<process name="gamesAccessContractHandling">
        targetNameSpace=http://abc.com/simpleContractProcessing
        xmlns:lns="http://contracts.org/wsdl/contract-establishment"
        ......................
        ...................... />
        <partners>
        <partner name="gamePlayerManager"
                serviceLinkType="lns:contractApproveLinkType"
                myRole="approver"/>
          <partner name="subscriptionManager"
        ............
        ......... />
        <partners>
        <sequence>
        <receive name="receiveSelection" partner="gamePlayerManager"
                portType="….."
        operation="receiveGamesSelection"
        ......... />
        </receive>
        <invoke name="invokedatachecker"
        partner="subscriptionManager"
        portType="…."
        ...... />
        </invoke>
        ......
        ......
        </sequence>
<process>
```

phases. By identifying business and software services on a phase-basis, as a result, at the lowest specification level, we get a number of independent service contracts and behavior specifications. This enhances the flexibility for combining services at different stages of a collaboration. To capture the information for possible orderings, for instance for the business services such as "delivery of goods" and "payment management", both the business model and the system model may be extended to include the information of interrelated services. However, this may be counter-productive from the service coupling perspective. Another possibility is to define the service interrelations by means of business rules and then relate those to business service definitions.

CONCLUSION

In this chapter, we have introduced a MDD-based method for designing business-aligned software services, which may be implemented using Web services or some other related technology.

In the model driven development, a clear understanding of the usability of all the employed models is of a high importance. In our approach, business value models play a major role in the service identification, because they offer some important advantages compared to other types of enterprise models. They can illustrate a high-level description of a whole business in a single and easy-understandable view. Here, we have shown that using the three layered REA/Open-edi framework, the business modeler can elicit an explorative business service portfolio conducting business transactions to use and produce economic values along all the phases of a business transaction lifecycle (i.e. planning, identification, negotiation, actualization and post-actualization). This model forms the basis at the top level, which is further extended by modeling the behaviour and rules for of every elicited business service. After, using a well-defined set of mappings, business model is transformed to a system model, which in detail specifies the structure and behavior of the software services, using UML 2. Such a formed model can be then easily transformed to an executable service specification and service coordination. We have illustrated the use of our method on the case of an on-line game provider.

The benefit of the proposed method is twofold. First, it enables a systematic and explorative identification of value-founded software services, which improves the overall performance of a network of actors in business value constellations. Secondly, the method describes a straightforward approach for development of software services and their coordinations. Using MDD as a cornerstone, the method enables traceability of low-level executable services toward economic value offerings, justifying thus the economic viability of these services.

REFERENCES

Ambler, S. (2004). *The object primer: Agile model-driven development with UML 2.0.* Cambridge University Press. doi:10.1017/CBO9780511584077

Amsden, J., Gardner, T., Griffin, C., & Iyengar, S. (2003). *IBM draft UML 1.4 profile for automated business processes with a mapping to BPEL 1.0.* Retrieved March 15, 2009, from http://www.ibm.com/developerworks/rational/library/content/04April/3103/3103_UMLProfileForBusinessProcesses1.1.pdf

Anderssson, B., Johannesson, P., & Zdravkovic, J. (2007). *Aligning goals and services through goal and business modeling. The International Journal of Information Systems and e-Business Management,* 7, 143–169.

Baida, Z., Gordijn, J., Saele, H., Akkermans, H., & Morch, A. (2005). An ontological approach for eliciting and understanding needs in e-services. In O. Pastor & J.F. Cunha (Eds.), *17th Conference on Advanced Information Systems Engineering* (LNCS) (vol. 3520, pp. 400-414). Springer-Verlag. doi:10.1007/11431855_28

Boerner, R., & Goeken, M. (2009). Identification of business services literature review and lessons learned. In *Proceedings of 15th Americas Conference on Information Systems 2009.* Retrieved February 15, 2014, from http://d-nb.info/103476697X/34#page=28

Cherbakov, L., Galambos, G., Harishankar, R., Kalyana, S., & Rackham, G. (2005). Impact of service orientation at the business level. *IBM Systems Journal, 44*(4), 653–668. doi:10.1147/sj.444.0653

Curtis, B., Kellner, M., & Over, J. (1992). Process modeling. *Communications of the ACM, 35*(9), 75–90. doi:10.1145/130994.130998

Davenport, T. (1992). *Process innovation: Reengineering work through information technology.* Harvard Business School.

Derzsi, Z., Gordijn, J., & Tan, Y. (2008). Towards model-based assessment of business-IT alignment in e-service networks from multiple perspectives. In *Proceedings of 16th European Conference on Information Systems*. Retrieved March 15, 2009, from http://is2.lse.ac.uk/asp/aspecis/20080007.pdf

Estrada, H., Morales-Ramírez, I., Martínez, A., & Pastor, O. (2010). From business services to web services: An MDA approach. In J. Castro, X. Franch, & J. Mylopoulos (Eds.), *Fourth International iStar Workshop*, (vol. 586, pp. 31-35). CEUR.

Fox, M. S. (1992). The TOVE project: Towards a common-sense model of the enterprise. *Enterprise Integration Laboratory Technical Report*. Retrieved May 2, 2009, from http://www.eil.utoronto.ca/enterprise-modelling/papers/fox-tove-uofttr92.pdf

Fritscher, B., & Pigneur, Y. (2011). Business IT alignment from business model to enterprise architecture. In C. Salinesi, & O. Pastor (Eds.), *Advanced information systems engineering workshops (LNBIP)* (Vol. 83, pp. 4–15). Springer. doi:10.1007/978-3-642-22056-2_2

Gailly, F., España, S., Poels, G., & Pastor, O. (2008). Integrating business domain ontologies with early requirements modelling. Lecture Notes in Computer Science, 5232, 282-291.

Gailly, F., & Poels, G. (2009) Using the REA ontology to create interoperability between e-collaboration modeling standards. In *Proc. of 21st International Conference on Advanced Information Systems Engineering* (CAiSE 09), (LNCS), (vol. 5565, pp. 395-409). Springer-Verlag. doi:10.1007/978-3-642-02144-2_32

Geerts, G., & McCarthy, W. E. (1999). *An accounting object infrastructure for knowledge-based enterprise models*. IEEE Intelligent Systems & Their Applications.

Gordijn, J. (2004). E-business modeling using the e3 value ontology. In W. Curry (Ed.), *E-business model ontologies* (pp. 98–127). Elsevier Butterworth-Heinemann. doi:10.1016/B978-075066140-9/50007-2

Gordijn, J., Akkermans, J. M., & van Vliet, J. C. (2000). Business modeling is not process modeling. In G. Goos, J. Hartmanis & van J. Leeeuwen (Eds.), Conceptual Modeling for e-Business and the Web (LNCS), (vol. 1921, pp. 40-51). Springer-Verlag.

Gordijn, J., van Eck, P., & Wieringa, R. (2008). Requirements engineering techniques for e-services. In D. Georgakopoulos, & M. P. Papazoglou (Eds.), *Service-oriented computing: cooperative information systems series* (pp. 331–352). Cambridge, MA: The MIT Press.

Hess, A., Humm, B., Voss, M., & Engels, G. (2007). Structuring software cities a multidimensional approach. In *Proceedings of 11th IEEE International Conference on Enterprise Distributed Object Computing Conference - EDOC 2007*. (pp. 122-122). IEEE.

Hruby, P. (2006). *Model-driven design of software applications with business patterns*. Springer Verlag.

Iacob, M. E., Meertens, L. O., Jonkers, H., Quartel, D. A. C., Nieuwenhuis, L. J. M., & Van Sinderen, M. J. (2012). From enterprise architecture to business models and back. *Software & Systems Modeling*, 1–25.

ISO. IEC 19502:2005(E). (2005). *Meta Object Facility (MOF) Specification, Version 1.4.1*. Retrieved March 08, 2009, from http://www.omg.org/cgi-bin/doc?formal/05-05-05.pdf

ISO. IEC 15944-4:2006 Information technology – Business Agreement Semantic Descriptive Techniques – Part 4: Open-EDI Business Transaction Ontology. (2006). Retrieved May 04, 2009, from http://www.itu.dk/~hessellund/REA2006/papers/McCarthy.pdf

Johannesson, P. (2007). The role of business models in enterprise modeling. In J. Krogstie, A. Opdahl, & S. Brinkkemper (Eds.), *Conceptual modeling in information systems engineering* (pp. 123–140). Springer-Verlag. doi:10.1007/978-3-540-72677-7_8

Johnston, S. (2005). UML 2.0 profile for software services. *IBM Cooperation*. Retrieved March 15, 2009, from http://www.ibm.com/developerworks/rational/library/05/419_soa/

Jones, S. (2005). *A methodology for service architectures*. Capgemini white paper. Retrieved February 15, 2014, from http://www.oasis-open.org/committees/download.php/15071

Kherraf, S., Lefebvre, E., & Suryn, W. (2008). Transformation from CIM to PIM using patterns and archetypes. In *Proceedings of the 19th Australian Software Engineering Conference* (pp. 338-346). IEEE Computer Society. doi:10.1109/ASWEC.2008.4483222

Kleppe, A., Warmer, J., & Bast, W. (2003). *MDA explained*. Addison-Wesley Professional.

Loniewski, G., Insfran, E., & Abrahão, S. (2010). A systematic review of the use of requirements engineering techniques in model-driven development. In Model driven engineering languages and systems (LNCS), (vol. 6395, pp. 213–227). Springer. doi:10.1007/978-3-642-16129-2_16

López-Sanz, M., Acuña, C. J., Cuesta, C. E., & Marcos, E. (2008). UML profile for the platform independent modelling of service-oriented architectures. Lecture Notes in Computer Science, 4758, 304-307.

Marshall, C. (2000). *Enterprise modeling with UML: Designing successful software through business analysis*. Addison-Wesley Professional.

McCarthy, W. E. (1982). REA accounting model: A generalized framework for accounting systems in a shared data environment. *Accounting Review*, *57*(3), 554–578.

OMG Meta Object Facility. (MOF) Core Specification. (2013). Retrieved February 04, 2014, from www.omg.org/spec/MOF/2.4.1/

OASIS - Web Services Business Process Execution Language Version 2.0., WS-BPEL. (2007). Retrieved May 04, 2009, from http://docs.oasis-open.org/wsbpel/2.0/OS/wsbpel-v2.0-OS.html

OMG - Business Process Modeling Notation (BPMN). OMG/Business Management Initiative. (2011). Retrieved February 04, 2014, from www.omg.org/spec/BPMN/2.0/

Osterwalder, A. (2004). *The business model ontology*. (Doctoral thesis). HEC Lausanne. Retrieved May 02, 2009, from http://www.hec.unil.ch/aosterwa/

Peltz, C. (2003). Web services orchestration and choreography. *IEEE Computer*, *36*(10), 46–52. doi:10.1109/MC.2003.1236471

Piccinelli, G., & Stammers, E. (2001). From e-processes to e-networks: An e-service-oriented approach. In *Proceedings of International Conference on Internet Computing*, (vol. 3, pp. 549-553). CSREA Press.

Poels, G. (2010). A conceptual model of service exchange in service-dominant logic. In J. Morin, J. Ralyte, & M. Snene (Eds.), *First International Conference on Exploring Services Science,* (LNBIP), (vol. 53, pp. 224-238). Springer. doi:10.1007/978-3-642-14319-9_18

Porter, M. (1998). *Competitive advantage: Creating and sustaining superior performance*. The Free Press.

Rosen, M. (2003, December). MDA, SOA and technology convergence. *MDA Journal*. Retrieved March 15, 2009, from http://www.bptrends.com/publicationfiles/12-03%20COL%20Frankel%20-%20MDA%20SOA%20-%20Rosen.pdf

Scheer, A., Thomas, O., & Adam, O. (2005). Process modeling using event-driven process chains: Process-aware information systems: Bridging people and software through process technology. Hoboken, NJ: Academic Press.

Sewing, J., & Rosemann, M. (2008). Assessing the potential impact of web services on business processes. In I. Lee (Ed.), *E-business models, services and communications* (pp. 221–249). Hershey, PA: Information Science Reference.

Sicilia, M. A., & Mora, M. (2010). On using the REA enterprise ontology as a foundation for service system representations. In Ontology, Conceptualization and Epistemology for Information Systems, Software Engineering and Service Science 2010 (LNBIP) (Vol. 62, pp. 135-147). Springer. doi:10.1007/978-3-642-16496-5_10

Stabell, C. B., & Fjeldstad, O. D. (1998). Configuring value for competitive advantage: On chains, shops, and networks. *Strategic Management Journal*, *19*(5), 413–437. doi:10.1002/(SICI)1097-0266(199805)19:5<413::AID-SMJ946>3.0.CO;2-C

UN/CEFACT Modeling Methodology (UMM) User Guide. (2006). Retrieved May 04, 2009, from http://www.unece.org/cefact/umm/UMM_userguide_220606.pdf

Vidales, M. A. S., García, A. M. F., & Aguilar, L. J. (2008). A new MDA approach based on BPM and SOA to improve software development process. *Polytechnical Studies Review*: *Tékhne*, *6*(9), 70–90.

Wang, Z., Chu, D., & Xu, X. (2010). Value network based service choreography design and evolution. In *Proceedings of IEEE 7th International Conference on e-Business Engineering (ICEBE),* (pp. 495-500). IEEE.

White, S. (2005, March). Using BPMN to Model a BPEL Process. *Business Process Management Trends*. Retrieved March 04, 2009, from http://www.businessprocess-trends.com/publicationfiles/03-05%20WP%20Mapping%20BPMN%20to%20BPEL-%20White.pdf

Zdravkovic, J., & Ilayperuma, T. (2012). Designing Consumer-aligned Services Using Business Value Modelling. *International Journal of Organisational Design and Engineering*, *2*(3), 317–342.

ADDITIONAL READING

Hruby, P. (2006). *Model-driven design of software applications with business patterns*. Springer Verlag.

Johannesson, P. (2007). The role of business models in enterprise modeling. In J. Krogstie, A. Opdahl, & S. Brinkkemper (Eds.), *Conceptual modeling in information systems engineering* (pp. 123–140). Springer-Verlag. doi:10.1007/978-3-540-72677-7_8

Stabell, C. B., & Fjeldstad, O. D. (1998). Configuring value for competitive advantage: On chains, shops, and networks. *Strategic Management Journal*, *19*(5), 413–437. doi:10.1002/(SICI)1097-0266(199805)19:5<413::AID-SMJ946>3.0.CO;2-C

KEY TERMS AND DEFINITIONS

Business Process Model: An ordered set of business activities.

Business Service: A business activity offered by a service provider to its environment.

Business Transaction: Reciprocal economic events that transfer economic resources among the actors involved in a business model.

Business Value Model: A business model that describe the transfer of economic values taking place among the involved actors.

Open-EDI: An ISO standard for defining the phases in a business collaboration.

REA: An ontology for defining a business value model, including three core concepts: *resource* (economic value), *event* (transfer), and *agent* (actor).

Software Service: The provisioning of a business service over an electronic network, such as the Internet.

Web Service: A technology for realising software services.

Chapter 5
Cloud Computing Economics

Stamatia Bibi
Aristotle University of Thessaloniki, Greece

Dimitrios Katsaros
University of Thessaly, Greece

Panayiotis Bozanis
University of Thessaly, Greece

ABSTRACT

Cloud services and technologies are currently receiving increased attention from the industry mostly due to business-driven promises and expectations. Significant innovations in virtualization and distributed computing, as well as improved access to high-speed Internet and a weak economy, have accelerated interest in cloud computing. However, is the migration to the Cloud the most profitable option for every business? Enterprise adoption of cloud computing often requires a significant transformation of existing Information Technology (IT) systems and processes. To justify such a change, a viable business case must be made based on the economics of transformation. This chapter presents a study of the basic parameters for estimating the potential infrastructure and software costs deriving from building and deploying applications on cloud and on-premise assets. Estimated user demand and desired quality attributes related to an application are also addressed in this chapter as they are aspects of the decision problem that also influence the choice between cloud and in-house solutions.

INTRODUCTION

Cloud computing has become the buzzword in the industry today. Cloud computing enables the use of common business applications online using the providers' software and hardware resources and finally paying on-demand Although it is not an entirely new concept significant innovations in virtualization and distributed computing, as well as improved access to high-speed Internet and a weak economy, have accelerated the interest in cloud computing. This model opens a new horizon of opportunity for enterprises as it introduces new business models that allow customers to pay for the resources they effectively use instead of making upfront investments. This fact raises the

DOI: 10.4018/978-1-4666-6359-6.ch005

question of whether such a technology reduces IT costs and the situations under which cost is actually a motive for migrating to cloud computing technologies.

As cloud computing services are maturing, they are becoming an attractive alternative to traditional in-house or on premise development.. Cloud computing promises to increase the velocity with which applications are deployed, increase innovation, and lower costs, all while increasing business agility.The variable costs calculated on scalable use of resources, the support of enterprise growth through on demand instant infrastructure provisioning and the shift of maintenance, administration and monitoring operations to third parties are among the compelling benefits of the cloud. Still a quantitative analysis of the relevant aspects of the potential IT problem is required before making a decision on the appropriate development and infrastructure model.

IT managers are recently faced with the problem of making a selection between cloud computing and on-premise development and deployment. Cloud computing option is attractive, especially if the quality delivered and the total cost is satisfying and the risks are reasonable. The real question for many IT departments is whether the cost of transition to an external computing cloud will be low enough to benefit from any medium-term savings (Armbrust et al., 2008), (Cloud Computing Congress, 2010). In order to be able to provide answers to the above question, a formal cost analysis of cloud and on-premise deployment should be performed in order to compare thoroughly the two alternatives.

A thorough analysis of the estimated costs and quality associated with the two alternatives will help an IT manager define the pros and cons of each solution. Such an analysis will point out which is the right combination of cloud and premise based assets and can indeed provide the optimal solution. As mentioned by Knight, (2009) the key is not choosing between the two solutions but being strategic about where to deploy various hardware and software components of a total solution.

Although there is a lot of research dedicated to cloud computing software engineering issues, economics and cost estimation drivers for adopting such a technology are not systematically addressed. This chapter presents basic parameters for estimating the potential benefits from Cloud computing and provides an estimation framework for determining if it is a technology that offers a long term profitable solution to IT business problems. Basic parameters for estimating the potential costs deriving from building and deploying applications on cloud and on premise assets are presented.

The assessment of cloud computing costs is more evident compared to the assessment of on premises development and deployment. The cost of cloud computing services initially depends on the usage of three types of delivery models; namely, software-as-a-service, platform-as-a-service and infrastructure-as-a-service. The usage is counted and billed based on the committed resources per hour or the number of users per hour. As the cloud technology is offered from types of providers from giants like Amazon to small re-sellers, measurement standards are not yet fully defined and consistent for each model. The usage metrics should be carefully selected in order to provision and receive effective services (Dikaiakos et al., 2009). The metrics that nowadays are frequently used are bandwidth, CPU, memory and applications usage, per hour. These metrics will also be used to estimate the cost of an application moving or being developed over the cloud. Other important parameters that should be taken into account in order to evaluate cloud computing adoption is the business domain and objectives of the application considered, demand behaviour in the particular field and technical requirements (Klems et al., 2009). Of course this estimation would help in order to approximately predict the cost of cloud computing adoption, but still one should be able to estimate the costs of the alternative privately owned solution in order to compare them and make a justifiable choice.

Estimating the cost of software development and deployment based on on-premise assets is a more complex procedure. On–premises application development includes a variety of different costs associated with IT infrastructure and software development. Estimating in-house development and deployment of software is a difficult task, as there are different cost drivers related to personnel, product, process, hardware and operation expenses. Developing applications on privately owned IT infrastructure comprise, apart from software development and maintenance costs which remain the same in both cases, a series of cost drivers associated with physical attributes, performance factors and functional expenses (McRitsie et.al., 2008). Physical attributes, that may affect the in-source development, are related to the operating environment such as facility requirements, systems hardware and software costs and end users equipment. Performance attributes involve the technical non-functional requirements of the application relevant to the required reliability, transaction- rate, safety, accuracy. The non-functional requirements have an impact on the selected infrastructure. Finally the functional expenses of the company may involve years of operation, labor rates, size of the development and support team and replacement and upgrade policies.

These factors affect the total cost of an IT investment and may define the feasibility of a certain application development and the potential benefits of developing it in-sourcing or out-sourcing over the cloud.

This chapter is an overview of possible billing measures and metrics related to infrastructure and software either they are deployed in the cloud or in house. It is addressed to IT managers that face the dilemma of selecting to deploy applications on the cloud or on premise, to cloud providers that want to effectively bill their provisions and to Independent Service Vendors that want to offer to potential customers both of the two alternatives, clarifying long term benefits of each of the two. Specifically, in the sequel we pursue three main goals:

1. To analyze the different types of costs related to adopting cloud technologies and in house development. Our approach is based on the discussion of general cost categories that are taken into account by "cloud" providers and the traditional cost drivers considered in estimating in-source software and systems applications;
2. To provide an analytic comparison example for the deployment of a CRM system based on current economic status. The analysis is based using commercial data from software development coming from the International Standards Benchmarking Group (ISBSG, 2010) and from (Yankee, 2005) report;
3. To define quality attributes and levels of demand behaviour that may affect the final choice. User demand is an indicator of the load of a system and the estimated traffic that greatly affects infrastructure costs. Desired quality attributes and the level these attributes are incorporated into on premise and on cloud solutions can also affect the final decision.

The rest of the chapter is organized as follows: The next Section provides an analysis of the background and the related work. Section entitled "Choose the right deployment model" describes cloud computing and traditional software and system costs and provides a three step procedure that will assist IT managers to understand the benefits of each solution. The two last sections discuss future work and conclude the Chapter.

BACKGROUND

There is fairly broad general interest on the benefits and drawbacks of moving or deploying an application to the cloud. Cost is recognized as an important factor that may motivate the transitioning of IT operations to cloud computing. Practitioners show an increased interest on the costs related to cloud computing however monetary cost- benefits are not yet fully recorded, assessed and analyzed by the scientific community.

Armbrust et. al. (2009) in their technical report, include a chapter devoted to cloud computing economics. Three issues are mentioned in (Armbrust et al., 2009) that should participate in cloud computing economic models. These issues are related to long-term cost benefits, hardware resource costs declines and resource utilization. A host service in the cloud should offer benefits over the long term. This means that one has to estimate the utilization over the cloud for a significant period of time. In these estimations the "pay as you go" billing system offered by cloud computing providers is evaluated in terms of elasticity measured in resource utilization. An IT manager will predict daily average and peak demand measured for example as the number of servers required and then he will be able to compare utility computing versus privately owned infrastructure. Also hardware expenditures should be taken into consideration into economic models. Hardware resource costs decline at variable rates a fact that may lead to unjustifiable expenditures compared to actual resource usage. Cloud computing can track changes to hardware costs and pass them through the client more cost effectively.

Klems et al. (2009) propose a framework for determining the benefits of cloud computing as an alternative to privately owned IT infrastructure. The model presented is based on the business scenario and the comparison of costs between the two alternatives. The business scenario is defined by the business domain and objectives, the demand behavior and the technical requirements. For example, the business domain defines whether an application will be used at a Business to Business level or Business to Client level, or for internal use. The business goals will point out particular benefits coming from web hosting in the cloud such as short time to market, reduced costs, and software licenses violations. Demand behavior also is an important factor that affects the performance of services and applications in the Web according to Kleims (2009). Demand behavior can be seasonal, temporary or caused by batch processing jobs.

In Bibi et.al (2010) the cost factors of on premise and hosted solutions are addressed while in Bibi et al. (2012) a cost model is introduced for assessing costs of on premise, SaaS and hybrid solutions (IaaS). In the last study a case study is presented utilizing data from a company that assessed all three solutions. The TCO analysis pointed that the SaaS solution has benefits with respect to the in-house solution, but the gain tends to decrease over a 20-year period, while the IaaS solution benefits over the in-house solution remain practically stable.

The key factors that must be considered in determining the economic soundness of any transformation to cloud computing are presented by Beaty et al (2011). The paper discusses the aspects that should be taken into consideration for performing sensible ROI analysis that captures the relevant factors affecting the economics of cloud transformation. The type of IT costs considered are: infrastructure and software costs, energy costs and labor for system management.

A few studies addressed the issue of pricing models that would help cloud providers be competitive and challenge potential customers. Samimi and Patel (2011) introduced a review and comparison of the recent pricing models in grid and cloud computing and their economic models. They also highlighted the differences in grid and cloud computing by comparing their usage, standardization, virtualization, and SLAs. They studied pricing models thoroughly in grid computing and compared them to those in cloud computing.. Sharma et al., (2012) suggested a financial model for cloud providers capable of bringing high level of QoS to customers with competitive price. The authors employed the financial option theory and captured the realistic value of cloud resources. The price appointed by this model represented the optimal price that the service provider should charge its customers to recover the initial costs. The financial option theory gave a lower boundary of the price that should be charged to customers. The upper boundary of the price was determined using Moore's law. The authors suggested that, if the price was set between these two boundaries, it would be beneficial for both customers and service providers.

Related studies that discuss the cost of familiar to cloud computing models like grid computing are (Kondol et. al., 2009) and (Optitz et al., 2008). Performance trade- offs and monetary costs of cloud computing compared to desktop grids are analyzed in (Kondol et. al., 2009). The above comparison involves two relevant architectural platforms, cloud computing and volunteer computing, that present similar principles. Performance comparison is quantified in terms of execution, platform construction, application deployment and completion times. Cost comparison is performed in terms of technical requirements such as project resource usage. The costs of relevant aspects of cloud computing such as grid computing is addressed also in (Optitz et al., 2008). The study analyzes different types of costs and determines the total costs of a resource provider. Relevant cost for resource providers include hardware, business premises, software, personnel and data communication expenses.

Practitioners on the other hand seem to be bigot supporters of utility computing. Miller (2009) states that cloud computing is a type of web-based computing that allows easy and constant access to applications and data from all over the world through an internet connection and facilitates group collaboration. Though he mentions that cloud computing is not suitable for any case, stressing the advantages and disadvantages of cloud computing. Regarding costs he refers that cloud computing reduces hardware and software costs and increases the productivity of the employees as they have access to their files and applications from home as well. Among the disadvantages of cloud computing related to costs Miller (2009) mentions that cloud computing requires fast and instant internet connections. Also data confidentiality in the cloud is a subject under examination that may cause economic loss (McGowan, 2009). Gupta et al. (2013) analyze five factors that affect the decision of an SME to adopt cloud services: usability, convenience, security, privacy and costs. According to the findings of the study, contrary to the generic belief, cost reduction is not among the top two factors for SMEs to move to cloud. Usability and convenience are the two main factors that can urge the migration to the cloud. Reliability seems to be the main concern of SMEs that prevents sharing and collaboration to the cloud.

Knight (2009) argues that the dilemma between cloud computing and on-premise development is wrong and should be substituted by the question of which is the right combination of cloud and premise based assets. The combination of the two approaches can indeed exploit the best of both worlds.

CHOOSE THE RIGHT DEPLOYMENT MODEL

In this Section our goal is to clarify which services are offered by cloud computing and how they are related to on-premise software and system costs. We record and analyze thoroughly all relevant costs related to cloud deployment and in-house development and finally suggest a three step decision model that will support the decision of migrating or not to the clouds.

Cloud Utilities

The main purpose of Cloud Computing is to provide a platform to develop, test, deploy and maintain Web-scale applications and services. A formal definition of cloud computing is not found in literature but most resources refer to this term for anything that involves the delivery of hosted services over the Internet. These services are broadly divided into three categories (Dikaiakos et al., 2009), (Lenk et al., 2009): Software-as-a-Service (SaaS), Platform-as-a-Service (PaaS) and Infrastructure-as-a-Service (IaaS). Figure 1 depicts the services offered by the cloud.

Software as a Service

Software as a Service is a software distribution and usage model that is available via a network to the customers. Both horizontal and vertical market software are offered by SaaS. Typical examples of horizontal SaaS are subscription management software, mail servers, search engines and office suites. Examples of vertical SaaS are more specialized software such as Accounting software, Management Information systems and Customer Relationship Management systems.

SaaS software is leased through Service Level Agreements (SLAs). An SLA (SLA definition, 2010) is a contractual service commitment. An SLA is a document that describes the minimum performance criteria a provider promises to meet while delivering a service. It typically also sets out the remedial action and any penalties that will take effect if performance falls below the promised standard. It is an essential component of the legal contract between a service consumer and the provider. SaaS investment is typically limited to the subscription fee. This pricing model provides a predictable investment that follows a pay per usage billing scheme. Usually costs are calculated considering user licenses, customizations costs and end user support and training costs (CRM Landmark, 2009). The last three types of cost refer mostly to software for vertical needs. All these costs are determined in SLAs that define the pay-on-demand rates.

Defining the billing model of SaaS is a challenging task for potential customers, providers and Independent Software Vendors. Many Independent Software Vendors (ISVs) have developed their SaaS solutions offered in parallel with the corresponding commercial products. Among the challenges ISVs are confronted is the re-

Figure 1. Cloud services

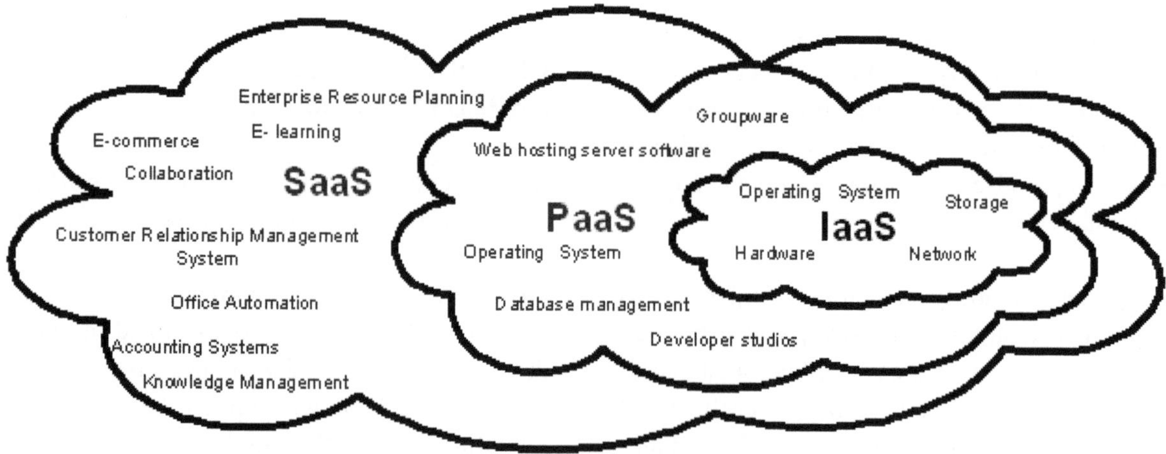

structuring of pricing models. In order to establish attractive pay- as- you go subscription fees, the understanding of the differences in cost between software products and services is required. These differences need also to be clearly presented to candidate customers.

Major SaaS providers bid very low prices hoping that perpetual licensing will lead to upfront earnings. SaaS providers usually provide scalable types of licensing based on the number of users or on the number of applications accessible to the user. One pricing model may not be appropriate for all types of applications and software services. For example, eCommerce or supply-chain SaaS solutions could be priced based on the number of transactions or volume of data transmitted. Customer relationship management (CRM) or Salesforce Automation (SFA) solutions can be priced based on the number of accounts, prospects, or bookings they support. Determining customers' price-sensitivity when it comes to SaaS is especially difficult for providers who need to balance their new solution pricing against existing product pricing schedules. (Le Cayla, 2006).

SaaS providers are faced with the problem of metering and billing their services in order to establish competitive offers that will at first attract potential customers, and offer long term benefits to both of the two parties. A provider is faced with the following three problems:

- Which usage data to collect and record?
- Based on which metrics to charge?
- Should process and ratings be flexible per customer? Per contract?

Answering the first question we can say that the relevant data collected so far by providers generally falls into three categories, resource data, transactional data and workflow data.

Resource data most of the times describe the customers usage of the premises offered by the provider. Relevant data that can be recorded is the number of users, or connections to the application that can be 'per use' or per 'concurrent use'. The number of registered users of a product per month is an increasingly popular method of pricing SaaS. SalesForce, (2010) is a major SaaS provider that use among others this model for most of its offerings. This billing model has different prices for each level usage based on the number of users. The payment per user is appropriate for software that serves internal needs of the customers company. In that case the customer needs to isolate and record the number of employees that will actually utilize the SaaS software. The number of registered users is a good indicator of the value that a group derives from the product (Rothbart, 2009). Risks deriving from this method involve possible user's abandonment. The customer company needs to control, manage and remove users that do not regularly use the software.

Another way of pricing resource usage is based on per- user page view fees counted as the number of users that access a page. This kind of pricing model is mostly appropriate for products that are destined for large external customer and partner communities. In that case, the number of users that access and browse a website is recorded as the basis to charge customers. Theoretically this metric is indicative of the number of users that visit a website and actually may use or buy a product, but still there is no guarantee that a high page view presents the proportional benefits to the SaaS customer and its clients. The page view does not always reflect how much users are using a product. The "concurrent use" on the other hand can be an alternative metric in the cases of SaaS products that require concurrent user intensive functions. Examples of such SaaS products may be teleconferencing applications, discussion forums, calendars, or even information portals. Concurrent user is an industry standard term that refers to the total number of people (as measured by network connections), that are connected to a server or online service at any one point in time. The term "concurrent user" is analogous to "port" or "line" with respect to a telephone branch exchange (Nefsis, 2010). In general, the pricing based on number of users or user licences may be combined with additional fees for extra bandwidth and storage.

Transactional data refer to the interaction between a subscribed customer and the SaaS provider and usually are one –time fees based on the needs of the customer. For example, SaaS Optics (2010) define several types of transaction items within the subscription life cycle. In essence, these transaction items are the events that can occur with regard to a term agreement over time. Such transactions may involve *New Subscription, Upgrade, Downgrade, Adjustment, Renewal, Cancellation*. New Subscription service is a one time fee that can break down to license and professional services fees. License costs are related to the initial subscription to the SaaS service. Professional services fees may include consultancy, training, user support and several other customer needs that may occur. Upgrade, Downgrade or Adjustment are three services that can be offered to a single customer subscription that allow the customization of the application to the customer's needs. The fees charged are based on the level, the costs and the time required for the incorporated changes. Renewal charges include the fees related to the continuation of the services to the customer while cancellation fees include penalties to the customer in case of cancelling the contract based on the time period of the notification.

Workflow data may involve usage metrics involving process oriented activities. Such metrics are relative to the specific SaaS application and are forced by the business goals. For example an E-commerce system may count the number of sales or invoices send, an Advertising& Marketing system may count the number of emails or forms received. The usage of a document management system is reflected by the number of documents download or uploaded. Workflow metrics are defined by the procedures and user tasks incorporated in the SaaS software and are indicators of the level of successful usage of a system. A high level of workflow metrics is associated with relevant economic benefits of the SaaS customer.

We mentioned possible data and metrics that can be used to bill SaaS based on the type of the application and the customer's needs. As with any variation of products available to market there should be differences in pricing taking into consideration the basic marketing mix: the four P's of product, price, promotion, and place (Lovelock, 2007). Depending on the potential customer the SaaS services might be different, the price might be different, the hosted place and the product might be different. Table 1 summarises the metrics that are currently used by SaaS providers to charge their services. Still the pricing models of SaaS are in their infancy at a lot of research is devoted to capturing the correct price model that will better reflect the usage and value of SaaS.

Platform as a Service

Platform as a Service (PaaS) includes the delivery of operating systems and associated desktop services over the Internet without download or installation. PaaS is an outgrowth of Software as a Service targeted to middleware distribution. Platform as a service is a development platform hosted to the cloud and accessed via a network. The functionality that PaaS offers involves at least the following: operating systems, developer studios that include all necessary tools to build a web application, seamless deployment to hosted runtime environment and management and monitoring tools. PaaS offers the potential for general developers to build web applications without having any tools installed in their own space. PaaS applications are hosted to infrastructure offered as a service by cloud computing providers.

Table 1. SaaS billing metrics

Type of Metric	Metric	Explanation	Unit of Measurement	Charges and Current SaaS Vendors
Resource metrics				
	Number of users	Internal enterprise employees	# of licences	Based on ranges of # licences www.salesforce.com www.salesboom.com
	Pay per user	External community users, potential customers	# of page views per month	Based on usage per search http://www.ppcsaas.com/ (for a Search Engine SaaS is the number of searches per month)
	Pay per concurrent user	Systems of high concurrence	# of concurrent users per month	Teleconferecing and knowledge sharing systems http://www.nefsis.com
	Number of user + additional bandwidth and storage	Low prices for small number of users because of additional bandwidth and storage charging	# of users + infrastructure charges	Based on ranges of # number of users + ranges of infrastructure usage
Trasactional metrics				
	New Subscription	Licence fees + Professional services	Standard subscription fee, training costs, consultancy costs, user support costs	Subjective monetary costs by SaaS provider
	Upgrade	Cost of upgrading current application	Based on the level of upgrade. (time, infrastructure, labour costs are counted)	Subjective monetary costs by SaaS provider
	Downgrade	Cost of downgrading current application	Based on the level of degrade	Subjective monetary costs by SaaS provider
	Adjustment	Cost of adjustment of current application	Based on the level of adjustment	Subjective monetary costs by SaaS provider
	Renewal	Cost of renewing SaaS agreement	Subjective monetary costs by SaaS provider	Subjective monetary costs by SaaS provider
	Cancellation	Penalty costs of cancelling a SaaS SLA		
Workflow metrics				
	Successful business scenarios that show the benefit of the customer using a SaaS	Invoices (proofs of sales), Emails (proof of marketing and advertisment)	# business metric/ month	Measure business successful usage http://www.verticalresponse.com/ http://www.zoho.com/invoice/index.html

Therefore, the costs of PaaS are connected to the costs of Infrastructure as a Service and will be analytically addressed in the next section.

Infrastructure as a Service

Infrastructure as a Service is a provision model in which the customer outsources the equipment used to support operations, including storage, hardware, servers and networking components. In that case the provider is the owner of the hardware equipment and all relevant resources and expenses related to housing, constant operation and maintenance are his own responsibility. The client typically pays on a per-use basis. Infrastructure as a Service involves the physical storage space and processing capabilities that enable the use of SaaS and PaaS if wanted otherwise these services are used autonomously by the customer. Virtualization enables IaaS providers to offer almost unlimited instances of servers to customers and make cost-effective use of the hosting hardware.

IaaS can be exploited by enterprises that chase quick time to market. The customer enterprise can accelerate the development time required to build new versions of applications or environments without having to worry about ordering, waiting, paying and configuring new hardware equipment. The most popular use of IaaS is website hosting. Website hosting is a convenient way for enterprises to shift the relevant IT resources away from an internal infrastructure whose primary purpose is to run the business, not the website. In this case the availability and the monitoring of the website are in the concerns of the IaaS provider.

IaaS offers relatively simple infrastructure as it includes basic hardware and operating services. Customers select software servers with operating systems that match their needs and then they load up their own libraries, applications and data and finally configure them themselves. This process requires that the in-house personnel possess considerable IT skills. In the case that the customer enterprise personnel is relatively inexperienced IaaS may not be enough to cover the needs of the customer and can be combined with PaaS. IaaS is then enriched with platform services such as database management systems, web hosting server software, batch processing software and application development environments that are installed in the relevant infrastructure. PaaS and IaaS costs in that case are interrelated.

IaaS and PaaS are billed based on the services delivered to the customer. The billing model is produced considering the level of usage of hardware, application, storage and networking components. Hardware and application components are usually charged simultaneously. These costs most of the times are calculated as on-demand instances per hour. On-Demand instances refer to the number of servers used. The prices differ according to the operating systems and middleware applications loaded to the offered servers. The payment is then processed based on per use instances that are indicative of the compute capacity. Additional metrics that can be used derive from the technical attributes of the server such as the hard disk size of the server, the cpu and the memory capacity. The usage of the servers may also be charged measured in bandwidth or as a daily percentage usage, along with additional IP generation. Also full back ups of cloud servers may be charged separately. PaaS services that may be included in the prices involve databases, web servers, application development environments and servers and video encoding and streaming software.

Storage services are billed based on the hard disk demands, the data transfer and the requests. Initially the data storage is measured in terabytes committed in the hard disk. The price depends on the level of hard disk usage. Data transfer involves transferring the data into databases. Data transfer may be charged autonomously, or is included in data storage fees or may be for free based on the regions of transfer. Data requests involve operations such as copy, get, put, list and other requests regarding the data. Data requests involve inquiries in the data set.

Networking services involves the possibility of establishing a virtual private cloud (Amazon, VPC) that will be the bridge between a company's existing IT infrastructure and the cloud. A private cloud enables enterprises to connect their existing infrastructure to a set of isolated cloud compute resources via a Virtual Private Network (VPN) connection, and to extend their existing management capabilities such as security services, firewalls, and intrusion detection systems to include their cloud resources. The billing of such services is based on the number of VPN connections per hour and the data transferred.

The metrics used to bill IaaS and PaaS services are presented in Table 2.

Traditional Software and Systems Costs

This Section discusses the costs related to IT infrastructure and software development for an application based on on–premise assets. Companies that possess their own IT department have the dilemma of selecting between in-house and hosted SaaS solutions will find very useful to predict software development costs, as these

Table 2. IaaS and PaaS billing metrics

Type of Metric	Metric	Explanation	Charges and Current SaaS Vendors
Hardware and application metrics			
	No Instances of servers	Number of servers.	The prices are based on the operating system and the software installed on the server. The pricing models depend on the provider and can be calculated based on the usage per hour or per month.
	CPU	Level of CPU usage	The CPU usage may is calculated in hours or cores.
	Bandwidth	Incoming, outgoing bandwidth	The gigabytes transferred from and to the cloud measured in gb/ per unit of time
	RAM	Megabytes, Gigabytes	RAM memory committed measured in MB or GB /per unit of time
Storage metrics			
	Data Storage	Hard disk storage, Terabytes	GB or TB/ per unit of time
	Data transfer	Amount of data transferred in different regions	GB or TB/ per unit of time
	Data requests	Copy, get, put, list	Number of requests per month
Networking services			
	No of VPN connections	Virtual Private Network that will bridge the cloud to private infrastructure	Number of VPN connections per hour
	Monitoring operations	Monitor the cloud computing resources, statistics	A charge based on the number of instances monitored per hour
	IP addresses	Additional public IP adresses	Number of IP addresses generated

costs define all relevant on-going costs such as maintenance, training, upgrades and also costs related to infrastructure.

IT Infrastructure Costs

When estimating software development and maintenance costs, IT infrastructure costs should also be accounted. IT costs are non-negligible as usually they stand up to 60% of Total Ownership costs (Gray, 2003), (McRitsie, 2008). Unlike software development estimation, IT estimation is a simpler process as infrastructure and services are more tangible. The cost drivers that influence IT costs as mentioned in (McRitsie, 2008), (Optitz, 2008) and (TechAmerica, 2008) can be operational attributes and business premises.

Operational attributes refer to hardware costs, software and system license fees. Hardware costs include new resources acquisition, replacement and maintenance of existing resources. Hardware acquisition costs depend on the infrastructure hardware list (servers) and the end user hardware list (laptops, CPU, printers). Hardware maintenance costs usually are estimated using measures that compute the Mean Time To Failure (MTTF) or Mean Time Between Failures (MTBF). Software, system and database license fees refer to operational software that will be installed in computer systems necessary for the operation of the new application. License costs are defined by the number of inbound and outbound workstations in which the new application will be installed. The number of users usually affects cost mainly through the number of software licenses needed and recruitment and training costs.

Several performance factors are associated with the non-functional requirements of an application that apart from the need to incorporate them in the software also rise the need for business premises. The average transaction rate, the storage needs, security issues and reliability factors require computational power and capacities. Computational power in low level is related to electricity costs. Other business premises that are necessary for IT development and are associated to total costs involve labor rates, outsourcing agreements and operational locations. Labor rates are related to the personnel expenses and training procedures. Outsourcing agreements may include hardware/software leasing or development. Different physical locations of the organization and different access points to the application are associated to rental or leasing expenses. Tables 3 and 4 summarize in-house infrastructure costs.

Table 3. Operational drivers

	Drivers
	Operational Drivers
New resources	Servers, Laptops, PCs
	Peripheral devices, CPU, memory
	WAN/LAN equipment
Maintenance and replacement costs	CPU
	Hard Disk
	Power supply
	CPU Cooler
License fees	Application Software (office applications, mail)
	System Software (Operating system)
	Database (Licences for end users)

Table 4. Business premises

	Drivers
	Business Premises
Personnel Expenses	Labor Rates
	Training expenses
Electricity costs	Electricity consumption
Physical Locations	Rental expenses

Software Costs

Software development costs are divided into four groups. Product, platform, process and personnel drivers are pointed out by literature (Boehm, 1981) as the most important aspects that determine software costs. Tables 5 to 8 summarize in-house software development cost drivers.

Product attributes related to a software project include descriptive variables and size indicators. The aggregation of variables of both categories is indicative of the complexity of the new projects and the expected difficulties that might rise. Descriptive variables provide information regarding the development type of the project, the application type (IT project type ERP, MIS, CRM or Web applications, etc.) and the user type of the application (professional, amateur, concurrent, casual. In order to estimate size attributes an initial assessment of functional requirements is necessary. From functional requirements we can provide a size estimate measured in function points (Albrecht, 1979) or in Lines of Code (Boehm, 1981). Accurate size estimation is a very important task as it is considered to directly affect the amount of effort required to complete a software project.

Table 5. Product drivers

	Drivers	
	Product Drivers	**Metric**
Type of project	Application Type	ERP, Telecommunications, Logistics, etc.
	Business Type	Medical, Public Sector, Transports, Media, etc.
	Development Type	New Development, Re-development, Enhancement
User type	Level of usage	Amateur, Professional, Casual
	Number of Users	1-50, 50-200, 200-1000, >1000
Size	Source Code Lines	Lines of Code (LOC)
	Function Points	Number of Function Points

Table 6. Platform drivers

Table Head	**Drivers**	
	Platform Drivers	**Metric**
Technical attributes	Distributed Databases	1-5 Scale that depicts the necessity of the attribute.
	On-line Processing	1-5 Scale
	Data communications	1-5 Scale
	Back-ups	1-5 Scale
	Memory constraints	1-5 Scale
	Use of new or immature technologies	1-5 Scale
Non-functional requirements	Reliability	1-5 Scale
	Performance	1-5 Scale
	Installation Ease	1-5 Scale
	Usability	1-5 Scale
	Security	1-5 Scale

Table 7. Process drivers

Table Head	Drivers	
	Process Drivers	**Metric**
Use of Case Tools	Versioning tools	% of usage
	Analysis & Design Tools	% of usage
	Testing Tools	% of usage
Management Process	Use of lifecycle models	Yes or No
	Managed development Schedule	1-5 Scale
Methodologies	Existance of best practices	1-5 Scale
	Software Reuse	% of the total LOC

Table 8. Personnel drivers

Table Head	Drivers	
	Personnel Drivers	**Metric**
Experience	Analysts cababilities	1-5 Scale
	Programmers experience	1-5 Scale
	Familiarity with the problem domain	1-5 Scale
Cultural issues	Reward mechanism	1-5 Scale
	Collaboration	1-5 Scale
	Cabable leadership	1-5 Scale

Non-functional requirements affect the values of platform drivers and can oppose certain constraints or lead to conflicting interests. Examples of non-functional requirements are software reliability, database size, security issues, performance standards, usability issues and transaction rates. Other drivers that directly affect platform costs are incremented memory needs, increased storage facilities and maintenance of back up files. All the above parameters capture platform complexity of the software under development.

Process attributes refer to all project supplements that may be used and enable the development and delivery of quality software within cost and time limitations. Among these characteristics the use of CASE (Computer Aided Software Engineering), the utilization of methods, techniques and standards are the main aspects that define the level of support and observation of the development procedure. Productive development teams usually follow a well-defined and guided process. Proven best practices, methodologies and the selection of the appropriate lifecycle processes are aspects that a development team should rely on to complete a project. The success of a project, the time and cost required for its completion depends on the existence of a well-managed process.

Software costs are also dependant on personnel team attributes. Typical examples of this group of cost drivers are the experience of the team, the analysts' capabilities, the familiarity with the programming language and the application.

Recent studies also point out that cultural characteristics also determine software costs. Well structured teams that encourage communication allow knowledge exchange and support reward mechanisms are more productive compared to impersonal teams. The capabilities of the personnel and the motivation of the environment affect directly the productivity of a development team thus the total developments costs.

Estimating Cloud Computing Migration

IT managers are faced with the problem of selecting how and where to develop and deploy their applications. The requirements of an application will determine the choice between cloud computing and development on premises or even a combination of both (Armbrust, 2008). Each of the two different options presents advantages and disadvantages on various fields. The business goals and priorities of the application will determine the level of usage of cloud or premise assets. IT decision making often requires trading between innovation and time-to-value advantages of cloud computing against performance and compliance advantages of development on-premise. For this reason we propose a three step procedure that will assist in decision making:

1. Assess software and infrastructure development costs.
2. Define quality characteristics.
3. Estimate user demand.

The issue of deciding whether to develop and deploy the applications in the cloud was also addressed in (Klems et al., 2009), but our three-step process is somewhat more generic as it includes detailed recording of relevant parameters.

1. Assess Software and Infrastructure Development Costs

This procedure involves costs assessment of the two alternative solutions. The previous sections will be useful to keep in mind all the relevant aspects of the problem. A five year total cost of ownership projection will be useful to determine long-term benefits of each solution.

We will discuss the deployment of Customer Relationship Management Systems; a common business application that is becoming popular on the cloud. We will focus on software development costs of such an application.

Customer Relationship Management (CRM) is an information industry term for methodologies, software, and Internet capabilities that help an enterprise manage customer relationships in an organized and efficient manner (Laudon & Laudon, 2009). CRM functionality may include product plans and offerings, customer notifications, design of special offers, e.t.c.

Development and cost data for CRM applications built in-house can be found in the International Standards and Benchmarking Group (ISBSG, 2010) data base. Based on data coming from ISBSG, CRM systems on the average require 1867 total effort hours for completion. Keeping in mind average US salaries (4141 US$), 1867 effort hours correspond to 233 workdays, 11,65 months and 48242$. Analyzing the projects that include development data we can see that 56% of the projects require development teams larger than 9 people. All CRM projects developed in-house followed a particular methodology while only 33% of projects that presented values for that field were supported by the use of CASE tools. Cost and development data for CRM applications developed in-house are presented in tables 9 and 10.

Table 9. Cost data statistics for on-premise CRM applications

Cost Data	Average Value
Effort (hours)	1867 h.
Size (function points)	181.5 fp
Cost (US $)	48242 $

On the other hand CRM cloud applications with Zoho (Zoho, 2010) and Salesforce (Salesforce, 2010) leading providers charge based on the number of users and the number of applications accessed. The prices range from 12$ per month to 75$ per month, per user. Considering in that case 5 potential users that will use a sublist of the product features charged 50$ per month the annual costs are calculated to be 3000$.

In both cases analyzed previously costs associated to software development and usage are recorded. In order to calculate infrastructure, maintenance and deployment costs we consider certain assumptions made by the analysis presented in (Yankee, 2005). In Table 11 we present a five year cost analysis including infrastructure and software costs for in-house and hosted to the cloud solution for a CRM application; the costs presented are only indicative and they may vary from case to case. Figure 2 summarizes the 5year costs.

We make the following assumptions (These assumptions and costs cannot be generalized in all possible deployment models but still provide an initial support to enterprises that want to calculate relevant costs):

- The number of end users of the CRM application is 10. This number was selected in order to simulate real world situation for a Small Medium Enterprise (SME). Keeping in mind that each employee serves from 50 to 100 clients we consider that the guest list of a SME is 500-1000 people.

Table 10. Development data statistics for on-premise CRM applications

Development Data	Values and Percentages
Development Team Size	> 9 people. (56%)
Use of CASE tools	Yes (33%)
Programming Languages	C, C#, Cobol, Visual basic and Oracle (65%)
Platform	PCs (39%), clients and servers (15%).
Database	Oracle (41,1%.

- The functionalities of the CRM support Sales, Marketing and Relationship management.
- The price per user for the hosted solution is calculated based on the Professional support offer of Salesforce 65$ per user per month. (The prices of other providers present slight differences that do not distort the results).
- The number of in-house servers is considered to be three; data base server, application server and web server. Three- tier architecture is a popular model adopted by many similar applications, therefore selected in this study. In all of the servers the appropriate middleware is installed and the relevant costs should be considered. Considering that the middleware can be either open source software or commercial solutions, the total infrastructure costs can range from 9000$ (3000$ per server machine considering no costs for middleware) to 70000$ when using commercial middleware (for example Oracle database server (47500$) and Windows (400$) or other commercial products). An average price considered in the analysis is 30000$.
- Application support and maintenance costs in an on premise solution are calculated as 18% of the development costs. Professional

Table 11. 5 year cost analysis of hosted and on premise software deployment

	Cost Category	Cost driver	Year 1	Year 2	Year 3	Year 4	Year 5
Hosted	Infrastructure Costs		included	included	included	included	included
	Software Costs	Number of Users	7800$	7800$	7800$	7800$	7800$
		Professional Services	5850$	1950$	1950$	1950$	1950$
		Customization	5850$	780$	780$	780$	780$
TOTALS			19500$	10530$	10530$	10530$	10530$
On premise	Infrastructure costs	Hardware + middleware	30000$	1500$	1500$	1500$	1500$
		Network Infrastructure (including internet)	19000$	19000$	19000$	19000$	19000$
		Power, Electricity	12000$	12000$	12000$	12000$	12000$
		Floor Space	12000$	12000$	12000$	12000$	12000$
	Software Costs	Development costs	48242$	0	0	0	0 $
		Application support and maintenance	8683$	8683$	8683$	8683$	8683$
		Customization and Integration	36182$	4824$	4824$	4824$	4824$
		User Training	1500$	750$	750$	750$	750$
TOTALS			167607$	58757$	58757$	58757$	58757$
TCO Hosted							61620$
Tco On premise							402635$

Figure 2. TCO for on premise and hosted solution

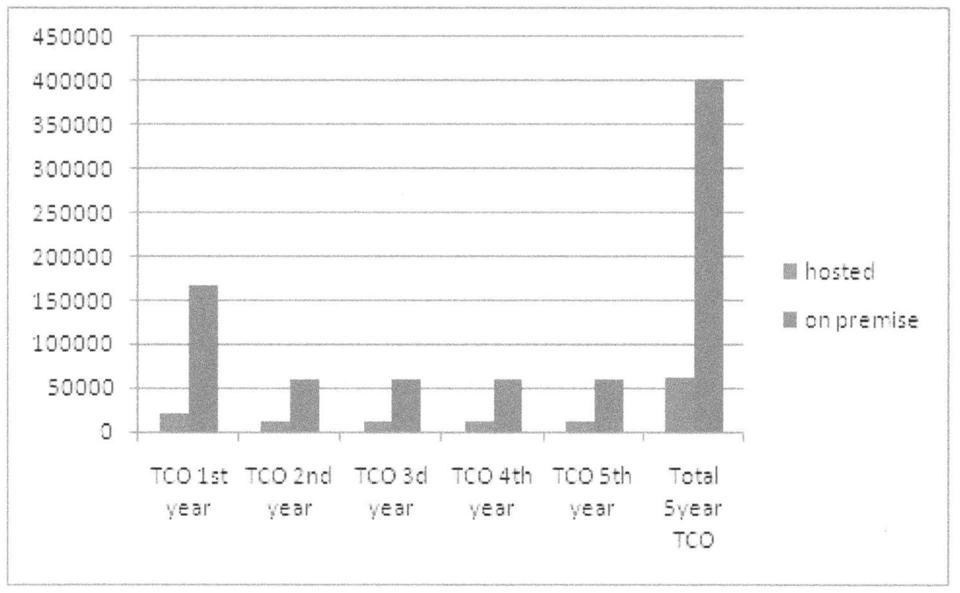

Services are calculated as 75% of the development costs. For the next four years they are calculated as 25% of the development costs. Customization and integration costs for the first year are calculated as 75% of the development costs and for the next four years they are calculated as 10% of the development costs. The percentages used in the calculations are based on the analysis of the Yankee Group(Yankee, 2006).

- Hardware costs for the second to the fifth year are calculated as 5% of the costs of the first year.
- Training costs varies based on the number of users.

2. Define Quality Characteristics

Quality characteristics are closely associated to business goals and most of the times are defined as non-functional requirements. An initial assessment involves the definition of non functional requirements and their priority. Table 12 summarizes quality attributes and which of the two solutions best incorporates them.

Among the quality characteristics that are incorporated in cloud computing is improved performance. Computers in a cloud computing system boot and run faster because they have fewer programs and processes loaded into memory (Miller, 2009). Compatibility is another

Table 12. Quality characteristics

Quality Attribute	Cloud vs. On premise?
Reliability	Reliability is an indicator of the ability of system to perform its required functions. Cloud-based providers are usually better equipped to recover from a failure. Most providers guarantee their uptime and have built-in continuity systems to ensure continuity of the operations.
Availability	Cloud solutions offer instant and universal access to the data and the applications of the customer thorough an internet connection. On the other hand cloud computing is impossible if you can't connect to the Internet or you have low connection speed.
Flexibility & Customization	Customization and integration are considered to be better addressed in on premise solutions. With the software running on its premises, a business retains complete control over its entire hardware and software environment, including the flexibility to select the peripherals and third-party applications that best complement and support its processes (McGowan, 2006).
Data confidentiality	The biggest advantage of on-premise software is that businesses have complete control over their critical business data. This data is physically located on a business's premises and does not require the transmission and storage of data off-site. Owning the hardware and supporting systems provides a business with maximum control.
Back ups	Cloud-based solutions are generally considered to ensure a more secure backup of data and data recovery as data stored in the cloud are replicated across multiple machines. Still there are arguments in case of data loss in cloud you have no physical or local backup.
Interoperability	The ultimate cloud computing advantage is device independence (McGowan,). Existing applications and documents are visible even if local systems and devices alter.
Maintenance and upgrades	Maintenance and upgrade is an intensive and time consuming task especially for web applications where servers, storage, software, backup systems and network are in constant operation. In case of hosted applications this burden is transferred to the provider and usually agreed upon SLAs.
Usability	McGowan states that many web-based applications do not provide the same functionality and features compared to their desktop-based brethren. Users that are tight with existing desktop applications might find interesting the learning curve of the web based corresponding applications.

attribute that is supported by cloud computing. Documents created in a Web application can be read and processed without any special installation on the users PCs. Increased data reliability is also ensured as cloud is considered the ultimate back-up. Interoperability and availability are two other quality characteristics of cloud computing. Interoperability and availability allow user to have access to the system any time, anywhere by any computer or network.

On premise software advantages involve data accessibility, ownership and safety. The biggest advantage of on-premise software is that businesses have complete control over their critical business data (MacGowan, 2006). This is also a main benefit for data intensive applications that should support high volumes of transactions. Other advantage of the on-premise software is that it allows integration with existing software/hardware resources. Customization is one more quality characteristic of in–premise software.

CRM systems usually store, handle and process sensitive private data of customers that should not in any case leak to competitors. Therefore safety is an important non functional requirement. Other important features involve the back-up file storage, and online any-time, any where immediate access to the system. Usability is another important feature for such an application. A customer should be able to navigate through different functionalities and access the information he needs easily and quickly. Prioritizing non functional requirements is an indicator that will help managers take a decision regarding the development and deployment of a system.

3. Estimate User Demand

Estimating the expected demand of the application is also very important in order to assess costs. Expected demand is associated with the number of users. The number of users affects licensing costs and hardware costs. Licensing costs are considered for users that access the applications and make changes of any kind. On the other hand, for hardware as the number of users increases, the hardware must also be improved or performance becomes unacceptable. Centralized database models present reasonable costs for 5-10 users, but present exponential growth of costs as the number of users increases. Distributed models are a solution to such problems shifting costs to PCs. Administration fees are also affected by the number of users as normally one administrator is considered every 5-10 users.

While estimating the number of users according to (Klems et al., 2009), one should keep in mind four types of demand.

- **Expected Demand - Seasonal demand:** This type of demand is associated with consumers' interest in particular products only during a specific period within the calendar year. For example, Christmas ornaments and snow ski equipment are subject to seasonal demand.
- **Expected Demand - Temporary effect:** Expected temporary demand may be caused due to offers, or low prices, or clearance period.
- **Expected Demand - Batch processing:** Batch processing demands involve computational intensive tasks that demand execution of a series of programs. Usually such batch processing procedures may be cost, time consuming or even unfeasible tasks when in house resources are considered.
- **Unexpected Demand - Temporal Effect:** The unexpected demand as mentioned by Klems et al, (2009) is similar to Expected temporary effect but the demand behavior cannot be predicted at all or only in short time in advance.

For the CRM system seasonal demand refers to sales and retails periods that usually present increased demand volume. In that case the number of in-house users may increase as the sales are increased. Temporary effect may refer to clearance period or possible relocation that are seldom events that may cause extra demands. Expected demands: Batch processing may involve for the CRM a period that massive advertisements are shifted. Finally, unexpected demands for the CRM may occur when a new product of the company becomes very popular unexpectedly.

FUTURE WORK

As future work we aim to evaluate the proposed model on real world applications deployment and compare the three alternatives (cloud, on–premise, a combination of the two) based on data coming from both in-house development and cloud hosting. In particular for the hybrid of the two worlds, we plan to elaborate on the cases where it is more profitable and derive appropriate "rules-of-thumb", since we argue that this model will be the one that will finally dominate the market.

In general, for companies it will be a big mind change to give up the convenience and comfort of local deployment, control, and operation to cloud computing vendors but the advantages of cost reduction, scalability, speed to market and high powered computing will allow them to return to their core business and differentiate themselves from their competitors. For the cloud computing vendor the key success factors will be to get the variable pricing right, ensure sustainability of the services provided, coordinate a smooth evolution of the services and that the quality of the services needs to be of a high value. Based on these, we understand that a broad horizon of research topics open up as described in the June 2009 issue of ACM SIGACT News magazine.

CONCLUSION

In this chapter we have taken a first step towards identifying all relevant costs of cloud computing and on-premises infrastructure and software. We proposed a three step decision model for evaluating the two alternatives. Software development and infrastructure costs, desired quality characteristics of the application and expected number of users are the main aspects that a software manager has to consider. The final choice may be the deployment of an application on the cloud, on business premises or by adopting a combination of the two aforementioned alternatives.

A thorough analysis of the costs of cloud computing solutions has been performed. All costs, metrics and measurements related to Software as a Service, Platform as a Service and Infrastructure as a Service has been recorded in order to help potential providers and ISVs bill and provision their services and potential customers calculate their expenses. SaaS costs do not only include the subscription fee but the customization and other professional services fees as well. The subscription fee can be charged based on the number of users, on number of page views or based on metrics coming from business oriented goals. PaaS and IaaS costs are related to the infrastructure and middleware utilized. The level of data storage and transfer, networking, server and middleware utilization are some of the measurements used by providers to charge a customer.

On premise costs on the other hand are split into software development costs and infrastructure costs. Software development costs are related to product drivers, such as the type of the application, the process maturity, ability of the development team to follow standard procedures, platform drivers, related to non functional requirements of the applications and personnel capabilities drivers. Companies possessing their own IT department and have the dilemma of selecting between in-house and hosted SaaS solutions will find very useful to predict software development costs, as these costs define all relevant on-going costs such as maintenance, training, upgrades and also costs related to infrastructure. Infrastructure costs are split into operational costs such as hardware, maintenance and networking and business premises costs such as personnel, physical locations and electricity costs. Infrastructure costs are tangible assets and can be estimated more accurately compared to software costs.

The choice of selecting between in house development and cloud deployment is a dilemma that nowadays concerns an increasing number of companies. Cloud computing is a term covering a wide range of online services and seems an attractive proposition for small medium companies that seek to exploit IT services at lower costs, instant time to market and limited risk. As mentioned the initial investment remains to relatively low levels compared to on premise development, the total cost of ownership is reduced and maintenance burden is shifted to providers. On the other hand on premise supporters argue about security, systems' redundancy, functionality and data privacy as obstacles to cloud computing. Aspects that can point out the way to IT deployment are potential costs, user demand and desired quality attributes. User demand is an indicator of the load of a system and the estimated traffic that greatly affects infrastructure costs. A thorough five year cost analysis will enlighten potential long term cost benefits of both solutions. Desired quality attributes on the other hand and the level these attributes are incorporated into on premise and on cloud solutions can also affect the final decision.

Today, most organizations tend to adopt exclusively one of the two solutions limiting the possibilities that a combined solution can offer. An hybrid approach can provide the best of both worlds by allowing the customer organizations to maximize the benefits of both a hosted delivery model and those of the on-premise model. Such a model may exploit just IaaS combined with on premise software applications to avoid infrastructure costs. An alternative is to use SaaS on VPNs to minimize potential data privacy risks. Or even a company can use PaaS service to build each own applications and deploy them using IaaS or private infrastructure. Services offered by the cloud cover a wide variety of IT needs. A potential customer can find the optimal development and deployment solution keeping in mind all relevant aspects of his own specific IT problem and how these are incorporated in the two models.

Closing, as future work we aim to evaluate the proposed model on real world applications deployment and compare the three alternatives (cloud, on–premise, a combination of the two) based on data coming from both in-house development and cloud hosting. In particular for the hybrid of the two worlds, we plan to elaborate on the cases where it is more profitable and derive appropriate "rules-of-thumb", since we argue that this model will be the one that will finally dominate the market.

REFERENCES

Aggarwal, S. (2005). *TCO of on-demand applications is significantly better for SMBs and mid-market enterprises*. Yankees Group Report. Retrieved March 10, 2010 from http://www.intente.net/pdfs/Yankee___On_Demand_vs_On_Premises_TCO_1_.pdf?ID=13165

Albrecht, A. J. (1979). Measuring application development productivity. In *Proceedings of the Joint SHARE, GUIDE, and IBM Application Development Symposium*. Monterey, CA: IBM Corporation.

Amazon Elastic Cloud. (2010). *Amazon Platform as a service*. Retrieved March 10, 2010, from Amazons website http://aws.amazon.com/ec2/

Armbrust, M., Fox, A., Griffith, R., Joseph, A. D., Katz, R. H., Konwinski, A., et al. (2008, February). *Above the clouds: A Berkeley view of cloud computing* (Technical Report EECS-2009-28). Berkeley, CA: University of California at Berkeley.

Bibi, S., Katsaros, D., & Bozanis, P. (2010, June), Application development: fly to the clouds or stay in-house? In *Proceedings of the 19th IEEE International Workshop on Enabling Technologies: Infrastructures for Collaborative Enterprises (WETICE)*, (pp. 60-65). IEEE. doi:10.1109/WETICE.2010.16

Bibi, S., Katsaros, D., & Bozanis, P. (2012). Business application acquisition: On-premise or SaaS-based solutions? *IEEE Software*, *29*(3), 86–93. doi:10.1109/MS.2011.119

Boehm, B. (1981). *Software engineering economics*. Englewood Cliffs, NJ: Prentice-Hall.

Cayla, L. (2006). *A white paper for independent software vendors*. Retrieved March 10 2010, from http://www.opsource.net/

Cloud Computing Congress. (2010). Retrieved March 10, 2010, from http://www.cloudcomputingchina.org/

Dikaiakos, M. D., Katsaros, D., Mehra, P., Pallis, G., & Vakali, A. (2009). Cloud computing: Distributed internet computing for IT and scientific research. *IEEE Internet Computing*, *13*(5), 10–13. doi:10.1109/MIC.2009.103

Gray, J. (2003, March). *Distributed computing economics* (Technical Report MSR-TR-2003-24). Microsoft Research.

International Software Benchmarking Group. (2010). *ISBSG dataset release 10*. Retrieved March 10 from, http://www.isbsg.org

Klems, M., Nemis, J., & Tai, S. (2009). *Do clouds compute? A framework for estimating the value of cloud computing*. Springer-Verlang.

Knight, D. (2009). *Why cloud vs. premise is the wrong question*. Retrieved March 10, 2010, from Cisco's blog website http://blogs.cisco.com/collaboration/comments/why_cloud_vs._premise_is_the_wrong_question/

Kondol, D., Bahman, J., Malecot, P., Cappello, F., & Anderson, D. (2009). Cost-benefit analysis of cloud computing versus desktop grids. In *Proceedings of the 18th International Heterogeneity in Computing Workshop*. Academic Press.

Landmark, C. R. M. (2009). *SaaS total cost of ownership*. Retrieved March 10, 2010, from CRM Landmark website http://www.crmlandmark.com/saasTCO.htm

Laudon, K., & Laudon, J. (2009). *Management information systems*. Pearson.

Lenk, A., Klems, M., Nimis, J., Tai, S., & Sandholm, T. (2009). What's inside the cloud? An architectural map of the cloud landscape. In *Proceedings of the International Conference on Software Engineering (ICSE) Workshop on Software Engineering Challenges of Cloud Computing (CLOUD)*, (pp. 23-31). ICSE.

Lovelock, C., & Wirtz, J. (2007). *Services marketing: People, technology, strategy* (6th ed.). Pearson International - Pearson/Prentice Hall.

MacGowan, G. (2006). *Helping small businesses choose between on-demand and on-premise software*. Retrieved March 10, 2010, from http://www.computerworld.com/s/article/9002362/Helping_small_businesses_choose_between_On_demand_and_On_premise_software

McRitchie, K., & Accelar, S. (2008). A structured framework for estimating IT projects and IT support. In *Proceedings of Joint Annual Conference ISPA/SCEA Society of Cost Estimating and Analysis*. ISPA/SCEA.

Miller, M. (2009). *Cloud computing pros and cons for end users*. Retrieved March 10, 2010, from http://www.informit.com/articles/article.aspx?p=1324280

Nefsis. (2010). *Pricing model*. Retrieved March 10, 2010, from http://www.nefsis.com/Pricing/concurrent-user.html

Opitz, A., König, H., & Szamlewska, S. (2008). What does grid computing cost. *Journal of Grid Computing*, *6*(4), 385–397. doi:10.1007/s10723-008-9098-8

Rothboard, J. (2009). *Linking SaaS software pricing to value*. Retrieved March 10 from, 2010, http://www.readwriteweb.com/enterprise/2009/01/linking-saas-software-pricing-to-value.php

SaaS Optics. (2010). *SaaS Optics Deep Dive*. Retrieved March 10, 2010, from http://www.saasoptics.com/saas_operations_operating_model/saas_metrics_management_deep_dive/saas_metrics_management_deep_dive.html

CRM SaaS Salesforce. (2010). Retrieved March 10, 2010, from http://www.salesforce.com/platform/platform-edition/

SLA Definition. (2009). *Definition of service level agreement*. Retrieved March 10 2010, from http://looselycoupled.com/glossary/SLA

TechAmerica. (2008). *Software Cost Estimating*. Retrieved March 10, 2010, http://www.techamerica.org/

CRM SaaS Zoho. (2010). Retrieved March 10, 2010, http://www.zoho.com/

ADDITIONAL READING

Barroso, L. A., & Holzle, U. (2009). *The Datacenter as a Computer: An Introduction to the Design of Warehouse-scale Machines. In Synthesis Lectures on Computer Architecture*. Morgan & Claypool Publishers.

Beaty, K. A., Naik, V. K., & Perng, C.-S. (2011, November). Economics of cloud computing for enterprise IT. *IBM Journal of Research and Development*, *55*(6), 456–468. doi:10.1147/JRD.2011.2172254

Brantner, M., Florescu, D., Graf, D., Kossmann, D., & Kraska, T. (2008). Building a database on S3. In *Proceedings of the ACM SIGMOD Conference on Management of Data*, (pp. 251-263). ACM.

Buyya, R., Yeo, C. S., Venugopal, S., Broberg, J., & Brandic, I. (2009). Cloud computing and emerging IT platforms: Vision, hype, and reality for delivering computing as the 5th utility. *Future Generation Computer Systems*, *25*(6), 599–616. doi:10.1016/j.future.2008.12.001

Cohen, J. (2009). Graph twiddling in a MapReduce world. *IEEE Computational Science & Engineering*, *11*(4), 29–41. doi:10.1109/MCSE.2009.120

Foster, I., Zhao, Y., Raicu, I., & Lu, S. (2008). Cloud computing and grid computing 360-degree compared. In *Proceedings of the IEEE Grid Computing Environments Workshop (GCE)*. IEEE. doi:10.1109/GCE.2008.4738445

Geng Lin, , Fu, D., Jinzy Zhu, , & Dasmalchi, G. (2009). Cloud computing: IT as a service. *IT Professional*, *11*(2), 10–13. doi:10.1109/MITP.2009.22

Grossman, R. L. (2009). The case for cloud computing. *IT Professional*, *11*(2), 23–27. doi:10.1109/MITP.2009.40

Gupta, P., Seetharaman, A., & Raj, J. R. (2013, October). Seetharaman, John Rudolph Raj, The usage and adoption of cloud computing by small and medium businesses. *International Journal of Information Management*, *33*(5), 861–874. doi:10.1016/j.ijinfomgt.2013.07.001

Kandukuri, B. R., Paturi, V. R., & Rakshit, A. (2009). Cloud security issues. In *Proceedings of the IEEE International Conference on Services Computing (SCC)*, (pp. 517-520). IEEE.

Kaufman, L. M. (2009). Data security in the world of cloud computing. *IEEE Security and Privacy*, *7*(4), 61–64. doi:10.1109/MSP.2009.87

Kaufman, L. M. (2009, August). Cloud computing and the common man. IEEE Computer, 106-108.

Keahey, K., Tsugawa, M., Matsunaga, A., & Fortes, J. (2009). Sky computing. *IEEE Internet Computing*, *13*(5), 14–22. doi:10.1109/MIC.2009.94

Lasica, J. D. (2009). *Identity in the age of cloud computing: The next-generation Internet's impact on business, governance and social interaction*. The ASPEN Institute.

Lin, J., & Dyer, C. (2010). *Data-intensive text processing with mapreduce. In Synthesis Lectures on Human Language Technologies*. Morgan & Claypool Publishers.

Mather, T., Kumaraswamy, S., & Latif, S. (2009). Cloud security and privacy: An enterprise perspective on risks and compliance. O'Reilly Media.

Miller, M. (2008), *Cloud computing: Web-based applications that change the way you work and collaborate online*. Que.

Ohlman, B., & Eriksson, A. (2009). What networking of information can do for cloud computing. In *Proceedings of the 18th IEEE International Workshops on Enabling Technologies: Infrastructures for Collaborative Enterprises*, (pp. 78-83). IEEE. doi:10.1109/WETICE.2009.27

Reese, G. (2009). *Cloud application architectures: Building applications and infrastructure in the cloud*. O'Reily Media.

Rhoton, J. (2009). *Cloud computing explained: Implementation handbook for enterprises*. Recursive Press.

Samimi, P., & Patel, A. (2011), Review of pricing models for grid & cloud computing. In *Proceedings of IEEE Symposium on Computers & Informatics (ISCI)*, (pp. 634-639). IEEE. doi:doi:10.1109/ISCI.2011.5958990doi:10.1109/ISCI.2011.5958990

Sotomayor, B., Montero, R. S., Llorente, I. M., & Foster, I. (2009). Virtual infrastructure management in private and hybrid clouds. *IEEE Internet Computing*, *13*(5), 14–22. doi:10.1109/MIC.2009.119

Stonebraker, M., Abadi, D., DeWitt, D., Madden, S., Paulson, E., Pavlo, A., & Rasin, A. (2010). MapReduce and parallel DBMSs: Friends or foes? *Communications of the ACM*, *53*(1), 64–71. doi:10.1145/1629175.1629197

Storage Networking Industry Association and the Open Grid Forum. (2009). *Cloud storage for cloud computing*. Author.

Thomas, D. (2008). Next generation IT – Computing in the cloud: Life after jurassic OO middleware. *Journal of Object Technology*, *7*(1), 27–33. doi:10.5381/jot.2008.7.1.c3

Varia, J. (2008). *Cloud Architectures*. Amazon White Paper.

Voas, J., & Zhang, J. (2009). Cloud computing: New wine or just a new bottle? *IT Professional*, *11*(2), 15–17. doi:10.1109/MITP.2009.23

Zehua Zhang., & Xuejie Zhang (2009). Realization of open cloud computing federation based on mobile agent. In *Proceedings of the IEEE International Conference on Intelligent Computing and Intelligent Systems (ICIS)*, (vol. 3, pp. 642-646). IEEE. doi:doi:10.1109/ICICISYS.2009.5358085 doi:10.1109/ICICISYS.2009.5358085

Zhang, L.-J., & Zhou, Q. (2009). CCOA: Cloud computing open architecture. In *Proceedings of the IEEE Conference on Web Services (ICWS)*, (pp. 607-616). ICWS.

KEY TERMS AND DEFINITIONS

IaaS: Infrastructure as a Service is a provision model in which the customer outsources the equipment used to support operations, including storage, hardware, servers and networking components.

Infrastructure Costs: Hardware, networking, and physical location costs.

PaaS: Platform as a Service (PaaS) includes the delivery of operating systems and associated desktop services over the Internet without download or installation.

SaaS: Software as a Service is a software distribution and usage model that is available via a network to the customers.

SLA: Service Level Agreements (SLA) is a contractual service commitment.

Software Development Costs: Development costs that are affected by the process, the product, the platform the personnel.

TCO: Total Cost of Ownership, direct and indirect costs and benefits related to the purchase of any IT component.

Chapter 6
Object-Oriented Cognitive Complexity Measures:
An Analysis

Sanjay Misra
Covenant University, Nigeria

Adewole Adewumi
Covenant University, Nigeria

ABSTRACT

This chapter presents the analysis of ten recently proposed object-oriented metrics based on cognitive informatics. The metrics based on cognitive informatics use cognitive weight. Cognitive weight is the representation of the understandability of the piece of software that evaluates the difficulty experienced in comprehending and/or performing the piece of software. Development of metrics based on Cognitive Informatics (CI) is a new area of research, and from this point of view, for the analysis of these metrics, it is important to know their acceptability from other existing evaluation and validation criteria. This chapter presents a critical review on existing object-oriented cognitive complexity measures. In addition, a comparative study based on some selected attributes is presented.

INTRODUCTION

Software metrics play a crucial role in the process of software development. Among other things, they assist the developer in assuring quality in software. Developers utilize metrics in the different phases that make up the life cycle of software development to better understand and assess the quality of systems they have built. Developing an absolute measure is a non-trivial activity as observed in literature (Fenton, 1994). Software engineers instead, attempt to derive a set of indirect measures that lead to metrics that provide an indication of quality of some representation of software. The quality objectives may include maintainability, reliability, performance, and availability (Somerville, 2001) which are all closely related to software complexity. Software complexity is defined as "the degree to which a system or component has a design or implementation that is difficult to understand and verify" (IEEE, 1990). Software complexity can be grouped

DOI: 10.4018/978-1-4666-6359-6.ch006

into two namely: computational and psychological complexities (Fenton, 1997). Computational complexity refers to the complexity of algorithms and also evaluates the time and memory requirements for executing a program. Psychological complexity refers to the cognitive complexity. This focuses on evaluating the human effort required to perform a software task. There are several definitions of cognitive complexity. For instance, Henderson-Sellers (1996) defines cognitive complexity as 'referring to those characteristics of software that affect the level of resources used by a person performing a given task on it.' Fenton (1997) defines cognitive complexity as the measure of effort required to understand software. Zuse (1998) defines it as the difficulty of maintaining, changing and understanding software. At this point, it is worth noting that metrics and measures are often used interchangeably in software engineering. This is due to the fact that both terms have approximately similar definitions. Pressman (2001) explains 'measure' in software engineering context as 'one that provides a quantitative indication of the extent, amount, dimension, capacity, or size of some attributes of a product or process'. A metric is defined by IEEE as 'a quantitative measure of the degree to which a system, component, or process possesses a given attribute''.

Cognitive informatics (CI), is an emerging area of research that is multidisciplinary in nature. It includes researches in the field of cognitive science, computer science, informatics, mathematics, neurobiology, physiology, psychology and software engineering (Wang, 2002, 2004, 2005, 2006, 2007, 2009). The importance of the CI research is the fact that, it attempts to address the common problems of two related areas in a bi-directional and multidisciplinary approach (Wang, 2004). CI utilizes the computing technique to solve the problem of cognitive science, neurobiology, psychology, and physiology and on the other hand uses the theories of cognitive science, neurobiology, psychology, and physiology to investigate the issues in informatics, computing, and software engineering as well as their solution. For instance, measurement in software engineering is still evolving and needs a lot of efforts to standardize it (i.e. the measurement techniques for software engineering). In the last few years, a number of researchers have tried to address these problems by combining the principles of cognitive science and measurement in software engineering. The number of proposals of object-oriented cognitive complexity measures (Kushwaha & Misra, 2006; Misra & Akman, 2008; Arockiam et al., 2009; Misra et al., 2011; Misra & Cafer, 2011; Arockiam & Aloysius, 2011; Misra et al., 2012; Aloysius & Arockiam, 2012) are the results of these efforts.

Cognitive Complexity refers to the human effort required to perform a task or the difficulty experienced in understanding a piece of code or the information packed in it (Misra & Kushvaha, 2006). Understandability of code is also referred to as program comprehension and is a cognitive process that relates to cognitive complexity. In other words, cognitive complexity is the mental burden on the user who deals with the code, for example the developer, tester and maintenance staff. Cognitive complexity provides valuable information for the design of systems. High cognitive complexity indicates poor design, which sometimes can be unmanageable (Briand, Bunse & Daly, 2001). In such cases, the maintenance effort increases significantly. In this respect, cognitive complexities are important in evaluating the performance of software system; they refer to those characteristics of software which affect the level of resources used by a person performing a given task on it (Zuse, 1998). A system with reduced cognitive complexity will not only improve the quality of the code but also reduce the future comprehension as well as maintenance efforts.

The objective of this chapter is to review and compare all the available object-oriented cognitive complexity metrics that are based on cognitive informatics. These metrics include: Total Complexity of Object-Oriented Software Product (Kushwaha & Misra, 2006), Weighted Class Complexity (WCC) (Misra & Akman, 2008), Extended Weighted Class Complexity (EWCC) (Arockiam et al., 2009), Inheritance Complexity Metric (Misra et al., 2011), Software Metric for Python (SMPy) (Misra & Cafer, 2011), Attribute Weighted Class Complexity (Arockiam & Aloysius, 2011), Suite of Cognitive Complexity Metrics (Misra et al., 2012), Cognitive Weighted Coupling Between Objects (Aloysius & Arockiam, 2012). In the sections that follow, we describe the features of the complexity measures and then evaluate each complexity metric based on different criteria and attributes. These criteria and attributes are selected based on the standard evaluation methodology for software complexity measures. For example, we check whether or not these proposals are evaluated and validated through proper theoretical, practical and empirical validation process? Finally we compare them based on their pros and cons. This comparative study provides essential information regarding these measures which can be useful for future work as well as for selecting an appropriate metric.

This chapter is organized in the following way. In the next section, we provide the background of object-oriented cognitive complexity metrics, and their relation to cognitive informatics. We go on to discuss the available object-oriented cognitive complexity metrics. Advantages and limitations of Object-Oriented Cognitive Complexity Measures are discussed in a separate section. We evaluate and compare object-oriented cognitive complexity metrics in a later section. A brief discussion on the observations and conclusion drawn form the last section of this chapter.

BACKGROUND OF OBJECT-ORIENTED COGNITIVE COMPLEXITY MEASURES

In cognitive informatics, the functional complexity of software in design and comprehension depends on three key factors namely: internal processing, its input and output (Wang & Shao, 2003). Initially three basic control structures (BCS), sequence, branch and iteration were identified (Hoare et al., 1987). Later, Wang & Shao (2003) modified these BCS's and introduced ten BCS's which are summarized in the Table 1. These BCS's are the basic

Table 1. Basic control structures and their cognitive weight

Category	BCS	Weight
Sequence	Sequence (SEQ)	1
Branch	If-Then-Else (ITE)	2
	Case	3
Iteration	For-do	3
	Repeat-until	3
	While-do	3
Embedded Component	Function Call (FC)	2
	Recursion (REC)	3
Concurrency	Parallel (PAR)	4
	Interrupt (INT)	4

logic building blocks of software. The cognitive weight of software is the extent of difficulty or relative time and effort for comprehending given software modeled by a number of BCS's.

There are two different architectures for calculating WBCS: either all the BCS's are in a linear layout or some BCS's are embedded in others. For the former case, sum of the weights of all n BCS's; are added and for the latter, cognitive weights of inner BCS's are multiplied with the weights of external BCS's. The cognitive weights for different Basic Control Structures are as given in Table 1. Actually, these weights are assigned on the classification of cognitive phenomenon as discussed by Wang. He proved and assigned the weights according to the complexity of the functions. For example, weight for lowest cognitive function is assigned as 1 for sequence structure of the program and weights for concurrency and interrupts are assigned as 4, the most complex structure of the programs. These weights also show the structure of the program and can be easily represented by the graph. We refer authors to read Wang & Shao (2003) paper for the details of the cognitive weights.

EXISTING OBJECT-ORIENTED COGNITIVE COMPLEXITY MEASURE

Cognitive complexity based on cognitive informatics is an emerging field of research. In this section we are providing all existing object-oriented cognitive complexity measures based on cognitive informatics.

Total Complexity of Object-Oriented Software Product (TCOOSP)

Kushwaha & Misra (2006) proposed a metric for finding the total complexity of object-oriented software calculated as:

$$TCOOSP = PUIV + CCI + CICM$$

where PUIV is the probability of the use of instance variable. Suppose a class contains "i" number of methods and "j" number of instance variables per class, let Mi be the method using Nj number of instance variables. The probability of method Mi using Nj number of instance variables is Nj/j.

Probability of use of instance variable for all the methods is:

PUIV =

$$PUIV = \sum_{k=1}^{i} (Nj / j)_k$$

CCI is the cognitive complexity of inheritance for all objects/classes in an inheritance tree and is given as:

$$CCI = [\sum_{o=1}^{k} \{(x / n)\log(x / n)\}_o$$

where o = number of objects O1, O2 ... Ox, x = number of messages related to object Ox, and n = total number of messages.

CICM is the cognitive information complexity measure of classes given as WICS * SBCS.

WICS is defined as

$$WICS = \sum_{k=1}^{LOCS} WICL_k$$

SBCS is defined as

$$SBCS = \sum_{i=1}^{n} W_i$$

where W1, W2 ... Wn are the cognitive weights of the basic control structures (Kushwaha & Misra, 2006b).

WICL is defined as ICSk / [LOCS - k], where

$$ICS = \sum_{k=1}^{LOCS} I_k$$

where Ik = Information contained in kth line of code, and LOCS = total lines of code in the software.

Since a class consists of a number of methods, the complexity of a class is calculated by finding the complexity of each method contained in a class.

Let M1, M2, M3 ... Mn be the methods in a class.

Let CICM1, CICM2, ..., CICMn be the CICM of each method.

Then CICM of the class is defined as:

$$CICM = \sum_{i=1}^{n} (CICM)_i$$

Weighted Class Complexity (WCC)

Misra & Akman (2008) proposed a metric on class level of OO systems. The proposed metric computes the structural and cognitive complexity of class by associating a weight to the class, and is referred to as Weighted Class Complexity (WCC). The proposed metric includes the complexity of operations and messages in a method in terms of cognitive weights. It also considers the complexity due to data members (attributes). The stages involved in computing the metric is described as follows:

The proposed metric is first interested in calculating the complexity of operations by considering corresponding cognitive weights. The cognitive weights are used to measure the complexity of the logical structures of the software. These logical structures reside in the method (code) and are classified as sequence, branch, iteration and call (message in OO). The corresponding weights of these basic control structures are one, two, three and two (Wang & Shao, 2003). Actually, the weights are assigned on the classification of cognitive phenomenon as discussed by Wang (Wang & Shao, 2003). He proved and assigned the weights for sub conscious function, meta cognitive function and higher cognitive function as 1, 2 and 3 respectively.

The second and third stages of the proposed metric calculate the complexity of each class and find the complexity of the entire code respectively. Accordingly, the weight of individual method in a class is first calculated by associating a number (weight) with each member function (method), and then adding all the weights of all methods. This gives the complexity (weight) due to methods. The total weight of a single method, called method complexity (MC) is defined as the sum of cognitive weights of its q linear blocks composed in individual BCS's. Since each block may consists of m layers of nested BCS's, and each layer with n linear BCS's, the total cognitive weight of a method can be calculated by:

$$MC = \sum_{j=1}^{q} \left[\prod_{k=1}^{m} \sum_{i=1}^{n} W_c(j,k,l) \right]$$

where Wc is the cognitive weight of the concerned Basic Control Structure (BCS). If there are s methods in a class, then complexity due to all methods of the class is given by total method complexity

$$= \sum_{p=1}^{s} MC_p$$

Further, we count the total number of attributes in that class. It reflects the complexity due to data members (attributes). In other words, the complexity due to data members for a class equals to total number of data members in that class. The attributes are not local to one procedure but local to objects and can be accessed by several procedures.

We represent the complexity due to attributes as Na. Using this consideration; we suggest a formula for calculating the complexity of a single class, called Weighted Class Complexity (WCC),

$$WCC = N_a + \sum_{p=1}^{s} MC_p$$

If there are y classes in an object oriented code, then the total complexity of the code is given by the sum of weights of individual classes.

$$TotalWeightedClassComplexity = \sum_{x=1}^{y} WCC_x$$

The unit of WCC is defined as the cognitive weight of the simplest software component i.e. only a linear structure BCS is taken as one Weighted Class Complexity unit (WCCU).

One thing worthy of note is that this approach includes the complexity of the class due to messages, automatically. In the case of a message between two classes, the complexity of the message is the sum of the weight of the called procedure and the weight due to that call (i.e. two). Messages between the classes are the indication of coupling. Although, WCC is not a measure of coupling and cohesion; it provides some indication for the level of coupling. If the number of messages between the classes increases, the overall complexity increases. Clearly, a high complexity value represents the high coupling between classes because of greater number of messages, which is undesirable according to quality design principles (Coad & Yourdon, 1991).

Extended Weighted Class Complexity (EWCC)

Arockiam et al. (2009) proposed a metric called Extended Weighted Class Complexity (EWCC). It is an extension of WCC. EWCC is the sum of cognitive weights of attributes and methods of the class and that of the classes derived. It also includes the cognitive complexity due to Inheritance.

If there are n methods in a class and the class can be derived from m number of classes then, the EWCC of that class can be derived using the equation given as follows:

$$EWCC = N_a + \sum_{i=1}^{n} \mathrm{MC}_{\mathrm{i}} + \sum_{j=1}^{m} \mathrm{ICC}_{\mathrm{j}}$$

Where Na is the total number of attributes, MC is the method complexity, and ICC is the inherited class complexity.

The Method complexity (MC) is calculated as shown in the previous section (WCC) while ICC can be calculated using the equation given as follows

$$ICC = \left(DIT \times C_L\right) \times \sum_{k=1}^{s} RMC_k + RN_a$$

where s is the number of inherited methods, RNa is the total number of reused attributes, RMC is the reused method complexity, ICC is the inherited class complexity, DIT is the Depth of Inheritance Tree, and CL is the cognitive complexity of Lth Level.

CL is the cognitive complexity of Lth level which will differ from person to person according to the cognitive maturity level (Wang, 2002). Here, the value of CL is assumed to be 1.

Inheritance Complexity Measure (ICM)

Misra et al., (2011) proposed a metric based on Inheritance – which is an important feature of object-oriented systems. It calculates the complexity at method level considering internal structure of methods, and also considers inheritance to calculate the complexity of class hierarchies.

The steps in computing the metric is described as follows:

The proposed metric is first interested in calculating the complexity of methods considering corresponding cognitive weights for each method of the class of the system (MC). Cognitive weights are used to measure the complexity of the logical structures of the software in terms of Basic Control Structures (BCSs). These logical structures reside in the method (code) and are classified as sequence, branch, iteration and message call with the corresponding weights of one, two, three and two, respectively. Actually, these weights are assigned on the classification of cognitive phenomenon as discussed by Wang & Shao (2003). They proved and assigned the weights for subconscious function, meta cognitive function and higher cognitive function as 1, 2 and 3, respectively.

The complexity due to method calls is also considered at this stage. If there is a message call to one of the methods of other classes, the complexity of that message in the method is the sum of the weights of the called method and the weight due to that call. On the other hand, if the message call is for a method in the same class, we only assign the weight due to the call. More formally, the method complexity (MC) is calculated as

$$MC = \sum_{j=1}^{q} \left[\prod_{k=1}^{m} \sum_{i=1}^{n} W_c(j,k,l) \right]$$

where Wc is the cognitive weight of the concerned basic control structure (BCS). The method complexity of a software component is defined as the sum of cognitive weights of its q linear blocks composed of individual BCSs, since each block may consist of m layers of nested BCSs, and each layer with n linear BCSs. Some methods in an object-oriented code may include recursive method calls. Each recursive method call is considered as a new call and taken into account during the calculation of method complexity. If the recursively called method is inside the same class of method which initiates the first call, then we add only the complexity arisen because of method calls, not the complexity of called method. If the recursively called method is from another class, we include the method complexity only once. Because, the cognitive complexity burden to developers/programmers by recursive method is not repetitive.

The second stage (Class Complexity) of the proposed metric calculates the complexity of each class. MC gives the complexity of the single method. If there are several methods in a class then complexity of an individual class is calculated by the summation of the weights of all methods.

Accordingly the class complexity (CC) is given by:

$$Class\,complexity(CC) = \sum_{p=1}^{s} MC_p$$

where s is the number of methods in a class

The third stage (Cognitive code complexity) of the proposed metric calculates the complexity of the entire code by identifying the existing relations between classes. The complexity of the entire system (if the system consists of more than one class) is calculated considering the following two cases in the OO architecture:

1. If the classes are in the same level then their weights are added.
2. If they are children of a class then their weights are multiplied due to inheritance property. If there are m levels of depth in the OO code and level j has n classes then the cognitive code complexity (CCC) of the system is given by

$$Cognitive\,code\,complexity\left(CCC\right)=\prod_{j=1}^{m}\left[\sum_{k=1}^{n}CC_{jk}\right]$$

If there are more than one class hierarchies in a project, then the CCCs of each hierarchy are added to calculate the complexity of the whole system. The Class Complexity Unit (CCU) of a class is defined as the cognitive weight of the simplest software component (having a single class which includes single method and also the method includes only a linear structure). This corresponds to sequential structure in BCS and hence its cognitive weight is taken as 1. CCU is used as the basic unit for complexity.

Software Metric for Python (SMPy)

Misra & Cafer (2011) proposed a metric for evaluating the complexity of Python code. The metric takes into consideration all the factors which may play important roles in the complexity of the code-this includes the complexities of the classes and the main program. The complexity factors identified include:

Complexity due to classes: Class is a basic unit of object oriented software development. All the functions are distributed in different classes. Further classes in the object-oriented code either are in inheritance hierarchy or distinctly distributed. Accordingly, the complexity of all the classes is due to classes in inheritance hierarchy and the complexity of distinct classes.

Complexity due to global factors: The second important factor, which is normally neglected in calculating complexity of object-oriented codes, is the complexity of global factors in main program.

Complexity due to coupling: Coupling is one of the important factors for increasing complexity of object oriented code.

The other factors like cohesion and methods are considered the complexity factors inside the class. Accordingly, we propose that the Complexity of the Python code is defined as:

$$SMPy = CIclass + CDclass + Cglobal + Ccoupling$$

when CIclass = Complexity due to Inheritance, CDclass = Complexity of Distinct Class, Cglobal = Global Complexity, and Ccoupling = Complexity due to coupling between classes.

Before calculating the complexity of Inheritance and distinct classes, we will estimate the complexity of a class, which will later become the part of inheritance hierarchy or of distinct classes. Accordingly, we will first compute the complexity of a simple class named as Cclass. Cclass can be defined as:

$$Cclass = weight\left(attributes\right) + weight\left(variables\right) + weight\left(structures\right) + weight\left(objects\right) - weight\ \left(cohesion\right)$$

Here, weight of attributes W(attributes) is defined as:

$$W\left(attributes\right) = 4 * AND + MND$$

Here, AND = Number of Arbitrarily Named Distinct Variables/Attributes and MND = Number of Meaningfully Named Distinct Variables/Attributes.

Weight of variable W(variables) is defined as:

$$W\left(variables\right) = 4 * AND + MND$$

Table 2 shows the value of the structures.

Arbitrary and Meaningful Variables and Attributes are one of the causes of complexity. Further, if a variable's name is arbitrarily given, then the comprehensibility of that code will be lower (Kushwaha & Misra, 2006). Therefore, variables and attributes of classes should have meaningful names. Although, it is suggested that the name of the variables should be chosen in such a way that it is meaningful in programming, there are developers who do not follow this advice strictly. If the variable names are taken arbitrarily, it may not be a grave problem if the developer himself evaluates the code.

However, it is not the case in real life. After the system is developed, especially during maintenance time, arbitrarily named variables may increase the difficulty in understanding four times more (Kushwaha & Misra, 2006) than the meaningful names.

Weight of structure W(structures) is defined as:

$$W\left(structures\right) = W(BCS)$$

Here, BCS are basic control structure.

According to Wang & Shao (2003) Sequences' complexity depends on its mathematical expres-

Table 2. Value of structures

Category	Value	Flow Graph
Sequence	1	
Condition	2	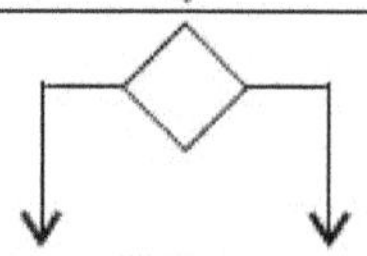
Loop	3	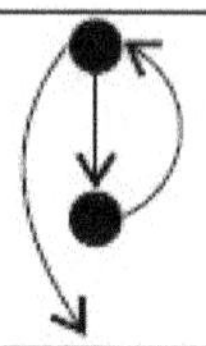
Nested Loop	3	-
Function	2	
Recursion	3	
Exception	2	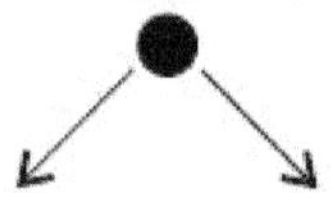

sion. Functions help tidiness of a code. Also, they may increase the reusability of the code. However, each function call disturbs the fluency of reading a code. Loops are used to repeat a statement for more than one time, although, they decrease computing performance. Especially, the more nested loops there are, the more time it takes to run the code. In addition, human brain has similarities with computers in interpreting a data. Conditional statements are used to make a program dynamic. On the other hand, by presenting more combinations they decrease the easiness of grasping the integrity of a program. Therefore conditional statements can be thought to be sequences built up in different possible situations. If the conditional situations are nested, then the complexity becomes much higher. The situation in exceptions is similar. We are assigning the weights for each basic control structure followed by the similar approach of Wang (Wang & Shao, 2003). Wang proved and assigned the weights for subconscious function, meta cognitive function and higher cognitive function as 1, 2 and 3 respectively. Although we followed the similar approach with Wang, we made some modifications in the weights of some Basic Control Structures as shown in Table 1.

Weight of objects W(object) is defined as:

$$W\left(object\right) = 2$$

Creating an object is counted as 2, because while creating a function constructor is automatically called. Therefore, it is the same as calling a function or creating an object. Here it is meant to be the objects created inside a class.

Weight of cohesion is defined as:

$$W\left(cohesion\right) = MA \, / \, AM$$

Here, MA= Number of methods where attributes are used and AM= Number of attributes used inside methods While counting the number of attributes there is no importance of AND or MND.

Notes:

- **Function Call:** During inheritance, calling super class's constructor is not counted.
- **Global Variable:** Static attribute is counted as a global variable.

$$Cglobal = W(variables + structures + objects)$$

Weight of variable W(variable) is defined as:

$$W\left(variables\right) = 4 * AND + MND$$

The variables are defined globally. Weight of structure W(structure) is defined as:

$$W\left(structures\right) = W\left(BCS\right) + obj.method$$

Here, BCS are basic control structure, and those structures are used globally. 'obj.method' calls a reachable method of a class using an object. 'obj.method' is counted as two, because it calls a function written by the programmer.

Weight of objects W(object) is defined as:

$$W\left(objects\right) = 2$$

Creating an object is counted as 2, as it is described above. Here it is meant to be the objects created globally or inside any function which is not a part of any class.

Notes: Exception: while calculating try catch statement, only the numbers of "catch"es are counted as 2. "try" itself is not counted.

There are two cases for calculating the complexity of the Inheritance classes depending on the architecture:

If the classes are in the same level then their weights are added.

If they are children of a class then their weights are multiplied due to inheritance property. If there are levels of depth in the OO code and level has classes then the complexity of the system due to inheritance is given as:

$$CIclasses = \prod_{j=1}^{m} \left[\sum_{k=1}^{n} Cclass_{jk} \right]$$

CDclass can be defined as:

$$CDclass = Cclass(x) + Class(y) + \ldots$$

Note: all classes, which are neither inherited nor derived from another, are part of CDclass even if they have caused coupling together with other classes.

Coupling is defined as:

$$Coupling = 2^{c}$$

where c=Number of connections.

Attribute Weighted Class Complexity (AWCC)

In 2011, Arockiam and Aloysius proposed a metric that can be used to calculate the complexity of the class using the method complexity, attribute complexity of the class, and the inherited members' complexity. The calculation is such that if there are n attributes, m methods in a class and the class is derived from m1 number of classes then, the AWCC of that class is given as follows:

$$AWCC = \sum_{i=1}^{n} AC_i + \sum_{j=1}^{m} MC_j + \sum_{k=1}^{m_1} ICC_k$$

where AC is the attribute complexity, MC is the method complexity, and ICC is the inherited class complexity.

Attribute complexity (AC) is used to calculate the complexity of the attribute in the class, by using the following equation:

$$AC = (PDT * W_b) + (DDT * W_d) + (UDDT * W_u)$$

where PDT is the number of Primary Data Type attributes, DDT is the number of Derived Data Type attributes, UDDT is the number of User Defined Data Type attributes, Wb is the cognitive weights of the PDT attributes, Wd is the cognitive weights of the DDT attributes, and Wu is the cognitive weights of the UDDT attributes.

The weighting factor of attribute is based on the classification of cognitive phenomenon as described by Wang (Wang, 2002), is as shown in Table 3.

The Method Complexity (MC) is calculated by assigning the cognitive weights proposed by Wang et. al, to control structures in the method. ICC can be calculated as follows:

$$ICC = (DIT * C_L) * \sum_{k=1}^{s} RMC_k + RN_a$$

where s is the number of inherited methods, RNa is the total number of reused attributes, RMC is the Reused Method Complexity, IC is the Inherited Complexity, DIT is the Depth of Inheritance Tree, and CL is the Cognitive Load of Lth level.

Table 3.

	Weights
Sub-Conscious Cognitive Attribute (PDT)	1
Meta Cognitive Attribute (DDT)	2
Higher Cognitive Attribute (UDDT)	3

Suite of Cognitive Complexity Measures (SCCM)

Furthermore, Misra et al. (2012) have proposed a suite of cognitive complexity measures for object oriented programs. They discovered that after the CK metric suite, no further attempts had been made seriously in that direction to develop a more effective suite of metrics for OO languages (Cherniavsky & Smith, 1991). All the metrics in CK metric suite are straight forward and simple to compute. On the other hand, these metrics did not cover the following issues:

1. The overall complexity of a class due to all possible factors
2. The internal architecture of the class
3. The impact of the relationship due to inheritance in the class hierarchy
4. The number of messages between classes and their complexities (CK metrics suite counts only the methods coupled with other classes)
5. Cognitive complexity, which is a measure of understandability and therefore has a great impact on maintainability of the system

The lack of the above features in CK metric suite motivated them to produce the new suite of metrics, which can be a complimentary set of the CK metric suite. In fact, their proposed metrics suggest examining the OO properties in more detail. For example, CBO (one of metrics in CK metric suite) is a measure to show interactions between objects by counting the number of other classes to which the class is coupled. In their proposal, coupling is computed by considering the message calls to other classes and the weight of the called methods. One class may have "1" for CBO showing that it interacts with only one class, but may include many messages to that class which causes a more complex code (which is considered in our metric). Therefore, they believed that their metric gave more accurate information about coupling of a class.

The complexity metrics developed for object-oriented languages prior to this suite were mainly based on the complexity of individual classes like number of methods, number of messages etc. However, not only the numbers of different components were important, but also the internal complexities of these components were equally important. Furthermore, in calculating the complexity of the entire system, it was needed to consider the special features of OO programs and type of the relations between classes. Accordingly, they proposed the following suite of metrics:

Method Complexity (MC): Method complexity is calculated by considering corresponding cognitive weights of structures in a method of a class. Cognitive weights are used to measure the complexity of the logical structures of the software in terms of Basic Control Structures (BCSs). These logical structures reside in the method (code) and are classified as sequence, branch, iteration and call with the corresponding weights of one, two, three and two, respectively. Actually, these weights are assigned on the classification of cognitive phenomenon as discussed by Wang (Wang & Shao, 2003). We calculate method complexity in a class by associating a number (weight) with each member function (method), and then simply add the weights of all the methods. More formally, the method complexity (MC) is calculated as;

$$MC = \sum_{j=1}^{q}\left[\prod_{k=1}^{m}\sum_{i=1}^{n}W_c(j,k,l)\right]$$

where, Wc is the cognitive weight of the concerned Basic Control Structure (BCS). The method complexity of a software component is defined as the sum of cognitive weights of its q linear blocks composed of individual BCSs, since each block may consist of m layers of nested BCSs, and each layer with n linear BCSs. MC gives the complexity of a single method.

Message complexity (Coupling Weight for a Class (CWC)): Two classes are coupled when there is a message call in one class for the other class. In our proposal, if there are message calls for other classes, we not only count the total number of such messages, but also we add the weight of the called methods. Accordingly, complexities due to message calls are the sum of weights of call and the weight of called methods. i.e.

$$CWC = \sum_{i=1}^{n} (2 + MC_i)$$

where, 2 is weight of the message to an external method and Wi is the weight of the called method. If there are n numbers of external calls, then the CWC is calculated as the sum of weights of all message calls.

Attribute Complexity (AC): It reflects the complexity due to data members (attributes). We simply assign the total number of attributes associated with class as the complexity due to data members. The attributes are not local to one procedure but local to objects and can be accessed by several procedures. Accordingly, the attribute complexity of a class (AC) is given by:

$$AC = \sum_{i=1}^{n} 1$$

where n is the total number of attributes.

Weighted Class Complexity (WCC): OO software development is based on classes and subclasses whose elements are attributes and methods (including messages). These elements are identified in class declarations and are responsible for the complexity of a class. Therefore, the complexity of a class is a function of the methods and the data attributes. More formally, we suggest the following formula to calculate the Weighted Class Complexity (WCC):

$$WCC = AC + \sum_{y=1}^{n} MC_y$$

WCC is the sum of the attribute complexity and the sum of all the method complexities of a class.

Code Complexity (Inheritance): For calculating the complexity of the entire system, we have to consider not only the complexity of all the classes, but also the relations among them. That is, we are laying emphasis on the inheritance property because classes may be either parent or children classes of others. In the case of a child class, it inherits the features from the parent class. By keeping this property of OO paradigm, we propose to calculate the code complexity of an entire system as follows:

- If the classes are of the same level then their weights are added.
- If they are subclasses or children of their parent then their weights are multiplied.

If there are m levels of depth in the object-oriented code and level j has n classes then the Code Complexity (CC) of the system is given by,

$$CC = \prod_{j=1}^{m} \left[\sum_{k=1}^{n} WCC_{jk} \right]$$

The unit of CC is defined as the cognitive weight of the simplest software component (having a single class which includes single method having only a sequential structure). This corresponds to sequential structure in BCS and hence its unit is taken as 1 Code Complexity Unit (CCU).

In addition to these metrics, we are also proposing the associated metrics which are extracted from the above metrics. These metrics may be useful indications for general information regarding the projects.

- **Average Method Complexity (AMC):** It gives an average method complexity for a class and is calculated by dividing the sum of complexities of all the methods of a class to the total number of methods in that class.

$$AMC = \sum_{y=1}^{n} MC_y \,/\, n$$

where MC is the complexity of a particular method, n is total number of methods in a class.

- **Average Method Complexity per Class (AMCC):** It is defined as the average method complexity for the entire system.

$$AMCC = \sum_{y=1}^{m} AMC \,/\, m$$

where, m is total number of classes in a project.

- **Average Class Complexity (ACC):** It is the average complexity of classes in a project and it is calculated by dividing the sum of the complexity of the classes to the total number of classes.

$$ACC = \sum_{y=1}^{m} WCC \,/\, m$$

where WCC is the complexity a class and m is total number of classes.

- **Average Coupling Factor (ACF):** It is defined as the complexity of all the external method calls (i.e. coupling weights) to the total number of messages.

$$ACF = \sum_{i=1}^{k} CWC \,/\, k$$

where, k is number of messages to other classes.

- **Average Attributes per Class (AAC):** It shows the average number of attributes per class in a project and it is calculated by dividing the sum of attribute complexity of all classes to the total number of classes.

$$AAC = \sum_{i=1}^{m} AC \,/\, m$$

where, m is the total number of classes.

Cognitive Weighted Coupling between Objects (CWCBO)

This metric was proposed by Aloysius & Arockiam. As of the time of developing this metric, several coupling metrics existed but there was none that was cognitive weighted (Aloysius & Arockiam, 2012). The proposed metric takes into consideration the various types of coupling namely: control coupling, global data coupling, internal data coupling, data coupling and lexical content coupling. It is calculated as follows:

$$CWCBO = (CC * WFCC) + (GDC * WFGDC) + (IDC * WFIDC) + (DC * WFDC) + (LCC * WFLCC)$$

where CC is the total number of modules that contains Control Coupling, GDC is the count of Global Data Coupling, IDC is the count of Internal Data Coupling, and LCC is the count of Lexical Content Coupling.

The Weighting Factor of each type of coupling is calibrated as shown in Table 4.

Advantages and Limitations of Object-Oriented Cognitive Complexity Measures

In the previous section, we have shown the formulation of the different object-oriented cognitive complexity measures based on cognitive informatics. In this section, (in Table 5), we are providing the specific features and the limitation of the each measure under consideration.

EVALUATION OF OBJECT ORIENTED COGNITIVE COMPLEXITY MEASURES AND COMPARATIVE STUDY

In the previous section we have demonstrated the features and limitation of existing object-oriented complexity measures. In this section we are evaluating and comparing each measure based on different attributes. We include all those attributes for evaluation and comparison purpose which are commonly used by researchers in software engineering community.

- **Theoretical Validation:**
  - Measurement theory.
  - Weyuker's properties.
  - Briand Properties for Complexity measures.
- **Practical Validation:**
  - GQM approach (Basili, Caldiera & Rombach(1994)).
  - Caner's Framework.
  - Any other criteria.
- **Empirical Validation:**
  - Small examples.
  - Case study.
  - Big projects from the web.
  - Real projects from the Industry.
- **Theoretical Validation:** It is very easy to find numbers of theoretical evaluation criteria in the literature. However, evaluation through measurement theory (Briand, Emam & Morasca, 1996; Briand, Morasca & Basili, 1996) and Weyuker's (1988) properties is more common and used for evaluating complexity measures. In analyzing all the object oriented cognitive complexity measures, we found that WCC, ICM, SCCM and CWCBO used either or both of Weyukers' properties and measurement theory. None of the others reported using any of the theoretical validation methods. Actually, there are some

Table 4. Weighting factor for the types of coupling

Weighting Factor of Control Coupling	WFCC	1
Weighting Factor of Global Data Coupling	WFGDC	1
Weighting Factor of Internal Data Coupling	WFIDC	2
Weighting Factor of Data Coupling	WFDC	3
Weighting Factor of Lexical Content Coupling	WFLCC	4

Table 5. Features and limitations of existing object-oriented cognitive complexity measures

Measure	Features and Advantages	Limitations
1.TCOOSP(2006)	The measure is computationally simple and can be used by practitioners at all stages of software development process. It reduces rework and backtracking thus saving effort and time.	The measure does not capture all key features of object orientation such as cohesion and coupling.
2.WCC(2008)	It can be used for the cognitive complexity of class by methods and attributes and thereof understandability of the code. It can be used to evaluate efficiency of the design. Low complexity value gives better design information and less maintenance effort. This metric not only sees the complexity of the procedure in method but it also considers the attributes and message between the classes. In other words, it measures the important concepts of OOPs like methods, class and coupling. It is language independent complexity metric since it uses cognitive weights and attributes which are the same in all programming languages. The metric is on the ratio scale, a fundamental requirement for a measure from the measurement theory perspective. Therefore, the proposed metric can be implemented for calculating the cognitive complexity of OO systems.	The present method gives the complexity value in number, which are generally high for large programs. High complexity values are not desirable. It is difficult to assign the upper bound for the complexity values. It is not possible to identify the underlying source of complexity with the proposed measure since it depends on several factors such as number of methods, their internal architectures, number of attribute and the number of message calls.
3.EWCC(2009)	The complexity of the class included the internal complexity of the class and the inherited classes' complexity. It also includes the cognitive complexity due to internal architecture of the methods, attributes and the inherited class complexity. This makes EWCC to be a better indicator of the class level complexity metric.	Cognitive Load has been assigned for Lth level inheritance which is not clearly defined; it simply assigned the value of 1. It therefore needs to be well defined and more specific for the inheritance level.
4.ICM(2011)	It is a simple metric and fulfills the requirements of a good metric since it also considers the internal architecture of the member function (method) unlike other complexity metrics on method level. It can be used to evaluate efficiency of a design. A low complexity value gives an indication of better design. A good design reduces the maintainability efforts. It can also be used as component level design metrics. It is capable of calculating the complexity and coupling (to a certain extent) of the module. It can be used to select the best design when more than one design alternatives are available for a software project. It can be used to evaluate the performance of designers and developers. It calculates the cognitive complexity of the OO programs. Low cognitive complexity indicates a good design; therefore less maintenance efforts. It can be used for the complexity of class by methods and thereby understandability of the code. It is obvious that more complex classes are less understandable and require more maintenance efforts. This metric not only sees the complexity of the structure in method but it also considers the messages between the classes and inheritance property. In other words, it measures the important concepts of OO programs. It is a language independent complexity metric since it uses cognitive weights, and cognitive weights of basic control structures are the same in all programming languages. The metric is on the ratio scale, a fundamental requirement for a measure from the perspective of the measurement theory.	The present method gives the complexity value in numerical terms, which are generally high for large programs. High complexity values are not desirable. It is difficult to assign the upper and lower boundaries for the complexity values. It is not possible to identify the underlying source of complexity with the proposed measure since it depends on several factors, such as; the number of methods, their internal architectures and the number of message calls.

continued on following page

Table 5. Continued

Measure	Features and Advantages	Limitations
5.SMPy(2011)	It is a super set of all the measures proposed by Chidamber & Kermer (2004) Unifies the factors responsible for complexity into one single metric.	The present method gives the complexity value in numerical terms, which are generally high for large programs. High complexity values are not desirable. The metric is language dependent.
6.AWCC(2011)	The metric differentiates from the CK metrics because none of the CK metrics provides the total complexity of the class by considering the complexity due to internal architecture of the code (methods and attributes). The metric is a better indicator than EWCC in that it considers the complexity that arises due to the data type of attributes. It takes cognitive weights into consideration A tool was developed to evaluate the metric	The proposed metric focuses only on the data type.
7.SCCM(2012)	A suite of object-oriented metrics were proposed in this study. These metrics are capable of capturing most of the features existing in object-oriented codes such as method, attribute, class, inheritance and coupling. The objective of such a metric suite is to combine most of the features responsible for complexity. These metrics calculate the complexity at each level of the code and the code complexity represents the structural and cognitive complexity of an OO system	The suite does not capture all the features of object orientation such as polymorphism.
8.CWCBO(2012)	When compared to the CBO metrics from CK metric suite, CWCBO is better in that it takes into consideration the complexity that arises due to the various types of Coupling Between Object. It takes into consideration cognitive weights.	Metric values are higher compared to the CBO metrics.

misunderstandings amongst the developers of complexity measures that a measure should satisfy all Weyuker's properties. However, it is not the case. If a measure is a sensible measure, it should not satisfy all the Weyuker's properties (Cherniavsky, & Smith, 1991) otherwise it may violate the rules of measurement theory. It is also known that some of Weyuker's properties contradict each other (e.g. Weyuker's property 5 and 6). In this chapter, our aim is not to check the applicability of Weyuker's properties on these measures.

- **Practical Evaluation:** Kaner's (2004) framework is a more appropriate choice for most developers of object-oriented cognitive complexity measures. Kaner has proposed a set of definitions/questions, which evaluates the practical utility of the proposed measures. WCC was the only reported metric to be evaluated practically using Kaner's framework. None of the other metrics use practical validation. It is important to note that Kaner's framework only evaluates the practical utility from theoretical point of view; however, it is possible that even after satisfying these conditions a measure will not fit or be appropriate in real life applications.
- **Empirical Validation:** It is the real evaluation of any complexity measure. It evaluates the practical applicability of any new

measure in real life applications. In other words, a new metric must be applied to the software industry to evaluate its practical applicability. However, the conditions of empirical validations for measurement models /metrics are not very good. To the best of our knowledge, none of the object-oriented cognitive complexity metrics are applied to industry till date. All the proposed metrics have used programs either from a book or from the Internet. The applicability of measures/metrics on these programs only proves the partial empirical validation. In other words, all the object-oriented cognitive complexity metrics are not evaluated or tested for their practical implementations in real life, i.e. in industry. It is the task for future work. In fact, there is a practical problem behind this. Most of the metrics are developed by academicians and it is very difficult for them to apply their new model of metric to the industry, if they are not associated with industry. Further, most of the medium and small scale software industries do not care for quality aspects and particularly the use of software metrics in these organizations is very limited. Of course, there are several constraints in small and medium scale companies like budget, time pressure and less number of software developers. For big and established companies, it is very difficult for the developer of a new metric to promote the benefits of his measure. As a result, most of the proposed metrics lack in their real empirical validation. In fact this is the major problem for developers of new measures. To implement new metrics in industry, the academicians should seek out ways to collaborate with industry. In this way they can solve the problem of real empirical validation.

DISCUSSION

All the object-oriented cognitive complexity measures under consideration are based on the concept of cognitive weight. They all used cognitive weight as a basic unit and added other terms for better representation of cognitive complexity. In cognitive informatics the functional complexity of software depends on input, output and internal architecture and therefore inheritance property is considered in the formulation of ICM i.e. Wang's work was modified by taking consideration of cognitive weights and the inheritance property of object-oriented systems. Further, by considering the importance of calculating class complexity in object-oriented systems, in WCC, EWCC and AWCC it is proposed that the cognitive complexity also depends on complexity of operations and messages in a method as well as complexity due to data members (attributes). In SMPy, the complexity of an object-oriented language – Python – is determined by identifying all the factors which play important roles in the complexity of the code – including the main program. AWCC differentiates from the CK metrics by considering the complexity due to methods and attributes of code and thus providing a comprehensive complexity for class that takes cognitive weights into consideration. SCCM is a suite that takes into consideration in addition to the cognitive complexity: the overall complexity of a class due to all possible factors; the internal architecture of the class; the impact of the relationship due to inheritance in the class hierarchy; as well as the number of messages between classes and their complexities. CWCBO takes into consideration all the possible coupling that can occur in object-oriented system and also factors in the cognitive weights of the different types of coupling.

In software engineering and especially in software development process, maintenance of the software takes a lot of efforts and money. In maintenance process, the comprehension of the software is the major factor which increases the maintenance cost. Further, comprehension of the code is cognitive process, which is related to cognitive complexity. In summary, if the code will be complex, it will be hard to comprehend and as a result its maintenance increases. To reduce the maintenance we must have to control the complexity. Cognitive complexity measures are one of the ways through which we can control the complexity of the code. Eight different types of object-oriented cognitive complexity measures are discussed in this chapter. However, again a question arises which one is better and how can we select the best? Our suggestion is that first we have to see what we want to measure. If anybody is interested to find overall class complexity, WCC, EWCC and AWCC are available. WCC is however the better option, because it is validated theoretically using Weyukers' properties and measurement theory; practically using Kaner's framework and empirically though case study making it a robust measure for the task. Furthermore, if anybody is specifically interested in computing cognitive complexity based on a specific language then he can choose SMPy which is for evaluating Python code. All the other metrics are language independent. However, in particular each one of them has their own advantages and disadvantages as summarized in Table 5.

CONCLUSION

Object-oriented cognitive complexity metrics based on cognitive informatics are analysed and compared. Object-oriented cognitive complexity metrics play a crucial role in maintaining the quality of software, which is one of the most important issues in any object-oriented software system. Cognitive complexity metrics can be applied at the design level to reduce the complexity and can be further used for evaluating programs during software review and testing phase. We have analysed all the available object-oriented cognitive complexity metrics in terms of their features. For comparison, we have selected some significant and common attributes, to find a comparative view of all available object-oriented cognitive complexity measures. All these metrics are based on the concept of cognitive weight. Furthermore, these metrics use cognitive weights, operators and /or operands in different ways, i.e. the way of interaction between them are different in these metrics. If we closely observe all the papers in which these metrics are proposed, we can easily observe that their trends in graphs (when applied on different examples) are similar. This is an advantageous point in these measures and therefore the organisations have flexibility to adopt them as per availability of tool.

REFERENCES

Aloysius, A., & Arockiam, L. (2012). Coupling complexity metric: A cognitive approach. *International Journal of Information Technology and Computer Science*, *4*(9), 29–35. doi:10.5815/ijitcs.2012.09.04

Arockiam, L., & Aloysius, A. (2011). Attribute weighted class complexity: A new metric for measuring cognitive complexity of OO systems. *World Academy of Science, Engineering and Technology*, *58*, 963–968.

Arockiam, L., Aloysius, A., & Selvaraj, J. C. (2009). Extended weighted class complexity: A new software complexity for object oriented system. In *Proceedings of International Conference on Semantic E-business and Enterprise computing (SEEC)*, (pp. 77-80). SEEC.

Basili, V. R., Caldiera, G., & Rombach, H. D. (1994). The goal question metric paradigm. In Encyclopedia of software engineering. John Wiley.

Briand, L., El Emam, K., & Morasca, S. (1996). On the application of measurement theory in software engineering. *Journal of Empirical Software Engineering, 1*(1), 61-88.

Briand, L. C., Bunse, C., & Daly, J. W. (2001). A controlled experiments for evaluating quality guidelines on the maintainability of object-oriented design. *IEEE Transactions on Software Engineering, 27*(6), 513–530. doi:10.1109/32.926174

Briand, L. C., Morasca, S., & Basili, V. R. (1996). Property based software engineering measurement. *IEEE Transactions on Software Engineering, 22*(1), 68–86. doi:10.1109/32.481535

Cherniavsky, J. C., & Smith, C. H. (1991). On Weyuker's axioms for software complexity measures. *IEEE Transactions on Software Engineering, 17*(6), 636–638. doi:10.1109/32.87287

Coad, P., & Yourdon, E. (1991). *Object oriented analysis* (2nd ed.). Prentice-Hall.

Fenton, N. (1994). Software measurement: A necessary scientific basis. *IEEE Transactions on Software Engineering, 20*(3), 199–206. doi:10.1109/32.268921

Fenton, N. (1997). *Software metrics a rigorous and practical approach*. Boston: PWS Publishing Company.

Henderson-Sellers, B. (1996). *Object-oriented metrics: Measures of complexity*. Prentice-Hall.

Hoare, C. A. R., Hayes, I. J., Jifeng, H., Morgan, C. C., Roscoe, A. W., & Sanders, J. W. et al. (1987). Laws of programming. *Communications of the ACM, 30*(8), 672–686. doi:10.1145/27651.27653

IEEE Computer Society. (1990). *IEEE standard glossary of software engineering terminology, IEEE Std. 610.12 – 1990*. IEEE.

Kaner, C. (2004). Software engineering metrics: What do they measure and how do we know? In *Proc. Int. Soft. Metrics Symp. Metrics,* (pp. 1-10). Academic Press.

Kushwaha, D. S., & Misra, A. K. (2006). Cognitive information complexity measure of object-oriented software – A practitioner's approach. In *Proceedings of the 5th WSEAS Int. Conf. on Software Engineering*, (pp. 174-179). WSEAS.

Kushwaha, D. S., & Misra, A. K. (2006b). *A modified cognitive information complexity measure of software. ACM SIGSOFT Software Engineering Notes, 31*, 1.

Misra, S. & Akman, I. (2008). Weighted class complexity: A measure of complexity for object oriented systems. *Journal of Information Science and Engineering, 24*, 1689–1708.

Misra, S., Akman, I., & Koyuncu, M. (2011). An inheritance complexity metric for object-oriented code: A cognitive approach. *Sadhana, 36*(3), 317–337. doi:10.1007/s12046-011-0028-2

Misra, S., & Cafer, F. (2011). Estimating complexity of programs in Python language. *Tehnički Vjesnik, 18*(1), 23-32.

Misra, S., Koyuncu, M., Crasso, M., Mateos, C., & Zunino, A. (2012). A suite of cognitive complexity metrics. In Computational Science and Its Application ICCSA 2012 (LNCS), (vol. 7336, pp. 234–247). Springer. doi:10.1007/978-3-642-31128-4_17

Pressman, R. S. (2001). *Software engineering: A practitioner's approach* (5th ed.). McGraw Hill.

Sommerville, I. (2001). *Software engineering* (6th ed.). Addison-Wesley.

Wang, Y. (2004). On the cognitive informatics foundation of software engineering. In *Proc. 3rd IEEE Int. Conf. Cognitive Informatics (ICCI'04)*, (pp. 1-10). IEEE.

Wang, Y. (2005), Keynote: Psychological experiments on the cognitive complexities of fundamental control structures of software systems. In *Proc. 4th IEEE International Conference on Cognitive Informatics (ICCI'05)*, (pp. 4-5). IEEE.

Wang, Y. (2007). The theoretical framework of cognitive informatics. *International Journal of Cognitive Informatics and Natural Intelligence*, *1*(1), 1–27. doi:10.4018/jcini.2007010101

Wang, Y., & Shao, J.(2003). A new measure of software complexity based on cognitive Weights. *Can .J. Elec. Comput. Engg,* 69-74.

Wang, Y., & Shao, J. (2009). On the cognitive complexity of software and its quantification and formal methods. *International Journal of Software Science and Computational Intelligence*, *1*(2), 31–53. doi:10.4018/jssci.2009040103

Weyuker, E. (1988). Evaluating software complexity measures. *IEEE Transactions on Software Engineering*, *14*(9), 1357–1365. doi:10.1109/32.6178

Yingxu Wang, (2002). On cognitive informatics: Keynote lecture. In *Proc. 1st IEEE Int. Conf. Cognitive Informatics (ICCI'02)*, (pp. 34–42). IEEE. doi:10.1109/COGINF.2002.1039280

Yingxu Wang., (2006). On the informatics laws and deductive semantics of software. *IEEE Transactions on Systems, Man and Cybernetics. Part C, Applications and Reviews*, *36*(2), 161–171. doi:10.1109/TSMCC.2006.871138

Zuse, H. A. (1998). *Framework of software measurement*. Berlin: Walter de Gruyter. doi:10.1515/9783110807301

KEY TERMS AND DEFINITIONS

Basic Control Structures: Basic building blocks of the software.

Cognitive Complexity: Refers to the human effort required to perform a task.

Cognitive Informatics (CI): Is multidisciplinary research area which combines the researches in the field of cognitive science, computer science, informatics, mathematics, neurobiology, physiology, psychology and software engineering.

Cognitive Weight: Is the extent of difficulty or relative time and effort for comprehending given software modeled by a number of BCS's.

Object Oriented Metrics: Metrics specially developed for object oriented programs.

Software Complexity: The degree to which a system or component has a design or implementation that is difficult to understand and verify.

Software Metrics: Measures quality attributes of software.

Chapter 7

QSE:
Service Elicitation with Qualitative Research Procedures

Ville Alkkiomäki
Lappeenranta University of Technology, Finland

Kari Smolander
Lappeenranta University of Technology, Finland

ABSTRACT

The chapter introduces QSE, the Qualitative Service Elicitation method. It applies qualitative research procedures in service elicitation. Service engineering practice lacks lightweight methods to identify service candidates in projects with tight schedules. The QSE provides a systematic method to analyze requirement material in service-oriented systems development with feasible effort by utilizing the procedures of the grounded theory research method to elicit service candidates from business process descriptions and business use case descriptions. The chapter describes the method with examples and a case study.

INTRODUCTION

The promise of service-oriented architecture (SOA) and enterprise service bus (ESB) for enterprises is in eliminating technical barriers for business development and process streamlining (Papazoglou and Van Den Heuval, 2007). SOA has a built-in philosophy to design autonomous and reusable units of software representing business-complete work, which can be used as a part of business processes (Papazoglou and Van Den Heuval, 2007).

Service-oriented computing can provide a way to make great changes in smaller portions by componentizing both the business and the IT and by incrementally building on top of existing assets (Bieberstein, Bose, Fiammante, Jones, & Shah, 2006; Cherbakov et al., 2005). Transforming an enterprise into a service-oriented one is a complex task and the role of IT is no longer supportive, but has often a key role in the change. Alignment between the business and IT is the key towards a service-oriented enterprise, and the implementation of the services should be prioritized to support

DOI: 10.4018/978-1-4666-6359-6.ch007

the incremental transformation of the enterprise. (Bieberstein et al., 2006; Cherbakov et al., 2005)

In this chapter, we propose Qualitative Service Elicitation, QSE, a new systematic method to be used in service elicitation. QSE provides practical means to prioritize and identify reusable service candidates in an enterprise context. The method is presented with an example of how to apply it in a sample project. The method is also tested in a real world project, and a case study of the project is provided.

THE CHALLENGE OF SERVICE ELICITATION

The service oriented approach differs fundamentally from the conventional development paradigms in the key concept of dynamically accessible services. The scope and performance of services are under constant development to support an increasing number of consumers. Components and objects do not provide this kind of run-time flexibility. Likewise, traditional requirement engineering practices do not support service composition nor do they encourage the identification of reusable services. (Papazoglou, Traverso, Dustdar, Leymann, & Kramer, 2006; Van Nuffel, 2007; Zimmermann, Schlimm, Waller, & Pestel, 2005)

Papazoglou et al. (2006) have listed the main challenges of the service-oriented engineering domain in their research roadmap. Novel approaches are required in service engineering to match the rate and pace of the business. Also the survey of Razavian et al (2011) suggests that the current service engineering practices fit poorly to the SOA migration challenges enterprises have and there is a need for successful yet cost-efficient approaches to elicit both the To-Be state as well as sufficient knowledge of the legacy applications.

The QSE approach addresses some of the challenges and provides practical means to build an enterprise level service catalogue only to the level of detail needed to be used in gap analysis. Additionally, the catalogue provides a ground for refining the right granularity of the services. The method itself does not provide automation in the analysis, but provides systematic procedures for the analysis, thus helping to reduce human errors. To enable systematic analysis, we have taken ingredients from research methodology literature. We believe service elicitation resembles by nature qualitative research.

The identification of services has been studied for some time and various methods already exist, but they focus on specific areas and the elicitation of specific types of services. A survey by Ramollari et al. (2007) lists ten different methods with varying coverage of the SOA project life cycle. Arsanjani (2005) classifies the SOA approaches into six categories: business process driven, tool-based MDA, wrap legacy, componentized legacy, data driven and message driven approaches.

Razavian et al. (2010) conducted systematic literature review of 39 SOA migration approaches resulting SOA-MF framework dividing the approaches into eight different families following two basic themes: modernizing the legacy system and facilitating reuse during service-based development.

QSE borrows elements suitable for top-down analysis from several of the approaches above. QSE is a top-down analysis method, which starts from business process descriptions and digs down to the essentials of the service candidates with the help of business use cases. Elements from the existing process driven, data driven and message driven methods have been included in QSE.

QSE is meant only to analyze business processes, not to design them. Completely different approaches, such as The MIT Process Handbook (Walker, 2006), are needed for designing business processes.

Process Driven Services

Process driven SOA is a popular approach, and business processes can be seen as an ideal source for reusable services (Papazoglou et al., 2006; Van Nuffel, 2007). Various different methods have been proposed to map and align services with business processes, but the field is somewhat dispersed with various engineering approaches and a vast number of different business process and workflow modeling languages.

The survey conducted by Papazoglou et al. (2004) identified two basic classes for complex web services: programmatic and interactive web services. Programmatic services encapsulate atomic business logic functionality to be used by other applications to build new applications. Interactive services include the logic for interacting with a user through the presentation service of a web application. The logic can contain the multi-step behavior of an interactive business process.

Patterns can be used to identify services in generic problem areas as long as they fit into the pre-defined scenarios. Different levels of patterns have been proposed in the area. For example Endrei at al. (2004) propose business patterns to be used to identify services in common business scenarios, while Zdyn et al. (2007) use more primitive software patterns to build processes out of building blocks.

SOMA (service-oriented modeling and architecture) is a software development method for SOA-based solutions containing a set of methods to support all phases of the SOA development (A. Arsanjani et al., 2008). SOMA provides several complementary methods to identify flows by analyzing business goals, business processes, as well as existing IT assets. However, details of the method have not been published.

Lo et al. (2008) propose a reference catalogue approach, which consists of two parts: a set of reference business models and a set of business service patterns. The needed business services are cataloged and used to identify services to be implemented.

There are also several methods using elements from product line engineering to manage the service specifications and production of new service variants based on analyzed needs. In these approaches, the services are seen as reusable application elements, which can be used to build new applications. (Adam & Doerr, 2008; Moon, Hong, & Yeom, 2008)

Overall, the methods above try to identify common process elements within the enterprise, some utilizing also familiar patterns from other enterprises to support the work.

Data Driven Services

The basic idea behind the data driven SOA or "Information as a Service" (IaaS) approach (Dan, Johnson, & Arsanjani, 2007) is to decouple the data and the business logic allowing systems to share the same data and data access logic. This approach has gained a great deal of interest lately, and also the market for IaaS tools is growing rapidly. Forrester predicts the market to exceed Enterprise Information Integration (EII), Enterprise Application Integration (EAI) and replication markets in size in the future (Forrester, 2008).

A survey by Papazgolou et al. (2004) lists three types of informational services: content services, information aggregation services and third-party information syndication services.

SOMA also provides several complementary methods to analyze information, a method called "domain decomposition" being the most interesting from our point of view (Arsanjani et al., 2008). In this method, the enterprise is first partitioned into functional areas, and then, business entities are identified within the areas. Different variations of the business entities are identified to ensure the reusability of the service design.

Data warehousing is another approach where data is gathered across the enterprise into a centralized database from where it can be read for business intelligent purposes. Having a unified view to the enterprise data can be very beneficial for the enterprise, and virtually all large enterprises are using this technique (Watson, Goodhue, & Wixom, 2002). For reporting needs, it is sufficient to have read-only access to the master data, making it possible to use a replica of the data instead of providing full master data functionalities (Walker).

Messaging Based Approach and Business-to-Business Communication

The message-driven approach to SOA focuses on the messages being transmitted between the systems (Arsanjani, 2005). This approach is well supported by many current BPM platforms, as they rely on messaging technologies to facilitate interactions between organizations running potentially heterogeneous systems (Sadiq, Orlowska, & Sadiq, 2005).

The message-based approach is popular in Business-to-Business (B2B) communication, where several standardization organizations are developing domain specific message standards. B2B communication consists of public and private processes and the connections between these two. Public processes can utilize B2B standards, which consist not only of the message format, but also of the process of how these messages can be used in inter-enterprise communication. (Bussler, 2001)

True B2B collaboration requires more sophisticated logic than a simple request-response approach provided by web services, and B2B communication is often based on a business agreement between the parties. Models for B2B communication typically require specified sequences of peer-to-peer message exchanges between the parties following stateful and long lasting business protocol used to orchestrate the underlying business process. These protocols define the messages as well as the behavior of the parties without revealing their internal implementation. (Bussler, 2001; Papazoglou & Dubray, 2004).

Messaging can also be used to implement private processes within an enterprise (Bussler, 2001; Sadiq et al., 2005). Services and web service technology can also be used to provide access to the existing messaging infrastructure by replacing the messaging adapters with web service wrappers (Harikumar, Lee, Hae Sool, Haeng-Kon, & Byeongdo, 2005).

QSE ANALYSIS

QSE is based on two principles. Firstly, it uses procedures from qualitative research to conceptualize and to categorize the service candidates. Secondly, it uses known characteristics of reusable services and the Zachman Framework (1987) as core categories for the analysis.

The grounded theory was originally introduced by Glaser and Strauss in 1967 and is now widely used in qualitative research (Robson, 2002; Strauss & Corbin, 1998). Grounded theory has been proposed to be used in the requirement engineering practice in other studies (Galal & Paul, 1999; Mattarelli, Bertolotti & Macrì, 2013) and applications in information systems research has been pushing the boundaries of grounded theory in general (Birks et al., 2013). The use of predefined core categories is against the principles of the original grounded theory, but is necessary to reuse the knowledge of known characteristics of enterprises and services. Therefore, QSE relies on the assumption that the enterprise fits into the Zachman Framework (1987) and that the reusable services in the enterprise have similar characteristics as identified in earlier research.

The QSE analysis consists of three phases:

- Conceptual analysis of the business process descriptions.
- Conceptual analysis of the project business use cases.
- Identification and prioritization of the service candidates using the outcomes of the analyses.

Core Categories

The Zachman Framework is used as a basis to discover all of the important aspects of an enterprise. John Zachman (1987) developed the framework in the 1980's and it "represents the logical structure for identifying and organizing the descriptive representations that are important in the management of the enterprises and to the development of systems".

The columns defined in the Zachman Framework (1987) act as core categories for an enterprise, and relevant elements from the service elicitation point of view should fall into these categories. The core categories are further divided into sub-categories based on the service candidate type characteristics derived from the existing approaches discussed in Section 3. The predefined categories are merged in Figure 2, and the service candidate types and characteristics used are listed in Table 1.

QSE Process Phases

Development projects implement services, and the identification of the services is often based on the analysis for that particular project only. This does not enforce that the services created are reusable in following projects. To provide a wider context for the service candidates, QSE analysis (Figure 2) starts with a conceptual analysis of the business process descriptions, creating a skeleton for the service categories of the enterprise.

In the next phase, this skeleton is complemented with details from the project material describing the use cases being implemented in the actual project.

In the final phase, the service candidates are prioritized based on how often similar needs were identified at the business process level and how likely they are to be re-used later. Both conceptual analysis phases are conducted by applying the basic procedures of the grounded theory (Strauss & Corbin, 1998) to elicit the basic concepts of an enterprise and to link them together at the conceptual level.

Conceptual Analysis Phases

Conceptual analysis uses the three coding phases of grounded analysis: open, axial and selective coding (Strauss & Corbin, 1998). Open coding is used to find the codes and their categories from the business data. During the axial coding, the identified categories are refined, differentiated and categories related to others are organized into sub-categories. Finally, the relations of the categories interesting from the service elicitation point of view are refined in the selective coding phase. Several iterations may be required to process the data and the phases should not be seen as distinguishable, but rather as different ways of handling the data than in grounded theory (Flick, 1998; Robson, 2002).

The purpose of the conceptual analysis is to find the essential business elements (categories) of the enterprise; especially the ones falling under the "Data", "Function" and "People" core categories. The categories under the core categories are identified and abstracted independently from each other, allowing the elements in each column to develop and saturate separately. The actual service candidates are identified from the codes under the numbered categories, and their granularity is

Table 1. Service candidate types

Service Candidate Type	Characteristics
Data driven services Both the information as a service and data warehousing approaches use centralized data models and data stores to provide access to enterprise information. The key issues are identifying the right information to be published through the service interface and the granularity of the services.	
1. Content services (RW)	Provides programmatic access to simple information content. (Papazoglou & Dubray, 2004)
2. Reporting content services (RO)	Provides read-only access to the replica of enterprise data. (Walker) Like content services, but the data is used only for reporting purposes and no real-time access to the data is needed. Can be merged into type 1 services if the same data is needed elsewhere in an operative manner.
3. Information aggregation services	Provides seamless aggregation of several information sources. (Papazoglou & Dubray, 2004) This is a variant of the service types 1 and 2, providing information using several simple content services as a source.
4. Non-electronic master data.	Information stored solely on paper or in other non-electronic forms. This category was identified during the case study. (These can be transformed into content service candidates if the business processes are further developed.)
Process driven services Process driven methods try to identify common process elements within the enterprise, some utilizing also general patterns from other enterprises. The key aspect of finding reusable services is the shared logic needed in several places within the enterprise.	
5. Programmatic services	Programmatic services encapsulate atomic business logic functionality to build new applications. A service is an atomic and independent part of logic within the process, which returns a concrete result. (Papazoglou & Dubray, 2004)
6. Interactive services	Interactive services include stateful logic for interacting with a user through the presentation layer of an application. It can contain the multi-step behavior of an interactive business process. (Papazoglou & Dubray, 2004)
Message based communication Includes the logic needed in business conversations to bind public and private processes and messages together. This logic can be wrapped behind a service. (Bussler, 2001; Harikumar et al., 2005)	
7. Third-party information syndication	Information sources and services provided by an external party. (Papazoglou & Dubray, 2004)
8. Business-to-business communication services	The logic needed in complex electronic business-to-business conversations. Often based on a contract between the enterprises. The service can contain stateful communication logic with the business partner, possibly following a standard such as ebXML or RosettaNet. (Papazoglou & Dubray, 2004) Additionally, the service can act as a translator transforming the source data format to the target data format. (Harikumar et al., 2005)

dependent of the relations to other categories. For example, service candidates accessing data (content services) are identified from the codes under the "Function" core category, but their granularity is determined from their relations to the categories in the "Data" core category. In this case, also the level in hierarchy is important; if the relation is made to a category with sub-categories, the service candidate is an information aggregation service candidate instead of a content service candidate.

During the open coding, the raw data is divided into discrete parts and interpreted into codes or labels describing the parts of the data (Robson, 2002). This division depends on the raw material; parts can be parts of drawings in process descriptions, words or sentences in business use case descriptions, and so on. Each part is given a label or code describing for what the part stands. See Table 3 for an example.

Figure 1. Core categories for an enterprise in service elicitation

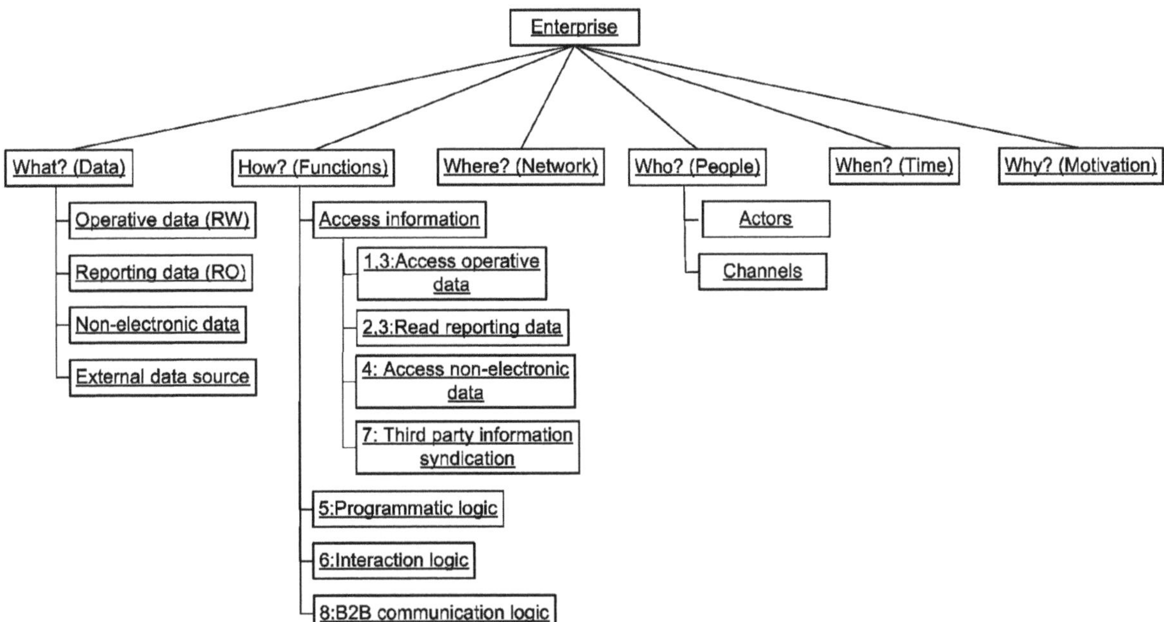

Figure 2. Phases of the Qualitative Service Elicitation (QSE) method

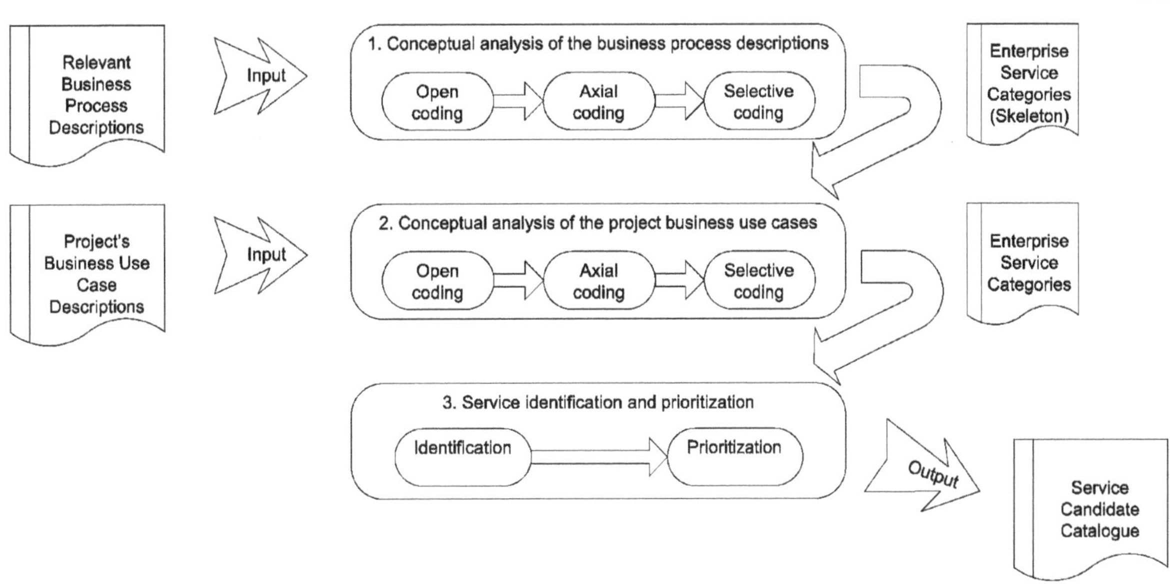

To help thinking of the codes during the open coding, the seven questions of the Zachman Framework (1987) can be used repeatedly during the analysis as a catalyst (See Table 2). Codes can be seen as labels or names defining for what the part in question stands. The wording used in the material being analyzed can be used sometimes, but often the analyst needs to invent a descriptive name for a code. Categories are concepts, which can be used to group several codes together. For

Table 2. Analysis core categories and catalyst questions for open coding

Zachman Column	Core Question	Detailed Questions
Data	What?	• Is the data accessed for reporting purposes only? (Are related services type 1 or 2?). • Is the data aggregation of other data? Is the data actually a category containing other categories or codes? (Related services are type 3). • Is the data available only in non-electronic form? (Type 4). • Is the data received directly or indirectly from any external source? (Related services are type 7).
Function	How?	• Is any data being accessed, processed, validated, generated or searched? How and which data? (Details for types 1, 2, 3, 7). • Is there a logic, which is atomic, independent and resulting in a concrete result? (Type 5). • Is stateful interaction needed between human beings and the IT system? (Type 6). • Is there any stateful communication with external parties? (Type 8). • Is data format transformation needed in communication? (Type 8).
Network	Where?	
People	Who?	Who is using the system and with what kind of channel or device? (Reusability of type 6 services).
Time	When?	
Motivation	Why?	Why is the data processed in non-electronic form? (Is there need for type 1 or 2 services?).

Table 3. Example business use case

Order Entry for ADSL Product (Relevant Code Sources Marked with Superscript)	Identified Codes
Goal and triggers: The goal of the use case is to *get the customer and payment data checked and updated*[1], *verify the availability of the product in the delivery address*[2] and *to enter the sales order*[3] to the IT system *according to the customer's wishes*[4]. The use case is triggered when a customer calls the contact center and wishes to order an ADSL product.	Why: *flawless customer data*[1], *order validation*[2], *order entry*[3] *customer need clarification*[4],
Actors: Contact center agent (user)	Who: Contact center agent
Basic course of events: **The user opens the system using a web browser**[1] and selects the ADSL purchase function from the main menu. The user asks for the *installation address*[2] from **the customer**[3] and enters the address into the system. The system **checks *the possibility to install*[4,5]** the *ADSL line*[6] in the given address and **returns *a list of possible speeds and add-ons*[7,5].** **The user selects the ADSL add-ons one by one based on the customer's wishes and the system guides this selection by removing all incompatible add-ons after each addition[8].** The system **shows *the price*[9,10]** after the add-ons have been entered. If the customer agrees on the price, the customer is identified and the system user **searches for existing customer data from the system with the *customer name*[11,12]**. The user verifies the validity of the *customer's social security number (SSN), phone number and billing address*[11]. If the customer data is not found, the user **adds a new customer into system with the data[13]** queried from the customer. The system **checks the validity of the given SSN[14] and stores the customer data[15].** **The system conducts a *credit check*[16] for the customer using an external credit check agency[17].** The system shows if the credit check fails. In this case, **all data is stored[15]**, but no *ADSL order*[18] is created. Instead, the customer is asked to come to the store and provide a *collateral deposit*[19]. If the credit check succeeds, the system **creates an *ADSL order*[18,20]** and **creates a related *installation order*[21] for a subcontractor[22]**. The system returns to the main menu and informs the user of a successful sales order creation.	**Who: Contact center agent with browser[1], customer[3]** *What: installation address[2], availability[4], product[6], product configuration[7], product price[9], customer basic data[11], customer credit standing[16], sales order[18], assurance deposit[19], service order[21]* **How: Get available product configurations with address[5], Guide configuration of ADSL product[8], get product configuration price[10], search for customer by name[12], create customer[13], validate customer SSN[14], update customer data[15], get customer credit standing[17] (external), create sales order[20], create service order[22] (external)** **Other codes: Communication with the customer, main menu**

example both "toothbrush" and "toothpaste" can be grouped under the "dental care products" category, which can be seen as a sub-category for the "product" category.

Additional notes should be written down for each identified code to help divide the codes into categories. The questions in the note column of Table 2 are derived from the characteristics of the sub-categories defined in Table 1.

The purpose of the axial coding is to link together the findings of the open coding (Robson, 2002). In this phase, the codes are grouped into categories containing similar codes and categories into sub-categories. If different wording has been used for the same phenomenon during the open coding phase, then these codes should be merged, as well. Additionally any relationships between codes under the same categories should be identified. The questions in this phase are, for example:

- Are there any codes which mean the same thing and could be merged?
- Are there similar codes which could be grouped under a common category?
- Can any categories be seen as an aggregate of two or more categories?

In the last phase, selective coding is performed on the data identified in the previous phases. In this phase, the identified categories and codes are sorted into core categories based on the Zachman Framework and the sub-categories based on Table 1. The hierarchy of the categories is presented in Figure 1.

The use of partly pre-defined categories as *a priori* categories is against the inductive nature of the grounded theory research methodology. However, the recurring analysis of similar data, such as in service elicitation, will probably benefit from a set of pre-defined categories. The pre-defined categories and their characteristics are needed to identify the service types known to be potentially reusable. Additional categories and sub-categories can be created inductively, if needed.

The actual service candidates are identified after the use case analysis and are generated from the codes under the "Function" core category with their relations to the codes and categories in the "Data" and "People" core categories.

Service candidate types 1, 2, 3 and 7 are identified from the codes under the "Access information" categories. The granularity of the candidate is determined with the relation to the codes and categories in the "Data" core category. The abstraction level is the one identified from the business process analysis, if available. Codes in the "Access non-electronic data" category can be transformed into content services if the business process itself is revised, as well.

Service candidate types 5 and 8 are identified from the codes under equivalent categories. If these codes have relations to other core categories, then these relations can be used to determine the correct granularity. For example data transformation logic services should use the granularity of the data category, such as the service candidates under the "Access information" category.

Interaction logic candidates (Type 6) are identified from the codes under the equivalent category. These codes should have relations to the "People" core category, which can help to estimate the reusability. If the same interaction logic is needed with several different actors or the actors are using different channels to access the same logic, then these services are more likely to be reusable.

Candidate Identification and Prioritization Phase

The scope of a service can vary from a simple request to a complex system that can access and combine information from other sources. Enterprises can use simple services to accomplish a specific business task, while several smaller services can be combined to support more complex processes. The services should represent functionality that is meaningful from the business perspective. (Papazoglou & Dubray, 2004)

After the analysis, the codes from the analysis of the use cases are transformed into service candidates. All of the codes under the "Function" core categories are service candidates and are given a descriptive name using the categories they represent and to which they are related.

With the help of the business process analysis, the service candidates can be prioritized based on how often they are mentioned in the business process descriptions. In our case study, we simply sorted the services into two classes: local and global service candidates. A service candidate is global if it belongs to any category identified from the business process analysis and should be thus reusable in other projects, as well. Otherwise, the candidate is local and is not likely to be reused in other projects.

EXAMPLE

As an example, we use an imaginary "Order-to-Cash" composite business process and a project implementing an IT system to support the "Order Entry" business process in a contact center. The "Order Entry" process is merely one stage within the "Order-to-Cash" composite process, and thus, the use case analysis of the project will cover only this stage. However, the scope of the business process analysis can cover the whole "Order-to-Cash" process, giving a more extensive view to the enterprise and providing a conceptual skeleton of the categories to be enhanced with the use case analysis.

The analysis of the composite business process reveals concepts such as customers, leads, products, sales orders, contracts, service orders, service resources, resource schedules, installed base and sales forecasts. The outcome of the business process analysis produces categories and codes such as those presented in Figure 2 with lower a case.

An example product in this project could be, for example, an ADSL connection, and thus, the business use case "Order Entry for ADSL Product" would be implemented in the project. The details of the example use case are presented in Table 3 with identified codes and categories. The codes and categories identified from the use case analysis are appended to the hierarchy presented in Figure 2. These additions are in bold font.

The service candidates are underlined in Figure 3. In this analysis, all of the identified candidates have relationships with a concept identified from business process analysis, and therefore, they would be classified as "global" and reusable in other projects, as well.

CASE STUDY

As a proof of the concept, a set of real world business process descriptions and a set of business use case descriptions from a large IT project were analyzed using QSE.

The case project core team included a program manager, a chief architect and a few persons with a mixed role of a requirement engineer and a sub-project manager. The key persons of the case project were all experts with sufficient knowledge of the business domain. The core team was complemented with several temporal advisors especially for security, technology and legal issues.

The goal of the case study was to test how well QSE would uncover the service candidates in a real project and to compare the produced service catalogue against the actual solution architecture made in the project with traditional methods by the experts. From the project point of view, this review acted as an additional verification for the

Figure 3. The category hierarchy appended with categories and codes from the use case analysis

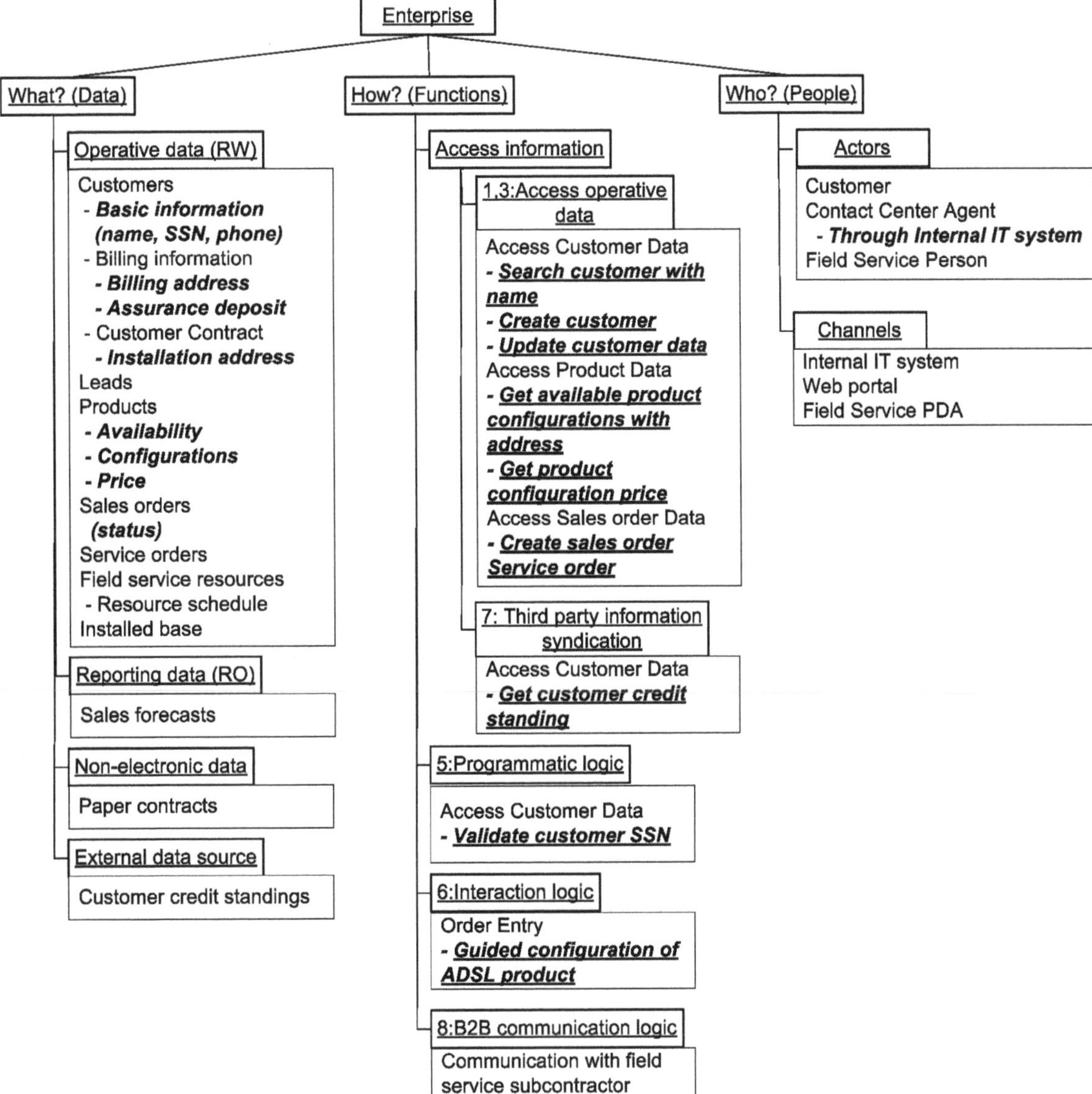

solution architecture, and for the research, this comparison gave an opportunity to validate the outcome against similar analysis made by the experts.

The planned changes to the actual business processes were minor in the case project, as the main driver was technical renewal. Respectively, the needed interfaces and connections to the external systems were carefully identified by the project, as the existing solution provided a good basis for the project design. Similarly, the business process and use case descriptions were more or less up-to-date and solid, providing a good basis for QSE analysis.

A total of 47 business process descriptions were analyzed covering the main operative processes of one business line. The analyzed project scope included 16 business level use cases and the use case analysis resulted in 17 global and 14 local service candidates. These service candidates were modeled using the Integration Use Case method (Alkkiomäki & Smolander, 2007), catalogued and compared to the solution architecture created by the project.

The comparison showed that QSE analysis was able to reveal all the services identified by the project with traditional methods. The scope and grouping of the service candidates were different compared to the project, but it was possible to map each elicited service candidate to the project design. On the other hand, the work made by the project was thorough and thus QSE analysis did not uncover any completely new services compared to the project findings.

Additionally, the feasibility of the prioritization model was evaluated by comparing how well the categorization matched with assumed reusability of each service candidate. Service candidates were assumed to be reusable only if the key project personnel were able to name either a system or another active project where the service could be used as well. As a result, 12 out of 17 global service candidates were seen reusable in other projects as well and further analysis showed that the scope of the case project itself included a new operative system to support all four processes from where the remaining five global service candidates where identified. Similarly only one out of 14 local service candidates was estimated to be reusable outside the project scope.

In this case study, QSE was able to provide a service catalog comparable with the one made by experts with traditional means. Also the concept of estimating the reusability of services based on their occurrences in the process descriptions seemed to be promising in the case project. As a result, QSE seems to provide a promising way of doing service elicitation in early phases of the project, at least when used with high quality raw material.

FUTURE RESEARCH DIRECTIONS

Various different tools are available to automate some parts of the service modeling and implementation tasks, but the most difficult part remains manual. The elicitation of the business needs and componentization of the business itself is not something one can really automate. Current approaches to SOA migration and service elicitation seem to fit poorly to the practical issues faced in enterprises (Razavian & Lago, 2011). Even when the service engineering research is slowly shifting towards empirical studies (Seth, Singla & Aggarwal, 2012), there is still little empirical evidence on what the enablers for successful SOA adoption are and what the value of SOA for enterprises is.

Similarly to qualitative research, QSE depends purely on the material being analyzed. Thus, faulty or incomplete source material will produce a faulty and incomplete analysis. In real life, the business process descriptions rarely cover all of the processes and should not be used as the only source for service prioritization. However, intensive use of business process descriptions may motivate business stakeholders to prepare the descriptions with more enthusiasm.

After all, even when the pace of change is getting faster in business, the basic concepts of business don't change quite as quickly allowing definition of somewhat stable service interfaces defining also boundaries between organizations. Stable boundaries provide loose coupling between different parts of the enterprise, thus allowing these parts to be developed more or less independently. And as a result, the additional agility can make a difference nowadays.

CONCLUSION

In this chapter, we have introduced QSE, a method for Qualitative Service Elicitation that applies the qualitative research approach to service elicitation. The use of QSE in service-oriented systems development allows more consistent quality of analysis and enforces developers to concentrate on reusability aspects of services.

Based on the experiences from the case study, it is feasible to use QSE as a systematic and practical method for service elicitation with results comparable to similar analysis carried out by experts with traditional methods. The use of business process level concepts and vocabulary in the service candidates made it easy for requirement engineers to pinpoint other usages for the service candidates outside the case project context.

Also the idea of prioritization of services based on how often the related concepts appear in the business processes seemed to be promising, although it should be enhanced to take the relationships between categories better into account. Prioritization pinpoints the services with potential reusability outside of the project scope, giving the project a possibility to check the other business processes for potential new requirements for the services being implemented.

REFERENCES

Adam, S., & Doerr, J. (2008). The role of service abstraction and service variability and its impact on requirement engineering for service-oriented systems. In *Proceedings of Annual IEEE International Computer Software and Applications Conference*. IEEE. doi:10.1109/COMPSAC.2008.54

Alkkiomäki, V., & Smolander, K. (2007). *Integration use cases – An applied UML technique for modeling functional requirements in service oriented architecture.* Paper presented at the Requirements Engineering: Foundation for Software Quality, 13th International Working Conference, REFSQ 2007. Trondheim, Norway.

Arsanjani, A. (2005). *Toward a pattern language for service-oriented architecture and integration, part 1: Build a service eco-system.* Retrieved 01/19, 2010, from http://www.ibm.com/developerworks/webservices/library/ws-soa-soi/

Arsanjani, A., Ghosh, S., Allam, A., Abdollah, T., Ganapathy, S., & Holley, K. (2008). SOMA: A method for developing service-oriented solutions. *IBM Systems Journal*, *47*(3), 377–396. doi:10.1147/sj.473.0377

Bieberstein, N., Bose, S., Fiammante, M., Jones, K., & Shah, R. (2006). *Service-oriented architecture compass: Business value, planning and enterprise roadmap.* Upper Saddle River, NJ: IBM Press.

Birks, D. F., Fernandez, W., Levina, N., & Nasirin, S. (2013). Grounded theory method in information systems research: Its nature, diversity and opportunities. *European Journal of Information Systems*, *22*(1), 1–8. doi:10.1057/ejis.2012.48

Bussler, C. (2001). The role of B2B protocols in inter-enterprise process execution. In Technologies for E-Services (pp. 16-29). Springer. doi:10.1007/3-540-44809-8_2

Cherbakov, L., Galambos, G., Harishankar, R., Kalyana, S., & Rackham, G. (2005). Impact of service orientation at the business level. *IBM Systems Journal*, *44*(4), 653–668. doi:10.1147/sj.444.0653

Dan, A., Johnson, R., & Arsanjani, A. (2007). Information as a service: Modeling and realization. In *Proceedings of the International Workshop on Systems Development in SOA Environments.* Washington, DC: Academic Press. doi:10.1109/SDSOA.2007.5

Endrei, M., Ang, J., Arsanjani, A., Chua, S., Comte, P., & Krogdahl, P. et al. (2004). *Patterns: Service-oriented architecture and web services.* IBM Press.

Flick, U. (1998). *An introduction to qualitative research*. London: Sage.

Galal, G. H., & Paul, R. J. (1999). A qualitative scenario approach to managing evolving requirements. *Requirements Engineering*, *4*(2), 92–102. doi:10.1007/s007660050016

Harikumar, A. K., Lee, R., Hae Sool, Y., Haeng-Kon, K., & Byeongdo, K. (2005). *A model for application integration using web services*. Paper presented at the Computer and Information Science, 2005. New York, NY. doi:10.1109/ICIS.2005.12

Lo, A., & Yu, E. (2008). From business models to service-oriented design: A reference catalog approach. In Proceedings of Conceptual Modeling - ER 2007 (Vol. 4801, pp. 87-101). Springer.

Mattarelli, E., Bertolotti, F., & Macrì, D. M. (2013). The use of ethnography and grounded theory in the development of a management information system. *European Journal of Information Systems*, *22*(1), 26–44. doi:10.1057/ejis.2011.34

Moon, M., Hong, M., & Yeom, K. (2008). Two-level variability analysis for business process with reusability and extensibility. In Proceedings of Computer Software and Applications. Turku, Finland: IEEE.

Noel Yuhanna, M. G. (2008). *The Forrester wave: Information-as-a-service Q1 2008*. Retrieved 02/16, 2010, from http://www.forrester.com/rb/Research/wave%26trade%3B_information-as-a-service%2C_q1_2008/q/id/43199/t/2

Papazoglou, M. P., & Dubray, J.-J. (2004). *A survey of web service technologies*. Retrieved 02/16, 2010, from http://eprints.biblio.unitn.it/archive/00000586/

Papazoglou, M. P., Traverso, P., Dustdar, S., Leymann, F., & Kramer, B. J. (2006). Service-oriented computing: A research roadmap. In F. Cubera, B. J. Krämer & M. P. Papazoglou (Eds.), Service oriented computing (SOC) (Vol. 05462). Internationales Begegnungs- und Forschungszentrum für Informatik (IBFI).

Papazoglou, M. P., & Van Den Heuvel, W.-J. (2007). Service oriented architectures: Approaches, technologies and research issues. *The VLDB Journal*, *16*(3), 389–415. doi:10.1007/s00778-007-0044-3

Ramollari, E., Dranidis, D., & Simons, A. J. H. (2007). *A survey of service oriented development methodologies*. Paper presented at the 2nd European Young Researchers Workshop on Service Oriented Computing. Leicester, UK.

Razavian, M., & Lago, P. (2010). A frame of reference for SOA migration. In *Towards a service-based internet* (LNCS), (Vol. 6481, pp. 150–162). Springer.

Razavian, M., & Lago, P. (2011). A survey of SOA migration in industry. In Proceedings of Service-Oriented Computing (LNCS), (vol. 7084, pp. 618-626). Springer.

Robson, C. (2002). *Real world research* (2nd ed.). Oxford, UK: Blackwell Publishing.

Sadiq, S., Orlowska, M., & Sadiq, W. (2005). *The role of messaging in collaborative business processes*. Paper presented at the IRMA International Conference. San Diego, CA.

Seth, A., Singla, A. R., & Aggarwal, H. (2012). Service oriented architecture adoption trends: A critical survey. In Contemporary computing, communications in computer and information science (vol. 306, pp. 164-175). Springer.

Strauss, A. L., & Corbin, J. M. (1998). *Basics of qualitative research: Techniques and procedures for developing grounded theory* (2nd ed.). Thousand Oaks, CA: Sage Publications Inc.

Van Nuffel, D. (2007). Towards a service-oriented methodology: Business-driven guidelines for service identification. In On the move to meaningful internet systems 2007: OTM 2007 workshops (pp. 294-303). OTM.

Walker, D. M. (2006). *White paper - Overview architecture for enterprise data warehouses*. Retrieved 02/16, 2010, from http://www.datamgmt.com/index.php?module=documents&JAS_DocumentManager_op=downloadFile&JAS_File_id=29

Watson, H. J., Goodhue, D. L., & Wixom, B. H. (2002). The benefits of data warehousing: Why some organizations realize exceptional payoffs. *Information & Management*, *39*(6), 491–502. doi:10.1016/S0378-7206(01)00120-3

Zachman, J. A. (1987). A framework for information systems architecture. *IBM Systems Journal*, *26*(3), 276–292. doi:10.1147/sj.263.0276

Zdun, U., Hentrich, C., & Dustdar, S. (2007). Modeling process-driven and service-oriented architectures using patterns and pattern primitives. *ACM Transactions on the Web*, *1*(3), 14. doi:10.1145/1281480.1281484

Zimmermann, O., Schlimm, N., & Waller, G. (2005). *Analysis and design techniques for service-oriented development and integration.* Paper presented at the INFORMATIK 2005 - Informatik LIVE!. Bonn, Germany.

KEY TERMS AND DEFINITIONS

Core Category: Core categories represent the essential business elements of the enterprise. The pre-defined core categories represent typical elements of an enterprise.

Data Driven Service: Purpose of data driven service is to encapsulate and store business data.

Integration Use Case: An integration use case represents the abstract service interface between service provider(s) and service consumer(s). If an enterprise service bus (ESB), a messaging queue or other middleware system is used in the system integration, then the integration use case describes also the role and actions of the middleware between the systems.

Messaging Service: Purpose of messaging service is to encapsulate the logic needed in business conversations to bind public and private processes together.

Process Driven Services: Purpose of process driven service is to automate one or more activities of one or more business processes.

Service Consumer: The service consumer is an application, service, or some other type of software component that requires the functionality of the service. The service consumer executes the service by sending it a request according to the service interface.

Service Provider: The service provider is an application that executes requests from service consumers according to the service interface. A service provider can also be a service consumer.

Chapter 8
A Proposed Pragmatic Software Development Process Model

Sanjay Misra
Covenant University, Nigeria

M. Omorodion
Federal University of Technology – Minna, Nigeria

Amit Mishra
Federal University of Technology – Minna, Nigeria

Luis Fernandez
University of Alcala de Henares, Spain

ABSTRACT

The rapid growth in technology and the dynamism in our society today poses a lot of problems for Software Engineering practitioners. The result is a series of software development process methods that can be used to combat or meet up with the problems. What we can do is evolve, grow, and adapt to the changes that come along with development. This is the dynamism inherent in man—to adapt to change and improve ourselves and our existing systems—since the world is a far cry from what it was a few decades ago. On this basis lay the need to develop the model proposed in this chapter to meet the variations that exist as a result of technological development.

INTRODUCTION

In the process of developing software, as a result of rapid advancement in technology, there always seems to be difficulties in meeting up with the demands of consumers and time constraints. As such, various development models and techniques seem to have mutated from the three fundamental models viz; The Classic Software Lifecycle Model which is sequential, The Evolutionary Process Model which is iterative and the Rapid Application Development Model which is incremental in nature (Crnkovic, Larsson & Chaudron, 2006).

Fowler (2005) stated in an article that obtaining accurate sets of requirement does not necessarily solve the problem. Good sets of requirements become obsolete within short periods of time and fixing requirements doesn't mean the world will come to a halt because of that; many changes in the business world are completely unpredictable: and if you cannot get stable requirements you cannot get a predictable plan.

Consequently, a research conducted on various development models and techniques revealed that there is an average of about 40 models already available (Misra, Omorodion & Fernandez, 2012)

DOI: 10.4018/978-1-4666-6359-6.ch008

and yet a consensus has not been reached to agree on one perfect model. Although it could be quite impossible to arrive at a one perfect model, but from the research conducted, software developers seem to have come to terms with the Agile Software Development Methods which is a web of several development techniques applying similar methods to software development such as developing a team, lack of bureaucracy and debugging as the code is being developed so as to minimise time wasted in software checks.

This project/work in the present paper is carried out for the purpose of designing a development model that will put into consideration most of the benefits and limitations of all the models that were found and make their weak points its strong points while also taking advantage of the benefits of those models. Its objectives are:

- To design a software process based on practical activities carried out by developers.
- To carry out a comparative analysis between the benefits of the model and those of past models.
- To design and evaluate a functional model that can and possibly will be implemented for the benefit of all humanity.
- To propose metrics that will be useful for proper product and project evaluation after using the model.

In the next section, several development methods are discussed including a bit of their pros and cons. In forthcoming section we discusses the materials and methods applied in the process of developing the model including the processes applied. A comparative analysis between the model and a few others are discussed in later section. A brief conclusion is given in the last section.

LITERATURE SURVEY AND EXISTING MODELS

The software process models history begins with the introduction of a model called "Build and Fix Model". The model has only two steps:

1. Write the Code.
2. Fix problems in the code.

Thus, the main theme of the model was to write some code first and then think about different phases of development (Boehm, 1988; Gull et al, 2009).

Sometimes, software developers integrate these models so that they can utilize the benefits of each process and discard those attributes that may not be of use to them. Thus, there are several alternative models and methods used for software development.

Sequential Models

The Waterfall Model

This is the earliest and the most common approach employed in the process of developing software. It exhibits sequential characteristics and discourages iteration; it was developed in 1970 by Royce (1970) on noticing that the process of developing software was a different activity from the development of hardware products which required well defined requirements that do not change till after the product has been released into the market (Scacchi, 2001). Figure 1 shows a view of the waterfall chart showing the various stages involved and the arrows indicate the linearity of the model and indicates that no backtracking is allowed.

Figure 1. Cascading waterfall model

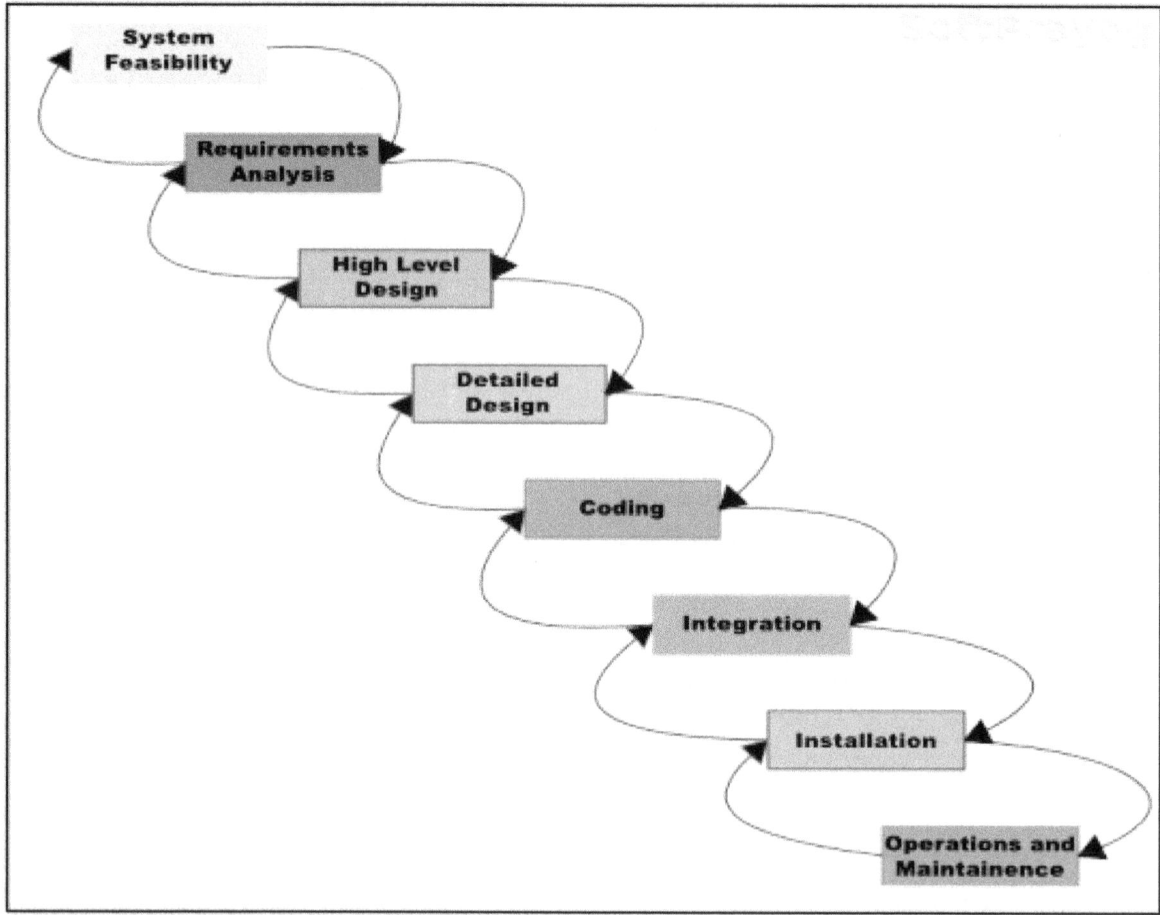

This model, sometimes called the classic software lifecycle model, has its stages broken down to as many as twelve in some reports (Scacchi, 2001; Buzzle, 2005b, Pressman, 2005; Sommerville, 2007). It has the advantages of simplicity, manageability as a result of rigidity, useful for small projects and not commencing a phase until the preceding phase is completed. Its disadvantages are adjusting scope during the life cycle can kill a project; the greatest disadvantage of the waterfall model is that until the final stage of the development cycle is complete, a working model of the software does not lie in the hands of the client. Thus, he is hardly in a position to mention if what has been designed is exactly what he had asked for and it cannot work well with long term projects.

The V-Model

Figure 2 illustrates the V-model and it is quite similar to the Waterfall Model. In describing the V-model, (Gull et al, 2009) stated that it is assumed to be the extension of Waterfall Model but exhibits its difference from the waterfall such that it doesn't move in a linear way instead its process steps bend upwards after the coding phase to form V-shape showing that each phase has an associated testing

Figure 2. The V-model

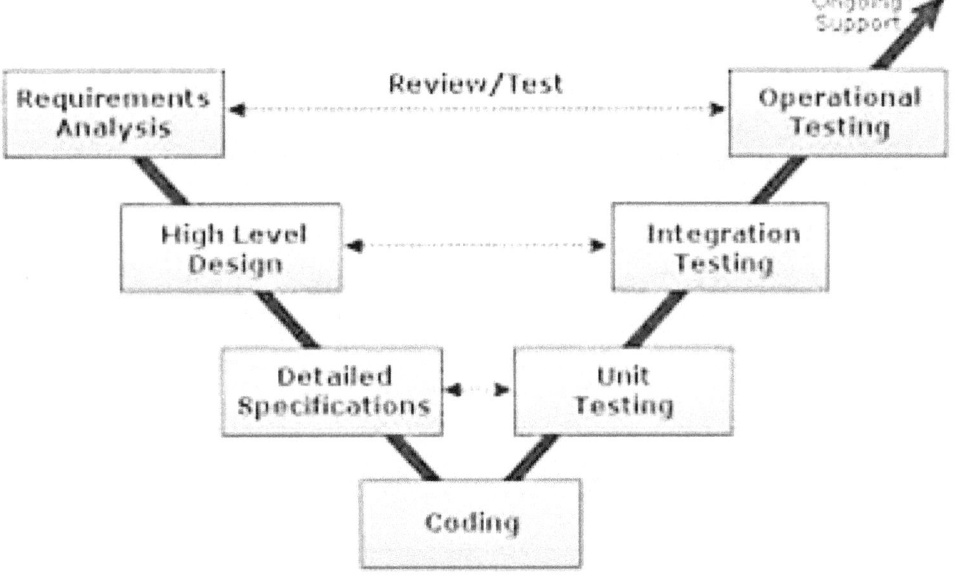

phase. Like the activities of the waterfall model, each activity has to be completed before moving on to the next activity (Sommerville, 2007).

(Software Experts), when describing the V-models indicated that "another idea evolved which was the traceability down the left side of the V. This means that the requirements have to be traced into the design of the system, thus verifying that they are implemented completely and correctly. The earlier versions of V-models used the first option. For later versions a series of subsequent V-cycles was defined.

The Evolutionary Process Model

These are the evolutionary models and are characterised in such a way that more complete versions of software are developed. The generic form of the evolutionary model is shown in Figure 3.

The Spiral Model

This is an evolutionary software process model that was proposed by (Boehm, 1987). It is divided into about six task regions and it couples the iterative methods with some methods in the linear sequential model. It provides the potential for rapid development of incremental versions of the software. Using the spiral model, software is developed in a series of incremental releases. During early iterations, the incremental release might be a paper model or prototype. During later iterations, increasingly more complete versions of the engineered system are produced (Pressman, 2005). A breakdown of the process activities include;

- **Customer Communication:** This step helps create an effective communication platform between the developer and client.

Figure 3. The generic evolutionary process model

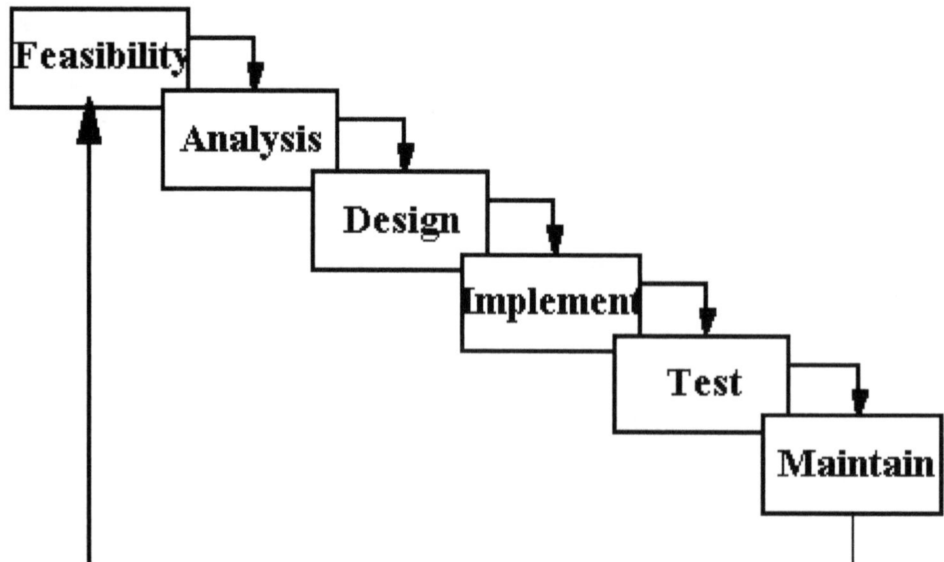

- **Planning:** Here the activities that are required to define resources, timelines, project related information, performance, functionality, ability to accommodate change and technology.
- **Risk Analysis:** At this stage the assessment of the risks involved technically and managerially are determined.
- **Engineering:** Tasks required to build one or more representations of the application.
- **Construction and Release:** This is similar to the verification and validation and maintenance stages of the linear models. It involves tasks needed to construct, test, install, and provide user support (Pressman, 2005; Buzzle, 2005a).

The Rapid Application Development Model (RAD)

The last model to be described is the RAD model. It is a model that combines the benefits of iterative and incremental models in the process of developing software. It is useful for development when the requirements are not well understood so that prototypes are developed to help the clients have a physical view of what they want. It is a merger of various structured techniques, especially the Data Driven Information Engineering with prototyping techniques to accelerate software systems development (Development Models). Sometimes the RAD model is referred to as Component Based Software Engineering (CBSE) used to assemble systems out of existing, independently developed components. Component Based Software Engineering entails more than mere reuse of components, though. It also aims to increase the flexibility of systems through improved modularization. Figure 4 illustrates the RAD model as a system reusability model.

Comparative Analyses of the Generic Models

A comparative analysis of the three generic models is carried out in Table 1. Only these three models have been analysed because all the other models and methodologies are variations of these three.

Figure 4. A system reuse model

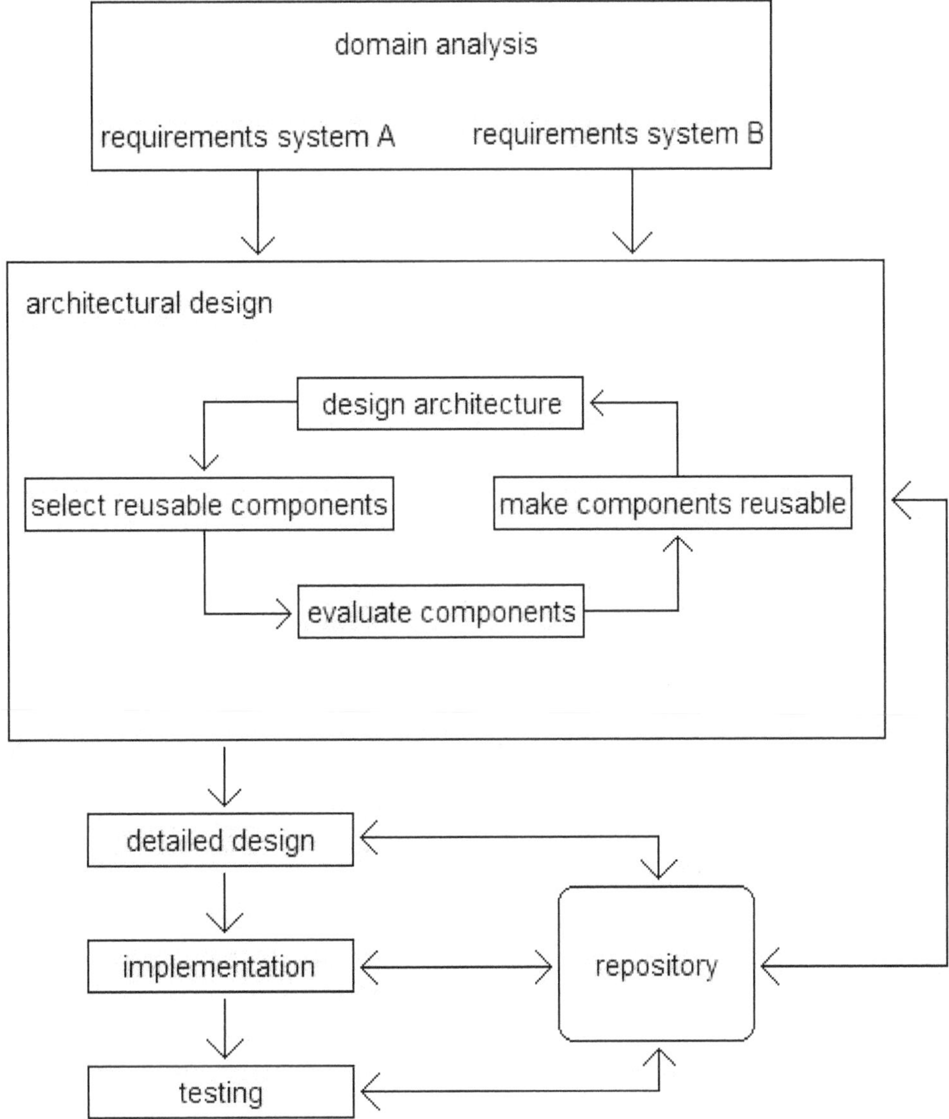

THE PRAGMATIC SOFTWARE DEVELOPMENT PROCESS

This model is designed based on suggestions made by a practitioner/software developer (Stein, D. 2009) on techniques he applied during the development of systems for his clients where he indicated that he uses Agile methods while meeting their needs for predictability;

- Make sure it is a project which can use Agile methodology.
- Propose a fixed burn-rate-propose a team that is right-sized to the skills and scale of the project.
- Propose a fixed sprint size (2 or 3 weeks is typical) for scrum and 6-8weeks releases composed of 3-4 2 week iterations.

Table 1. Comparison of the three generic models (Sommerville, 2007; Jawadekar, 2004)

Waterfall Model	Evolutionary Process Model	RAD
It lacks flexibility	It is very flexible	It is relatively flexible
It is useful when long life complex systems are being built	Useful mainly when small systems are being developed	Useful mainly for commercial systems
Delivery is relatively fast	Delivery is slow	It is characterized by rapid delivery
Very low risks	High risks	Low risks
Higher chances that user needs will not be met.	Needs are definitely met else the product will not be released	May not meet needs because of requirement compromise and time limit.
Badly structured systems	Poorly structured systems	Relatively well structured systems
It is simple and stable	Fairly clear but needs confirmation	Fairly clear, stable and large
It is static	It is dynamic	It is fairly dynamic
It is not cost effective because value for money is not achieved	It is not cost effective	It is relatively cost effective

- Propose a contract where the client can change anything they want for the next sprint or iteration and where they can accept/reject each story as it completes. In exchange the client can be sure there is a single voice (not a committee) who is available to (or embedded with) the team.
- Propose that the client can cancel at the end of any sprint/release with no penalty and will be left with shippable software that has been accepted.

He claims that he uses this approach in some of his engagements as well stating that it is a good compromise between time-and-materials and fixed-price models. The client can quickly receive value (and see the cost vs. value model emerge quickly from the results of each sprint/release). From initiative, we have applied our experience and knowledge to its development.

As is generally known, the human nervous system, as a whole, is sometimes considered as a computer system. Necessary features for development are made available at birth even when they are not really useful to the individual at that time and may never be useful to it at maturity. But considering the perfection and intelligence involved in the development of the nervous system, it can be seen that at the end of the day, from hindsight, nothing seems to be lacking for the individual provided he develops himself positively and the human software was designed in such a way that whatever paths an individual chooses to take, he can be totally different from (and similar to) the next individual. The problem of a clash of wills never comes to play or the possibility that the software cannot be adjusted to go in any direction.

After all software is supposed to be *soft;* so not just are requirements changeable, they ought to be changeable. It takes a lot of energy to get customers of software to fix requirements. It's even worse if they've ever dabbled in software development themselves, because then they "know" that software is easy to change (Fowler, 2005).

That is to say, if I choose to build cars today, am free to do so. Nothing binds me to being a farmer or something else I have been pre-programmed to do. In short, the system is very flexible; and funny enough, it is so flexible that it has the ability to change at any time even at old age without getting corrupted. Thus, this model is designed to exhibit such flexibility and dynamism that can be observed in humans. From the specification stage, it creates room for variation, improvement and increments. It has the ability to encourage development of the software in whatever direction – based on specifications made – that users want it to. It also involves team work both within the system and without. Though, it is not as perfect as the human nervous system, but it is a model that seems to want to put as much as is possible into consideration just as the nervous system does.

A point to note though is that one model or methodology cannot cut across different technologies. Some are useful for large systems, others for small systems and still others for systems for long term use. The different technologies, cultures, and project priorities call for different ways of working (Cockburn, 2001).

Developers must be able to make *all* technical decisions. XP gets to the heart of this where in its planning process it states that only developers may make estimates on how much time it will take to do some work. But the technical people cannot do the whole process themselves. They need guidance on the business needs. This leads to another important aspect of adaptive processes: they need very close contact with business expertise. This goes beyond most projects involvement of the business role. Agile teams cannot exist with occasional communication. They need continuous access to business expertise (Fowler, 2005).

Figure 5 shows an illustration of the Pragmatic Development Process model and the following sections give a description of each stage shown in the model. Take note that following the arrows, one can navigate from any one stage to whichever one he chooses to go to depending on the problems he comes across.

Figure 5. The pragmatic model

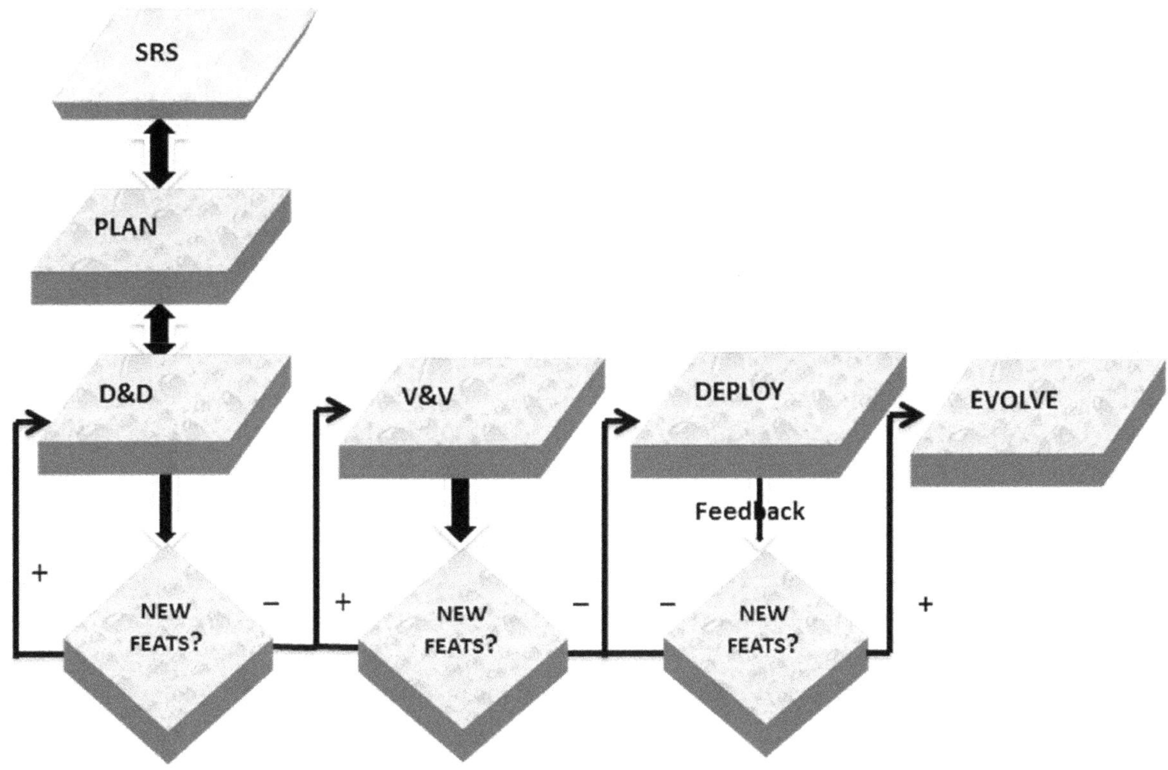

PROCESS SEQUENCE OF THE MODEL

Requirements and Specifications (SRS)

Specifications are gathered and negotiations are made on what they hope to achieve. The team (a group of experts useful for the development of the software) meets with the clients or end users to discuss whatever features can and cannot be considered and also they can make suggestions too on certain features the clients did not consider. Executing an adaptive process is not easy. In particular it requires a very effective team of developers. The team needs to be effective both in the quality of the individuals and in the way they blend together. There's also an interesting synergy: not just does adaptation require a strong team, most good developers prefer an adaptive process (Fowler, 2005). (Brooks, 1995) in his book also stated that the quality of the people on a project, and their organization and management, are more important factors in success than are the tools they use or the technical approaches they take.

They should also be informed that at any time they can come up with new specifications that will help to improve the features of the software. The clients should also fix a time frame for which the software should be ready to be delivered to the end users. To the clients' and team's convenience, they can fix meeting days and times within a week, preferably twice a week. They should meet the first time to collect requirements and the second time to not only collect more requirements but also show the clients the designs and if possible developments they have been able to come up with. This way in making more requirements their suggestions will be more in depth with understanding than the first time. All decisions made should be documented for reference purposes. A fruitful way to think about software development is to consider it as a cooperative game of communication and invention (Cockburn, 2001).

One primary goal of this model is to give room for flexibility not only to the development process but also to the developers themselves. In applying the methods suggested by this model, if somewhere along the line the developers discover that a path they are taking will probably lead to a dead end, they can come up with ideas of their own and modify the model to their own benefit. This is so that it can be useful for large systems as well as moderate and small systems. Fear should not come in when using this model for a large system. Remember that no matter how much your food is in a plate, all you need to do is take it one spoon after the other, and before you know it, you are done. Don't hesitate to document all the necessary processes no matter how many they are or how small and irrelevant they may seem to be; documentation is very vital in any process as all the ideas cannot be stuffed in the brain and remembered. This is an area where the Waterfall Model has an edge over the Agile Methods. Don't worry about them littering the place; put them in soft copies and you can easily delete the ones that are not needed.

Planning

The developer at this stage, after collecting requirements and specifications, should hold a meeting and decide on which methodology they want to use for the development process and they should pay attention to the size of the system they are about to develop (small or large systems). Time should not be wasted here; the meeting can last for at most an hour, but they should make sure that the opinion of every individual is considered before arriving at a final conclusion. If they meet problems somewhere along the line then they should come back to this stage and reconsider their position once again.

Design and Development (D&D)

As much as possible, the development of the software should commence as soon as a set of requirements and specifications have been made. Since they will be allowed to change specifications at any time, little or no time should be wasted on waiting for them to arrive at a consensus on what they might not ask for at the end of the day. This idea is coined from the Concurrent Process Model where rather than confining software engineering activities to a sequence of events; it defines a network of activities. Each activity on the network exists simultaneously with other activities. Events generated within a given activity or at some other place in the activity network trigger transitions among the states of an activity (Pressman, 2001). Research has shown that shorter iterations have lower complexity and risk, better feedback, and higher productivity and success rates (Larman, 2004).

At this stage, the source code should be developed inculcating features that will give room for development, changes, total removal from the system or increments. After this point, whatever changes they come up with will only be fixed in as additional features to the already designed features for such development. A maximum of four iterations can be used, if possible, less. After each design, the client should be consulted for possible changes, improvements, rejections and so on. Often the most valuable features aren't at all obvious until customers have had a chance to play with the software. Agile methods seek to take advantage of this, encouraging business people to learn about their needs as the system gets built, and to build the system in such a way that changes can be incorporated quickly (Fowler, 2005).

Verification and Validation (V&V)

This stage can be divided into three sub-stages viz; unit testing, integration and testing and review. After each development, tests should be carried out on each unit developed to ensure that flaws, errors and omissions are corrected. This process is quite a difficult one as errors cannot easily be noticed especially by the programmer. Suggestions are either two programmers develop their programmes independently and exchange their work to check for errors or interns, being eager to learn, excited about their new job and probably, being youths, are agile and can easily notice any errors, should be allowed to go through their work as they go along so that such errors can be corrected.

As soon as an adequate number of units that can be integrated have been built, they should be integrated and tested to verify that they can function together; making sure also that the emergent properties suit the needs of the clients. After three iterations, the clients should be notified that there is the need for a final validation of the software so that it can finally be released into the market. At this stage, there is still room for an extra iteration. Informing them about moving on to the verification and validation stage will help to ensure that no more changes are made after the fourth iteration. At this stage final tests should be carried out with the clients present agreeing that all needs have been met and are satisfied, else, if there is need for more variations or additions then they should be carried out and then reviewed again.

From practice data indicates that many times clients stop development at around 85-90% of the original budget because the product is good enough to be shipped thereby saving costs for the company (Boehm, 1988).

Operations and Maintenance

This stage is also divided into three parts – deployment, feedback and evolution. At this stage, a complete functional and acceptable system should be delivered to the client for shipping. The complaints of customers and possible suggestions on improvements they may have should be considered and implemented for another release. Problems they may have should also be considered and modifications made to improve the product.

Advantages of the Model

1. Flexibility.
2. Lesser risks.
3. Adaptive.
4. Rationality.
5. Less Iterative.
6. Supports Backtracking.
7. Client's need is a priority.
8. Team work is supported.
9. Interactive.
10. Supports Documentation.

Limitations

1. Major changes in requirements could render the product useless.
2. Client may take advantage of flexibility.

COMPARATIVE ANALYSES BETWEEN THE PRAGMATIC MODEL AND OTHERS

This section analyses the model with respect to the way it improves on some of the shortcomings of some of the mostly used models. Only the three Generic Models are used for comparison since all other models described earlier in Chapter Two are offshoots from them, but the Agile Methodology being a more recent, far removed methodology from the others and the Spiral Model because of its uniqueness in terms of risk assessment will be added. The weaknesses of the models mentioned were gotten from reports, textbooks, and web posts and sometimes by observation.

Tables 2, 3, 4, 5 and 6 show the uniqueness of the model over the waterfall, RAD, Evolutionary Process and the Spiral Models; the care and effort put into the development of the Agile Methodologies makes it a bit difficult to come up with its shortcomings and as such only a few will be mentioned with respect to the Agile Methodologies.

Table 2. Differences between the waterfall model and the pragmatic model

The Waterfall Model	The Pragmatic Model
Very bureaucratic	Very flexible
It was built as a flawed and non-working model	It is based on practices carried out on the field
The client has no idea of what is being built and cannot make variations until the project is completed	The client is worked with closely and can make changes as the work progresses
When a stage is completed, it discourages backtracking in spite of errors that may be present	Clients are encouraged to make changes whenever they come up with them

Table 3. Differences between the RAD model and the pragmatic model

The RAD Model	The Pragmatic Model
Due to time constraints the product may not be at top quality	It is aimed at producing high quality, shippable product
It burns out good technicians at an alarming rate	They are free to make modifications to suit their needs
Risks are low	Risks are avoided by trying to ensure that needs are met to minimize backtracking
Unknown cost of product alleviated by amount of rework in the process.	Cost of product is determined from the onset.
It may be difficult for many important users to commit the time required for success of the RAD process	Not much time is consumed
Due to time constraints the product may not be at top quality	Aimed at producing high quality, shippable product
The client usually gets a shell of what they want with several sections to be added in future projects (if you get to them) (Moore, 1997).	Clients declare they are content with the product before shipping
It burns out good technicians at an alarming rate.	They are free to make modifications on the model to suit their needs
Initial project requirements are usually under estimated	Under estimation is anticipated at the requirement stage
Not all types of applications are appropriate for RAD.	Can be applied to virtually any system
RAD is not appropriate when technical risks are high	

Table 4. Differences between the evolutionary process model and the pragmatic model

The Evolutionary Model	The Pragmatic Model
High risk	Risks are controlled and monitored
It is used as an excuse for hacking to avoid documenting requirements even if they are well understood (Development Models).	It involves proper documentation and is not an excuse for crime
Users/acquirers do not understand the nature of the approach and can be disappointed when the results are unsatisfactory	The nature of the software may not be understood at first but all these would be eliminated before final delivery
Systems are often poorly structured (Sommerville, 2007).	Systems are well structured

Table 5. Differences between the spiral model and the pragmatic model

The Spiral Model	The Pragmatic Model
The risk assessment is rigidly anchored in the process and in some cases the risk assessment may not be necessary in this detail (Software Experts).	Risks are avoided by trying to ensure that needs are met to minimize backtracking
Demands considerable risk assessment expertise and relies on this expertise for success	A risk assessment expert is not needed
If major risks are uncovered and managed, problems will occur (Pressman, 2005).	If risks are uncovered and managed then the model can easily be modified to suit needs

Table 6. Differences between the agile methodologies and the pragmatic model

The Agile Methodologies	The Pragmatic Model
The ability to cope with corrections or deficiencies introduced into the product is difficult (Williams, 2007).	Appropriate measures are taken while designing the code for possible modifications and improvements
There is the possibility that the project will go off track because of lack of emphasis laid on documentation and designing	A lot of emphasis is laid on documentation to ease feedback processes
It is difficult to use these methodologies for large projects as time and effort can no longer be judged in such cases	This method understands that various projects exists and it creates room for modifications to accommodate them
If the customer representative is not sure, then the project going off track increases manifold. Only senior developers are in a better position to take the decisions necessary for the agile type of development, which leaves hardly any place for newbie programmers, until it is combined with the seniors' resources (Fowler, 2005).	Emphasis is laid on the team of developers meeting with a team from the clients' side

The Compared Models in Brief

Figure 1 shows the pictorial representation of the waterfall model which is one of the oldest models used by software engineers to develop software packages. It was presented as a non-practicable model with many flaws and its advantages resulted in it becoming widely used. There is growing recognition that software, like all complex systems, evolves over a period of time Gilb, 2006), hence the need to design a model that will serve to accommodate an evolving product. In response to that, the evolutionary process model was developed; Evolutionary models are iterative and are characterized in a manner that enables software engineers to develop increasingly more complete versions of the software (Pressman, 2005). This model focuses on developing an implementation in small increments and although it is referred to as iterative it exhibits more of the incremental characteristics found in some models.

The RAD model is also referred to as the Component Based Software Engineering and it is an incremental method (Pressman, 2005) of software development process and it lays emphasis on an extremely short development cycle. It merges various structured techniques especially the data driven Information Engineering with Prototyping techniques to accelerate software systems development (Development Models).

The spiral model (Boehm, 1988) is an improvement on the evolutionary model. This model focuses on integrating the concepts of risk management, project objectives, and prototyping and project costs to the evolutionary model. The process begins at the centre position and then moves clockwise in transversals and each transversal result in a not clearly defined deliverable (software Experts).

Agile methodologies came into being when developers felt the need for change from the older bureaucratic methods which don't necessarily provide the customers with what they really want. In Agile methods, all software development processes are considered to be empirical rather than defined they are adaptive and feedback is required throughout the process of developing a system.

DISCUSSION

Figure 1 shows the pictorial representation of the waterfall model reflecting its linear features. The waterfall model is the oldest model used by software engineers to develop software packages. It was presented as a non-practicable model with many flaws but because of the advantages it presented, it soon became widely used in the field (Buzzle, 2005a). As indicated in Table 2, the new model overrides the Waterfall Model on the grounds that it is based on practice; not to mention that it also reduces bureaucracy to the barest minimum.

In Table 3 are highlighted the features that the Pragmatic Model have over the RAD Model. It showed that although the RAD Model method creates a situation where the products are delivered rapidly, it also posed the problem of not being able to meet the needs of consumers in the long run.

As shown in Table 5 the problem of risk assessment was taken advantage of during the design of the new model because it created the realization that the whole process is very risky and a lot of care has to be taken so as not to incur losses in the long run.

The ideas coined by the Agile Methods really served as a booster for the reasoning behind the Pragmatic Model. They introduced the idea of flexibility and less bureaucracy and the need for the process to be adaptive, not predictive which renders the work rigid and liable to failure. Although it has it shortcomings as indicated in Table 6, which were taken advantage of in this project, it has also played a vital role in the development processes practiced in the field.

A major shortcoming present in this project is the fact that the model could not be tested before its presentation because of lack of developers in the environment. For a cogent conclusion to be arrived at and an improvement on the beauty of the project, there is the need for the project to be put to test so that real life results can be obtained. For instance, the assumptions made about the edge it has over the older models are theoretical and for a fact, it is mentioned regularly that assumptions made theoretically are not necessarily practicable in real life situations not to mention that these practices are not necessarily carried out within the environment.

CONCLUSION

This paper briefly discussed a few software development process models, highlighted some of their weaknesses and strengths and went further to design a model based on practical events. The edge the new model has over the existing ones been also highlighted in tables and a brief discussion was carried out eventually.

The results show that some of the shortcomings of most of the models discussed were put into consideration and improved upon where necessary and changes were made when possible.

This model may not necessarily bring about the solution of the problems in the field and the wish of any designer is that someone else out there will learn from his mistakes and improve on them someday. Obviously, the model still possibly has a few weaknesses that passed unnoticed during the process of its design.

The aim of the paper so far was achieved as indicated in the report and there is hope that it will be useful to not just the Software Engineering Society but to all humanity.

REFERENCES

Boehm, B. (1987). A spiral model of software development and enhancement. *Computer, 20*(9), 61–72.

Boehm B. W. (1988, May). Model of software development and enhancement. *IEEE Computer*.

Brooks, F. P. (1995). *The mythical man-month, anniversary edition*. Harlow, UK: Addison-Wesley Publishing Company.

Buzzle. (2005a). *Spiral model-A new approach towards software development*. Author.

Buzzle. (2005b). *The waterfall model advantages and disadvantages*. Retrieved from http://www.buzzle.com/editorials/1-5-2005-63768.asp

Cockburn, A. (2001). *Agile software development*. Reading, MA: Addison Wesley Longman.

Crnkovic, I., Larsson, & Chaudron. (2006). *Component-based development process and component lifecycle*. A Technical Paper.

Development Models. (n.d.). Retrieved from http://myprojects.kostigoff.net/methodology/development_models/development_models.hm

Fowler, M. (2005). *The new methodology*. Retrieved from http://martinfowler.com/articles/newMethodology.html

Gilb, T. (2006). *Estimation or control? – Thesenpapier*. Retrieved from http://www.dasma.org/

Gull, H., Azam, F., Haider, W. B., & Iqbal, S. Z. (2009). A New Divide & Conquer Software Process Model World Academy of Science. *Engineering and Technology, 60*, 255–260.

Jawadekar, W. S. (2004). *Software engineering: Principles and practices*. Tata Mcgraw-Hill Publishing Company Limited.

Larman, C. (2004). *Agile and iterative development: A manager's guide*. Boston: Addison Wesley.

Misra, S, Omorodion, M., & Fernandez, L. (2012). *Brief overview on software process models, their benefits and limitations*. Accepted in a proposed book From IGI Global.

Moore, W. (1997). *About RAD*. Retrieved from http://wmoore.ca/demo/opinion/rad.htm

Pressman, R. S. (2001). *Software engineering, a practitioner's approach* (5th ed.). New York: McGraw-Hill.

Pressman, R. S. (2005). *Software engineering, a practitioner's approach* (6th ed.). McGraw Hill.

Royce, W. W. (1970). Managing the development of large software systems. In *Proc. 9th. Intern. Conf. Software Engineering*. IEEE.

Scacchi, W. (2001). *Process models in software engineering*. New York: John Wiley and Sons, Inc.

Software Experts. (n.d.). *Software process models*. Retrieved from http://www.the-software-experts.de/e_dta-sw-process.htm

Sommerville, I. (2007). *Software engineering* (8th ed.). Addison Wesley. Retrieved from http://www.buzzle.com/editorials/1-5-2005-63768.asp

Williams, L (2007). *A survey of agile development methodologies*. A Whitepaper.

KEY TERMS AND DEFINITIONS

Agile Software Development: Where requirements and solutions evolve through collaboration between development team and customers.

Evolutionary Process Model: Software models which are iterative in nature.

Process Models: Development methodologies used in software development.

Rapid Application Development Model: A model that combines the benefits of iterative and incremental models.

The Pragmatic Model: Introduced the idea of flexibility and appropriate measures are taken while designing the code for possible modifications and improvements.

The Spiral Model: An evolutionary software process model that was proposed by Boehm in 1987.

V & V: Verification and validation.

Waterfall Model: The Classic Software Lifecycle Model.

Section 2
Model–Driven Engineering

Chapter 9
Modelling, Simulation, and Analysis for Enterprise Architecture

Tony Clark
Middlesex University, UK

Balbir Barn
Middlesex University, UK

Vinay Kulkarni
Tata Consultancy Services, India

ABSTRACT

Modern organizations need to address increasingly complex challenges including how to represent and maintain their business goals using technologies and IT platforms that change on a regular basis. This has led to the development of modelling notations for expressing various aspects of an organization with a view to reducing complexity, increasing technology independence, and supporting analysis. Many of these Enterprise Architecture (EA) modelling notations provide a large number of concepts that support the business analysis but lack precise definitions necessary to perform computer-supported organizational analysis. This chapter reviews the current EA modelling landscape and proposes a simple language for the practical support of EA simulation including business alignment in terms of executing a collection of goals against prototype execution.

INTRODUCTION

Business and IT alignment has remained an ongoing concern for organizations since the 1980s (Luftman, 2000). Throughout this period, researchers have addressed the importance of alignment and in particular the need for congruence between business strategy and IT strategy (Chan & Reich, 2007). While there are multiple definitions for business and IT alignment (BIA) including integration, linkage, bridge, fusion or even fit, most are consistent with the definition derived from the *Strategic Alignment Model* (SAM) (Henderson & Venkatraman, 1993). They state

DOI: 10.4018/978-1-4666-6359-6.ch009

that alignment is the degree of fit and integration among business strategy, IT strategy, business infrastructure, and IT infrastructure.

Enterprise Architecture (EA) aims to capture the essentials of a business, its IT and its evolution, and to support analysis of this information: *it is a coherent whole of principles, methods, and models that are used in the design and realization of an enterprise's organizational structure, business processes, information systems and infrastructure.* (Lankhorst, 2009). In addition to presenting a coherent explanation of the *what*, *why* and *how* of a business, EA aims to support specific types of business analysis including: alignment between business functions and IT systems, and business change describing the current state of a business (as-is) and a desired state of a business (to-be). Thus EA has the potential to serve as the basis of machinery that can be used to address BIA (Wang, Zhou & Jiang, 2008; Pereira & Sousa, 2005).

Alignment occurs in the context of an organization and it is relevant to explore the notion of an organization to better understand this context. Ours is an organizational society such that organizations are the dominant characteristic of modern societies. One rationale for the existence of organizations posited by Carley and Gassser is that they exist to overcome the cognitive, physical, temporal and institutional limitations of individual (Carley and Gasser, 1999). While there are many ways in which these limitations can be overcome and the structure, form or architecture of an organization contributes to such efforts, decades of research indicate that there is no optimal organizational design. Instead, the challenge morphs into one of adaptability and response to change. First we present here a necessarily brief overview of some of the key definitions and perspectives on organizations that underpin how we intend to articulate the concept of an organization in the context of the model driven enterprise. We first begin with a definition of the term organization recognizing that there are multiple definitions depending upon the perspective taken. The definition is reported from (Parsons, 1960).

Organizations are social units (or human groupings) deliberately constructed and reconstructed to seek specific goals.

We explore this definition further by considering how the study of organizations has generally investigated the constituent elements of an organization and three dominant theoretical perspectives informing research. Leavitt identifies some core features of organizations (Leavitt, 1964):

- **Social:** Structure: regularized aspects of relationships among participants in an organization that may be both normative (embodying what ought to be) or factual order (actual structures).
- **Participants:** Individuals who in return for a variety of inducements make contributions to the organization. Participants may belong to more than one organization.
- **Goals:** An organizational goal is a desired state of affairs that the organization attempts to realize. Goals are central to how an organization functions and are often vague or very specific.
- **Technology:** This is the means by which work is performed in an organization. Technology can be interpreted as a manufacturing plant, the software systems enabling workers to perform work or even technical knowledge and skills of participants.
- **Environment:** Organizations exist in a specific physical, socio-technical and cultural environment to which they must respond and adapt. All aspects of an organization is influenced and contextualized by the environment. For example, software

systems are purchased from external providers or developed by technicians trained in some other organization.

These features are generic to organizations and can form the basis of extracting key concepts of an organization. (Carley and Gasser, 1999) presents a similar set. Note that these features may vary in some way when viewed through a particular perspective or metaphor. The last century has seen three dominant perspectives (and overlaps) dominating research in organization theory: Organizations as Rational Systems; Organizations as Natural Systems and Organizations as Open Systems. A rational system perspective denotes a focus on efficiency and optimization and ultimately presents a reductionist model. The open systems perspective is of most relevance to us as it ranges from a simple clockwork view (a dynamic system with predetermined motions), cybernetic view (a system capable of self-regulation in terms of externally prescribed criterion such as a thermostat) to an open system (a system capable of self-maintenance based on throughputs of resources such as a living cell) (Buckley, 1967). These models lend themselves to solutions based on technologies around EA.

From this understanding of organizations we can observe three opportunities: Firstly, goals are inherently part of an organization and a model-based solution must support this feature. Secondly, the behavioral aspects of an organization present opportunities for simulation. Technologies such those described in later sections of this chapter are candidate approaches for simulation based systems. Thirdly there is a necessity for structuring a model representation of an organization along dimensions consistent with the characteristics observable of an organization. Our proposal addresses this requirement.

Various informal frameworks have been proposed for expressing EA, business goals and BIA including SAM, TOGAF, ArchiMate, BMM, KAOS and i*. In general these methods and technologies support a wide range of business facing modelling concepts that are appropriate for the business analyst, but that presents problems in terms of a precise analysis of business alignment.

In general, BIA involves comparing business goals with business design. Goals express the *why* of an organization in terms of requirements, motivations, policies and regulations. Business designs express the *how* of an organization either in terms of business processes and information structures, or in terms of configurations of software components. As such, BIA can be viewed as verifying that the operational aspects of a business are correct with respect to the required behaviour.

The view of BIA raises similar issues to software verification where a system implementation must be shown to be correct with respect to a system requirement. Many formal and informal techniques have been developed over the last 40 years that aim to support this process for software development. Our proposal is that these techniques are appropriate for BIA, however they must be modified in order to accommodate the broader nature of organizational architecture.

In particular, it would be interesting to leverage the precise nature of software requirements expressed in formal logic. A significant problem with such an approach is that EA model tend to be discursive and business facing and therefore lack a precise semantics would be necessary for a logic-based language to be used to express the goals. Our proposal is to provide a small and well-defined collection of modelling concepts into which the business concepts can be mapped (Clark, Barn & Oussena, 2012). Given such a precise basis, business goals can then be expressed using a formal language.

Business goals fall into two different areas: behavioural requirements for an organization and non-functional requirements. Our claim is that a precise basis for an EA model is necessary to facilitate definitions and analysis of both of these types of goal. In order to effectively express non-functional business goals, the organizational model must be both precise and provide a means to measure a given non-functional property as a function of the model (or its semantics). For example, a quality based attribute such as reliability requires that the model associate each structural and behavioural feature of the organization with a reliability function such that a goal can be expressed in terms of an invariant over the value of the function, or a relative change in the case of an as-is and to-be business change. This chapter does not address non-functional goals, however our approach is described in (Barn & Clark, 2012).

Behavioural goals express a required behaviour for an organization. Work on intentional systems development such as KAOS has proposed a formal language for expressing behavioural goals similar to that used for specifying the dynamic behaviour of software systems. Having expressed the behavioural goal, the question arises: how to achieve BIA?

Having represented the goal in a precise way, it follows that the organizational architecture must be represented in a precise way to support BIA. However, there is a lack of consensus regarding a precise language for EA since, as described above, current EA languages tend to be business facing and to provide a rich collection of (often overlapping) business modelling concepts.

Furthermore, having such a precise basis for both what and how in EA does not guarantee an effective method for automatic BIA since computer based formal verification is notoriously difficult to scale. There are two important reasons for this related to the size of the search space generated by non-trivial system definitions. Firstly, in order to control a search engine that seeks out an alignment proof, the human engineer requires great skill in expressing the verification criteria. Often the results of a verification proof need to be interpreted by an expert. Secondly, in general automatic verification is undecidable which means in practice that it is not possible to know a priori whether an automatic proof system will terminate or not. Whilst formal verification techniques may be very successful for very specific areas, it is difficult to see how they could be applied to current BIA problems in general. Although fully automatic verification may not be immediately applicable for BIA, partial techniques may be useful.

Our approach, called LEAP, provides such a precise basis for both goals and architectures. Rather than providing an automated proof that the goals and architecture are aligned, LEAP supports the construction of executable models of a system such that the goals can be measured against a prototype simulation. As the simulation is executed using concrete data, the goals are discharged thereby providing a trace of the system execution including evidence that the system is behaving correctly. Incorrect behaviour shows up as an unsatisfied goal and can be traced back through the simulation.

Our contribution is to provide a precise basis for both goals and architectures and an approach to BIA based on simulation. This chapter reviews technologies for EA and for intentional modelling, introduces LEAP and the mechanisms for BIA and shows how the approach works using a simple case study.

BACKGROUND

Enterprise Architecture

Enterprise Architecture (EA) aims to capture the essentials of a business, its IT and its evolution, and to support analysis of this information. A key objective of EA is being able to provide a holistic understanding of all aspects of a business, connecting the business drivers and the surrounding business environment, through the business processes, organizational units, roles and responsibilities, to the underlying IT systems that the business relies on. In addition to presenting a coherent explanation of the *what*, *why* and *how* of a business, EA aims to support specific types of business analysis including

(Ekstedt, Johnson, Plazaola, Silva, & Lilieskold, 2004; Reige & Aier, 2009; Niemann, 2006; Butcher, T., Fischer, Kurpjuweit & Winter, 2006): *alignment* between business functions and IT systems; *business change* describing the current state of a business (*as-is*) and a desired state of a business (*to-be*); *maintenance* the de-installation and disposal, upgrading, procurement and integration of systems including the prioritization of maintenance needs; *quality* by managing and determining the quality attributes for aspects of the business such as security, performance to ensure a certain level of quality to meet the needs of the business; *acquisition and mergers* describing the alignment of businesses and the effect on both when they merge; *compliance* in terms of a regulatory framework, e.g. Sarbanes-Oxley; *strategic planning* including corporate strategy planning, business process optimization, business continuity planning, IT management.

EA has its origins in Zachman's original EA framework (Zachman, 1999) while other leading examples include the Open Group Architecture Framework (TOGAF) (Spencer, 2004) and the framework promulgated by the Department of Defense (DoDAF) (Wisnosky & Vogel, 2004). In addition to frameworks that describe the nature of models required for EA, modelling languages specifically designed for EA have also emerged. One leading architecture modelling language is ArchiMate (Lankhorst, Proper & Jonkers, 2010).

A modern enterprise can be thought of as being constructed of three key layers and three key aspects as shown in Figure 1 (Jonkers, Lankhorst, Buuren, Bonsangue & Van Der Torre, 2004). The business layer contains intentional features such as business goals, the essential information required by the organization and the high-level structure of the organizational units. The application layer describes the data, resources and functionality necessary to realize the business directives, and the infrastructure layer describes the physical systems on which the organization runs.

EA Modelling

The analysis of modern organizations is supported by the construction of EA models that describe various features of the organization shown in Figure 1. Figure 2 shows an idealized EA model that includes many features supported by current technologies. Intentional modeling is used to capture the goals of an organization and is shown in Figure 2 as a goal decomposition tree. Each goal refers to models of the information, resources and organization structure necessary to express the requirements.

The goal tree is rooted at the high-level requirements of the CXO including the view of the organization information and structures that are appropriate at this level. As the goal tree is decomposed, the requirements become more specific and detailed. The detail increases until the goals become operational in the form of business processes that initially span the organizational structure, but are increasingly refined until they are localized within specific technology units.

The models shown in Figure 2 are idealized in the sense that they are intended to cover all aspects of the organization from top-level management to the operational systems that run the business. The intention is that each level of decomposition represents a view of the business. They are interdependent so that information from the technology

Figure 1. Enterprise architecture concepts

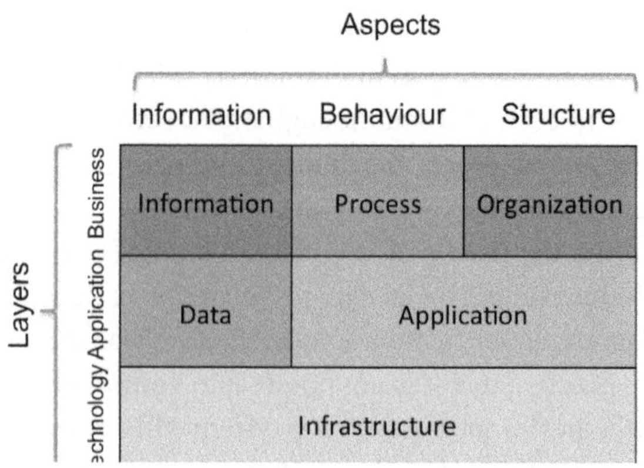

Figure 2. A model driven enterprise

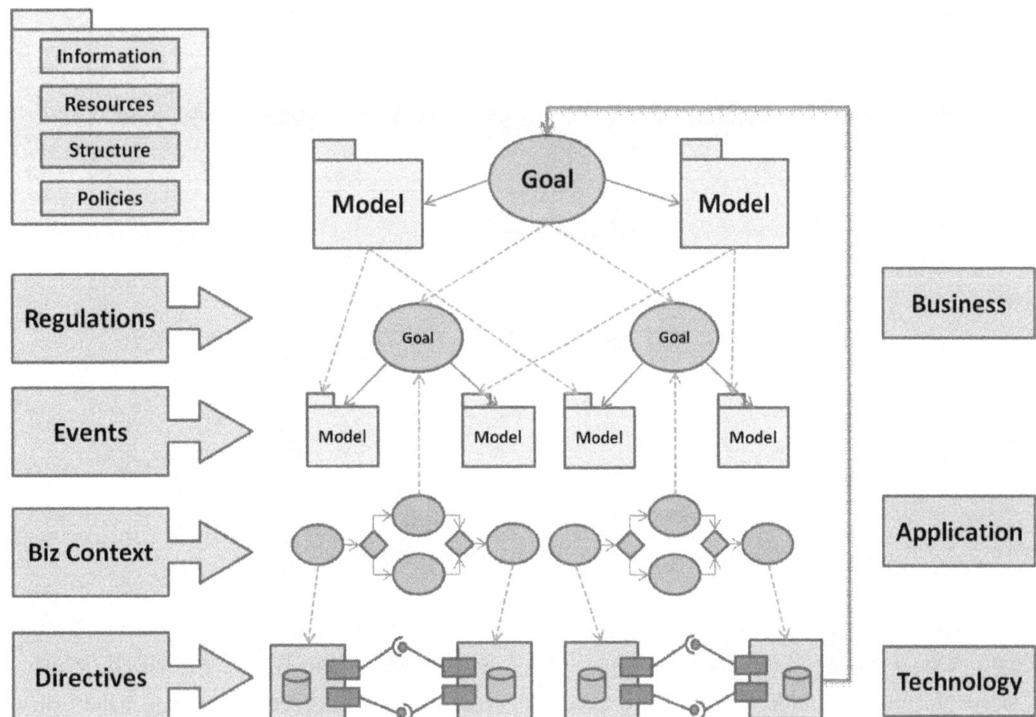

layer can be reported back to the CXO in terms that reflect the goals that the CXO initially expressed.

The rest of this section provides an overview of the current technologies for EA modeling.

ArchiMate

ArchiMate (Lankhorst, Proper & Jonkers, 2010) is a standard managed by the Open Group http://www.opengroup.org/archimate. It consists of a framework of layers and aspects similar to the Zachman framework (Zachman, 1999) that defines a theory or `world view' about the way enterprises are structured. The aspects are described using a set of modelling concepts that constitute a DSML for EA. The framework is described in Figure 3 and is taken from (Engelsman, Quartela, Jonkers & van Sinderen, 2010). The framework distinguishes between the business layer (concerned with products and services offered to customers), the application layer (concerned with the application services that the company implements internally), and the technology layer (concerned with the infrastructure services necessary to run the applications). To model each layer, ArchiMate provides modelling concepts in each of the three layers:

1. Business: actor; role; collaboration; interface; object; process; function; interaction; event; service; representation; meaning; value; product; contract.
2. Application: component; collaboration; interface; object; function; interaction; service.
3. Technology: node; device; network; communication path; interface; software; service; artifact.

Clearly there is a great deal of overlap between the modelling concepts in the different layers; for example, *interface* occurs in all three layers, and *function* occurs in the first two. There are con-

Figure 3. ArchiMate structure

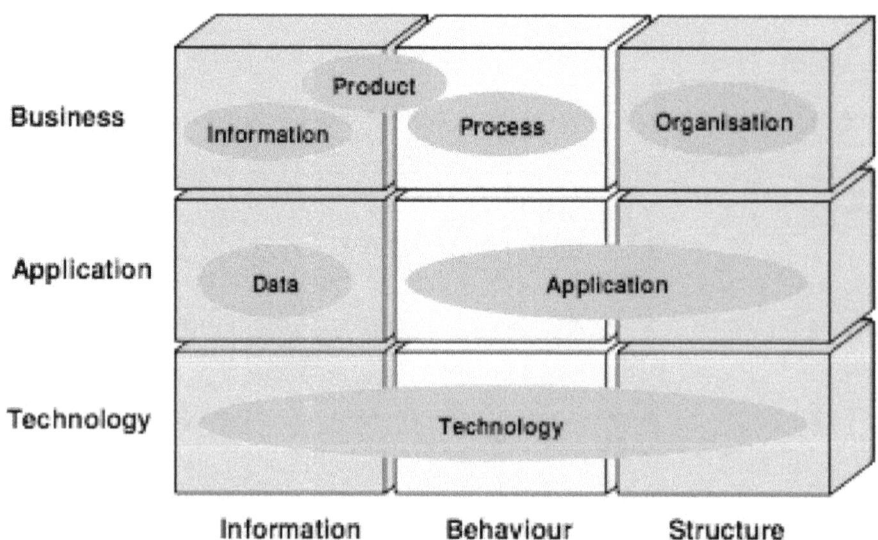

cepts whose meaning would seem to overlap, for example *process*, *service* and *function*. Archimate provides a notation for each of the modelling concepts. The notation has a syntax definition in the form of well-formedness constraints, however there is no semantics in the sense of axiomatic, denotational or operational definitions.

There is a proposal for a UML profile for ArchiMate (Iacob, Jonkers & Wiering, 2004). An overview of the proposal is shown in Figure 4 where the business layer is modelled using class diagrams, the application layer using component diagrams and the technology layer using deployment diagrams. However this does not constitute a semantics since UML itself does not have a precise semantics. The lack of semantics makes it difficult to compare model elements for similarity, difference and redundancy. Furthermore, the lack of semantics makes it difficult to determine the meaning of extensions to the language as proposed below.

The original definition of ArchiMate did not support business motivation. The ARMOR language (Engelsman, Quartela, Jonkers & van Sinderen, 2010) has been proposed as an extension to ArchiMate. The extension introduces goals as shown in Figure 5 and is based on languages such as KAOS, i* and BMM described below. As the model shows, the extension is based on adding goals to use-case actors.

The ARMOR language supports a structural representation of business goals. The authors describe several forms of EA analysis that are supported by the ArchiMate extension including traceability and impact analysis that follows from the structural relationships between goals and other aspects of the ArchiMate model. The details of the goals themselves are expressed using natural language and as such have no semantics that can be processed by a machine.

BMM

The Business Motivation Model (BMM) has been developed by the Business Rules Group[1]. It provides a way of capturing the relationships between what a business aims to achieve, how it proposes to achieve its aims and the issues that will influence the outcome in a positive and negative way. The BMM is essentially an ontology of terms and relationships that would be used by a business analyst when structuring the aspirations

Figure 4. UML profile for Archimate

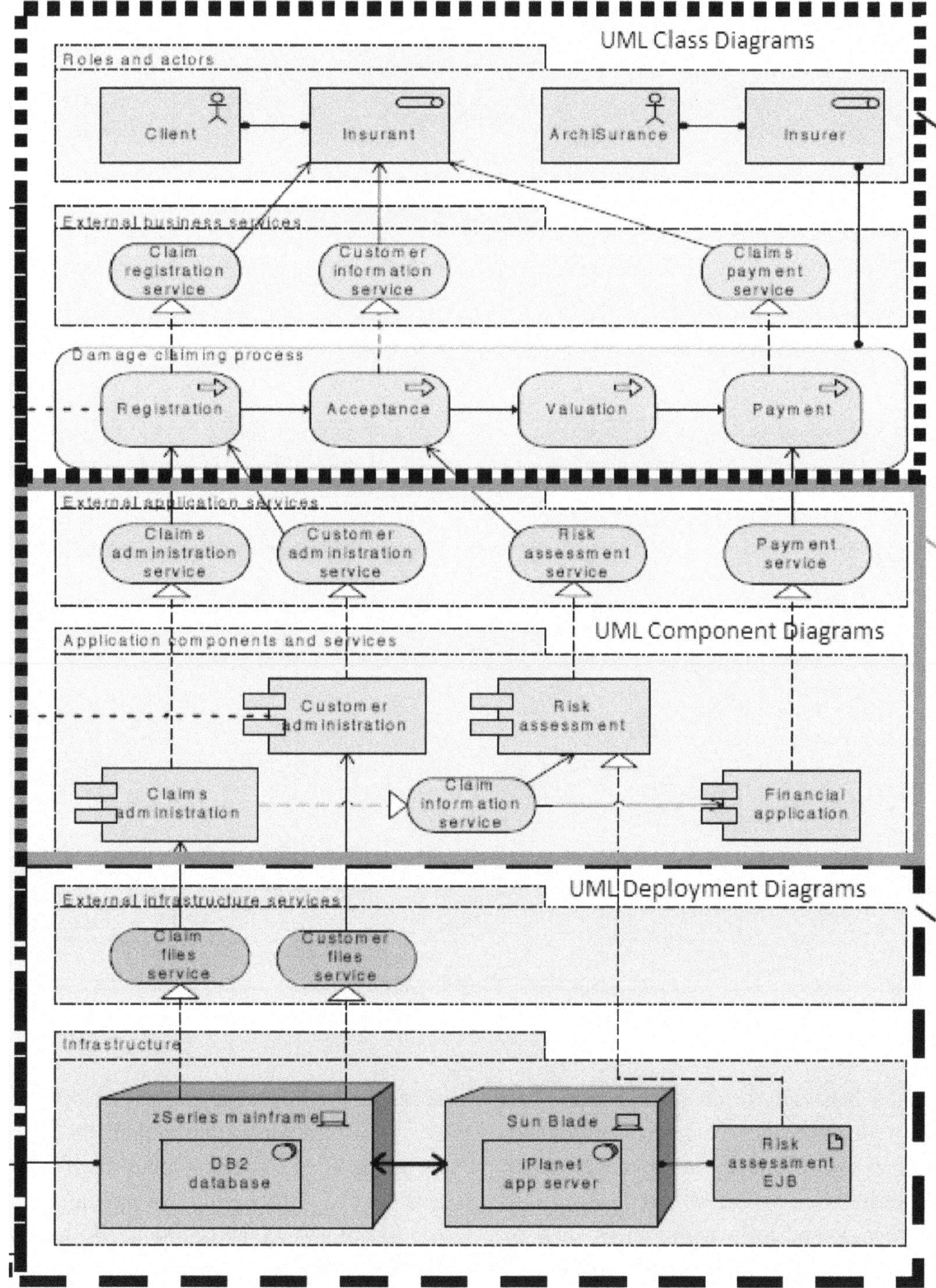

Figure 5. ARMOR extension to ArchiMate

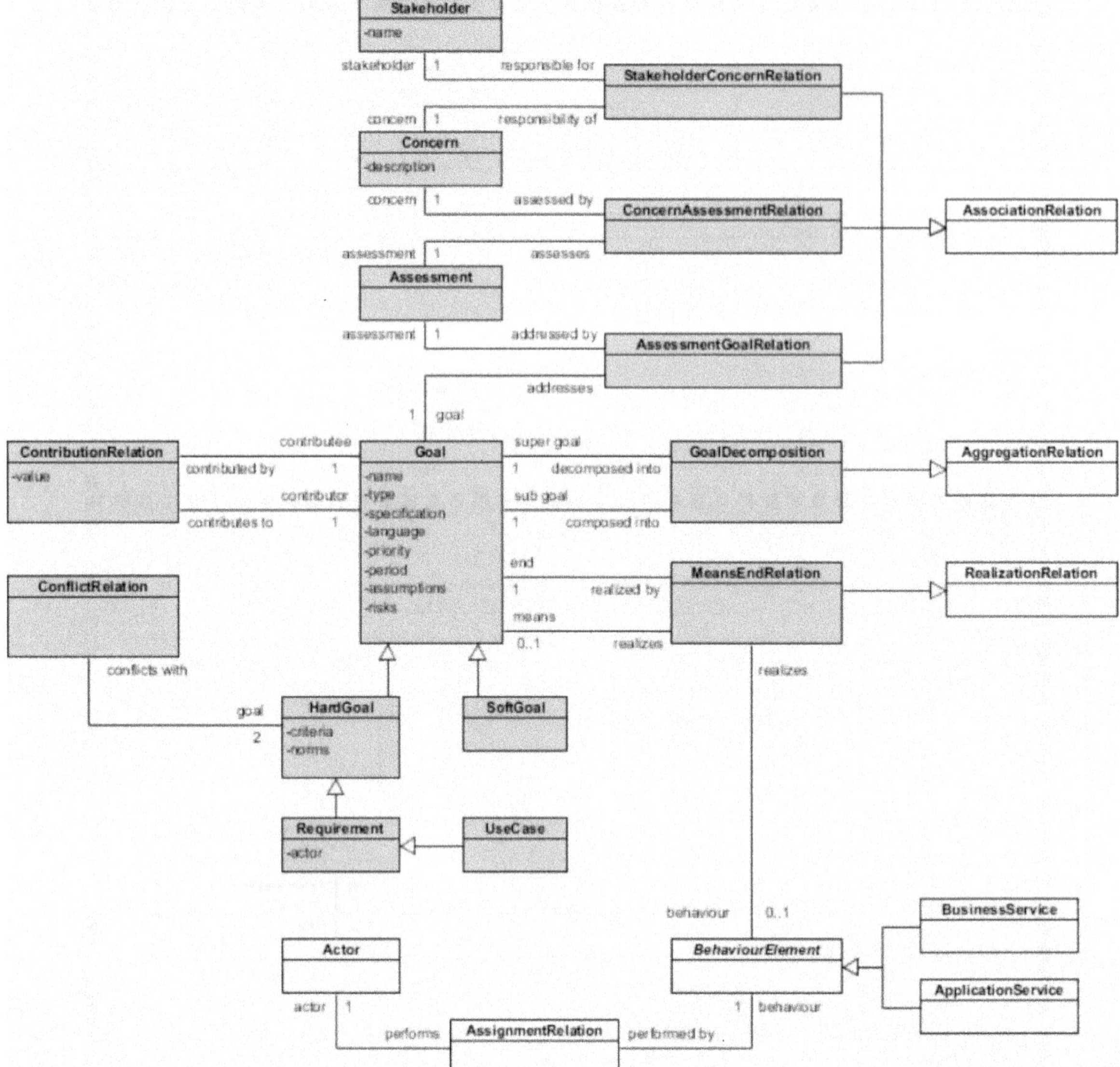

and planned behavior for an organization. For example it distinguishes between aspirational terms such as *ends*, *visions*, *goals* and *objectives*; planning terms such as *means*, *missions*, *strategies* and *tactics*; and influencing terms such as *opportunities*, *threats*, *strengths* and *weaknesses*.

The BMM provides a useful structuring mechanism for other modeling approaches (for example it is one of the technologies that influences the ARMOR language described above). It is a useful structuring mechanism that can be used as the basis of structural analysis of intentional aspects of EA modeling, for example an *end* is *realized* by a *means* and is *impacted* by a *weakness*. However, there is no precisely defined meaning to these terms and relationships: the detail is left to the individual BMM application, or is left up to user interpretation.

TOGAF

TOGAF[2] is a large-scale EA meta-model and modeling method that consists of six main parts as described in Figure 6 (Ernst, Matthes, Ramache & Schweda, 2009). TOGAF includes the Architecture Development Method (ADM) that describes how to derive an organization-specific EA that addresses business architecture. Various frameworks are provided including the Architecture Content Framework that describes deliverables, artifacts; the Enterprise Continuum that provides a repository for EA reuse; the Architecture Capability Framework containing resources to help the architect establish EA practice within an organization.

As such is a huge integrated resource that supports all aspects of the EA process. The language and processes are very detailed, but lack the precision that would be necessary to perform computer aided BIA.

KAOS

KAOS[3] is a language for expressing system requirements. It is organized as a goal decomposition tree where the goals are linked to agents that are responsible for achieving their functional and non-functional specifications. Like BMM, KAOS includes a representation for conflicting goals and issues such as obstacles to goal satisfaction.

KAOS has an associated tool called Objectiver that can be used to construct KAOS models and to analyse various structural properties. Figure 6 shows an example KAOS model (Ponsard & Devroey, 2011). The model shows a goal decomposition tree rooted at the Maintain[SafeOperationofMine] goal. The goals are linked to agents (for example the PumpController) that are responsible for achieving or maintaining the requirements expressed by the goal.

The authors (Ponsard & Devroey, 2011) observe that many behavioural goals can be expressed

Figure 6. TOGAF architectural development method cycle

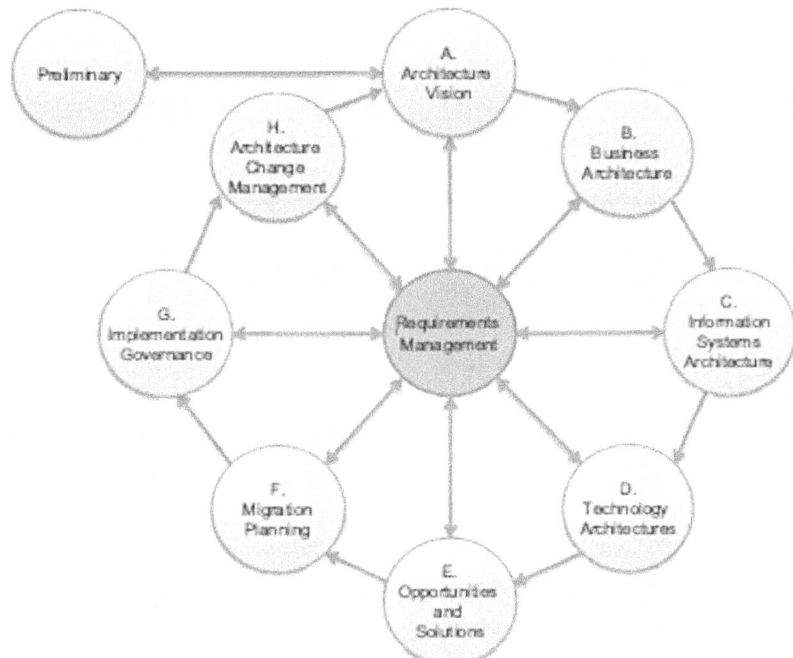

Figure 7. An example KAOS model

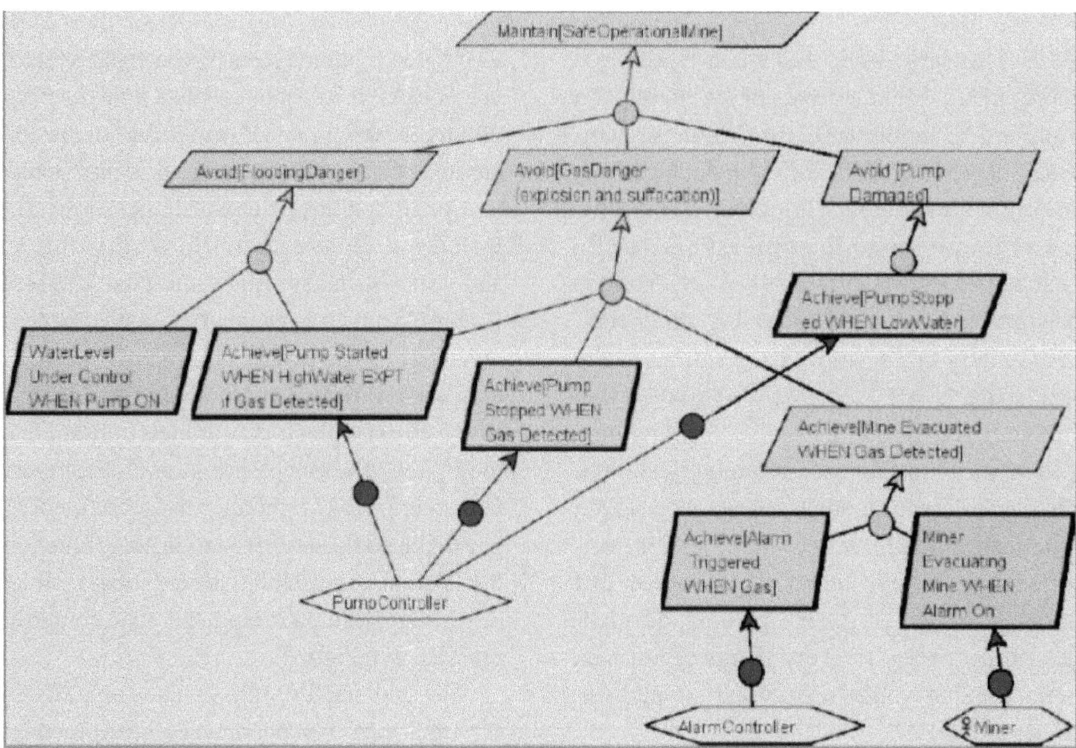

using temporal logic that expresses constraints over the ongoing behavior of the agents. Although KAOS does not provide explicit support for any formal languages, the authors show how temporal logic formulas can be added to KAOS models and subsequently translated into the B language that provides support for formal verification. This is a very attractive approach since the B language and its associated tooling is mature and supports a wide range of analysis. However this approach seems to be related to systems requirements and works at the general level. It is not clear how this approach will scale as over large EA models.

i*

i* (Liu, Yu & Myopoulos, 2003) is a goal-oriented requirements engineering notation and method that, unlike KAOS above, includes a description of who interacts with a system and answers the question: *what do they want to achieve?* Each actor in a system has goals that they want to achieve (unlike KAOS where there is a single goal that is decomposed and linked to agents that are responsible for achieving the leaf goals). Like KAOS, goals may be hard or soft meaning that they either refer to system behaviour or refer to non-functional requirements such as system quality attributes. Like KAOS, i* goals are decomposed and ultimately linked to tasks that are responsible for accomplishing the goal.

Like the other modeling approaches described above, i* supports structural analysis that shows which actors are related to which tasks, which actors are involved in the system, their inter-dependencies and what their respective expectations are.

LEAP

LEAP is an executable modelling language and associated tool that aims to provide a basis for component-based development. LEAP is based on a collection of simple concepts that are intended to span the development life-cycle from requirements through analysis, animation and eventually deployment. LEAP is currently in development (Clark & Barn, 2012; Clark, Barn & Oussena, 2012; Clark, Barn & Oussena, 2011) and has been applied to case studies including the design of an information system to support universities comply with UK Border Agency regulations, organizational change in universities in order to achieve non-functional requirements, and modelling of a crisis management system[4].

Our aim with LEAP is to support both enterprise models and system models using the same collection of features. Our view is that such systems can be represented as hierarchically organized collaborating components expressed using a suitable collection of modelling languages. Therefore, a specification language is provided that expresses conditions over static and dynamic features of component models. Components manage their own internal state as a form of *knowledge base* and a deductive theory language is provided together with a functional language for expressing behaviour. Declarative component behaviour can be achieved using a state-machine language together with a language for event driven rules. Our purpose in this chapter is to show how a simple and precise definition of components together with behavioural goals can provide a basis for architecture alignment.

LEAP takes the form of a textual modeling language and an associated tool. Figure 8 is a snapshot of the tool that shows the key features. The top-left panel is a view of the elements in a LEAP model that has been loaded into the tool. The user can browse models, edit properties and invoke tool functionality from this panel. The bottom left panel shows a view of the file system showing LEAP source code. A LEAP model consists of one or more source files that can be loaded from this panel.

Two top-right panels show diagram views of the loaded model. The left diagram panel shows goals and the right diagram panel shows an information model. Below that is a text editor panel that contains the source code of part of the LEAP model. The editor provides syntax support for the LEAP language. Below the editor is a property editor for LEAP model elements and a console window for output.

LEAP models are organized as one or more components. A component has a message interface and can consume messages sent to its input ports and produce messages on its output ports. Connectors from output ports to input ports are used to link components together. Components are viewed as black boxes that independently consume and produce messages.

Internally, components manage a state that consists of a list of data terms. Message handlers can change the state of a component and produce output messages. Rules monitor the state of a component and fire actions when rule-patterns are satisfied. Messages are handled using either state machines (when the behaviour lends itself to such a structure) or a collection of operations (when behaviour is complex).

Components are used to describe system architecture. In the degenerate case, a system can be viewed as a single LEAP component whose message interface implements the system functionality and its observable outputs. Multiple components can be used to represent a system at increasing levels of detail, where each component represents groupings such as logical system functionality, physical IT systems, organizational units, people, etc.

The state of a component is expressed in terms of a collection of data terms that are instances of an information model owned by the component. An information model consists of classes and associations. The model is a data type for a col-

Figure 8. LEAP tool

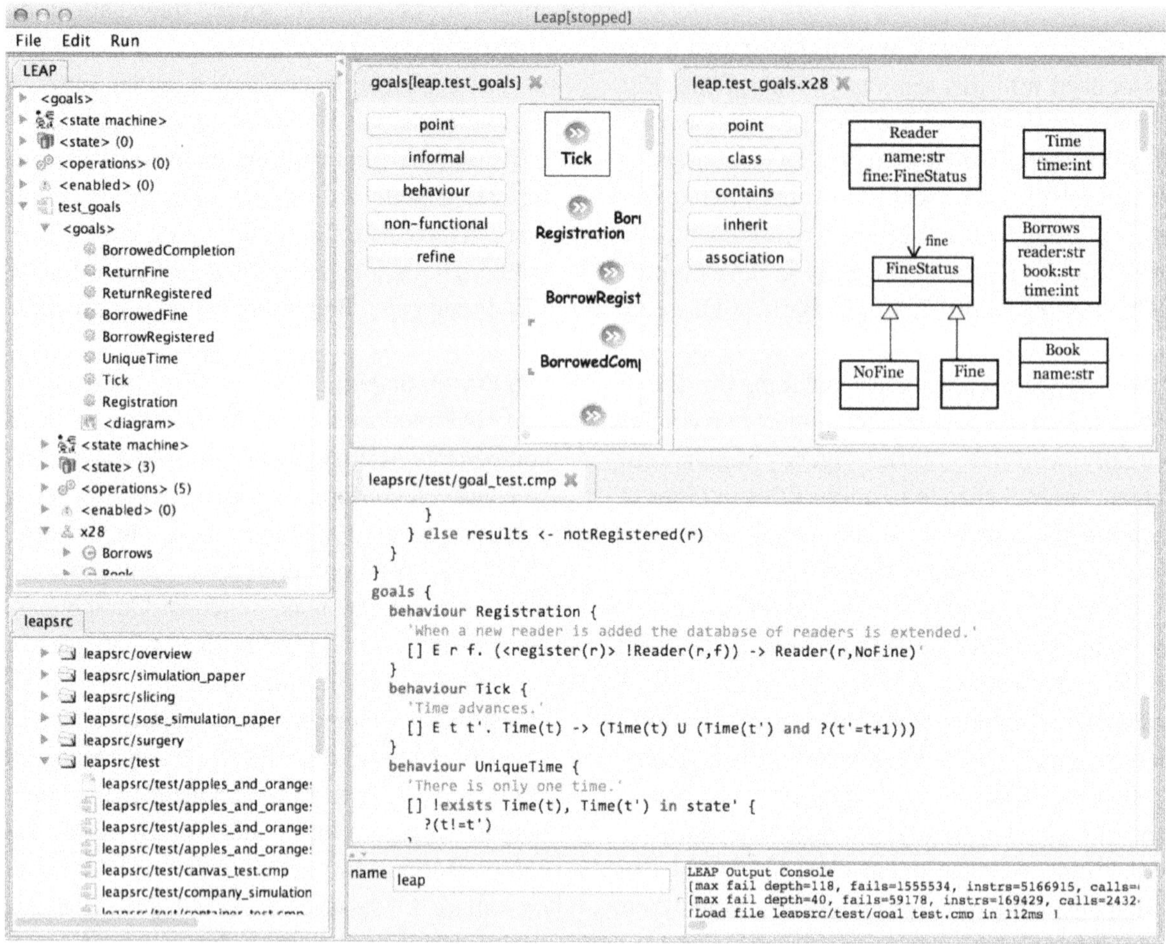

lection of data values that are *terms*. A term is equivalent to a row in a relational database table and the intention is that LEAP will be able to interface to databases in the future. The information model defines a structure over the database tables so that the list of raw terms can be viewed as structured data.

The behaviour of a component is implemented in a number of ways, the least structured of which is as an operation. An operation is a named function that will be invoked when a message with the same name is processed. The body of the function can access and update the state of the component and can produce output messages. LEAP provides a rich collection of expression language for implementing operation bodies. The state of a component is available to an operation as a list of terms and therefore LEAP provides a rich collection of list-processing expressions including list-comprehensions.

The required behaviour of a component is specified using goals. Like other systems for intentional modelling, LEAP goal models are organized as a decomposition tree where the leaves of the tree are specific requirements that must be achieved by components. LEAP supports non-functional and functional goals. This chapter deals only with functional goals.

Functional goals can be expressed using a temporal logic that places constraints on the behaviour of components. Each component is a self-contained black box that processes messages received at input ports and produces messages at output ports. Multiple components are connected so that messages sent to their output ports are transferred to the input ports of one or more target components. Messages are processed from the input port one at a time. Operations, state machines or data driven rules can control the behaviour of a component. The examples in this chapter use operations to control a component and the principles apply to all other modes of behaviour definition.

When a message is processed, it is removed from the input queue and matched against an operation with the same name. The operation arguments are bound from the contents of the message and the body of the operation is performed. The operation body has access to the internal state of the component and may change it and may produce output messages. An output message may be *synchronous* or *asynchronous*. A synchronous message causes the active component to halt and wait for the response from the message; an asynchronous message is added to the output queue and execution continues without waiting for the result. All operations produce a result. In the case of an asynchronous message the result is ignored. In the case of a synchronous message, the source of the message is a component whose execution is resumed.

A functional goal is a condition on the behaviour of a component. The behaviour is a sequence of state transitions that are caused by messages being consumed and produced. We use a temporal logic that can express properties over sub-sequences of behaviour; allowing, for example, the condition that after a given message is processed then the component will eventually achieve a satisfactory state. The rest of this section introduces the key features of LEAP using some simple examples.

Invariants

Figure 9 shows a simple example of a goal being used to define an invariant over the state of a component. A component definition consists of a collection of optional sub-clauses that contain different aspects of the component. The example initialises the state of the component to contain a single term of the form Value(0). Each term has a type (in this case Value) and some argument values (in this case 0). The tree-view on the left shows the model after it is loaded and the state contains the single term.

A component defines any number of input and output ports. In the example there is a single input port called actions. A port has an interface that defined the type signatures of the messages that can be processed by the port. In this case there are two asynchronous messages called add and sub respectively.

The example goals clause defines the functional requirements for the component. In this case it is an invariant that requires the state of the component to contain an event integer. We know it is an invariant because of the form of the logical expression: []P. The [] operator applies to a logical statement P and states that P must hold *at all times from this time on*. Time is measured in terms of message processing, when a component handles a message it moves from one time frame to the next. If a statement holds at all times from now on then it must hold no matter what messages are processed. Since the goal named Inv_even has no qualifier before the [] operator then it holds at time 0, therefore it always holds, i.e. it is an *invariant*.

The operations clause defines the behaviour of the component. A component should define operations for all messages that it can handle, but may also define auxiliary operations that are used as helpers. In this case the component defines operations that add and subtract 2 from

Figure 9. Example invariant

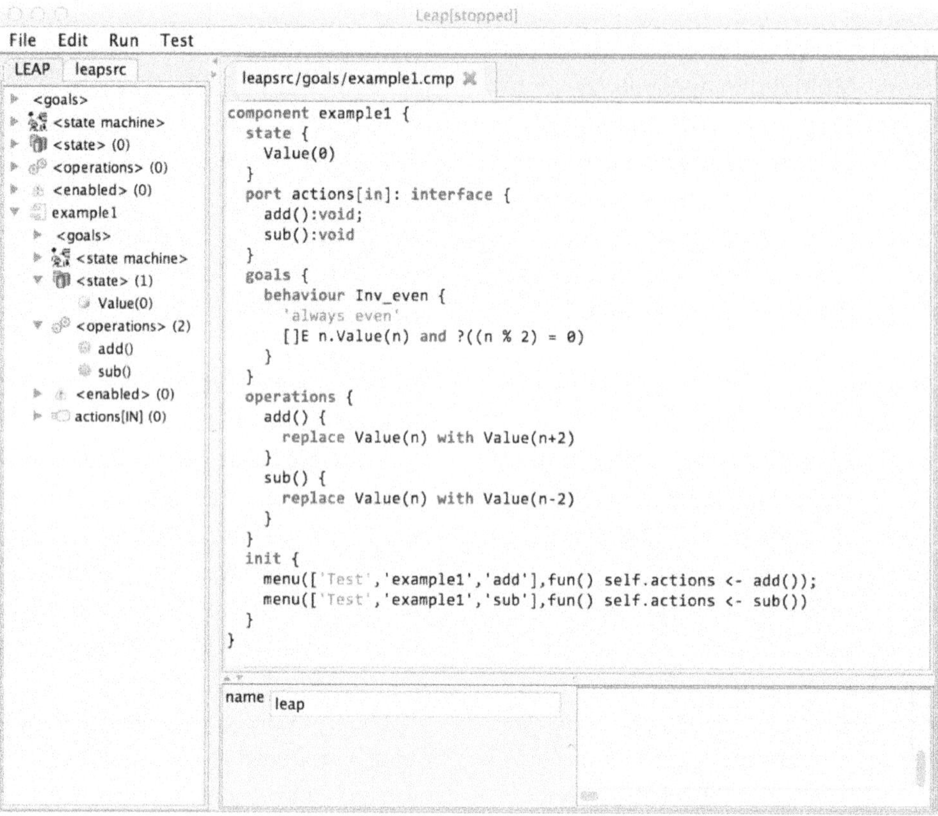

the integer value in its local state. The body of the operations use a *replace* command (an expression whose value is ignored) to remove the current value and add a new value.

LEAP uses pattern matching to process lists of values. The state of a component is managed as a list of terms and a replace command uses a pattern Value(n) to match against the list and to extract the value n. Operationally, the pattern is matched against every term in the list until a match is found. In this case the component's state is always a list with a single element.

The final clause is used to initialize the component. It is evaluated when the component is loaded. In this case it is used to add two items to the LEAP tool menu bar that allow us to test the component by sending it messages. The function menu takes two arguments: a list of strings that name the menu item using nested menus and a function to be called when the menu item is selected. In both cases the function sends a message to an input port, where self is used by a component to refer to itself.

Figure 10 shows a screenshot after the message add (selected via the menu Test) is processed. The state change can be seen in the browser window on the left. In addition to processing the message, LEAP has applied the goals to the simulation. This is shown in the output window in the bottom right where the message delivery is recorded and the reduction of the invariant is shown.

Initially, each goal is in an *outstanding* state. This means that the goal has yet to be satisfied or *discharged*. When a message is processed a state change occurs. All outstanding goals are processed by checking that they hold with respect to the state change. If a goal is fully satisfied by the state change then it becomes *discharged* and

Figure 10. Processing a message

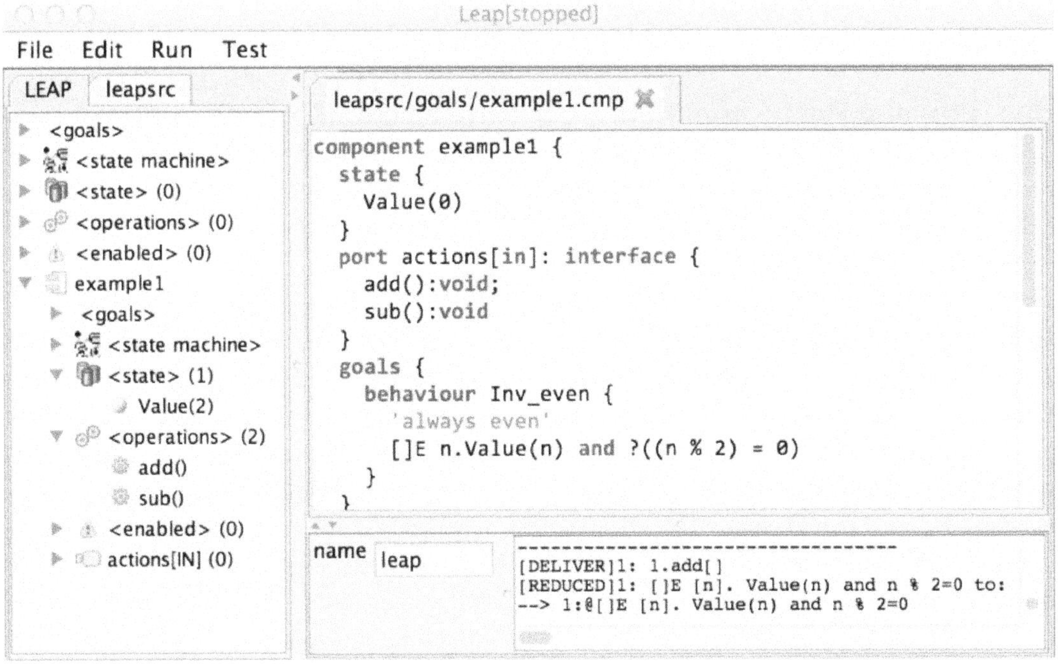

will take not further part in the component execution. If the goal is false then it *fails*, which means that the component cannot satisfy its initial set of goals. Otherwise, it may be the case that the goal cannot be fully satisfied because it needs to know about future state changes. If this is the case then the goals is *reduced* by transforming it into a simpler form that is then outstanding with respect to future message processing.

Consider the Inv_even goal. It has the form [] P which means that it must hold for the current state change. In order to work out how to apply this goal, it is transformed into the following equivalent form P and @[]P. Which states that P must hold now and in the next state change []P must hold. The temporal logic operator @ applies to condition Q and requires Q to hold in the next state change.

In order to check P and @[]P we can check each half of the conjunction separately. In this case P is the formula E n.Value(n) and ?((n % 2) = 0). A formula of the form E n.Q is used to require that the variable n is completely new and cannot be confused with any other variable called n in Q. The formula Q is a conjunction that can be tested in the current state change. The term Value(n) requires that there is a term that matches the pattern in the state before the change occurs. The formula ?((n % 2) = 0) requires that the value of n is even. Given the current state of the component is Value(0) before the state change, the left hand of the conjunction is discharged.

That leaves the other half of the conjunction: @[]P. Since this formula starts with an @, it is not possible to check it with respect to the first state change. Therefore the formula @[]P is reduced to []P as shown in the LEAP output console. This is the original goal, therefore it will be checked in the next and all subsequent state changes, requiring that the component always contains an even value. Testing via the menu operations will verify that no matter ow many add and sub messages are sent to the component the formula Value(n) and ?((n % 2) = 0) is always satisfied.

If we modify the definition one of the operations to be incorrect then the console will flag this up (shown in Box 1).

Actions, Pre- and Post-Conditions

Components perform state changes in response to handling messages. A behavioural goal that expresses a condition in terms of such a change is a formula of the form <m>P -> Q where m is a pattern that matches the message that is being handled, P is a pre-condition and Q is post-condition. Generally, a pre-condition is a formula that relates m to the state of the component before the corresponding operation is invoked. A post-condition is a formula that expresses a condition on the state of the component after the operation has completed. If a pre-post condition holds at all times then the formula has the form []<m>P -> Q.

Figure 11 shows an example of a behavioural goal that specifies a single operation. The goal Pre_post_add contains a formula of the form []<m>P -> Q where m is the message pattern add(), P is a state pattern Value(n) and Q is a conjunction Value(m) in state' and ?(m=n+1). The formula applies every time the component processes an add() message. The pre-condition requires that there is a value n in the state and the post-condition requires that the value has increased by 1. A state formula has the complete form p in e where p is a pattern and e is an expression that evaluates to produce a list of values. The formula is true when the pattern matches a value in the list. There are two special expressions that denote lists of values: state and state'. They both denote the list of terms that is the state of the immediately enclosing component. A goal is checked each time a state transition occurs in a component and the expression state refers to the component's state before the operation is performed and state' refers to the state after the operation has completed. Therefore the formula Value(m) in state' and ?(m=n+1) requires that there is a new value m that is 1 greater than n after the operation add has completed.

Box 1.

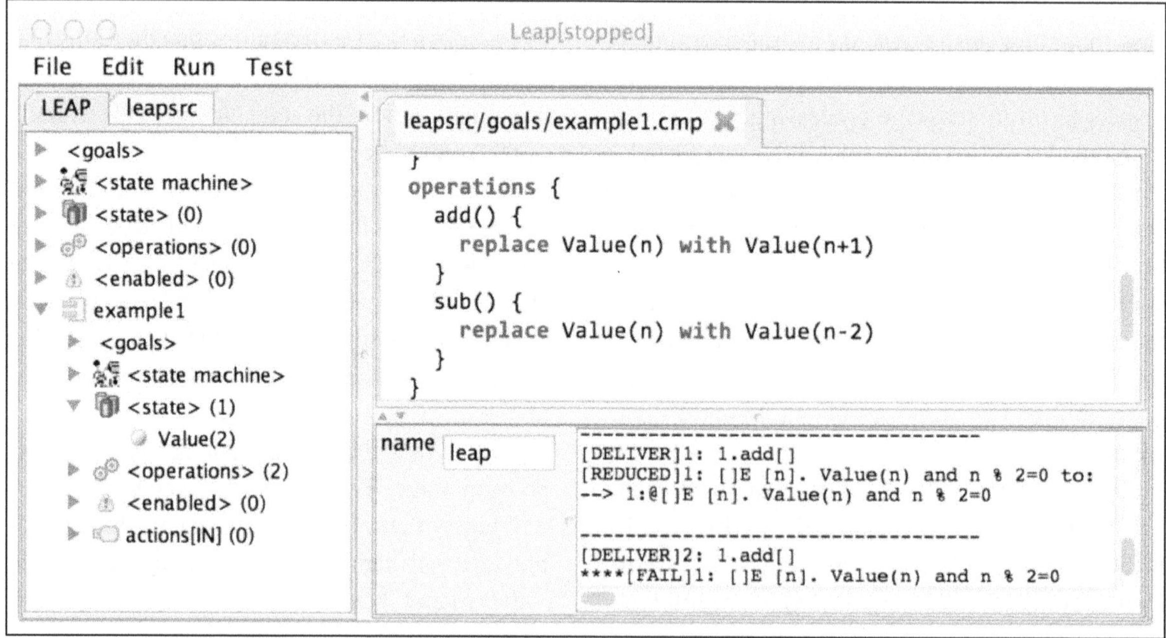
Leap[stopped]
File Edit Run Test
LEAP leapsrc
leapsrc/goals/example1.cmp
<goals>
<state machine>
<state> (0)
<operations> (0)
<enabled> (0)
example1
<goals>
<state machine>
<state> (1)
Value(2)
<operations> (2)
<enabled> (0)
actions[IN] (0)
operations {
add() {
replace Value(n) with Value(n+1)
}
sub() {
replace Value(n) with Value(n-2)
}
}
name leap
[DELIVER]1: 1.add[]
[REDUCED]1: []E [n]. Value(n) and n % 2=0 to:
--> 1:@[]E [n]. Value(n) and n % 2=0
[DELIVER]2: 1.add[]
****[FAIL]1: []E [n]. Value(n) and n % 2=0

Figure 11 shows the state of the component after two messages have been processed. The first message is add() and therefore the goal is checked and reduced. The second message is sub() in which case the goal does not apply to the transition, however it is still reduced because of the operator [].

The Future

The previous sections have shown how behavioural goals express formulas that must always hold and which hold over a single state transition in a component. Sometimes an action will occur in a situation where we require a situation to be achieved *at some time in the future*. A formula that can express such a condition has the form <>P. In this case the formula P may hold immediately, may hold after the next state transition, after two more state transitions etc. Once P is achieved, the formula <>P is discharged.

Suppose that we want a component that manages a numeric value that is increased and decreased in response to messages. For each increase we would like to ensure that the value is eventually decreased to return to its current value. Figure 12 shows an example of a goal that requires each add() message to be followed by a sub() message at some time in the future. The formula takes the form of a pre-post condition, there the post-condition is @(<>Value(n)) meaning that in the next state (i.e. not immediately), after any number of state transitions, the integer managed by the component will return to its current value n.

Figure 11. Actions with pre and post-conditions

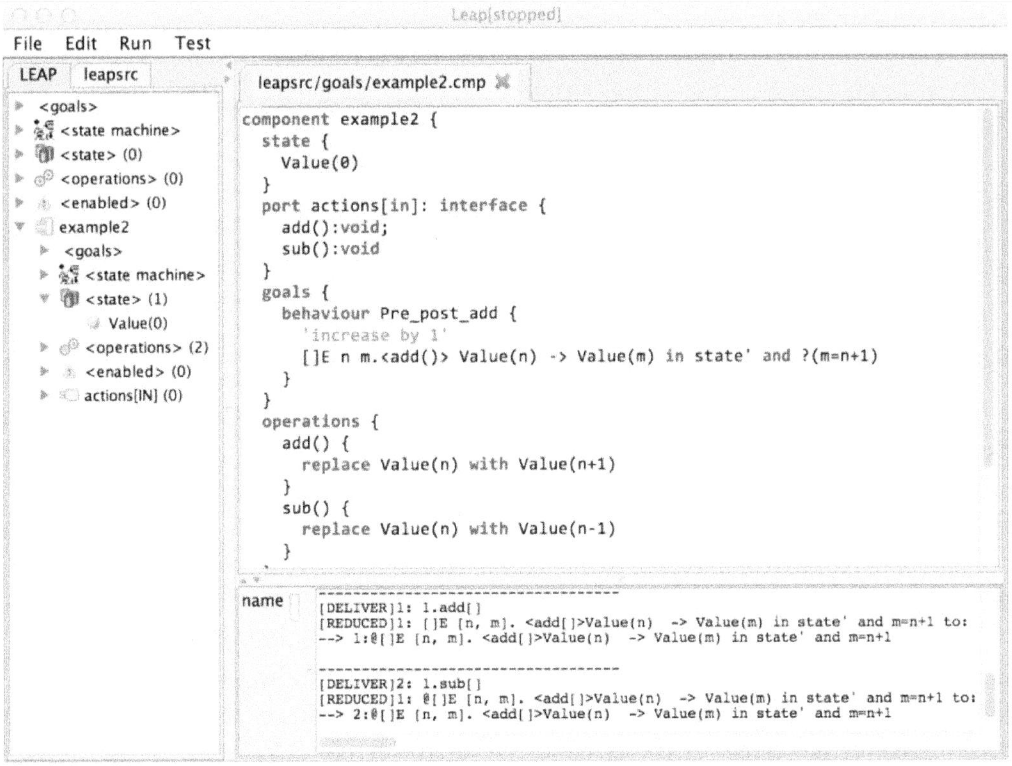

```
component example2 {
  state {
    Value(0)
  }
  port actions[in]: interface {
    add():void;
    sub():void
  }
  goals {
    behaviour Pre_post_add {
      'increase by 1'
      []E n m.<add()> Value(n) -> Value(m) in state' and ?(m=n+1)
    }
  }
  operations {
    add() {
      replace Value(n) with Value(n+1)
    }
    sub() {
      replace Value(n) with Value(n-1)
    }
```

```
----------------------------------
[DELIVER]1: 1.add[]
[REDUCED]1: []E [n, m]. <add[]>Value(n)  -> Value(m) in state' and m=n+1 to:
--> 1:@[]E [n, m]. <add[]>Value(n)  -> Value(m) in state' and m=n+1

----------------------------------
[DELIVER]2: 1.sub[]
[REDUCED]1: @[]E [n, m]. <add[]>Value(n)  -> Value(m) in state' and m=n+1 to:
--> 2:@[]E [n, m]. <add[]>Value(n)  -> Value(m) in state' and m=n+1
```

Figure 12. Expressing conditions that eventually hold

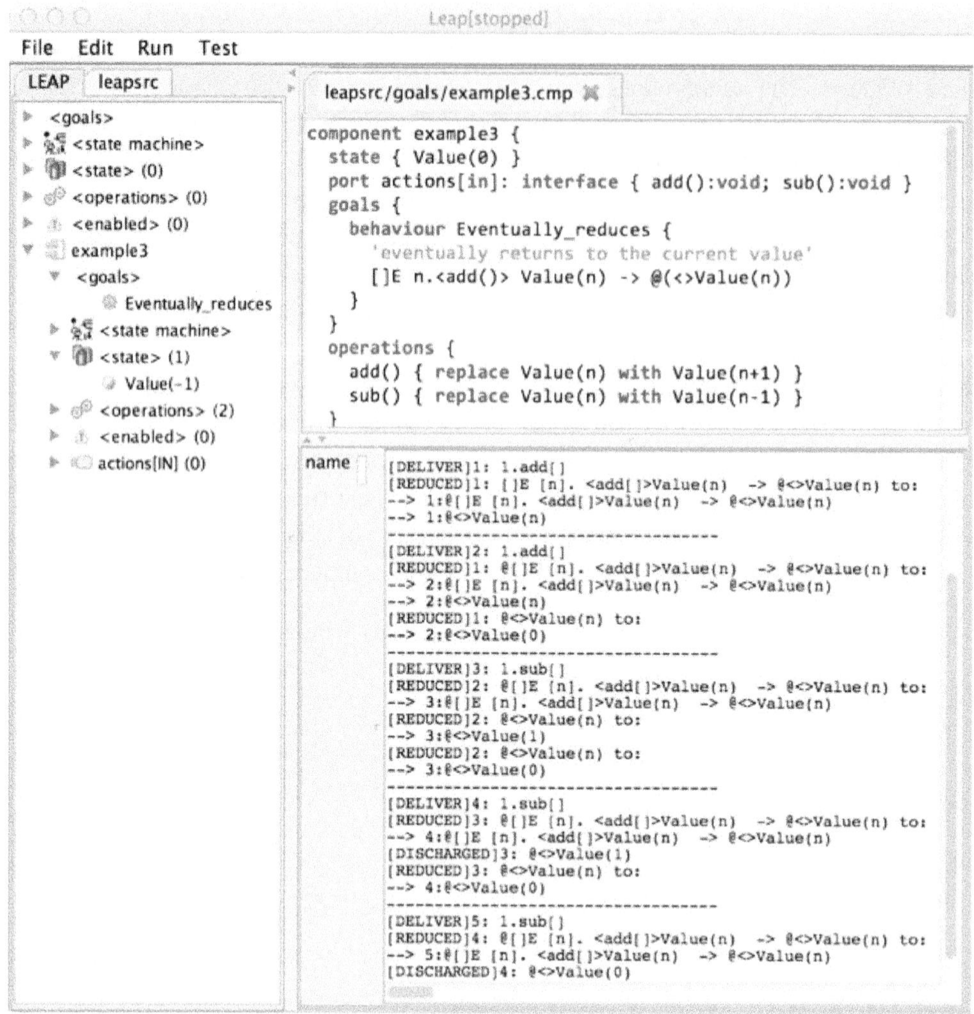

The goal can be seen in action via the LEAP console window. The component is sent two add() messages and then two sub() messages. After each sub() message the outstanding goals are discharged.

Duration

The previous section has shown how a formula can be required to hold at some time in the future. It is useful to be able to express that a formula holds during the interim. This requires the ability to express time durations. The formula P U Q requires that P holds *until* Q holds (after which we do not care whether P holds or not).

Figure 13 shows an example of a formula that, like example 3, requires the value in the component to increase and then return to its original value. The added requirement is that in the interim, the value must always be greater than n, i.e. the value cannot skip over n to become less and then approach n from below.

Figure 13. Time duration

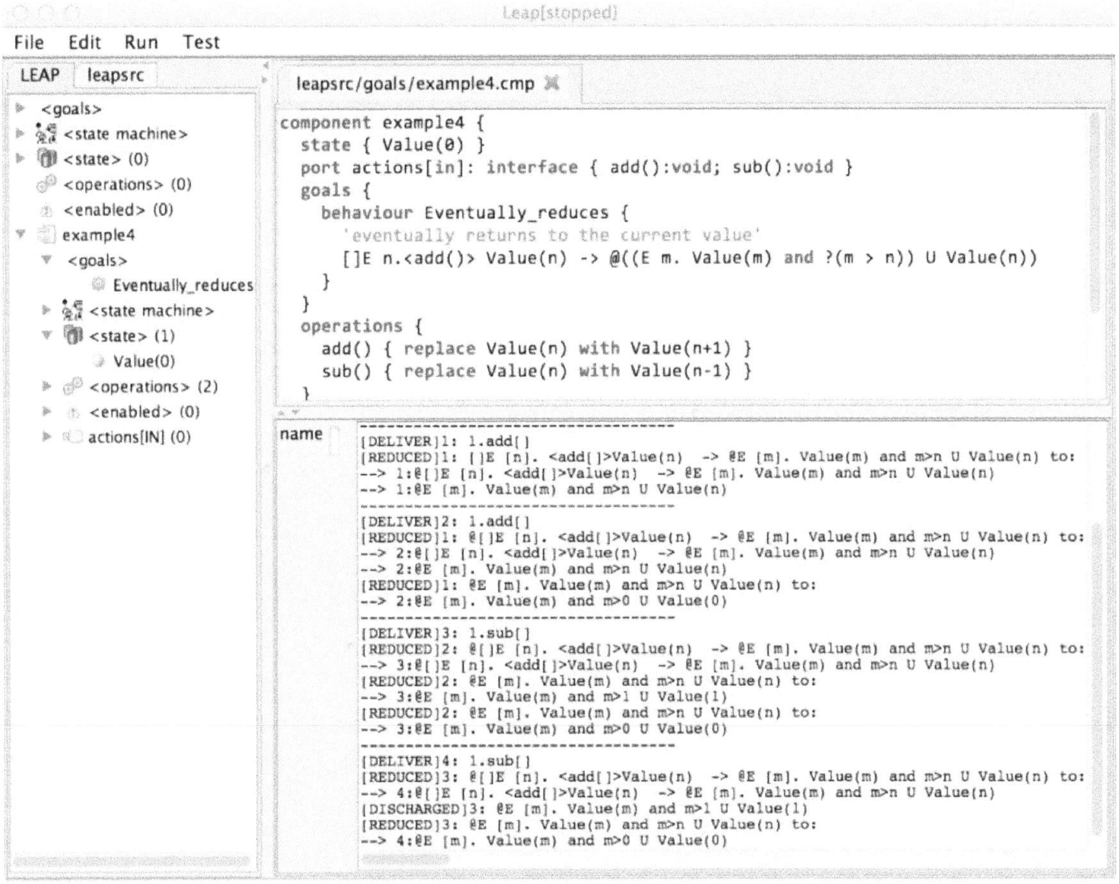

```
component example4 {
  state { Value(0) }
  port actions[in]: interface { add():void; sub():void }
  goals {
    behaviour Eventually_reduces {
      'eventually returns to the current value'
      []E n.<add()> Value(n) -> @((E m. Value(m) and ?(m > n)) U Value(n))
    }
  }
  operations {
    add() { replace Value(n) with Value(n+1) }
    sub() { replace Value(n) with Value(n-1) }
  }
```

Output Messages

Component state transitions involve an input message that is matched to an operation. When the operation is invoked the internal state of the component may change and some output messages may be produced. A goal may with to specify a condition on the output messages. The formula [m] requires that the message pattern m matches an output message in the current time frame. The message pattern may be asynchronous in which case it specifies no return value or synchronous in which case it has the form [p=m] where p is a pattern that is required to match the value returned by the target component.

Figure 14 shows an example of a component that manages an integer value and which specifies a limit on the value. The value may be incremented until the limit is reached when an event is raised by sending a message to the output port named events. The console window shows the result of three increments. The component implementation does not match its specification (shown by printing a message instead of raising the event) and the goal fails.

Nested Components

The examples given above have used goals to specify the behaviour of single components. In general, an enterprise will be organized as a hierarchically decomposed collection of interrelated components. In addition, there needs to be a development method for constructing executable

Figure 14. Asynchronous output messages

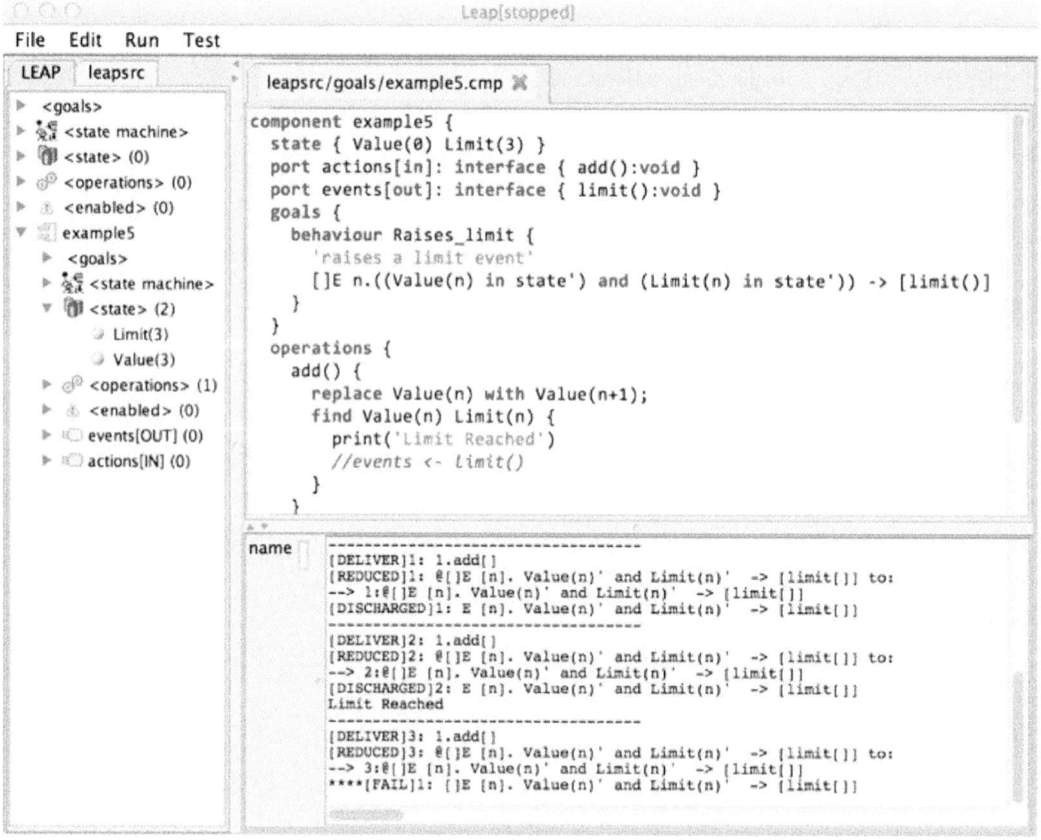

models for organizations. One such method is to start with a single high-level component that uses a single information model to capture the essential features of the organization and then to develop a more sophisticated model by step-wise refinement. This method leads to a requirement for parent goals to place constraints on the behaviour of their children. Furthermore, if we are use LEAP to address the 3-layers for an organization described in Figure 1 then the business layer must be able to control the behaviour of components defined at the technology layer.

Each LEAP goal is owned by a component and may refer to the component's children. Any state change in a child causes the goals of its parent (transitively) to be checked. A parent can refer to the state of its children by name. If a child is called c then the parent may refer to its pre-state as c.state and its post-state as c.state'.

Consider a simple example that requires a parent component to keep two children in sync. Each child maintains a counter and the parent can change each child independently by sending it messages. This example also provides an opportunity to explain another feature of LEAP: higher-order components. Although the parent component has two children, they have the same structure and behaviour. Therefore it makes sense to have a single definition for a child component that is parameterized with respect to the differences.

Figure 15 shows an example LEAP function definition. The function maps a component name

Figure 15. A component template

```
Leap[stopped]
File  Edit  Run
leapsrc/goals/example6/mk_child.op
mk_child(name) {
  component {
    state { Value(0) }
    port commands[in]: interface { add():void }
    operations {
      add() { replace Value(n) with Value(n+1) }
    }
    init {
      menu(['Example6',name,'add'],fun() self.commands <- add())
    }
  }
}
```

and returns a new component. The supplied name is used as a menu label. The component that is returned manages a single integer value and provides a single operation that is used to increment the value.

Figure 16 shows the definition of a component that uses the mk_child template function. The behavioural goal expresses a condition that whenever the state of the parent or the children changes, the value in child2 eventually becomes the same value as that in child1. To complete the specification we should also add a goal that states that if the value in child2 changes, the value in child1 eventually synchronizes. The implementation of the inc operation sends a message to both children and thereby satisfies the goal.

Figure 16. A parent goal

```
Leap[stopped]
File  Edit  Run
leapsrc/goals/example6/example6.cmp
component example6 {
  goals {
    behaviour Nested_inv {
      'same values'
      [] E n. Value(n) in child1.state -> <>(Value(n) in child2.state)
    }
  }
  port commands [in]: interface {
    inc():void
  }
  operations {
    inc() {
      child1.commands <- add();
      child2.commands <- add()
    }
  }
  init {
    menu(['Example6','inc'],fun() self.commands <- inc())
  }
  child1 = mk_child('child1')
  child2 = mk_child('child2')
}
```

IMPLEMENTATION

LEAP is implemented as a Java engine that constructs component models and executes them. This section provides a brief overview of the Java classes that are used to represent and execute the models including how BIA is achieved by executing goals against running simulations.

Figure 17 shows part of the LEAP component model. The class Value is used to represent all values that can be denoted in user-models. A component is a value that consists of the following elements:

- A state that is represented as a list of terms. The state can be modified by adding and removing terms, but individual terms cannot be modified.
- A collection of ports. Each port has a queue of messages and is either used for input or output. At any given time, a component has a number of input messages that are pending. A transition occurs when a message is removed from the head of the input queue.
- A collection of definitions contained in a record. A record is a value that maps names to values via bindings. Both operations and components are values and therefore a component contains its children and the operations that implement its messages via the record. Note that components may contain any types of value in its record. The abstract class Atom is the root of a collection of classes that define basic value types such as integer. Note also that the body of an operation is defined by the abstract class Exp that is the root of a class of expression syntax classes.
- A component manages a trace consisting of a sequence of transitions. Each transition records the state change that occurs when a message is processed from one of the input queues.
- A component contains a collection of goals. A goal consists of a formula that defines a constraint over the trace of the component. Each formula may contain *free variables* that can take values from elements in the trace. A formula together with bindings for each of its free variables is called an *fclosure*. A component manages three collections of fclosures: *outstanding* that are

Figure 17. LEAP implementation model

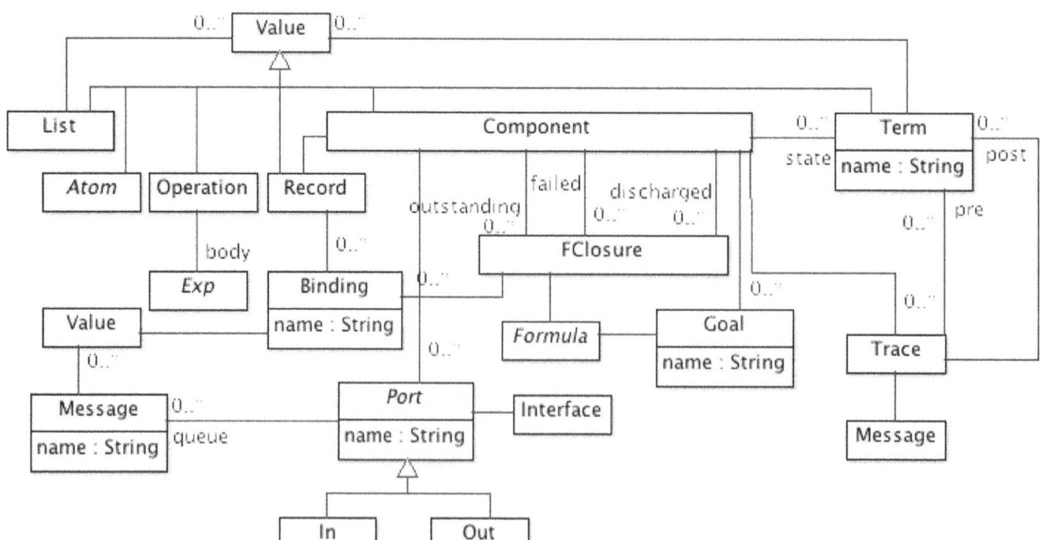

formulas yet to be established; *failed* that are formulas that have evaluated to false; *discharged* that are formulas each of which have evaluated to true.

An evaluation step at a component is described by Algorithm 1.

The reduction step uses unification over values in the trace to calculate the variable bindings. Where the reduction involves choice the fclosure records the choice point in case backtracking is required at a later stage. An fclosure can be fully reduced if there are no temporal operators that require more trace than is available. For example a formula @P requires access to the next step in the trace. If this is available then the formula reduction can continue, otherwise the formula reduces to P and the algorithm will add it to the collection of outstanding fclosures.

CASE STUDY

This section provides a simple example of a single module application to show how goals can specify the behavior of an IT component. The application is a library in which time limits are imposed on borrowings so that a fine must be paid if a borrowing exceeds the limit.

Figure 18 shows the required IT component and its interfaces. A reader must register before using the library and subsequently may borrow and return books. At regular intervals a clock ticks and time advances. The results interface shows events that are raised in response to library state changes. Registering the same reader twice results in a readerExists event, attempting to use the library when the reader has a fine results in a fineOutstanding event, attempting to use the library before registering results in a notRegistered

Algorithm 1.

```
let m(v1,…,vn) be the next input message
    pre be the current state
    M1 be the current set of output messages
    o be the operation record.m
in call o(v1,…,vn);
   let post be the state after the call
       M2 be the current set of output messages
       O = M2 - M1
       outstanding' = emptyset
   in extend trace with (pre,post,O);
      for f in outstanding do
        case reduce f with respect to trace of
          false -> add f to failed
          true -> add f to discharged
          f' -> add f to outstanding'
        end
      end;
      outstanding:= outstanding'
   end
end
```

Figure 18. Library component

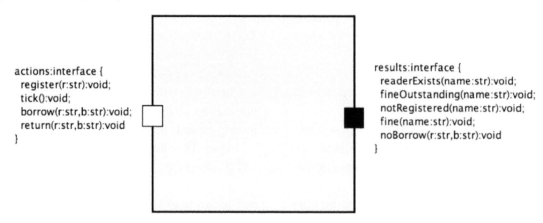

event, attempting to return a book that the reader has not borrowed results in a noBorrow event.

The information model used to represent the state of the library is shown in Figure 19. In LEAP an information model defines a collection of term types such that the state of the component consists of lists of terms of the declared types. Associations, such as fine, represent nested terms and are shown both as an association and a property of the type.

The specification of the library is shown in Figure 20. The goal Registration requires that new readers are added to the state. The goal Tick is interesting because it specifies that time must be increasing: given time currently at t, it will stay at t until it increases by 1 time unit. The goal UniqueTime requires that there can be no two time terms with different values in any given state. The goals BorrowRegistered, BorrowedFine, returnRegistered and ReturnFine all define situations where illegal actions are attempted that consequently that lead to events being raised. The final goal, BorrowedCompletion specifies that if a book is successfully borrowed by a reader then eventually the reader will return the book or a fine event will be raised.

The implementation of the library is defined in Figure 21. Having defined both the goals and the design for the software component, LEAP allows the alignment to be checked by running the goals against a simulation of the design. This provides confidence that the goals and the IT design are aligned.

DISCUSSION AND FUTURE DIRECTIONS

This chapter has discussed the issues relating to aligning business goals with aspects of an Enterprise Architecture model. We have proposed an approach to modeling the key features and

Figure 19. Library information model

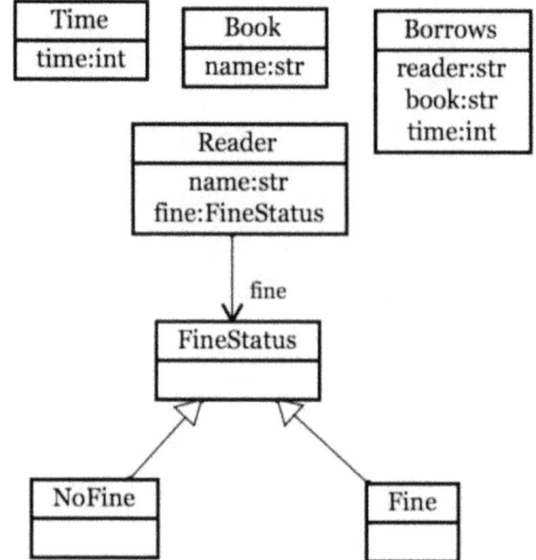

Figure 20. Library specification

```
goals {
  behaviour Registration {
    'When a new reader is added the database of readers is extended.'
    [] E r f. (<register(r)> !Reader(r,f)) -> Reader(r,NoFine)'
  }
  behaviour Tick {
    'Time advances.'
    [] E t t'. Time(t) -> (Time(t) U (Time(t') and ?(t'=t+1)))
  }
  behaviour UniqueTime {
    'There is only one time.'
    [] !exists Time(t), Time(t') in state' {
      ?(t!=t')
    }
  }
  behaviour BorrowRegistered {
    'To borrow a book the reader must be registered.'
    [] E r b s. (<borrow(r,b)> !Reader(r,s)) -> [notRegistered(r)]
  }
  behaviour BorrowedFine {
    'To borrow a book the reader must be fine free.'
    [] E r b. (<borrow(r,b)> Reader(r,Fine)) -> [fineOutstanding(r)]
  }
  behaviour ReturnRegistered {
    'To return a book the reader must be registered.'
    [] E r b s. (<return(r,b)> !Reader(r,s)) -> [notRegistered(r)]
  }
  behaviour ReturnFine {
    'To return a book the reader must be fine free.'
    [] E r b. (<return(r,b)> Reader(r,Fine)) -> [fineOutstanding(r)]
  }
  behaviour BorrowedCompletion {
    'After borrowing successfully, return or fine.'
    [] E t. (<borrow(r,b)> and Borrow(r,b,t)') ->
      <>(<return(r,b)> or [fine(r)])
  }
}
```

shown that these can be implemented in a tool. However, significant challenges remain to be addressed. In particular, we lack a method for addressing real-world situations that are complex and in which much knowledge and information is tacit. Furthermore, the issue of goal and IT alignment in an enterprise is just one aspect of the challenges that face a modern organization that wishes to achieve agility with respect to a dynamic environment. To address this challenge we have proposed the notion of a Model Driven Enterprise (MDE):

def: A Model Driven Organization uses models in the analysis, design, simulation, delivery, operation, and maintenance of systems to address its strategic, tactical and operational needs and its relation to the wider environment. (Clark et al., 2014)

Figure 22 taken from (Clark et al., 2013) shows an instance of an MDO that includes a model of the organization given in a platform independent (or domain specific) notation, a platform specific model of the organization in terms of the technologies and processes necessary to realize its goals, and a general purpose platform for running an organization of a particular type (perhaps financial or telecoms).

This can be viewed as generalizing the notion of Model Driven Architecture (MDA) to the level of organizations, where the platform-independent

Figure 21. Library implementation

```
operations {
  register(r) {
    find Reader(r,_) in state {
      results <- readerExists(r)
    } else new Reader(r,NoFine)
  }
  tick() {
    replace Time(t) with Time(t+1);
    for Borrow(r,_,t') when (time()) = t' + 3 {
      results <- fine(r);
      replace Reader(r,_) with Reader(r,Fine)
    }
  }
  borrow(r,b) {
    find Reader(r,s) {
      case s {
        Fine -> results <- fineOutstanding(r);
        NoFine -> new Borrow(r,b,time())
      }
    } else results <- notRegistered(r)
  }
  time() {
    find Time(t) {
      t
    } else 0
  }
  return(r,b) {
    find Reader(r,s) {
      case s {
        Fine -> results <- fineOutstanding(r);
        NoFine -> find Borrow(r,b,t) {
          delete Borrow(r,b,t)
        } else results <- noBorrow(r,b)
      }
    } else results <- notRegistered(r)
  }
}
```

model (PIM) contains features from the strategic and tactical layers and the platform-specific model (PSM) is the IT platform that runs the organization. An MDO requires models of the organization and its IT platform that support multiple perspectives on different levels of abstraction that are used for communication and collaboration among various groups of stakeholders. Models of enterprise systems integrated with models of the organizational action system contribute to IT Business alignment. Organizational agility is promoted by empowering advanced users to apply changes to models that in turn result in a modification of the enterprise software system.

The idea is that the model of the organization allows the various business-facing stakeholders in the organization to specify their requirements in ways in which are meaningful to their role. In addition, stakeholders can interact with the organization in order to perform their various roles using domain-specific interfaces (i.e., languages). The platform independent models are transformed (variously off-line or dynamically) into a platform-specific language that controls a domain-specific platform that can be shared across multiple organizations of the same type.

The business case for such an approach includes companies that wish to supply platforms across a range of organizations in much the same way as ERP systems are currently supplied. In many ways the MDO can be viewed as providing the next generation of business solutions. Partial-MDO solutions can be added to existing platforms.

There are significant technological challenges in achieving an MDO. A key challenge is the ability to support multiple domain specific languages required by different stakeholders. A promising approach is the use of meta-modeling technologies that can be used to provide multiple modeling languages all of which share the same meta-model. However, meta-modeling is not without its own problems as described in (Frank, 2012). Further work is required in order to ensure that multiple languages to be developed at the meta-level in such a way as they freely integrate and a promising approach is described in (Henderson-Sellers, 2013). Given the requirements for language engineering we might be temped to use a standard approach based on the technologies defined and promoted by the Object Management Group (OMG). This approach to language engineering involves four levels:

M0: Containing only instances of classes. Elements at this level are represented in UML Object Diagrams in terms of objects, slots and links;

Figure 22. A model driven enterprise

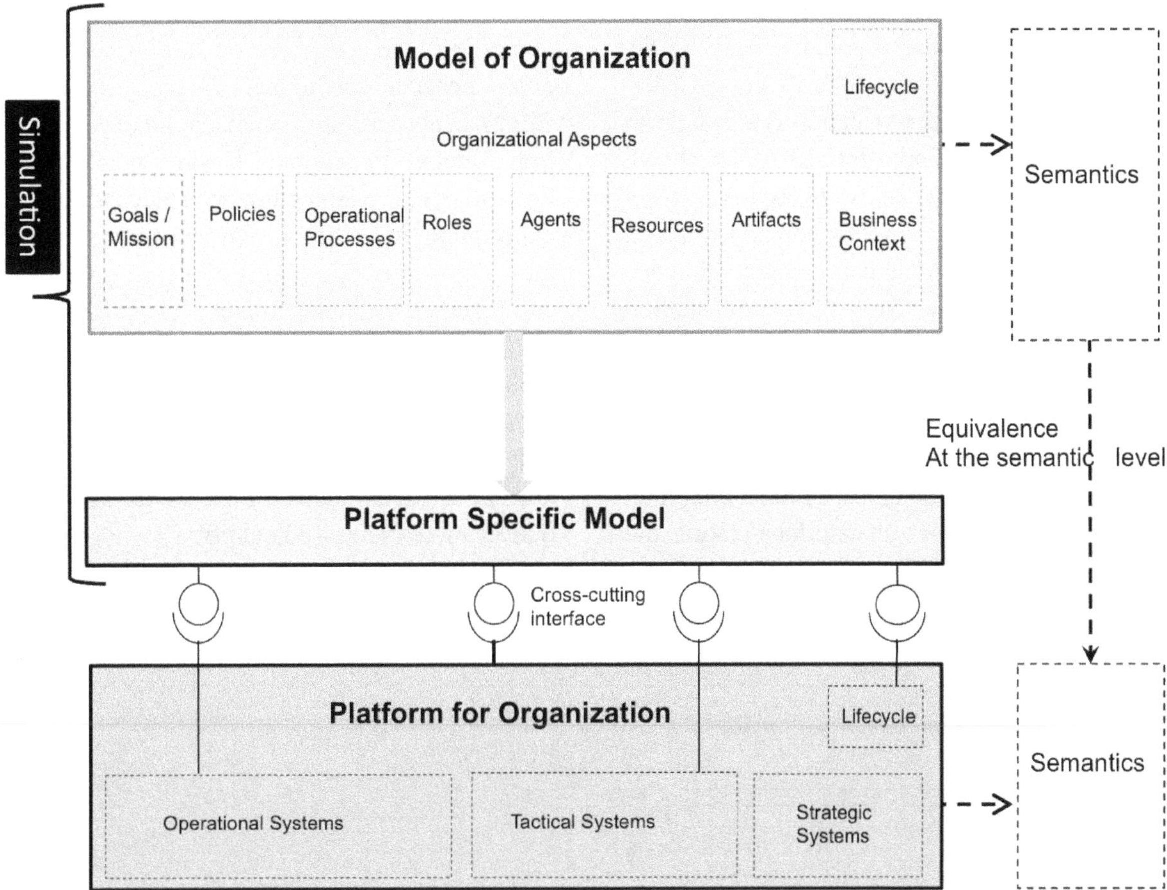

M1: Containing system models involving classes, associations, state machines, use-case scenarios *etc*;

M2: Containing modelling language definitions for the UML family of languages. This level contains meta-classes such as Class and Association;

M3: Containing the language that is used to express M2 language definitions. This is called the *Meta Object Facility* (MOF).

The **M0-M3** organization is *strict* in the sense that elements from one level may not be used at a different level. This restricts the expressive power of the language; for example, it is not possible to define a class at **M1** that defines a canonical default instance. Furthermore, it prevents type level information from being expressed and specialized in user models, for example by introducing an ordered sequence as a specialization of a sequence.

The reflection aspect of MOF is not integrated with the type-level features and must go through some form of translation thereby forcing *strictness*. This restricts the expressive power and introduces an unnecessary dichotomy that compromises meta-circularity. XMF (Clark & Willans, 2012) is based on the *golden braid* language architecture whereby instances, types and meta-types are first-class citizens and allow for an arbitrary number of classification layers and mixed-level languages. This type of approach would be appropriate for the platform independent languages required by the MDO whilst the LEAP approach would be appropriate for the platform specific languages.

The LEAP approach requires many of the features of an organization to be expressed using a lowest-common representation (i.e., platform specific) based on components. LEAP has shown that this approach can be useful, however it is a particular implementation of the component-based representation for EA elements and therefore we should seek to abstract from the implementation details of LEAP to provide a general purpose component ontology for EA. A candidate conceptual model for component-based EA is shown in Figure 23. A component is a self-contained functional unit with high coherence and low external coupling. A component exposes an interface stating the externally observable goals, expectations from the environment, mechanisms to interact with the environment, and encapsulates an implementation that describes how the exposed goals are met. A component can make use of several contained components in order to meet the promised goals. Components participate in hierarchical composition structure to accomplish wider goals of the enterprise, e.g., a larger unit or an enterprise. The expectations of a component from its environment are accompanied by a quality of service guarantee and together both constitute a negotiating lever. Thus, a component is in fact a family of (member) components where all family members have the same goal and inter- action specifications but differ only in terms of the quality of service delivered and the expectations from the environment for delivering the promised quality.

The LEAP language presented in this chapter contains a rich collection of features that are

Figure 23. Conceptual component model for EA

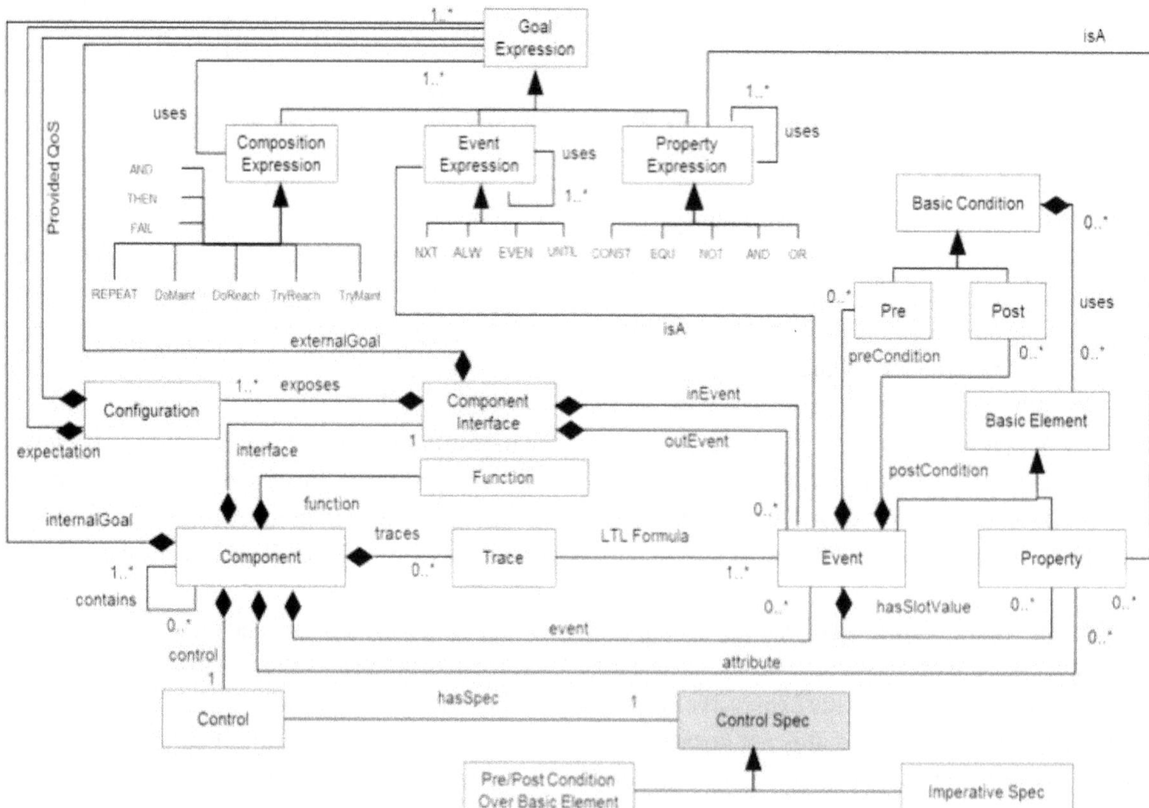

Figure 24. Domain specific languages target kernel

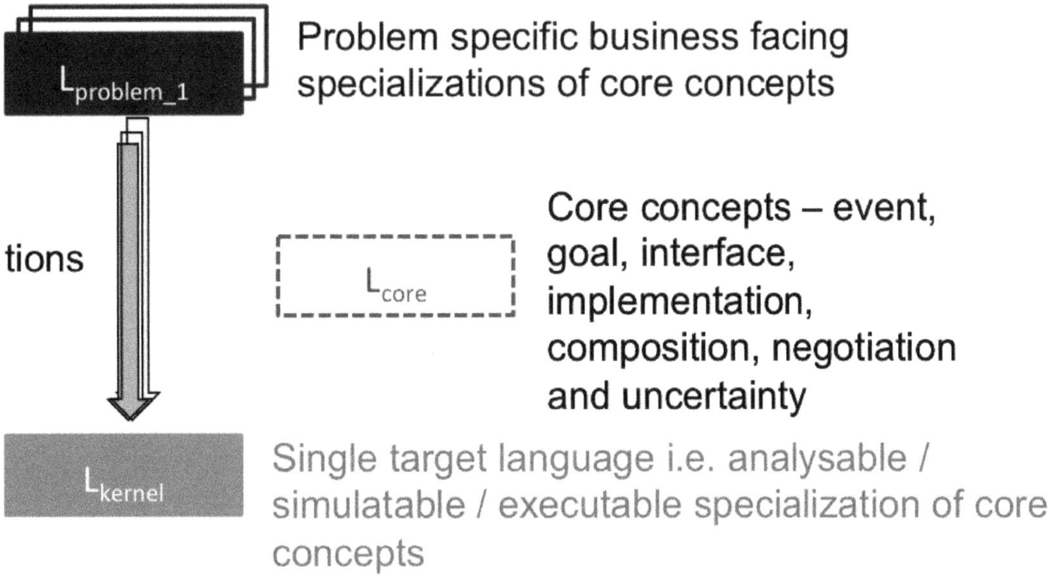

used to create and manage component-models. Our aim is to provide a basis for simulating organizations and therefore it is important that the LEAP language supports the user with high-level features. However, we would like to extend LEAP in a number of ways. Firstly, we would like to understand the fundamental core features required by LEAP such that all high-level features can be constructed from a kernel language. The kernel language will characterize the domain and provide a basis for analysis. Our hypothesis is that the kernel language should provide the following features: adaptability; modularity; autonomy; distribution; intent; composition; extensibility; events. An initial version of the kernel language is described in (Clark and Barn, 2014).

The kernel language will be the target of a collection of domain specific languages (DSLs) that support the representation, simulation and analysis of specific business problems. Figure 24 shows the proposed approach whereby a high-level DSL is translated into core concepts that are supported by the Kernel.

Secondly, we would like to introduce more realistic features to simulations that allow real-world architectures to be represented and for simulations to solve real-world problems faced by organizational stakeholders. Such features might include stochastic simulation and distribution. Finally, we would like to make components within an organization both knowledge-based and driven by their own internal goals.

Figure 25 shows the proposed interface for a model-driven platform that supports the domain specific representation and analysis of organizations. The plug-in architecture for the tool supports a wide variety of business domains all of which map to the kernel. The platform can be constructed once and applied in many different scenarios to support analysis and decision-making. Each new application involves the construction of a mapping from a DSL to the Kernel that is used to populate the platform, to express queries and simulation data, and to express results.

Our work in this direction has led us to identify two related research directions for LEAP. The first uses Actor Theory (Hewitt, 2010) to provide a sound basis for a kernel language. Actors are similar to components, but provide scope for safe concurrency that is key to supporting realistic

Figure 25. Simulation and analysis

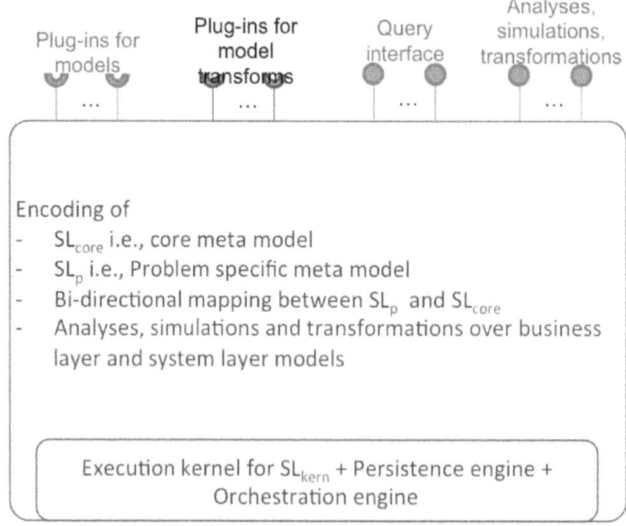

Expertise and past experience captured in the form of ready-to-use actionable knowledge, Reusable across problem instances e.g. Business-IT alignment, M&A, data-driven decision making etc, Configurable, Extensible, No lock-ins

simulations. Furthermore, Hewitt shows how this approach can be applied to organizations in (Hewitt, 2009). The second direction is based on Multi-Agent Systems where agents are autonomous, state-based autonomous entities. Typically, an agent uses knowledge-based techniques to reason using their internal knowledge of the world in order to make decisions. This is exactly how we would expect elements of an organization to behave. We intend to merge Actors and MAS into a single kernel language that forms the basis of LEAP-like component language features in order to represent and simulate organizations.

The LEAP tool supports the design of goals and executable designs, and has been used to construct models of systems including alignment of business goals from the UK Higher Education sector and engineering crisis management. Goal alignment is achieved by simultaneously checking the goals against a running prototype of the system in terms of the models. There are several areas for future tool development:

- LEAP systems consist of collections of components. A suitable development method is step-wise refinement of components starting with a single component with a high-level information model and developing the system through a number of elaborations involving increasing numbers of collaborating components and increasingly complex information models. Each layer developed by such an approach will be linked to the previous layer via a refinement relationship. For the approach to be practical, support must be provided for recording the refinement relationship and checking that it holds.
- The LEAP goal language provides temporal operators that are based on the notion of future that involves an arbitrary number of steps. Many applications require a specific notion of time (albeit relativized to each individual component) and the ability to express conditions such as *within the*

next 10 time units P must hold. Indeed the library example shown above uses an explicit representation of time to achieve this kind of condition. The goal language can be extended to systematically encode time as part of the temporal operators.

- As it stands, LEAP goals can only be shown to hold against specific execution of the models. This choice was made because more general approaches such as model checking and theorem proving do not scale well. However, these techniques may be useful for specific types of application or in restricted circumstances, in which case more general properties of LEAP models can be established.
- LEAP provides a technology for linking to external applications. The LEAP system is written in Java and provides a Java interface definition that allows any Java program to be integrated as a LEAP component. This mechanism can be used to link to external IT systems such as databases and provide a route to linking LEAP goals with existing systems.
- The LEAP language for expressing executable models is simple and has been designed to allow analysis and transformation. Once a LEAP system model has been developed and checked and aligned with the system goals should be possible to run the LEAP models against the systems in an organization and thereby show that the organization is aligned with the LEAP model.

CONCLUSION

This chapter has reviewed the need for business alignment and EA simulation. It has reviewed the current state of the art in Enterprise Architecture modelling languages. Our claim is that these languages are generally business facing and provide good support for the business analyst, but otherwise provide little or no support for precise analysis that is required to establish alignment. Systems that aim to provide such support are often based around requirements definition and do not contain modelling elements suitable for architectural definition. Furthermore, systems that provide support for precise analysis of alignment tend to be limited in scope of application because of the state space explosion.

LEAP has been designed to provide a simple basis for constructing executable architectural models and has been shown elsewhere to support many of the features defined by EA modelling languages. As such it is proposed as a basis for EA modelling, simulation and analysis. LEAP includes a language for expressing both behavioural and non-functional goals and as such is proposed as a basis for testing architectural alignment. The approach taken is not to establish global system properties because of the limitation of current approaches, but to provide confidence in alignment by running goals against the executable system models and to record the successes and failures.

This chapter has provided an overview of the LEAP language and toolset in terms of the different types of goals that can be expressed. We have defined the alignment algorithm used by LEAP and given a simple standard example in terms of the ubiquitous library information system.

Our aim is to provide a precise practical basis for EA analysis including alignment and LEAP is the technology platform we are currently developing. Further work is needed to integrate with existing technologies for EA and to strengthen the analysis provided by LEAP. As described in the previous section we are seeking a kernel language that characterizes EA in terms of modelling, analysis and simulation. The kernel language is to support the existing component-based features of LEAP, but will also include features for stochastic modelling, distribution and intelligent goal-directed behaviour.

REFERENCES

Barn, B., & Clark, T. (2012) Goal based alignment of enterprise architectures. In *Proceedings of the 7th International Conference on Software Paradigm Trends*, (pp 230-236). SciTePress.

Buckley, W. (1967). *Sociology and modern systems theory*. Prentice-Hall.

Butcher, T., Fischer, R., Kurpjuweit, S., & Winter, R. (2006). Analysis and application scenarios of enterprise Architecture: An exploratory study. In *Proceedings of 10th IEEE International Enterprise Distributed Object Computing Conference Workshops*. IEEE.

Carley, K. M., & Gasser, L. (1999). Computational organization theory. In Multiagent systems: A modern approach to distributed artificial intelligence, (pp. 299–330). Academic Press.

Chan, Y. E., & Reich, B. H. (2007). IT alignment: What have we learned? *Journal of Information Technology, 22*(4), 297–315. doi:10.1057/palgrave.jit.2000109

Clark, T., & Barn, B. (2012). A common basis for modelling service-oriented and event-driven architecture. In *Proc of the 5th Annual India Software Engineering Conference, ISEC 2012*. ACM.

Clark, T., Barn, B., & Oussena, S. (2011) LEAP: A Precise Lightweight Framework for Enterprise Architecture. *In Proceedings of the 4th Annual India Software Engineering Conference*. ACM.

Clark, T., Barn, B., & Oussena, S. (2012). A method for enterprise architecture alignment. In *Proceedings of the 4th Working Conference on Practice-Driven Research on Enterprise Transformation,* (pp 48-76). Springer.

Clark, T., & Barn, B. S. (2014). Outsourcing service pro- vision through step-wise transformation. In *Proceedings of the 7th India Software Engineering Conference*. ACM.

Clark, T., Frank, U., Kulkarni, V., Barn, B., & Turk, D. (2013, July). Domain specific languages for the model driven organization. In *Proceedings of the First Workshop on the Globalization of Domain Specific Languages* (pp. 22-27). ACM. doi:10.1145/2489812.2489818

Clark, T., Kulkarni, V., Barn, B., France, R., Frank, U., & Turk, D. (2014). Towards the model driven organization. In *Proceedings of 47th Hawaii International Conference on System Sciences* (pp 4817-4826). IEEE.

Clark, T., & Willans, J. (2012). *Software language engineering with XMF and XModeler. In Formal and practical aspects of domain specific languages: Recent developments*. IGI Global.

Ekstedt, M., Johnson, P., Lindstrom, A., Gammelgard, M., Johansson, E., & Plazaola, L. et al. (2004). Consistent enterprise software system architecture for the CIO - A utility-cost based approach. In *Proceedings of the 37th Annual Hawaii International Conference on System Sciences*. IEEE. doi:10.1109/HICSS.2004.1265519

Engelsman, W., Quartel, D., Jonkers, H., & van Sinderen, M. (2011). Extending enterprise architecture modelling with business goals and requirements. *Journal of Enterprise Information Systems, 5*(1), 9–36. doi:10.1080/17517575.2010.491871

Ernst, M., Matthes, F., Ramacher, R., & Schweda, C. (2009). Using enterprise architecture management patterns to complement TOGAF. In *Proceedings of the Enterprise Distributed Object Computing Conference*. IEEE.

Frank, U. (2012). Multi-perspective enterprise modeling: Foundational concepts, prospects and future research challenges. *Software & Systems Modeling*, 1–22.

Henderson, J. C., & Venkatraman, N. (1993). Strategic alignment: Leveraging information technology for transforming organizations. *IBM Systems Journal*, *32*(1), 4–16. doi:10.1147/sj.382.0472

Henderson-Sellers, B., Clark, T., & Gonzalez-Perez, C. (2013, January). On the search for a level-agnostic modelling language. In *Advanced information systems engineering* (pp. 240–255). Springer. doi:10.1007/978-3-642-38709-8_16

Hewitt, C. (2009). Norms and commitment for iOrgs (TM) information systems: Direct logic (TM) and participatory grounding checking. *arXiv preprint arXiv:0906.2756.*

Hewitt, C. (2010). Actor model of computation: Scalable robust information systems. *arXiv preprint arXiv:1008.1459.*

Iacob, M., Jonkers, H., & Wiering, M. (2004). *Towards a UML profile for the ArchiMate language*. Retrieved from https://doc.telin.nl/dscgi/ds.py/Get/File-47276

Jonkers, H., Lankhorst, M., Buuren, R., Bonsangue, M., & Van Der Torre, L. (2004). Concepts for modeling enterprise architectures. *International Journal of Cooperative Information Systems*, *13*(3), 257–287. doi:10.1142/S0218843004000985

Lankhorst, M. (2009). *Introduction to enterprise architecture.* Springer-Verlag.

Lankhorst, M., Proper, E., & Jonkers, J. (2010). The anatomy of the archimate language. *International Journal of Information System Modeling and Design*, *1*(1), 1–32. doi:10.4018/jismd.2010092301

Leavitt, H. J. (1964). Applied organization change in industry: structural, technical and human approaches. *New Perspectives in Organizational Research*, *55*, 71.

Liu, L., Yu, E., & Mylopoulos, J. (2003). Security and privacy requirements analysis with a social setting. In *Proceedings of the 11th IEEE International Conference on Requirements Engineering*. IEEE. doi:10.1109/ICRE.2003.1232746

Luftman, J. (2000). Assessing business-IT alignment maturity. *Strategies for Information Technology Governance*, *4*(14), 99.

Niemann, K. (2006). *From enterprise architecture to IT governance: Elements of elective IT management.* Vieweg+ Teubner Verlag.

Parsons, T., & Jones, I. (1960). *Structure and process in modern societies* (Vol. 3). New York: Free Press.

Pereira, C. M., & Sousa, P. (2005). Enterprise architecture: Business and IT alignment. In *Proceedings of the 2005 ACM Symposium on Applied Computing* (p. 1345). ACM.

Ponsard, C., & Devroey, X. (2011). Generating high-level event-b system models from KAOS requirement models. In *Proceedings of Actes du XXIX eme Congres INFORSID*. Academic Press.

Reige, C., & Aier, S. (2009). A consistency approach to enterprise architecture method engineering. In Proceedings of Service-Oriented Computing, ICSOC Workshops (pp. 388–399). Springer.

Spencer, J. (2004). *TOGAF enterprise edition version 8.1.* Academic Press.

Wang, X., Zhou, X., & Jiang, L. (2008). A method of business and IT alignment based on enterprise architecture. In *Proceedings of IEEE International Conference on Service Operations, Logistics and Informatics* (pp. 740-745). IEEE. doi:10.1109/SOLI.2008.4686496

Wisnosky, D. E., & Vogel, J. (2004). *DoDAF wizdom: A practical guide to planning, managing and executing projects to build enterprise architectures using the department of defense architecture framework* (DoDAF). Academic Press.

Zachman, J. (1999). A framework for information systems architecture. *IBM Systems Journal, 38*(2/3), 454–470. doi:10.1147/sj.382.0454

KEY TERMS AND DEFINITIONS

CEP: Complex Event Processing allows multiple arbitrarily structured temporally related events to drive computation.

Component: A collection of logically consistent information and behaviour with state. Typically a component offers up a collection of services via a public interface.

Connector: A conduit for messages between components.

Domain Specific Language: A language that has been tailored to support concepts from a specific application domain. To be compared with a General Purpose Language.

EDA: An Event Driven Architecture is driven by events that trigger behavior in software components.

Invariant: A condition that must hold throughout the execution of a system or for some well-defined period of the system lifetime.

Message: The key mechanism by which behavior is triggered in component-based systems. A message may be sent synchronously or asynchronously.

Model Driven Enterprise: Using modeling approaches and technologies to address enterprise-wide use cases, for example to establish strategic business alignment.

Reification: Is a process of moving static or otherwise inaccessible information into user-supplied dynamic data and using it to affect the execution of a system.

SOA: A Service Oriented Architecture requires software components to publish logically coherent groups of system functionality.

Temporal Logic: A language that can be used to express conditions over system execution by making statements about the future or the past.

ENDNOTES

1 Business Rules Group, 2008. The business motivation model – business governance in a volatile world [online]. Release 1.3. Available from: bmm.shtml [Accessed 27 May 2010].

2 The Open Group, "Togaf "enterprise edition" version 9," 2009.

3 A KAOS tutorial, V1.0.

Chapter 10
Quality-Driven Database System Development within MDA Approach

Iwona Dubielewicz
Wrocław University of Technology, Poland

Zbigniew Huzar
Wrocław University of Technology, Poland

Bogumila Hnatkowska
Wrocław University of Technology, Poland

Lech Tuzinkiewicz
Wrocław University of Technology, Poland

ABSTRACT

The chapter presents an extended version of a quality-driven, MDA-based approach for database system development. The extension considers the relationship between successive models in the MDA approach. In particular, it gives rise to the introduction of domain ontology as a model preceding the CIM model as well as allows assessment of the extent to which the successive model is conformant with the preceding model. The chapter consists of four parts. The first part gives a short presentation of quality models and basic MDA concepts. The second one discusses the specific relationships between software development and quality assessment processes. The third part presents the Q-MDA framework and the proposal of a new quality characteristic (model conformance) with some measures for assessing the quality of a specific model in the context of other models. The last part contains an example of the framework application limited to the proposed quality model extension.

INTRODUCTION

Information systems become more complex and widespread, their quality becomes a more and more important concern in their development. Therefore, requirements for software product quality should be treated in the same way as functional requirements, however it involves additional effort and extra costs. To ensure product quality two basic approaches can be considered: the first basing on evaluation of the quality of the final product, and the second basing on evaluation of the quality of the process by which the product is developed. The quality of software development process influences positively on a quality of a software product.

Many modern approaches to software development are based on modeling paradigm and follow

DOI: 10.4018/978-1-4666-6359-6.ch010

the Model Driven Architecture (MDA) approach. Developers are encouraged to build a sequence of models, in which the following is a refined or transformed version of the previous one. In such model-driven development approaches the requirements to the models at the different levels of abstraction are clearly identified and specified. MDA focuses on functionality. It means that developers during building a model concentrate on specification of its functionality, and next on transformation that preserves functionality into a subsequent model. MDA is a very promising approach, however quality aspect is not explicitly considered by it.

This chapter presents a quality-driven framework for model-based software development. The framework integrates two complementary processes. The first – based on MDA approach (Miller & Mukerji, 2003) – is used for development purposes while the second – based on the quality specification and evaluation process defined by International Organization for Standardization (ISO) and the International Electrotechnical Commission (IEC) in ISO/IEC 25000 series of standards – is used for verification and validation of the output artifacts from the former one. In the paper we present the Extended Q-MDA which refines the Q-MDA framework presented in (Dubielewicz, Hnatkowska, Huzar, & Tuzinkiewicz, 2011). Motivation for the enhancement is to enable software developers more complete quality assessment of MDA models, i.e. an assessment of a given MDA model in the context of other model. Moreover, we propose for the assessment purposes of CIM model to use a domain ontology describing the same reality as the CIM does. We are convinced that such extension is useful and allows to gain high quality software product.

Similarly to the previous framework the new one can be refined for specific purposes. We present its adaptation to quality-driven database system development but this presentation is limited to the extension part only. The adaptation forms a systematic approach to data modeling at different level of abstraction and evaluation of their quality that adheres to MDA and ISO standards.

The chapter is organized as follows. The background part contains basic notions relating to MDA approach and to quality specification and evaluation models. Next, we give a brief outline of Extended Q-MDA framework, and then more detailed description of using the framework for database system development is presented and illustrated by a simple example which is however restricted to consideration on CIM and PIM data models only. The chapter is summarized by conclusions and an outline of future research within the Extended Q-MDA approach.

BACKGROUND

As a software system is a kind of a product which is developed in a production process therefore its quality may be considered in two perspectives: the product quality and the development process quality. The perspectives are strongly interrelated, for example, in shipbuilding industry, which is more matured discipline compared to software engineering, the controlled quality over the design and building process is necessary to guarantee the quality of a ship – the final product. In software engineering the quality of software development process also influences positively on a quality of a software product but does not guarantee expected quality of the product. The software development process may be considered as a sequence of activities that deliver different artifacts. At the beginning of the process software requirements, both functional and nonfunctional, are defined usually on the base of the business model. At the end a final software product is delivered. Other activities deliver intermediate artifacts. The quality of the intermediate artifacts influence the quality of the final software product. The chapter abstracts from the quality of software development process, and concentrates on the quality of the software product and its relationship to the quality of intermediate artifacts.

How to get high quality software becomes nowadays more and more important question. The question concerns two sub-questions: how to develop software and how to control its quality within the development process.

In further, we consider MDA as a modern approach to the development of software systems.

OMG document (Miller & Mukerji, 2003) describes MDA as an approach to system "development…[that]… provides a means for using models to direct the course of understanding, design, construction, deployment, operation, maintenance and modification."

MDA provides a frame for structuring the modeling process. The frame defines models and their transformations. Three kind of models are introduced: Computation Independent Model (CIM), Platform Independent Model (PIM) and Platform Specific Model (PSM), each representing different viewpoint. The different viewpoints enable separation of the specification of system's functionality from the specification of its implementation on a specific platform.

The CIM focuses on the environment of the future information system, and the requirements for the system; the details presenting system structure and behavior are hidden or not yet determined. The PIM focuses on the operation of a system while hiding the details necessary for a particular platform. The PIM shows that part of the complete specification that remains unchanged for different platforms. The PSM combines the platform independent viewpoint with an additional focus on the details of a specific platform. For example, in database system design the details are related to specific data models and the languages for their specification, e.g. relational, object, XML models.

System development is seen as a transformation of models that represent different viewpoints. In the transformation process mainly functional requirements are taken into account. Those stated by CIM should be maintained by PIM, next by PSM model, and finally by complete software product implemented in selected programming language. However, functionality of the developed system is the main but not the only requirement. Non-functional (quality) demands should be also considered. Unfortunately, up to now, specification of quality requirements and their transformation within modeling is not considered. Therefore, further shows how quality aspect may be integrated into the MDA approach.

The most complete definition of the quality and evaluation of product can be found in newly elaborated series of ISO/IEC 25000 standards – Software product Quality Requirements and Evaluation (SQuaRE). SQuaRE series has replaced ISO/IEC 9126 Software Product Quality and ISO/IEC 14598 – Product Evaluation standards. Its goal is to deliver logically organized, unified series covering two main processes: software quality requirements specification and software quality evaluation, supported by a software measurement process (SQuaRE, 2005).

The standard ISO/IEC 25010:2011 concerning a quality of software product defines this notion as *the degree to which the software product satisfies stated and implied needs when used under specified conditions*. This quality is evaluated on the base of measurement of (software) product quality attributes, i.e. measurable physical or abstract properties. Software quality attributes are classified into quality characteristics that are further subdivided into subcharacteristics. ISO/IEC 25010 standardizes the terminology concerning the definition of quality characteristics and subcharacteristics for the products (understood as software intensive computer system, final software as well as intermediate artifacts that are produced in a software process development).

A quality of a product is not defined in an unique way, it may be defined and evaluated from different perspectives. Currently there are three quality models in the ISO SQuaRE 25000 series: the quality-in-use model, the product (external/

internal) quality models in ISO/IEC 25010, and the data quality model in ISO/IEC 25012. There are also other approaches to quality model definition, for example, Garvin (Garvin, 1984) defines five different quality views: transcendent view, product view, user view, manufacturing view, and value-based view. The ISO models could be mapped into Garvin views, e.g. ISO quality-in-use model could be mapped into user view. In (Wagner & Deissenboeck 2007) authors propose a three level architecture for quality models that allows to define all (except transcendent) views in one solution.

The ISO/IEC 25010 quality-in-use model represents the perspective of a final user which uses the system with software product in specified environment and a specific context of use. External quality model represents common perspective of a developer that delivers and a customer that acquires the software product. The external quality model should be agreed as an essential element of the contract between developer and customer. These participants evaluate the product when it is used in simulated customer environment, usually in productive environment. Internal quality model represents the perspective of a software developer and relates to the artifacts that are produced during software development process (e.g. data model).

In further, we will use the product quality perspective defined in the ISO/IEC 25010 and thus two kinds of quality models for product: external and internal quality models.

The quality models representing the mentioned above perspective are strongly interrelated. The relationships may be explained in the context of software development process.

Explicit and implicit user needs (implicit needs are those not expressed directly) prompting a software product development are transformed into system requirements that are the base for quality-in-use model. This model is used to define users' quality expectations and it is used to asses quality of the product when used in specific environment and specific context of use. It means that the quality-in-use model is strongly dependent on a specific user.

Next, the external quality model is defined with the intension that the system (and final software product) satisfying it will also satisfy the quality-in-use model. So, the external quality model is derived from the quality-in-use model. The model is separated from direct influence of particular users.

The established external quality model is the base for internal quality models that are used to assess the artifacts generated within software development process. That is a decision of software developer which artifacts to select for quality evaluation. In general, only the artifacts which influence on the quality of the final software product should be considered. So, the internal quality models are means to help software developer to assure quality of the final software product.

For quality models representing different perspectives ISO/IEC 25010 defines two separate sets of quality characteristics: one set for quality-in-use perspective and another common set for external and internal perspectives. The scope of our further consideration is limited to external and internal quality models. We ascertain only that quality-in-use model relates to the capability of product to enable specified users to achieve specific goals with the effectiveness, efficiency, satisfaction, safety and context comprehensiveness.

In ISO/IEC 25010 the set of characteristics (subcharacteristics) for external and internal quality contains eight characteristics: functional suitability, compatibility, performance efficiency, usability, reliability, security, maintainability and portability. All these characteristics (and their subcharacteristics) are defined informally.

- *Functional suitability* characteristic (with functional completeness, functional correctness, functional appropriateness subcharacteristics) is defined as *the degree to which the product provides functions that meet stated and implied needs when the product is used under specified condition.*

- *Compatibility* characteristic (with co-existence and interoperability subcharacteristics) is understood *as the degree to which two or more systems or components can exchange information and/or perform their required functions while sharing the same hardware or software environment.*
- *Performance efficiency* characteristic (with time behavior and resource utilization subcharacteristics) means "the performance relative to the amount of resources used under stated conditions".
- *Reliability* characteristic (with maturity, availability, fault tolerance and recoverability subcharacteristics) is defined as *the degree to which a system or component performs specified functions under specified conditions for a specified period of time.*
- *Usability* characteristic (with appropriateness recognisability, learnability, operability, user error protection, user interface aesthetics and accessibility subcharacteristics) is determined as *the extent to which a product can be used by specified users to achieve specified goals with effectiveness, efficiency and satisfaction in a specified context of use.*
- *Security characteristic* (with confidentiality, non-repudiation, accountability, integrity, authenticity subcharacteristics) is defined as *the degree to which information and data are protected so that unauthorized persons or systems cannot read or modify them and authorized persons or systems are not denied access to them.*
- *Maintainability* characteristic (with modularity, reusability, analysability, modifyability and testability subcharacteristics) is defined as *the degree of effectiveness and efficiency with which the product can be modified.*
- The last one, *portability* characteristic (with adaptability, installability and replaceability subcharacteristics) is defined as *the degree to which a system or component can be effectively and efficiently transferred from one hardware, software or other operational or usage environment to another.*

To enable quantitative interpretation of characteristics, the notion of measure is introduced. Measures are functions defined over the values of measurable software attributes yielding results from usually a numerical set of values. Many measures may be assigned to a given quality characteristic or subcharacteristic. How to define measures and to assign them to characteristics of the quality model are serious and independent research problems to be solved.

A set of selected quality characteristics and subcharacteristics together with the assigned measures forms the quality model. The quality model provides the basis for specifying quality requirements and evaluating quality.

To evaluate quality, quality assessment functions have to be defined. An assessment function rates the quality of a software artifact on the base of its measurement. The measurement brings values of defined measures. The assessment functions may be defined to rate the quality of the whole software products, a set of selected artifacts or even separate artifacts. The functions may also be defined to give complete or partial evaluation of a artifact or set of artifacts. Complete evaluation takes into account all characteristics and subcharacteristics of the quality model while partial evaluation takes into account only selected quality characteristic or subcharacteristic from the quality model.

The scale rating quality of a software product can be divided into categories corresponding to different degrees of requirements satisfaction – the set of recommended values contains: *exceeding* requirements, *target*, *minimal* and *non-acceptable*.

A quality model and assessment functions form so called quality and evaluation model. Summarizing, the model is defined by three elements:

- A family of quality characteristics and subcharacteristics that are hierarchically ordered;
- A quality measures that are assigned to the characteristics or subcharacteristics; and
- At least one assessment function.

Software quality is a subject of many research, for example (Deissenboeck, Juergens, Lochmann & Wagner, 2009; Ho-Won, Seung-Gweon & Chang-Shin, 2004). An interesting review of research results is given in (Mohagheghi, Dehlen, & Neple, 2009). The paper proposes the quality model dedicated only to model (artifact) itself. This quality model called 6C consists of six quality characteristics: completeness, consistency, comprehensibility, correctness, confinement, changeability. Completeness is defined as having all the necessary information that is relevant and being detailed enough according to the purpose of modeling. Confinement is understood as a agreement with the purpose of modeling and the type of system (e.g. using relevant diagrams and being at the right abstraction level). Consistency is defined as no contradictions within the model as well as between models that represents the same aspect (e.g. data) but at different abstraction levels. Comprehensibility means understandability by the intended users (either human users or tools). Correctness is relative to the language and modeling rules or conventions. Changeability is defined as a feature supporting changes or improvements and it is important for maintainability purposes.

Another formalized version of quality model definition can be found in (Lamouchi, Cherif & Levy, 2008). In general the model defined there is very similar to ours, however the notions used in (Lamouchi, Cherif & Levy, 2008) are different from those defined in ISO 25010 (e.g. quality goal is equivalent to characteristic, quality factor – to subcharacteristic, criterion – to subcharacteristic that is not further decomposed, measure – to measure, rule – assessment function).

The topics that are important in the context of software development process, e.g. how to construct quality and evaluation models suitable for a given product and development process; which artifacts select to evaluation as indicators for the quality of final product, are not covered neither in ISO 25000 series nor in works mentioned above. There is at least one more objection to the research in the software quality area. In almost all works we have reviewed it is assumed indirectly that a quality of a given artifact is considered independently of its designing context. The exception is the 6C quality model (Mohagheghi, Dehlen, & Neple, 2009) where some of the characteristics refer (however indirectly) to the context of assessed artifacts. This context-independent quality assessment within MDA approach would mean that a quality of PSM model could be assessed independently of its relationship to the PIM model, similarly a quality of PIM model independently of CIM model, whilst the PSM model strongly depends on PIM model, and similarly PIM model on CIM model.

We have found the existing quality models and particularly ISO view are not sufficient to assess the quality of MDA models. In the presented approach we propose a new quality characteristic – *conformance* understood as the extent to which one MDA model (target) is consistent with another MDA model (source). The introduction of this new characteristic results from the fact that there is strong dependency between the source and target models – the source model is to be transformed into the target model. We expect that during the transformation that all information contained in the source model (starting form CIM) will be maintained by the target model, and elements of the target model and their corresponding elements in the source model will be consistent.

For the conformance characteristic we introduce two quality subcharacteristics: completeness and compliance. The first one is defined as the degree to which each element from the target model has adequate element in the source model. The second one is understood as the degree to which each element from the target model corresponds semantically to an element or elements in the source model.

Note that this proposed quality characteristic, conformance, is applicable only for an internal quality model, but not for an external quality model. The external perspective abstracts from models and their transformations.

EXTENDED Q-MDA

The Extended Q-MDA (Extended Quality-driven MDA) is a framework for information system development, which integrates the process of software development and the process of software quality specification and evaluation. Software development process follows MDA approach which means that the CIM, PIM, PSM models, and code are considered as intermediate artifacts. Software quality specification and evaluation process is based on ISO/IEC 25010 standard which entails application of external and internal quality and evaluation models. An information system is usually embedded in an enterprise system in which there are actors constituting a direct environment of the information system. Information systems consist of parts that are hardware with operating systems, application software, databases. Therefore, concentrating on quality-driven software development, the context where the software is placed should be taken into account. It means that quality requirements for the software are derived from the quality requirements for the information system, and the quality of the software influence on the quality of the whole information system. Further, only database systems are considered as software product.

In this Section, we explain the background for the framework assuming that a database system is considered as a software product. Figure 1 presents the basic structure of Extended Q-MDA framework. The structure of Extended Q-MDA framework consists of MDA models and associated quality and evaluation models, further called quality models for the shortcut, represented in form of UML packages.

There are dependency relationships between some elements in the figure. Except for standard trace dependency <<trace>> there are two new stereotypes of dependency relationships: <<spec>> and <<ass>>.

The trace dependency reflects transformation between two subsequent models. The dependency between models is a result of trace dependencies that exist between elements of these models. The trace dependencies between these elements are the base for the evaluation of completeness and compliance measures within conformance quality characteristic.

The specification dependency <<spec>> means that a dependent element is defined on the base of an independent element. For example, Internal Quality Model – PIM is elaborated on the base of the External Quality Model for Information System and the PIM model. The assessment dependency <<ass>> links a quality model as independent element with a MDA model or Information System and means that the model or product is assessed with respect to the specific quality model.

The root of the basic structure of Extended Q-MDA framework is External Quality Model for Information System. On the base of this model, internal quality models for PIM, PSM and code are defined. It is worth to note that internal quality model for CIM is independent from the external quality model. The reason is that the most important quality characteristics for any CIM model are

Figure 1. The structure of dependencies between MDA quality models

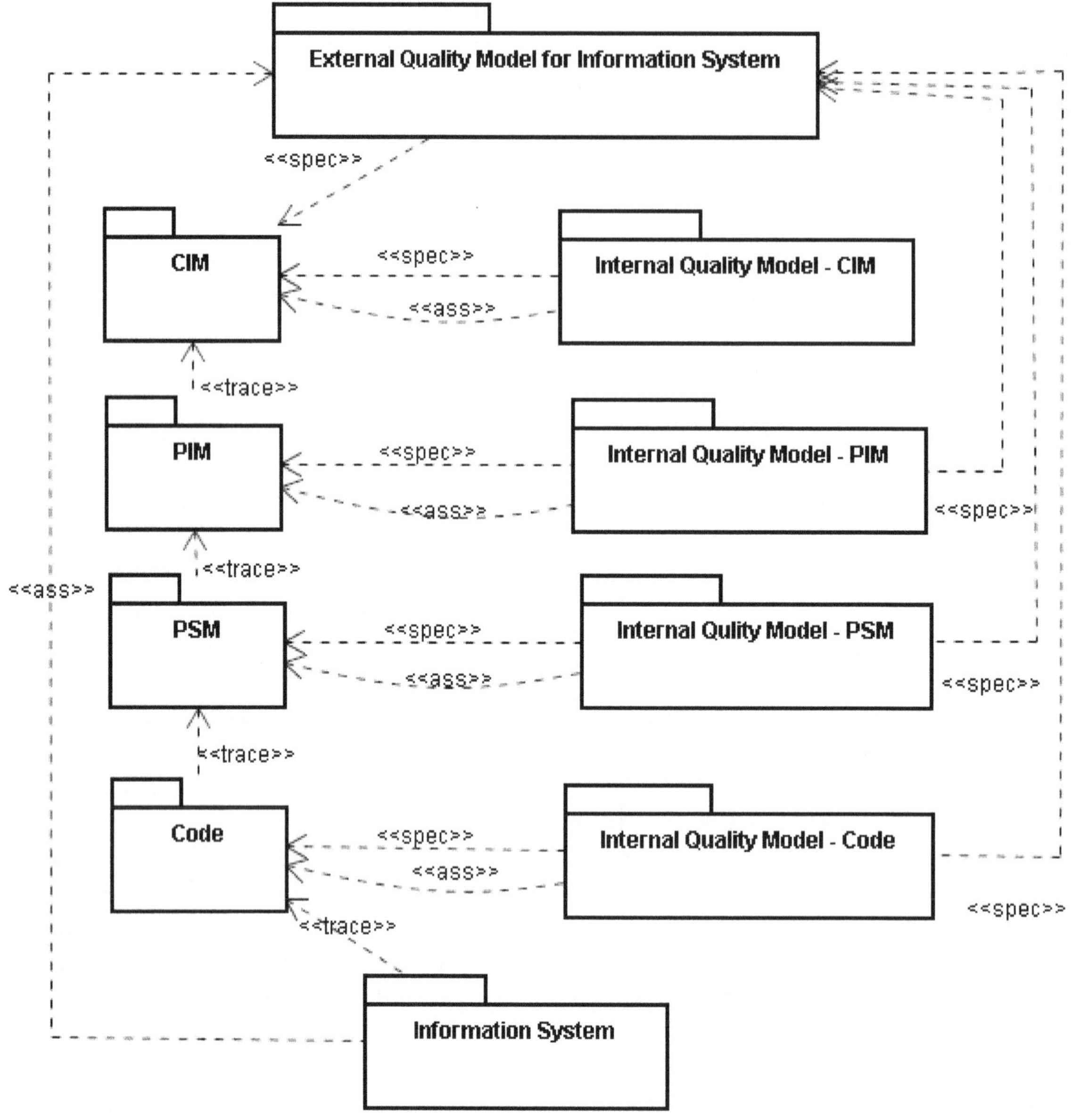

not ISO characteristics. The CIM model should be compliant and complete with respect to its application domain. The assessment of CIM compliance and completeness is usually done by a domain expert. In some cases the assessment may be done by comparison the CIM model to domain ontologies.

The quality of the final software product – Information System – is evaluated with respect to its external quality model, and the quality of intermediate artifacts – CIM, PIM, PSM and code – with respect to their internal quality models.

Now, we explain in more detail relationship between quality models. The relationship between the models results from the relationship between elements of those models, i.e. quality characteristics, measures and assessment functions.

Each quality characteristics from the external quality model should be present, if possible, in an internal quality model. The idea behind the rule is that when evaluating any intermediate artifact all characteristics concerning the final software product should be taken into account. This is not always possible because evaluated intermediate artifacts may have not attributes suitable for a given characteristic. However, some extra characteristics may be included to the internal quality models. The inclusion may ensue, for example, from the experience that specific extra characteristics will improve the quality of the final product, or may be result of quality policy applied by the software manufacturer.

There is no direct relationships between quality assessment functions in external and internal quality models. Only simple rule of thumb may be recommended: the quality assessment function in the internal quality model should be defined in such a way that negative evaluation of the quality of the intermediate artifact should be a credible forecast of a negative evaluation of the quality of the final software product. Similar rule may also be applied to the relationship between internal quality models for two subsequent MDA models. For example, negative evaluation of the quality of PIM model should be a credible forecast of a negative evaluation of the quality of PSM model.

DATABASE SYSTEM DEVELOPMENT USING QUALITY-DRIVEN MDA

Data Models and Their Relation to MDA

Database development, similarly to software development, can be conducted using bottom-up or top-down approach. In the first approach, firstly attributes for all entities are identified, next functional dependencies between attributes are defined, and finally, basic on normalization process, the schemata of database is elaborated. This approach is effective only for small databases. If the number of attributes goes back hundreds or even thousands, it excludes the possibility of identifying all the relationships between attributes even for domain experts. The second approach, similarly to MDA, is based on data models that are created on different levels of abstraction. Subsequent models are derived more or less automatically from the previous ones. In general, data models are defined at three abstraction levels: conceptual, logical and physical resulting in three different data models: conceptual data model, logical data model and physical data model.

Conceptual data model describes entities (for example patient, service) from a considered domain, properties of these entities (e.g. first name, second name, birth date) and relationships between entities (e.g. a patient *orders* service). The model is platform independent, that is, it abstracts from all details relating to a specific database environment. Conceptual data model can be expressed by Entity Relationship Diagrams (Connolly & Begg, 2005, pp. 342–385) or, what recently is more popular, by UML class diagrams (Elmasri & Navathe, 2007, pp. 121–123). As conceptual data model concentrates on interesting entities in a given domain, it can be easily understood and verified by domain experts.

Logical data model describes how data are organized within specific technology. Many different logical models are distinguished, for example hierarchical, network, relational, object-relational, object-oriented (Connolly & Begg, 2005, pp. 461–490) The most popular is still relational data model, invented by E.F. Codd in 1970. So, our further considerations apply to that model only. Relations are the main element in logical data model. A relation is defined as a subset of the Cartesian product of n domains. It consists of a schema and a body. A schema is a set of attributes, where an attribute is an ordered pair of attribute name and attribute type. A body of n-ary relation is a set of n-ary tuples, where a tuple is an unordered set of attribute values. Tuples in relation should be identified by so called (primary) key. A key is defined as a minimal subset of relation's attributes for which each two tuples have distinguishable values. Relationships between relations are usually expressed with the concept of foreign keys. A foreign key is an attribute in relation A that holds values of the (primary or alternative) key in relation B. A table is an accepted visual representation of a relation. Relational data model could be expressed in many ways. Usually the database supporting tools propose their own notation for that purpose, for example Enterprise Architect. Some (e.g. Rational Rose Data Modeler) propose to use a specific profile of the UML language, dedicated for database modeling. Using a standardized version of SQL 2003 language (ISO/IEC 9075, 2003) or Common Warehouse Metamodel (CWM) Specification (CWM, 2003) could be also considered as an acceptable way of expressing relational database model.

Physical data model describes how data are organized within a specific database management system (DBMS), for example Oracle, MS SQL 2005 or eXist. This knowledge is needed for database programmers who are responsible for database schemata definition. Of course physical data model should be consistent with logical data model (e.g. still should be relational one). However, a specific DBMS usually offers native capabilities that can be used by database programmers (e.g. specific types, views). We assume, that physical data model can also contain realization of part of business logic delegated to DMBS like stored procedures or transaction definitions. Physical data model is usually represented by SQL scripts accepted in the target environment. It is also possible to define these models directly in DMBS using available tools.

Sometimes, prior to conceptual data model elaboration, an additional domain data model is created. This model facilitates stakeholders to understand the considered domain. Like the conceptual data model, the domain model shows the entities that exist in a given domain and the relationships between them.

There is a clear correspondence between database models and MDA models (Dubielewicz, Hnatkowska, Huzar, &Tuzinkiewicz, 2006). Domain data model can be considered as a part of CIM model, conceptual data model – because of its platform independence – as a part of PIM model, logical data model – as a part of PSM model, while physical data model – as a part of code.

Quality in the Context of Database Systems

Database system is important, executable component of information system. It is usually controlled by database management system, for example Oracle or MS SQL. Database system is understood here as a set of data (database) with a set of database operations (insert, update, delete), and specification of access permissions.

Database system can be viewed as a software product itself, and can be evaluated against external quality model derived from the external quality model defined for the information system. Database system is not the complete product perceived by the end-users, so it can be evaluated against quality-in-use perspective.

We have analyzed the external quality characteristics proposed in ISO/IEC 25010 in respect to their applicability for database system quality assessment. In result we formulate the following conclusions.

For external quality model all quality characteristics except usability characteristic are applicable. The reason for excluding usability is that this characteristic deals with end-user oriented features like understandability, easiness to learn and attractiveness (database system does not include end-user interface).

We share opinion of many researchers (Kifer, Brenstein & Lewis, 2006, pp. 383–455; Lightstone, Teorey & Nadeau, 2007, pp. 32–50), that among applicable quality characteristics maintainability, performance efficiency and security characteristics are the most important. The reason for maintainability is that software maintenance is the most expensive stage in the software life cycle (between 67% and 90% of total life cycle costs is consumed in this stage). Performance efficiency of database system has very often crucial influence on efficiency of the whole information system. Data stored in databases as assets owned by companies or individuals need to be secured.

We have also analyzed the internal quality characteristics proposed in ISO/IEC 25010 in respect to their applicability for different data models quality assessment. The conclusions of our analysis are presented in Table 1. This Table contains the newly proposed *conformance* characteristic.

The notion 'partially applicable' means that for a given characteristic not all its subcharacteristics are possible to be applied. For example *portability* characteristic, described by three subcharacteristics (installability, adaptability, replaceability) is partially applicable at PSM level as only adaptability (measured with the number of data structure changes) can be estimated. The other subcharacteristic, for example, installability cannot be applied as it is inadequate for PSM data model (PSM data model has static nature). The characteristic *portability* is applicable at code level as all their subcharacteristics can be measured.

Usability characteristics is assumed to be not applicable for any data models. The reason is that usability is perceived by end-users only.

In contrast to usability maintainability characteristic is applicable for all data models. In opinion of (Piattini, Calero, Sahraoui & Lounis, 2001; Piattini & Genero, 2001) the most important subcharacteristics of maintainability is analyzability measured by complexity measure. Complexity can be defined and evaluated for data models expressed either by UML class diagrams (Piattini & Genero, 2001) or relational schema

Table 1. Internal quality characteristics applicability to data models

MDA/ data model	**Quality characteristic**								
	Functional suitability	**Reliability**	**Usability**	**Compatibility**	**Security**	**Performance Efficiency**	**Portability**	**Maintainability**	**Conformance**
CIM/domain	NA	NA	NA	NA	NA	NA	NA	A	A*
PIM/conceptual	NA	NA	NA	NA	NA	PA	NA	A	A
PSM/logical	PA	NA	NA	NA	PA	A	PA	A	A
Code/physical	PA	PA	NA	NA	PA	A	A	A	A

Note. All quality characteristics come from ISO/IEC 25010. The meaning of used abbreviations is as follows: A – fully applicable, A* (fully applicable under specific conditions), NA – not applicable, PA – partially applicable.

(Piattini, Calero, Sahraoui & Lounis, 2001), so it can be applied for domain, conceptual, logical as well as physical data models.

Functional suitability characteristic is partially applicable to physical model because all its subcharacteristics could be evaluated at that level provided that system functions are implemented by DBMS (e.g. stored procedures).

Analyzing two performance efficiency subcharacteristics time behavior and resource utilization, the first one could only been estimated taking into account specification of database system operations, while the second one can be assessed for example with measures taken from ISO/IEC 9126-3 (ISO/IEC 9126-3, 2003) at PSM and code levels.

Security characteristic is partially applicable to PSM and physical models when, for example, grants are defined at these levels.

Characteristics of both reliability and compatibility are not applicable to data models because all their subcharacteristics are "behavior–oriented" e.g. availability, maturity, recoverability, fault tolerance, co-existence or interoperability.

The new proposed characteristic, conformance, with two subcharacteristics: completeness and compliance is applicable to CIM provided that an ontology exists for considered domain. It is fully applicable when considering other models.

Background for Model Conformance

Introduction

The considerations below illustrate how to compare two subsequent database models within MDA approach in order to assess their conformance. Limitation of this illustration bases on the assumption that the models are represented by UML diagrams. In the case of database design they are class diagrams.

MDA approach assumes a manual or automatic transformation of one model into the next model. We abstract of the way the source model is transformed into the target model, but we assume that tracing information is given. The tracing information is expressed in the form of UML dependency relationship stereotyped by <<trace>>.

The trace dependencies are assumed to be defined already by a modeler. This dependency is a statement of relationship between two elements or set of elements in different models. The elements from the source model, called suppliers, are independent, and the elements from the target model, called clients, are dependent. The trace dependency indicates a connection between two elements that represent the same concept at different levels of meaning. We assume that semantics of the client is compliant to semantics of the supplier but we skip the question how it is decided.

Notation

For a relation $R \subseteq X \times Y$, we will use standard notation $dom(R)$, $ran(R)$ for the relation domain and codomain, and $R(A)$, $R^{-1}(B)$ for the image of a set $A \subseteq X$, and preimage of a set $B \subseteq Y$ under R. Cardinality of the finite set X is denoted by $|X|$.

Assumptions

- Two models are considered: the first one, called the source model *SM*, and the second one, called target model *TM*.
- The models are represented as class diagrams expressed in UML. The models consist of classes with their attributes, and relationships (associations and generalizations) among classes. By C_{SM}, R_{SM} and C_{TM}, R_{TM}, respectively, we denote the set of classes and the set of relationships for *SM* and *TM* models. For the sake of simplicity we assume that the set of classes contains also association classes.
- There is a general trace dependency relationship between these models meaning

that the source model was the base for an elaboration of the target model. The trace dependencies are assumed to be defined already by a modeler.

- Apart the general trace dependency there are specific trace dependencies between elements from these models. The set of all specific traces define a binary tracing relationship $TR = TR_C \cup TR_R$ where TR_C and TR_R have the signatures:

$TR_C \subseteq C_{TM} \times (C_{SM} \cup R_{SM})$, and

$TR_R \subseteq R_{TM} \times (C_{SM} \cup R_{SM})$.

The first relation TR_C represents a tracing of classes and the second one TR_R – a tracing of relationships from the target to the source model.

The pair $<e_{TM}, e_{SM}> \in TR$ represents an arrow with stereotype <<trace>> leading from the element $e_{TM} \in TM$ to the element $e_{SM} \in SM$. The arrow means that a model developer has decided that semantics of the element e_{TM} (the client) is compliant with semantics of the element e_{SM} (the supplier).

We compare the source and target models. The aim of the comparison is an assessment of one model with respect to the another. Both assessment perspectives – assessment the target model with respect the source model and vice versa – are reasonable at different stages of software development. At the stage of a CIM model elaboration it is crucial to keep consistency with the description of the application domain. If the description of the domain is represented by an ontology, the CIM should be assessed with respect to the ontology. At further stages of software development, for example at a PIM model elaboration, it is crucial to keep consistency of the PIM with respect with the CIM model as well as to check that all information in the CIM model is maintained in the PIM model. In this latter case it means that the CIM model may be assessed with respect to the PIM model.

We will assess the target model with respect to the source model taking into account conformance quality characteristic. The assessment will be based on measures that are defined for its subcharacteristics: completeness and compliance. The total completeness means that the domain of the relation *TR* is included in the set of elements of the source model, i.e. $dom(TR) = C_{TM} \cup R_{TM}$. Complete compliance means that each element $e \in C_{TM} \cup R_{TM}$ from the target model should correspond semantically to an element or elements $TR(e) \subseteq C_{SM} \cup R_{SM}$ from the source model.

Completeness

The measures of completeness may be defined at different abstraction levels. We distinguish two levels: classes and relationships. At both levels the measures are defined in similar way:

$$ct_C(TM, SM) = \frac{|\, dom(TR_C)\,|}{|\, C_{TM}\,|}$$

and

$$ct_R(TM, SM) = \frac{|\, dom(TR_R)\,|}{|\, R_{TM}\,|}$$

By definition, the value of completeness measure of the target model *TM* with respect to the source model *SM* at class level and relationship level is not greater than 1. The value less than 1 means there are extra elements in the target model that have no corresponding elements in the source model. The values:

$$\frac{|C_{TM}| - |dom(TR_C)|}{|C_{TM}|}, \frac{|R_{TM}| - |dom(TR_R)|}{|C_{TM}|}$$

are the measures of the extension of the target model with respect to the source model at the level of classes and relationships.

Note that the completeness may be also considered in similar way from the view of the source model. Namely, the measures:

$$ct_C(SM,TM) = \frac{|ran(TR_C)|}{|C_{SM}|}$$

and

$$ct_R(SM,TM) = \frac{|ran(TR_R)|}{|R_{SM}|}$$

inform about the degree to which the source concepts are covered by the target model. The value less than 1 means that the target model *TM* is incomplete, and needs to be improved.

Compliance

The measures of compliance is also considered at different abstraction levels: classes level, classes' attributes level, and relationships level.

At the classes level the compliance of the target model *TM* with respect to the source model *SM* is defined as:

$$cp_C(TM,SM) = \Big(\sum_{c \in dom(TR_C)} |TR_C(c)|^{-1} \Big) / |dom(TR_C)|$$

The value of the measure is not greater 1. The value is less than 1 if $|TR_C(c)| > 1$ for some $c \in dom(TR_C)$ which means that the class *c* from *TM* represents at least two concepts from *SM*. So, the *TM* is not entirely compliant to *SM*, and needs to be improved.

It is worth to note that it is reasonable to consider an inverted compliance of the source model *SM* with respect to the target model *TM* defined as:

$$cp_C(SM,TM) = \Big(\sum_{e \in ran(TR_C)} |TR_C^{-1}(e)|^{-1} \Big) / |ran(TR_C)|$$

The value of the measure is not greater 1. The value is less than 1 if $|TR_C^{-1}(e)| > 1$ which means that the concept *e* from the *SM* is represented by at least two classes in the *TM*.

At the classes' attributes level the compliance of the target model *TM* with respect to the source model *SM* is defined in the following way.

For the class $c \in dom(TR_C)$ by *c.Att* we denote the set of its attributes, and by $TR_C(c).Prop$ the set of properties of the image of this class in the *SM*. We compare two sets *c.Att* and $TR_C(c).Prop$. We say that $a \in c.Att$ corresponds to the property $p \in TR_C(c).Prop$ if *a* and *p* are semantically equivalent and the domain (a set of values) of *a* is a subset of the domain of *p*. By

$$|c.Att \cap TR_C(c).Prop|$$

we denote the number of attributes from *c.Att* that correspond to properties in $TR_C(c).Prop$. The value:

$$cp_{Att}(c) = \frac{|c.Att \cap TR_C(c).Prop|}{|c.Att|}$$

is the measure of compliance of attributes of the class $c \in dom(TR_C)$ from the target model *TM* with respect to the source model *SM*. The value of the measure is not greater 1. If the class *c* has not attributes then, by definition, $cp_{Att}\left(c\right)=1$.

Finally, the measure of compliance of attributes of all classes from the target model *TM* with respect to the source model *SM* is defined as:

$$cp_{Att}(TM,SM)=\sum_{c\in dom\left(TR_C\right)} cp_{Att}(c)/\mid dom\left(TR_C\right)\mid$$

The value of this measure is also normalized to the [0, 1] range.

The definition of the compliance at the relationships level is more complex. Let $r \in R_{TM}$ be relationship from the target model. By *r.Ends* we denote a set of classes from the target model that are arguments of this relationship.

To define the measure $cp_{Rel}\left(r\right)$ of the compliance at the relationship level for a given $r \in R_{TM}$, we have to consider two cases.

The first: if the relationship $TR_R(r)$ is defined then we demand that $TR_R(r).Ends \subseteq TR_C(r.Ends)$. If it is satisfied then $cp_{Rel}\left(r\right)=1$, and $cp_{Rel}\left(r\right)=0$ otherwise.

The second: if the relationship $TR_R(r)$ is not defined then we demand that in the set of source model elements $TR_C(r.Ends)$ there exists at least one element $e \in SM$ semantically equivalent to *r*. If it is satisfied then $cp_{Rel}\left(r\right)=1$, and $cp_{Rel}\left(r\right)=0$ otherwise.

The compliance of the target model *TM* with respect to the source model *SM* at the relationship level is defined as:

$$cp_{Rel}(TM,SM)=\sum_{r\in dom\left(TR_R\right)} cp_{Rel}(r)/\mid dom\left(TR_R\right)\mid$$

The value of this measure, similarly to the previous ones, is normalized to the [0, 1] range. The value determines a percentage of relations in the target model *TM* for which there are semantically equivalent concepts in the source model *SM*.

Background for Model Quality Assessment

Remember that to asses a quality of a model three elements have to be defined: a set of quality characteristics and subcharacteristics (Table 1.), quality measures that are assigned to them, and an assessment function. It should be noted that ISO characteristics and the proposed new characteristic conformance play different roles in the assessment of a model. Namely, positive assessment of a model with respect to conformance characteristic is necessary condition for the assessment of the model with respect to other characteristics.

So, the first step in model quality assessment is to introduce the function *Conform(TM, SM)* evaluating the *TM* model with respect to the *SM* model at the conformance characteristic. The proposed function may be of the form:

$$\begin{aligned}&Conformance\left(TM,SM\right)=\\&\min(Completness\left(TM,SM\right),\\&Compliance\left(TM,SM\right))\end{aligned}$$

where

$$\begin{aligned}&Completness\left(TM,SM\right)=\\&\min(ct_C\left(TM,SM\right),ct_R(TM,SM))\end{aligned}$$

$$\begin{aligned}&Compliance\left(TM,SM\right)=\\&\min(cp_C\left(TM,SM\right),\\&cp_{Att}\left(TM,SM\right),cp_{Rel}(TM,SM))\end{aligned}$$

If *Conform(TM, SM)* =1 then the *TM* model is fully conformed with the *SM* model, and it is reasonable to evaluate the quality of the TM model with respect to other characteristics. In the opposite case, the value *Conform(TM, SM)* < 1 indicates the problem that the model *TIM* is not conformed to the *SM* model. Then the problem is to be analyzed and the reason for nonconformance should be detected. Next, the *TM* model is improved or accepted by domain experts. In the latter case the decision is the result of a comprehensive comparison of semantics of these two models.

Now, if the *TM* model is accepted the total quality assessment function *TQ* may be computed. The function is a composition of the functions $PQ_{c1}, PQ_{c2}, \ldots, PQ_{ck}$ that assess partially the quality of the model with respect to a set of selected characteristics or subcharacteristics{*c1, c2,..., ck*}. Each of these functions operates on values of measures defined for a given characteristic and yields, similarly to *TQ*, one of the assessment values {*unacceptable, minimal, target, excided*}.

Comparison of semantics of two models is a real problem. The modeler developing an information system is faced with the problem, first time, during models transformation, and next during models comparison. Comparison of two models is based on the assumption that a set of trace dependencies between the target and source models is given.

There are two kinds of trace dependencies: first – when clients are classes from the target model and suppliers are sets of elements from the source model, and second – when clients are relations from the target model and suppliers are also sets of elements from the source model. In both cases we expect that the clients and suppliers are semantically equivalent. How to check the equivalence is a separate problem which is not discussed here. Only some examples of semantically possible transformations are presented in Figure 2.

EXAMPLE OF QUALITY-DRIVEN MDA APPLICATION

This section is an illustration of the application of the proposed enhancement to Q-MDA framework. The considered software product is a Hotel Management database system. This system was selected as a fairly simple, and related to commonly known matter.

The presentation starts with the concise description of user needs. Next, CIM and PIM models are presented, and their quality is evaluated with the usage of proposed metrics. CIM is evaluated against an ontology (presented in a separated subchapter), while PIM – against CIM.

Needs Description

The system is going to support a hotel staff in its business activities. Internet is a typical medium of selling products nowadays, so it is crucial for any hotel manager to provide the offer that way in order to be able to compete in the market. A potential hotel client should be able to get to know hotel information including hotel rooms, room equipment, room availability and prices. The client also should be able to make a reservation or cancel it. On the other hand, the system should support the hotel staff in their duties, particularly the hotel manager and receptionists. Hotel manager is responsible for preparing an interesting offer which is adjusted to clients needs, and is economically viable. The manager decides about room prices, promotions, room facilities, and room renovations. To do this the manager should have a relevant information, e.g. about planned hotel arrivals or about history guest stays. The reception desk is managed by trained personnel. The responsibilities of the receptionists include informing clients about

Figure 2. Possible semantically equivalent trace dependencies

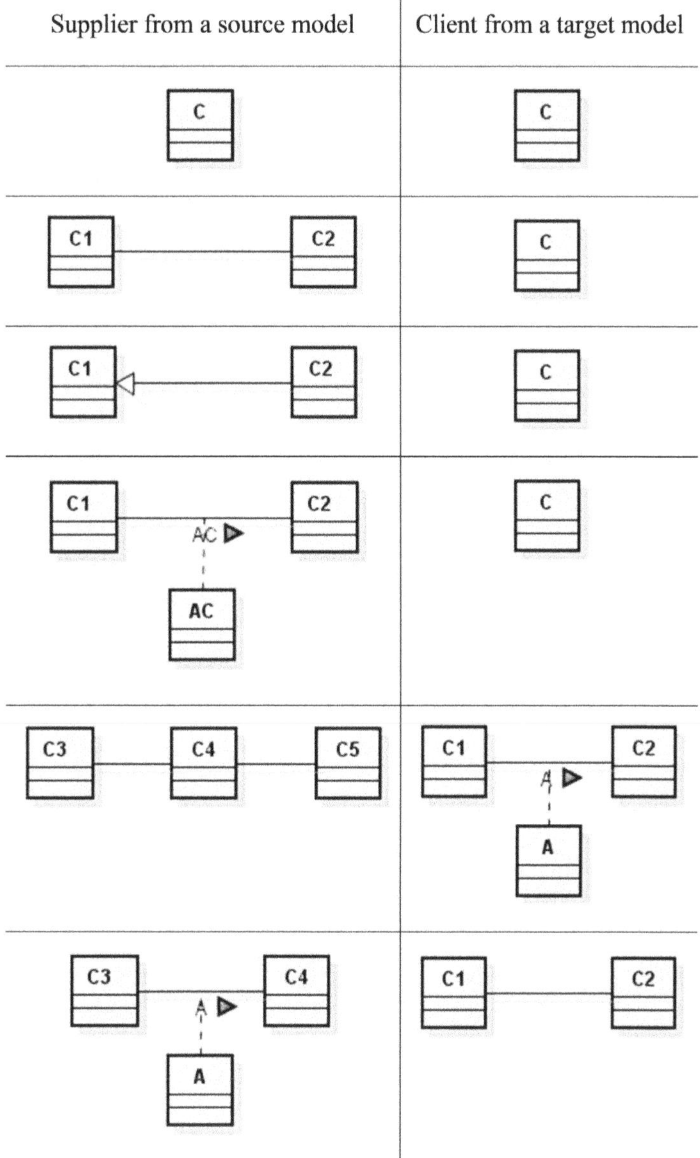

hotel services, manage reservations, checking in and out of the hotel, accepting payments and preparing receipts (payments are out of scope of further considerations). Reservations' details are used to an analysis of planned hotel occupancy, schedule of rooms renovation, and adjustment the offer to the real needs. Stays' details are used to an analysis of financial incomes and also allow to adjust the offer to the market expectation.

The hotel is characterized by the following quantities:

- 10 000 potential clients per year;
- 65 rooms of 5 types;
- Two reception desks with a processing time of five minutes per client.

The following main problems are identified within considered domain:

- Current lack of the room reservation by Internet results in clients' dissatisfaction and choosing another offer.
- Time consuming preparation of analytical reports.

Having to improve the quality of delivered hotel services and clients satisfaction, the following needs were established:

- From the perspective of hotel clients:
    - Quick and simple reservations.
- From the perspective of hotel manager:
    - Effective management of hotel resources (rooms), and assurance of high clients' satisfaction.
    - Support for analytical reports preparation.

CIM Model

Typically CIM consists of four components: a domain model with business rules, and a use-case model with supplementary specification. We limit our presentation to the domain model with business rules, as only that part will be compared to ontology definition.

The starting point for business modeling is business rules identification. We defined the business rules belonging to different groups. We followed classification of business rules elaborated by von Halle (Halle, 2001). We started from terms and facts definition, and after that we identified a set of invariants – all mentioned types of business rules can be directly expressed on a UML class diagram.

- Terms (in alphabetic order):
    - **Customer:** A person who makes a reservation, and stays at a hotel.
    - **Disclosure:** A period for which a hotel room is unavailable.
    - **Feature:** An amenity of rooms belonging to a specific room type.
    - **Hotel:** A building with hotel rooms to be hired.
    - **Hotel Name:** A name of a hotel.
    - **Hotel Address:** A post address of a hotel.
    - **Hotel Room:** A separate place in a hotel that can be reserved and hired.
    - **Hotel Room Number:** A unique number to identify a hotel room.
    - **Hotel Room State:** Description of room state (enumeration: occupied, free, disclosed).
    - **Hotel Standard:** A standard, typically expressed with a number of stars, of a hotel.
    - **Price List Item:** A value in a specific currency expressing how much a customer has to pay for a room of specific type hired for specific period.
    - Price List Item Currency.
    - Price List Item Value.
    - **Price List Item Period:** dateFrom, dateTo.
    - **Reservation (As a Term):** An agreement between a customer and a hotel owner about hiring a specific room in the hotel for specific period on specific conditions (prices).
    - **Reservation Period:** dateFrom, dateTo.
    - **Reservation State:** Description of reservation state (enumeration: submitted, cancelled, closed, overdue).
    - **Room Type Capacity:** The maximal number of person who can live in a room of that type.
    - **Room Type:** A model of a room describing the room equipment.

  - **Stay:** An information who (guests) checked-in to a hotel room maybe according to a specific reservation.
- Facts (in alphabetic order):
  - **SF/01:** Hotel has a name, an address, and standard defined.
  - **SF/02:** Hotel consists of hotel rooms.
  - **SF/03:** Hotel room has a number and a room state.
  - **SF/04:** Hotel offers different room types.
  - **SF/05:** Room type has capacity.
  - **SF/06:** Room type is equipped with features.
  - **SF/07:** Room type has price list items.
  - **SF/08:** Price list item has a value, a currency and a period (dateFrom, dateTo) it takes effect.
  - **SF/09:** Hotel room is of a specific room type.
  - **SF/10:** Customer makes a reservation on a hotel room.
  - **SF/11:** Reservation has a period (dateFrom, dateTo) and a reservation state.
  - **SF/12:** Reservation can result in a stay.
  - **SF/13:** Customer is a guest within a stay.
  - **SF/14:** Hotel room can be planned for disclosure.
  - **SF/15:** Disclosure has a period (dateFrom, dateTo).
- Invariants (must be true for all entities):
  - **I/1:** Hotel room must have at least 1 hotel room.
  - **I/2:** Stay must depict at least 1 guest.
  - **I/3:** Room type must have at least 1 price list item defined.
  - **I/4:** The price list items assigned with a specific room type must cover the continuous period.
  - **I/5:** In every entity dateFrom must preceed dateTo.

On the base of presented above business rules a domain model was elaborated – see Figure 3.

Most invariants can be expressed formally with the use of OCL language (shown in Box 1).

Hotel Ontology

We found a hotel ontology, created by Karen Joy Nomorosa (Nomorosa, 2011), describing different concept prevalent in the hotel domain, which is distributed on GNU General Public Licence [???]. We study carefully this ontology, trying to find equivalences for our terms. When a notion was not presented directly in hotel.kif we look for it in upper ontologies, e.g. merge.kif. Table 2. presents the mapping between terms and facts from our UML CIM model and ontology entities.

We also proposed a translation of SUMO ontology to UML class diagram (only the part we were interested in) – see Figure 4.

CIM Evaluation against Ontology Definition

Completeness

In order to assess our CIM model against existing ontology we calculated most of measures proposed in preceding section, starting from completeness at class level.

$$ct_C\left(CIM, Ontology\right) = \frac{\left|dom\left(TR_C\right)\right|}{\left|C_{CIM}\right|} = \frac{7}{9}$$

Two classes of CIM model were not traced from ontology definition, i.e. *Disclosure* and *Feature*, what influenced on ct_c measure result. *Disclosure* is not presented in hotel ontology what can mean that this ontology is incomplete (or that this notion is out of ontology scope). We also didn't find any ontology representation for *Feature* class understood as a room equipment

Figure 3. CIM for hotel management system

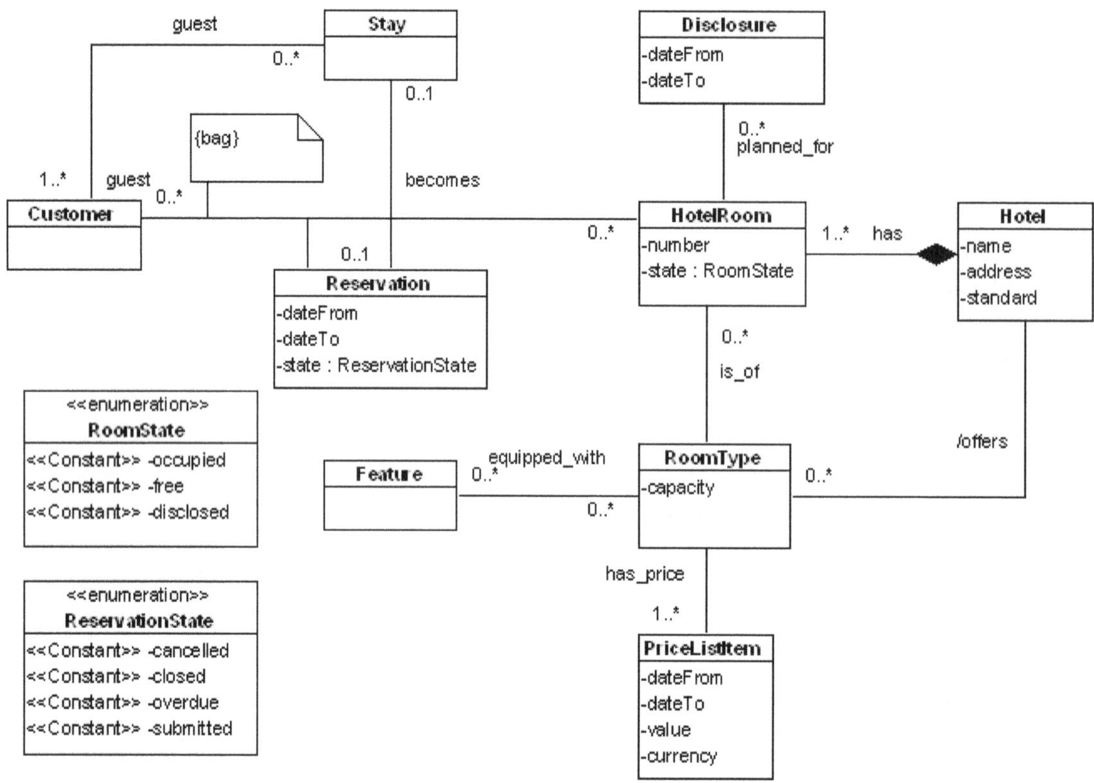

which is better than *Physical* (analysis of room amenity relationship). But, in our opinion, such mapping is unacceptable, as *Physical* class is too general (has to many meanings). We expect the ontology to be more specific.

We decided to trace *Price List Item* (in CIM) from *Formula* from hotels ontology. Formula is a domain for *rateDetails* predicate, which "gives the price detail associated with each item in the reservation", *Stay* class was traced from *stays* association.

After that we calculated the completeness measure at relationship level.

Box 1.

```
context Disclosure inv: dateFrom < dat eto
context Reservation inv: dateFrom < dateTo
context RoomType inv: capacity > 0
context PriceListItem inv: dataFrom <dataTo
context RoomType inv:
   let sortedPrices: Sequence = self.priceListItem.sortedBy(dateFrom) in
   sortedPrices→forAll(p | p <> sortedPrices.last() implies
   p.dateTo = sortedPrices→at(sortedPrices→indexOf(p) + 1).dateFrom + 1)
```

Table 2. CIM - SUMO ontology mapping

Term in CIM	Entity in Hotel Ontology
Customer	CognitiveAgent
Disclosure	-
Feature	-
Hotel	HotelBuilding
Hotel name	Entity: fullName
Hotel address	PostalPace: postAddressText
Hotel standard	-
Hotel room	HotelRoom
Hotel room number	-
Hotel room state	-
Price List Item	Formula
Price list item currency	-
Price list item value	-
Price list item dateFrom	TimePoint
Price list item dateTo	TimePoint
Reservation	HotelReservation
Reservation state	-
Reservation dateFrom	TimePoint
Reservation dateTo	TimePoint
Room type	HotelUnit
Room type capacity	StacionaryArtefact: MaxRoomCapacity
Stay	Stays: Human x TemporaryResidence
SF/01 (hotel attributes)	PostalPlace: postAddressText
SF/02 (has: Hotel x Hotel room)	properPart: Object x Object (+hotel axioms)
SF/03 (hotel room attributes)	-
SF/04 (offers: hotel x room type)	-
SF/05 (room type attributes)	StacjonaryArtefact: MaxRoomCapacity
SF/06 (equipped_with: room type x feature)	roomAmenity: HotelUnit x Physical
SF/07 (has_price: room type x price list item)	rateDetails: Reservation x Formula
SF/08 (price list item attributes)	-
SF/09 (is_of: hotel room x room type)	subclass HotelRoom HotelUnit
SF/10 (reservation: customer x room)	ReservingEntity: Agent x Reservation ReservedRoom: HotelReservation x HotelUnit
SF/11 (reservation attributes)	Reservation end: HotelReservation x TimePoint Reservation start: HotelReservation x TimePoint
SF/12 (becomes: reservation x stay)	-
SF/13 (guest: stay x customer)	Guest: CognitiveAgent x CognitiveAgent
SF/14 (planned_for: hotel room x disclosure)	-
SF/15 (disclosure attributes)	-

Figure 4. UML representation of Hotel ontology with selected entities from Upper ontologies

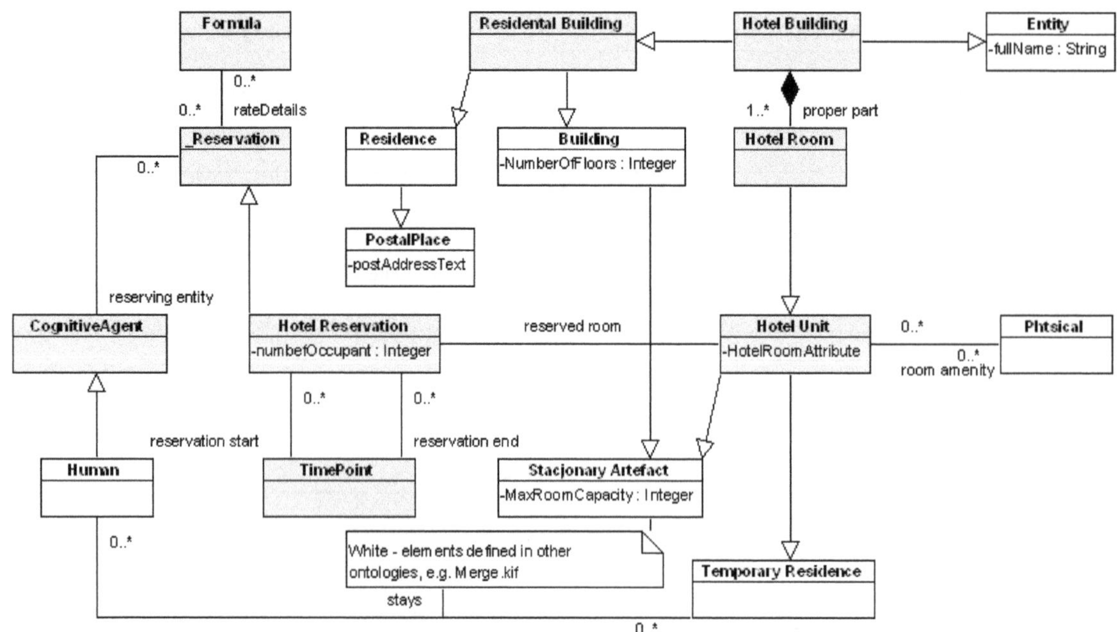

$$ct_R\left(CIM, Ontology\right) = \frac{\left|dom\left(TR_R\right)\right|}{\left|R_{CIM}\right|} = \frac{6}{9} = \frac{2}{3}$$

66% of CIM relationships were traced from ontology. We couldn't trace three associations:

- SF/04 – which is a derived association in our model, meaning that it can be removed without losing important information,
- SF/12 (becomes association) – which is completely absent in ontology, so we can say in this area hotel ontology is incomplete,
- SF/14 (planned_for) – as above, this association (similarly to one of classes it links) is absent in ontology (ontology incompleteness).

Compliance

Having completeness assessed, we can consider element compliance, first at class level.

$$cp_C\left(TM, SM\right) = \frac{\sum_{c \in dom\left(TR_C\right)} \left|TR_C\left(c\right)\right|^{-1}}{\left|dom\left(TR_C\right)\right|} =$$

$$\frac{1+1+1+1+1+1+1}{7} = 1$$

Each class which was traced from ontology, was traced from exactly one ontology element. This is an ideal case meaning that the granularity level of notion is the same in CIM and in ontology.

After that we calculated the value of compliance measure for attributes.

$$cp_{Att} = \frac{\sum_{c \in dom(TR_C)} cp_{Att}(c)}{\left|dom\left(TR_C\right)\right|} = \frac{1 + \frac{2}{3} + \frac{0}{2} + \frac{0}{4} + \frac{2}{3} + \frac{1}{1} + 1}{7} = 0,62$$

There were 2 classes in our model without attributes, so the assessment function for them returned 1. *Hotel room* and *Price list items* were classes for which neither of attributes were found in ontology. *Reservation* attributes and *Hotel* attributes were traced partially (2 attributes from 3). The value of cp_{Att} less than 1 can suggest two possible problems:

- Target model is not simple refinement of source model; it introduced some new concepts, maybe closed to implementation.
- Ontology incompleteness, where some key notions were omitted (e.g. it seems that hotel room number should be present in ontology definition).

The last measure we calculated was compliance for relationships.

$$cp_{Rel} = \sum_{r \in dom(TR_R)} cp_{Rel}(r) / \mid dom\left(TR_R\right) = \frac{1+1+0+0+1+0}{6} = 0,5$$

Three from six relationships in our model was not compliant with their origins, e.g. cp_{Rel}(*has_price*) = cp_{Rel}(*is_of*)=cp_{Rel}(*guest*) = 0.

RateDetails predicate in hotel ontology being the source of *has_price association* connects completely different entities (*Reservation* and *Formula*) than in domain model (*Room type* and *Price List Item*). However, CIM allows to navigate from a reservation instance to an instance of hotel room, and next to its type and associated price list items. So we can say, that this relationship was model in CIM and ontology in different ways. That can be changed easily at CIM level.

Guest predicate, which definition in ontology is very close to our, relates two *CognitiveAgents* not *Stay* and *Customers* as in our solution. Semantics of this notion is different in both models.

Very interesting case is about *is_of* association linking hotel room and hotel type in CIM. The equivalent relationship in SUMO is inheritance hierarchy, which can be suggested also by our model (hotel room is of a room type).

Reservation association class in CIM is represented with Hotel Reservation class inheriting from Reservation class and two associations: reserved room and reserving entity. This is a classical equivalent relationship between different UML models.

PIM Model

On the base of functional requirements for Hotel Management system, traced from needs, but not presented here, PIM model was developed – see Figure 5.

Traceability for PIM elements to CIM elements are gathered in Table 3.

PIM Evaluation Against CIM

Completeness

Below the results for particular measures of completeness are given.

$$ct_C\left(PIM, CIM\right) = \frac{\left|dom\left(TR_C\right)\right|}{\left|C_{PIM}\right|} = \frac{9}{9}$$

$$ct_C\left(CIM, PIM\right) = \frac{\left|ran\left(TR_C\right)\right|}{\left|C_{CIM}\right|} = \frac{8}{8}$$

Figure 5. PIM model for Hotel management system

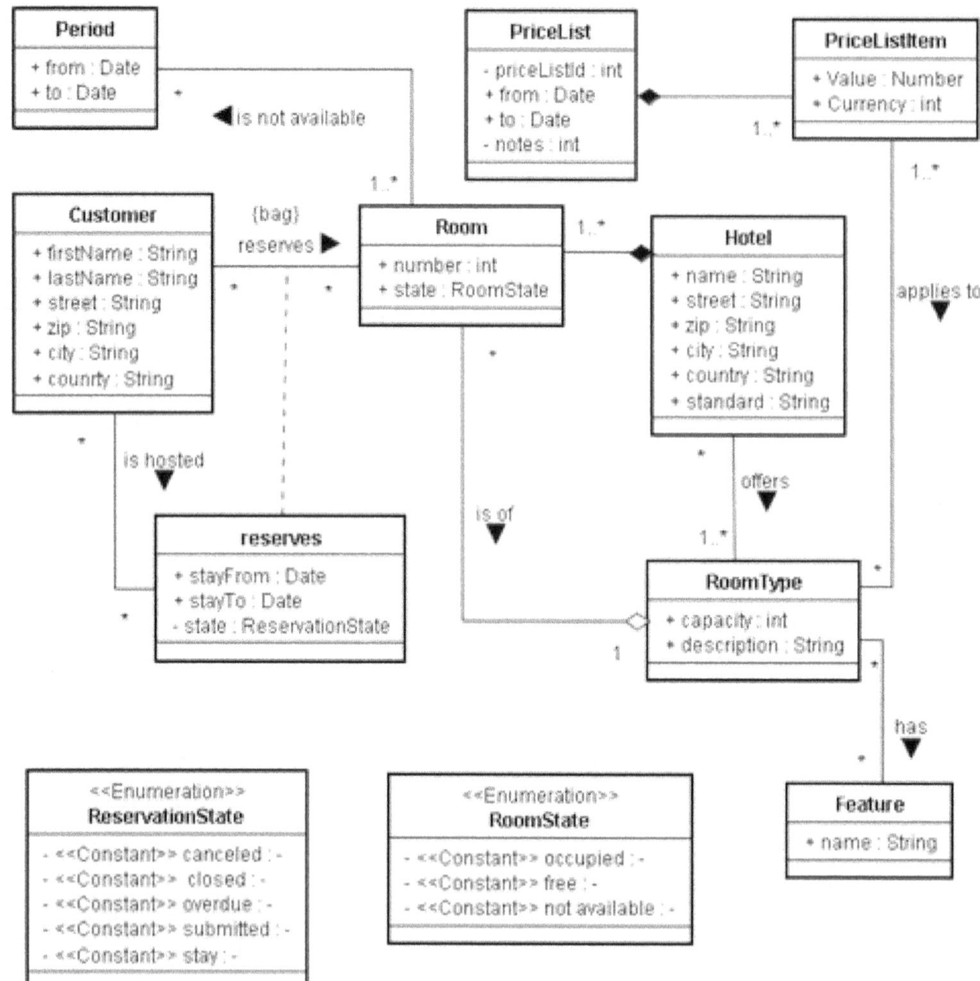

Completeness can be evaluated from two perspectives (CIM, and PIM). We can say that at class level both models are complete.

$$ct_R\left(PIM,CIM\right)=\frac{\left|dom\left(TR_R\right)\right|}{\left|R_{PIM}\right|}=\frac{8}{9}=0.89$$

$$ct_R\left(CIM,PIM\right)=\frac{\left|ran\left(TR_R\right)\right|}{\left|R_{CIM}\right|}=\frac{9}{9}=1$$

Similarly to classes, completeness of relationships can be evaluated from two perspectives (CIM, and PIM). PIM model introduced one new relationship.

Compliance

Below the results for particular measures of compliance are given.

$$cp_C(PIM,CIM)=(\frac{\sum_{c\in dom(TR_C)}\left|TR_C\left(c\right)\right|^{-1})}{\left|dom\left(TR_C\right)\right|}=$$

$$\frac{1+1+1+1+1+1+1+1+1}{9}=1$$

Table 3. PIM - CIM mapping

No	PIM Model (Target Model)	CIM Model (Source Model)
Classes and their attributes		
C01	**Customer**	**Customer**
2.	firstName, lastName, Street, Zip, city, country (6)	-
C02	**Hotel**	**Hotel**
7.	Name	Name
8.	street	Address
9.	zip	
10.	city	
11.	country	
12.	standard	Standard
C03	**Room**	**HotelRoom**
3.	Number	Number
4.	state	State
C04	**PriceList**	**PriceListItem**
7.	priceListId	-
8.	from	dateFrom
9.	to	dateTo
10.	notes	-
11.	-	Currency
12.	-	Value
C05	**PriceListItem**	**PriceListItem**
5.	Value	Value
6.	currency	Currency
7.		dateFrom
8.		dateTo
C06	**RoomType**	**RoomType**
3.	capacity	Capacity
4.	description	
C07	**Period**	**Disclosure**
3.	from	dateFrom
4.	to	dateTo
C08	**Feature**	**Feature**
2.	name	
C09	**Reserves**	**Reservation**
4.	stayFrom	dateFrom
5.	stayTo	dateTo
6.	State	State

continued on following page

Table 3. Continued

No	PIM Model (Target Model)	CIM Model (Source Model)
Relationships		
10.	reserves (Customer [*]: [*] Room; {bag})	Reservation (Customer [*]: [*] HotelRoom; {bag})
11.	is not available (Room [1..*]: [*] Period)	planned_for (Disclosure [1..*]: [1] HotelRoom)
12.	consists of (Hotel [1]: [1..*] Room)	has (Hotel [1]: [1..*] HotelRoom)
13.	consists of (PriceList [1]: [1..] PriceItem)	
14.	offers (Hotel [*]: [1..*] RoomType)	offers (Hotel [*]: [1..*] RoomType)
15.	Is hosted (Customer [*]: [*] reserves)	guest (Customer [1..*]: [*] Stay) becomes (Stay [0..1]: [0..1] Reservation)
16.	applies to (PriceItem [1..*]: [*] RoomType)	has_price (RoomType [1]: [1..*] PriceListItem)
17.	has (RoomType [*]: [*] Feature)	equipped_with (RoomType [*]: [*] Feature)

$$cp_C(CIM, PIM) = (\frac{\sum_{e\in ran(TR_C)} \left|TR_C^{-1}(e)\right|^{-1})}{\left|ran\left(TR_C\right)\right|} = \frac{1+1+1+\frac{1}{2}+1+1+1+1}{8} = 0.94$$

There are some classes in CIM model that were refined and decomposed into more elements (PriceListItem from CIM is now represented by two classes: PriceList and PriceListItem in PIM).

$$cp_{Att}\left(PIM, CIM\right) = \frac{\sum_{c\in dom(TR_C)} cp_{Att}\left(c\right)}{\left|dom\left(TR_C\right)\right|} = \frac{0+1+1+1+1+\frac{1}{2}+1+0+1}{9} = \frac{6.5}{9} = 0.72$$

Three classes at PIM level were refined (new attributes were added).

$$cp_{Rel}\left(PIM, CIM\right) = \frac{\sum_{r\in dom(TR_R)} cp_{Rel}\left(r\right)}{\left|dom\left(TR_R\right)\right|} = \frac{1+1+1+0+1+1+1+1+1}{9} = 0.89$$

One association at PIM level was added what caused decreasing of cp_{Rel}.

Defined measures can be used as acceptance ratio of the compared models. Each value of the measure that is less than 1 is the information about the need to verify the indicated parts of the model. A designer can accept these parts of the model and mark them as a correct (arbitrarily) or he/she can decide to improve some elements in the target model.

CONCLUSION

In the chapter we presented extended Q-MDA framework to software system development which combines MDA approach with quality specification and evaluation. The framework enhances quality model presented in (Dubielewicz, Hnatkowska, Huzar, Tuzinkiewicz 2011). The extended framework takes into account that there is a strong dependency relationship between two subsequent models in software development process. The dependency imposes a necessity to compare semantics of two consecutive models and, in consequence, to decide if the target model is conformed to the source model. The proposed measures for the newly introduced quality characteristic – conformance – with its two subcharacteristics – completeness and compli-

Table 4. Summary of completeness and compliance measures

Measure	Value	Acceptance	Comments
$ct_C(PIM, CIM)$	1.0	Ok	Completeness at class level
$ct_C(CIM, PIM)$	1.0	Ok	Completeness at class level (opposite direction)
$ct_R(PIM, CIM)$	0.89	Verify	Completeness at relationship level
$ct_R(CIM, PIM)$	1	OK	Completeness at relationship level (opposite direction)
$cp_C(PIM, CIM)$	1.0	Ok	Compliance at class level
$cp_C(CIM, PIM)$	0.94	Verify	Compliance at class level (opposite direction)
$cp_{Att}(PIM, CIM)$	0.72	Verify	Compliance of attributes of all classes
$cp_{Rel}(PIM, CIM)$	0.89	Verify	Compliance at relationship level

ance – enable to compare the developed models and analyze sources of possible inconsistencies. The conformance of the target model with respect to the source model is necessary condition for evaluation of the quality of the model in terms of quality characteristics defined by ISO. The Q-MDA framework enables early examination and evaluation of developed models in the context of software development process what results in controlled quality of final software product and also improves efficiency of development process. The framework is general and can be adopted for different kinds of applications, for example for database systems.

Additional advantage of the extended Q-MDA is possibility to assess CIM models with respect to domain ontologies. Domain ontologies play more and more important role in software development aimed at supporting of many application domains, and therefore they should be taken into account in the software development process.

A simple example of database system development illustrates an application of the extended framework. The example is concentrated on explanation how to compare a CIM model with a domain ontology, and how to compare PIM model with the CIM model. An illustration how to define software quality demands and how to assess the quality of database models with respect to this demands is presented in (Dubielewicz, Hnatkowska, Huzar, Tuzinkiewicz 2011).

The considerations presented in the chapter reveal the need for specific methods of ontologies' presentation and their use in the software development process.

REFERENCES

Common Warehouse Metamodel (CWM) Specification Version 1.1. (2003). Retrieved from http://www.omg.org/technology/documents/formal/cwm_2.htm

Connolly, T., & Begg, C. (2005). *Database systems: A practical approach to design, implementation, and management* (4th ed.). New York: Pearson Education, Inc.

Deissenboeck, F., Juergens, E., Lochmann, K., & Wagner, S. (2009). Software quality models: Purposes, usage scenarios and requirements. In *Proc. Seventh Workshop on Software Quality* (pp. 9–14). IEEE Computer Society. doi:10.1109/WOSQ.2009.5071551

Dubielewicz, I., Hnatkowska, B., Huzar, Z., & Tuzinkiewicz, L. (2006). Feasibility analysis of MDA-based database design. In ZamojskiW. (Ed.), *Proceedings of International Conference on Dependability of Computer Systems. DepCoS – RELCOMEX* (pp. 19–26). Los Alamitos, CA: IEEE Computer Society Press.

Dubielewicz, I., Hnatkowska, B., Huzar, Z., & Tuzinkiewicz, L. (2011). Quality-driven database system development. In J. Osis, & E. Asnina (Eds.), *Model-driven domain analysis and software development: Architectures and functions* (pp. 201–231). Hershey, PA: Information Science Reference.

Elmasri, R., & Navathe, S. B. (2007). *Fundamentals of database systems (5th ed.).* New York: Pearson Education, Inc.

García, F., Serrano, M., Cruz-Lemus, J., Ruiz, F., & Piattini, M. (2007). Managing software process measurement: A metamodel-based approach. *Information Sciences, 177*(12), 2570–2586. doi:10.1016/j.ins.2007.01.018

Garvin, D. A. (1984). What does "product quality" really mean? MIT Sloan Management Review, 26(1), 25–43.

Guide to the Software Engineering Body of Knowledge (SWEBOK). (2004). Retrieved from http://www.computer.org/portal/web/swebok/about

Halle von, B. (2001). *Business rules applied: Building better systems using the business rules approach.* Willey Publ.

Halpin, T., & Morgan, T. (2008). *Information modelling and relational databases* (2nd ed.). Burlington, MA: Morgan Kaufman Publisher.

Ho-Won, J., Seung-Gweon, K., & Chang-Shin, Ch. (2004). Measuring software product quality: A survey of ISO/IEC 9126. *IEEE Software, 21*(5), 88–92. doi:10.1109/MS.2004.1331309

ISO/IEC 9126-3:2003 (E). (2003). *Software engineering – Product quality – Part 3: Internal metrics.*

ISO/IEC 9075:2003 (part 1, 2). (2003). *Information technology – Database languages-SQL.*

ISO/IEC 25000:2005 (E). (2005). *Software engineering – Software quality and requirements evaluation (SQuaRE) guide to SQuaRE.*

ISO/IEC 25010:2011 (E). (2011). *Systems and Software engineering – Software quality and requirements evaluation (SQuaRE) - Systems and software quality models.*

Kifer, M., Brenstein, A., & Lewis, P. M. (2006). *Database systems: An application-oriented approach* (2nd ed.). New York: Addison Wesley.

Kroll, P., & Kruchten, P. (2003). *Rational Unified Process Made Easy, A Practitioner's Guide to the RUP.* Boston, MA: Addison-Wesley Professional.

Lamouchi, O., Cherif, A. R., & Levy, N. (2008). A Framework Based Measurements for Evaluating an IS Quality. In *Proc. Fifth Asia-Pacific Conference on Conceptual Modelling* (pp. 39–47). Wollongong, Australia: CRPIT.

Leffingwell, D., & Widrig, D. (2003). *Managing Software Requirements: A Use Case Approach.* Boston, MA: Addison-Wesley.

Lightstone, S., Teorey, T., & Nadeau, T. (2007). *Physical Database Design. The Database Professional's Guide to Exploiting Indexes, Views, Storage, and More*. San Francisco, CA: Morgan Kaufman Publisher.

Miller, J., & Mukerji, J. (2003). *MDA Guide version 1.0.1*. Retrieved from http://www.omg.org/

Mohagheghi, P., & Dehlen, V. (2008). *Developing a Quality Framework for Model-Driven Engineering. In Models in Software Engineering* (pp. 275–289). Heidelberg, Germany: Springer.

Mohagheghi, P., Dehlen, V., & Neple, T. (2009). Definitions and approaches to model quality in model-based software development – A review of literature. *Information and Software Technology*, *51*(12), 1646–1669. doi:10.1016/j.infsof.2009.04.004

Nomorosa, K. Y., (2011). *Hotel ontology*. Rearden Commerce Inc. Retrieved from http://sigmakee.cvs.sourceforge.net/viewvc/sigmakee/KBs/Hotel.kif

Piattini, M., Calero, C., Sahraoui, H., & Lounis, H. (2001). Object-relational database metrics. *L'Object Edition Hermès Sciences*, *17*(4), 477–498.

Piattini, M., & Genero, M. (2001). *Empirical validation of measures for class diagram structural complexity through controlled experiments*. Retrieved from http://www.iro.umontreal.ca/~sahraouh/qaoose01/genero.pdf

UML Profile for Modeling Quality of Service and Fault Tolerance Characteristics and mechanisms, v 1.1. (2008). Retrieved from http://www.omg.org/technology/documents/formal/QoS_FT.htm

Wagner, S., & Deissenboeck, F. (2007). An Integrated Approach to Quality Modelling. In *Proceedings of the 5th International Workshop on Software Quality* (pp. 1). Washington, DC: IEEE Computer Society.

ADDITIONAL READING

Ambler, S. (2006). *Refactoring Database: Evolutionary Database Design*. NY: Addison Wesley Professional.

Behkamal, B., Kahani, M., & Akbari, M. K., (2009). Customizing ISO 9126 quality model for evaluation of B2B applications. *Information and Software Technology* 51, 599–609, Available online 26 September 2008

Bombardieri, M., & Fontana, F., A., (2009). Software aging assessment through a specialization of the SQuaRE quality model, In: *Proc. Seventh Workshop on Software Quality* (pp. 33–38), IEEE Computer Society.

Calero, C., Sahraoui, H. A., Piattini, M., & Lounis, H. (2002) Estimating Object-Relational Database Understandability Using Structural Metrics. From www.springerlink.com/index/04jldq2uwenn5v90.pdf

Cherfi, S. S., Akoka, J., & Comyn-Wattiau, I. (2007). Perceived vs. Measured Quality of Conceptual Schemas: An Experimental Comparison. In Grundy, J., Hartmann, S., Laender, A. H. F., Maciaszek, L. and Roddick, J. F. (Ed.), *Proc. Tutorials, posters, panels and industrial contributions at the 26th International Conference on Conceptual Modeling – ER 2007* (pp. 185–190), Auckland, New Zealand. CRPIT, 83, ACS

Cockburn, A. (2001). *Writing Effective Use Cases.* Boston: Addison Wesley.

Cortellessa, V., Di Marco, A., & Inverardi, P. (2007) Non-Functional Modeling and Validation in Model-Driven Architecture. from www.plastic.paris-rocquencourt.inria.fr/dissemination/wicsa2007_cr-2.pdf

Dubielewicz, I., Hnatkowska, B., Huzar, Z., & Tuzinkiewicz, L. (2006). An approach to evaluation of PSM. MDA database models in the context of transaction performance. *International Journal on Computer Systems and Network Security, 10*(6), 179–186.

Dubielewicz, I., Hnatkowska, B., Huzar, Z., & Tuzinkiewicz, L. (2006). An approach to software quality specification and evaluation (SPoQE). In K. Sacha (Ed.), *Software engineering techniques: design for quality* (pp. 155–166). New York, Boston: Springer. doi:10.1007/978-0-387-39388-9_16

Dubielewicz, I., Hnatkowska, B., Huzar, Z., & Tuzinkiewicz, L. (2006). Software Quality Metamodel for Requirement, Evaluation and Assessment, In: *Proceedings of Information, Simulation, Modeling. ISIM'06 Conference.* pp. 115–122. Prerov, Czech Republic:Acta Mosis No. 105.

Dubielewicz, I., Hnatkowska, B., Huzar, Z., & Tuzinkiewicz, L. (2007). Quality-driven software development within MDA approach. *International Review on Computers and Software, 6*(2), 573–580.

ISO/IEC 14598-5:1998 (E), Software engineering – Product evaluation – Part 5: Process for evaluators.

ISO/IEC 14598-3:2000 (E), Information technology – Product evaluation – Part 3: Process for developers.

ISO/IEC 9126-2:2003 (E), Software engineering – Product quality – Part 2: External metrics.

Kleppe, A., Warmer, J., & Bast, W. (2004). *MDA Explained: The Model Driven Architecture: Practice and Promise.* Boston, MA: Pearson Education, Inc.

Lange, C. F. J., & Chaudron, M. R. V. (2005). Managing Model Quality in UML-based Software Development. *Proceedings of the 13th IEEE International Workshop on Software Technology and Engineering Practice (STEP'05)* (pp. 7–16), IEEE Compter Society, Washington, DC, USA. doi:10.1109/STEP.2005.16

MacDonell, S. G., Shepperd, M. J., & Sallis, P. J. (1997). Metrics for Database Systems: An Empirical Study. METRICS '97: Proceedings of the 4th International Symposium on Software Metrics (pp. 99), IEEE Compter Society, Washington, DC, USA. doi:10.1109/METRIC.1997.637170

Mendling, J., Reijers, H. A., & van der Aalst, W. M. P. (2010). Seven process modeling guidelines (7PMG). *Information and Software Technology, 52*(2), 127–136. doi:10.1016/j.infsof.2009.08.004

Mohagheghi, P., & Aagedal, J. (2007). Evaluating Quality in Model-Driven Engineering. *International Workshop on Modeling in Software Engineering* (pp. 6), IEEE Computer Society, Washington, DC, USA. doi:10.1109/MISE.2007.6

Naiburg, E. J., & Maksimchuk, R. A. (2002), UML for Database Design, Boston, Addison Wesley.

Pham, H. N., Mahmoud, Q. H., Ferworn, A., & Sadeghian, A. (2007). Applying Model-Driven Development to Pervasive System Engineering. *29th International Conference on Software Engineering Workshops* (pp. 7), IEEE Computer Society, Washington, DC, USA. doi:10.1109/SEPCASE.2007.2

Piattini, M., & Genero, M. (2002). *An empirical study with metrics for object-relational databases* (pp. 298–309). Lecture Notes in Computer Science Volume Software Quality – ECSQ.

Rawashdeh, A., & Matalkah, B. (2006). A new software quality model for evaluating COTS components. *Jordan Journal of Computer Science*, *2*(4), 373–381. doi:10.3844/jcssp.2006.373.381

Rech, J., & Bunse, C. (Eds.). (2008). *Model-Driven Software Development: Integrating Quality Assurance*. Information Science Reference. doi:10.4018/978-1-60566-006-6

Reingruber, M. C., & Gregory, W. W. (1994). *The Data Modeling Handbook: A Best-Practice Approach to Building Quality Data Models*. New York: John Wiley & Sons, Inc.

Rosenberg, D., & Scott, K. (1999). *Use Case Driven Object Modeling With UML: A Practical Approach*. Reading, MA: Addison Wesley Longman, Inc

Ross, R. G. (1997). *The Business Rule Book* (2nd ed.). Houston, Texas: Business Rules Solutions, Inc.

Röttger, S., & Zschaler, S. (2004). Lecture Notes in Computer Science: Vol. 3273. *Model-Driven Development for Non-functional Properties: Refinement Through Model Transformation. Book: The Unified Modelling Language* (pp. 275–289). Heidelberg: Springer Berlin.

Shasha, D., & Bonet, P. (2003). *Database Tuning, principles, experiments and troubleshooting techniques*. San Francisco: Morgan Kaufmann Publisher.

Skene, J., & Emmerich, W. (2003) A Model-Driven Approach to Non-Functional Analysis of Software Architectures. from http://eprints.ucl.ac.uk/720/1/9.9.5ase03.pdf

Unhelkar, B. (2005). *Verification and Validation for Quality of UML 2.0 Models*. Hoboken, NY: Wiley-Interscience. doi:10.1002/0471734322

Wagner, S., Lochmann, K., Winter, S., Goeb, A., & Klaes, M. (2009). Quality Models in Practice: A Preliminary Analysis, In: *Proc. 3rd International Symposium on Empirical Software Engineering and Measurement* (pp. 464–467). IEEE Computer Society, Lake Buena Vista, FL, USA. doi:10.1109/ESEM.2009.5316003

KEY TERMS AND DEFINITIONS

Conceptual Data Model: A model of a database expressed at platform independent level; describes entities from a considered domain, properties of these entities, and the relationships between entities.

External Quality Model: A kind of *quality model* which represents the perspective of a final user which uses the software product in a specified environment and a specific context of use.

Internal Quality Model: A kind of *quality model* which represents the perspective of a software developer and relates to the intermediate artifacts that are produced during software development process.

Logical Data Model: A model of a database expressed at platform dependent level; depending on the used technology hierarchical, network, relational, object-relational, and object-oriented logical models are distinguished. Among aforementioned models, relational logical model is the most popular. The relational logical data model describes relations (that can be perceived as tables), and relationships between them.

Ontology: An explicit description of a domain. It introduces a common vocabulary which enables to uniform interpretation of domain knowledge and understanding and explaining the concepts of domain. Most ontologies describe individuals (instances) classes (concepts), attributes, and relations.

Physical Data Model: Model of a database expressed at platform dependent level in the way accepted by a specific database management system. Beside the data it can also contain implementation of business logic in the form of stored procedures or transaction definitions.

Quality and Evaluation Model: A *quality model* with *assessment functions.*

Quality Model: A set of selected quality characteristics and subcharacteristics together with the assigned *measures*. The quality model provides the basis for specifying quality requirements and evaluating quality.

Quality-Driven MDA Framework: A framework for model-based software development aiming at producing high quality software products; It integrates two complementary processes: MDA approach and quality specification and evaluation process, defined mainly in the ISO/IEC 9216 series of standards.

Chapter 11
Rule-Based Domain-Specific Modeling for E-Government Service Transactions

Guillermo Infante Hernández
Universidad de Oviedo, Spain

Benjamín López Pérez
Universidad de Oviedo, Spain

Aquilino A. Juan Fuente
Universidad de Oviedo, Spain

Edward Rolando Núñez-Valdéz
Universidad de Oviedo, Spain

ABSTRACT

There is an explosion of different software platforms and protocols used to achieve systems interoperation. Among those platforms are the e-government transactions systems used mainly by public sector organizations to deliver demanded services to citizens. This scenario brings the appearance of communications gap among public organizations that share common processes, services, and regulations. Therefore, to find a solution to integrate these platforms becomes a relevant issue to be treated. This chapter proposes a rule-based domain-specific modeling environment for public services and process integration formed by common public service elements and a set of process integration rules. This approach provides a mechanism to integrate the conforming pieces of public transactions among different platforms. In addition, a service and a process meta-model is proposed in order to formalize the information structures. A set of process integration rules is also presented to complete the proposed model.

INTRODUCTION

The objective behind Information Technology (IT) projects in e-government contexts as argued in (Buhl & Löffler, 2011) are: simplification and realization of information, communication, and transaction processes within and between public administrations and citizens by using digital information and communication technology. There have been an increased research activity on e-government field in recent years and the development of theoretical and conceptual models to understand its different aspects (Dawes, Pardo, & Cresswell, 2004; Gilgarcia & Pardo, 2005; Gupta, 2003). This recent interest in this domain is caused by the increased government's reliance on information and communication technologies (ICT) in their everyday transactions. One of the

DOI: 10.4018/978-1-4666-6359-6.ch011

particular fields of interest in this domain is the study of the different relations established among the e-government actors to achieve service transactions. In (Abramson & Means, 2001) there is a classification of three major categories or relationships called Government-to-Government (G2G), Government-to-Citizen (G2C), and Government-to-Business (G2B). This chapter mainly focuses on Government-to-Citizen relationship where the information sharing between Public Administrations' (PAs) processes and services takes place. These information interchanges or interoperability between PA organizations have been classified as a relevant subject and a critical prerequisite for the adequate performance of PA systems (Klischewski, 2004; Peristeras, Loutas, Goudos, & Tarabanis, 2007; Tambouris, Manouselis, & Costopoulou, 2007).

The European Interoperability Framework for Pan-European e-Government Services (EIF) (Overeem, Witters, & Peristeras, 2007) of the European Commission defines interoperability as the ability of information and communication technology (ICT) systems and of the business processes they support to exchange data and to enable sharing of information and knowledge.

EIF defines three interoperability types such as the technical level, semantic level and organizational level where this chapter focuses on. The interaction among different business processes and services is addressed. At this level the following aspects are covered:

1. **Domain Specific Integration Modeling:** This includes the definition of the metamodel that contains common processes and services elements to undertake their integration.
2. **Business Rules Integration:** This describes the construction of the integration knowledge base used to validate instances of the defined model both in modeling time and runtime.
3. **Domain Specific Modeling Editor Development:** This address the description of the necessary steps to undertake the development of a domain specific modeling tool as proof of concept for the proposals introduced in this chapter.

BACKGROUND

Process modeling has gained a lot of attention over the past decade involving process reengineering and innovation (Wang & Wang, 2006). The use of Service Orientated Architectures (SOAs) has changed the process orientation to service orientation modeling approach. These architectures are mainly dedicated to issues related to advertise, discover, invoke, compose and monitor services available from multiple providers over the web. This change resulted in the development of the Web Services (Alonso, Casati, Kuno, & Machiraju, 2004; Moitra & Ganesh, 2005).

There are discussions on different approaches to undertake process-service integration modeling. The workflow and SOA approaches are discussed in (Gortmaker, Janssen, & Wagenaar, 2005) presenting two reference models: Workflow Reference Model (Eder & Liebhart, 1996) and the SOA reference model (Papazoglou & Georgakopoulos, 2003). Relevancy of these models in the implementation of service-process integration in e-government is questioned. According to (Gortmaker et al., 2005), the workflow reference model is mainly focused on technology and therefore fails to address the non-technical integration issues. Instead the SOA reference model manages to address several of these issues in a rather descriptive way. Hence the SOA model manages the required functionality but does not indicate how this should be implemented. Therefore, the conclusion from this works is that a new domain specific process-service integration model is needed to facilitate process integration in e-government context.

There are a number of generic process models proposed for e-government domain. Amongst this models can be found the Federal Enterprise Architecture Business Reference Model (Chief, 1999) and the SAP Public Sector Solution Map (Draijer & Schenk, 2004). These models represent generic representations of e-government domain and do not address the process-service integration issue.

By the other hand the IMPULSE project (IMPULSE, 2002) addresses public administration services integration based on processes distributed over different information and workflow systems. These kinds of services are usually composed by a number of available processes which reside on single PA managed workflow systems. Some authors (Pasic, Diez, & Espinosa, 2002) argue that this approach is more suitable for virtual enterprises and similar applications, and less to PAs with hierarchical structures of rationalized procedures. There is a need therefore to build new models for the integration of various kinds of PA systems from the process modeling perspective where the internal workflow implementation details are transparent to other PAs systems. A process-service integration metamodel is suggested in this chapter to address this deficit.

DOMAIN SPECIFIC PROCESS-SERVICE MODELING INTEGRATION

A successful approach to reduce the development complexity of large software systems is the use of abstraction of the underlying system into models (Fowler, 2010; Selic, 2003). These models can be used as documentation to the underlying system, but these abstractions may become outdated as the system changes. Model-driven development (MDD) fosters the use of models as first-class citizens in the development process, where the system may be automatically generated from its model (Selic, 2003). Modeling is particularly beneficial for rapidly-evolving domains, as a modeled system is less sensitive to the changes in its underlying platforms. When a system is effectively modeled against a well-defined modeling language, the model may also be used to predict the behavior of the system, and at a significantly lower cost than the implementation of the modeled system (Selic, 2003).

These modeling benefits can be taken into e-government domain to formalize this very changing context and to gain an abstract representation of repetitive tasks in order to automatize them. Figure 1 describes an activity diagram that depicts a common notification process in an e-government transaction. As shown in Figure 1 there are some repeated actions that implicitly encapsulates an external service call, e.g. (Sign Publication or Notification calls an electronic signature service to perform the action). However the single use of models in this context may not be completely suitable to address all the changes caused by different policies, regulations and laws enactments. One of the alternatives to address this issue is to use validation tools to show design errors in model instances so they can be fix it. The drawback of validation is that there is not a simple way to get the big picture of the entire design quality corresponding to defined constraints. These constraints in e-government domain come from the mentioned public regulations and may significantly vary from one territory, organization or country to another. As the variations on process model requirements takes place, the services that support their transactions over the web must be adapted to guarantee a proper interoperability functioning. There is a need then to count on an updating or self-constructing integrated mechanism that evaluates the process model instances and adapt external services integration into modeled processes. This mechanism is called in this chapter as *model adapting* and is described below as a component.

Service Integration Metamodel

This section includes the definition of the service integration metamodel (ServInt) that contains common processes and services elements to undertake their interoperation. The idea behind the

Figure 1. UML activity diagram of a common notification process

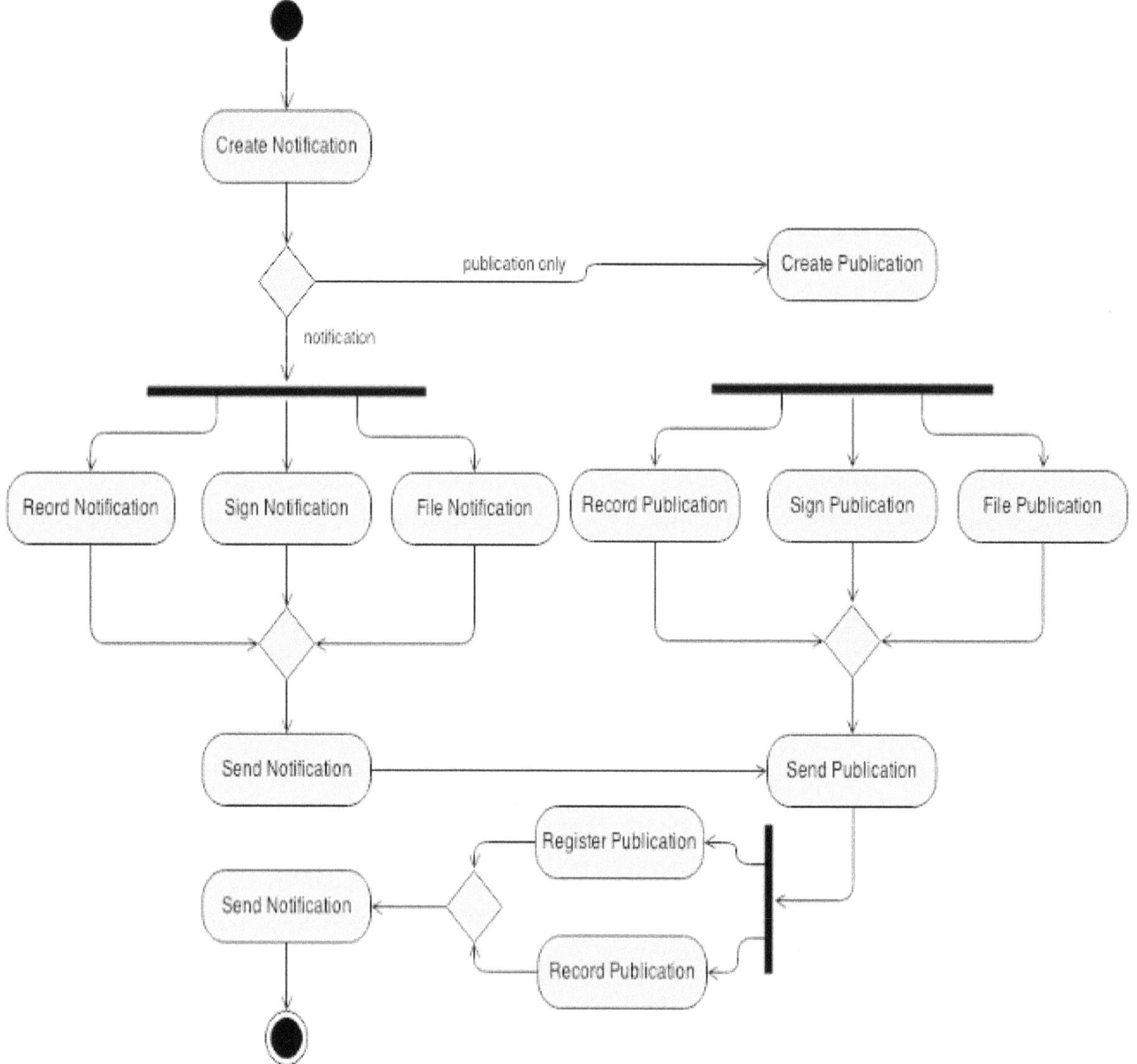

definition of the metamodel in this context is to provide the binding elements amongst processes and services that can be used to ease the integration of both. This point of view places the domain expert at the modeler role when defining process models, this way it can use its knowledge of the e-government domain without been aware of the services needed for the transactions execution in the modeled process. Figure 2 describes a fragment of the proposed metamodel.

Here is a brief description of the main metamodel elements:

Figure 2. Process-Service integration metamodel excerpt

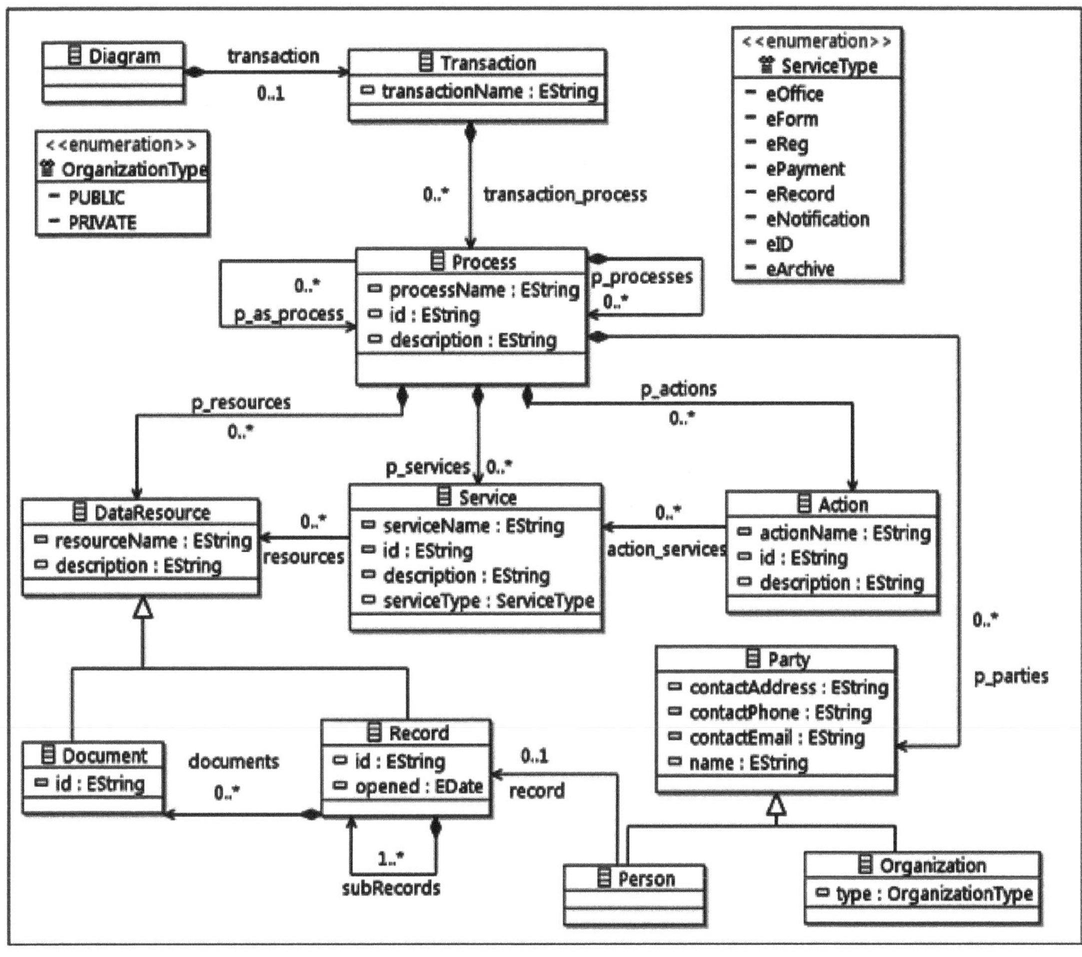

- **Transaction:** Represents the containment element of all the modeled processes. A transaction, e.g. (a driving license application) represents a specific process or set of them to achieve a final result.
- **Process:** Central element into a transaction formed by a set of related input actions which execution determines its final result or output.
- **Action:** Represents an operation performed to attain a specific goal. It is the triggering element for service integration.
- **Service:** Exposed and external technology intended to process incoming requests that gives a correspondent response. In this context this element takes the form of a public web service offered by some PA or government, e.g. (electronic ids, payments, signatures, etc.).
- **Data Resource:** Any data used in process transactions. It can be a *Document* that belongs to some *Person*'s or *Organization*'s *Record.*

Interoperation Modeling

The definition of domain models is an effort intensive activity that requires coordination amongst different backgrounds and skills: from modeling experts to master model driven environments and resources; and from the domain experts to deepen into the application domain as stated in (Bertolino, De Angelis, Di Sandro, & Sabetta, 2011). The definition of models is also a critical activity. Since models usually are the starting point for many subsequent transformations, faults that are possibly introduced in this stage can have detrimental impacts. Therefore, ensuring that the model is correct becomes of crucial importance. In the case of e-government domain models (e.g. process transaction models), the accuracy which they have been defined determines for example the compliance with a specific regulation or mandate as the context of their usage is usually the public sector. Therefore the models validation becomes of crucial importance in this domain since it can prevent from failing in unlawful procedures. As mentioned before this approach places the domain expert in the modeler role. The idea is to have an editor with semiautomatic model validation to model processes that can be integrated with the services they need to function properly. The implementation of the editor involves the development and integration of two components: model adapting and service integration, as well as the underlying model instances and ServInt metamodel itself. An overall summary of these components and their integration is provided in Figure 3 as an UML component diagram.

The ServInt metamodel component is implemented as a single component using Eclipse Modeling Framework (EMF) (Steinberg, Budinsky, Paternostro, & Merks, 2008). This component internally depends on two external components to provide the metamodels for XSD and Ecore.

The decomposition of the ServInt model component is provided in Figure 4. This component is made up of two sub-components: a model instance component and a model transformation component.

The former component provides the functionality to store, interact and serialize a given

Figure 3. UML component diagram of the proposed implementation

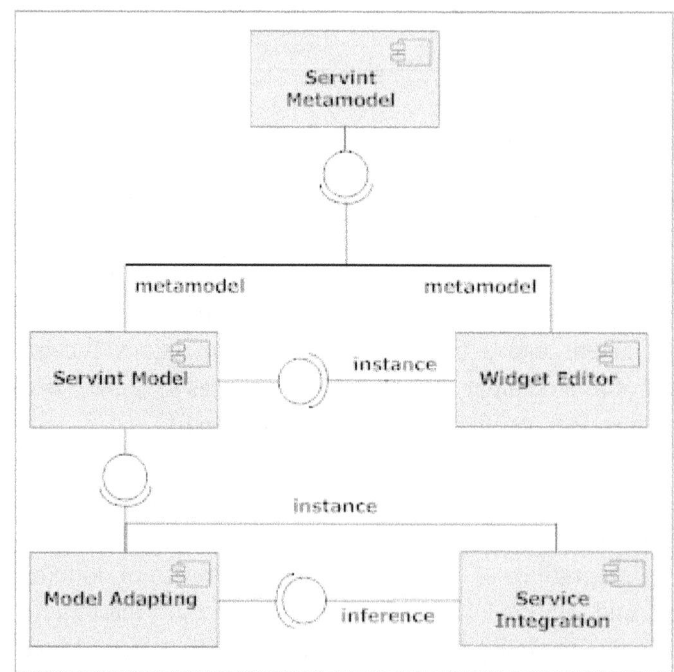

Figure 4. ServInt model UML component diagram

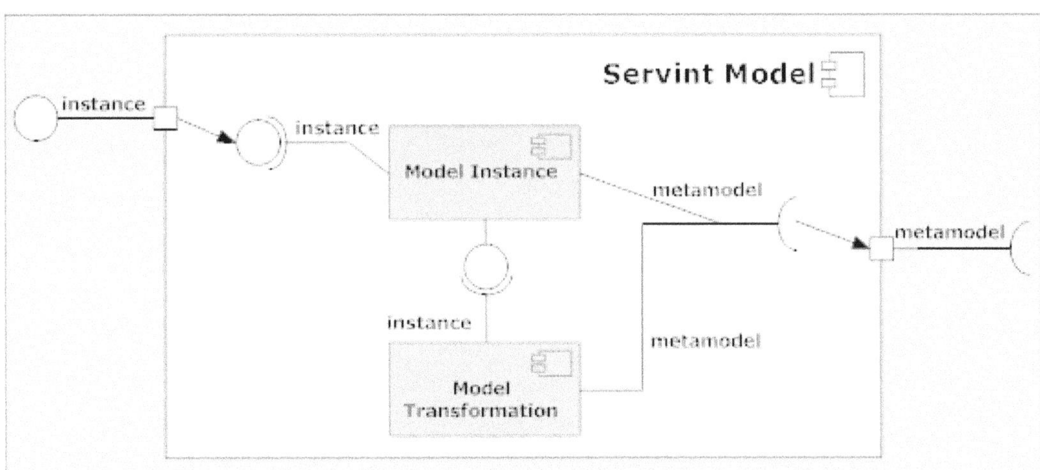

ServInt model instance, with respect to the ServInt metamodel; and the latter component provides the functionality to transform model instances between different metamodel versions.

The *model instance component* interacts with all other components in the system as they all use ServInt model instances to function. The implementation of this component, however, is simply the generated source code from EMF from the given Ecore-based metamodel. As described by (Steinberg et al., 2008), this involves automatically creating a genmodel model for a given metamodel source and then using this genmodel instance to generate the relevant source codes. ServInt model instances are therefore stored as XMI representations within *servint* files. The *model transformation component* is implemented with the single purpose of testing the implementation with existing model instances according to changes in the underlying ServInt metamodel.

Domain Specific Integration Modeling Editor

As mentioned before, to exploit domain expert's knowledge at modeling time along with the usability of a visual editor that *speaks* his/her language, a domain specific integration modeling editor is proposed. The UML component diagram of the developed Widget Editor is shown in Figure 5.

Part of the implementation of EMF is EMF. Edit Support, which provides a basic user interface for editing model instances, by combining the generated model plugin with the Eclipse UI Framework JFace (Steinberg et al., 2008). An Edit plugin may be generated automatically from the genmodel model instance.

This generated plugin includes a tree-based or widget-based viewer of a model instance derived automatically from the metamodel structure, and a properties-based element viewer allowing a model instance developer to modify the attributes and references of selected model elements. Although the generated implementation of this component is fairly incomplete, it can be the start point to extend its behavior and implement a rapid prototyping editor, also is a necessary requirement for future diagram editor construction. The extended implementation of a widget-based editor for editing ServInt model instances is shown in Figure 6.

As discussed earlier in this chapter there is a need of updating or self-constructing integrated mechanism that evaluates the process model instances and adapts external services integration into modeled processes. This mechanism called *model adapting* is implemented as a component

Figure 5. Widget Editor UML component diagram

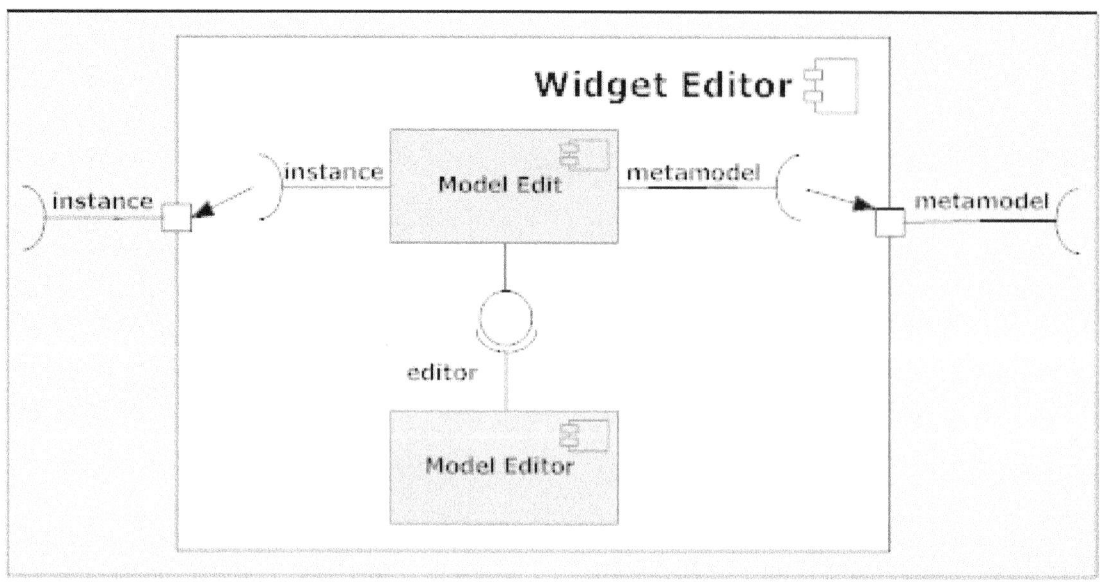

and is described in Figure 7. The model adapting component defines the implementation of the model adapting process, based on the argumentation proposed by (Wright & Dietrich, 2010).

The underlying rule engine behind the implementation of model adapting in ServInt model instances is Drools (Sottara, Mello, & Proctor, 2010). Drools, also known as JBoss Rules, is an

Figure 6. Implementation of a widget-based editor for ServInt model instances using EMF

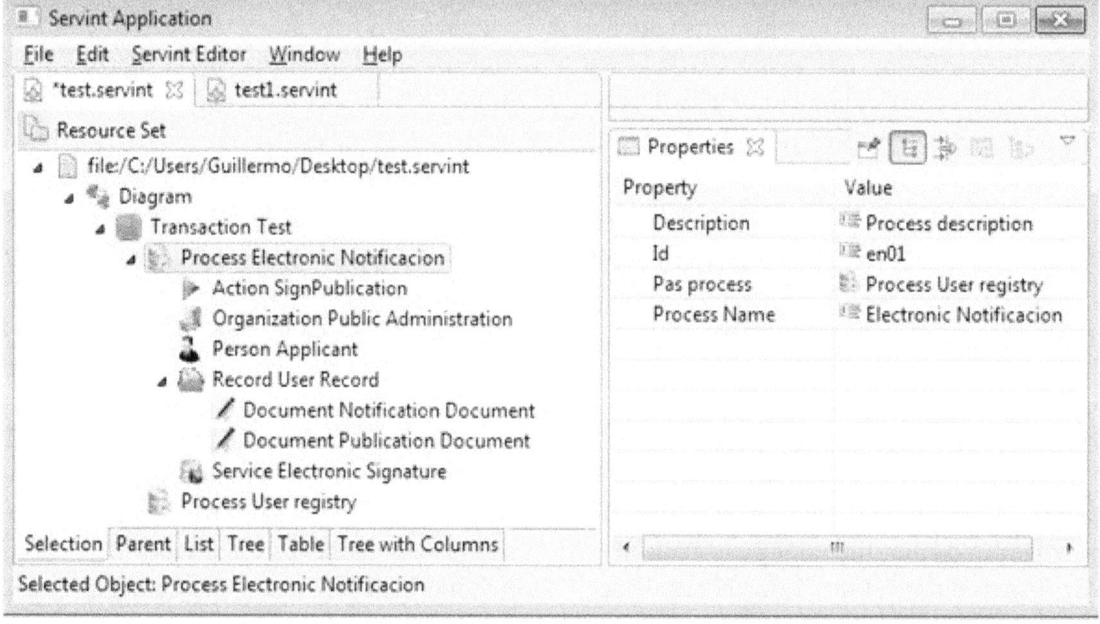

Figure 7. Model Adapting UML component diagram

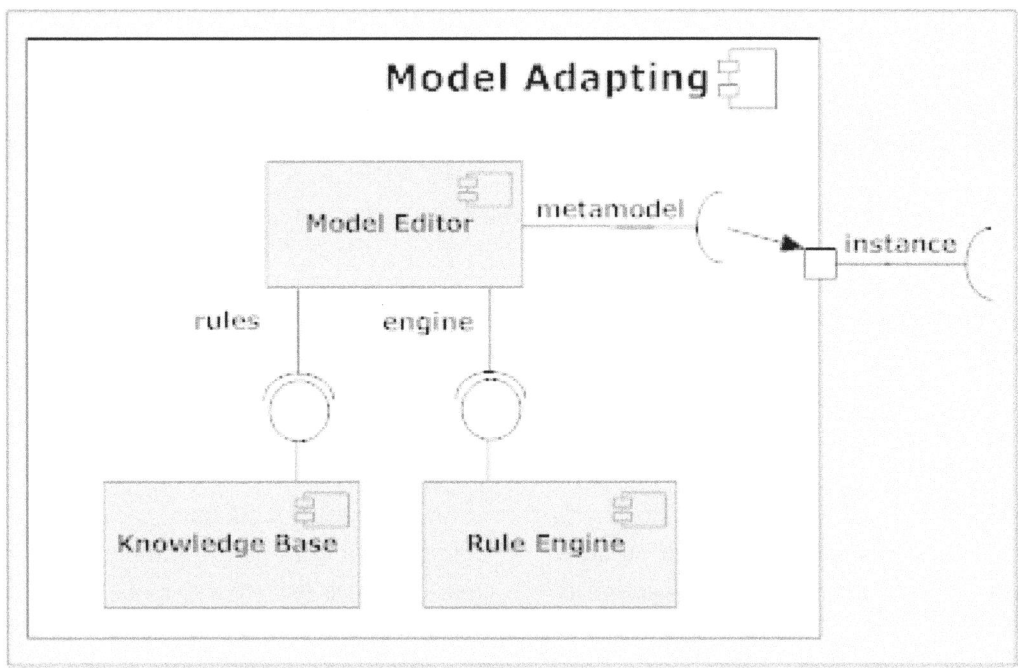

open source business rule management system and inference rule engine implemented in Java that supports an implementation of the JSR-94 specification. Inference rules are evaluated using an enhanced implementation of the Rete algorithm (Sottara et al., 2010). Drools natively provides an expressive textual language for defining inference rules, but also supports the integration of a custom rule DSL to improve the productivity of defining rules within certain domains.

The underlying model that Drools operates within is simple POJOs, making it easy to integrate into an existing Java-based software system, this structure do not need to be defined as part of the rule base; this means that all metamodel properties and operations are always accessible to a Drools rule. Alternatively, metamodel reflection is possible using the EMF API. A model adapting rule is implemented in Drools to adapt a modeled process as described in Figure 8.

FUTURE RESEARCH DIRECTIONS

There are some research lines related to this work that needs to be mentioned. Model driven engineering has gained a lot of attention from the research community and its applications nowadays may vary significantly from different domains. E-government domain can be one of the contexts where MDE can be successfully applied as argued in this chapter due to its straightforward methods to transform domain models in executable software. The code generation of e-government application platforms as a way to achieve standardization in respect to interoperability issues can be a promising research field. Also the administrative process modeling with graphical editors in order to improve the understanding of the modeled processes semantics from domain experts constitute a viable research direction. Another interesting direction of research can be the use of standards like

Figure 8. Model adapting rule implemented in Drools

```
rule "Adapt process to interoperate with eNotification"
    no-loop
    when
        $service: Service(serviceType == ServiceType.ENOTIFICATION)
        $action: Action(action_services contains $service)
        $process: Process(p_actions contains $action)
    then
        modify($process){
    getP_services().add($service)
    }
end
```

SBVR (OMG & Specification, 2008) along with MDE model transformation techniques in order to obtain semantically enriched e-government specifications.

CONCLUSION

In this chapter a rule based domain-specific modeling environment for public services and process integration is proposed. This environment is composed by the definition of the ServInt metamodel where the most relevant elements involved in e-government transactions domain were formalized. This formalization was taken as a starting point to gain an abstract representation of repetitive tasks in order to automatize them, as well as the information structure needed to integrate administrative processes and services. A known issue related to this integration is also argued in this chapter, the one referring to the constant changes in this domain caused by different policies, regulations and laws enactments. These variations on process model requirements have to deal with the corresponding changes in services interoperation mechanisms that support their transactions over the web. As a solution to this issue this work suggests a *model adapting component* as part of the proposed solution that evaluates the process model instances and adapts external services integration into modeled processes to guarantee a proper interoperability functioning. Along with model adapting there is another important use of rules integration in the modeling environment: the model instance validation that in this domain can be used to prevent from failing in unlawful procedures. Finally this chapter places the domain expert in modeler role and proposed a domain specific modeling editor as a proof of concept implementation that encompasses all previous argumentations. It can be considered that this proposal eases the task of modeling public processes performed by public employees without been aware of the intrinsic mechanisms to achieve that task and in a friendly environment that *speaks* his/her language. Can be concluded also that this work aids the interoperation of public processes and services since it provides a mechanism that tackles the semantics of this integration in a form of a rule based knowledge base that can be changed without affecting the information contained in both processes and services structures.

REFERENCES

Abramson, M. A., & Means, G. E. (2001). E-government 2001. *The PricewaterhousCoopers Endowment Series on The Business of Government*. Rowman & Littlefield Publishers. Retrieved from http://books.google.com/books?hl=de&lr=&id=WGbqZN4M5j8C&pgis=1

Alonso, G., Casati, F., Kuno, H., & Machiraju, V. (2004). *Web Services: Concepts, Architectures and Applications*. Springer. Retrieved from http://www.amazon.com/dp/3642078885

Bertolino, A., De Angelis, G., Di Sandro, A., & Sabetta, A. (2011). Is my model right? Let me ask the expert. *Journal of Systems and Software, 84*(7), 1089–1099. Retrieved October 15, 2012, from10.1016/j.jss.2011.01.054

Chief, T. (1999, September). Federal Enterprise Architecture Framework. *Architecture,* 80. Retrieved from http://www.cio.gov/documents/fedarch1.pdf

Dawes, S. S., Pardo, T. A., & Cresswell, A. M. (2004). Designing electronic government information access programs: a holistic approach. *Government Information Quarterly, 21*(1), 3–23. Retrieved from http://www.sciencedirect.com/science/article/B6W4G-4B71BC0-1/2/0ffcef06875aa7c64fdf9b510e62466b

Draijer, C., & Schenk, D. (2004). Best practices of business simulation with SAP R/3. *Journal of Information Systems Education, 15*(3), 261. Retrieved from http://findarticles.com/p/articles/mi_qa4041/is_200410/ai_n9464918/pg_5/

Eder, J., & Liebhart, W. (1996). Workflow Transactions. In *Workflow Handbook 1997* (pp. 195–202). John Wiley & Sons, Inc. Retrieved from http://citeseerx.ist.psu.edu/viewdoc/summary?doi=10.1.1.21.7110

Fountain, J. E. (2001). Building the virtual state: Information technology and institutional change. *Information Systems Research, 7*, xii. Retrieved from http://isr.journal.informs.org/cgi/content/abstract/7/1/22

Fowler, M. (2010). Domain specific languages. *International Journal of Computer Applications IJCA, 1*, 39–60.

Gilgarcia, J., & Pardo, T. (2005). E-government success factors: Mapping practical tools to theoretical foundations. *Government Information Quarterly, 22*(2), 187–216. Retrieved July 3, 2011, from http://linkinghub.elsevier.com/retrieve/pii/S0740624X05000158

Gortmaker, J., Janssen, M., & Wagenaar, R. W. (2005). Towards requirements for a reference model for process orchestration in e-government. In M. Böhlen, J. Gamper, W. Polasek, & M. A. Wimmer (Eds.), *EGovernment towards electronic democracy* (Vol. 3416, pp. 169–180). Springer. Retrieved from http://springerlink.metapress.com/(hgp11niu3o1t4b552xj3zy55)/app/home/contribution.asp?referrer=parent&backto=issue,16,28;journal,526,3824;linkingpublicationresults,1:105633,1

Gupta, M. (2003). E-government evaluation: A framework and case study. *Government Information Quarterly, 20*(4), 365–387. Retrieved July 11, 2011, from http://linkinghub.elsevier.com/retrieve/pii/S0740624X03000790

Halchin, L. E. (2004). Electronic government: Government capability and terrorist resource. *Government Information Quarterly, 21*(4), 406–419. doi:10.1016/j.giq.2004.08.002

IMPULSE. (2002). *Project IST-1999-21119*. Retrieved from http://cordis.europa.eu/search/index.cfm?fuseaction=proj.document&PJ_LANG=PL&PJ_RCN=4850507&pid=270&q=D67BEC82A602A23FF8B013B7DA527238&type=pro

Klischewski, R. (2004). Information integration or process integration? How to achieve interoperability in administration. *Electronic Government, 3183*, 57–65. Retrieved from http://www.springerlink.com/index/cndhp3plq6pt05x3.pdf

Means, G., & Schneider, D. (2000). *Meta-Capitalism: The e-Business Revolution and the Design of 21st-Century Companies and Markets*. Wiley. Retrieved from http://www.amazon.ca/exec/obidos/redirect?tag=citeulike09-20&path=ASIN/0471393355

Moitra, D., & Ganesh, J. (2005). Web services and flexible business processes: Towards the adaptive enterprise. *Information & Management, 42*(7), 921–933. Retrieved from http://linkinghub.elsevier.com/retrieve/pii/S0378720604001338

OMG, & OMGA Specification. (2008). *Semantics of business vocabulary and business rules*. Author.

Papazoglou, M. P., & Georgakopoulos, D. (2003). Service-oriented computing. *Communications of the ACM, 46*(10), 24–28. Retrieved from http://ieeexplore.ieee.org/lpdocs/epic03/wrapper.htm?arnumber=1607964

Pasic, A., Diez, S., & Espinosa, J. (2002). IMPULSE: Interworkflow Model for e-Government. In R. Traunmüller & K. Lenk (Eds.), Electronic Government (Vol. 2456, pp. 53–79). Springer.

Peristeras, V., Loutas, N., Goudos, S., & Tarabanis, K. (2007). Semantic interoperability conflicts in pan-european public services. In H. Österle, J. Schelp, & R. Winter (Eds.), *15th European Conference on Information Systems ECIS 2007* (pp. 2173–2184). University of St. Gallen. Retrieved from http://is2.lse.ac.uk/asp/aspecis/20070128.pdf

Selic, B. (2003). The pragmatics of model-driven development. *IEEE Software, 20*, 19–25. Retrieved from http://ieeexplore.ieee.org/lpdocs/epic03/wrapper.htm?arnumber=1231146

Sottara, D., Mello, P., & Proctor, M. (2010). A configurable rete-OO engine for reasoning with different types of imperfect information. *IEEE Transactions on Knowledge and Data Engineering, 22*(11), 1535–1548. doi:10.1109/TKDE.2010.125

Steinberg, D., Budinsky, F., Paternostro, M., & Merks, E. (2008). *EMF: Eclipse modeling framework*. Addison-Wesley Professional. Retrieved from http://portal.acm.org/citation.cfm?id=1197540

Tambouris, E., Manouselis, N., & Costopoulou, C. (2007). Metadata for digital collections of e-government resources. *The Electronic Library, 25*(2), 176–192. doi:10.1108/02640470710741313

Van Overeem, A. V. O. A., Witters, J. W. J., & Peristeras, V. P. V. (2007). *An Interoperability Framework for Pan-European E-Government Services (PEGS)*. IEEE. Retrieved from http://ieeexplore.ieee.org/lpdocs/epic03/wrapper.htm?arnumber=4076384

Wang, M., & Wang, H. (2006). From process logic to business logic—A cognitive approach to business process management. *Information & Management*, *43*(2), 179–193. doi:10.1016/j.im.2005.06.001

Wright, J. M., & Dietrich, J. B. (2010). Non-monotonic model completion in web application engineering. In *Proceedings of 2010 21st Australian Software Engineering Conference*, (pp. 45–54). IEEE. Retrieved December 3, 2012, from http://ieeexplore.ieee.org/lpdocs/epic03/wrapper.htm?arnumber=5475055

ADDITIONAL READING

Alpar, P., & Olbrich, S. (2005). Legal Requirements and Modelling of Processes in e-Government. Electronic. *Journal of E-Government*, *3*(3), 107–116. Retrieved from http://www.ejeg.com/volume-3/vol3-iss3/v3-i3-art2.htm

Badri, M., & Alshare, K. (2008). A path analytic model and measurement of the business value of e-government: An international perspective. *International Journal of Information Management*, *28*(6), 524–535. doi:10.1016/j.ijinfomgt.2006.10.004

Buhl, H. U., & Löffler, M. (2011). *The Role of Business and Information Systems Engineering in E-Government*. Business & Information Systems Engineering.

Gil-Garc, ía, J., & Pardo, T. (2005). E-government success factors: Mapping practical tools to theoretical foundations. *Government Information Quarterly*, *22*(2), 187–216. doi:10.1016/j.giq.2005.02.001

Indihar Stemberger, M., & Jaklic, J. (2007). Towards E-government by business process change—A methodology for public sector. *International Journal of Information Management*, *27*(4), 221–232. doi:10.1016/j.ijinfomgt.2007.02.006

Karagiannis, D., Utz, W., Woitsch, R., & Leutgeb, A. (2008). Business Processes and Rules An eGovernment Case-Study. *Artificial Intelligence*, 5.

Muller, P.-A., Fondement, F., Baudry, B., & Combemale, B. (2010). Modeling modeling modeling. *Software & Systems Modeling*. doi: doi:10.1007/s10270-010-0172-x

Murzek, M., & Specht, G. (2010). *Model-Driven Development of Interoperable, Inter-Organisational Business Processes*. Interoperability in Digital.

Norman Andersen, K. (2010). Electronic Government and the Information Systems Perspective. First International Conference, EGOVIS 2010 Bilbao, Spain, August 31 – September 2, 2010.

Peristeras, V., Tarabanis, K., & Goudos, S. K. (2009). Model-driven eGovernment interoperability: A review of the state of the art. *Computer Standards & Interfaces*, *31*(4), 613–628. doi:10.1016/j.csi.2008.09.034

Riss, U. V., Weber, I., & Grebner, O. (2009). Business Process Modelling, Task Management, and the Semantic Link. In K. Hinkelmann (Ed.), AAAI Spring Symposium AI Meets Business Rules and Process Management (pp. 99–104). AAAI Press. Retrieved from https://www.aaai.org/Papers/Symposia/Spring/2008/SS-08-01/SS08-01-013.pdf

Salhofer, P., & Stadlhofer, B. (2012). Semantic MDA for E-Government Service Development. 2012 45th Hawaii International Conference on System Sciences. IEEE. Retrieved from http://ieeexplore.ieee.org/lpdocs/epic03/wrapper.htm?arnumber=6149279

Shareef, M. A., Kumar, V., Kumar, U., & Dwivedi, Y. K. (2011). e-Government Adoption Model (GAM): Differing service maturity levels. *Government Information Quarterly*, *28*(1), 17–35. doi:10.1016/j.giq.2010.05.006

Zampou, E., & Eliakis, S. (2010). Measuring the Benefit of Interoperability: A Business Process Modelling Approach. Interoperability in Digital, 321–338. doi:10.4018/978-1-61520-887-6.ch017

KEY TERMS AND DEFINITIONS

Domain Specific Modeling Language (DSML): Modeling language of limited expressiveness focused on a particular domain.

E-Government: Use of technology, especially web-based applications to enhance access to and efficiently deliver government information and services.

Interoperability: Ability of ICT systems and of the business processes they support to exchange data and to enable sharing of information and knowledge.

Model-Driven Development (MDD): Approach that promotes the idea that models should be adopted as part of systems development using the essentials of models automation and modeling standards.

Public Administrations: Organizations that delivers public services to citizens, other administrations and businesses.

Service Oriented Architecture (SOA): Software architecture that defines the usage of services to support business requirements.

Web Service: Technology that uses a set of protocols and standards to exchange data among applications that differs in programing languages, platforms and operating systems.

Chapter 12
Developing Software with Domain-Driven Model Reuse

Audris Kalnins
University of Latvia, Latvia

Elina Kalnina
University of Latvia, Latvia

Tomasz Straszak
Warsaw University of Technology, Poland

Edgars Celms
University of Latvia, Latvia

Michał Śmiałek
Warsaw University of Technology, Poland

Wiktor Nowakowski
Warsaw University of Technology, Poland

ABSTRACT

This chapter presents an approach to software development where model-driven development and software reuse facilities are combined in a natural way. It shows how model transformations building a Platform Independent Model (PIM) can be applied directly to the requirements specified in RSL by domain experts. Further development of the software case (PSM, code) is also supported by transformations, which in addition ensure a rich traceability within the software case. Alternatively, the PSM model and code can also be generated directly from requirements in RSL, thus providing fast development of the final code of at least a system prototype in many situations. The reuse support relies on a similarity-based comparison of requirements for software cases. If a similar part is found in an existing software case, a traceability link-based slice of the solution can be merged into the new case. The implementation of the approach is briefly sketched.

INTRODUCTION

Some of the most significant cornerstones for state-of-the art software development are model driven development (MDD) and software reuse. There is a lot of success in applying them separately, but only very few approaches try to combine them. The proposed approach provides a tight natural integration of both – "a model driven reuse". The third equally important cornerstone is an adequate facility for specifying requirements to the software system being developed. Only in this way a complete MDD life cycle can be supported, where the use of models starts from the "very beginning". This approach is based on a special Requirements Specification Language (RSL).

DOI: 10.4018/978-1-4666-6359-6.ch012

This language is semiformal in the sense that it is close to a natural language and understandable to non-IT specialists, but on the other hand it has a meaning precise enough to be processed by model transformations and reuse mechanisms. Consequently, a true model driven development is possible, where the initial version of the next model in the chain is built from the previous one by model transformations. In totality, these models form a software case. Thus, there is an automatic transformation supported path from requirements to code. All these models play an important role in the reuse process.

More precisely, requirements in RSL consist of two related parts. The domain concepts to be used in the requirements are described in a domain vocabulary. This domain vocabulary serves as a semiformal easy readable equivalent of the domain class model. The meaning of domain elements can be specified by means of links to corresponding WordNet (Fellbaum, 1998) entries. The domain model serves as the basis for the other part of requirements – the required system behaviour description. This description is centred on use cases. The distinctive feature of RSL is that a use case is refined by one or more scenarios in a simple controlled language. Each noun within a scenario sentence must be defined in the domain vocabulary, thus the whole sentence gets a precise meaning. In addition to use cases, non-functional requirements to the system can be described by natural language sentences, using hyperlinks to the same vocabulary. The precise syntax of RSL is described by a metamodel. It will be described in more detail in the next section.

Due to separation of notions and their operations from use cases containing sequences of imperative Subject-Predicate sentences containing only links to the phrases in the vocabulary, RSL models capture the domain logic of the system at a high level of abstraction. At the same time, the domain logic is the foundational basis to specify the application logic describing the observable interaction of the users with the system. Requirements models expressed with the RSL characterize the essential (inherent) complexity of the software system, while accidental (technical) complexity comes from implementation aspects of these requirements (Nowakowski, Śmiałek, Ambroziewicz & Straszak, 2013). In the classical MDA model chain (Object Management Group, 2003) a requirements model in RSL can be treated as a Computional Independent Model (CIM).

When the software case development starts, the requirements model is transformed into the initial version of the Platform Independent Model (PIM) and the Platform Specific Model (PSM) in the selected subset of UML. The static structure of these models is generated from the domain vocabulary within requirements. Consequently, the whole structure of the system, especially its business logic and data access layers, depend on this domain. Thus a true domain driven design is supported. An initial version of the behaviour is obtained by transformations analyzing the use case scenarios, thus aspects of use case driven design are also present. Having the PSM models generated, the initial code for the system can be produced. The precise contents of the generated models depend on the selected transformation profile for the software system to be developed. Model transformation profiles supporting several architecture styles have been developed. More details on the transformation-assisted software case development will be given in section "Definition of software cases". For software systems with a relatively simple behaviour, the proposed transformations can generate a nearly complete code of the system, at least at the prototype level. Thus a "smart definition" of requirements in RSL comes close to the usage of RSL as a sort of domain specific language (DSL) based on controlled natural language for the development of simple web-based information systems. The possibilities to describe the system behaviour in RSL are, for example, much richer than those of DSL examples in Brambilla, Cabot & Wimmer (2012).

One more important aspect of the approach is strong support for traceability in the form of mapping links between the models. Since the initial version of the next model is generated by transformations, a rich set of mapping links between consecutive models can be easily supported. The starting point for this traceability is always the requirements model in RSL. In particular, the domain vocabulary is the starting point for traceability to models describing the static structure of the system to be built.

Traceability is the key element for reuse of software cases in the approach. If a set of software cases has been already built using the approach, just the requirement models of these cases must be compared to the requirements of a new case to be created. If a similar part is found in the requirements of an existing case, the whole chain of model parts traceable from this one can serve as the basis for reuse. This chain is called a "slice" in the approach.

In order to reuse artefacts included in a software case, requirements specifications written in RSL need to be compared through formulating a query. The query is based on a newly specified requirements specification which might be partial (requirements sketch). This "new" specification is compared with the "old" specifications taken from the repository of software cases. Appropriate domain-driven similarity metrics are applied which are discussed in more detail in section "Reuse of software cases". After finding similar requirements, slices leading from these requirements are calculated. This slice can then be copied into the current software case for adaptation of the contained model elements to the current problem. Thus a true domain driven reuse of software cases is supported.

The proposed approach has been implemented in the form of a tooling environment called the ReDSeeDS Engine (www.redseeds.eu). The implementation and practical validation of the approach will be briefly described in section "Implementation and validation".

REQUIREMENT SPECIFICATION LANGUAGE

The Requirements Specification Language (RSL) (Smiałek, Bojarski, Nowakowski, Ambroziewicz & Straszak, 2007; Kaindl et al., 2007) is a semi-formal language for specifying requirements of a software system.

RSL employs use cases for defining precise requirements of the system behaviour. As traditionally for requirements, a use case corresponds to a targeted interaction between an actor and the system to be specified. Related use cases can be grouped into a package. An essential difference from traditional requirement elicitation methods is that use case behaviour can be precisely defined in RSL. Each use case is detailed by one or more scenarios, one of which is the main (describes the typical behaviour of the use case) and the others provide various alternatives.

A scenario in turn consists of special controlled natural language sentences. The main type of sentences is the SVO(O) sentence (Kaindl et al., 2007), which consists of a subject, a verb (or a predicate) and a direct object (optionally, also an indirect object). These sentences express the actions to be performed in the scenario, for example, *System* reserves *facility* for *customer*. On the one hand, the SVO(O) sentences can be read informally as simple conventional natural language sentences, thus readability for non-IT professionals is maintained. On the other hand, links to domain elements (see below) permit to perform formal analysis and transformations of these sentences. SVO(O) sentences can contain also some other syntactic elements, such as modifiers (adjectives or participles) associated to a subject or object. In addition to SVO(O), there can be also conditions, rejoin sentences (shift of control to a point in the same or another scenario) and invocation sentences (invoking other use cases). The precise invocation relation between a scenario and another use case in RSL replaces the rather vague inclusion and extension relationships between use cases, found in UML.

Alternatively, the set of scenarios for a use case can be visualized in a natural way as a profile of UML activity diagrams. SVO(O) sentences serve as the nodes of the diagram, and conditions and rejoins as control flows (in addition to the natural "next sentence" control flow).

Another part of RSL is the domain definition which consists of actors (e.g. system users), system elements and notions. Notions correspond to elements (classes) of the conceptual domain model of the future system. It is possible to define also notion generalization and simple associations between notions. Thus the essential part of the domain model can be specified in requirements. From the syntax point of view, a notion is a single noun (e.g., *facility*) or a "complex noun" (e.g., *reservable facility list*).

The behaviour and domain parts in a valid RSL requirements model must be strictly related. The subject of an SVO(O) sentence must be an actor or system element. An object (direct or indirect) must be a notion. The informal meaning of each noun and verb must be defined in a vocabulary (currently, WordNet (Fellbaum, 1998)).

In WordNet, each term (a noun or a verb) has a set of predefined meanings. The most appropriate one of these meanings is selected for the given term, but if none matches, it is possible to extend the used copy of the WordNet vocabulary. New complex nouns can also be added to the vocabulary.

There are also informal requirements in RSL, describing additional functional or non-functional properties of the system in plain natural language, but with hyperlinks to notions. Complete description of RSL is available in Kaindl et al. (2007).

An RSL example is demonstrated in Figure 1. In this diagram, a small example from fitness club application is demonstrated. The user selects a facility from a reservable facility list, which she wants to reserve. The scenario is shown both in the form of a sentence list and an activity diagram. For each element of the SVO sentences (subject or object) arrows show the corresponding domain element.

The precise syntax of RSL is defined by means of a metamodel (Kaindl et al., 2007). This metamodel has been built with the goal to provide a convenient abstract syntax specification of RSL. Another goal was to facilitate usability for model transformation definition and ReDSeeDS engine development.

As already mentioned, RSL is a language for requirements specification. The main class in the metamodel is RequirmentsSpecification. Each specification contains a RequirementsPackage hierarchy with RSLUseCases. Each RSLUseCase is represented by one or more ConstrainedLanguageScenario. ConstrainedLanguageScenario*s* consist of ordered sentences. The main type of sentences is the SVOSentence. However there are also InvocationSentence*s* and RejoinSentence*s*. An InvocationSentence is used to invoke another RSLUseCase. A RejoinSentence is used to describe loops in sentence execution order. An SVOSentence consists of a Subject and a Predicate (a verb together with objects). The Subject is (more precisely, is defined by) a NounPhrase, but the predicate is a VerbPhrase. This part of the metamodel can be seen in Figure 2.

Each *SVOSentence* is refined for further analysis by specifying links to the terminology used in this sentence. This is illustrated in Figure 3. A subject must be a *NounPhrase* containing (more precisely, referencing uniquely to) a *Noun*. A predicate is a *VerbPhrase*. There are *SimpleVerbPhrase*s and *ComplexVerbPhrase*s. *SimpleV-*

Figure 1. RSL example

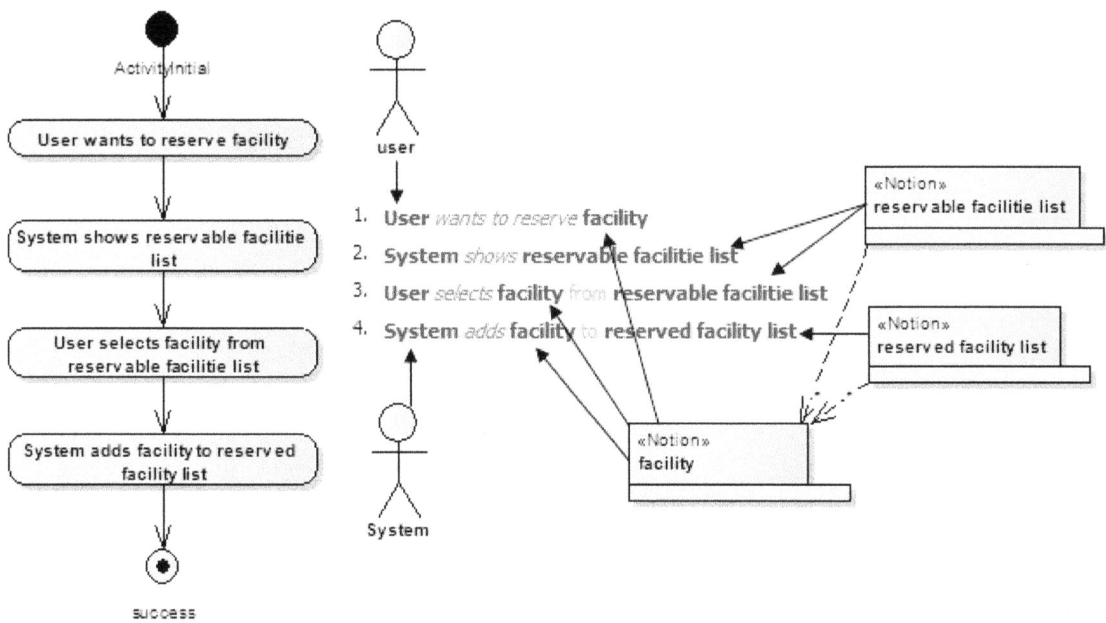

Figure 2. RSL use case MM

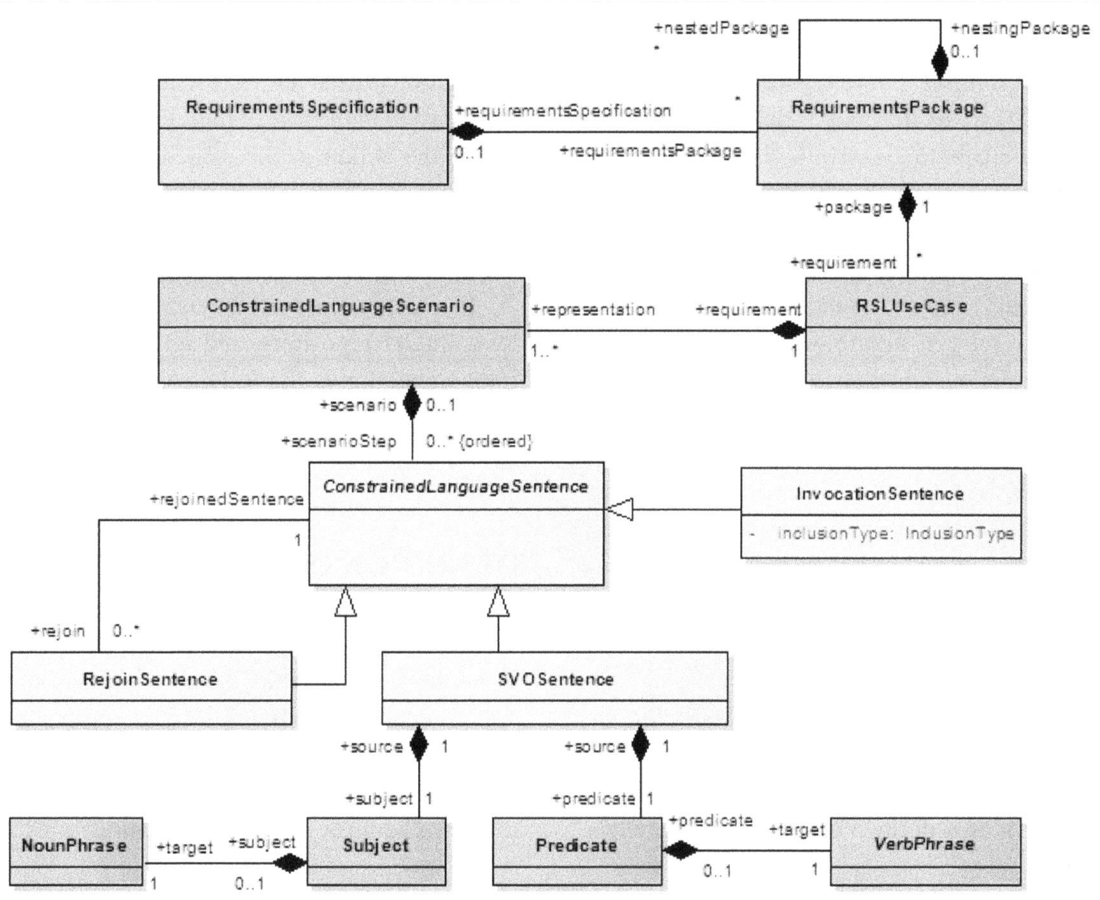

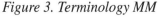

Figure 3. Terminology MM

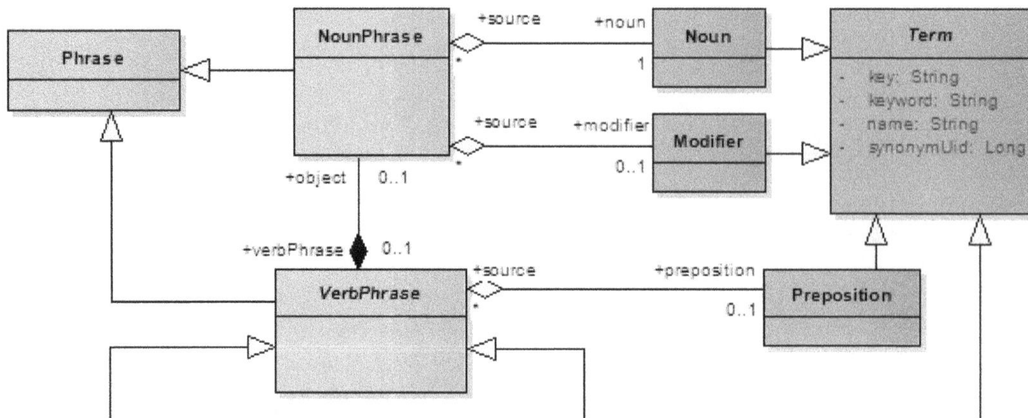

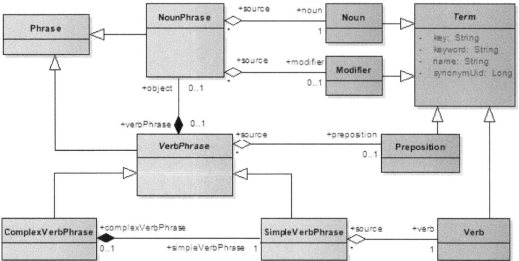

erbPhrases contains a *Verb* and a direct object – a *NounPhrase*. *ComplexVerbPhrases* contain a *SimpleVerbPhrase* and an indirect object – also a *NounPhrase*. A *Preposition* is also contained in a *ComplexVerbPhrase*. A *NounPhrase* can also include a *Modifier*. For every term used, a mapping to a WordNet meaning is defined. It is done using the attribute *synonymUid*. The WordNet vocabulary is not directly part of the model repository, therefore this attribute is used to reference the relevant WordNet element.

The main element of the domain part is the *Notion*, as seen in Figure 4. There can be two types of relationships between *Notions*: *NotionSpecalisations* and *NotionRelationships*. The *NotionSpecalisation* corresponds to the UML generalization, the *NotionRelationship* corresponds to the UML association. Notions are used as objects in *SVOsentences*. The notion name is defined using a *NounPhrase* which in turn contains a *Noun*.

There are also *Actors* and *SystemElements* in the domain. They are used as *subjects* of *SVOSentences*. There can be *DomainElementRelationships* between *Actors* and *SystemElements* as well.

The mapping between *Notions* and objects in *SVOsentences* is defined using *Nouns*. It means that an object maps to a *Notion* if they both map to the same *Noun*. The same is true for *Actors* and *SystemElements*.

An additional *recipient* association links an *Actor* or *SystemElement* to an SVOSentence. This association is used for SVO sentences with a *SystemElement* in the role of the subject. It describes where the action in the sentence is directed to (whether it is a system response to the actor or a system internal action) and is explicitly set by the scenario writer.

This metamodel can be used for building an RSL model repository and editor. The current implementation is the ReDSeeDS Engine (Rein et al., 2008) available for download from www.redseeds.eu.

DEFINITION OF SOFTWARE CASES

When requirements for a software system have been specified in RSL, the development of the system can start. In the described approach, the development is done in a model driven way. This means that a sequence of models finally leading to code is being developed. These models in total-

Figure 4. Notion MM

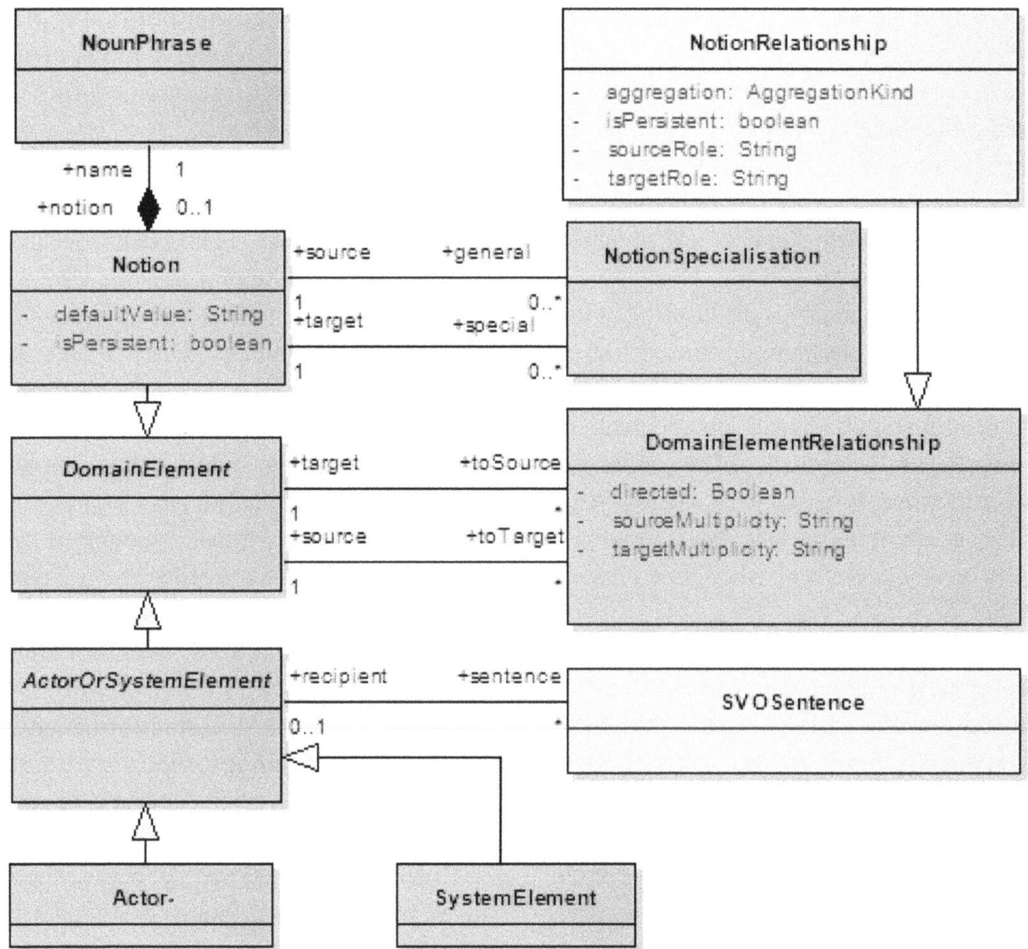

ity form a software case. For all steps, automated model transformations assist in the creating of the next model in the sequence. This section explains what models constitute a software case, how they are chosen and what the role of transformations is.

Software Case

For the MDD life cycle, the terminology coming from the early days of MDA has been chosen. The requirements model in RSL is treated as a concrete version of the Computation Independent Model (CIM) (MDA documents (Object Management Group, 2003) provided no explanation what in fact CIM should be). The next model is the Platform Independent Model (PIM) in a selected subset of UML. It is followed by the Platform Specific Model (PSM) model, again in another subset of UML, where implementation-specific details can be specified. Finally, the code comes. Thus, it can be said that in the described approach a *software case* is a sequence of the corresponding CIM (requirements), PIM, PSM and code, with all the required relationships between them.

However, the MDA or MDD standards do not specify what the exact contents of each model in the MDD lifecycle should be. It is completely up to the chosen development strategy. The contents of the models in the described approach are thus determined by the concept called the architectural style.

The *architectural style* includes the chosen system and the model structure, the related set of design patterns (with indications where they should be used), general design principles and finally, the way model elements are obtained from the models preceding in the development chain. Thus, the style includes the layering of the system, by specifying what should be in each layer and how they interact. A very important part of an architectural style is the chosen coherent set of design patterns. Patterns should be applied for all consecutive models in the chain and all layers. That is because patterns provide strict guidelines what kind of model elements should be created in each situation.

A definition of the architectural style in fact provides precise requirements for creating the set of model transformations which support the chosen development process of a software case. The style provides clear guidelines as to what elements should be created in the target model of each transformation step and how they depend on the corresponding source model. In addition, the style defines also the sequence of steps. A set of transformations supporting the given architecture style is called the *transformation profile* for it. Thus the architecture style describes the model-driven system development process at a high abstraction level and has the most value for transformation developers, certainly the methodology user guide is also based on the style as an explanation of the model chain appearing in the process. The transformation profile which implements the given style is the artefact which is really used by system developers when they apply the corresponding transformations in an appropriate order to get from RSL to code.

It should be noted that an architecture style can be implemented via different transformation profiles, for example, an intermediate model not significant for manual extension can be created just internally and not shown to users, by directly passing it to the next transformation in the chain. In such a way, for example the PIM model may be hidden by a transformation profile, directly creating PSM from RSL.

The goal is to ensure that transformations can create a significant part of the target model. Certainly, a manual extension of the model (in the relevant subset or profile of the UML) is then done. Transformations are provided also for the step from requirements (CIM) to PIM since RSL has sufficient formality to enable this.

Obviously, the required set of model transformations heavily depends on the chosen architecture style and implementation technology. Currently three architecture styles are supported by ready to use transformation profiles that are described in the next sections. Two of these styles are relatively similar and more or less follow the classical MDD approach, they are supported by "RSL to UML" and "RSL to JAVA" transformation profiles respectively. According to the chosen transformation profile, the target models and in particular the structure and notation are generated.

It should be noted that the part of the system to be created automatically by transformations significantly depends on how sophisticated is the analysis of requirements in RSL. Therefore an advanced requirements analysis method, which is based on the use of keywords in SVO sentences and extended features of notions is briefly described. An appropriate extended architecture style which can take into account the results of this analysis and the corresponding transformation profile "RSL with Keywords" is also sketched.

RSL to UML Transformation Profile

The "RSL to UML" transformation profile implements the MDA concepts with the requirements specification as the CIM (Computation Independent Model), 4-layer solution architecture as the PIM (Platform Independent Model) and detailed design based on abstract factory in Java as the PSM.

A detailed description of transformation rules will be given for the CIM to PIM transition since this transformation seems to be the most interesting. PIM defines the static structure of the system to be built by means of classes, components and interfaces. Draft behaviour of the system is described by means of sequence diagrams.

According to the chosen transformation profile, four-layer architecture is used with the following layers: *Data Access*, *Business Logic*, *Application Logic* and *User Interface*. Additionally, *Data Transfer Objects (DTOs)* are used as data containers for data exchange between layers. Component and interface based design style is used at all layers. Components encapsulate groups of related elements of the system. Interfaces appear as provided interfaces of the respective components. The main patterns used in this architectural style are data access objects (DAO) for the Data Access layer and MVC for the Application Logic layer.

There are seven static structure packages in the PIM, one for each layer, one for the DTOs, one for the Interfaces and one for the Actors. The package *Actors* contains actors of the system to be built. They are directly copied from the requirements. The package *Data Transfer Objects* contains DTOs created from notions. Each notion is transformed into one DTO class. Thus this package serves also as a sort of conceptual domain model.

The package *Data Access* contains data access objects (DAO) for the persistence related operations. Each lowest level notion package is transformed in one DAO component. Each Notion contained in this package is transformed into an interface of this component. For each interface the relevant CRUD (create-read-update-delete) operations are added.

The package *Business Logic* contains business level components and interfaces. Components and interfaces are created in the same way as in Data Access layer. However, only notions participating in business level operations are used therein. In other words, only interfaces containing business level operations are created. Business level operation creation will be described together with the behaviour sequence diagram creation.

Packages *Application Logic* and *UI* are based on the MVC (model-view-controller) pattern. Components in application logic are created from use case packages which are of the lowest level in the package tree. Provided interfaces of these components are created from use cases written in RSL. For each use case one interface is created. Methods of these interfaces are created by analyzing the system behaviour. This will be described together with the sequence diagram creation. Currently, only a placeholder for the UI part is created. It could be replaced by a real UI support, but it is out of the scope of this chapter.

The above rules for generating the static structure of the system introduced in Figure 1 are illustrated in Figure 5.

Certainly, the most complicated part is the description of system behaviour. The sequence diagrams describing system behaviour are created by analyzing scenario sentences. There can be three types of SVO sentences. The first one is an actor – system sentence. In this case the subject of SVO sentence is an actor. For two other sentence types the subject of sentence is a system element. Sentence types are distinguished using the recipient link. Recipient is an SVO sentence element; it defines where the behaviour described in sentence is directed. The second kind of sentence is system – actor. In this case the subject is system and the recipient is actor. The third kind of sentence is system – system. In this case the subject and recipient is the system. It is used to describe system internal actions. The type of the particular message generated in the sequence diagram depends on the type of sentence.

Figure 6 illustrates the behaviour sequence diagram for the previously described example. It shows that the operations in the business logic layer are created only for the system – system sentences. From actor-system sentences the application logic methods are created. From system – actor sentences UI methods are created.

Figure 5. Static structure example

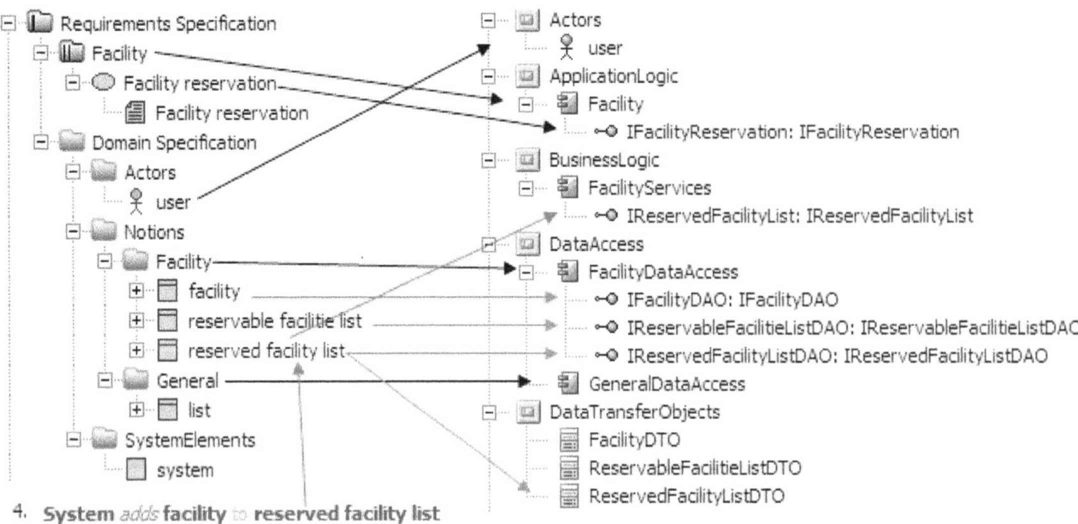

Figure 6. Behaviour example

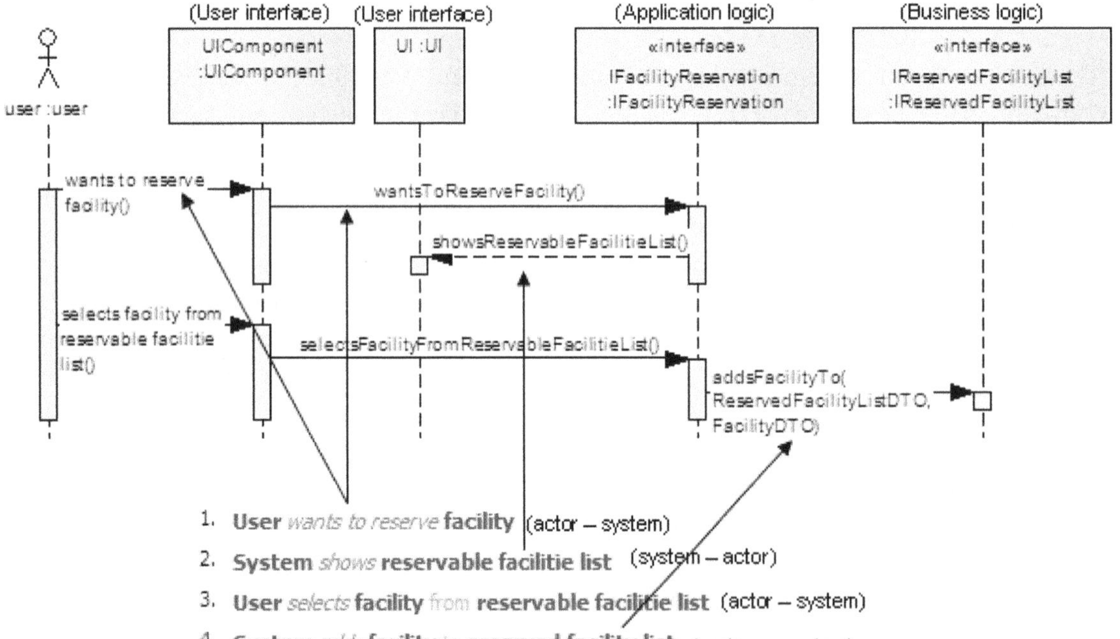

The PIM can be manually extended after the initial generation. Then it is transformed to the PSM. The same four layers and DTOs are used. In this model, the factory pattern is used. It enables the management of classes and interfaces. Each component in the PIM is transformed into a package and a factory class in the PSM. Every interface is transformed into an interface and an implementing class. Classes and interfaces are located in packages created from components.

Factory classes created from components have methods for getting provided interfaces. For each layer, one more factory class is created. It manages all other factory classes in this layer.

The platform specific model can be extended manually in the same way as the platform independent one. Then this model can be transformed to code.

RSL to JAVA Transformation Profile

In the second transformation profile, the formal architecture model is omitted. The main aim is to transform a CIM in the form of RSL requirement specification into a PSM containing classes and then into code in JAVA. In this approach, the architectural style is implemented in the transformation rules. It is based on the MVP (Model-View-Presenter) architectural pattern (Potel, 1996). The output of the transformation is a UML model consisting of classes with code, attributes and relations. This model is the input for the code generator. The output system in the MVP architecture is based on the Echo framework (Echo Framework, 2014).

Most of the system code is automatically generated with complete View, Presenter, Data access layers and stubs in the Model layer. Each generated class consist of the source object's name and a predefined prefix that emphasizes the layer affinity:

- M for the model layer classes. They are created based on the business objects stored in the system and contain all the operations that can be performed on those objects;
- V for the view layer classes. The view layer classes are GUI elements responsible for presenting information and interacting with the user;
- C for the controller/presenter layer classes. The controller/presenter classes are responsible for conducting the system's observable behaviour;
- X for the data transfer object (DTO) classes. They are used to transfer data between layers, therefore they contain only attributes and no operations (except for the constructor).

During the transformation, the static class structure and system behaviour in the form of class operations are generated. Each notion from the domain specification, is transformed into one data transfer object class and one model layer class (see Figure 7). To maintain the consistency of specification and code, the generated model classes are arranged in packages named as in the source model (cf. the *Books* package).

The notions that represent UI elements are placed in a special *!UIElements* package. They are transformed differently to "normal" domain elements as shown in Figure 8. Each such notion transforms into one class in the view layer. It is worth mentioning that notions from the *!Buttons* package do not transform into any new classes because buttons are always part of some window or form. Additionally a class representing the application's main window is generated.

The Figure 9 presents an example transformation of use cases into classes. Each use case transforms into one class in the controller/presenter layer. The name of the class consists of the "C" prefix and the source use case's name.

The example of complete structure of classes generated on the base of notions and use cases is presented in Figure 10

Scenarios do not transform directly into any objects, but their sentences are the basis for generating class operations, as shown in Figure 11.

Depending on the direction of control flow between an actor and a system, the target class for generating the appropriate operation's code is chosen according to the following general rules:

- Actor-to-System (subject is an actor) SVO sentence generates an operation in the controller/presenter layer class. The opera-

Figure 7. Generation of the model layer classes

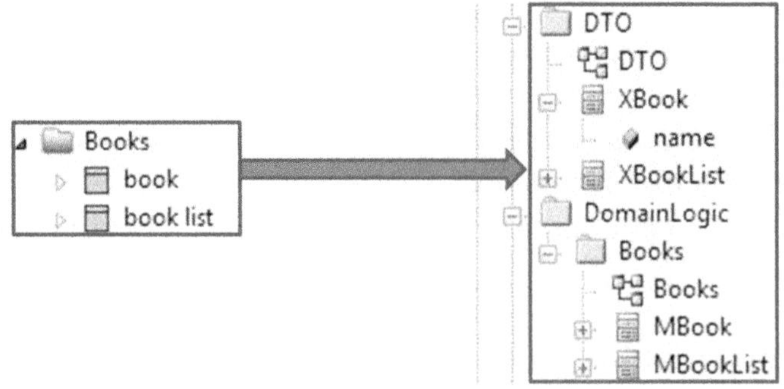

Figure 8. Generation of the view layer classes

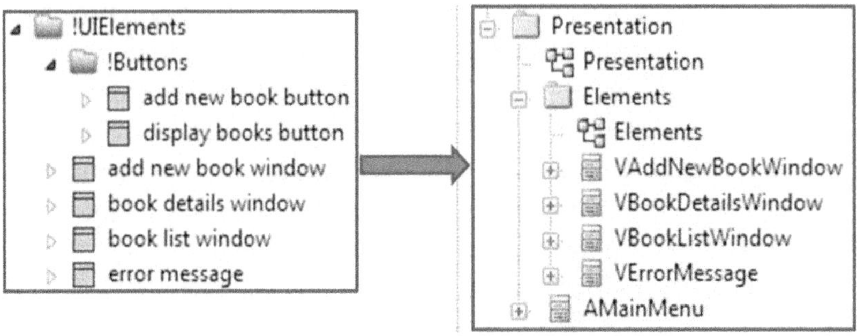

Figure 9. Generation of the controller/presenter layer classes

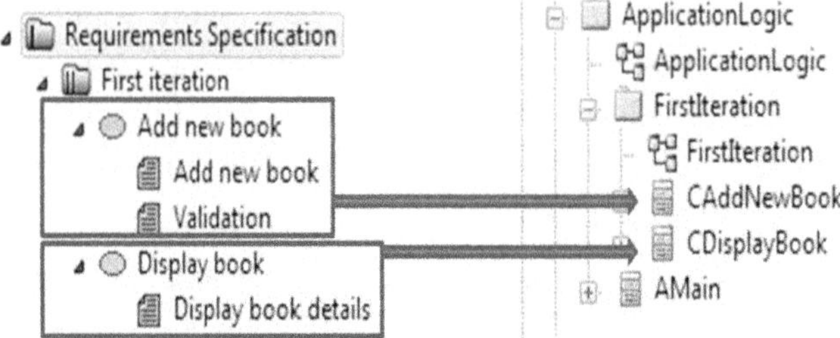

tion's name is constructed from the verb phrase pointed-to by the predicate of the sentence. SVOO sentence is transformed in the same way as the SVO sentence, but additionally the operation's parameter (based on the indirect object) is added;

- System-to-Actor (subject is a system, direct object in a UI element) sentence generates an operation in the view layer class;
- System-to-System (subject is a system, direct object is a regular domain notion) sentence generates an operation in the model layer class;
- Condition sentence is transformed into the "if-else" structure where operations created from the basic scenario sentences are added to the "if" structure and the opera-

Figure 10. General structure of the generated code

JFrame
Elements::
VErrorMessage
+ displays() : void
+vErrorMessage
+cAddNewBook
CAddNewBook
+ aBook: XBook {bag}
+ _ClicksAddNewBookButton() : void
+ FillsAddNewBookWindow(pBook :XBook) : void
+ init() : void
+cAddNewBook
+mBook
Books::MBook
+ getResult() : int
+ saves(aBook :XBook) : void
+ validates(aBook :XBook) : void
+cAddNewBook
JFrame
Elements::
VAddNewBookWindow
+ displays() : void
+vAddNewBookWindow

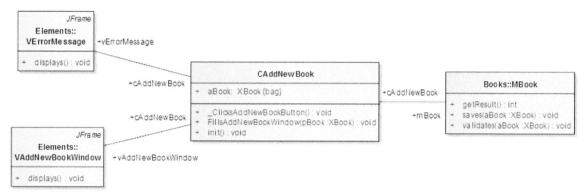

tions created from the alternative scenario sentences are added to the "else" structure.

Figure 11 presents two examples of code generated for SVOO sentences. The first example shows code generated for an Actor-to-System sentence. The operation name is constructed from a verb phrase and the (optional) operation parameter from an indirect object. Then the *XBook* object is assigned to a local *aBook* variable and passed to the "validates" operation in the *MBook* class. The second example shows code for a System-to-Actor sentence. The system constructs a new *VBookListWindow* object and then displays it with a previously fetched *XBookList* data (cf. *aBookList*).

In an example presented in Figure 12, the controller/presenter class assigns the result of validation to a local variable and then, depending on the validation result, the "if-else" structure decides whether to save the *XBook* object or to display an error message.

The next step is to export the above described UML model and generate code with a code generation tool. ReDSeeDS currently supports export of UML models and code generation using Enterprise Architect (Sparx Systems) and Modelio (Modelio). Full code generated from the requirements specification includes classes that contain all the necessary declarations, imports, constructors and operations. It also includes appropriate references between the model, the view and the presenter classes.

A more detailed description of use case scenario translational semantics can be found in Śmiałek, Jarzebowski & Nowakowski (2012)

Figure 11. Dynamic code generated for SVO sentences

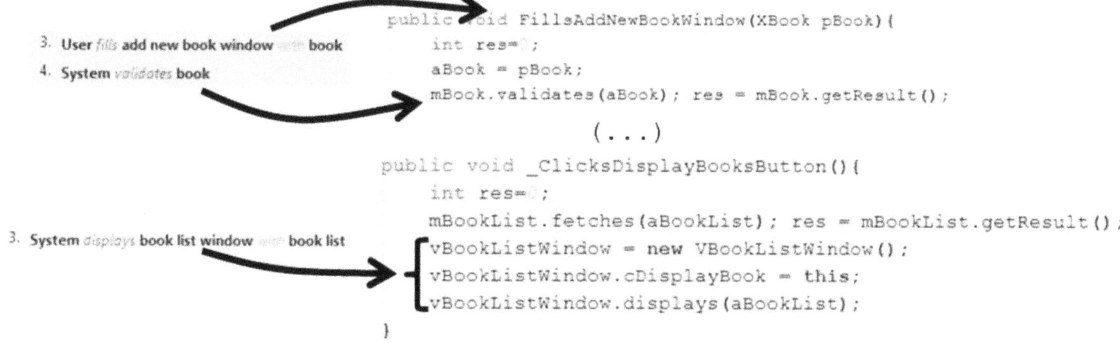

Figure 12. Dynamic code generated for condition sentences

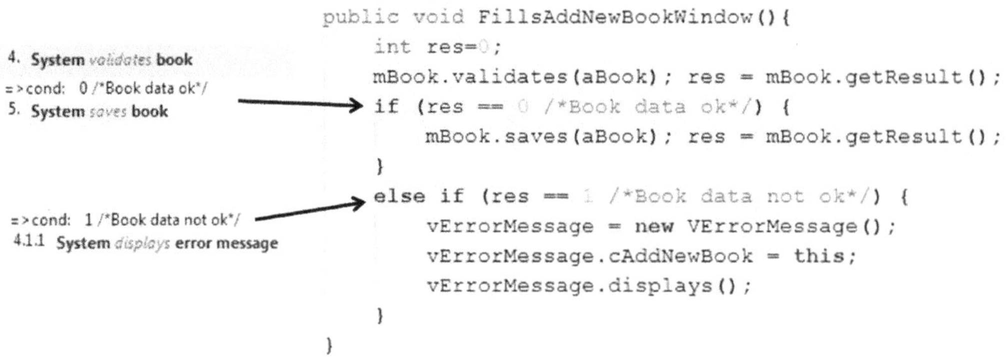

4. System *validates* book
=>cond: 0 /*Book data ok*/
5. System *saves* book

=>cond: 1 /*Book data not ok*/
4.1.1 System *displays* error message

```
public void FillsAddNewBookWindow(){
    int res=0;
    mBook.validates(aBook); res = mBook.getResult();
    if (res == 0 /*Book data ok*/) {
        mBook.saves(aBook); res = mBook.getResult();
    }
    else if (res == 1 /*Book data not ok*/) {
        vErrorMessage = new VErrorMessage();
        vErrorMessage.cAddNewBook = this;
        vErrorMessage.displays();
    }
}
```

and Śmiałek, Nowakowski, Jarzębowski & Ambroziewicz (2012).

Transformation algorithms for RSL to UML and RSL to JAVA transformation profiles were implemented in the model transformation language MOLA (Kalnins, Barzdins & Celms, 2005). The sample example of transformation procedure implemented in MOLA can be found in Figure 13.

Traceability

In order to support reuse, links between elements in different models within a software case are required. It must be possible to trace what elements in the PIM, PSM and code are created from which elements in the requirements. It is important, if it is supposed to reuse parts of the requirements

Figure 13. Transformation example

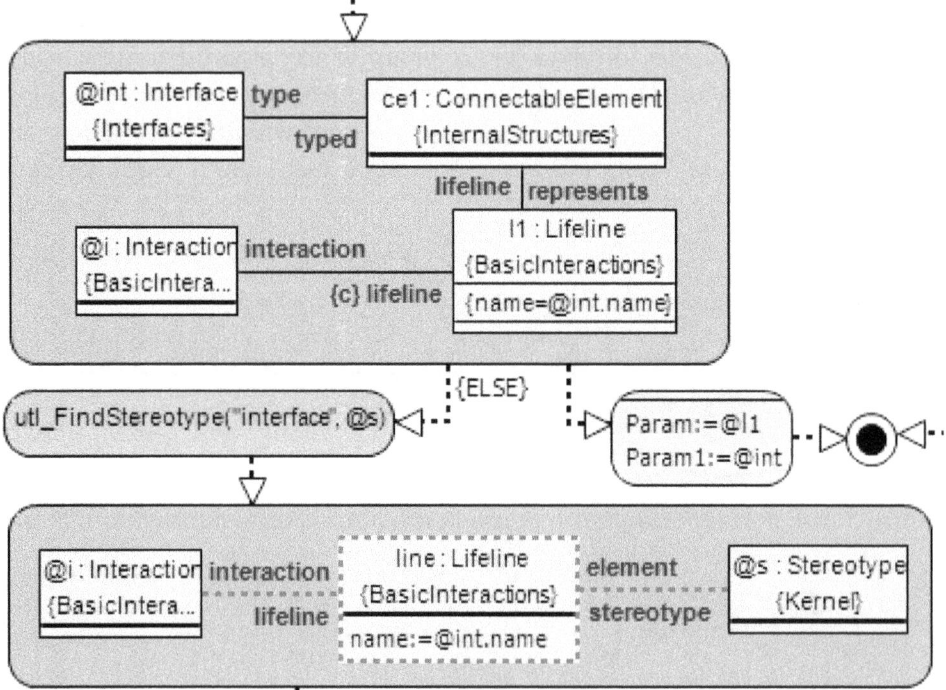

specification. In such case it should be possible to identify which elements in other models are created from particular elements of the specifications. To ensure such possibilities, traceability links are introduced. They show which elements in the next model are created from which elements in the previous model. Traceability links are created automatically when creating models using model transformations. It ensures that traceability links are really present. If the user should create them manually, he could easily forget to create some links. In such case it would cause problems in analyzing which elements are created from which.

It should be noted that in using model transformation language MOLA traceability links serve also as the base for easy definition of transformation rules.

To save traceability links they should be stored in a software case. Therefore, the traceability meta-model is created. There are two types of traceability links *IsAllocatedTo* from RSL to UML and *IsDependentOn* from UML to UML. In the transition from PSM to code, traceability links are treated differently, because code is a text and it is not defined through a meta-model. The traceability metamodel can be seen in Figure 14.

Figure 14. Traceability metamodel

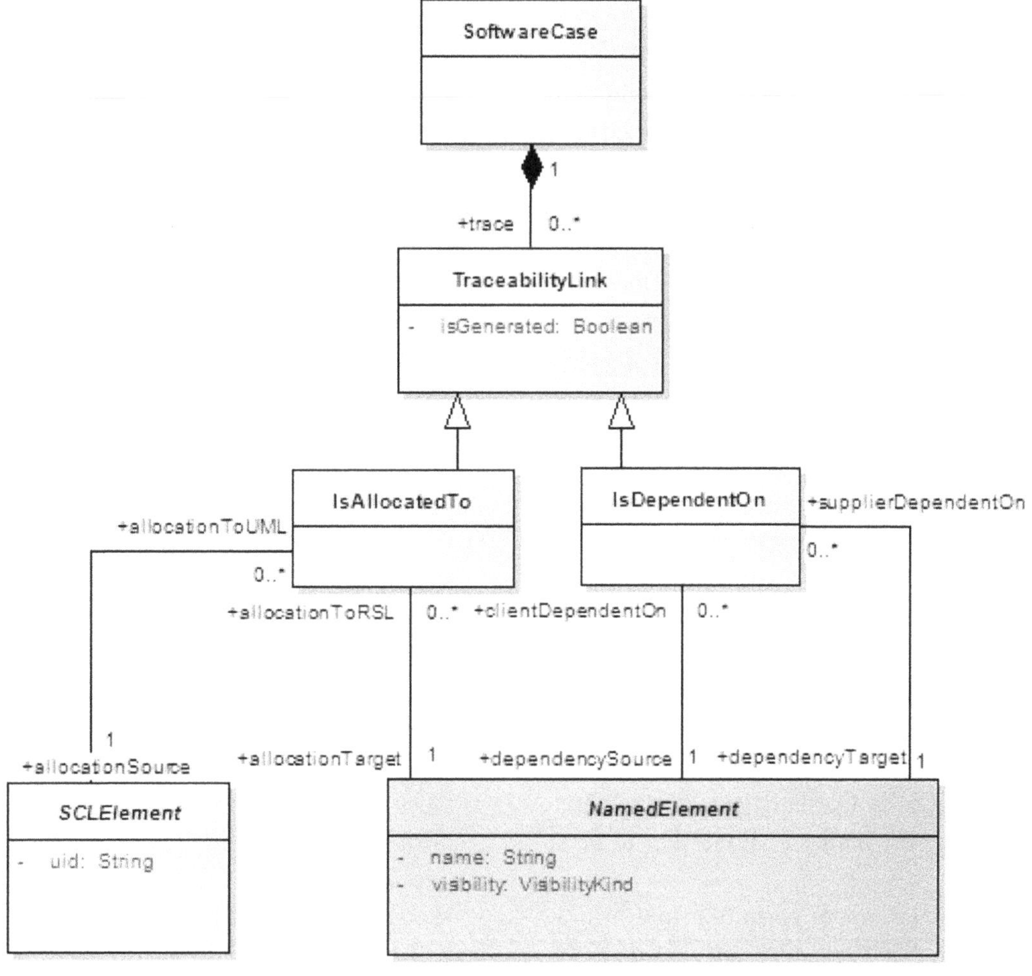

Profile Based on Keywords and Extended Domain

As it was shown in previous subsections, the basic domain based analysis of RSL scenarios and the basic architecture style supports transformation based development for all steps within a software case. However, the part of business logic layer, which can be generated automatically in the PSM model (and consequently, in code), is not always sufficiently large.

More advanced solutions are available here. Taking under consideration the SVO sentences:

System shows *reservable facility list*

User selects *facility* from *reservable facility list*,it is clear that more can be inferred from them. The first sentence clearly means displaying a form (containing reservable facility list – a list of rows showing facility data). The second one means that the user has selected a facility from this list. This intuitive reasoning can be made formal with the simple concept of keywords. It can be decided that verbs *show* and *display* will mean the action of displaying a form (as it in fact always is). These verbs can be declared to be syntactic forms of the keyword *show* with the above described semantics. Similarly, *select* can be defined as a keyword for a user action which means a selection of one element in a previously displayed list (not specifying exactly the technique used – be it a list-box or data grid or something else). A noun (more typically, one part of a complex noun) can also be defined as a keyword. Thus, *list* (within the complex noun "reservable facility list") should be defined as a keyword specifying that a list with elements being the notions defined by the remaining part of the complex noun (here – reservable facility) is being used. Examples of other verb keywords are *build, add, remove, save*, another noun keyword could be *form* (or its alternative *window* with the same meaning) for marking an element to be a GUI form.

The use of keywords permits to perform a significantly more "semantic" analysis of SVO sentences. Another possibility is to use the notion concept in RSL to its full capacity. The metamodel in Figure 4 shows that notions can be marked as being persistent, a notion can be an attribute of another notion, and notion relationships can have all basic features of associations. Thus, by means of analyzing notions together with scenario sentences, a more adequate domain model (a class diagram with appropriate stereotypes) can be created where persistent notions are distinguished from various temporary concepts such as lists and forms; nontrivial associations can also be created.

The stereotype set used in such a class diagram is sufficient for generating an ORM-based persistence framework and simple but adequate database schema. On the other hand, the basic usage of data elements (simple entities and lists of them) in a form can be inferred in a similar way. Figure 15 shows an example of a domain model which can be obtained from an RSL similar to that in Figure 1 if extended notion features and keyword based analysis is used.

However, the main advantage of this approach is that significantly more detailed behaviour can be generated in the PIM model. Frequently, operations to be performed within the business logic layer can be inferred without being explicitly specified as SVO sentences.

Certainly, this smarter analysis of sentences requires also an extension of the architectural style. More design patterns (manager, façade, POJO instead of DTO, abstract ORM) are used in this style. These patterns provide guidelines how data-related operations should be assigned to interfaces in a standard way during the behaviour specification in PIM by means of sequence diagrams. In the result, model transformations can be built which generate a realistic behaviour in PSM on the basis of requirements in RSL similar to those in Figure 1, but with keywords used in a consistent way.

Similarly, a more "practical" architectural style can be used for PSM. For example, patterns specific to Spring and Hibernate frameworks can

Figure 15. Fragment of an extended domain model

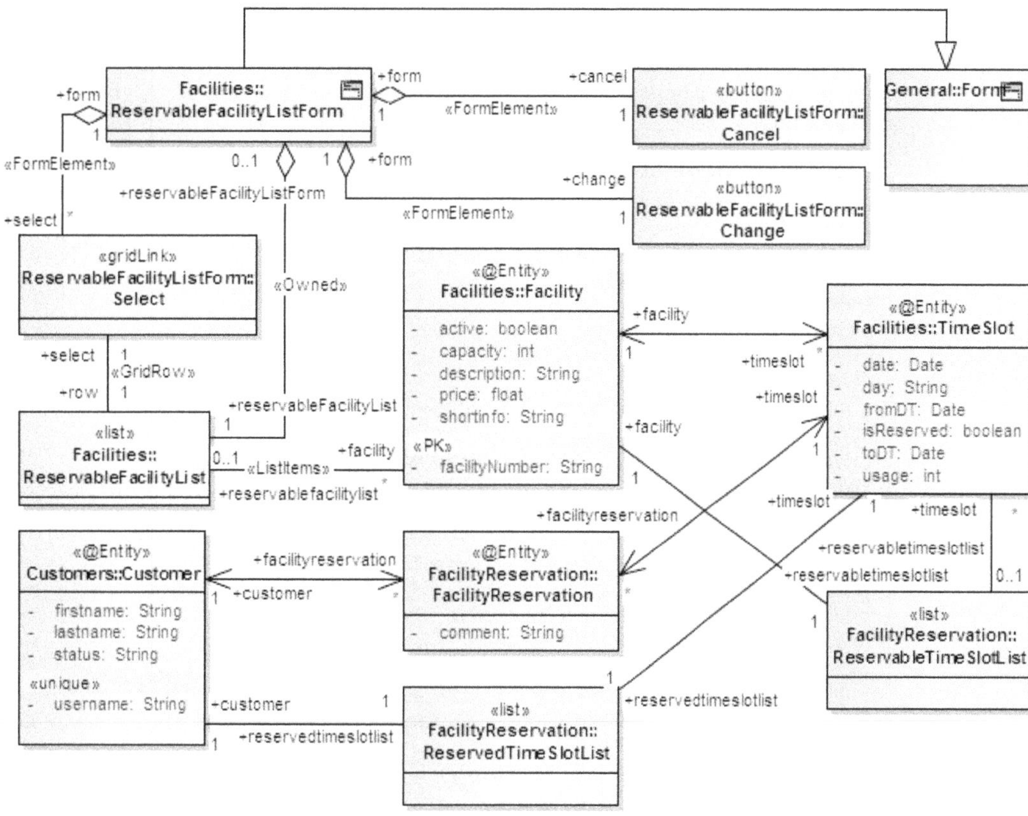

be included, and one of Java MVC GUI frameworks can be chosen. This way a quite realistic PSM, and even more, an executable Java code which serves as a draft prototype for the system can be built by transformations. Alternatively, Java Enterprise Edition code containing EJB and persistence support via JPA could also be built. In the result, a lot of non-trivial code in method bodies can be generated. The approach briefly described here has been supported by an appropriate transformation profile "RSL with keywords" built in MOLA. See a more detailed description of this profile in Kalnins, Kalnina, Celms & Sostaks (2010 a) and Kalnins, Kalnina, Celms & Sostaks (2010 b). The Java code examples generated this way from an RSL similar to that in Figure 1 are shown in Figure 16 – fragments of the code for entity class Facility and application logic class ReservationsService.

In simple cases this profile can generate complete system code in Java, certainly, if notions and behaviour are described to a sufficient detail in the RSL model. In addition, the transformations in the profile may be chained so that the PSM model or even Java code can be obtained directly from RSL. Thus in a sense such extended use of RSL comes close to possibilities of domain specific languages (DSL) for simple web-based system development, such as those in Brambilla et al. (2012) and Zviedris, Barzdins, Romane & Čerāns

Figure 16. Generated Java code fragments

```
@Entity
@Table((name="facility")
public class Facility {
private Boolean active;
private Boolean capacity;
private String description;
private String facilityNumber;
private String id;
@Column(name = "active", nullable = false)
public Boolean get_Active(){
return active;
}
...
@Service("ReservationsService")
public class ReservationsService implements IReservationsService {
@Autowired
private IChangeDisplayCriteriaService iChangeDisplayCriteriaService_;
@Autowired
private IFacilityService iFacilityService_;
@Autowired
private IReservedTimeSlotListService iReservedTimeSlotListService_;
private List<Facility> reservableFacilityList;
private List<TimeSlot> reservableTimeSlotList;
private List<TimeSlot> reservedTimeSlotList;
...
public void reservations(){
reservableFacilityList=iFacilityService_.
buildsReservableFacilityList();
}
...
```

(2013). The use of behaviour scenarios in RSL gives the possibilities to support richer system behaviour than in those references.

However, code for non-trivial business logic (e.g., what Reservation actually means) is difficult to build automatically this way. Therefore, in more complicated cases the created code then has to be manually extended to a real system, especially the business logic part.

REUSE OF SOFTWARE CASES

In the previous section, the process of developing software cases in the MDD way was described. This section describes activities and techniques that extend the above process in order to enable the reuse of software cases.

Figure 17 shows general overview of activities in the process of creating and reusing software cases in the ReDSeeDS approach. To enable reuse process, a repository that stores software cases created during past projects is needed. The whole process begins when the initial requirements model (CIM) for a new software system is formulated. According to the chosen transformation profile, this model can be transformed into PIM and PSM models or into PSM only and finally into code, as it was described earlier. Then a query the repository for similar software cases can be run. This is done by comparing actual requirements model with requirements models of past software cases. As a result of this comparison, also design models (PIM and PSM or PSM only) and code being a solution to the software problem expressed by requirements are found, thanks to the traceability

Figure 17. Reuse overview

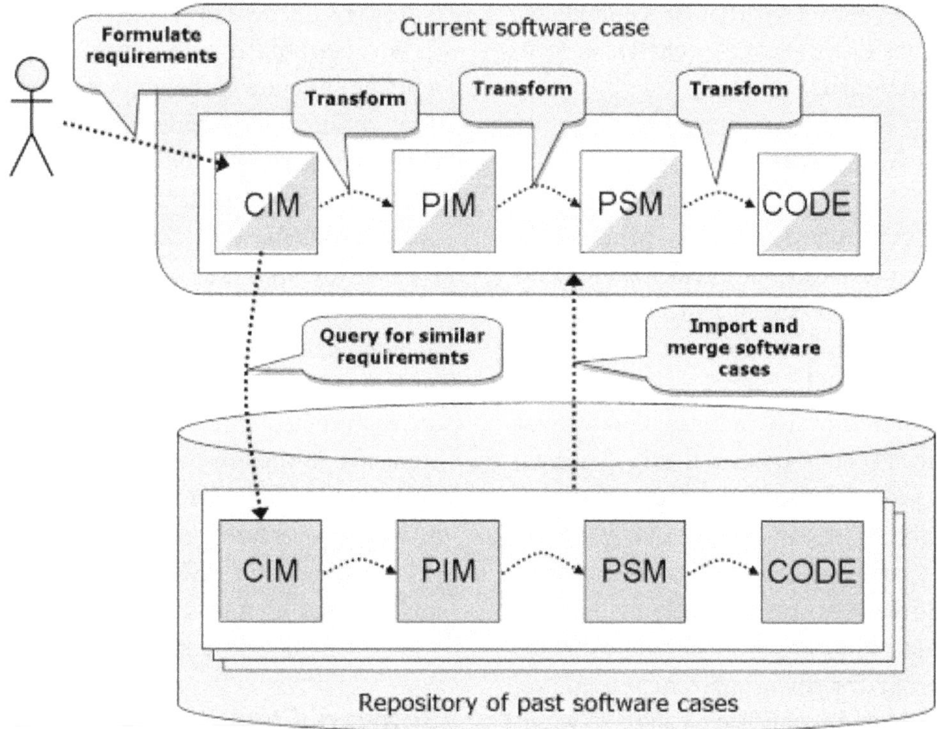

links connecting all these artefacts. The whole past software case found in the repository or just selected, usually the most similar, part of it, called slice, can be then imported and merged with the current software case. The remaining part of this section provides more details of reuse-related issues.

Querying for Similar Software Cases

Initially specified requirements model for the currently built system can serve as a basis for querying a repository of past software cases in order to find solutions manifested by requirements models similar to the current one. In the ReDSeeDS approach, the initial requirements model is the query itself. Therefore, the time-consuming task of specifying separate queries can be omitted. Querying for a similar software cases is performed by comparison of two graphs – the one representing requirements specification of the prospective system and the one which represents requirement specification of the past software case stored in the repository. For these two graphs a special similarity measure is calculated. The similarity measure takes into account many factors as it is a combination of several measures commonly used in the processes of information retrieval, case based reasoning and description logic. These measures are described in more details further in this section.

From the point of view of the user, the query is performed by running a special query engine which takes the current requirements specification as the input parameter. As the result of a query, the query engine returns the list of similar software cases found in the repository along with the values indicating the degree of similarity. The returned values can range from 0, meaning no similarity at all, to 1, denoting that the current requirements model is completely contained in the past software case. As the result of the query, also similarities between particular requirements representations like use cases scenarios are calculated and returned.

Similarity Measures

In order to construct a similarity measure appropriate for comparing different requirements representations expressed in RSL, several local similarity measures from different research domains were combined.

Information retrieval techniques allow for texts comparison and can be applied to all representations. They provide lexicographic term matching – textual artifacts are equal if the same words occur with the same frequency. This approach does not take into account structural information. For example, when there are two scenarios using the same words but describing opposing procedures, they are considered equal. The meaning of words is also not considered – there is no distinction between homonyms.

In addition to information retrieval techniques also WordNet-based similarity measures for comparing synsets (synsets in WordNet is a synonym set that group synonymic words or sequences of words, i.e., words having the same defined meaning) are used. These measures are based mainly on path lengths between synsets defined by semantic relations. Two synsets are more similar, the shortest distance there is between them. This approach can handle with synonyms and homonyms but cannot compare sentences or whole paragraphs of text.

Structure-based similarity measures cope with the structure of the artifacts to be compared. Two different structure-based measures were used to construct the global similarity measure: Graph-based and Description Logics. Both approaches handle with the structure of artifacts. Basically, graphs are compared using both taxonomic comparison of elements and their relations to other elements. In this approach, two artifacts are considered equal when the same elements are represented with the same relations to other elements. Structure-based similarity measures gives good results when comparing artifacts with a flexible structure like requirements specifications expressed in RSL and are not suitable for unstructured elements like plain text in RSL's natural language hypertext sentences.

Software Case Slicing

What is very important in the ReDSeeDS' approach to reuse is the possibility of reusing specific parts of software cases. Such a partial software case contains all the artefacts that are related with some selected elements from the requirements specification. It is illustrated in Figure 18.

A complete software case contains elements of requirements specification, elements of design models (PIM and PSM models) and, finally, pieces of code generated from design models. As it was

Figure 18. The idea of software case slicing

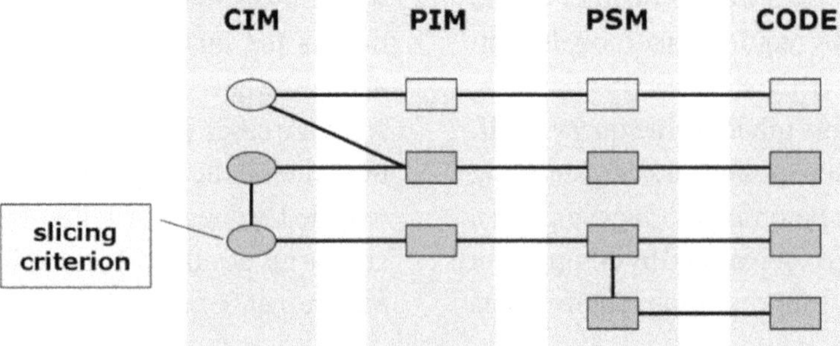

described in one of the previous sections, all elements of the model on one level can be traced from elements of the model on contiguous levels, thanks to traceability links created during models transformations. In order to create a software case slice, a slicing criterion has to be chosen. A slicing criterion is a selected set of requirements (use cases) along with interlinked elements from the domain vocabulary. Following traceability links outgoing from the selected elements from requirements specification, all the artefacts from the following levels can be determined. Rephrasing the definition of program slicing (Weiser, 1984), the software case slicing can be defined as follows:

Software Case slicing is a decomposition technique that extracts from a Software Case, artifacts relevant to a particular set of requirements. Informally, a slice provides the answer to the question "What artifacts realize the system behavior described by given set of functional requirements?"

For a particular software case, starting with the same slicing criterion, it is possible to create few different slices varying by the scope of elements from the source software case that will be included in a slice. The minimal slice is composed of selected requirements, their nested elements intra-level dependencies (i.e. traces between elements from contiguous levels, e.g. interfaces on the PIM level trace from requirements-level use cases) and inter-level dependencies (i.e. dependencies between elements from the same level, e.g. use case scenarios relate to vocabulary elements) of selected requirements. This kind of slice usually is not sufficient for reuse, as elements used by elements present in such a slice would not be selected, having the whole solution incomplete (e.g. missing some vocabulary elements). The maximal slice incorporates any elements related in any degree to the elements already present in slice. Such a slice is, in most cases, nearly identical to the source software case (especially in case of incorrectly decomposed system). An optimal slice is a compromise between minimal and maximal slice, where dependencies among elements are broken or left untouched depending on their type and according to the advanced set of rules.

Some of the slicing principles described above are exemplified in Figure 19. If *Use Case 1* from *Use Case Package 1* is taken as a slicing criterion, the elements from the requirements tier to be also included in the slice would be: *Use Case 3* (linked by RSL's invocation relation), *Notion 3*, *Notion 8* (these notions are used in a scenario or description of *Use Case 1*). Please note that *Notion 1* (related to *Notion 3*) would not have to be included (it is not directly connected with any of the slicing criteria).

Already selected *Use Case 3* has some subsequent elements: it links to *Notion 7* and *Notion 5*. Therefore, *Notion 5* and *Notion 7* would also have to be included in the computed slice, but e.g. *Notion 9*, a child in generalization relationship between *Notion 7* and *Notion 9*, would not be the part of the minimal slice. The elements from other tiers that would form the minimal slice are: *UCInterface1* and *UCInterface3* (as linked by *Use Case 1* and *Use Case 3*), *NotionInterface3*, *NotionInterface5*, *NotionInterface7*, *NotionInterface8* (from Architecture layer) along with parent components *Logic Layer Component 1*, *Business Layer Component 1* and *Logic Layer Component 2* and their implementations in Detailed Design: (*UCInterface1*, *UCImpl1*, *UCInterface3*, *UCImpl3*, *NotionInterface3*, *NotionInterface5*, *NotionInterface7*, *NotionInterface8*, *NotionImpl3*, *NotionImpl5*, *NotionImpl7*, *NotionImpl8* with *LogicFactory1*, *BusinessFactory1* and *BusinessFactory2* as parent elements. The result of such a slicing operation would be a CIM model containing the requirements specification, elements of PIM and PSM tiers corresponding to the functionality contained in use cases selected as the slicing criterion.

Figure 19. Detailed slicing example

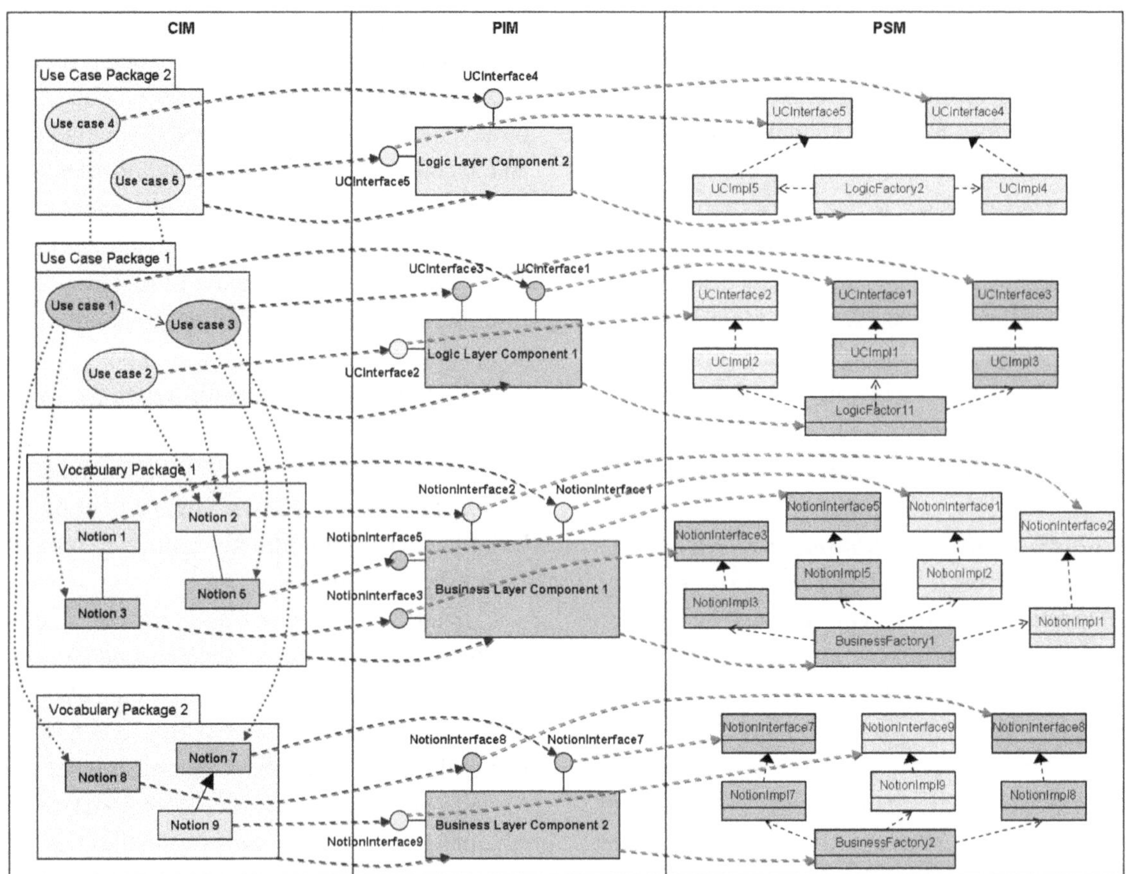

Merging Slices

The selected slices from the past software cases can be reused in the currently built software case. To include the slice into the current software case, import and merge operations should be applied. The Clipboard – special temporary space is used for import operation. It is a waiting room for slices which had been selected to reuse in the current software case. A selected slice is imported into the Clipboard, not directly into the main software case. Every import operation causes new Clipboard creation – one software case would then have many Clipboards. Although the Clipboard is an integral part of an software case, it is logically separated on the level of:

- **Terminology:** E.g. the word "car" in the main software case and in the Clipboard have separable meanings;
- **Structure:** Both Clipboard and main software case have CIM-PIM-PSM structure, but with separate sub-package structure;
- **Transformation:** All Clipboards should be excluded from the transformations.

Such a separation gives the opportunity to make pre-merge changes in the imported slice as well as in the current software case in order to avoid merge conflicts. These conflicts affect names, semantics and structure. To support the user in a repetitive conflict resolution during the merge operation, simple "skip/override/auto-solve" mechanisms have been introduced. In general, each element of the software case, which is not a package, should have a unique name. Uniqueness of packages must hold on the level of the parent package. To avoid hyponym occurrence, each notion can have only one meaning.

If conflicts touching the above constraints occur, the user may decide how the conflict should be resolved (skip, override or auto-solve), and applicable operations should be applied. The skip option in the conflict resolution mechanism leaves untouched the element in the target software case. The override option erases the element's characteristics and content in the target software case and puts a new one from the imported slice. The auto-solve option adds a suffix to the requirements specification element name with the name of the slice's clipboard. When the imported slice is not needed any more, it can be simply deleted.

IMPLEMENTATION AND VALIDATION

The domain-driven reuse of software design models is fully supported by a set of tools integrated in one complete environment called the ReDSeeDS Engine. The engine allows for editing and validating requirements, storing current and past software cases, querying for similar software cases, merging slices from past software cases into the current one and performing transformations.

Component based architecture, which was chosen for ReDSeeDS, gives the opportunity for replacement of particular parts of the engine according to further changes of technical requirements and needs. Considering such a style of the architecture, the Eclipse framework as the integration platform and its dynamic plug-in model that accomplish above functionalities – were chosen to build the complete ReDSeeDS environment (see Figure 20). The user interface, business and application logic are divided into several plug-ins, which are enclosed in the ReDSeeDS Eclipse Perspective. The layout and function of the Eclipse-based application is under fine-grained control of its developer, but also a subject to easy customisation by an end-user.

The main part of the ReDSeeDS Engine is the RSL editor. It allows for viewing and editing all elements of the requirements specification through individual editors for Requirements, Use Cases, Notions, Domain Statements, Actors and

Figure 20. ReDSeeDS engine architecture

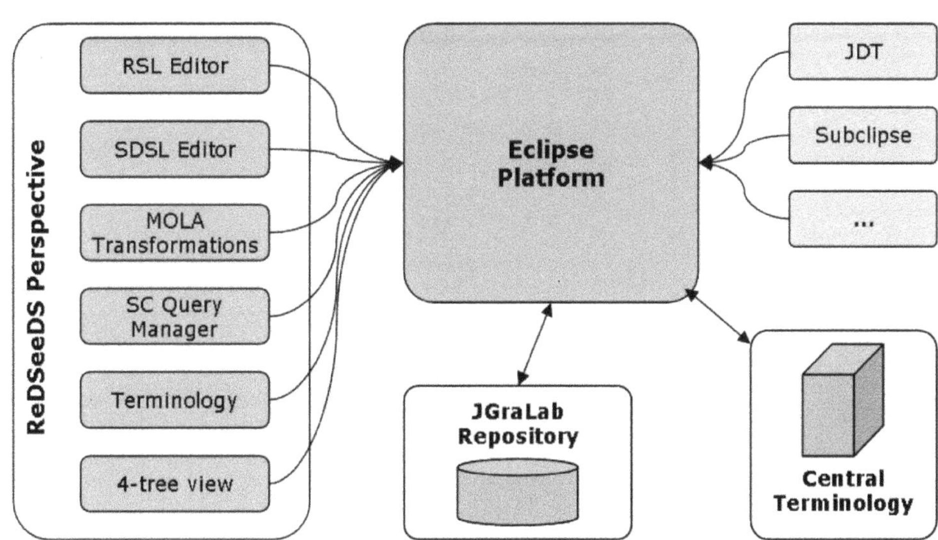

System Elements, which have similar layout and functionality. The user can edit element's description, name and relations to other requirements specification elements.

Very important feature of the software case is the central domain vocabulary, which includes all notions and its operations in the form of domain statements used in use case scenarios and other requirements definitions. Domain statements are in fact noun or verb phrases, whose descriptions can be linked to other notions. Every notion from the domain vocabulary can be edited in the Notion Editor. Beside notion details, it allows for editing domain statements. Usually, domain statements are added automatically when the user writes use case scenario sentences but, if needed, domain statements can be also added manually at any time by using the Domain Statement Editor.

For the purpose of determining similarity between different requirements specifications, notions are referred to a central terminology within the WordNet framework (i.e., the chosen software cases should rely on a common WordNet vocabulary copy). Term sense assignments can be managed in the special property view, which can be used for all term occurrences in the domain based requirements specification (see Figure 21). The user has an opportunity to expand the central terminology with new terms as well as new relations (synonym, antonym, hyponym, meronym) in order to make possible further similarity measures.

The Use Case Editor is the most sophisticated editor in the ReDSeeDS Engine. It is a multipage editor, where the first page is similar to other editors, and other pages contains scenarios for the particular use case and visualisation of all

Figure 21. ReDSeeDS perspective with scenario editor and term assignment property view

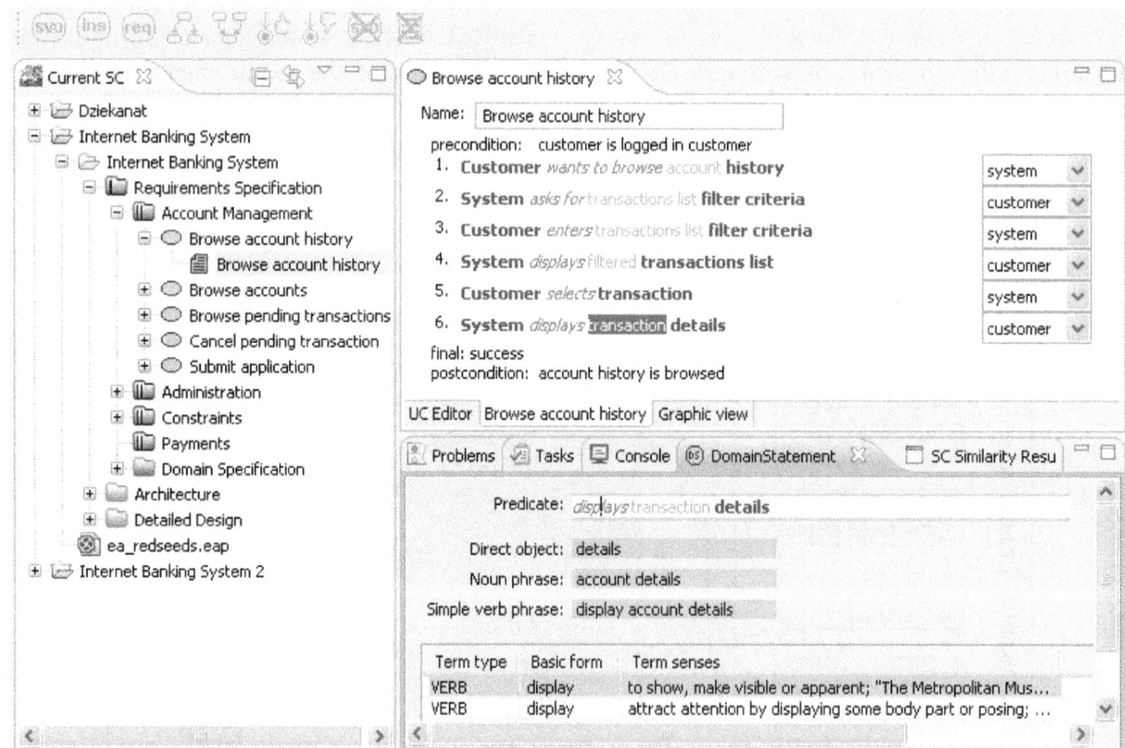

scenarios in the form of an activity diagram. The Scenario Editor, which is a part of the Use Case Editor can be seen in Figure 21.

While writing the SVO sentences, the user may tag words as specific parts of the sentence. It can be done by clicking a mouse on a chosen word and selecting one of the available sentence parts. As it was stated above, when writing a scenario, notions and domain statements which do not exist in the domain vocabulary can be created. When marking parts of the SVO sentence, the system checks if appropriate sentence parts exist in the domain vocabulary. These sentence parts are displayed in the property view below the scenario tab and if any of them is not present in the model, the tool suggests to add it.

The Scenario Editor allows for forking scenarios (alternate scenarios) and rejoining them (including loops) thanks to condition sentences. Sentences which are common with the main scenario are marked. Changes made in these sentences will take effect in all scenarios where they occur.

In order to make sure that the specification written by the user conforms to all RSL rules and is fully coherent, the tool offers validation mechanisms for the created specifications. While writing a requirement specification, the user can run the validation mechanism at any point and for any part of the specification. If there are any incoherencies or any of the RSL rules is broken, the tool will display a listing of all encountered problems. Problems are grouped in three levels of severity: Errors, Warnings and Informations. Errors are critical problems and they should be corrected immediately in order to make the specification conform to the RSL rules. Problems listed in Warnings group are not critical problems but it is strongly advisable to correct them. Problems classified as Informations are just suggestions what can be done to make use of all the features offered by RSL.

Transformations between models in the ReDSeeDS Engine are performed with an integrated transformation engine, which uses the transformation language MOLA. A user of the ReDSeeDS Engine can run any transformation from the list of predefined transformation profiles. There is also a possibility to modify existing transformation rules or create new ones.

To PIM and PSM models, the SDSL Editor is used. As these models are expressed in UML, an existing CASE tool (Enterprise Architect created by Sparx Systems) is used. The implemented functionality of the SDSL Editor includes invoking Enterprise Architect (EA) for viewing the existing UML models. The transformation engine converts ReDSeeDS models into internal EA model and back. Such synchronisation mechanism can be easily adopted for other CASE tools.

All models, which constitute a software case, are stored in the central repository. As these models are in fact graphs, the repository is based on JGraLab – a Java implementation of TGraph (Ebert, Riediger, & Winter, 2008). This solution provides easy storing and querying of graphs, which structure reflects the MOF models. Any well defined partial software case requirements specification can be used as an input for a query.

To query the past software case repository, the Query Manager should be used. A current software case requirements specification is an input for the query, where it is compared with past software cases to find similarities. The user can browse the results of the query, view particular similarities on the level of the software case, the use cases and even the scenario sentences (see Figure 22). In order to view slices based on selected requirements specification elements, the user can use a multi tree view, which contains a complete CIM-PIM-PSM structure tree browsers (see Figure 22). To obtain a slice of a past software case, the generated traceability links are used. These traceability links lead to the PIM and PSM parts that were generated from selected requirements.

The multi tree view provides reuse of selected past software case slices in the current project. The ReDSeeDS Engine fully supports merging slices from a past software case into the current

Figure 22. ReDSeeDS Engine perspective with multi tree view, and similarity results for use cases and scenarios

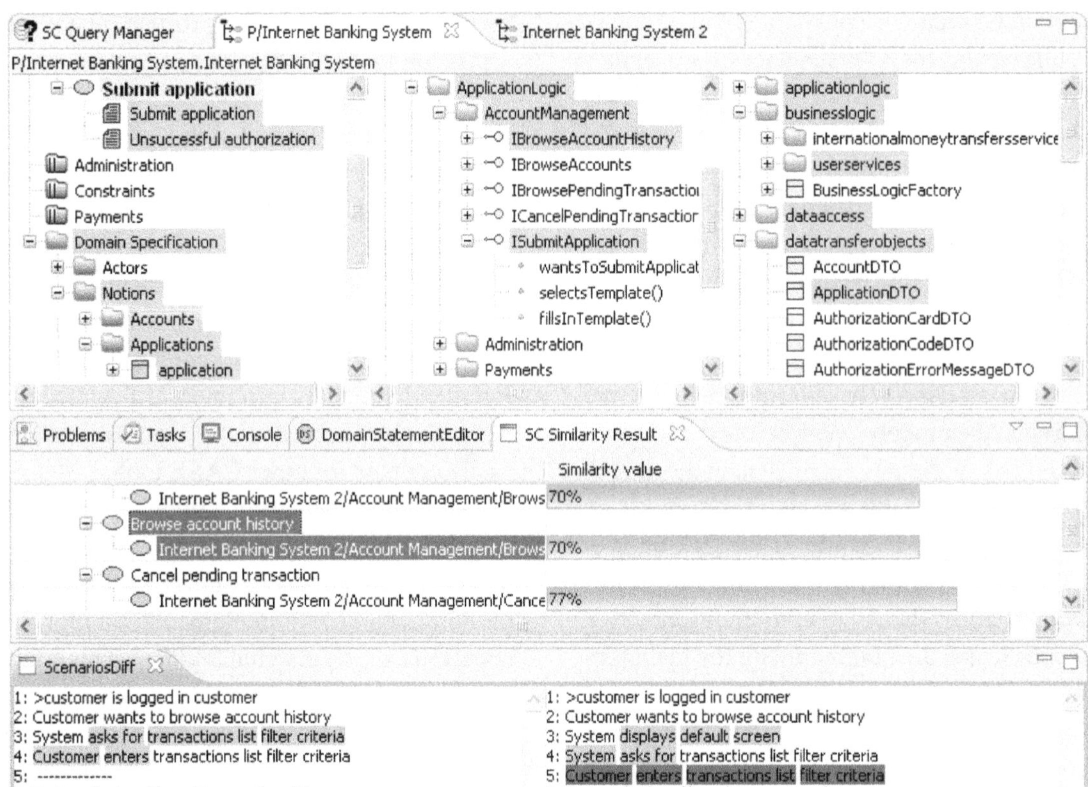

one by implementation of the import and merge functionality described in the previous section.

In order to confirm applicability of the presented ideas and usability of the tool, a comprehensive validation cycle in the industrial context is currently being conducted. This cycle is led by Fraunhofer IESE with the participation of four software development teams. The current validation outcomes show, that the whole system can be used in real industrial environments and that it reduces effort associated with formulating requirements and building complete software cases. Validation results point that requirements analysts accept the RSL. At the same time applicability of automatically generated design models was confirmed by software architects. Finally, the initial evaluation results of reuse activities prove that the effort to construct a new software case with the slices of existing ones is noticeably smaller than predicted.

RELATED WORK

There are two essential innovative aspects in the proposed approach to system development. One is the use of requirements language which can be processed in a formal way. The Computation Independent Model (CIM) in the classical MDA methodology (OMG 2003) means requirements for the system, understandable by domain experts.

Typically requirements are written as a free text, but a strong intention is to apply transformations also to CIM. Therefore a natural approach is to specify requirements in a controlled natural language (which can be used both as a formal and informal language), as is done in this chapter. A similar kind of requirements are used as a starting point in Leal, Pires, & Campos (2006), Leonardi & Mauco (2004), Bryant et. al. (2003), Osis, Asnina & Grave (2007). The approach closest to ours is Leal et al. (2006), where the Natural MDA language is proposed for behaviour description. This language uses a large set of keywords therefore it is much closer to programming languages than RSL, and the transformation based approach there is only partial. The approach in Leonardi & Mauco (2004) is based on the Language Extended Lexicon and does not use the behaviour description thoroughly. An interesting approach is proposed in Osis et al. (2007) where the initial requirements in natural language are manually converted into a list of semiformal functional features which then can be transformed formally using the topological functioning model. The approach proposed in Bryant et. al. (2003) also requires an initial semi-manual transformation of requirements. Thus, though the idea of using controlled natural language for requirements has been used before, the approach in this chapter (where scenarios are linked to a domain model) permits to apply formal transformations directly to the requirements specified by domain experts.

Another innovative aspect is the reuse based on requirements. An early attempt to provide a requirements language comprising a rigorous use case notation valid for reuse (but without formal transformations) is given in Biddle, Noble, & Tempero (2002). The reuse aspect is crucial for product line approach which also extensively uses model transformation and requirements modelling but solves the reuse issues differently by trying to generalize the problem statements (see e.g. Moon, Yeom, & Chae (2005)).

CONCLUSION

This chapter has shown how to combine model driven development and software reuse in a natural way. The basis for all of this is the semiformal requirements language RSL. The requirements in RSL consist of use cases refined by scenarios in a simple controlled language and the domain vocabulary containing the domain concepts. The meaning of each noun in a scenario sentence is defined in the domain vocabulary thus giving a precise meaning for the whole sentence. The requirements language is simple enough to be used directly by domain experts.

On the other hand, the specification of requirements to a system in RSL permits to apply model transformations directly to the original requirements. A non-trivial PIM model can be obtained by these transformations which after a manual extension can be transformed to PSM and further to code thus building an initial version of a complete software case. The transformations provide all necessary traceability links between the generated models.

The reuse aspect is also based on requirements in RSL. Requirements for a new software case are compared for similarity to the requirements of existing ones. Similar parts in requirements which are found this way are extended to slices on the basis of traceability links. These slices can then be imported into the current software case and adapted accordingly. Thus reuse is supported for all the development artefacts.

The presented approach has been implemented within a tool (ReDSeeDS Engine) developed during an EU 6FP project. This allowed to perform validation to confirm usability of the approach. The experiments have shown that nontrivial parts of a software system can be generated by transformations from appropriately defined requirements. However, this automatically generated part can be increased even more. One of the future research directions is to add more formality to requirements by means of keyword based analysis, as introduced in this chapter. It can be noted that this extension does not compromise understandability of requirements by domain experts. Another direction of future research is to refine the definition of similarity and building of slices, in order to provide a more targeted reuse of software case elements, with less manual adaptation required.

REFERENCES

Biddle, R., Noble, J., & Tempero, E. (2002). Supporting reusable use cases. In C. Gacek (Ed.), *Proceedings of the 7th International Conference on Software Reuse: Methods, Techniques, and Tools (ICSR-7)* (LNCS), (vol. 2319, pp. 210-226). Springer-Verlag.

Brambilla, M., Cabot, J., & Wimmer, M. (2012). *Model-driven Software Engineering in Practice*. San Rafael, CA: Morgan & Claypool Publishers.

Bryant, B. B., Lee, B. S., Cao, F., Zhao, W., Burt, C. C., Gray, J., et al. (2003). From Natural Language Requirements to Executable Models of Software Components. In *Proceedings of the Monterey Workshop on Software Engineering for Embedded Systems 2003* (pp. 51-58). Academic Press.

Ebert, J., Riediger, V., & Winter, A. (2008). Graph Technology In Reverse Engineering, The TGraph Approach. In *Proceedings of 10th Workshop Software Reengineering (WSR 2008)* (LNI) (vol. 216, pp. 67-81). Bonn: Springer.

Echo Framework. (n.d.). Retrieved February 26, 2014, from http://echo.nextapp.com/

Fellbaum, C. (Ed.). (1998). *WordNet: An electronic lexical database*. MIT Press.

IMCS. (n.d.). *MOLA pages*. Retrieved June 17, 2009, from http://mola.mii.lu.lv/

Kaindl, H., Smiałek, M., Svetinovic, D., Ambroziewicz, A., Bojarski, J., Nowakowski, W., et al. (2007). *Requirements specification language definition*. Retrieved February 26, 2014 from www.redseeds.eu

Kalnins, A., Barzdins, J., & Celms, E. (2005). Model transformation language MOLA. In *Proceedings of MDAFA 2004* (LNCS), (vol. 3599, pp. 62-76). Springer.

Kalnins, A., Kalnina, E., Celms, E., & Sostaks, A. (2010 a). From requirements to code in a model driven way. In *Proceedings of Associated Workshops and Doctoral Consortium of the 13th East European Conference, ADBIS 2009* (LNCS), (vol. 5968, pp. 161-168). Springer.

Kalnins, A., Kalnina, E., Celms, E., & Sostaks, A. (2010 b). Model driven path from requirements to code. *Scientific Papers University of Latvia. Computer Science and Information Technologies, 756*, 33–57.

Leal, L. N., Pires, P. F., Campos, M. L. M., & Delicato, F. C. (2006). Natural MDA: Controlled Natural Language for Action Specifications on Model Driven Development. In R. Meersman & Z. Tari (Eds.), *OTM Conferences* (vol. 1, pp. 551-568). Springer.

Leonardi, M. C., & Mauco, M. V. (2004). Integrating natural language oriented requirements models into MDA. In *Proceedings of Workshop on Requirements Engineering (WER) 2004*, (pp. 65-76). WER.

Modelio. (n.d.). Retrieved February 26, 2014, from http://www.modelio.org/

Moon, M., Yeom, K., & Chae, H. S. (2005). An approach to developing domain requirements as a core asset based on commonality and variability analysis in a product line. *IEEE Transactions on Software Engineering*, *31*(7), 551–569. doi:10.1109/TSE.2005.76

Nowakowski, W., Śmiałek, M., Ambroziewicz, A., & Straszak, T. (2013). Requirements-Level Language and Tools for Capturing Software System Essence. *Computer Science and Information Systems*, *10*(4), 1499–1524. doi:10.2298/CSIS121210062N

Object Management Group. (2003). *MDA Guide Version 1.0.1, omg/03-06-01*. Author.

Object Management Group. (2004). *Reusable Asset Specication: Final Adopted Specification, ptc/04-06-06*. Author.

Object Management Group. (2006). *Meta Object Facility Core Specification, version 2.0, formal/2006-01-01*. Author.

Object Management Group. (2009). *Unified Modeling Language: Superstructure, version 2.2, formal/09-02-02*. Author.

Osis, J., Asnina, E., & Grave, A. (2007). Computation Independent Modeling within the MDA. In *Proceedings of ICSSTE07*, (pp. 22–34). ICSSTE.

Potel, M. (1996). *MVP: Model-view-presenter the taligent programming model for C++ and Java. Technical report*. Taligent Inc.

Rein, M., Ambroziewicz, A., Bojarski, J., Nowakowski, W., Straszak, T., Kalnins, A., et al. (2008). *Initial ReDSeeDS Prototype*. Project Deliverable D5.4.1, ReDSeeDS Project. Retrieved June 17, 2009, from www.redseeds.eu

Requirements Driven Software Development System (ReDSeeDS). (n.d.). Retrieved February 26, 2014 from http://www.redseeds.eu

Śmiałek, M., Bojarski, J., Nowakowski, W., Ambroziewicz, A., & Straszak, T. (2007). Complementary use case scenario representations based on domain vocabularies. In Proceedings of *Model Driven Engineering Languages and Systems, (LNCS), (vol. 4735*, pp. 544–558). Berlin: Springer. doi:10.1007/978-3-540-75209-7_37

Śmiałek, M., Jarzebowski, N., & Nowakowski, W. (2012). Translation of use case scenarios to Java code. *Computer Science*, *13*(4), 35–52. doi:10.7494/csci.2012.13.4.35

Śmiałek, M., Nowakowski, W., & Ambroziewicz, A. (2012). From use cases and their relationships to code. In *Proceedings of Second IEEE International Workshop on Model-Driven Requirements Engineering MoDRE* (pp. 9–18). Chicago: IEEE doi:10.1109/MoDRE.2012.6360084

Sparx Systems. (n.d.). *Enterprise architect tool*. Retrieved February 26, 2014, from http://www.sparxsystems.com/products/ea/

Weiser, M. (1984). Program Slicing. *IEEE Transactions on Software Engineering*, SE-*10*(4), 352–357. doi:10.1109/TSE.1984.5010248

Zviedris, M., & Barzdins, G. Romane & A., Čerāns. K. (2014). Ontology-based information system. In *Proceedings of JIST 2013* (LNCS), (vol. 8838, pp. 33-47). Springer International Publishing.

KEY TERMS AND DEFINITIONS

Domain-Driven Development: Software producing approach focused on reflecting the reality in models of the system.

MDA: Model Driven Architecture, software design approach where all design artefacts in form of models should be integrated into the software lifecycle by automatic transformations that are used to convert one model into another.

Metamodel: Rules, constraints, models and theories applicable for modeling a predefined class of problems; is basis for automatic model transformations.

Model Transformation: Derivation of one model from another.

ReDSeeDS: Requirements Driven Software Development.

RSL: Requirements Specification Language.

Software Reuse: An approach of using once produced software artifacts in the new projects.

Chapter 13
Quantitative Productivity Analysis of a Domain-Specific Modeling Language

Joe Hoffert
Indiana Wesleyan University, USA

Douglas C. Schmidt
Vanderbilt University, USA

Aniruddha Gokhale
Vanderbilt University, USA

ABSTRACT

Model-Driven Engineering (MDE), in general, and Domain-Specific Modeling Languages (DSMLs), in particular, are increasingly used to manage the complexity of developing applications in various domains. Although many DSML benefits are qualitative (e.g., ease of use, familiarity of domain concepts), there is a need to quantitatively demonstrate the benefits of DSMLs (e.g., quantify when DSMLs provide savings in development time) to simplify comparison and evaluation. This chapter describes how the authors conducted quantitative productivity analysis for a DSML (i.e., the Distributed Quality-of-Service [QoS] Modeling Language [DQML]). The analysis shows (1) the significant quantitative productivity gain achieved when using a DSML to develop configuration models compared with not using a DSML, (2) the significant quantitative productivity gain achieved when using a DSML interpreter to automatically generate implementation artifacts as compared to alternative methods when configuring application entities, and (3) the viability of quantitative productivity metrics for DSMLs.

INTRODUCTION

Model-driven engineering (MDE) helps address the problems of designing, implementing, and integrating applications (Hästbacka, 2011)(Lukman, 2010)(Schmidt, 2006)(Hailpern, 2006)(Atkinson, 2003)(Kent, 2002). MDE is increasingly used in domains involving modeling software components, developing embedded software systems, and configuring quality-of-service (QoS) policies.

DOI: 10.4018/978-1-4666-6359-6.ch013

Key benefits of MDE include (1) raising the level of abstraction to alleviate accidental complexities of low-level and heterogeneous software platforms, (2) more effectively expressing designer intent for concepts in a domain, and (3) enforcing domain-specific development constraints. Many documented benefits of MDE are qualitative, *e.g.*, use of domain-specific entities and associations that are familiar to domain experts, and visual programming interfaces where developers can manipulate icons representing domain-specific entities to simplify development. There is a lack of documented quantitative benefits for domain-specific modeling languages (DSMLs), however, that show how developers are more productive using MDE tools and how development using DSMLs yields fewer bugs.

Conventional techniques for quantifying the benefits of MDE in general (*e.g.*, comparing user-perceived usefulness of measurements for development complexity (Abrahao and Poels, 2007, 2009)) and DSMLs in particular (*e.g.*, comparing elapsed development time for a domain expert with and without the use of the DSML (Loyall, Ye, Shapiro, Neema, Mahadevan, Abdelwahed, Koets, & Varner, 2004)) involve labor-intensive and time-consuming experiments. For example, control and experimental groups of developers may be tasked to complete a development activity during which metrics are collected (*e.g.*, number of defects, time required to complete various tasks). These metrics also often require the analysis of domain experts, who may be unavailable in many production systems.

Even though DSML developers are typically responsible for showing productivity gains, they often lack the resources to demonstrate the quantitative benefits of their tools. One way to address this issue is via productivity analysis, which is a lightweight approach to quantitatively evaluating DSMLs that measures how productive developers are, and quantitatively exploring factors that influence productivity (Boehm, 1987) (Premraj, Shepperd, Kitchenham, & Forselius, 2005). This chapter applies quantitative productivity measurement using a case study of the Distributed QoS Modeling Language (DQML), which is a DSML for designing valid QoS policy configurations and transforming the configurations into correct-by-construction implementations. Our productivity analysis of DQML shows significant productivity gains compared with common alternatives, such as manual development using third-generation programming languages. While this chapter leverages DQML as a case study, in general the productivity gains and analysis presented are representative of DSMLs' ability to reduce accidental complexity and increase reusability.

The remainder of this chapter includes the following objectives: highlighting related work; presenting an overview of DQML; outlining the DQML case study as a basis for DSMLs; describing productivity analysis for DSMLs leveraging the DQML case study; and presenting concluding remarks and lessons learned.

BACKGROUND

This section presents related work in the area of metrics for MDE and domain-specific technologies. We present work on quantitative analysis for MDE technologies as well as metrics to support quantitative evaluation.

Conway and Edwards (2004) focus on measuring quantifiable code size improvements using the NDL Device Language (NDL), which is a domain-specific language applicable to device drivers. NDL abstracts details of the device resources and constructs used to describe common device driver operations. The creators of NDL show quantitatively that NDL reduces code size of a semantically correct device driver by more than 50% with only a slight impact on performance. While quantifiable code size improvements are shown by using NDL, the type of improvement is applicable to DSLs where a higher level language is developed to bundle or encapsulate lower level, tedious, and error prone development. The productivity analysis for a DSL is easier to quantify since common units such as lines of source code are used. Conway and Edwards present compelling evidence of productivity gains of NDL although they do not encompass all the benefits of automatic code generation found with DSMLs such as the ease of a graphical user interface (GUI).

Bettin (2002) measures productivity for domain-specific modeling techniques within the domain of object-oriented user interfaces. Comparisons are made between (1) traditional software development where no explicit modeling is performed, (2) standard Unified Modeling Language (UML)-based software development, where UML is interpreted as a graphical notation providing a view into the source code, and (3) domain-specific notations to UML to support a higher-level abstraction that automatically generates large parts of the implementation. While the use of the domain-specific notations show a sharp reduction in the number of manually-written lines of source code as compared to traditional software development, the addition of modeling elements comes at some cost since no models are developed in traditional software development. The trade-off of the manual coding and modeling efforts is not clear quantitatively.

Balasubramanian, Schmidt, Molnar, & Ledeczi (2007) quantitatively analyze productivity gains within the context of the System Integration Modeling Language (SIML). SIML is a DSML that performs metamodel composition augmenting elements of existing DSMLs or adding additional elements. The productivity analysis of SIML focuses on the reduction of development steps needed for functional integration as compared to manual integration including design and implementation using native tools. The design and implementation steps are weighted more heavily (*i.e.*, are more expensive in development resources such as time and man-power) than using SIML which provides automated DSL integration. The analysis shows a 70% reduction in the number of distinct integration steps for a particular use case.

Genero, Piattini, Abrahao, Insfran, Carsi, & Ramos (2007) qualitatively measure ease of comprehension for class diagrams generated using various transformation rules via an experimental approach. From a given requirements model UML class diagrams were generated using 3 different sets of transformation rules. Human subjects were then asked to evaluate how easy the generated diagrams were to understand. While this experimental approach gleans valuable user feedback, this approach also incurs substantial experimental resources and time by involving human subjects and also targets the qualitative aspect of ease of understanding.

Abrahao and Poels (2007) have created OO-Method Function Points (OOmFP) which enhance function point analysis (FPA), originally designed for functional user requirements, to be applicable to object-oriented technologies. The metric generates a value related to the amount of business functionality a system provides to a user. Experimental procedures were conducted with students to compare FPA and OOmFP. The experiments showed that OOmFP consumed more time than FPA but the results were more accurate and more easily reproducible. Abrahoa and Poels (2009) then extended their OOmFP work into the area of Web applications which they termed OOmFPWeb. OOmFPWeb was designed to evaluate functionality of Web systems based on user-defined requirements encapsulated in the conceptual model of an application developed for the Web rather than based solely on implementation artifacts created once the application had been fully developed (Cleary, 2000)(Reifer, 2000).

Martínez, Cachero, & Meliá (2012) created and implemented empirical productivity studies when using a traditional code-centric approach, a UML model-based approach (describe what model-based means), and a model-driven engineering approach. The objective of the experiments was to compare the productivity of junior Web developers when developing the business layer of a Web 2.0 application. The experiments included 26 web application students that were grouped into six teams. The results of the experiments showed statistically significant increases in productivity when the subjects leveraged MDE practices. However, the results come with several caveats. While productivity improvements are empirically shown, the authors acknowledge that the results have not been extrapolated to a wider scope, *e.g.*, level of subject expertise, the domain of interest, number of developers. The results are only applicable to the scope stated in the research and quantifying the results for a different level of development expertise or for a different domain are non-trivial and challenging.

Papotti, do Prado, de Souza, Cirilo, & Pires (2013) developed an empirical experiment to compare a model-driven development approach where code is automatically generated to the classic lifecycle development approach where code is manually generated. The goal of the experiment was to conduct a comparative analysis of the amount of time spent in developing Create, Retrieve, Update, and Delete (CRUD) functionality for web systems using application entity classes described in UML class diagrams. In particular, the subjects were working on a medium to large size system to store academic information. In this experiment, the developers were 19 upper-level computer science and computer engineering students at the Federal University of São Carlos in Brazil. The subjects were divided into 9 homogeneous groups based on the level of development experience. The results showed that using automatic code generation decreases development time in a statistically significant way (*i.e.*, reduction of 90.98%). However, no results were presented as to other factors typically of interest (*e.g.*, quality of the code). The researchers also acknowledge that the results are limited to CRUD web applications using university students as software developers and that additional experiments would need to be conducted to gather relevant information for other developer populations (*e.g.*, larger or smaller groups, more or less experienced developers, different software development domains).

Mohagheghi, Gilani, Stefanescu, Fernandez, Nordmoen, & Fritzsche (2013) present experience reports from three large industrial regarding the benefits of model-driven engineering. The software applications involved range from SAP's large-scale enterprise business applications to Telefonica's network modeling to WesternGeco's simulation of seismic instrumentation to discover oil and gas below the sub-sea surface. The three participating organizations found benefits to using MDE techniques especially in the areas of providing abstractions of complex systems from different levels of abstraction and from different perspectives. The domain specific models also facilitated communication with non-technical experts and aided in simulation, testing, and performance analysis. The negative impacts of MDE were also noted such as the extra effort and negative impact on tools when developing reusable solutions. Moreover, merging several tools with one another required several transformations. The authors note that productivity improvements could not be measured although the potential exists based on feedback from the users. However, no approaches for quantitatively measuring the productivity improvements were proposed nor were classification of relevant factors for productivity improvements (*e.g.*, size of development team).

In contrast to the work outlined above, this chapter showcases (1) a quantitative productivity metric of developing DSMLs and (2) a quantitative productivity metric of DSML interpreters that transform models into implementation artifacts. These metrics are important since DSML developers and interpreter developers need to understand not only the quantitative benefit of DSMLs and interpreters but also the development effort for which the DSML and interpreter are justified.

QUANTITATIVE PRODUCTIVITY ANALYSIS

DSML Case Study: Overview of the Distributed QoS Modeling Language (DQML)

The *Distributed QoS Modeling Language* (DQML) is a DSML that addresses key inherent and accidental complexities of ensuring semantically compatible QoS policy configurations for publish/subscribe (pub/sub) middleware. Semantic compatibility is accomplished when the combination and interaction of the specified QoS policies produce the overall desired QoS for the system, *i.e.*, when the system executes with the QoS that is intended. DQML automates the analysis and synthesis of semantically compatible QoS policy configurations for the OMG *Data Distribution Service* (DDS), which is an open standard for QoS-enabled pub/sub middleware (Object Management Group, 2007). DQML was developed using the *Generic Modeling Environment* (GME) (Ledeczi, Bakay, Maroti, Volgyesi, Nordstrom, Sprinkle, & Karsai, 2001), which is a metaprogrammable environment for developing DSMLs.

This section provides an overview of DDS and the structure and functionality of DQML. Although DQML focused initially on QoS policy configurations for DDS, the approach can be applied to other pub/sub technologies, such as Web Services Brokered Notification (OASIS, 2006), Java Message Service (Sun Microsystems, 2002), CORBA Event Service (Object Management Group, 2004-1), and CORBA Notification Services (Object Management Group, 2004-2).

Overview of the OMG Data Distribution Service (DDS)

DDS defines a standard pub/sub architecture and runtime capabilities that enables applications to exchange data in event-based distributed systems. DDS provides efficient, scalable, predictable, and resource-aware data distribution via its *Data-Centric Publish/Subscribe* (DCPS) layer, which supports a global data store where publishers write and subscribers read data, respectively. Its modular structure, power, and flexibility stem from its support for (1) *location-independence*, via anonymous pub/sub, (2) *redundancy*, by allowing any numbers of readers and writers, (3) *real-time QoS*, via its 22 QoS policies, (4) *platform-independence*, by supporting a platform-independent model for data definition that can be mapped to different platform-specific models, and (5) *interoperability*, by specifying a standardized protocol for exchanging data between distributed publishers and subscribers.

As shown in Figure 1, several types of DCPS entities are specified for DDS. A *domain* represents the set of applications that communicate with each other. A domain acts likes a virtual private network so that DDS entities in different domains are completely unaware of each other even if on the same machine or in the same process. A *domain participant factory*'s sole purpose is to create and destroy domain participants. The factory is a pre-existing singleton object that can be accessed by means of the *get_instance()* class operation on the factory. A *domain participant* provides (1) a container for all DDS entities for an application within a single domain, (2) a factory for creating publisher, subscriber, and topic entities, and (3) administration services in the domain, such as allowing the application to ignore locally any information about particular DDS entities.

DDS is topic-based, which allows strongly typed data dissemination since the type of the data is known throughout the entire system.[1] As outlined in Table 1, DDS *topic* describes the type and structure of the data to read or write, a *data reader* subscribes to the data of particular topics, and a *data writer* publishes data for particular topics. Various properties of these entities can be configured using combinations of the 22 QoS policies that are described in Table 2. In addition,

Figure 1. Architecture of the DDS Data-Centric Publish/Subscribe (DCPS) layer

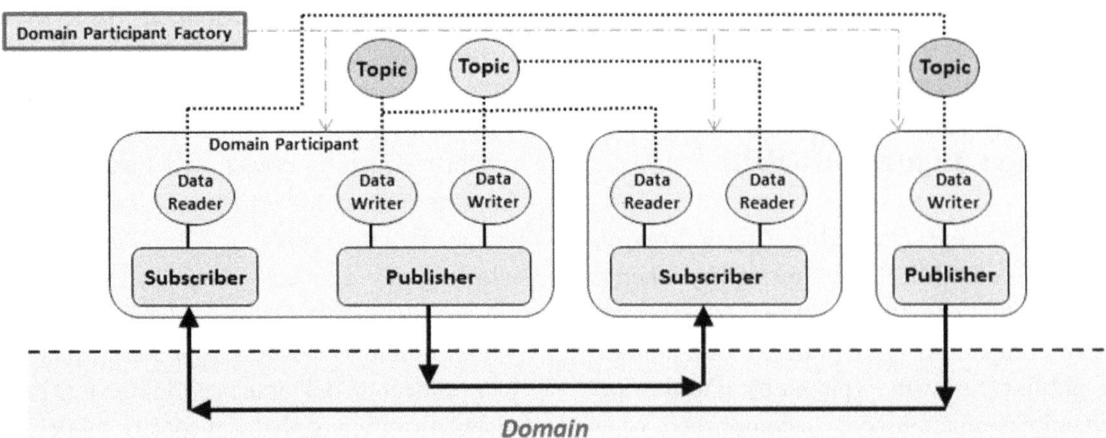

Table 1. DDS entities relevant to QoS properties

DDS Entity	Description
Data Reader	Subscribes to the data of particular topics
Data Writer	Publishes the data for particular topics
Domain Participant	Creates Publisher, Subscriber, and Topic entities
Domain Participant Factory	Creates and destroys domain participant entities
Publisher	Manages one or more data writers
Subscriber	Manages one or more data readers
Topic	Describes the type and structure of the data to read or write

publishers manage one or more data writers while *subscribers* manage one or more data readers. Publishers and subscribers can aggregate data from multiple data writers and readers for efficient transmission of data across a network.

Topic types are defined via the OMG Interface Definition Language (IDL) that enables platform-independent type definition. An IDL topic type can be mapped to platform-specific native data types, such as C++ running on VxWorks or Java running on real-time Linux. Below we show an example topic definition in IDL that defines an analog sensor with a sensor id of type *string* and a value of type *float*.

```
struct AnalogSensor {
   string sensor_id; // key
   float value; // other sensor data
};
```

DDS provides a rich set of QoS policies, as illustrated in Table 2. Each QoS policy has ~2 attributes, with most attributes having an unbounded number of potential values, *e.g.*, an attribute of type character string or integer. The DDS specification defines which QoS policies are applicable for certain entities, as well as which combinations of QoS policy values are semantically compatible. For example, if a data reader and data writer as-

Table 2. DDS QoS policies

DDS QoS Policy	Description
Deadline	Determines rate at which periodic data should be refreshed
Destination Order	Determines whether data writer or data reader determines order of received data
Durability	Determines if data outlives the time when written or read
Durability Service	Details how data that can outlive a writer, process, or session is stored
Entity Factory	Determines enabling of DDS entities when created
Group Data	Attaches application data to publishers, subscribers
History	Sets how much data is kept for data readers
Latency Budget	Sets guidelines for acceptable end-to-end delays
Lifespan	Sets time bound for "stale" data
Liveliness	Sets liveness properties of topics, data readers, data writers
Ownership	Determines if multiple data writers can write to the same topic instance
Ownership Strength	Sets ownership of topic instance data
Partition	Controls logical partition of data dissemination
Presentation	Delivers data as group and/or in order
Reader Data Lifecycle	Controls data and data reader lifecycles
Reliability	Controls reliability of data dissemination
Resource Limits	Controls resources used to meet requirements
Time Based Filter	Mediates exchanges between slow consumers and fast producers
Topic Data	Attaches application data to topics
Transport Priority	Sets priority of data transport
User Data	Attaches application data to DDS entities
Writer Data Lifecycle	Controls data and data writer lifecycles

sociated via a common topic want data to flow reliably, they must both specify reliable transmission via the reliability QoS policy.

The extensive QoS support of DDS and the flexibility of the QoS policies present the challenges of appropriately managing the policies to form the desired QoS configuration. These challenges not only include ensuring valid QoS parameter types and values but also ensuring valid interactions between the policies and the DDS entities. Moreover, managing semantic compatibility increases the accidental complexity of creating valid QoS configuration since not all valid combinations of QoS policies will produce the desired system behavior as outlined above with the flow of reliable data.

DSMLs can help address these challenges. DSMLs can reduce the variability complexity of managing multiple QoS policies and their parameters by presenting the QoS policies as modeling elements that are automatically checked for appropriate associations and whose parameters are automatically typed and checked for appropriate values. DSMLs can also codify constraints for semantic compatibility to ensure that data flows as intended. Moreover, DSMLs can automatically generate implementation artifacts that accurately reflect the design.

Structure of the DQML Metamodel

DDS defines 22 QoS policies shown in Table 2 that control the behavior of DDS applications. DQML models all of these DDS QoS policies, as well as the seven DDS entities (*i.e.*, *Data Reader*, *Data Writer*, *Topic*, *Publisher*, *Subscriber*, *Domain Participant*, and *Domain Participant Factory)* that can have QoS policies. Associations between the seven entities themselves and also between the entities and the 22 QoS policies can be modeled taking into account which and how many QoS policies can be associated with any one entity as defined by DDS. While other entities and constructs exist in DDS none of them directly use QoS policies and are therefore not included within the scope of DQML.

The constraints placed on QoS policies for *compatibility* and *consistency* are defined in the DDS specification. DQML uses the Object Constraint Language (OCL) (Warmer & Kleppe, 2003) (Cabot & Gogolla, 2012) implementation provided by GME to define these constraints. Compatibility constraints involve a single type of QoS policy (*e.g.*, reliability QoS policy) associated with more than one type of DDS entity (*e.g.*, data reader, data writer) whereas consistency constraints involve a single DDS entity (*e.g.*, data reader) with more than one QoS policy (*e.g.*, deadline and latency budget QoS policies). Both types of constraints are included in DQML.

Figure 2 shows an example of how OCL is used in DQML to determine if deadline properties between data readers and data writers are compatible. Line 1 determines if a deadline policy has been specified for a data reader. If so, then the period for that deadline is retrieved and stored in the variable dr_deadline (*i.e.*, period for data reader's deadline) on line 2. Line 4 determines if a deadline policy has been specified for a data writer. If so, then the period for that deadline is retrieved and stored in the variable dw_deadline (i.e., period for the data writer's deadline) on line 5. Lines 7 through 11 are comments meant to add clarification to the constraint code. Line 12

Figure 2. OCL example for checking deadline compatibility

```
1  if (dr_deadline_policies->size() = 1) then
2     let dr_deadline = dr_deadline_policies->theOnly().oclAsType(DeadlineQosPolicy).period in
3
4     if (dw_deadline_policies->size() = 1) then
5        let dw_deadline = dw_deadline_policies->theOnly().oclAsType(DeadlineQosPolicy).period in
6
7     -- The DDS specification defines compatibility such that the data writer's offered deadline
8     -- must be less than or equal to the data reader's requested deadline.
9     -- We have chosen -1 to represent infinity.
10    -- NOTE: A Topic can use this function as well since there is an implied DataWriter if
11    --        a Topic is associated with a DurabilityQosPolicy
12       dw_deadline <= dr_deadline or
13       dr_deadline = -1
14    else
15       -- Here compare dr_deadline <= infinity
16       dr_deadline = -1
17    endif
18 else
19    -- Here compare infinity <= infinity
20    true
21 endif
```

compares the period of the deadline for the data writer to the period of the deadline for the data reader and returns that values OR'ed with whether or not the data reader deadline was infinite as specified on line 13. We used the value of -1 as a convention to specify an infinite deadline period (which is the default value for a deadline period). If the data reader's deadline period is infinite then it is compatible with whatever deadline period the data writer specifies (per the DDS specification). Line 16 checks to see if the data reader's deadline period was infinite which will match the default data writer's deadline period of infinite since in this case no deadline property was associated with the data writer. Finally, line 14 returns true since no deadline property was specified for either the data writer or the data reader. In this case the deadlines are compatible since the default period values are infinite for both the data reader and data writer.

There are important differences between a programming language (*e.g.*, C++, Java, and Python) and a constraint language. The two types of languages address different needs (*i.e.*, specifying constraints vs. specifying program execution). However, while OCL is not a programming language OCL does provide programmers with common programming language features (*e.g.*, if/then/else code blocks) as illustrated in Figure 2. Moreover, it can be helpful for programmers to think of OCL as a language to define predicates (*i.e.*, functions to return either true or false) since predicates are a common programming language construct particularly with respect to generic/template programming (Sutton and Stroustrup, 2011). Therefore, codifying constraints using a constraint language like OCL is equivalent to codifying program execution in terms of the effort required and the complexity involved.

The OCL constraints for a DQML model are checked when explicitly initiated by the user. Programmatically checking these constraints greatly reduces the accidental complexity of creating valid QoS configurations. The DSML design decision to have constraint checking explicitly initiated by the user rather than automatically initiated by the DSML was made so that model developers could develop and save partial or incomplete models as development checkpoints.

Functionality of DQML

DQML allows DDS application developers to specify and control key aspects of QoS policy configuration in the following ways.

- **Creation of DDS Entities:** As illustrated in Figure 3, DQML allows developers to create the DDS entities involved with QoS policy configuration. DQML supports the seven DDS entities that can be associated with QoS policies.
- **Creation of DDS QoS Policies:** DQML allows developers to create the QoS policies involved with QoS policy configuration. DQML supports the 22 DDS policies that can be associated with entities to provide the required QoS along with the attributes, the appropriate ranges of values, and defaults. As shown in Figure 4, DQML ameliorates the variability complexity of

Figure 3. DDS entities supported in DQML

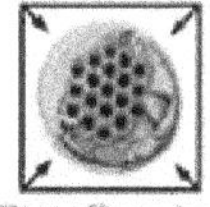

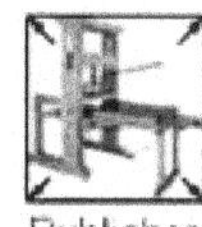

Figure 4. Example of DQML QoS policy variability management

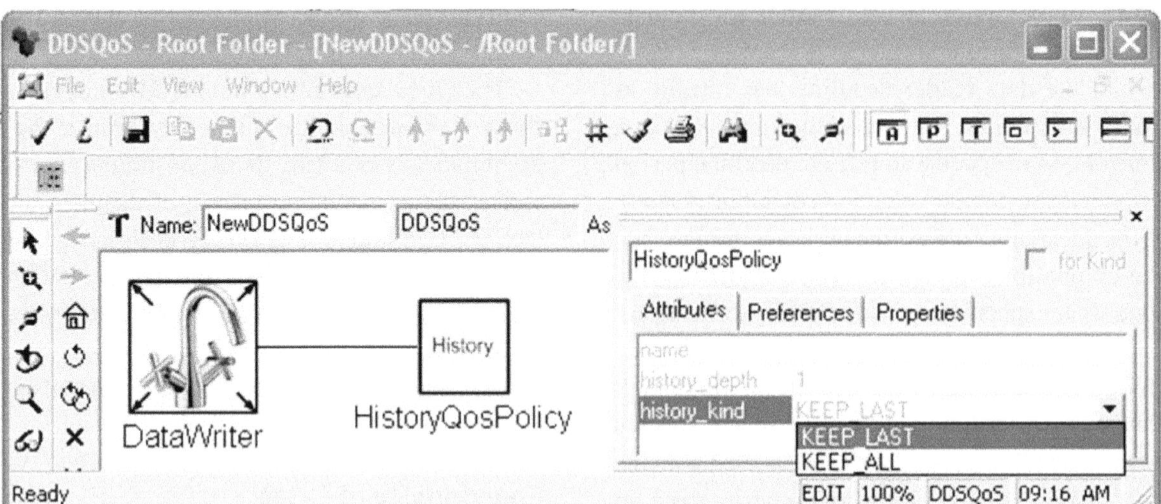

specifying (1) valid associations between QoS policies and DDS entities and (2) valid QoS policy parameters, parameter types, and values (including default values).

- **Creation of Associations between DDS Entities and QoS Policies:** As shown in Figure 5, DQML supports the generation of associations between the entities and the QoS policies and ensures that the associations are valid. DQML's support of correct associations is important since only certain types of entities can be associated with certain other entities and only certain types of QoS policies can be associated with certain types of entities.
- **Checking Compatibility and Consistency Constraints:** DQML supports checking for compatible and consistent QoS policy configurations. The user initiates this checking and DQML reports if there are any violations. Figure 6 shows DQML detecting and notifying users of incompatible reliability QoS policies while Figure 7 shows inconsistency between a deadline's period and a time based filter's minimum separation both associated with the same data reader.
- **Transforming QoS Policy Configurations from Design to Implementation:** DQML transforms QoS policy configurations into implementation artifacts via application specific interpreters. Figure 8 shows a representative implementation artifact for a data reader and two data writers. At runtime the DDS middleware will then read this XML while deploying and configuring the DDS entities.

DQML Case Study: DDS Benchmarking Environment (DBE)

Developing DDS applications is hard due to inherent and accidental complexities. The inherent complexities stem from determining appropriate configurations for the DDS entities. The accidental complexities stem from managing the variability, semantic compatibility, and transformation of QoS configurations. This section presents a case study highlighting development complexity to show how DQML can be applied to improve productivity compared to manual approaches.

Figure 5. Modeling entities, policies, and association in DQML

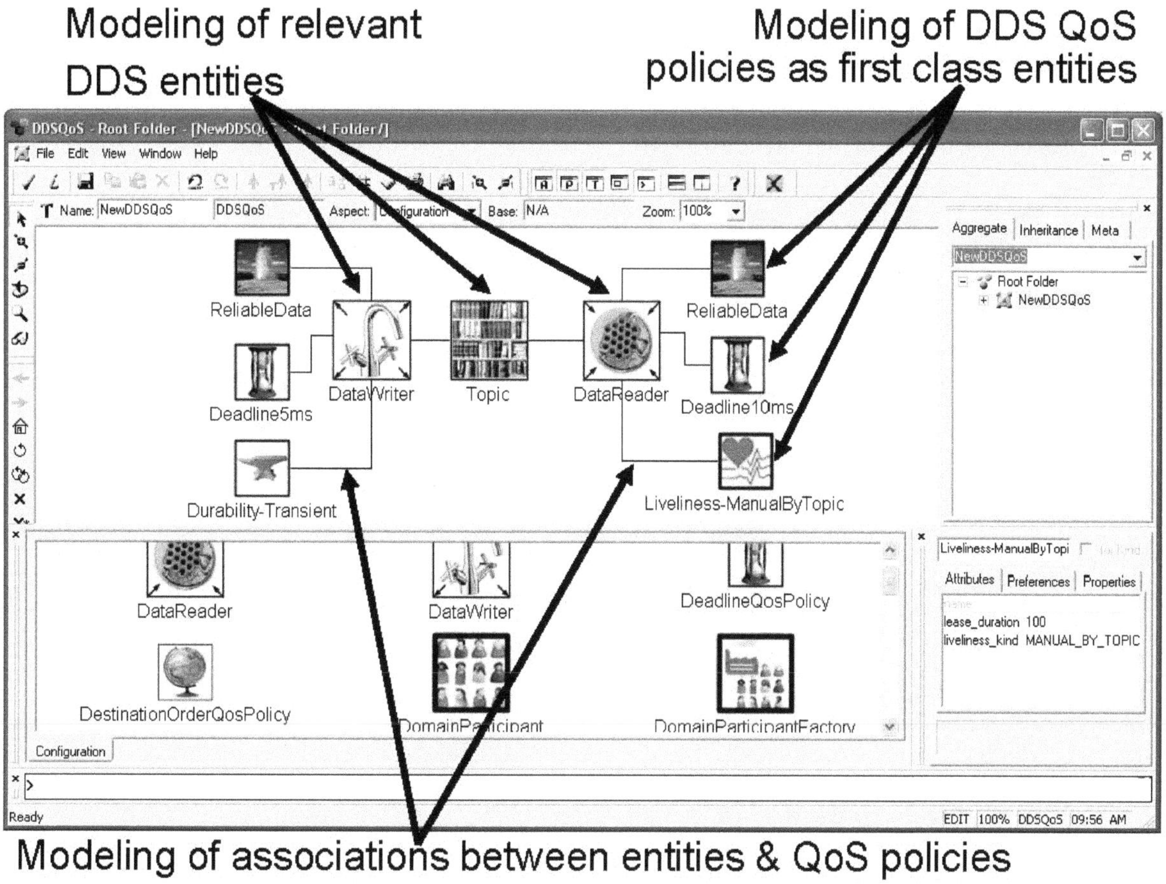

Modeling of relevant DDS entities

Modeling of DDS QoS policies as first class entities

Modeling of associations between entities & QoS policies

Figure 6. Example of DQML QoS policy compatibility constraint checking

Compatibility Constraint for Reliability - VIOLATED

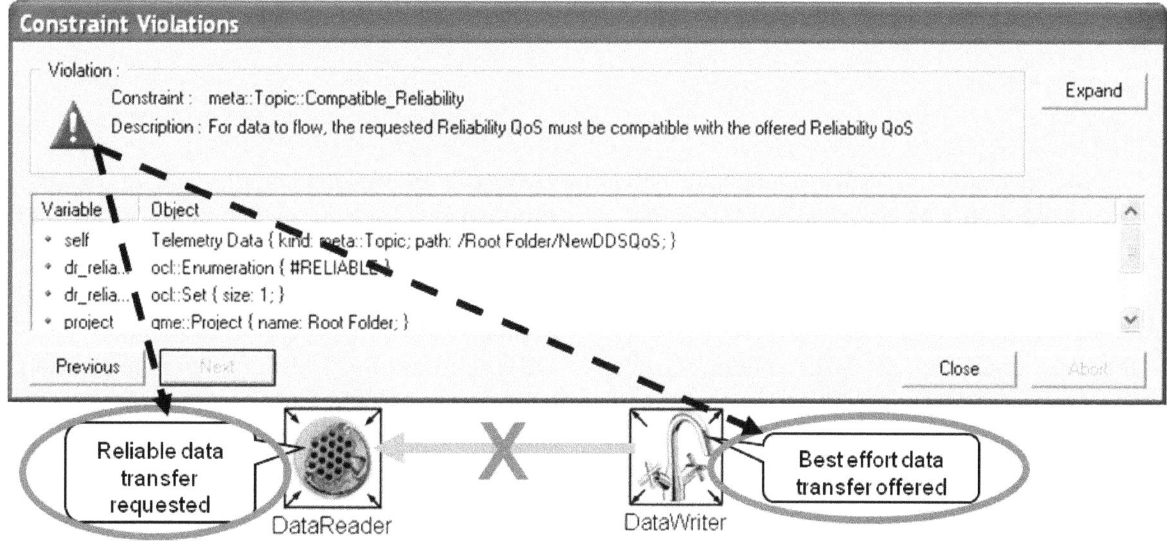

Figure 7. Example of DQML QoS policy consistency constraint checking

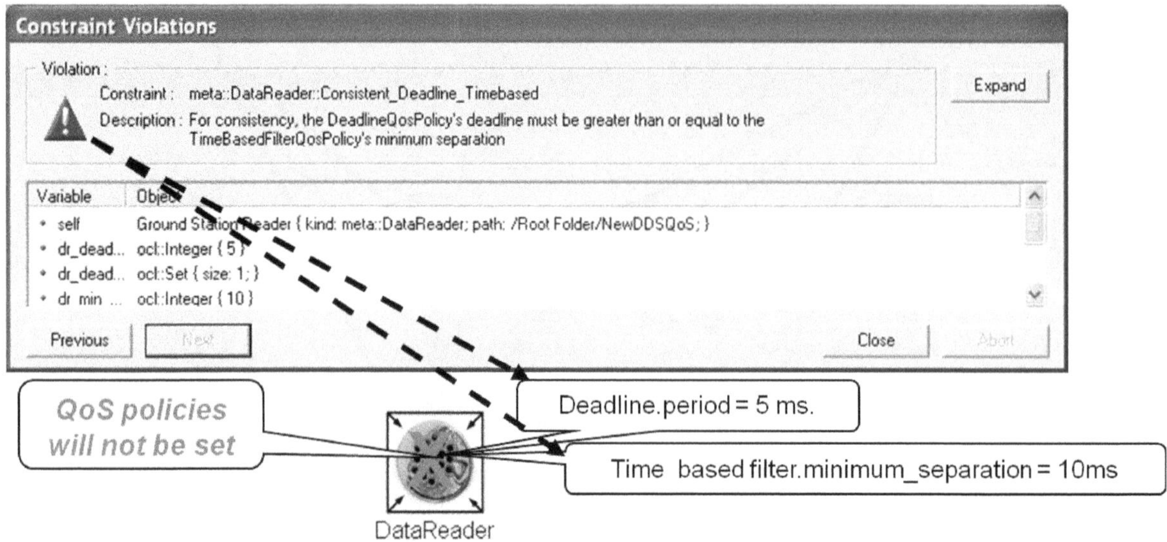

Figure 8. Example QoS policy configuration file

```
- <DQML>
  - <DataWriter name="DataWriter1">
      <deadline>period="50"</deadline>
    </DataWriter>
  - <DataReader name="DataReader1">
      <deadline>period="100"</deadline>
      <timebased_filter>min_separation="0"</timebased_filter>
    </DataReader>
  - <DataWriter name="DataWriter2">
      <reliability>kind="RELIABLE" max_blocking_time="100"</reliability>
    </DataWriter>
  </DQML>
```

At least eight different implementations of DDS are available each with its own set of strengths and market discriminators.[2] A systematic benchmarking environment is needed to objectively evaluate the QoS of these implementations. Such evaluations can also help guide the addition of new features to the DDS standard as it evolves. The *DDS Benchmarking Environment* (DBE) (www.dre.vanderbilt.edu/DDS/html/dbe.html) tool suite was developed to examine and evaluate the QoS of DDS implementations (Xiong, Parsons, Edmondson, Nguyen, & Schmidt, 2007). DBE is an open-source framework for automating and managing the complexity of evaluating DDS implementations with various QoS configurations. DBE consists of a repository containing scripts, configuration files, test ids, test results, a hierarchy of Perl scripts to automate evaluation setup and execution, and a shared C++ library for collecting results and generating statistics.

We use DBE as a case study in this chapter to highlight the challenges of developing correct and valid QoS configurations, as well as to analyze the productivity benefits of DQML. Although we focus on DBE in our case study, production DDS-based applications will generally encounter the same accidental complexities when implementing QoS parameter settings, *e.g.*, design-to-implementation transformation fidelity; valid, correct, compatible, and consistent settings. DDS QoS policy settings are typically specified for a DDS implementation programmatically by manually creating source code in a third-generation computer language, *e.g.*, Java or C++. Manual creation can incur the same accidental complexities as the DBE case study without the integration of MDE tools like DQML.

Since DDS has a large QoS configuration space (as outlined in the DDS overview above) there is an exponential number of testing configurations where QoS parameters can vary in several orthogonal dimensions. Manually performing evaluations for each QoS configuration, DDS implementation, and platform incurs significant accidental complexity. Moreover, the effort to manage and organize test results also grows dramatically along with the number of distinct QoS configurations.

DBE deploys a QoS policy configuration file for each data reader and data writer. As shown in Figure 9, the files contain simple text with a line-for-line mapping of QoS parameters to values, *e.g.*, *datawriter.deadline.period=10*. A file is associated with a particular data reader or data writer. For DBE to function properly, QoS policy settings in the configuration files must be correct to ensure that data flows as expected. If the QoS policy configuration is invalid, incompatible, inconsistent, or not implemented as designed, the QoS evaluations will not execute properly.

The DBE configuration files have traditionally been hand-generated using a text editor, which is tedious and error-prone since the aggregate parameter settings must ensure the fidelity of the QoS configuration design as well as the validity, correctness, compatibility, and consistency with respect to other values. Moreover, the configuration files must be managed appropriately, *e.g.*, via unique and descriptive filenames, to ensure the implemented QoS parameter settings reflect the desired QoS parameter settings. To address these issues, we developed an interpreter for DBE within DQML to automate the production of DBE QoS settings files.

When applying DQML to generate a QoS configuration for DBE we model (1) the desired DDS entities, (2) the desired QoS policies, (3) the associations among entities, and (4) the associations between entities and QoS policies. After an initial configuration is modeled, we then perform constraint checking to ensure compatible and consistent configurations. Other constraint checking is automatically enforced by the DQML metamodel as a model is constructed (*e.g.*, listing only the parameters applicable to a selected QoS when modifying values, allowing only valid values for parameter types).

We then invoke the DBE interpreter to generate the appropriate QoS settings files. These files

Figure 9. Example portion of a DBE QoS settings file

```
datareader.deadline.period=10
datareader.durability.kind=VOLATILE
datareader.liveliness.lease_duration=10
datareader.liveliness.kind=AUTOMATIC
datareader.reliability.kind=BEST_EFFORT
datareader.reliability.max_blocking_time=100
datareader.resource_limits.max_samples=-1
datareader.resource_limits.max_samples_per_instance=-1
datareader.resource_limits.max_instances=-1
datareader.timebased_filter.min_separation=0
```

contain the correct-by-construction parameter settings automatically generated by the interpreter as it traverses the model and transforms the QoS policies from design to implementation. Finally, we execute DBE to deploy data readers and data writers using the generated QoS settings files and run experiments to collect performance metrics.

DSML Productivity Analysis

This section provides a lightweight taxonomy of approaches to developing quantitative productivity analysis for a DSML. It also presents a productivity analysis for DQML that evaluates implementing QoS configurations for the DBE case study from the previous section.

Productivity Analysis Approach

When analyzing productivity gains for a given DSML, analysts can employ several different types of strategies, such as

- **Design Development Effort:** Comparing the effort (*e.g.*, time, number of design steps (Balasubramanian Schmidt, Molnar, & Ledeczi, 2007)) or number of modeling elements (Kavimandan & Gokhale, 2008) (von Pilgrim, 2007)) it takes a developer to generate a design using traditional methods (*e.g.*, manually) versus generating a design using the DSML,
- **Implementation Development Effort:** Comparing the effort (*e.g.*, time, lines of code) it takes a developer to generate implementation artifacts using traditional methods, *i.e.*, manual generation, versus generating implementation artifacts using the DSML,
- **Design Quality:** Comparing the number of defects in a model or an application developed traditionally to the number of defects in a model or application developed using the DSML (Kärnä, Tolvanen, & Kelly, 2009),
- **Required Developer Experience:** Comparing the amount of experience a developer needs to develop a model or application using traditional methods to the amount of experience needed when using a DSML, and
- **Solution Exploration:** Comparing the number of viable solutions considered for a particular problem in a set period of time using the DSML as compared to traditional methods or other DSMLs (White, Schmidt, Nechypurenko, & Wuchner, 2008).

Our focus is on the general area of quantitative productivity measurement (*e.g.*, number of entities and relationships to manage in a configuration, implementation development effort in terms of lines of code). The remainder of this section compares (1) number of DDS entities and relationships between those entities when considering development of a DSML and (2) the lines of configuration code manually generated for DBE data readers and data writers to the lines of C++ code needed to implement the DQML DBE interpreter, which in turn generates the lines of configuration code automatically.

Metrics and Productivity Analysis for Developing a DSML

In this section we analyze the effect on productivity and the breakeven point of developing a DSML. For this analysis we use the case study of DQML as a representative DSML. A DSML is used to design domain-specific elements such as configuring QoS for applications that are incorporating DDS to support QoS. However, the effort to develop a DSML is not without some cost and effort. We compare the effort to develop a DSML to designing the domain-specific elements without the use of a DSML. This analysis is helpful in determining whether or not to develop a DSML. Using the context of DQML as a case study this section specifically focuses on quantifying the effort to design QoS configurations with and without the use of a DSML. Using the DSML productivity analysis taxonomy outlined in the previous section, this section focuses on the category of *design development effort*.

To design domain-specific configurations the designer must be familiar with all the relevant elements in the domain. For the DDS case study of DQML, the seven relevant QoS entity elements are listed in Table 1. Knowledge of these seven DDS elements is needed to understand possible DDS QoS designs whether a DSML is being developed or not. Moreover, the designer needs to have familiarity with all seven entity elements even if not all the elements are used for a particular design. This familiarity ensures that all the relevant DDS entity elements are included in design considerations and that no relevant DDS entity elements are excluded.

The effort to incorporate knowledge of these DDS elements into the development of a DSML includes knowledge of the meta-modeling environment being used. In this case study GME was used to develop the DQML metamodel. However, the analysis performed for developing a DSML applies equally to other DSML development environments such as the Eclipse Modeling Framework (EMF) (Gronback, 2009) (Budinsky, Steinberg, Merks, 2009) since the general tasks of managing the types of entities and managing the valid associations between them must be performed regardless of any tool used. GME is a metaprogrammable development environment that is used to develop DSMLs. GME provides a GUI with drag-and-drop capabilities for creating relevant metamodel entities. The cost to learn a metamodel development tool is non-trivial. However, with the exception of simple point solutions as outlined below, a QoS designer will want to maintain designs in some electronic form (*e.g.*, utilizing a drawing package) since non-electronic forms are harder to manage (*e.g.*, copy, index, store). This management step will ensure that (1) design enhancements and modifications can be saved and archived and (2) design intent can be clearly communicated to the development team including the original designer.

A single developer creating QoS configurations for DDS might be able to manage all the relevant information without the use of external tools (*i.e.*, in his or her head). However, the threshold for the point at which a developer can manage all this information is typically quite low. Research has shown that the number of items a person can mentally manage is between 4 and 9 items (Miller, 1956)(Cowan, 2001)(Kamiński, Brzezicka, & Wróbel, 2011). For our analysis we use the more conservative value of 9 items. Therefore, if the single developer must manage more than 9 different items including, for example, any relevant DDS entities and DDS QoS policies then use of a DSML is warranted.

This threshold of 9 items applies to more than simply the unique types of entities (*e.g.*, 22 unique QoS polices in DDS) since it also applies to the total number of entities even if some entities are of the same type (*e.g.*, more than 9 instances of the Data Reader entity). The role that each entity plays in the overall design along with the relationships between these entities add to the inherent design complexity. Moreover, this threshold of 9 items also applies to the relationships that the entities can have. For example, as shown in Figure 6, a DDS reliability QoS policy is only applicable between a data reader entity and a data writer entity (or alternatively between a topic entity and a data reader entity or between a topic entity and a data writer entity). In this case, the QoS configuration developer must not only manage the three DDS entities but also the valid relationships between them.

If the developer is working in a team then the number of communication paths between the team members must also be managed to ensure correct information. As shown by Tsui, Karam, & Bernal (2013), the number of communication paths between members of a development team increases geometrically as the number of team members increases linearly. If the number of communication paths is more than 9 then a development tool with clearly defined semantics is warranted in order to clearly communicate the design being developed. For a group of 5 developers all working together the number of communication paths surpasses the threshold of 9 (*i.e.*, 10 communication paths).

If a simple electronic format is utilized (*e.g.*, a simple text file), the cost of developing a format to describe a design or the cost of unambiguously describing the design in text will surpass the effort to learn a metamodeling tool such as GME or EMF. This proposition will be true for all cases that involve any combination of more than 9 (1) types of entities, (2) modeled entities even of a single type, (3) relationships between the modeled entities, or (3) number of developers involved. Moreover, if the implementation artifacts are going to be maintained or modified then developing a DSML is warranted. Short-term memory ranges from minutes to hours while long-term memory ranges from days to years (Bailey, Bartsch, & Kandel, 1996). We use the conservative value of one week to denote the time by which short-term memory has been lost. Using this value of one week, a DSML is warranted if a design is going to be maintained beyond the timeframe of one week. Figure 10 outlines the decision process to determine if developing a DSML is warranted.

In the case of DDS, the specification is fairly straightforward as to how entities relate to each other and what QoS properties are applicable to which entities. The specification also provides UML class diagrams to document these relationships. Therefore, a DSML for DDS QoS configurations is quite amenable to development using a metamodeling tool such as GME or EMF. Other domains and specifications for those domains might not be as compatible with class diagrams. However, in general entities and relationships between those entities will be needed and which map well to classes and class diagrams.

Additionally, DDS provides 22 QoS property elements (as outlined in Table 2) with which the QoS designer must be familiar. As outlined previously regarding knowledge of all DDS entity elements, a QoS designer will need to have at least cursory knowledge of these 22 QoS property elements so that the relevant QoS property elements are included in the design and that no relevant QoS property elements are excluded. This knowledge is needed regardless if a DSML is being developed.

Recent research by Pati, Feiock, and Hill (2012) outlines how to incorporate proactive modeling so that the complexities of developing valid models can be ameliorated. This approach can reduce the overhead of developing models and make the creation of a DSML more appealing. This approach has not yet been analyzed for its quantitative benefit in model generation but is a promising area of research to explore in this regard.

Metrics and Productivity Analysis for Developing a DSML Interpreter

Once a DSML has been developed, analysis should be performed to determine if development of an interpreter for the DSML is warranted. Below we analyze the effect on productivity and the break-even point of using a DSML interpreter for QoS policy configurations. In particular, this section quantifiably analyzes the productivity of developing and using a DSML interpreter to generate implementation artifacts for DBE compared to manual generation. Although configurations can be *designed* using various methods as outlined in previous work (Hoffert, Schmidt, & Gokhale, 2007), manual *implementation* of configurations is applicable to these other design solutions since

Figure 10. DSML decision process

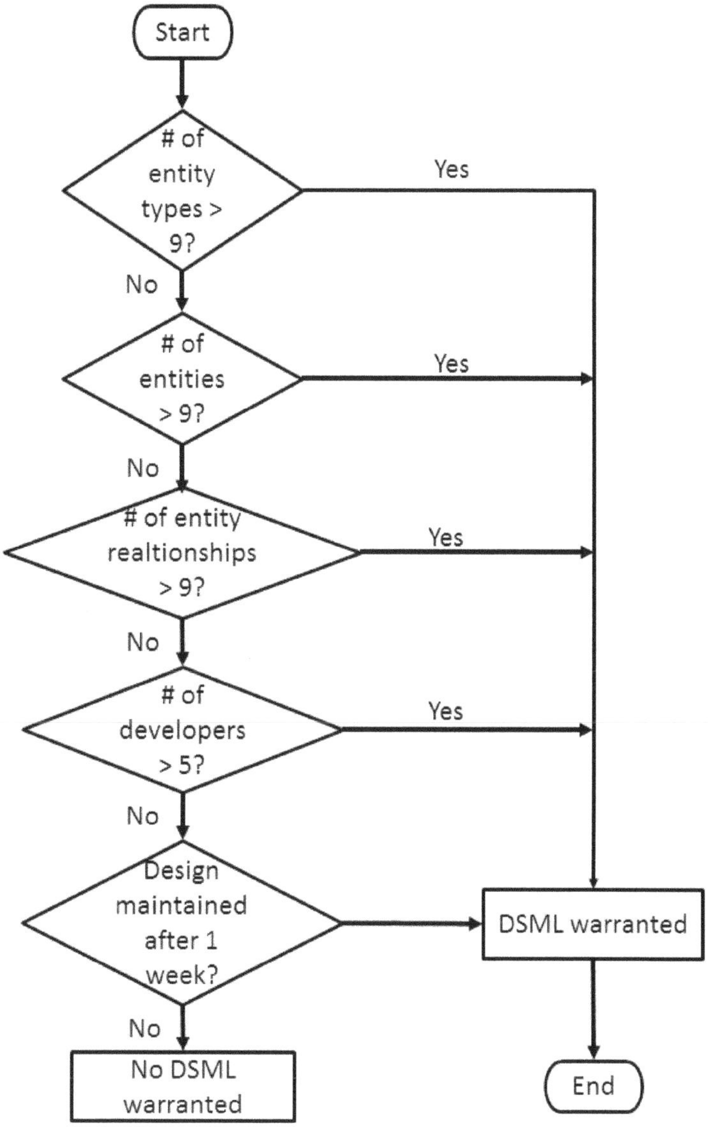

these solutions provide no guidance for implementation. Using the DSML productivity analysis taxonomy outlined in the previous section, this section focuses on the category of *implementation development effort*.

Within the context of DQML, we developed an interpreter specific to DBE to support DBE's requirement of correct QoS policy configurations. The interpreter generates QoS policy parameter settings files for the data readers and data writers that DBE configures and deploys. All relevant QoS policy parameter settings from a DQML model are output for the data readers and data writers including settings from default as well as explicitly assigned parameters.

As appropriate for DBE, the interpreter generates a single QoS policy parameter settings file for every data reader or data writer modeled. Care is taken to ensure that a unique filename is created since the names of the data readers and data writers modeled in DQML need not be unique. Moreover, the interpreter's generation of filenames aids in QoS settings files management (as described previously) since the files are uniquely and descriptively named. The following subsections detail the scope, development effort, and productivity analysis of DQML's DBE interpreter versus manual methods.

1. **Scope:** DBE uses DDS data readers and data writers. Our productivity analysis therefore focuses on these entities and, in particular, the QoS parameters relevant to them. In general, the same type of analysis can be performed for other DDS entities for which QoS policies can be associated. As shown in Table 3, 15 QoS policies with a total of 25 parameters can be associated with a single data writer.

Likewise, Table 4 shows 12 QoS policies with a total of 18 parameters that can be associated with a single data reader. Within the context of DBE, therefore, the total number of relevant QoS parameters is *18 + 25 = 43*. Each QoS policy parameter setting (including the parameter and its value) for a data reader or writer corresponds to a single line in the QoS parameter settings file for DBE.

2. **Interpreter Development:** We developed the DBE interpreter for DQML using GME's Builder Object Network (BON2) framework, which provides C++ code to traverse the DQML model utilizing the Visitor pattern. When using BON2, developers of a DSML interpreter only need to modify and add a small subset of the framework code to traverse and appropriately process the particular DSML model. More specifically, the BON2 framework supplies a C++ visitor class with virtual methods (*e.g.*, visitModelImpl, visitConnectionImpl, visitAtomImpl). The interpreter developer then subclasses and overrides the applicable virtual methods.

Table 3. DDS QoS policies for data writers

QoS Policy	Number of Parameters	Parameter Type(s)
Deadline	1	int
Destination Order	1	enum
Durability	1	enum
Durability Service	6	5 ints, 1 enum
History	2	1 enum, 1 int
Latency Budget	1	int
Lifespan	1	int
Liveliness	2	1 enum, 1 int
Ownership	1	enum
Ownership Strength	1	int
Reliability	2	1 enum, 1 int
Resource Limits	3	3 ints
Transport Priority	1	int
User Data	1	string
Writer Data Lifecycle	1	boolean
Total Parameters	**25**	

Table 4. DDS QoS policies for data readers

QoS Policy	Number of Parameters	Parameter Type(s)
Deadline	1	int
Destination Order	1	enum
Durability	1	enum
History	2	1 enum, 1 int
Latency Budget	1	int
Liveliness	2	1 enum, 1 int
Ownership	1	enum
Reader Data Lifecycle	2	2 ints
Reliability	2	1 enum, 1 int
Resource Limits	3	3 ints
Time Based Filter	1	int
User Data	1	string
Total Parameters	**18**	

The DDS entities relevant to DQML are referred to as *model implementations* in BON2. Therefore, the DBE interpreter only needs to override the *visitModelImpl()* method and is not concerned with other available virtual methods. When the BON2 framework invokes *visitModelImpl()* it passes a model implementation as an argument. A model implementation includes methods to (1) traverse the associations a DDS entity has (using the *getConnEnds()* method) and specify the relevant QoS policy association as an input parameter (*e.g.*, the association between a data writer and a deadline QoS Policy), (2) retrieve the associated QoS policy, and (3) obtain the attributes of the associated QoS policy using the policy's *getAttributes()* method.

The DQML-specific code for the DBE interpreter utilizes 160 C++ statements within the BON2 framework. We stress that any interpreter development is a one-time cost; specifically there is no development cost for the DBE interpreter since it is already developed. The main challenge in using BON2 is understanding how to traverse the model and access the desired information. After interpreter developers are familiar with BON2, the interpreter development is fairly straightforward. We detail the steps of developing the DBE interpreter below.

Figure 11 outlines the visitor class that has been created for the DBE interpreter for use within the BON2 framework. This class is the only class that needs to be implemented for the DBE interpreter. Line 1 determines the class name and its derivation from the BON2 Visitor class. Lines 3 and 4 declare the default constructor and destructor respectively. Lines 7 – 9 declare the abstract methods visitAtomImpl, visitModelImpl, and visitConnectionImpl inherited from the BON2 Visitor class that need to be defined for the DBE interpreter. Lines 11 and 12 declare methods to process data readers and data writers respectively. Lines 14 – 22 declare the main method that processes the QoS properties for a data reader or data writer and writes the QoS parameters to the appropriate file. Line 25 defines the debugging output file that had been used for debugging the DBE interpreter.

As is shown in Figure 11, the structure of the DBE visitor class is fairly simple and straightforward. Moreover, of the three methods inherited from the BON2 Visitor class and declared on lines

Figure 11. Visitor class for DBE interpreter

```
1  class DDSQoSVisitor : public Visitor {
2  public:
3      DDSQoSVisitor ();
4      ~DDSQoSVisitor ();
5
6  protected :
7      virtual void visitAtomImpl (const Atom& atom);
8      virtual void visitModelImpl (const Model& model);
9      virtual void visitConnectionImpl ( const Connection& connection);
10
11     void processDataReaderQos (const Model& dataReader);
12     void processDataWriterQos (const Model& dataWriter);
13
14     void outputDDSEntityQos (const Model& dds_entity,
15                              const std::string &entity_name,
16                              const std::string &entity_abbrev,
17                              const std::string &qos_connection_name,
18                              const std::string &qos_name,
19                              const std::map<std::string, std::string> &attribute_map,
20                              int entity_count,
21                              bool &file_opened,
22                              std::ofstream &out_file);
23
24 private:
25     std::ofstream out_file_;
26 };
```

7 – 9 only the visitModelImpl method declared on line 8 is a non-empty method. For DBE, the only DQML entities of interest are what GME terms the *model elements* which for DBE's interests are the data readers and data writers. The DBE interpreter is not concerned with traversing atom or connection elements since these elements will be addressed by processing the model elements.

We now focus on the implementations of the relevant methods particularly as they relate to complexity and required background knowledge. The default constructor and destructor simply open and close the file used for debugging which is not required functionality for the DBE interpreter. Therefore the implementations of these two methods (which total two C++ statements) are excluded to save space. The visitAtomImpl and visitConnectionImpl methods are defined (since the inherited methods are abstract) but empty (since they are not needed).

As shown in Figure 12, the visitModelImpl method determines the type of model element currently being processed and calls the appropriate method, *i.e.*, processDataReaderQos for a data reader on line 6 and processDataWriterQos for a data writer on line 12. The lines written to out_file_ are simply for debugging purposes and are not required by DBE. The DBE interpreter developer required familiarity with the DQML metamodel to know the names of the model elements of interest but the model elements in the metamodel were given intuitive names to reduce accidental complexity, *e.g.*, DataReader and DataWriter on lines 3 and 9 respectively.

Figure 13 outlines the processDataWriterQos method. For each QoS policy applicable to a data writer this method sets up a mapping of DQML QoS parameter names to DBE QoS parameters names. Then the method calls outputDDSEntityQoS method to write the QoS parameter values

Figure 12. visitModelImpl method

```
void DDSQoSVisitor::visitModelImpl( const Model& model )
{
    if (model->getModelMeta().name() == "DataReader")
    {
        out_file_ << "DDS DataReader Name: " << model->getName() << std::endl;
        processDataReaderQos(model);
        out_file_ << "...Done DDS DataReader Name: " << model->getName() << std::endl;
    }
    else if (model->getModelMeta().name() == "DataWriter")
    {
        out_file_ << "DDS DataWriter Name: " << model->getName() << std::endl;
        processDataWriterQos(model);
        out_file_ << "...Done DDS DataWriter Name: " << model->getName() << std::endl;
    }
}
```

to the appropriate file. The interpreter developer needed to have an understanding of the QoS parameter names for DBE, the QoS parameter names in the DQML metamodel, and the names of the associations between data readers/writers and QoS policies in the DQML metamodel. However, as with the model elements in the DQML metamodel, the QoS parameters were given intuitive names to reduce accidental complexity, *e.g.*, history_kind and history_depth on lines 25 and 26 respectively, as were the connection names, *e.g.*, dw_deadline_Connection and dw_history_Connection on lines 16 and 30 respectively.

Figure 13 shows the source code for processing the deadline and history QoS policies. The rest of the method which has been elided for brevity handles all the other QoS policies relevant to data writers. Finally, the method closes the QoS parameter file if one has been opened previously and increments the count of data writers processed so that unique filenames can be generated. Likewise, the processDataReaderQos method provides the same functionality for QoS policies and parameters relevant to data readers. Its source code is not included due to space constraints.

Figure 14 presents the outputDDSEntityQos method which traverses the connection that a data reader or data writer has to a particular QoS policy (*e.g.*, connections to QoS policies for data readers or data writers) and writes the QoS parameters out to the QoS settings file for that data reader or writer. Lines 14 – 21 and 54 – 57 provide error checking for the BON2 framework and have been elided for space considerations. Line 11 retrieves the associations that the data reader or writer has with a particular QoS policy, *e.g.*, all the associations between a data reader and the reliability QoS policy. Lines 24-27 retrieve the endpoint of the connection which will be the associated QoS policy of the type specified as the input parameter of line 4. Lines 29 and 30 retrieve the parameters of the associated QoS policy, lines 31 – 41 open a uniquely named DBE QoS settings file if one is not currently open, and lines 42 – 52 iterate through the QoS parameters and write them out to the opened file in the required DBE format using the attribute mapping passed as an input parameter on line 6.

Since the BON2 framework relies on the Visitor pattern, familiarity with this pattern can be helpful. This familiarity is not required, however, and developers minimally only need to implement relevant methods for the automatically generated Visitor subclass. In general, the DQML interpreter code specific to DBE (1) traverses the model to gather applicable information, (2) creates the QoS settings files, and (3) outputs the settings into the QoS settings files.

Figure 13. processDataWriterQos method

```
void DDSQoSVisitor::processDataWriterQos( const Model& dataWriter )
{
    static int dw_count = 1;
    const std::string dw_name("DataWriter");
    const std::string dw_prefix("DW");
    std::ofstream output_file;
    bool file_opened = false;
    std::map<std::string, std::string> attrib_map;

    // Handle Deadline QoS Policy
    attrib_map.clear ();
    attrib_map["period"] = "datawriter.deadline.period=";
    outputDDSEntityQos (dataWriter,
                        dw_name,
                        dw_prefix,
                        "dw_deadline_Connection",
                        "Deadline",
                        attrib_map,
                        dw_count,
                        file_opened,
                        output_file);

    // Handle History QoS Policy
    attrib_map.clear ();
    attrib_map["history_kind"] = "datawriter.history.kind=";
    attrib_map["history_depth"] = "datawriter.history.depth=";
    outputDDSEntityQos (dataWriter,
                        dw_name,
                        dw_prefix,
                        "dw_history_Connection",
                        "History",
                        attrib_map,
                        dw_count,
                        file_opened,
                        output_file);
    •
    •
    •
```

The C++ development effort for DQML's DBE interpreter is only needed one time. In particular, no QoS policy configuration developed via DQML for DBE incurs this development overhead since the interpreter has already been developed. The development effort metrics of 160 C++ statements are included *only* to be used in comparing manually implemented QoS policy configurations.

3. **Comparing Manually Developing DBE Implementation Artifacts:** To compare model-driven engineering approaches in

Figure 14. outputDDSEntityQos method

```
void DDSQoSVisitor::outputDDSEntityQos (const Model& dds_entity,
                                        const std::string &entity_name, // e.g., "DataReader"
                                        const std::string &entity_abbrev, // e.g., "DR"
                                        const std::string &qos_connection_name,
                                        const std::string &qos_name,
                                        const std::map<std::string, std::string> &attribute_map,
                                        int entity_count,
                                        bool &file_opened,
                                        std::ofstream &out_file)
{
    std::multiset<ConnectionEnd> conns = dds_entity->getConnEnds(qos_connection_name);
    if (conns.size() > 0)
    {
        if (conns.size() > 1){ ... }
        else
        {
            std::multiset<ConnectionEnd>::const_iterator iter(conns.begin ());
            ConnectionEnd endPt = *iter;
            FCO fco(endPt);
            if (fco)
            {
                std::set<Attribute> attrs = fco->getAttributes ();
                std::set<Attribute>::const_iterator attr_iter(attrs.begin());
                if (!file_opened)
                {
                    file_opened = true;
                    std::string filename;

                    char cnt_buf [10];
                    ::sprintf_s (cnt_buf, "%d", entity_count);
                    std::string cnt_str = cnt_buf;
                    filename = entity_abbrev + cnt_str + "_" + dds_entity->getName () + ".txt";
                    out_file.open(filename.c_str ());
                }
                for (; attr_iter != attrs.end (); ++attr_iter)
                {
                    Attribute attr = *attr_iter;
                    std::string attr_name = attr->getAttributeMeta ().name ();
                    std::map<std::string, std::string>::const_iterator map_iter =
                        attribute_map.find (attr_name);
                    if (map_iter != attribute_map.end ())
                    {
                        out_file << map_iter->second << attr->getStringValue () << std::endl;
                    }
                }
            }
            else{ ... }
        }
    }
}
```

general and the DQML DBE interpreter in particular, we outline the steps to generate the implementation artifacts of DBE QoS settings files given a manually generated QoS configuration design. Several areas of inherent and accidental complexity need to be addressed for manual development of DBE QoS settings files. To illustrate these complexities we follow the steps needed to transform a data reader entity associated with a reliability QoS policy from design into implementation. We assume the QoS configuration design is specified either in a text or graphics file or handwritten. We also assume that the QoS configuration design has been developed separately from the generation of implementation artifacts to separate these concerns and divide the labor.

a. **Variability Complexity:** Implementation developers must ensure the correct semantics for the association between the data reader and the reliability QoS policy. Developers cannot assume that the data reader, the reliability QoS policy, or the association between the two are valid and correctly specified since the configuration was manually generated. The data reader and reliability QoS policy must be cross-referenced with the DDS specification. This cross-referencing entails checking that (1) a data reader can be associated with a reliability QoS policy, (2) the parameter names specified for the reliability QoS policy are appropriate (*e.g.*, only kind and max_blocking_time are valid reliability QoS parameters), and (3) the values for the parameters are valid (*e.g.*, only RELIABLE and BEST_EFFORT are valid values for the reliability kind). Moreover, developers must manage the complexity of creating a separate QoS settings file for the data reader and ensuring a unique and descriptive filename that DBE can use.
b. **Semantic Compatibility Complexity:** Implementation developers must ensure the correct consistency semantics for the data reader's reliability QoS policy and the other QoS policies associated with the data reader. If QoS policies associated with the data reader are inconsistent then the policies cannot be used. Moreover, the developer must ensure correct semantics for the data reader's reliability QoS policy and data writers associated with the same topic. If QoS policies associated with the data reader are incompatible then the data will not be received by the data reader.

For the reliability QoS policy there are no inconsistency concerns. Developers must verify that this is the case, however, by checking the DDS specification for consistency rules. For the reliability QoS policy there are potential incompatibilities. If the reliability QoS policy kind for the data reader is specified as RELIABLE the developer must traverse the QoS configuration and check the reliability QoS policies for *all* data writers associated with the same topic. If no associated data writer has a reliability QoS kind set to RELIABLE (either explicitly or implicitly via default values) then the data reader can never receive any data thereby making the data reader superfluous. Default values for QoS parameters must therefore be known and evaluated for compatibility even if not explicitly specified. Manually traversing the QoS configuration to check for compatibility and accounting for default parameter values is tedious and error prone and greatly exacerbates the accidental complexity of generating implementation artifacts.

c. **Faithful Transformation:** Implementation developers must ensure that the QoS configuration design is accurately mapped to the implementation artifacts appropriate for DBE. As noted above, this transformation includes creating and managing a QoS settings file for each data reader and writer. Moreover, the developer must ensure that the syntax of QoS settings conform to what DBE requires. For example, the reliability's maximum blocking time of 10 ms must be specified as datareader.reliability. max_blocking_time=10 on a single line by itself in the QoS settings file for the particular data reader.

4. **Analysis:** The hardest aspect of developing DQML's DBE interpreter is traversing the model's data reader and data writer elements along with the associated QoS policy elements using the BON2 framework. Conversely, the most challenging aspects of manually implementing QoS policy configurations are (1) maintaining a global view of the model to ensure compatibility and consistency, (2) verifying the number, type, and valid values for the parameters of the applicable QoS policies, and (3) faithfully transforming the configuration design into implementation artifacts. On average, implementing a single C++ statement for the DBE interpreter is no harder than implementing a single parameter statement for the DBE QoS settings files. When implementing a non-trivial QoS policy configuration, therefore, development of the C++ code for the DBE interpreter is no more challenging than manually ensuring that the QoS settings in settings files are valid, consistent, compatible, and correctly represent the designed configuration. Below we provide additional detail into what can be considered a non-trivial QoS policy configuration.

The development and use of the DBE interpreter for DQML is justified for a *single* QoS policy configuration when at least 160 QoS policy parameter settings are involved. These parameter settings correlate to the 160 C++ statements for DQML's DBE interpreter. Using the results for QoS parameters in Table 3 and Table 4 for data readers and data writers, Figure 15 shows the justification for interpreter development. The development is justified with ~10 data readers, ~7 data writers, or some combination of data readers and data writers where the QoS settings are

Figure 15. Metrics for manual configuration vs. DQML's interpreter

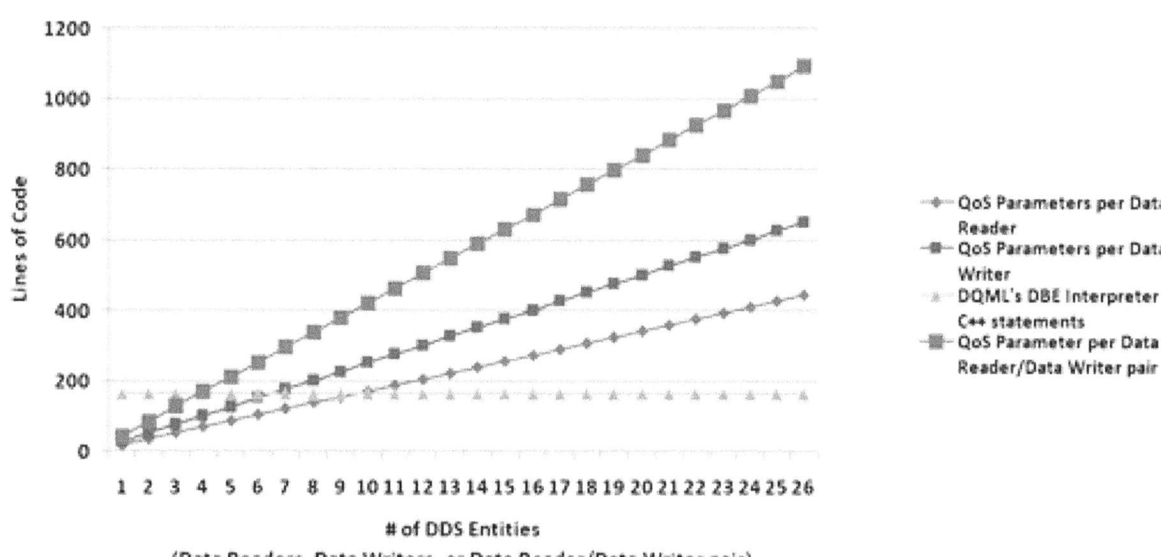

greater than or equal to 160 (*e.g.*, 5 data readers and 3 data writers = 165 QoS policy parameter settings). For comparison, the breakeven point for data reader/writer pairs is 3.72 (*i.e.*, 160/43).

We also quantified the development effort needed to support topics if the DBE interpreter required that functionality. Table 5 shows the DDS QoS policies and policy parameters applicable to topics. To support topics an additional 59 C++ statements would need to be added. Conversely, for manual generation 23 more QoS parameters need to be considered for each topic. The breakeven point for data reader/writer/topic triplets becomes 3.32 (*i.e.*, (160 + 59)/(43 + 23)) which is less than the breakeven point for data reader/writers alone (*i.e.*, 3.72).

This breakeven point is less because the additional source code to support topics can leverage existing code, in particular, the outputDDSEntityQos method outlined in Figure 14. The breakeven point can be applicable for *any* interpreter that leverages the commonality of formatting regardless of the entity type (cf. outputDDSEntityQos method). Moreover, the complexity of developing any DQML interpreter is lessened by having the DBE interpreter as a guide. The design and code of the DBE interpreter can be reused by another application-specific interpreter to navigate a DQML model and access the QoS policies.

Table 6 also shows productivity gains as a percentage for various numbers of data readers and data writers. The percentage gains are calculated by dividing the number of parameter values for the data readers and data writers involved by the number of interpreter C++ statements, *i.e.*, 160, and subtracting 1 to account for the baseline manual implementation (*i.e.*, ((# of data reader and writer parameters)/160)-1). The gains increase faster than the increase in the number of data readers and data writers (*e.g.*, the gain for 10 data readers and data writers is more than twice as much for 5 data readers and data writers) showing that productivity gains are greater when more entities are involved.

The interpreter justification analysis shown relates to implementing a single QoS policy configuration. The analysis includes neither the scenario of modifying an existing valid configuration nor the scenario of implementing new configurations for DBE where no modifications to the interpreter

Table 5. DDS QoS policies for topics

QoS Policy	Number of Parameters	Parameter Type(s)
Deadline	1	int
Destination Order	1	enum
Durability	1	enum
Durability Service	6	5 ints, 1 enum
History	2	1 enum, 1 int
Latency Budget	1	int
Lifespan	1	int
Liveliness	2	1 enum, 1 int
Ownership	1	enum
Reliability	2	1 enum, 1 int
Resource Limits	3	3 ints
Transport Priority	1	int
Topic Data	1	string
Total Parameters	**23**	

Table 6. Productivity gains using DQML's DBE interpreter

# of Data Readers and Data Writers (each)	Total # of Parameters	Productivity Gain
5	215	34%
10	430	169%
20	860	438%
40	1720	975%
80	3440	2050%

code would be required. Changes made even to an existing valid configuration require that developers (1) maintain a global view of the model to ensure compatibility and consistency and (2) remember the number of, and valid values for, the parameters of the various QoS policies being modified. These challenges are as applicable when changing an already valid QoS policy configuration as they are when creating an initial configuration. Moreover, the complexity for developing a new interpreter for some other application is ameliorated by having the DBE interpreter as a template for traversing a model in BON2.

In large-scale DDS systems (*e.g.*, shipboard computing, air-traffic management, and scientific space missions) there may be thousands of data readers and writers. As a point of reference with 1,000 data readers and 1,000 data writers, the number of QoS parameters to manage is *43,000* (*i.e.*, 18 * 1,000 + 25 * 1,000). This number does not include QoS parameter settings for other DDS entities such as publishers, subscribers, and topics. For such large-scale DDS systems the development cost of the DQML interpreter in terms of lines of code is amortized by more than 200 times (*i.e.*, 43,000 / 160 = *268.75*).

The productivity analysis approach taken for DQML's DBE interpreter is applicable to other DSMLs since the complexities involved will be similar. A break-even point for the development effort of an interpreter for any DSML will exist. We outline four areas that directly influence this break-even point: number of entities, complexity of the entities, complexity of associations between the entities, and level of maintainability needed.

The number of entities affects the break-even point for interpreter development since the more entities that are to be considered the less likely any one individual will be able to manage these entities appropriately as outlined in the previous section. The guideline of 4 to 9 items that a human can process at one time can be helpful in exploring the break-even point for interpreter development. If there are more than 9 entities to be considered then the accidental complexity increases since the developer must manage the entities using some tool or device (*e.g.*, a piece of paper, a database) external to the person. With this external management comes the possibility of introducing errors in the use of the management tool (*e.g.*, incorrectly transcribing the entities from the developer's head to the tool).

Likewise, this same analysis holds for the complexity of entities as determined by the number of fields or parameters. If an entity contains more than 9 fields then some external tool should be used to manage this complexity. The use of a tool introduces accidental complexity (*e.g.*, incorrectly transcribing the order, names, or types of the parameters). The same analysis can also be applied to the number of associations made between entities to determine that complexity as well as the number of times a configuration will need to be modified.

If any one of these four areas exceeds the threshold of 9 then an interpreter is warranted. If more than one of these areas exceeds the threshold (*e.g.*, more than 9 entities with more than 9 associations between the entities) then the break-even point for an interpreter is lowered. The exact determination for justifying interpreter development will vary according to the application but the guidelines presented can provide coarse-grained justification.

FUTURE RESEARCH DIRECTIONS

Our future work for DQML includes assembly and deployment support as an aid for complex QoS configurations. Additionally, future research work includes developing domain-specific QoS profiles for different types of applications within the domain. These profiles would ease development of QoS configurations since they would provide a template or starting point for an application-specific configuration

DQML is available as open-source software and is included as part of the Component Synthesis with Model Integrated Computing (CoSMIC) tool chain being developed and maintained at Vanderbilt University's Institute for Software Integrated Systems. Information regarding downloading, building, and installing CoSMIC can be found at www.dre.vanderbilt.edu/cosmic.

CONCLUSION

Although MDE and DSMLs have become increasingly popular, concrete evidence is needed to support the quantitative evaluation of DSMLs. This chapter described various approaches to quantitatively evaluating DSMLs via productivity analysis. We applied one of these approaches to a case study involving the *Distributed QoS Modeling Language* (DQML). The following is a summary of the lessons learned from our experience developing DQML and conducting productivity analysis using it for the DBE case study:

- *Trade-offs and the break-even point for DSMLs must be clearly understood and communicated.* There are pros and cons to any technical approach including DSMLs. The use of DSMLs may not be appropriate for every case and these cases must be evaluated to provide balanced and objective analysis. For a DSML product line the advantages of DSMLs will typically outweigh the development costs. For a one-time point solution the development of a DSML may not be justified, depending on the complexity of the domain.
- *The context for DSML productivity analysis should be well defined.* Broad generalizations of a DSML being "X" times better than some other technology is not particularly helpful for comparison and evaluation. A representative case study can be useful to provide a concrete context for productivity analysis.
- *Provide analysis for as minimal or conservative a scenario as possible.* Using a minimal scenario in productivity analysis allows developers to extrapolate to larger scenarios where the DSML use will be justified. This work highlighted the exponential benefit of automatically generating implementation artifacts from domain-specific models as the number of modeling elements increases linearly.
- *In general, the threshold for developing a DSML and accompanying interpreters is fairly low.* Several factors account for this low threshold including (1) the number of entities to be modeled, (2) the number of relationships between the modeled entities, (3) the number of developers involved, and (4) the likelihood of maintaining or modifying any one model. However, for situations where none of the above factors are relevant (e.g., the number of entities, relationships between entities, and number of developers is less than 7) then the overhead of learning a tool to develop a DSML and then developing the DSML might not be warranted.

REFERENCES

Abrahão, S., & Poels, G. (2007). Experimental evaluation of an object-oriented function point measurement procedure. *Information and Software Technology*, *49*(4), 366–380. doi:10.1016/j.infsof.2006.06.001

Abrahão, S., & Poels, G. (2009). A family of experiments to evaluate a functional size measurement procedure for web applications. *Journal of Systems and Software*, *82*(2), 253–269. doi:10.1016/j.jss.2008.06.031

Atkinson, C., & Kuhne, T. (2003). Model-driven development: A metamodeling foundation. *IEEE Software*, *20*(5), 36–41. doi:10.1109/MS.2003.1231149

Bailey, C.H., Bartsch, D., & Kandel, E. (1996). Toward a molecular definition of long-term memory storage. *Proceedings of the National Academy of Sciences of the United States of America*, *93*(24), 13445–13452. doi:10.1073/pnas.93.24.13445 PMID:8942955

Balasubramanian, K., Schmidt, D., Molnar, Z., & Ledeczi, A. (2007). Component-based system integration via (meta)model composition. In *Proceedings of the 14th Annual IEEE International Conference and Workshops on the Engineering of Computer-Based Systems* (pp. 93–102). Los Alamitos, CA: IEEE. doi:10.1109/ECBS.2007.24

Bergmann, G., Hegedus, A., Horvath, A., Rath, I., Ujhelyi, Z., & Varro, D. (2011). Implementing efficient model validation in EMF tools. In *Proceedings of the 2011 26th IEEE/ACM International Conference on Automated Software Engineering* (pp. 580–583). New York: ACM. doi:10.1109/ASE.2011.6100130

Bettin, J. (2002). Measuring the potential of domain-specific modeling techniques. In *Proceedings of 17th Annual ACM Conference on Object-Oriented Programming, Systems, Languages, and Applications*. Seattle, WA: ACM.

Boehm, B. (1987). Improving Software Productivity. *Computer*, *20*(9), 43–57. doi:10.1109/MC.1987.1663694

Budinsky, F., Steinberg, D., & Merks, E. (2009). *EMF: Eclipse Modeling Framework*. Boston: Pearson Education, Inc.

Cabot, J., & Gogolla, M. (2012). Object Constraint Language (OCL): A Definitive Guide. In *Proceedings of the 12th International Conference on Formal Methods for the Design of Computer, Communication, and Software Systems: Formal Methods for Model-Driven Engineering* (pp.58–90). Berlin: Springer-Verlag. doi:10.1007/978-3-642-30982-3_3

Carzaniga, A., Rutherford, M., & Wolf, A. (2004). A routing scheme for content-based networking. In *Proceedings of Twenty-Third Annual Joint Conference of the IEEE Computer and Communications Societies,* (vol. 2, pp. 918-928). Los Alamitos, CA: IEEE.

Cleary, D. (2000). Web-based development and functional size measurement. In *Proceedings of International Function Point Users Group Annual Conference*. San Diego, CA: Academic Press.

Conway, C., & Edwards, S. (2004). NDL: A domain-specific language for device drivers. In *Proceedings of the 2004 ACM SIGPLAN/SIGBED conference on languages, compilers, and tools for embedded systems* (pp. 30–36). New York: ACM. doi:10.1145/997163.997169

Cowan, N. (2001). The magical number 4 in short-term memory: A reconsideration of mental storage capacity. *The Behavioral and Brain Sciences*, *24*(1), 87–114. doi:10.1017/S0140525X01003922 PMID:11515286

Genero, M., Piattini, M., Abrahao, S., Insfran, E., Carsi, J., & Ramos, I. (2007). A controlled experiment for selecting transformations based on quality attributes in the context of MDA. In *Proceedings of First International Symposium on Empirical Software Engineering and Measurement* (pp. 498-498). Los Alamitos, CA: IEEE. doi:10.1109/ESEM.2007.64

Gronback, R. (2009). *Eclipse Modeling Project: A Domain-Specific Language (Dsl) Toolkit*. Boston: Pearson Education, Inc.

Hailpern, B., & Tarr, P. (2006). Model-driven development: The good, the bad, and the ugly. *IBM Systems Journal*, *45*(3), 451–461. doi:10.1147/sj.453.0451

Hästbacka, D., Vepsäläinen, T., & Kuikka, S. (2011). Model-driven development of industrial process control applications. *Journal of Systems and Software*, *84*(7), 1100–1113. doi:10.1016/j.jss.2011.01.063

Hoffert, J., Schmidt, D., & Gokhale, A. (2007). A QoS policy configuration modeling language for publish/subscribe middleware platforms. In *Proceedings of the International Conference on Distributed Event-Based Systems* (pp. 140–145). New York: ACM. doi:10.1145/1266894.1266922

Kamiński, J., Brzezicka, A., & Wróbel, A. (2011). Short-term memory capacity (7±2) predicted by theta to gamma cycle length ratio. *Neurobiology of Learning and Memory*, *95*(1), 19–23. doi:10.1016/j.nlm.2010.10.001 PMID:20951219

Kärnä, J., Tolvanen, J., & Kelly, S. (2009). Evaluating the use of domain-specific modeling in practice. In *Proceedings of 9th Workshop on Domain-Specific Modeling (OOPSLA 2009)*. New York: ACM.

Kavimandan, A., & Gokhale, A. (2008). Automated middleware QoS configuration techniques using model transformations. In *Proceedings of the 14th IEEE Real-Time and Embedded Technology and Applications Symposium* (pp. 93–102). Los Alamitos, CA: IEEE.

Kent, S. (2002). Model driven engineering. In *Proceedings of the 3rd International Conference on Integrated Formal Methods* (pp. 286–298). Berlin: Springer. doi:10.1007/3-540-47884-1_16

Ledeczi, A., Bakay, A., Maroti, M., Volgyesi, P., Nordstrom, G., Sprinkle, J., & Karsai, G. (2001). Composing domain-specific design environments. *Computer*, *34*(11), 44–51. doi:10.1109/2.963443

Li, G., & Jacobsen, H. (2005). Composite subscriptions in content-based publish/subscribe systems. In *Proceedings of the 6th International Middleware Conference* (pp. 249-269). New York: Springer-Verlag. doi:10.1007/11587552_13

Loyall, J., Jianming Ye., Shapiro, R., Neema, S., Mahadevan, N., Abdelwahed, S., et al. (2004). A Case Study in Applying QoS Adaptation and Model-Based Design to the Design-Time Optimization of Signal Analyzer Applications. In *Proceedings of Military Communications Conference (MILCOM)* (pp. 1700–1705). Los Alamitos, CA: IEEE. doi:10.1109/MILCOM.2004.1495193

Lukman, T., Godena, G., Gray, J., & Strmcnik, S. (2010). Model-driven engineering of industrial process control applications. In *Proceedings of the 2010 IEEE Conference on Emerging Technologies and Factory Automation* (pp. 1-16). Los Alamitos, CA: IEEE. doi:10.1109/ETFA.2010.5641224

Martínez, Y., Cachero, C., & Meliá, S. (2012). Article. In Evaluating the impact of a model-driven web engineering approach on the productivity and the satisfaction of software development teams (LNCS), (vol. 7387, pp. 223–237). Berlin: Springer-Verlag. doi:10.1007/978-3-642-31753-8_17

Miller, G.A. (1956). The magical number seven, plus or minus two: Some limits on our capacity for processing information. *Psychological Review*, *63*(2), 81–97. doi:10.1037/h0043158 PMID:13310704

Mohagheghi, P., Gilani, W., Stefanescu, A., Fernandez, M., Nordmoen, B., & Fritzsche, M. (2013). Where does model-driven engineering help? Experiences from three industrial cases. *Software & Systems Modeling*, *12*(3), 619–639. doi:10.1007/s10270-011-0219-7

OASIS. (2006). *Web services brokered notification 1.3*. Retrieved December 11, 2009 from http://docs.oasis-open.org/wsn/wsn-ws_brokered_notification-1.3-spec-os.pdf

Object Management Group. (2007). *Data distribution service for real-time systems, version 1.2*. Retrieved June 8, 2009, from http://www.omg.org/spec/DDS/1.2

Object Management Group. (2004a). *Event service specification version 1.2*. Retrieved December 11, 2009, from http://www.omg.org/cgi-bin/doc?formal/2004-10-02

Object Management Group. (2004b). *Notification service specification version 1.1*. Retrieved December 11, 2009, from http://www.omg.org/cgi-bin/doc?formal/2004-10-11

Papotti, P., do Prado, A., de Souza, W., Cirilo, C., & Pires, L. (2013). Article. In A quantitative analysis of model-driven code generation through software experimentation (LNCS), (vol. 7908, pp. 321–337). Berlin: Springer-Verlag. doi:10.1007/978-3-642-38709-8_21

Pati, T., Feiock, D., & Hill, J. (2012). Proactive modeling: auto-generating models from their semantics and constraints. In *Proceedings of the 2012 Workshop on Domain-specific modeling*, (pp. 7-12). New York: ACM. doi:10.1145/2420918.2420921

Pilgrim, J. (2008). *Measuring the level of abstraction and detail of models in the context of mdd. In Proceedings of Models in Software Engineering: Workshops and Symposia at MoDELS 2007* (pp. 105–114). Berlin: Springer-Verlag.

Premraj, R., Shepperd, M., Kitchenham, B., & Forselius, P. (2005). An empirical analysis of software productivity over time. In *Proceedings of the 11th IEEE International Symposium on Software Metrics* (pp. 37-46). Los Alamitos, CA: IEEE. doi:10.1109/METRICS.2005.8

Reifer, D. (2000). Web development: Estimating quick-to-market software. *IEEE Software*, *17*(6), 57–64. doi:10.1109/52.895169

Schmidt, D. (2006). Model-driven engineering. *IEEE Computer*, *39*(2), 25–31. doi:10.1109/MC.2006.58

Sun Microsystems. (2002). *Java Message Service version 1.1*. Retrieved December 11, 2009 from http://java.sun.com/products/jms/docs.html

Sutton, A., & Stroustrup, B. (2011). Design of concept libraries for c++. In *Proceedings of 4th International Conference on Software Language Engineering* (pp. 97-118). Los Alamitos, CA: IEEE.

Tsui, F., Karam, O., & Bernal, B. (2013). *Essentials of software engineering*. Burlington, MA: Jones and Bartlett Publishers, Inc.

Warmer, J., & Kleppe, A. (2003). *The object constraint language: getting your models ready for MDA*. Boston: Addison-Wesley Longman Publishing Co., Inc..

White, J., Schmidt, D., Nechypurenko, A., & Wuchner, E. (2008). Model intelligence: An approach to modeling guidance. *UPGRADE*, *9*(2), 22–28.

Wu, Y., Hernandez, F., Ortega, F., Clarke, P., & France, R. (2010). Measuring the effort for creating and using domain-specific models. In *Proceedings of 10th Workshop on Domain-Specific Modeling*. (pp. 1-6). ACM. doi:10.1145/2060329.2060360

Xiong, M., Parsons, J., Edmondson, J., Nguyen, H., & Schmidt, D. (2007). Evaluating technologies for tactical information management in net- centric systems. In *Proceedings of the Defense Transformation and Net-Centric Systems conference*. Academic Press. doi:10.1117/12.719679

KEY TERMS AND DEFINITIONS

Data Distribution Service (DDS): An open standard for QoS-enabled pub/sub middleware supported by the Object Management Group (OMG).

DDS Benchmarking Environment: An open-source tool suite developed to examine and evaluate the QoS of various DDS implementations.

Domain Specific Modeling Language (DSML): A computer language (typically graphical in nature) developed for a particular domain (*e.g.*, disease diagnosis, QoS configuration).

Middleware: A software abstraction layer that typically resides between the operating system and the application layer (*e.g.*, the Java Virtual Machine).

Productivity Analysis: Analyzing the use of various software system development techniques to show productivity gains or losses (*i.e.*, typically concerned with the productivity of the software developers).

Publish/Subscribe (Pub/Sub): An architectural paradigm for software systems that is data-centric (i.e., data is sent out and received) rather than call-centric (*i.e.*, request/response typically done by invoking a function and receiving a response).

Quality of Service (QoS): Properties of a software system related to non-functional aspects (*e.g.*, latency, reliability, usability).

ENDNOTES

1 In contrast, content-based pub/sub middleware, such as Siena (Carzaniga, Rutherford, & Wolf, 2004) and the Publish/subscribe Applied to Distributed REsource Scheduling (PADRES) (Li & Jacobsen, 2005), examine events throughout the system to determine data types.

2 The Object Management Group maintains a list of vendors supplying DDS implementations at http://portals.omg.org/dds/category/web-links/vendors.

Chapter 14

Developing Executable UML Components Based on fUML and Alf

S. Motogna
Babeş-Bolyai University, Romania

I. Lazăr
Babeş-Bolyai University, Romania

B. Pârv
Babeş-Bolyai University, Romania

ABSTRACT

Model-driven architecture frameworks provide an approach for specifying systems independently of a particular platform and for transforming such system models for a particular platform, but development processes based on MDA are not widely used today because they are in general heavy-weight processes: in most situations they cannot deliver (incrementally) partial implementations to be executed immediately. Executable UML means an execution semantics for a subset of actions sufficient for computational completeness. This chapter uses Alf as the fUML-based action language to describe the operations for iComponent: the proposed solution for a platform-independent component model for dynamic execution environments. Moreover, a UML profile for modeling components is defined and applied, following agile principles, to the development of service-oriented components for dynamic execution environments. The intended use of the proposed approach is enterprise systems.

INTRODUCTION

Some service-oriented component models support the dynamic availability of components at runtime and offer the possibility to build dynamically adaptable applications. However, building service-oriented components is a complex task due to the complexity of service-oriented frameworks. In this context today frameworks try to simplify the component development by allowing developers to concentrate only on implementing the business

DOI: 10.4018/978-1-4666-6359-6.ch014

logic of the component and then to configure declaratively the component deployment.

In this chapter, we describe our contribution to this domain, as a continuation to the *ComDeValCo* framework with updates regarding the Alf specification, that can be expressed in:

- A platform-independent component model, *iComponent* with a corresponding UML profile for constructing components as UML models according to MDA;
- An agile MDA approach for constructing executable models for service oriented components;
- Mappings of *iComponent* to some existing service-oriented component frameworks.

BACKGROUND

Why

Component-based approaches lead to applications developed and deployed as a set of components. The main benefits of these approaches consist of loose coupling among the application components, third-party component selection, and increased component reuse. In traditional component-based approaches the set of components is statically configured; this means that the benefits outlined above typically extend only to the development portion of the software system life-cycle, not to the run-time portion (Escoffier & Hall, 2007).

Nowadays, there are component models and frameworks which allow components unavailable at the time of application construction to be integrated into the application later into its life-cycle, i.e. after the application has been installed (OSGi, 2007). Such a framework should offer a dynamic execution environment, providing: (i) *dynamic availability of components* - the ability to install, update, and remove components at run-time, and to manage their provided and required interfaces; (ii) *dynamic reconfiguration* - the ability to change the configuration properties of a running component; (iii) *dynamic composition* - the ability to compose components from other existing components at runtime.

Most frameworks that support dynamic availability of components use the general principles of service-oriented component models (Cervantes & Hall, 2004), merging the concepts of service-oriented computing (Papazoglou & Georgakopoulos, 2003) into a component model.

Typically, a service-oriented component approach to build an application includes the following steps: (1) *Decompose the application into a collection of interacting services.* The semantics of these services are described independently of each other, and of any implementation. The service specifications will provide a basis for substitutability. (2) *Define a set of components implementing the application services.* A component may provide and require zero or more services. (3) *Define composite components that guide the application execution.* These composite components are described in terms of service specifications, and the concrete implementations of services will be resolved at run-time.

One of the main ideas for simplifying the construction of components is to separate the business logic of a component from the non-functional requirements related to the container in which the component execution will be managed. In such a context, developers concentrate first on implementing the business logic of the component, and then they configure declaratively the component deployment. Another important aspect of component models and frameworks refers to the development approach. Approaches in which modeling is at the core of the development activities also simplify the component construction process.

The success of using models (formal or not) is influenced in part by the availability and the degree of acceptance of modeling tools and techniques developed by the software development community. Those who build models need to perceive the usefulness of the models (Henderson & Walters, 1999), need to find a tradeoff between model complexity and its ease of use. It is convenient to build simple models, without great investments in time and intellectual effort. More important, the resulting models need to be accessible, easy to understand and analyze, and to have a reasonable degree of formality.

Executable models (Mellor & Balcer, 2002) improve even more the eficiency and reliability of an application: model excution will verify all the constraints on the model and the code will be generate only if the verification passed, and any modification of the model will be automatically reflected in the generated code.

What

As identified above, two important aspects for simplifying the construction of components consist of (1) *applying a model-driven development (MDD) approach* and (2) *separating the business logic of a component from the nonfunctional requirements.*

Model-Driven Development Approaches

The Model-driven Architecture (MDA) frameworks provide an approach for specifying systems independently of a particular platform and for transforming the system specification into one for a particular platform. MDA is considered the OMG approach to Model Driven Engineering (MDE) (Balasubramanian, Gokhale, Karsai, Sztipanovits & Neema, 2006; Batory 2006). MDE approaches can be based either on MDA, or on Domain Specific Modeling. MDE appeared as a solution to applications that have to deal with increased platform complexity and domain concepts, aiming to raise the level of abstraction in program specification and to increase automation in program development. The system can be developed based on models at different levels of abstraction, and then model transformations partially automate some steps of program development. But development processes based on MDA are not widely used today because most of them are viewed as heavy-weight processes - they cannot deliver (incrementally) partial implementations to be executed as soon as possible.

In this context, executing UML models became a necessity for development processes based on extensive modeling. For such processes, models must act just like code, and UML 2 and its Action Semantics (OMG, 2007) provide a foundation to construct executable models. In order to make a model executable, it must contain a complete and precise behavior description. Unfortunately, creating such a model is a tedious task or an impossible one because of many UML semantic variation points.

Executable UML (Mellor & Balcer, 2002) means execution semantics for a subset of actions sufficient for computational completeness. Two basic elements are required for such subsets: an action language and an operational semantics. The action language specifies the elements that can be used while the operational semantics establishes how the elements can be placed in a model, and how the model can be interpreted. Again, creating reasonable-sized executable UML models is difficult, because the UML primitives from the UML Action Semantics package are too low level.

The fUML standard (OMG, 2008) provides a simplified subset of UML Action Semantics package and it also simplifies the context to which the actions need to be applied. Alf (OMG, 2010) provides the necessary concrete textual syntax that eases the process of creating executable models.

An agile MDA process (Mellor, 2005) applies the main Agile Alliance principles (e.g. testing first, immediate execution) into a classical MDA process. In other words, "models are linked together, rather than transformed, and they are then all mapped to a single combined model that is then translated into code according to a single system architecture" (Mellor, 2005). The verification gap between a model and the corresponding code can be reduced by generating small parts of code as soon as possible, parts that are generated from the model, and that can be executed immediately.

Separation of the Business Logic and Non-Functional Requirements

This targets two important aspects in software development. First at all, the developer will concentrate on the functionality without concern for data access or presentation aspects. Secondly, such an approach will support reuse on a larger scale. Early comercial component models such as Component Object Model (COM) (Microsoft, 1995), Enterprise Java-Beans 2.1 (Sun, 2003), and CORBA Component Model (OMG, 2002) propose specific application programming interfaces, so they do not offer a clear separation between functional and non-functional requirements. These approaches increase the development costs and decrease the potential reuse of the components.

There are many other component models developed by the academic community which provide solutions for the separation problem but do not provide dynamic execution environment features (Lau & Wang, 2005). Some of these frameworks - such as iPOJO (Escoffier & Hall, 2007), OSGi framework (OSGi, 2007), SCA (OASIS, 2007) - which have similar features to the approach presented in this chapter, are discussed in more detail in the Related work section.

How: *ComDeValCo* Framework

MDA and Agile principles represent the driven principle of our proposal, a framework for Software Component Definition, Validation, and Composition, ComDeValCo (Pârv, Lazăr & Motogna, 2008; Pârv, Lazăr, Motogna, Czibula & Lazăr, 2009).

The framework is intended to cover component development and component-based system development. Component development starts with its definition, using an object-oriented modeling language, and graphical tools. Modeling language provides the necessary precision and consistency, and use of graphical tools simplifies developer's work. Once defined, component models are passed to a verification and validation (V&V) process, which is intended to check their correctness and to evaluate their performances. When a component passes V&V step, it is stored in a component repository, for later (re)use.

Component-based system development takes the components already stored in repository and uses graphical tools, intended to: select components fulfilling a specific requirement, perform consistency checks regarding component assembly and include a component in the already existing architecture of the target system. When the assembly process is completed, and the target system is built, other tools will perform V&V, as well as performance evaluation operations on it.

ComDeValCo consists of:

- A modeling language used to describe components models.
- A component repository, which stores and retrieves software components and systems, and represents the persistent part of the framework, containing the models of all fully validated components. After passing the verification and validation step, component models are store into the repository, from where they can be reuse in system development.
- A toolset aimed to help developers to define, check, and validate software components and systems, and to provide maintenance operations for the component repository. The toolset is intended to automate many tasks and to assist developers in performing component definition and V & V, maintenance of component repository, and component assembly.

The framework offers a solution to the current issues stated in the previous section. Its basic features can be summarizes in:

- **Supports Separation of Business Logic and Non-Functional Requirements:** Using a platform-independent component model developers concentrate only on defining the business logic, all dynamic execution environment features being managed by the proposed infrastructure.
- **Support MDA Using Executable Models:** The benefits of such an approach are: a higher level of abstraction (developers concentrate on the application level of abstraction), a clearer separtion of concerns, and a more direct translation from PIM to PSM. Actions are specified in an action language, and consequently the implementations code can be generated from such an UML model.
- **Supports Agile MDA:** Services, structure and deployment models are linked together and test-driven development is applied to simple components in order to obtain incrementally, small pieces of code that can be executed immediately.

EXECUTABLE UML ACTIVITIES

In order to offer a good support for agile MDA processes, a modeling language should provide a metamodel, together with graphical and textual notations for easy manipulation of language elements. All language constructs should be simple and easy to handle for both the developers and users of the model. Consequently, the syntax definition uses a procedural style.

Three requirements were imposed on the Action Language (AL): completeness, in the sense that all the required elements of the model can be described with the language constructs, minimality, i.e. AL omits all unnecessary details, and extensibility. It was defined in the initial phase, implementing the procedural paradigm, and then enhanced with modular issues. AL has the following features:

- All elements are objects, instances of classes defined at logical level, with no relationship to a concrete programming language; this means that component models are platform-independent, (PIM);
- Top-level language constructs cover both complete software systems - Program (the only executable) and concrete software components (not executable by themselves, but ready to be assembled into a software system) - Procedure, Function, Module, Class, Interface, Connector, Component;
- There is a 1:1 relationship between the internal representation of the component model - an aggregated object - and its external representation;
- The dimensions of extensibility are: the statement set, the component definition, the data type definition, and the set of components;
- It allows automatic code generation for component PIMs towards concrete programming languages, according to MDA specifications. One can define mappings from the modeling elements to specific constructs in a concrete programming language in a declarative way. Another extensibility dimension is the concrete programming language.

Also, AL needs to create the abstract representation for the statements and control structures as provided by programming languages, and it must support complex expressions and easy access to parameters and variables.

The features of our proposed action language (Motogna, Lazăr, Pârv, 2011) were very similar to those of Alf, so after Alf was adopted by OMG as the action language for foundational UML, it was an easy task to define models in Alf instead of our action language. The rest of the chapter assumes that the action language under discussion is Alf, and that the models can be described combining graphical with textual syntactical notations.

EXAMPLE

The example model consists of a POS (Point of Sale) class, which contains a list of Products and is the entry point of the system, as shown in Figure 1.a). The user can make a new Sale (stored in POS as the currentSale) by invoking the makeNewSale operation and by adding SaleItems to the current sale in the form of product code and quantity. The POS object finds the Product associated with the given product code by using a private findProduct activity, and, if present, passes the product and quantity to the currentSale. The Sale creates a new SaleItem instance and adds it to its list of sale items.

The findProduct activity is a private activity of the POS class. Figure 1.b) shows Alf concrete syntax of this activity, while Figure 1.c) shows the fUML abstract syntax of the findProduct activity. The activity has one in-parameter, for which there exists an input ActivityParameterNode; its value is exposed to the actions using a ForkNode. The activity has also a return parameter for which there exists an output ActivityParameterNode, named return. A MergeNode is placed before this parameter node, as argued in the previous section.

The activity will be structured in statements, using StructuredActivityNodes and ControlFlow edges to enforce the sequential flow between the statements (blocks of statements). The actions for each statement will be grouped inside one StructuredActivityNode. The only exception is represented by the ForkNodes that expose the variable/parameter values, and which are placed on the same level as the statement nodes, though no ControlFlow edges connect to them, only ObjectFlow edges.

The concrete syntax as presented in Figure 1.b) is quite simple, and easy to be followed. Line 2 shows how a multivalue property may be accessed (self.product) and line 3 shows how a simple property can be accessed (prod.code).

iCOMPONENT PROFILE

iComponent (injected component) (Lazăr, Pârv, Motogna, Czibula & Lazăr, 2008) has been designed as a platform-independent component model that can be used to develop service-oriented components for dynamic execution environments. This section describes the *iComponent* metamodel and its corresponding UML profile, and the next section presents how it can be used in an agile MDA approach.

The set of stereotypes used to model injected components are: Module, Component, Domain, Node, DynamicExecutionEnvironment, provides, requires, validate, invalidate, controller, and config, as shown in Figure 2.

- **Modules:** The Module stereotype extends the UML 2 DeployedArtifact metaclass and represents the unit of deployment. A Module may contain classes, interfaces, components, component instances, and other resources. The set of model elements that are manifested in the module (used in the construction of the module) is indicated by the manifestation property of the DeployedArtifact.
- **Component Types:** The Component stereotype extends the Class metaclass (from UML StructuredClasses) and represents a component type. A Component may define

Figure 1. Alf example and corresponding fUML representation

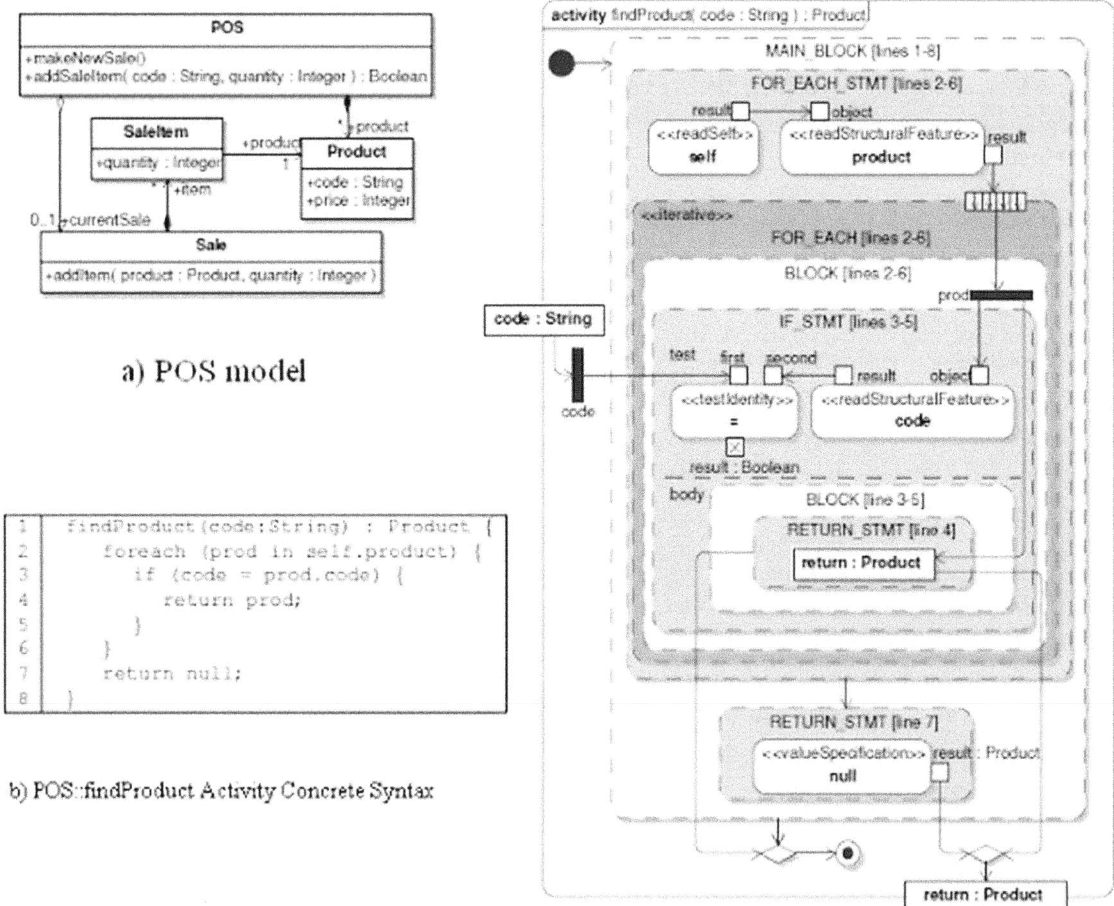

properties and methods since it is a structured class. The configuration properties of a component must be marked with the config stereotype, which contains an attribute for indicating a setter operation to be called when the component container injects the value for a given configuration property.

The provides stereotype is used for publishing services and their properties. This stereotype extends both UML InterfaceRealization and Port metaclasses in order to allow modeling of published services as simple classes that implement interfaces, as well as components that have attached ports. The property attribute can be used to export the service properties, expressed as a set of (key, value) pairs.

The requires stereotype can be used for requiring services. This stereotype extends both UML Association and Port metaclasses such that the required services may be modeled as simple classes that have unidirectional associations with interfaces, as well as components that have attached ports. The filter attribute can be used to filter the required services, based on their properties.

Figure 2. UML profile for iComponent

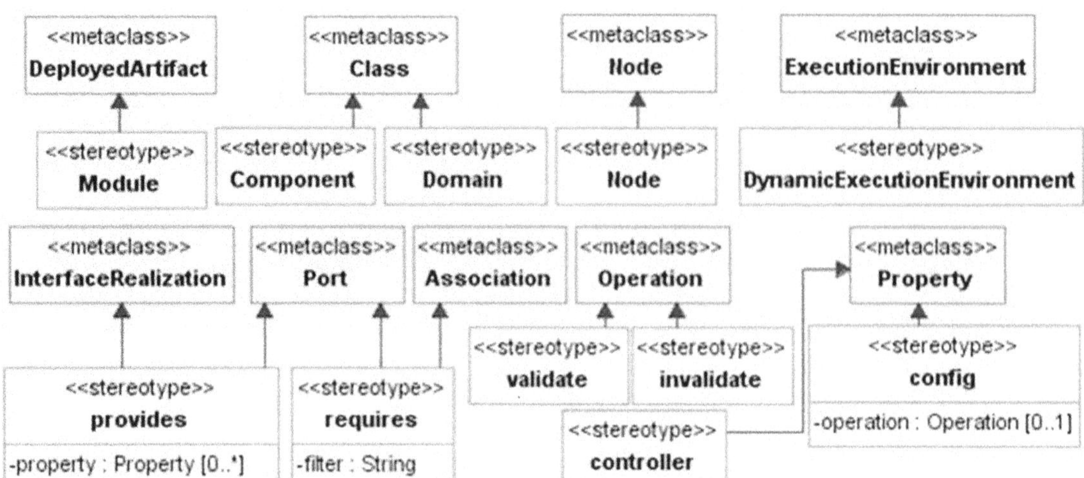

The UML provided/required interfaces do not contain such attributes, which explains why the provides and requires stereotypes were introduced. The two attributes are essential in the service-oriented component model because they contain information needed for component matching. For example, consider two components *EnglishDictionary* and *FrenchDictionary* implementing the same interface *Dictionary* and an *EnglishSpellChecker* component that requires a *Dictionary*. If the two concrete dictionary components are adnotated with a property representing the language (*language=English*, respectively *language=French*), then the spell checker component can choose which interface implementation to use: *filter=(language=English)*.

- **Composite Components:** UML 2.0 offers two ways of modeling subcomponents: subcomponents as parts and subcomponents as nested elements. The composites in iCOMPONENT use UML composite structures in order to indicate their internal structure. In this context, subcomponents modeled as parts are shared components which may be referenced by many composite components.
- **Component Instances:** The execution environment creates (target) component instances in two ways: (a) by creating the instances specified by Modules, and (b) by creating the instances specified as parts of composite Components. In case (a), the module containing the component definition indicates that a corresponding component instance must be created. In case (b), if a composite structure diagram attached to the component contains an instance specification with an interface type, then an instance of a component that implements the interface will be created when such a component type is available. After creation, the instance is bound to the composite instance. Moreover, if such a bound instance disappears, another compatible one can be instantiated to replace the missing service

required by the composite. This mechanism is called dynamic substitution of services. In both cases, the component instances are specified as InstanceSpecification objects of type Component. The values of the InstanceSpecification's slots are used to configure the component instance's properties (using member field injection). The component's required references (services) will be injected by the execution environment.

- **Component Binding:** The execution environment creates for each component instance a container, wrapping the instance, which automatically manages the activities of providing and requiring interfaces. When a component is added to the dynamic execution environment, it enters the *invalid* state. The component enters the *valid* state and its provided interfaces are published into a service registry when the container resolves its dependencies, i.e. the required interfaces.
- **Lifecycle Controllers:** *iComponent* proposes a simple notification mechanism between a component and its container: (a) After a module is installed it enters the *installed* state. When all the model elements required by a module (its module dependencies) are available, the module enters the *resolved* state. A resolved module can be started and the module enters the *active* state. (b) The component instances configured by the module will be created in the *active* state and destroyed when the module leaves this state. When a module becomes *active*, its components enter the *invalid* state; they become *valid* only after validation. A valid component can require its container to enter the invalid state; this is achieved by configuring a component boolean property as controller property using the controller stereotype.
- **Service Registries:** The execution environment offers a global service registry in which component instances publish their provided interfaces. Other component instances may automatically acquire references to these global services through their wrapper containers. In order to isolate the component instances and services of an application, the instances of a composite are not published globally by default. Each composite component has its own service registry which is used by all component instances of the same composite for providing and requiring services. Because a composite may contain other composites, a mechanism for importing and exporting services is needed; this way, a composite can export a service to its parent or can import a service from its parent.
- **Nodes and Dynamic Execution Environments:** Node stereotype extends UML Node metaclass. A node may deploy several modules and therefore possible several components instantiated by these modules. The DynamicExecutionEnvironment stereotype extends Node, in which you can use: (a) the properties associated to a service that is published by a component, and (b) dynamic binding using filters for selecting the services required by a component, in a similar way to the iPOJO approach (Escofier & Hall, 2007).
- **Domain:** A Domain represents the architecture - a complete configuration for system deployment, and consists of nodes and connectors between nodes. It may have several nodes, each containing several components. Here a node is seen as a process on a computer. The binding of the components in a specific domain does not depend of the nodes in which the components are deployed.

AGILE MDA APPROACH FOR SERVICE-ORIENTED COMPONENTS

The models can be constructed using any UML case tool, and their execution can be performed with any fUML-compliant tool (such as fUML plugin from MagicDraw (Model Driven Community, 2009)). As discussed above, ComDeValCo workbench is such a tool, being designed according to these requirements (Motogna, Lazăr, Pârv & Czibula, 2009; Lazăr, Pârv, Motogna, Czibula & Lazăr, 2007; 2009). The iComponent profile may be easily applied to develop service-oriented components for dynamic execution environments.

The proposed agile MDA approach consists of applying the following steps in the specified order: (1) the model is described on different layers: services, structure and deployment, then (2) for simple components proceed with test-first component development. The approach is applied for the following example: a case study that prints the product prices of a given store. The store has a product catalog containing product information (code, description, and price without taxes and discounts). The printing procedure must consider the discount strategies the store may have for each product and the application of VAT.

Services Model

The services model, typically defined by the system analyst, describes the services that will be provided by the system. The modules that refer to services model may include any data type, such as classes, interfaces, or components. The interfaces contain the operations provided by the services.

At this step, the model should be defined with the separation of responsibilities in mind. The modules will contain required operation or will simply delegate execution to corresponding operation from another module within the model.

Figure 3.a shows the services model, illustrating the separation of responsibilities. The StoreService interface contains the required operations for printing the product prices with taxes and discounts. StoreService's operations can simply delegate execution to their corresponding operations from ProductCatalog and PriceCalculator.

Figure 3. (a) Services model and (b) structural model

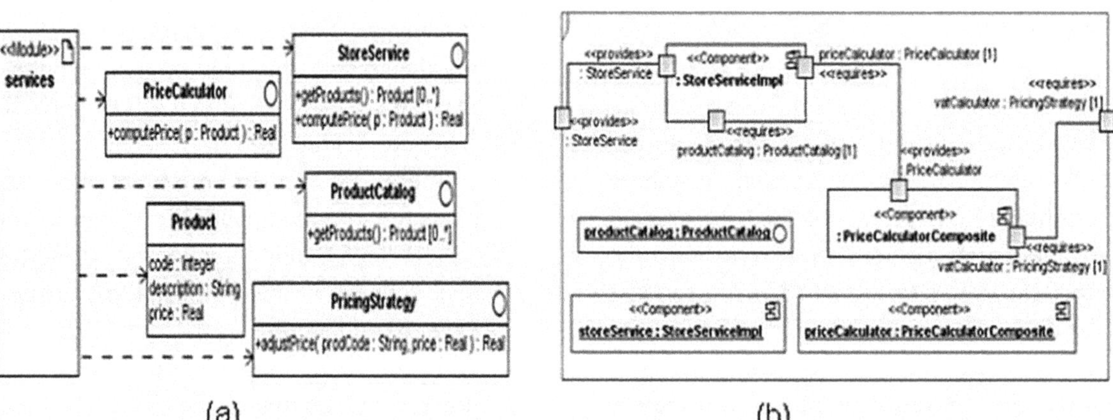

The Pricing-Strategy interface is designed to represent both discount and VAT price adjustments. The services module includes all these interfaces as well as the Product business entity.

Structural Model: Composite Components

The structural model, typically defined by the system architect, indicates component instances that implement the services. At this stage, the system is decomposed into a set of components, simple or composite. *Composite components* help the architect to decompose the system functionality in a hierarchical way. Each composite component has attached a composite structure diagram, describing its internal structure, using component parts (simple or composite) and connectors between ports, and specifying which components will be instantiated. The rules for the construction of the diagram are:

- The internal structure of a component uses instances of other components, connected through ports;
- The provided and required ports, as well as their multiplicity, should be specified;
- To select a certain service implementation satisfying some criteria, use the property attribute corresponding to provides and filter attribute corresponding to requires;
- The InstanceSpecification objects indicate which components should be created and their corresponding property values.

Instances will be created according to the rules specified by iComponent profile. The hierarchical composition works such that components acquire services from their parent, and provide services to their parent.

Figure 3.b shows the composite structure diagram of the Store composite component. Store uses three shared subcomponents; one of them, PriceCalculatorComposite, is a composite too. The provided and required interfaces are represented as ports and the components are linked using connectors.

Deployment Model

The deployment model is specified using UML Node and DynamicExecutionEnvironment constructs, as shown above. The dependencies in this model represent the required runtime dependencies between modules (see Figure 4(a)). All monolithic implementations reference only interfaces, but composite components may use other components as parts.

At this moment, the domain has to be specified, with its included nodes, and the deployment of modules within nodes – as shown in Figure 4(b). There are two nodes, corresponding to CatalogApp and TaxServices. Next, the module must indicate which components will be instantiated during execution and which nodes are involved in each instantiation process.

Coresponding to the domain specification above, Figure 5 shows the component instances created at runtime in their corresponding nodes. StoreComposite acquires vatCalculatorImpl service and publishes it for its part components, then creates instances for its parts.

Test-First Component Development

When the decomposition is complete, the next step is to define simple or monolithic components solving the initial problem. For each new feature of the system being developed, the proposed agile MDA process includes the sequence of following test-first design steps (Beck, 2002):

- **Add a Test:** Developers write the tests using either graphical or textual notations. Both are compiled into the same UML repository model. The tests are conformant with UML testing specifications (OMG, 2005). During the activity construction

Figure 4. Deployment model

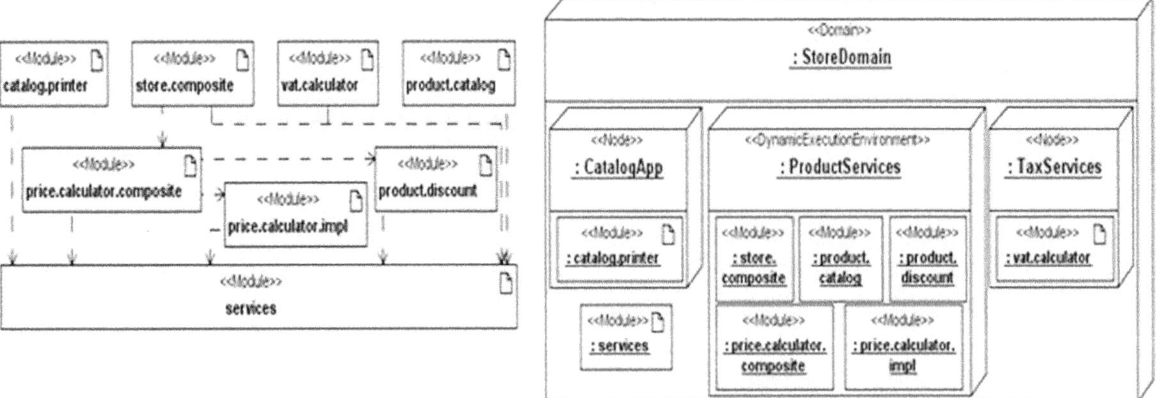

(a) Module dependencies

(b) Domain and nodes

Figure 5. Component instances

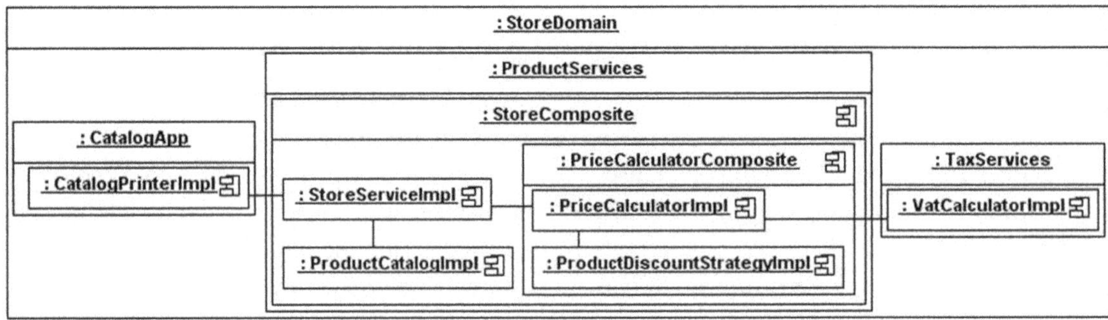

process, the framework allows the use of inline expressions, represented and evaluated according to the pull model for actions.

Figure 6a) shows how tests for ProductDiscount module are created, including initialization of the component properties productCode and discountPercentage. Using the action language, the implementation:

```
assert 90 = pricingStrategy.adjust-
Price(''3'',100);
```

```
assert 100 = pricingStrategy.adjust-
Price(''1'',100);
```

- **Run the Tests:** The methods of the components have an empty body, only the conditions are specified.
- **Add Production Code:** The third step is to update the functional code to make it pass the new test. Again, both graphical and textual syntax of AL can be used. By running the tests, the code is updated correspond-

Figure 6. a)Product discount tests; b) Product discount

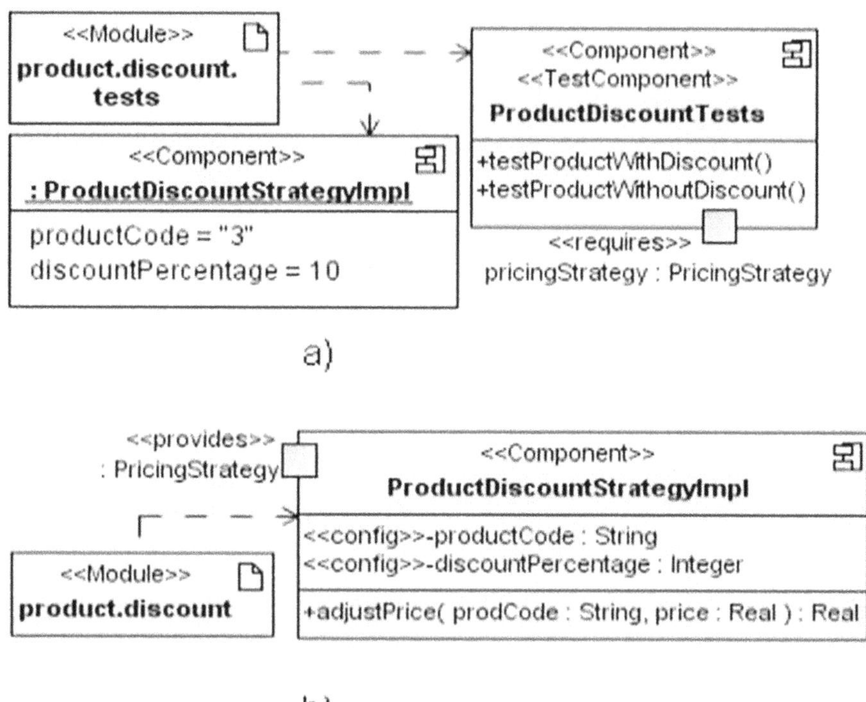

ingly. After the tests from Figure 6a) are run, the code is updated is in Figure 6b) with the following implementation for adjustPrice method:

```
if (productCode = self.productCode)
      return (1-discountPercent-
age/100)* price;
else
      return price;
```

- **Run the Tests:**This last step means running the tests again. Once the tests pass the next step is to start over implementing a new system feature.

In order to support the first step of this approach, we suggest that a graphical tool may be used to define the components of the model, and in order to avoid the low level primitives of fUML for operations' definitions, the body of the methods may be described using textuat syntactical constructions (from Alf). So, we have to extend Alf syntax with assert statement. We propose a Xtext[1]definition that can be used to create tests in concrete syntax. The definition is conformant with Alf syntax, and also with UML testing profile. The Xtext grammar is depicted in Figure 7.

Papyrus offers partial support for Alf (Cuccuru, 2013), in the sense that the project is under development, and the core grammar contains at this moment statements and expressions. That's why our grammar defines statements and Boolean expressions as Alf Statements, respectively Conditional-TestExpression from Papyrus. According to grammar definition, the body of the tested methods can contain zero or more Alf statements, and an assert clause that will return a verdict, specifying if the test passes or fails.

Figure 7. Xtext grammar for method's body

```
grammar org.xtext.example.testalf.Testalf with
                              org.eclipse.xtext.common.Terminals
import "http://www.eclipse.org/papyrus/alf/Alf" as alf
generate testalf "http://www.xtext.org/comdevalco/testalf/Testalf"

Body:
        '{'(Statements+=Statement)* Assert '}'
;
Statement:
        [alf::Statement]
;
Assert:
        'assert' [alf::ConditionalTestExpression]
;
```

RELATED WORK

As shown in the first section, two important issues for simplifying the construction of components are: (1) the separation of the business logic of a component from its non-functional requirements and (2) the application of a model-driven development (MDD) approach. Both are challenging research topics and several academic and commercial solutions targeting component models and service orientation are under development.

Among the MDA approaches which address the traditional component models (e.g. Corba Component Model), the standard specification for deployment and configuration of component-based distributed applications (OMG, 2006) should be mentioned.

Other MDA approaches referring to embedded systems (Cano, Martinez, Seepold, & Aguilar 2007) or pervasive systems (Bottaro, Bourcier, Escofier, & Lalanda, 2007; Bourcier, Chazalet, Desertot, Escofier & Marin, 2006; Munoz, Pelechano, & Fons, 2004) address the dynamic execution environment features and the separation problem.

Academic solutions, such as Fractal (Bruneton, Coupaye, Leclercq, Quema & Stefani, 2004) and SOFA 2.0 (Bures, Hnetynka & Plasil, 2006) are open component models that provide all dynamic features but do not offer a clear separation of the functional and non-functional requirements.

iPOJO (injected Plain Old Java Objects) (Escofier & Hall, 2007) is a service-oriented component framework supporting the service-oriented component model concepts and dynamic availability of components, following the POJO (Plain Old Java Object) approach. All service-oriented aspects, such as service publication, the required service discovery and selection are managed by an associated component container. The operations in iPOJO are similar to *iComponent* operations, but our approach is platform-independent, while iPOJO is restricted to Java.

Also, the current version of iPOJO does not provide a clear separation of the business logic and non-functional requirements for all operations discussed above. More precisely, only dynamic availability of components and composition of components are supported, while the dynamic reconfiguration of components can be performed only using the OSGi Configuration Admin service.

Another framework which supports dynamic availability and reconfiguration of components is the OSGi framework (OSGi, 2007), which offers a service-oriented component model. OSGi components are bound using a service-oriented interaction pattern, and their structure is described declaratively. However, OSGi does not offer a clear separation between business logic and the non-functional requirements.

Service Component Architecture (SCA) Assembly Model specification (OASIS, 2007) proposes a definition of composite components similar to iPOJO; in addition, the components may be distributed in several locations/nodes within the same domain. Another remarkable feature of SCA is that it allows specification of component implementations which are not necessary classes; they can be business processes also. However, there are also some drawbacks of SCA: it doesn't indicate any solution for controlling the lifecycle of components and does not allow the user to attach properties to a published service and to filter services specifying some conditions.

Table 1 enumerates the main elements used to develop service-oriented components for dynamic execution environments and gives the mapping between these elements from *iComponent*, iPOJO and SCA frameworks. These two frameworks were taken into consideration as specific target platforms for models created using our proposed UML profile.

As the table suggests, the main difference between *iComponent* and SCA on one hand, and iPOJO, on the other hand, is that iPOJO does not support distributed service architecture. *iComponent* supports it, by distributing the modules in the nodes of the dynamic execution environment. Comparing *iComponent* with SCA, one may observe that SCA does not have lifecycle controllers, i.e. a notification mechanism between a component and its container such that the component can participate to its lifecycle events.

In conclusion, *ComDeValCo* framework allows service-oriented applications to be modeled independently of any platform, then these models can be executed, and in the end, complete code is generated targeting such a platform (SCA, iPOJO), providing that the differences highlighted in the table were taken into consideration.

To our best knowledge, we haven't found agile MDA approaches based on fUML and Alf. The idea of test driven development for simple components may be compared with two research

Table 1. iComponent, iPOJO, and SCA mappings

iComponent	iPOJO	SCA
Domain	-	Domain
Node	-	Node
DynamicExecutionEnvironment	OSGi implementation	-
Module	Bundle	Contribution
Component	Component	Component
Composite component	Composite	Composite
provides	provides	Service
Requires	Requires	Reference
validate and invalidate	validate and invalidate	-
controller	controller	-
Config	Property	Property

ideas: i) to use fUML and Alf for testing UML components and ii) extend fUML and Alf for other purposes.

The Moliz project[2] offers a testing framework for UML activities, that includes a test specification language and a test interpreter. The test specification language is designed based on fUML constructs, and the extension covers assertions for execution order, runtime states and finally states. Their current approach does not provide the possibility to use the concrete syntax of Alf in component definition (Mijatov, Langer, Mayerhofer, Kappel, 2013).

Several approaches of defining DSML (Domain Specific Modelling Languages) based on fUML and Alf target different application domains: Lai & Carpenter (Lai, Carpenter, 2012) propose an approach to detect several corectness isssues based on a behavioral semantics defined in terms of fUML and Alf; T. Mayerhofer a.o. (Mayerhofer, Langer, Wimmer & Kappel. 2013) propose xMOF, as DSML that integrates Ecore with parts of fUML, and a methoology to use xMOF to support execution of models using a fUML virtual machine.

FUTURE RESEARCH DIRECTIONS

The development of our proposed methodology includes two main directions:

- To provide a complete integration with Alf: at this stage the implementation of Alf in Papyrus is not complete (only expressions and statements), and several constructions that exists in Alf specifications must be introduced. The integration will also take into consideration extensions related to tests, that should conform to UML Testing profile (OMG, 2005): TestContext, TestComponent and TestCase;
- To align our component definition according to the RFP issued by OMG related to composite structures (OMG, 2011). The request for proposals issued in December 2011 aims to define a "precise specification of the semantics for all the metaclasses supporting the ability of classifiers to have both an internal structure (comprising a network of linked parts) and an external structure (consisting of one or more ports)". Although the deadline passed for quite some time, at this moment there is no OMG standard for composite structures, but their inclusion in fUML would be benefic, since it will allow a more complex model definition.

CONCLUSION

This chapter describes *ComDeValCo* framework, made up of: *iComponent* - a platform-independent component model for dynamic execution environments, and an agile MDA approach for building executable models. To the best of our knowledge, no other existing works combines executable models, agile MDA, and platform-independent service-oriented component models for dynamic execution environments.

Our proposal is compared to other specific platforms, like iPOJO and SCA. By using *iComponent* profile, *ComDeValCo* models can be constructed with any UML tool and can be executed in any executable UML tool.

The intended use of *ComDeValCo* framework is twofold. The first target is component-based development, since *ComDeValCo* conforms to UML and MDA standards, providing a complete framework for executable service-oriented component models.

The second target is of an academic nature. *ComDeValCo* can be used in many Software Engineering courses as an example of applying model-driven principles in the software development process. At a beginner level, students get used earlier with model-based development, while at an advanced level the framework may be used for model-driven V&V tasks.

ACKNOWLEDGMENT

The research was partially supported by the grant ID 546, sponsored by NURC - Romanian National University Research Council (CNCSIS).

REFERENCES

Balasubramanian, K., Gokhale, A., Karsai, G., Sztipanovits, J., & Neema, S. (2006). Developing applications using model-driven design environments. *Computer*, *39*(2), 33–40. doi:10.1109/MC.2006.54

Batory, D. (2006). Multilevel models in model-driven engineering, product lines, and metaprogramming. *IBM Systems Journal*, *45*(3), 527–539. doi:10.1147/sj.453.0527

Beck, K. (2002). *Test-driven development by example*. Boston: Addison Wesley.

Bottaro, A., Bourcier, J., Escoffier, C., & Lalanda, P. (2007). Autonomic Context-aware service composition in a home control gateway. In: *Proceedings of IEEE International Conference on Pervasive Services* (pp. 223-231). Istanbul, Turkey: IEEE. doi:10.1109/PERSER.2007.4283920

Bourcier, J., Chazalet, A., Desertot, M., Escofier, C. & Marin, C. (2006). A dynamic-SOA home control gateway. In *Proceedings of IEEE International Conference on Services Computing* (pp. 463–470). Chicago: IEEE.

Bruneton, E., Coupaye, T., Leclercq, M., Quema, V., & Stefani, J.-B. (2004). An open component model and its support in java. In Component-Based Software Engineering, (LNCS) (vol. 3054, pp. 7-22). Springer.

Bures, T., Hnetynka, P., & Plasil, F. (2006). SOFA 2.0: Balancing advanced features in a hierarchical component model. In *Proceedings SERA* (pp. 40-48). Seattle, WA: IEEE Computer Society.

Cano, J., Martinez, N., Seepold, R., & Aguilar, F. L. (2007). Model-driven development of embedded system on heterogeneous platforms. In *Procedings of Forum on Specification and Design Languages* (pp. 243–248). Barcelona, Spain: ECSI.

Cervantes, H., & Hall, R. S. (2004). A Framework for Constructing Adaptive Component-Based Applications: Concepts and Experiences. In *7th Symposium on Component-Based Software Engineering* (LNCS), (vol. 3054, pp. 130-137), Berlin: Springer. doi:10.1007/978-3-540-24774-6_13

Cuccuru, A. (2013). *Papyrus Support for Alf.* Retrieved February 2014, from: http://www.omg.org/news/meetings/tc/agendas/va/xUML_pdf/Cucurru.pdf

Escofier, C., & Hall, R. S. (2007). Dynamically Adaptable Applications with iPOJO Service Components. In *Proc. 6th Conference on Software Composition*, (LNCS) (vol. 4829, pp. 113-128). Berlin: Springer. doi:10.1007/978-3-540-77351-1_9

Henderson, P., & Walters, R. J. (1999). System Design Validation Using Formal Models. In *Proceedings of 10th IEEE International Workshop in Rapid System Prototyping* (pp. 10-14), Clearwater, FL: IEEE Computer Society.

Lai, Q., & Carpenter, A. (2012). Defining and verifying behaviour of domain specific language with fUML. In *Proceedings of the 4th Workshop on Behaviour Modeling - Foundations and Applications (BM-FA) @ ECMFA 2012*, (pp. 1–7). ACM doi:10.1145/2325276.2325277

Lau, K.-K., & Wang, Z. (2005). A Taxonomy of Software Component Models. In: *Proceeding of 31st EUROMICRO Conference of Software Engineering and Advanced Applications* (pp. 88-95). IEEE Computer Society.

Lazăr, C.-L., Lazăr, I., Pârv, B., Motogna, S., & Czibula, I.-G. (2009). Using an fUML Action Language to Construct UML Models. In *Proceedings of 11th International Symposium on Symbolic and Numeric Algorithms for Scientific Computing*. Timisoara, Romania: Academic Press. doi:10.1109/SYNASC.2009.49

Lazăr, I., Pârv, B., Motogna, S., Czibula, I.-G., & Lazăr, C.-L. (2007). An Agile MDA Approach for Executable UML Structured Activities, Studia Univ. Babeş-Bolyai. *Informatica*, *52*(2), 101–114.

Lazăr, I., Pârv, B., Motogna, S., Czibula, I.-G., & Lazăr, C.-L. (2008). iComponent: A Platform-independent Component Model for Dynamic Execution Environments. In *Proceedings of 10th International Symposium on Symbolic and Numeric Algorithms for Scientific Computing* (pp. 257-264). Timisoara, Romania: IEEE Computer Society. doi:doi:10.1109/SYNASC.2008.71 doi:10.1109/SYNASC.2008.71

Mayerhofer, T., Langer, P., Wimmer, M., & Kappel, G. (2013). xMOF: Executable DSMLs based on fUML. In *Proceedings of the 6th International Conference on Software Language Engineering (SLE)* (LNCS), (vol. 8225, pp. 1 – 20). Springer.

Mellor, S. J. (2005). *Agile MDA*. Retrieved May 20, 2009, from: http://www.omg.org/mda/mda_files/Agile_MDA.pdf

Mellor, S. J., & Balcer, M. J. (2002). *Executable UML: A Foundation for Model-Driven Architecture*. Boston: Addison Wesley.

Microsoft. (1995). *Component object model*. Microsoft, Inc. Retrieved May 20, 2009, from: http://www.microsoft.com/com/

Microsystems, S. (2003). *Enterprise JavaBeans specification*. Retrieved October 2007, from: http://java.sun.com/products/ejb/docs.html

Mijatov, S., Langer, P., Mayerhofer, T., & Kappel, G. (2013). A Framework for Testing UML Activities Based on fUML. In *Proceedings of the 10th International Workshop on Model Driven Engineering, Verification and Validation co-located with 16th International Conference on Model Driven Engineering Languages and Systems (MODELS 2013)*. CEUR.

Model Driven Community. (2009). *fUML MagicDraw plugin*. Retrieved Oct, 2009, from: http://portal.modeldriven.org/content/fuml-reference-implementation-download

Motogna, S., Lazăr, I., & Pârv, B. (2011). An MDA Approach for Developing Executable UML Components. In J. Osis & E. Asnina (Eds.), Model-Driven Analysis and Software Development: Architectures and Functions, (pp. 254-273). IGI Global.

Motogna, S., Lazăr, I., Pârv, B., & Czibula, I. (2009). An Agile MDA Approach for Service-Oriented Components. In J. Happe & B. Zimmerova (Eds.), *6th International Workshop on Formal Engineering approaches to Software Components and Architectures* (FESCA) (pp. 2-17). York, UK: Electronic Notes in Theoretical Computer Science.

Munoz, J., Pelechano, V., & Fons, J. (2004). Model driven development of pervasive systems. *ERCIM News*, *58*, 50–51.

Niklaus, W. (1977). What can we do about the unnecessary diversity of notation for syntactic definitions?. *Communication of ACM, 20*(11), 822-823.

OASIS. (2007). *SCA Service Component Architecture: Assembly Model Specification, Version 1.1.* Retrieved October 2007, from: http://www.oasis-opencsa.org/sca

OMG. (2002). *CORBA Components Specification, Version 3.0.* Retrieved October 2007, from: http://www.omg.org/technology/documents/formal/components.htm

OMG. (2005). *UML 2.0 Testing Profile Specification.* Retrieved October 2007, from: http://www.omg.org/cgi-bin/apps/doc?formal/05-07-07.pdf

OMG. (2006). *Deployment and Configuration of Component-based Distributed Applications Specification, Version 4.* Retrieved October 2007, from: http://www.omg.org/technology/documents/formal/deployment.htm

OMG. (2007). *UML Superstructure Specification, Rev. 2.1.2.* Retrieved October 2007, from: http://www.omg.org/docs/formal/07-11-02.pdf

OMG. (2008). *Semantics of a Foundational Subset for Executable UML Models (FUML).* Retrieved April 2009, from: http://www.omg.org/spec/FUML/

OMG. (2010). *Concrete Syntax for UML Action Language (Action Language for Foundational UML - ALF).* Retrieved February 2014, from: http://www.omg.org/spec/ALF/1.0.1/

OMG. (2011). *Precise Semantics of UML Composite Structures. Request For Proposal.* Retrieved February 2014, from: http://www.omg.org/cgi-bin/doc?ad/11-12-07.pdf

OSGi Alliance. (2007). *OSGi Service Platform Core Specification, Release 4, Version 4.1.* Retrieved October 2007, from: http://www.osgi.org/

Papazoglou, M., & Georgakopoulos, D. (2003). Service-Oriented Computing. *Communications of the ACM*, *46*(10), 25–28.

Pârv, B., Lazăr, I., & Motogna, S. (2008). ComDeValCo Framework - the Modeling Language for Procedural Paradigm. *International Journal of Computers, Communications & Control*, *3*(2), 183–195.

Pârv, B., Lazăr, I., Motogna, S., Czibula, I.-G., & Lazăr, C.-L. (2009) ComDeValCo Framework - Procedural and Modular Issues. In *Proceedings of 2nd International Conference Knowledge Engineering: Principles and Techniques* (pp. 189-193). Cluj-Napoca, Romania: Studia Universitatis Babeş-Bolyai.

KEY TERMS AND DEFINITIONS

Action Language: Part of executable UML, uses only elements allowed by fUML standard and should create abstract representations for all the elements the model requires (Mellor & Balcer, 2002).

Agile MDA: Applies the main agile principles into a classical MDA process;"models are linked together, rather than transformed, and they are then all mapped to a single combined model that is then translated into code according to a single system architecture" (Mellor, 2005).

Component-Based Development: Software systems are developed and deployed as a set of components, providing loose coupling among the application components, third-party component selection, and increased component reuse (Escofier & Hall, 2007).

Executable UML: Represents an execution semantic for a subset of actions sufficient for computational completeness. Two basic elements are required for such subsets: an action language and an operational semantics (Mellor & Balcer, 2002).

Execution Environment: Manages application compositions based on service availability and provides deployment and integration (Cervantes & Hall, 2004).

Service-Oriented Component Model: Adopts the service oriented approach of late binding among components via services. Thus, the application is consists of component composition, and at run time it adapts based on availability of the services (Cervantes & Hall, 2004).

Test-Driven Development: Is a software development technique that relies on repeatedly apply small unit testing in order to detect system behavior and write the corresponding code (Beck, 2002).

ENDNOTES

1 www.eclipse.org/Xtext

2 http://www.modelexecution.org

Compilation of References

Aboelaze, M., & Aloul, F. (2005). Current and future trends in sensor networks: A survey. In *Proceedings of the Second IFIP International Conference on Wireless and Optical Communications Networks WOCN 2005*, (pp. 551–555). doi:10.1109/WOCN.2005.1436087

Abrahão, S., & Poels, G. (2007). Experimental evaluation of an object-oriented function point measurement procedure. *Information and Software Technology*, *49*(4), 366–380. doi:10.1016/j.infsof.2006.06.001

Abrahão, S., & Poels, G. (2009). A family of experiments to evaluate a functional size measurement procedure for web applications. *Journal of Systems and Software*, *82*(2), 253–269. doi:10.1016/j.jss.2008.06.031

Abramson, M. A., & Means, G. E. (2001). E-government 2001. *The PricewaterhousCoopers Endowment Series on The Business of Government*. Rowman & Littlefield Publishers. Retrieved from http://books.google.com/books?hl=de&lr=&id=WGbqZN4M5j8C&pgis=1

Abrial, J.R., Butler, M., Hallerstede, S., & Voisin, L. (2006, June). An open extensible tool environment for Event-B. In Proceedings of ICFEM 2006 (Vol. 4260, pp. 588-605). Berlin: Springer-Verlag.

Adam, S., & Doerr, J. (2008). The role of service abstraction and service variability and its impact on requirement engineering for service-oriented systems. In *Proceedings ofAnnual IEEE International Computer Software and Applications Conference*. IEEE. doi:10.1109/COMPSAC.2008.54

ADM. (2014). *Architecture-Driven Modernization Task Force*. Retrieved February 7, 2014, from http://www.omgwiki.org/admtf/doku.php

Aggarwal, S. (2005). *TCO of on-demand applications is significantly better for SMBs and mid-market enterprises*. Yankees Group Report. Retrieved March 10, 2010 from http://www.intente.net/pdfs/Yankee___On_Demand_vs_On_Premises_TCO_1_.pdf?ID=13165

AheadWorks. (2012). aheadWrks. *Magento Got a Third Slice of Pie*. Retrieved from http://blog.aheadworks.com/2012/09/magento-got-a-third-slice-of-pie/

Ahmed, S., & Ashraf, G. (2007). Model-based user interface engineering with design patterns. *Journal of Systems and Software*, *80*(8), 1408–1422. doi:10.1016/j.jss.2006.10.037

Akiki, P. A., Bandara, A. K., & Yu, Y. (2013). RBUIS: Simplifying enterprise application user interfaces through engineering role-based adaptive behavior. In *Proceedings of the 5th ACM SIGCHI symposium on Engineering interactive computing systems* (pp. 3-12). New York, NY: ACM. doi:10.1145/2494603.2480297

Aktug, I., & Naliuka, K. (2007). ConSpec: A Formal Language for Policy Specification. In *Proceedings of the First International Workshop on Run Time Enforcement for Mobile and Distributed Systems, REM 07* (pp. 107-109).

Aktug, I., & Naliuka, K. (2008). ConSpec - A Formal Language for Policy Specification. *Electronic Notes in Theoretical Computer Science*, *197*(1), 45–58. doi:10.1016/j.entcs.2007.10.013

Akyildiz, I. F., Su, W., Sankarasubramaniam, Y., & Cayirci, E. (2002). Wireless sensor networks: A survey. *Computer Networks*, *38*(4), 393–422. doi:10.1016/S1389-1286(01)00302-4

Albrecht, A. J. (1979). Measuring application development productivity. In *Proceedings of the Joint SHARE, GUIDE, and IBM Application Development Symposium.* Monterey, CA: IBM Corporation.

Alexander, C., Ishikawa, S., Silverstein, M., Jacobson, M., Fiksdahl-King, I., & Angel, S. (1977). *A Pattern Language: Towns, Building, Construction.* New York: Oxford University Press.

Alfalayleh, M., & Brankovic, L. (2004). An overview of security issues and techniques in mobile agents. In *Proceedings of Communications and Multimedia Security (CMS2004)* (pp. 59–78). Windermere, UK: Emerald Group Publishing Limited.

Aljuraidan, J., Fragkaki, E., Bauer, L., Jia, L., Fukushima, K., Kiyomoto, S., & Miyake, Y. (2012). *Run-time enforcement of information-flow properties on Android. Technical Report CMUCyLab-12-015.* Carnegie Mellon University.

Alkkiomäki, V., & Smolander, K. (2007). *Integration use cases – An applied UML technique for modeling functional requirements in service oriented architecture.* Paper presented at the Requirements Engineering: Foundation for Software Quality, 13th International Working Conference, REFSQ 2007. Trondheim, Norway.

Alonso, G., Casati, F., Kuno, H., & Machiraju, V. (2004). *Web Services: Concepts, Architectures and Applications.* Springer. Retrieved from http://www.amazon.com/dp/3642078885

Aloysius, A., & Arockiam, L. (2012). Coupling complexity metric: A cognitive approach. *International Journal of Information Technology and Computer Science, 4*(9), 29–35. doi:10.5815/ijitcs.2012.09.04

Alur, D., Crupi, J., & Malks, D. (2001). *Core J2EE Patterns: Best Practices and Design Strategies.* Prentice Hall / Sun Microsystems Press.

Amazon Elastic Cloud. (2010). *Amazon Platform as a service.* Retrieved March 10, 2010, from Amazons website http://aws.amazon.com/ec2/

Ambient Intelligence. (2005). Retrieved from http://www.itea-office.org/projects/facts_sheets/ ambience_fact_sheet.htm

Ambler, S. (2004). *The object primer: Agile model-driven development with UML 2.0.* Cambridge University Press. doi:10.1017/CBO9780511584077

Amsden, J., Gardner, T., Griffin, C., & Iyengar, S. (2003). *IBM draft UML 1.4 profile for automated business processes with a mapping to BPEL 1.0.* Retrieved March 15, 2009, from http://www.ibm.com/developerworks/rational/library/content/04April/3103/3103_UMLProfileForBusinessProcesses1.1.pdf

Anastasakis, K., Bordbar, B. & Kuster, J. (2007). *Analysis of Model Transformations via Alloy.* Modevva 2007.

Anastasakis, K., Bordbar, B., Georg, G. & Ray, I. (2010). On challenges of model transformation from UML to Alloy. *Software Systems Modelling, 9*(1).

Andersen, H. R. (1995). Partial Model Checking (Extended Abstract). In *Proceedings of the Tenth Annual IEEE Symposium on Logic in Computer Science* (pp. 398-407). doi:10.1109/LICS.1995.523274

Andersson, C., Freeman, D., James, I., Johnston, A., & Ljung, S. (2006). *Mobile media and applications, from concept to cash.* New York, NY: John Wiley & Sons, Inc. doi:10.1002/9780470028469

Anderssson, B., Johannesson, P., & Zdravkovic, J. (2007). *Aligning goals and services through goal and business modeling. The International Journal of Information Systems and e-Business Management,* 7, 143–169.

Andriessen, J. H. E. (2003). *Working with Groupware: Understanding and Evaluating Collaboration Technology.* London: Springer. doi:10.1007/978-1-4471-0067-6

Angyal, L., Lengyel, L., & Charaf, H. (2006). An Overview of the State-of-the-Art Reverse Engineering Techniques. In *Proceedings of7th International Symposium of Hungarian Researchers on Computational Intelligence* (pp. 507-516). Budapest, Hungary: Academic Press.

Antón, A. I. (1996). Goal-based requirements analysis. In Proceedings of*Second IEEE International Conference on Requirements Engineering (ICRE '96),* (pp. 136-144). IEEE. doi:10.1109/ICRE.1996.491438

Antoniou, J., Pinto, F. C., Simoes, J., & Pitsillides, A. (2010). Supporting context-aware multiparty sessions in heterogeneous mobile networks. *Mobile Networks and Applications*, *15*(6), 831–844. doi:10.1007/s11036-010-0235-9

Apache Derby. (2009). Retrieved June 10, 2009, from http://db.apache.org/derby/

Apple Inc. (2014). *iOS Security*. White Paper. Author.

Apple. (n.d.). *iOS Developer Library*. Retrieved from https://developer.apple.com/library/ios/documentation/general/conceptual/devpedia-cocoacore/MVC.html

Ardi, S., & Shahmehri, N. (2009) Introducing vulnerability awareness to common criteria's security targets. In *Proceedings of the fourth international conference on software engineering advances* (ICSEA 2009) (pp. 419-424). Porto, Portugal: IEEE Computer Society. doi:10.1109/ICSEA.2009.67

Ardi, S., & Shahmehri, N. (2009, September) *Secure software development for higher common criteria evaluation assurance levels*. Paper presented at the 10th International Common Criteria Conference & Exhibition. Tromsø, Norway.

Ardi, S., Byers, D., & Shahmehri, N. (2006). Towards a structured unified process for software security. In *Proceedings of the 2nd international workshop on software engineering for secure systems (SESS06)* (p. 3-9). Shanghai, China: IEEE Computer Society. doi:10.1145/1137627.1137630

Armando, A., & Compagna, L. (2008). Sat-based model-checking for security protocols analysis. *International Journal of Information Security*, *7*(1), 3–32. doi:10.1007/s10207-007-0041-y

Armando, A., Costa, G., & Merlo, A. (2013). Bring Your Own Device, Securely. In *Proceedings of the 28th Annual ACM Symposium on Applied Computing, SAC 13* (pp. 1852-1858). doi:10.1145/2480362.2480707

Armando, A., Merlo, A., Migliardi, M., & Verderame, L. (2012). Would You Mind Forking This Process? A Denial of Service Attack on Android (and Some Countermeasures). In *Proceedings of the 27th IFIP TC11 Information Security and Privacy Conference, SEC 2012* (pp. 13-24). doi:10.1007/978-3-642-30436-1_2

Armbrust, M., Fox, A., Griffith, R., Joseph, A. D., Katz, R. H., Konwinski, A., et al. (2008, February). *Above the clouds: A Berkeley view of cloud computing* (Technical Report EECS-2009-28). Berkeley, CA: University of California at Berkeley.

Armbrust, M., Stoica, I., Zaharia, M., Fox, A., Griffith, R., & Joseph, A. D. et al. (2010). A view of cloud computing. *Communications of the ACM*, *53*(4), 50–58. doi:10.1145/1721654.1721672

Arockiam, L., & Aloysius, A. (2011). Attribute weighted class complexity: A new metric for measuring cognitive complexity of OO systems. *World Academy of Science, Engineering and Technology*, *58*, 963–968.

Arockiam, L., Aloysius, A., & Selvaraj, J. C. (2009). Extended weighted class complexity: A new software complexity for object oriented system. In *Proceedings of International Conference on Semantic E-business and Enterprise computing (SEEC)*, (pp. 77-80). SEEC.

Arsanjani, A. (2005). *Toward a pattern language for service-oriented architecture and integration, part 1: Build a service eco-system*. Retrieved 01/19, 2010, from http://www.ibm.com/developerworks/webservices/library/ws-soa-soi/

Arsanjani, A., Ghosh, S., Allam, A., Abdollah, T., Ganapathy, S., & Holley, K. (2008). SOMA: A method for developing service-oriented solutions. *IBM Systems Journal*, *47*(3), 377–396. doi:10.1147/sj.473.0377

Asnina, E., & Osis, J. (2010). Computation independent models: bridging problem and solution domains. In J. Osis, & O. Nikiforova (Ed.), *Proceedings of the 2nd InternationalWorkshop on Model-Driven Architecture and Modeling Theory-Driven Development MDA & MTDD 2010, In conjunction with ENASE 2010, Athens, Greece, July 2010* (pp. 23-32). Portugal: SciTePress.

Asnina, E., & Osis, J. (2011). Topological Functioning Model as a CIM-Business Model. In E. Asnina, & J. Osis (Eds.), *Model-Driven Domain Analysis and Software Development: Architectures and Functions* (pp. 40–64). Hershey, PA: IGI Global.

ASTM. (2011). *Abstract Syntax Tree Metamodel, version 1.0, OMG Document Number: formal/2011-01-05*. Retrieved February 7, 2014, from http://www.omg.org/spec/ASTM

Atkinson, C., & Kuhne, T. (2003). Model-driven development: A metamodeling foundation. *IEEE Software*, *20*(5), 36–41. doi:10.1109/MS.2003.1231149

ATL. (2014). *AtlasTransformation Language (ATL) Documentation*. Retrieved February 7, 2014, from http://www.eclipse.org/atl/documentation/

AVANTSSAR Consortium. (2009, July). *ASLan v.2 with static service and policy composition*. Deliverable D2.2.

Baar, T., & Markovic, S. (2007). A graphical approach to prove the semantic preservation of UML/OCL refactoring rules, *Perspectives of Systems Informatics. LNCS*, *4378*, 70–83.

Bagci, F., Schick, H., Petzold, J., Trumler, W., & Ungerer, T. (2005). Communication and security extensions for a ubiquitous mobile agent system (UbiMAS). In *Proceedings of the 2nd Conference on Computing Frontiers (CF'05)* (pp. 246–251). Ischia, Italy: ACM. doi:10.1145/1062261.1062302

Bahl, P., Han, R. Y., Li, L. E., & Satyanarayanan, M. (2012). Advancing the state of mobile cloud computing. MCS '12 In *Proceedings of the third ACM workshop on Mobile cloud computing and services* (pp. 21-28). doi:10.1145/2307849.2307856

Baida, Z., Gordijn, J., Saele, H., Akkermans, H., & Morch, A. (2005). An ontological approach for eliciting and understanding needs in e-services. In O. Pastor & J.F. Cunha (Eds.), *17th Conference on Advanced Information Systems Engineering* (LNCS) (vol. 3520, pp.400-414). Springer-Verlag. doi:10.1007/11431855_28

Bailey, C.H., Bartsch, D., & Kandel, E. (1996). Toward a molecular definition of long-term memory storage. *Proceedings of the National Academy of Sciences of the United States of America*, *93*(24), 13445–13452. doi:10.1073/pnas.93.24.13445 PMID:8942955

Balasubramanian, K., Gokhale, A., Karsai, G., Sztipanovits, J., & Neema, S. (2006). Developing applications using model-driven design environments. *Computer*, *39*(2), 33–40. doi:10.1109/MC.2006.54

Balasubramanian, K., Schmidt, D., Molnar, Z., & Ledeczi, A. (2007). Component-based system integration via (meta) model composition. In*Proceedings of the 14th Annual IEEE International Conference and Workshops on the Engineering of Computer-Based Systems* (pp. 93–102). Los Alamitos, CA: IEEE. doi:10.1109/ECBS.2007.24

Baldauf, M., Dustdar, S., & Rosenberg, F. (2007). A survey on context-aware systems. *International Journal of Ad Hoc and Ubiquitous Computing*, *2*(4), 263–277. doi:10.1504/IJAHUC.2007.014070

Balfe, S., Yau, P., & Paterson, K. G. (2010). A guide to trust in mobile ad hoc networks. *Security and Communication Networks*, *3*(6), 503–516. doi:10.1002/sec.147

Ballagas, R., Borchers, J., Rohs, M., & Sheridan, J. G. (2006). The smart phone: A ubiquitous input device. *IEEE Pervasive Computing / IEEE Computer Society [and] IEEE Communications Society*, *5*(1), 70–77. doi:10.1109/MPRV.2006.18

Ballendat, T., Marquardt, N., & Greenberg, S. (2010). Proxemic interaction: designing for a proximity and orientation-aware environment. In *Proceedings of ACM International Conference on Interactive Tabletops and Surfaces* (pp. 121–130). New York, NY: ACM Press. doi:10.1145/1936652.1936676

Barbier, F., Deltombe, G., Parisy, O., & Youbi, K. (2011). Model Driven Engineering: Increasing Legacy Technology Independence. In *Proceedings ofSecond India Workshop on Reverse Engineering (IWRE, 2011) in The 4th India Software Engineering Conference* (pp. 5-10). Thiruvanantpuram, India: CSI ed.

Barn, B., & Clark, T. (2012) Goal based alignment of enterprise architectures. In *Proceedings of the 7th International Conference on Software Paradigm Trends*, (pp 230-236). SciTePress.

Barthe, G., Beringer, L., Crégut, P., Grégoire, B., Hofmann, M., Müller, P., … Vétillard, E. (2007). MOBIUS: Mobility, ubiquity, security - objectives and progress report. In *Trustworthy Global Computing: Revised Selected Papers from the Second Symposium TGC 2006,* (LNCS), (vol. 4461, pp. 10-29). Springer-Verlag.

Basili, V. R., Caldiera, G., & Rombach, H. D. (1994). The goal question metric paradigm. In Encyclopedia of software engineering. John Wiley.

Basin, D., Mödersheim, S., & Viganò, L. (2005). OFMC: A symbolic model checker for security protocols. *International Journal of Information Security*, *4*(3), 181–208. doi:10.1007/s10207-004-0055-7

Bass, L., Clements, P., & Kazman, R. (1998). *Software architecture in practice*. Reading, MA: Addison-Wesley.

Batory, D. (2006). Multilevel models in model-driven engineering, product lines, and metaprogramming. *IBM Systems Journal*, *45*(3), 527–539. doi:10.1147/sj.453.0527

Beaudouin-Lafon, M. (2000). Instrumental Interaction: An Interaction Model for Designing Post-WIMP Interfaces. In *Proceedings of ACM Human Factors in Computing Systems (CHI)* (pp. 446-453). New York, NY: ACM Press. doi:10.1145/332040.332473

Becker, M., Singh, G., Wenning, B., & Gorg, C. (2007). On mobile agents for autonomous logistics: An analysis of mobile agents considering the fan out and sundry strategies. *International Journal of Services Operations and Informatics*, *2*(2), 114–130. doi:10.1504/IJSOI.2007.014515

Beck, K. (2002). *Test-driven development by example*. Boston: Addison Wesley.

Bellifemine, F. L., Caire, G., & Greenwood, D. (2007). *Developing Multi-Agent Systems with JADE*. New York, NY: John Wiley & Sons, Inc. doi:10.1002/9780470058411

Bergmann, G., Hegedus, A., Horvath, A., Rath, I., Ujhelyi, Z., & Varro, D. (2011). Implementing efficient model validation in EMF tools. In *Proceedings of the 2011 26th IEEE/ACM International Conference on Automated Software Engineering* (pp. 580–583). New York: ACM. doi:10.1109/ASE.2011.6100130

Bertolino, A., De Angelis, G., Di Sandro, A., & Sabetta, A. (2011). Is my model right? Let me ask the expert. *Journal of Systems and Software, 84*(7), 1089–1099. Retrieved October 15, 2012, from10.1016/j.jss.2011.01.054

Bettin, J. (2002). Measuring the potential of domain-specific modeling techniques. In *Proceedings of 17th Annual ACM Conference on Object-Oriented Programming, Systems, Languages, and Applications*. Seattle, WA: ACM.

Bibi, S., Katsaros, D., & Bozanis, P. (2010, June), Application development: fly to the clouds or stay in-house? In*Proceedings of the 19th IEEE International Workshop on Enabling Technologies: Infrastructures for Collaborative Enterprises (WETICE)*, (pp. 60-65). IEEE. doi:10.1109/WETICE.2010.16

Bibi, S., Katsaros, D., & Bozanis, P. (2012). Business application acquisition: On-premise or SaaS-based solutions? *IEEE Software*, *29*(3), 86–93. doi:10.1109/MS.2011.119

Biddle, R., Noble, J., & Tempero, E. (2002). Supporting reusable use cases. In C. Gacek (Ed.), *Proceedings of the 7th International Conference on Software Reuse: Methods, Techniques, and Tools (ICSR-7)* (LNCS), (vol. 2319, pp. 210-226). Springer-Verlag.

Bidoit, M., & Mosses, P. (2004). *CASL User Manual- Introduction to Using the Common Algebraic Specification Language*. Heidelberg, Germany: Springer-Verlag.

Bieberstein, N., Bose, S., Fiammante, M., Jones, K., & Shah, R. (2006). *Service-oriented architecture compass: Business value, planning and enterprise roadmap*. Upper Saddle River, NJ: IBM Press.

Bi, J., & Bennet, K. P. (2003). Regression error characteristics curves. In *Proceedings of the 20th International Conference on Machine Learning (ICML-2003)* (pp. 43-50). ICML.

Birks, D. F., Fernandez, W., Levina, N., & Nasirin, S. (2013). Grounded theory method in information systems research: Its nature, diversity and opportunities. *European Journal of Information Systems*, *22*(1), 1–8. doi:10.1057/ejis.2012.48

Bisbal, J., Lawless, D., Wu, B., & Grimson, J. (1999). *Legacy Information Systems: Issues and Directions. Journal IEEE Software, 16 (5)*, 103–111.

Biswas, S., & Morris, R. (2005). ExOR: Opportunistic multi-hop routing for wireless networks. *Computer Communication Review*, *35*(4), 133–144. doi:10.1145/1090191.1080108

Boehm B. W. (1988, May). Model of software development and enhancement. *IEEE Computer*.

Boehm, B. (1981). *Software engineering economics*. Englewood Cliffs, NJ: Prentice-Hall.

Boehm, B. (1987). A spiral model of software development and enhancement. *Computer*, *20*(9), 61–72.

Boehm, B. (1987). Improving Software Productivity. *Computer*, *20*(9), 43–57. doi:10.1109/MC.1987.1663694

Boerner, R., & Goeken, M. (2009). Identification of business services literature review and lessons learned. In *Proceedings of 15th Americas Conference on Information Systems 2009*. Retrieved February 15, 2014, from http://d-nb.info/103476697X/34#page=28

Borchers, J. O. (2000). *A Pattern Approach to Interaction Design*. New York, NY: John Wiley & Sons.

Borodin, Y., Mahmud, J., & Ramakrishnan, I. V. (2007). Context Browsing with Mobiles - When Less is More. In *Proceedings of the 5th international conference on Mobile systems, applications and services (MobiSys '07)*. ACM. doi:10.1145/1247660.1247665

Boronat, A., Heckel, R., & Meseguer, J. (2009). Rewriting logic semantics and verification of model transformations. *FASE*, *2009*, 18–33.

Bosch, J. (2000). Design & Use of Software Architectures: Adopting and Evolving a Product Line Approach. Pearson Education Limited, .

Bottaro, A., Bourcier, J., Escoffier, C., & Lalanda, P. (2007). Autonomic Context-aware service composition in a home control gateway. In: *Proceedings of IEEE International Conference on Pervasive Services* (pp. 223-231). Istanbul, Turkey: IEEE. doi:10.1109/PERSER.2007.4283920

Boubeta-Puig, J., Ortiz, G., & Medina-Bulo, I. (2014). A model-driven approach for facilitating user-friendly design of complex event patterns. *Expert Systems with Applications*, *41*(2), 445–456. doi:10.1016/j.eswa.2013.07.070

BouncyCastle API. (n.d.). Retrieved June 24, 2009, from http://www.bouncycastle.org/

Bourcier, J., Chazalet, A., Desertot, M., Escofier, C. & Marin, C. (2006). A dynamic-SOA home control gateway. In *Proceedings of IEEE International Conference on Services Computing* (pp. 463–470). Chicago: IEEE.

Brambilla, M., Cabot, J., & Wimmer, M. (2012). *Model-driven Software Engineering in Practice*. San Rafael, CA: Morgan & Claypool Publishers.

Braun, P., & Rossak, W. (2005). *Mobile Agents: Basic Concepts, Mobility Models, and the Tracy Toolkit*. Amsterdam, Netherlands: Morgan Kaufmann.

Bresciani, P., Perini, A., Giorgini, P., Giunchiglia, F., & Mylopoulos, J. (2004). Tropos: An agent-oriented software development methodology. *Autonomous Agents and Multi-Agent Systems*, *8*(3), 203–236. doi:10.1023/B:AGNT.0000018806.20944.ef

Briand, L., El Emam, K., & Morasca, S. (1996). On the application of measurement theory in software engineering. *Journal of Empirical Software Engineering, 1*(1), 61-88.

Briand, L. C., Bunse, C., & Daly, J. W. (2001). A controlled experiments for evaluating quality guidelines on the maintainability of object-oriented design. *IEEE Transactions on Software Engineering*, *27*(6), 513–530. doi:10.1109/32.926174

Briand, L. C., Langley, T., & Wieczorek, I. (2000, June). A replicated assessment and comparison of common software cost modeling techniques. In *Proceedings of the 22nd international conference on Software engineering* (pp. 377-386). ACM. doi:10.1145/337180.337223

Briand, L. C., Morasca, S., & Basili, V. R. (1996). Property based software engineering measurement. *IEEE Transactions on Software Engineering*, *22*(1), 68–86. doi:10.1109/32.481535

Brooks, F. P. (1995). *The mythical man-month, anniversary edition*. Harlow, UK: Addison-Wesley Publishing Company.

Brouwers, N., Corke, P., & Langendoen, K. (2008). Darjeeling, a Java compatible virtual machine for microcontrollers. In *Proceedings of the ACM/IFIP/USENIX Middleware '08 Conference Companion*, (pp. 18–23). New York, NY: ACM. doi:10.1145/1462735.1462740

Brown, A. (2004). Oops! Coping With Human Error in IT. *ACM Queue – System Failures, 2*(8), 34-41.

Brucker, A., & Wolff, B. (2008). *HOL-OCL: A formal proof environment for UML/OCL. In Proceedings of FASE 2008, (LNCS),*(Vol. 4961). Springer.

Bruneliere, H., Cabot, J., & Dupé, G. (2012). How to Deal with your IT Legacy: What is Coming up in MoDisco? *ERCIM NEWS, 88*, 43-44. Retrieved February 7, 2014, from http://ercim-news.ercim.eu/images/stories/EN88/EN88-web.pdf

Bruneton, E., Coupaye, T., Leclercq, M., Quema, V., & Stefani, J.-B. (2004). An open component model and its support in java. In Component-Based Software Engineering, (LNCS) (vol. 3054, pp. 7-22). Springer.

Bruno, R., Conti, M., & Gregori, E. (2005). Mesh networks: Commodity multihop ad hoc networks. *IEEE Communications Magazine, 43*(3), 123–131. doi:10.1109/MCOM.2005.1404606

Bryant, B. B., Lee, B. S., Cao, F., Zhao, W., Burt, C. C., Gray, J., et al. (2003). From Natural Language Requirements to Executable Models of Software Components. In *Proceedings of the Monterey Workshop on Software Engineering for Embedded Systems 2003* (pp. 51-58). Academic Press.

Buchholz, T., Kupper, A., & Schiffers, M. (2003). Quality of context: What is it and why we need it. In *Proceedings of 10th Workshop of the HP OpenView University Association* (OVUA'03). Geneva, Switzerland: OVUA.

Buckley, W. (1967). *Sociology and modern systems theory*. Prentice-Hall.

Budinsky, F., Steinberg, D., & Merks, E. (2009). *EMF: Eclipse Modeling Framework*. Boston: Pearson Education, Inc.

Buonadonna, P., Gay, D., Hellerstein, J. M., Hong, W., & Madden, S. (2005). Task: Sensor network in a box. In *Proceedings of European Workshop on Sensor Networks*, (pp. 133–144). Istanbul, Turkey: Academic Press.

Burd, B. (2011). *Android Application Development All-in-One For Dummies*. John Wiley & Sons.

Bures, T., Hnetynka, P., & Plasil, F. (2006). SOFA 2.0: Balancing advanced features in a hierarchical component model. In *Proceedings SERA* (pp. 40-48). Seattle, WA: IEEE Computer Society.

Buschmann, F., Meunier, R., Rohnert, H., Sommerland, P., & Stal, M. (1996). *Pattern-oriented Software Architecture. A System of Patterns*. John Wiley & Sons.

Bussler, C. (2001). The role of B2B protocols in inter-enterprise process execution. In Technologies for E-Services (pp. 16-29). Springer. doi:10.1007/3-540-44809-8_2

Butcher, T., Fischer, R., Kurpjuweit, S., & Winter, R. (2006). Analysis and application scenarios of enterprise Architecture: An exploratory study. In *Proceedings of 10th IEEE International Enterprise Distributed Object Computing Conference Workshops*. IEEE.

Buttner, F., Cabot, J., & Gogolla, M. (2011). On validation of ATL transformation rules by transformation models. In *Proceedings of MoDeVVa 2011*. MoDeVVa.

Buzzle. (2005a). *Spiral model-A new approach towards software development*. Author.

Buzzle. (2005b). *The waterfall model advantages and disadvantages*. Retrieved from http://www.buzzle.com/editorials/1-5-2005-63768.asp

Byers, D. (2013). *Improving software security by preventing known vulnerabilities*. (Doctoral dissertation). Linköping Studies in Science and Technology, Linköping University, Sweden.

Byers, D., & Shahmehri, N. (2007). Design of a process for software security. In *Proceedings of the Second International Conference on Availability, Reliability and Security* (ARES07). Washington, DC: IEEE Computer Society.

Byers, D., & Shahmehri, N. (2008). A cause-based approach to preventing software vulnerabilities. In S. T. Stefan Jakoubi & E. R. Weippl (Eds.), *Proceedings of the the third international conference on availability, reliability and security* (ARES08) (pp. 276-283). Washington, DC: IEEE Computer Society.

Byers, D., & Shahmehri, N. (2009). Prioritisation and selection of software security activities. In *Proceedings of the fourth international conference on availability, reliability and security* (ARES09) (pp. 201-207). Washington, DC: IEEE Computer Society.

Byers, D., Ardi, S., Shahmehri, N., & Duma, C. (2006). Modeling software vulnerabilities with vulnerability cause graphs. In *Proceedings of the International Conference on Software Maintenance* (ICSM06) (p. 411-422). Washington, DC: IEEE Computer Society.

Byers, D., & Shahmehri, N. (2010). Unified modeling of attacks, vulnerabilities and security activities. In *Proceedings of the 6th international workshop on software engineering for secure systems (SESS10)*. Cape Town, South Africa: IEEE Computer Society. doi:10.1145/1809100.1809106

Byers, D., & Shahmehri, N. (2011). Modeling security goals and software vulnerabilities. In L. Petre, K. Sere, & E. Troubitsyna (Eds.), *Dependability and computer engineering: Concepts for software-intensive systems* (pp. 171–198). IGI Global. doi:10.4018/978-1-60960-747-0.ch009

Cabot, J., Clariso, R., Guerra, E., & De Lara, J. (2010). Verification and Validation of Declarative Model-to-Model Transformations Through Invariants. *Journal of Systems and Software*, *83*(2), 283–302. doi:10.1016/j.jss.2009.08.012

Cabot, J., Clariso, R., & Riera, D. (2007). UMLtoCSP: A tool for the verification of UML/OCL models using constraint programming. *Automated Software Engineering*, *7*, 547–548.

Cabot, J., & Gogolla, M. (2012). Object Constraint Language (OCL): A Definitive Guide. In *Proceedings of the 12th International Conference on Formal Methods for the Design of Computer, Communication, and Software Systems: Formal Methods for Model-Driven Engineering* (pp.58–90). Berlin: Springer-Verlag. doi:10.1007/978-3-642-30982-3_3

Calegari, D., Luna, C., Szasz, N., & Tasistro, L. (2011). *A type-theoretic framework for certified model transformations*, in FM 2011. *LNCS*, *6527*, 112–127.

Calvary, G., Coutaz, J., Thevenin, D., Limbourg, Q., Bouillon, L., & Vanderdonckt, J. (2003). A Unifying Reference Framework for Multi-Target User Interfaces. *Interacting with Computers*, *15*(3), 289–308. doi:10.1016/S0953-5438(03)00010-9

Canfora, G., & Di Penta, M. (2007). New Frontiers of reverse Engineering. In Future of Software Engineering, (pp. 326-341). IEEE Press.

Cano, J., Martinez, N., Seepold, R., & Aguilar, F. L. (2007). Model-driven development of embedded system on heterogeneous platforms. In *Procedings of Forum on Specification and Design Languages* (pp. 243–248). Barcelona, Spain: ECSI.

Cánovas Izquierdo, J., & García Molina, J. (2009a). Model driven architecture - Foundations and applications. In A domain specific language for extracting models in software modernization. (LNCS), (vol. 5562, pp. 82–97). Berlin: Springer-Verlag.

Cánovas Izquierdo, J., & García Molina, J. (2009b). Extracción de modelos en una modernización basada en ADM. *Actas de los Talleres de las Jornadas de Ingeniería de Software y BBDD*, *3*(2), 41-50. Retrieved February 7, 2014, from http://www.sistedes.es/ficheros/actas-talleres-JISBD/Vol-3/No-2/DSDM09.pdf

Capra, L. (2004). Engineering human trust in mobile system collaborations. In *Proceedings of the 12th International Symposium on the Foundations of Software Engineering, SIGSOFT 2004/FSE-12* (pp. 107-116). New York, NY: ACM Press. doi:10.1145/1029894.1029912

Cardei, M., Yang, S., & Wu, J. (2008). Algorithms for fault-tolerant topology in heterogeneous wireless sensor networks. *IEEE Transactions on Parallel and Distributed Systems*, *19*(3).

Carley, K. M., & Gasser, L. (1999). Computational organization theory. In Multiagent systems: A modern approach to distributed artificial intelligence, (pp. 299–330). Academic Press.

Carroll, J. M. (2000). *Making Use: Scenario-Based Design of Human-Computer Interactions*. Cambridge, MA: MIT Press. doi:10.1145/347642.347652

Cartwright, M. H., Shepperd, M. J., & Song, Q. (2003). Dealing with missing software project data.*In Proceedings of the 9th IEEE International Metrics Symposium (METRICS'03)* (pp. 154-165). IEEE. doi:10.1109/METRIC.2003.1232464

Carzaniga, A., Rutherford, M., & Wolf, A. (2004). A routing scheme for content-based networking. In *Proceedings of Twenty-Third Annual Joint Conference of the IEEE Computer and Communications Societies,* (vol. 2, pp. 918-928). Los Alamitos, CA: IEEE.

CASE MDA. (2014). *Committed Companies And Their Products*. Retrieved February 7, 2014, from www.omg.org/mda/committed-products.htm

Castrucci, A., Martinelli, F., Mori, P., & Roperti, F. (2008). Enhancing Java ME Security Support with Resource Usage Monitoring. In *Proceedings of the 10th International Conference on Information and Communications Security (ICICS08), Lecture Notes in Computer Science 5308* (pp. 256-266). Springer Verlag. doi:10.1007/978-3-540-88625-9_17

Cayla, L. (2006). *A white paper for independent software vendors*. Retrieved March 10 2010, from http://www.opsource.net/

Cengarle, M., & Knapp, A. (2009). Interactions. In UML 2 Semantics and Applications. Wiley.

Center for Strategic and International Studies. (2013, July). *The economic impact of cypercrime and cyber espionage*. Retrieved from http://www.mcafee.com/us/resources/reports/rp-economic-impact-cybercrime.pdf

Ceri, S., Gottlob, G., & Tanca, L. (1989). What you always wanted to know about datalog (and never dared to ask. *IEEE Transactions on Knowledge and Data Engineering*, *1*(1), 146–166. doi:10.1109/69.43410

Cervantes, H., & Hall, R. S. (2004). A Framework for Constructing Adaptive Component-Based Applications: Concepts and Experiences. In *7th Symposium on Component-Based Software Engineering* (LNCS), (vol. 3054, pp. 130-137), Berlin: Springer. doi:10.1007/978-3-540-24774-6_13

Chalon, R., & David, B. (2005). IRVO: An Interaction Model for Designing Collaborative Mixed Reality Systems. In *Proceedings of 11th International Conference on Human-Computer Interaction*. London: LEA.

Champalle, O., David, B., Chalon, R., & Masserey, G. (2006). Ordinateur Porté Support de Réalité Augmentée pour des Activités de Maintenance et de Dépannage. In Proceedings of UbiMob, Paris, France.

Chan, Y. E., & Reich, B. H. (2007). IT alignment: What have we learned? *Journal of Information Technology*, *22*(4), 297–315. doi:10.1057/palgrave.jit.2000109

Chen, J., & Hsu, A. (2006). Implementing a banking front end processor in Taiwan using SOA. In *Proceedings ofIEEE International Conference on e-Business Engineering* (pp. 522-527). IEEE. doi:10.1109/ICEBE.2006.61

Cherbakov, L., Galambos, G., Harishankar, R., Kalyana, S., & Rackham, G. (2005). Impact of service orientation at the business level. *IBM Systems Journal*, *44*(4), 653–668. doi:10.1147/sj.444.0653

Cherniavsky, J. C., & Smith, C. H. (1991). On Weyuker's axioms for software complexity measures. *IEEE Transactions on Software Engineering*, *17*(6), 636–638. doi:10.1109/32.87287

Chief, T. (1999, September). Federal Enterprise Architecture Framework. *Architecture,* 80. Retrieved from http://www.cio.gov/documents/fedarch1.pdf

Chihani, B., Bertin, E., & Crespi, N. (2012). Enhancing M2M Communication with Cloud-Based Context Management. In *2012 Sixth International Conference on Next Generation Mobile Applications, Services and Technologies* (pp. 36–41). Paris: IEEE Press. doi:10.1109/NGMAST.2012.17

Chimia-Opoka, J., Felderer, M., Lenz, C., & Lange, C. (2008). Querying UML models using OCL and Prolog: A performance study. *ICSTW, 2008*, 81–88.

Choi, Y. J., Choi, J. G., & Bahk, S. (2007). Upper-level scheduling supporting multimedia traffic in cellular data networks. *Computer Networks*, *51*(3), 621–631. doi:10.1016/j.comnet.2006.05.007

Choppy, C., Hatebur, D., & Heisel, M. (2005). Architectural patterns for problem frames. In *Proceedings - Software,* (pp. 198-208). Washington, DC: IEEE Computer Society.

Choppy, C., Hatebur, D., & Heisel, M. (2006). Component composition through architectural patterns for problem frames. In *Proceedings of the Asia Pacific Software Engineering Conference (APSEC)* (pp. 27-36). Washington, DC: IEEE Computer Society. doi:10.1109/APSEC.2006.27

Chung, C. (2011). *Pro Objective-C Design Patterns for iOS*. Apress. doi:10.1007/978-1-4302-3331-2

Cicchetti, A., Di Ruscio, D., & Di Salle, A. (2007). Software customization in model driven development of web applications. In *Proceedings of the 2007 ACM symposium on Applied computing* (pp. 1025-1030). New York, NY: ACM. doi:10.1145/1244002.1244224

Clark, T., & Barn, B. (2012). A common basis for modelling service-oriented and event-driven architecture. In *Proc of the 5th Annual India Software Engineering Conference, ISEC 2012*. ACM.

Clark, T., & Barn, B. S. (2014). Outsourcing service provision through step-wise transformation. In *Proceedings of the 7th India Software Engineering Conference*. ACM.

Clark, T., Barn, B., & Oussena, S. (2011) LEAP: A Precise Lightweight Framework for Enterprise Architecture. *In Proceedings of the 4th Annual India Software Engineering Conference*. ACM.

Clark, T., Barn, B., & Oussena, S. (2012). A method for enterprise architecture alignment. In *Proceedings of the 4th Working Conference on Practice-Driven Research on Enterprise Transformation,* (pp 48-76). Springer.

Clark, T., Kulkarni, V., Barn, B., France, R., Frank, U., & Turk, D. (2014). Towards the model driven organization. In *Proceedings of47th Hawaii International Conference on System Sciences* (pp 4817-4826). IEEE.

Clarke, E. M., Emerson, E. A., & Sistla, A. P. (1986). Automatic verification of finite-state concurrent systems using temporal logic specifications. *ACM Transactions on Programming Languages and Systems*, *8*(2), 244–263. doi:10.1145/5397.5399

Clark, T., Frank, U., Kulkarni, V., Barn, B., & Turk, D. (2013, July). Domain specific languages for the model driven organization. In *Proceedings of the First Workshop on the Globalization of Domain Specific Languages* (pp. 22-27). ACM. doi:10.1145/2489812.2489818

Clark, T., & Willans, J. (2012). *Software language engineering with XMF and XModeler. In Formal and practical aspects of domain specific languages: Recent developments*. IGI Global.

ClearSy. (2012). Retrieved from http://www.atelierb.eu

Cleary, D. (2000). Web-based development and functional size measurement. In *Proceedings of International Function Point Users Group Annual Conference*. San Diego, CA: Academic Press.

Cloud Computing Congress. (2010). Retrieved March 10, 2010, from http://www.cloudcomputingchina.org/

Coad, P., & Yourdon, E. (1991). *Object oriented analysis* (2nd ed.). Prentice-Hall.

Cockburn, A. (2001). *Agile software development*. Reading, MA: Addison Wesley Longman.

Colby, C., Lee, P., & Necula, G. C. (2000). A Proof-Carrying Code Architecture for Java. In *Proceedings of the 12th International Conference on Computer Aided Verification* (pp. 557-560).

Common Warehouse Metamodel (CWM) Specification Version 1.1. (2003). Retrieved from http://www.omg.org/technology/documents/formal/cwm_2.htm

Conan, D., Rouvoy, R., & Seinturier, L. (2007). Scalable processing of context information with COSMOS. In *7th IFIP International Conference on Distributed Applications and Interoperable Systems* (pp. 210–224). Paphos, Cyprus: Springer. doi:10.1007/978-3-540-72883-2_16

Conficker Working Group. (n.d.). *Conficker infection tracking*. Retrieved from http://www.confickerworkinggroup.org/wiki/pmwiki.php/ANY/InfectionTracking

Connolly, T., & Begg, C. (2005). *Database systems: A practical approach to design, implementation, and management* (4th ed.). New York: Pearson Education, Inc.

Conti, M., Crispo, B., Fernandes, E., & Zhauniarovich, Y. (2012). CRêPE: A System for Enforcing Fine-Grained Context-Related Policies on Android. *IEEE Transactions on Information Forensics and Security*, *7*(5), 1426–1438. doi:10.1109/TIFS.2012.2204249

Conti, M., Nguyen, V. T. N., & Crispo, B. (2010). CRêPE: Context-Related Policy Enforcement for Android. In *Proceedings of the 13 Information Security Conference, ISC10* (pp. 331-345)

Conway, C., & Edwards, S. (2004). NDL: A domain-specific language for device drivers. In *Proceedings of the 2004 ACM SIGPLAN/SIGBED conference on languages, compilers, and tools for embedded systems* (pp. 30–36). New York: ACM. doi:10.1145/997163.997169

Coplien, J. O. (1992). *Advanced C++ programming styles and idioms*. Reading, MA: Addison-Wesley.

Costa, G., Martinelli, F., Mori, P., Schaefer, C., & Walter, T. (2010a). Runtime Monitoring for Next Generation Java ME Platform. *Computers & Security, 29*, 74-87.

Costa, G., Dragoni, N., Lazouski, A., Martinelli, F., Massacci, F., & Matteucci, I. (2010). Extending Security-by-Contract with Quantitative Trust on Mobile Devices. In *Proceedings of the fourth International Conference on Complex, Intelligent and Software Intensive Systems* (pp. 872-877). doi:10.1109/CISIS.2010.33

Côté, I., Hatebur, D., Heisel, M., Schmidt, H., & Wentzlaff, I. (2008). A systematic account of problem frames. In *Proceedings of the European Conference on Pattern Languages of Programs* (EuroPLoP) (pp. 749-767). Universitätsverlag Konstanz.

Couto, D., Aguayo, D., Bicket, J., & Morris, R. (2005). A high-throughput path metric for multi-hop wireless routing. *Wireless Networks*, *11*(4), 419–434. doi:10.1007/s11276-005-1766-z

Cowan, N. (2001). The magical number 4 in short-term memory: A reconsideration of mental storage capacity. *The Behavioral and Brain Sciences*, *24*(1), 87–114. doi:10.1017/S0140525X01003922 PMID:11515286

CRM SaaS Salesforce. (2010). Retrieved March 10, 2010, from http://www.salesforce.com/platform/platform-edition/

CRM SaaS Zoho. (2010). Retrieved March 10, 2010, http://www.zoho.com/

Crnkovic, I., Larsson, & Chaudron. (2006). *Component-based development process and component lifecycle*. A Technical Paper.

Cuccuru, A. (2013). *Papyrus Support for Alf*. Retrieved February 2014, from: http://www.omg.org/news/meetings/tc/agendas/va/xUML_pdf/Cucurru.pdf

Curtis, B., Kellner, M., & Over, J. (1992). Process modeling. *Communications of the ACM*, *35*(9), 75–90. doi:10.1145/130994.130998

Czarnecki, K. (1998). *Generative Programming: Principles and Techniques of Software Engineering Based on Automated Configuration and Fragment-Based Component Models*. (Doctoral dissertation). Technical University of Ilmenau.

Dahlman, E., Parkvall, S., & Skol, J. (2013). *4G: LTE/LTE-Advanced for Mobile Broadband*. Waltham, MA: Academic Press.

Damopoulos, D., Kambourakis, G., & Gritzalis, S. (2011). iSAM: An iPhone Stealth Airborne Malware. In Future Challenges in Security and Privacy for Academia and Industry, IFIP Advances in Information and Communication Technology, 354, 17-28.

Dan, A., Johnson, R., & Arsanjani, A. (2007). Information as a service: Modeling and realization. In *Proceedings of the International Workshop on Systems Development in SOA Environments*. Washington, DC: Academic Press. doi:10.1109/SDSOA.2007.5

Dardenne, A., van Lamsweerde, A., & Fickas, S. (1993). Goal-directed requirements acquisition. *Science of Computer Programming*, *20*(1-2), 3–50. doi:10.1016/0167-6423(93)90021-G

Davenport, T. (1992). *Process innovation: Reengineering work through information technology*. Harvard Business School.

David, B., & Chalon, R. O., Masserey, G., & Imbert, M. (2006). ORCHESTRA: Formalism to Express Mobile Cooperative Applications. Lecture Notes in Computer Science, 4154, 163-178.

David, B., Chalon, R., Vaisman, G., & Delotte, O. (2003). Capillary CSCW. In *Proceedings of HCI International* (vol. 2, pp. 879-883). London: LEA.

David, B., Delotte, O., & Chalon, R. (2005). Model-Driven Engineering of Cooperative Systems. In *Proceedings of 11th International Conference on Human-Computer Interaction*. London: LEA.

David, B., Yin, C., & Chalon, R. (2008). Contextual Mobile Learning for Repairing Industrial Machines: System Architecture and Development Process. In *Proceedings of ICELW*. New York, NY: ICELW. doi:10.3991/ijac.v1i2.559

Davis, J., & Chang, E. (2011a). Variant Logic Meta-data Management for Model Driven Applications Applications - Allows Unlimited End User Configuration and Customisation of All Meta-data EIS Application Features. In *13th International Conference on Enterprise Information Systems* (pp. 395-400). SciTePress.

Davis, J., & Chang, E. (2011c, October). Automatic application update with user customization integration and collision detection for model driven applications. In *Proceedings of the World Congress on Engineering and Computer Science* (pp. 1081-1086). Newswood Limited.

Davis, J., & Chang, E. (2011d). Temporal Meta-data Management for Model Driven Applications - Provides Full Temporal Execution Capabilities throughout the Meta-data EIS Application Lifecycle. In *13th International Conference on Enterprise Information Systems* (pp. 376-379). SciTePress.

Davis, J., Tierney, A., & Chang, E. (2004). Meta Data Framework for Enterprise Information Systems Specification - Aiming to Reduce or Remove the Development Phase for EIS Systems. In *6th International Conference on Enterprise Information Systems* (pp. 451-456). SciTePress.

Davis, J. (2013a). Runtime Integration Capability for Distributed Model-Driven Applications. In V. Díaz, J. Lovelle, B. García-Bustelo, & O. Martínez (Eds.), *Progressions and Innovations in Model-Driven Software Engineering* (pp. 147–180). IGI Global. doi:10.4018/978-1-4666-4217-1.ch005

Davis, J., & Chang, E. (2011b). Lifecycle and generational application of automated updates to MDA based Enterprise Information Systems. In *Proceedings of the Second Symposium on Information and Communication Technology* (pp. 207-216). New York, NY: ACM. doi:10.1145/2069216.2069255

Davis, J., & Chang, E. (2013b). Variant Logic for Model Driven Applications. In V. Díaz, J. Lovelle, B. García-Bustelo, & O. Martínez (Eds.), *Advances and Applications in Model-Driven Software Engineering* (pp. 1–34). IGI Global. doi:10.4018/978-1-4666-4494-6.ch001

Davis, J., Tierney, A., & Chang, E. (2005). Merging Application Models in a MDA Based Runtime Environment for Enterprise Information Systems. In *3rd International Conference on Industrial Informatics, Frontier Technologies for the Future of Industry and Business* (pp. 605-610). Washington, DC, USA: IEEE Computer Society. doi:10.1109/INDIN.2005.1560445

Dawes, S. S., Pardo, T. A., & Cresswell, A. M. (2004). Designing electronic government information access programs: a holistic approach. *Government Information Quarterly*, *21*(1), 3–23. Retrieved from http://www.sciencedirect.com/science/article/B6W4G-4B71BC0-1/2/0ffcef06875aa7c64fdf9b510e62466b

de Alwis, B., & Sillito, J. (2009). Why are software projects moving from centralized to decentralized version control systems? In *Proceedings of the 2009 ICSE Workshop on Cooperative and Human Aspects on Software Engineering* (pp. 36-39). Washington, DC, USA: IEEE Computer Society. doi:10.1109/CHASE.2009.5071408

de Jode, M. (2004). *Programming the Java 2 micro edition for Symbian OS: A developer's guide to MIDP 2.0.* John Wiley & Sons.

Debbabi, M., Saleh, M., Talhi, C., & Zhioua, S. (2005). Security analysis of mobile Java. In *Proceedings of the Sixteenth International Workshop on Database and Expert Systems Applications* (pp. 231- 235). IEEE Computer Society.

Debbabi, M., Saleh, M., Talhi, C., & Zhioua, S. (2005a). Java for Mobile Devices: A Security Study. In *Proceedings of the 21st Annual Computer Security Applications Conference, ACSAC05* (pp. 235-244). IEEE Computer Society. doi:10.1109/CSAC.2005.34

Debbabi, M., Saleh, M., Talhi, C., & Zhioua, S. (2006). Security evaluation of J2ME CLDC embedded Java platform. *Journal of Object Technology*, *5*(2), 125–154. doi:10.5381/jot.2006.5.2.a2

Deissenboeck, F., & Ratiu, D. (2006). A Unified Meta Model for Concept-Based Reverse Engineering. In *Proceedings of 3rd International Workshop on Metamodels, Schemes, Grammars, and Ontologies for Reverse Engineering*. Retrieved September 24, 2012, from http://planet-mde.org/atem2006/atem06Proceedings.pdf

Deissenboeck, F., Juergens, E., Lochmann, K., & Wagner, S. (2009). Software quality models: Purposes, usage scenarios and requirements. In *Proc. Seventh Workshop on Software Quality* (pp. 9–14). IEEE Computer Society. doi:10.1109/WOSQ.2009.5071551

Delomier, F., David, B., Benazeth, C., & Chalon, R. (2012). Situated and colocated Learning Games. In *Proceedings of6th European Conference on Games Based Learning* (pp. 139-151). Sonning Common, UK: Academic Conferences and Publishing International Limited.

Deng, Y. & Wang, J. & Tsai, J. J. P. & Beznosov, K. (2003). An approach for modeling and analysis of security system architectures. *IEEE Transactions on Knowledge and Data Engineering, 15*(5).

Department of Electrical and Electronic Engineering (University of Cagliari). (2012). *SIoT*. Retrieved December 17, 2013, from http://platform.social-iot.org/

Derzsi, Z., Gordijn, J., & Tan, Y. (2008). Towards model-based assessment of business-IT alignment in e-service networks from multiple perspectives. In *Proceedings of 16th European Conference on Information Systems*. Retrieved March 15, 2009, from http://is2.lse.ac.uk/asp/aspecis/20080007.pdf

Desmet, L., Joosen, W., Massacci, F., Naliuka, K., Philippaerts, P., Piessens, F., & Vanoverberghe, D. (2007). A Flexible Security Architecture to Support Third-party Applications on Mobile Devices. In *Proceedings of the 2007 ACM workshop on Computer security architecture* (pp. 19-28). doi:10.1145/1314466.1314470

Desmet, L., Joosen, W., Massacci, F., Naliuka, K., Philippaerts, P., Piessens, F., & Vanoverberghe, D. (2009). The S3MS.NET Run Time Monitor. *Electronic Notes in Theoretical Computer Science*, *253*(5), 153–159. doi:10.1016/j.entcs.2009.11.021

Desmet, L., Joosen, W., Massacci, F., Philippaerts, P., Piessen, F., Siahaan, I., & Vanoverberghe, D. (2008). Security-by-contract on the. NET platform. *Information Security Technical Report*, *13*(1), 25–32. doi:10.1016/j.istr.2008.02.001

Development Models. (n.d.). Retrieved from http://myprojects.kostigoff.net/methodology/development_models/development_models.hm

Dey, A. (2001). Understanding and Using Context. *Personal and Ubiquitous Computing*, *5*(1), 4–7. doi:10.1007/s007790170019

Dey, A. K., & Abowd, G. D. (1999). Towards a Better Understanding of Context and Context-Awareness. In *Proceedings of the 1st international symposium on Handheld and Ubiquitous Computing* (pp. 304–307). London, UK: Springer-Verlag.

Di Lucca, G., Fasolino, A., & De Carlini, U. (2000). Recovering Use Case models from Object-Oriented Code: a Thread-based Approach. In *Proceedings of the Seventh Working Conference on Reverse Engineering (WCRE 2000)*, (pp.108-117). doi:10.1109/WCRE.2000.891458

Digia. (2003). *Programming for the Series 60 Platform and Symbian OS*. John Wiley & Sons.

Dikaiakos, M. D., Katsaros, D., Mehra, P., Pallis, G., & Vakali, A. (2009). Cloud computing: Distributed internet computing for IT and scientific research. *IEEE Internet Computing*, *13*(5), 10–13. doi:10.1109/MIC.2009.103

Dittrich, Y., Vaucouleur, S., & Giff, S. (2009). ERP Customization as Software Engineering: Knowledge Sharing and Cooperation. *IEEE Software*, *26*(6), 41–47. doi:10.1109/MS.2009.173

Donins, U. (2012b). *Topological Unified Modeling Language: Development and Application*. (Doctoral Thesis). RTU, Riga, Latvia.

Donins, U. (2013). *Formal Analysis of Problem Domain Workflows. Databases and Information Systems VII: Selected Papers from the Tenth International Baltic Conference (DB&IS 2012): Tenth International Baltic Conference on Databases and Information Systems (Baltic DB&IS 2012), Lithuania, Vilnius, July 8-11, 2012* (pp. 135-148). Amsterdam: IOS Press.

Donins, U., & Osis, J. (2011). Topological Modeling for Enterprise Data Synchronization System: A Case Study of Topological Model-Driven Software Development. In *Proceedings of the 13th International Conference on Enterprise* (vol. 3, pp. 87-96). Beijing, China: SciTePress.

Donins, U. (2012a). Semantics of Logical Relations in Topological Functioning Model. In *Proceedings of the 7th International Conference on Evaluation of Novel Approaches to Software Engineering (ENASE 2012)*, (pp. 217-223). ENASE.

Dragoni, N., Martinelli, F., Massacci, F., Mori, P., Schaefer, C., Walter, T., & Vetillard, E. (2008). Security-by-Contract (SxC) for Software and Services of Mobile Systems. In At your service: Service Engineering in the Information Society Technologies Program (pp. 429-455). MIT Press.

Dragoni, N., Massacci, F., Naliuka, K., & Siahaan, I. (2007). Security-by-Contract: Toward a Semantics for Digital Signatures on Mobile Code. In Proceedings of Public Key Infrastructure, Theory and Practice (pp. 297-312). Academic Press.

Dragoni, N., Massacci, F., Naliuka, K., & Siahaan, I. (2007). Security-by-contract: Toward a semantics for digital signatures on mobile code. *Lecture Notes in Computer Science*, *4582*, 297–312. doi:10.1007/978-3-540-73408-6_21

Draijer, C., & Schenk, D. (2004). Best practices of business simulation with SAP R/3. *Journal of Information Systems Education*, *15*(3), 261. Retrieved from http://findarticles.com/p/articles/mi_qa4041/is_200410/ai_n9464918/pg_5/

Dreslinski, R., Wieckowski, M., Blaauw, D., Sylvester, D., & Mudge, T. (2010). Near-Threshold Computing: Reclaiming Moore's Law Through Energy Efficient Integrated Circuits. *Proceedings of the IEEE*, *98*(2), 253–266. doi:10.1109/JPROC.2009.2034764

Dubielewicz, I., Hnatkowska, B., Huzar, Z., & Tuzinkiewicz, L. (2006). Feasibility analysis of MDA-based database design. In ZamojskiW. (Ed.), *Proceedings of International Conference on Dependability of Computer Systems. DepCoS – RELCOMEX* (pp. 19–26). Los Alamitos, CA: IEEE Computer Society Press.

Dubielewicz, I., Hnatkowska, B., Huzar, Z., & Tuzinkiewicz, L. (2011). Quality-driven database system development. In J. Osis, & E. Asnina (Eds.), *Model-driven domain analysis and software development: Architectures and functions* (pp. 201–231). Hershey, PA: Information Science Reference.

Dutta, P., Hui, J., Chu, D., & Culler, D. (2006). Securing the deluge network programming system. In *Proceedings of the 5th International Conference on Information Processing in Sensor Networks* (pp. 326–333). Nashville, TN: ACM doi:10.1109/IPSN.2006.243821

Ebert, J., Riediger, V., & Winter, A. (2008). Graph Technology In Reverse Engineering, The TGraph Approach. In *Proceedings of10th Workshop Software Reengineering (WSR 2008)* (LNI) (vol. 216, pp. 67-81). Bonn: Springer.

Economics, C. (2002, September). *Malicious code attacks had $13.2 billion economic impact in 2001*. Retrieved from http://www.computereconomics.com/article.cfm?id=133

Economics, C. (2003, August). *August 2003 – worst virus season ever?* Retrieved from http://www.computereconomics.com/article.cfm?id=867

Eder, J., & Liebhart, W. (1996). Workflow Transactions. In *Workflow Handbook 1997* (pp. 195–202). John Wiley & Sons, Inc. Retrieved from http://citeseerx.ist.psu.edu/viewdoc/summary?doi=10.1.1.21.7110

Egea, M., & Rusu, V. (2010). Formal executable semantics for conformance in the MDE framework. *Innovations in System Software Engineering*, *6*(1-2), 73–81. doi:10.1007/s11334-009-0108-1

Ekstedt, M., Johnson, P., Lindstrom, A., Gammelgard, M., Johansson, E., & Plazaola, L. et al. (2004). Consistent enterprise software system architecture for the CIO - A utility-cost based approach. In *Proceedings of the 37th Annual Hawaii International Conference on System Sciences*. IEEE. doi:10.1109/HICSS.2004.1265519

El Emam, K., & Birk, A. (2000). Validating the ISO/IEC 15504 measure of software requirements analysis process capability. *IEEE Transactions on Software Engineering*, *26*(6), 541–566. doi:10.1109/32.852742

Ellis, C., Gibbs, S. J., & Rein, G. L. (1991). Groupware: Some Issues and Experiences. *Communications of the ACM*, *34*(1), 39–58. doi:10.1145/99977.99987

Ellis, C., & Wainer, J. (1994). A Conceptual Model of Groupware. In *Proceedings of CSCW* (pp. 79-88). New York, NY: ACM Press.

Elmasri, R., & Navathe, S. B. (2007). *Fundamentals of database systems (5th ed.)*. New York: Pearson Education, Inc.

Endrei, M., Ang, J., Arsanjani, A., Chua, S., Comte, P., & Krogdahl, P. et al. (2004). *Patterns: Service-oriented architecture and web services*. IBM Press.

Engelsman, W., Quartel, D., Jonkers, H., & van Sinderen, M. (2011). Extending enterprise architecture modelling with business goals and requirements. *Journal of Enterprise Information Systems*, *5*(1), 9–36. doi:10.1080/17517575.2010.491871

Erlingsson, U. (2004). *The inlined reference monitor approach to security policy enforcement.* (PhD thesis). Cornell University, Ithaca, NY.

Ernst, M., Matthes, F., Ramacher, R., & Schweda, C. (2009). Using enterprise architecture management patterns to complement TOGAF. In *Proceedings of the Enterprise Distributed Object Computing Conference*. IEEE.

Escofier, C., & Hall, R. S. (2007). Dynamically Adaptable Applications with iPOJO Service Components. In *Proc. 6th Conference on Software Composition*, (LNCS) (vol. 4829, pp. 113-128). Berlin: Springer. doi:10.1007/978-3-540-77351-1_9

Estrada, H., Morales-Ramírez, I., Martínez, A., & Pastor, O. (2010). From business services to web services: An MDA approach. In J. Castro, X. Franch, & J. Mylopoulos (Eds.), *Fourth International iStar Workshop*, (vol. 586, pp. 31-35). CEUR.

Etherios. (2008). *Etherios*. Retrieved February 21, 2014, from http://www.etherios.com/

European Parliament and the Council of the European Union. (1995). DIRECTIVE 95/46/EC of the European parliament and of the council of 24 October 1995 on the protection of individuals with regard to the processing of personal data and on the free movement of such data. *Official Journal of the European Communities*, (L 281), 31–39.

EVRYTHNG. (2012). *EVRYTHNG*. Retrieved February 21, 2014, from https://www.evrythng.com/

Exosite. (2013). *Exosite*. Retrieved February 21, 2014, from http://exosite.com/

Fabian, B., Gürses, S., Heisel, M., Santen, T., & Schmidt, H. (2010). A comparison of security requirements engineering methods. *Requirements Engineering*, *15*(1), 7–40. doi:10.1007/s00766-009-0092-x

Fabra, J., Pe, J., Ruiz-Cort, A., & Ezpeleta, J. (2008). Enabling the Evolution of Service-Oriented Solutions Using an UML2 Profile and a Reference Petri Nets Execution Platform. In *Proceedings of the 3rd International Conference on Internet and Web Applications and Services*. (pp. 198-204). Washington, DC, USA: IEEE Computer Society. doi:10.1109/ICIW.2008.63

Fairley, R., & Willshire, M. J. (2011). Teaching software engineering to undergraduate system engineering students. In *Proceedings of the 24th IEEE-CS Conference on Software Engineering Education and Training* (CSEE&T 2011) (pp. 219-226). Honolulu, HI: IEEE.

Fais, D., Colombo, M., & Lazouski, A. (2009). An Implementation of Role-Base Trust Management Extended with Weights on Mobile Devices. *Electronic Notes in Theoretical Computer Science*, *244*, 53–65. doi:10.1016/j.entcs.2009.07.038

Falvo, M. C., Lamedica, R., & Ruvio, A. (2012). An environmental sustainable transport system: A trolley-buses Line for Cosenza city. In *Proceedings ofInternational Symposium on Power Electronics Power Electronics, Electrical Drives, Automation and Motion* (pp. 1479–1485). IEEE. doi:10.1109/SPEEDAM.2012.6264625

Favre, L. (2009). Reliable Software Technologies. In A Formal Foundation for Metamodeling (LNCS), (vol. 5570, pp. 177–191). Heidelberg, Germany: Springer-Verlag. doi:10.1007/978-3-642-01924-1_13

Favre, L., Martinez, L., & Pereira, C. (2009). MDA-Based Reverse Engineering of Object-Oriented Code. In *Proceedings EMMSAD 2009*, (LNBIP), (*Vol. 29*, pp. 251-263). Springer-Verlag.

Favre, L. (2006). A Rigorous Framework for Model Driven Development. In K. Siau (Ed.), *Advanced Topics in Database Research* (Vol. 5, pp. 1–27). Hershey, PA: Idea Group Publishing. doi:10.4018/978-1-59140-935-9.ch001

Favre, L. (2010). *Model Driven Architecture for Reverse Engineering Technologies: Strategic Directions and System Evolution*. IGI Global. doi:10.4018/978-1-61520-649-0

Favre, L., Pereira, C., & Martinez, L. (2009). Foundations for MDA CASE Tools. In M. Khosrow-Pour (Ed.), *Encyclopedia of Information Science and Technology* (2nd ed., pp. 159–166). Hershey, PA: IGI Global.

Feiler, P. H., Sullivan, K., Wallnau, K. C., Gabriel, R. P., Goodenough, J. B., Linger, R. C., & Schmidt, D. (2006). *Ultra-large-scale systems: The software challenge of future*. Pittsburgh, PA: Software Engineering Institute, Carnegie Mellon University.

Fellbaum, C. (Ed.). (1998). *WordNet: An electronic lexical database*. MIT Press.

Felt, A. P., Finifter, M., Chin, E., Hanna, S., & Wagner, D. (2011). A Survey of Mobile Malware in the Wild. In *Proceedings of of the 1st ACM Workshop on Security and Privacy in Smartphones and Mobile Devices* (pp. 3-14). ACM. doi:10.1145/2046614.2046618

Fenton, N. (1994). Software measurement: A necessary scientific basis. *IEEE Transactions on Software Engineering*, *20*(3), 199–206. doi:10.1109/32.268921

Fenton, N. (1997). *Software metrics a rigorous and practical approach*. Boston: PWS Publishing Company.

Ferber, J. (1999). *Multi-agent systems: an introduction to distributed artificial intelligence*. London, UK: Addison-Wesley.

Fernandez, E. B., la Red, M. D. L., Forneron, J. Uribe, V. E., & Rodriguez, G. G. (2007). A secure analysis pattern for handling legal cases. In *Proceedings of Latin America Conference on Pattern Languages of Programming*. Retrieved June 24, 2009, from http://sugarloafplop.dsc.upe.br/wwD.zip

Fisler, K., Krishnamurthi, S., Meyerovich, L. A., & Tschantz, M. C. (2005). Verification and change-impact analysis of access-control policies. In *Proceedings of the 27th international conference on software engineering* (pp. 196-205). New York: ACM.

Fleurey, F., Breton, E., Baudry, B., Nicolas, A., & Jézéquel, J. (2007). Model-Driven Engineering for Software Migration in a Large Industrial Context. In G. Engels, B. Opdyke, D. C. Schmidt, & F. Weil (Eds.), MoDELS 2007 (LNCS), (vol. 4735, pp. 482–497). Springer-Verlag. doi:10.1007/978-3-540-75209-7_33

Flick, U. (1998). *An introduction to qualitative research*. London: Sage.

Foley, J. D., Wallace, V. L., & Chan, P. (1984). The Human Factors of Computer Graphics Interaction Techniques. *IEEE Computer Graphics and Applications*, *4*(11), 13–48. doi:10.1109/MCG.1984.6429355

Foss, T., Stensrud, E., Kitchenham, B., & Myrtveit, I. (2003). A simulation study of the model evaluation criterion MMRE. *IEEE Transactions on Software Engineering*, *29*(11), 985–995. doi:10.1109/TSE.2003.1245300

Fountain, J. E. (2001). Building the virtual state: Information technology and institutional change. *Information Systems Research*, *7*, xii. Retrieved from http://isr.journal.informs.org/cgi/content/abstract/7/1/22

Fowler, M. (2005). *The new methodology*. Retrieved from http://martinfowler.com/articles/newMethodology.html

Fowler, M. (2003). *Patterns of enterprise application architecture*. Addison-Wesley.

Fowler, M. (2010). Domain specific languages. *International Journal of Computer Applications IJCA*, *1*, 39–60.

Fox, M. S. (1992). The TOVE project: Towards a common-sense model of the enterprise. *Enterprise Integration Laboratory Technical Report*. Retrieved May 2, 2009, from http://www.eil.utoronto.ca/enterprise-modelling/papers/fox-tove-uofttr92.pdf

Fragkaki, E., Bauer, L., Jia, L., & Swasey, D. (2012). Modeling and enhancing android's permission system. In *Proceedings of ESORICS 2012,* (LNCS), (vol. 7459, pp. 1-18). Springer-Verlag. doi:10.1007/978-3-642-33167-1_1

Framework, E. (n.d.). Retrieved February 26, 2014, from http://echo.nextapp.com/

France, R., & Rumpe, B. (2007). Model-driven Development of Complex Software: A Research Roadmap. In *Future of Software Engineering* (pp. 37–54). Washington, DC, USA: IEEE Computer Society. doi:10.1109/FOSE.2007.14

Frank, K., Robertson, R., Mcburney, S., Kalatzis, N., Roussaki, I., & Marengo, M. (2009). A Hybrid Preference Learning and Context Refinement Architecture. In *Proceedings ofWorkshop on Intelligent Pervasive Environments* (pp. 6-9). Edinburgh, UK: SSAISB.

Frank, U. (2012). Multi-perspective enterprise modeling: Foundational concepts, prospects and future research challenges. *Software & Systems Modeling*, 1–22.

Fritscher, B., & Pigneur, Y. (2011). Business IT alignment from business model to enterprise architecture. In C. Salinesi, & O. Pastor (Eds.), *Advanced information systems engineering workshops (LNBIP)*(Vol. 83, pp. 4–15). Springer. doi:10.1007/978-3-642-22056-2_2

Frohlich, N., Moller, T., Rose, S., & Schuldt, H. (2010). A benchmark for context data management in mobile context aware applications. In *Proceedings of the4th International Workshop on Personalized Access, Profile Management, and Context Awareness in Databases* (PersDB2010). Singapore: Academic Press.

Fundación Telefónica. (2014). La sociedad de la información en españa 2013. Author.

Gailly, F., & Poels, G. (2009) Using the REA ontology to create interoperability between e-collaboration modeling standards. In *Proc. of 21st International Conference on Advanced Information Systems Engineering* (CAiSE 09), (LNCS), (vol. 5565, pp. 395-409). Springer-Verlag. doi:10.1007/978-3-642-02144-2_32

Gailly, F., España, S., Poels, G., & Pastor, O. (2008). Integrating business domain ontologies with early requirements modelling. Lecture Notes in Computer Science, 5232, 282-291.

Galal, G. H., & Paul, R. J. (1999). A qualitative scenario approach to managing evolving requirements. *Requirements Engineering*, *4*(2), 92–102. doi:10.1007/s007660050016

Gamma, E., Helm, R., Johnson, R. E., & Vlissides, J. (1995). *Design patterns - elements of reusable object-oriented software*. Reading, MA: Addison Wesley.

Gamma, E., Helm, R., Johnson, R., & Vlissides, J. (1995). *Design patterns: Elements of reusable object-oriented software*. Addison-Wesley.

Gamma, E., Helm, R., Johnson, R., & Vlissides, J. (1995). *Design Patterns: Elements of Reusable Object-Oriented Software*. Upper Saddle River, NJ: Addison-Wesley.

Ganzha, M., Paprzycki, M., & Omicini, A. (2013). *Software Agents: Twenty Years and Counting*. IEEE Computing Now. Retrieved March 10, 2014 from http://www.computer.org/portal/web/computingnow/archive/november2013

García, F., Serrano, M., Cruz-Lemus, J., Ruiz, F., & Piattini, M. (2007). Managing software process measurement: A metamodel-based approach. *Information Sciences*, *177*(12), 2570–2586. doi:10.1016/j.ins.2007.01.018

Garcia-Crespo, A., Ruiz-Mezcua, B., Lopez-Cuadrado, J. L., & Gonzalez-Carrasco, I. (2011). Semantic model for knowledge representation in e-business. *Knowledge-Based Systems*, *24*(2), 282–296. doi:10.1016/j.knosys.2010.09.006

Gartner Inc. (2013). *Gartner Says Smartphone Sales Accounted for 55 Percent of Overall Mobile Phone Sales in Third Quarter of 2013*. Retrieved from http://www.gartner.com/newsroom/id/2623415

Garvin, D. A. (1984). What does "product quality" really mean? MIT Sloan Management Review, 26(1), 25–43.

Gaynor, M., & Bradner, S. (2004). A real options framework to value network, protocol, and service architecture. *SIGCOMM Comput. Commun.*, *34*(5), 31–38. doi:10.1145/1039111.1039121

Geerts, G., & McCarthy, W. E. (1999). *An accounting object infrastructure for knowledge-based enterprise models*. IEEE Intelligent Systems & Their Applications.

Genero, M., Piattini, M., Abrahao, S., Insfran, E., Carsi, J., & Ramos, I. (2007). A controlled experiment for selecting transformations based on quality attributes in the context of MDA. In *Proceedings ofFirst International Symposium on Empirical Software Engineering and Measurement* (pp. 498-498). Los Alamitos, CA: IEEE. doi:10.1109/ESEM.2007.64

Georgitzikis, V., Akribopoulos, O., & Chatzigiannakis, I. (2012). Controlling physical objects via the internet using the arduino platform over 802.15.4 networks. *IEEE Transactions on Latin America, 10*, 1686–1689. doi:10.1109/TLA.2012.6222571

Gilb, T. (2006). *Estimation or control? – Thesenpapier*. Retrieved from http://www.dasma.org/

Gilgarcia, J., & Pardo, T. (2005). E-government success factors: Mapping practical tools to theoretical foundations. *Government Information Quarterly, 22*(2), 187–216. Retrieved July 3, 2011, from http://linkinghub.elsevier.com/retrieve/pii/S0740624X05000158

Gogolla, M., Bohling, J., & Richters, M. (2005). Validating UML and OCL models in USE by automatic snapshot generation. *Software & Systems Modeling*, *4*(4), 386–398. doi:10.1007/s10270-005-0089-y

Gokhale, S., & Dasgupta, P. (2003). Distributed authentication for peer-to-peer networks. In *Proceedings of the 2003 Symposium on Applications and the Internet Workshops* (p. 347). Washington, DC: IEEE Computer Society. doi:10.1109/SAINTW.2003.1210184

González García, C., Pelayo G-Bustelo, B. C., Pascual Espada, J., & Cueva-Fernandez, G. (2014). Midgar: Generation of heterogeneous objects interconnecting applications: A domain specific language proposal for internet of things scenarios. *Computer Networks*, *64*(C), 143–158. doi:10.1016/j.comnet.2014.02.010

Google. (n.d.). *Android developers guide*. Retrieved from http://developer.android.com/guide/index.html

Gordijn, J., Akkermans, J. M., & van Vliet, J. C. (2000). Business modeling is not process modeling. In G. Goos, J. Hartmanis & van J. Leeeuwen (Eds.), Conceptual Modeling for e-Business and the Web (LNCS), (vol. 1921, pp. 40-51). Springer-Verlag.

Gordijn, J. (2004). E-business modeling using the e3 value ontology. In W. Curry (Ed.), *E-business model ontologies* (pp. 98–127). Elsevier Butterworth-Heinemann. doi:10.1016/B978-075066140-9/50007-2

Gordijn, J., van Eck, P., & Wieringa, R. (2008). Requirements engineering techniques for e-services. In D. Georgakopoulos, & M. P. Papazoglou (Eds.), *Service-oriented computing: cooperative information systems series* (pp. 331–352). Cambridge, MA: The MIT Press.

Gorman, B. L., Resseguie, D. R., & Tomkins-Tinch, C. (2009). Sensorpedia: Information sharing across incompatible sensor systems. In *Proceedings of2009 International Symposium on Collaborative Technologies and Systems*, (pp. 448–454). Academic Press. doi:10.1109/CTS.2009.5067513

Gortmaker, J., Janssen, M., & Wagenaar, R. W. (2005). Towards requirements for a reference model for process orchestration in e-government. In M. Böhlen, J. Gamper, W. Polasek, & M. A. Wimmer (Eds.), *EGovernment towards electronic democracy* (Vol. 3416, pp. 169–180). Springer. Retrieved from http://springerlink.metapress.com/(hgp11niu3o1t4b552xj3zy55)/app/home/contribution.asp?referrer=parent&backto=issue,16,28;journal,526,3824;linkingpublicationresults,1:105633,1

Grandon, E., & Pearson, M. (2004). Electronic commerce adoption: An empirical study of small and medium US businesses. *Information & Management*, *42*(1), 197–216. doi:10.1016/j.im.2003.12.010

Gray, J. (2003, March). *Distributed computing economics* (Technical Report MSR-TR-2003-24). Microsoft Research.

Greenberg, S., Marquardt, N., Ballendat, T., Diaz-Marino, R., & Wang, M. (2011). Proxemic interactions. *Interaction*, *18*(1), 42–50. doi:10.1145/1897239.1897250

Grisogono, A.-M. (1999). *What those killer kangaroos really fired*. Defense Systems Daily.

Gronback, R. (2009). *Eclipse Modeling Project: A Domain-Specific Language (Dsl) Toolkit*. Boston: Pearson Education, Inc.

Grusec, J. E., & Hastings, P. D. (2007). *Handbook of Socialization: Theory and Research*. New York: Guilford Press.

GSMA Intelligence. (2014). *Industry custom report: The mobile economy*. Retrieved February 20, from http://www.gsmamobileeconomy.com/GSMA_ME_Report_2014_R2_WEB.pdf

Gu, H., & Wang, D. (2009). A content-aware fridge based on RFID in smart home for home-healthcare. In *Proceedings of Advanced Communication Technology*, (Vol. 2, pp. 987–990). Phoenix Park.

Guerra, E., de Lara, J., Kolovos, D., Paige, R., & Marchi dos Santos, O. (2010). transML: A family of languages to model model transformations. In Proceedings of MODELS 2010 (LNCS), (vol. 6394). Springer-Verlag.

Guide to the Software Engineering Body of Knowledge (SWEBOK). (2004). Retrieved from http://www.computer.org/portal/web/swebok/about

Gull, H., Azam, F., Haider, W. B., & Iqbal, S. Z. (2009). A New Divide & Conquer Software Process Model World Academy of Science. *Engineering and Technology*, *60*, 255–260.

Gupta, M. (2003). E-government evaluation: A framework and case study. *Government Information Quarterly*, *20*(4), 365–387. Retrieved July 11, 2011, from http://linkinghub.elsevier.com/retrieve/pii/S0740624X03000790

Gürses, S., Jahnke, J. H., Obry, C., Onabajo, A., Santen, T., & Price, M. (2005). Eliciting confidentiality requirements in practice.*InProceedings of the Conference of the Centre for Advanced Studies on Collaborative Research (CASCON)*, (pp. 101-116). New York: IBM Press.

Gu, T., Pung, H. K., & Zhang, D. Q. (2005). A service-oriented middleware for building context-aware services. *Journal of Network and Computer Applications*, *28*(1), 1–18. doi:10.1016/j.jnca.2004.06.002

Guttman, M., & Parodi, J. (2007). *Real-life MDA: solving business problems with model driven architecture*. New York: Morgan Kaufmann Publishers.

Hagen, C., & Brouwers, G. (1994). Reducing Software Life-Cycle Costs by Developing Configurable Software. In *Proceedings of the Aerospace and Electronics Conference*, Vol 2 (pp. 1182-1187). Washington, DC, USA: IEEE Press. doi:10.1109/NAECON.1994.332908

Hailpern, B., & Tarr, P. (2006). Model-driven development: The good, the bad, and the ugly. *IBM Systems Journal*, *45*(3), 451–461. doi:10.1147/sj.453.0451

Halchin, L. E. (2004). Electronic government: Government capability and terrorist resource. *Government Information Quarterly*, *21*(4), 406–419. doi:10.1016/j.giq.2004.08.002

Haley, C. B., Laney, R., Moffett, J., & Nuseibeh, B. (2004). Picking battles: The impact of trust assumptions on the elaboration of security requirements. In C. D. Jensen & S. Poslad & T. Dimitrakos (Eds.), *Proceedings of the International Conference on Trust Management* (iTrust) (LNCS) (vol. 2995, pp. 347-354). Berlin: Springer.

Haley, C. B., Laney, R., Moffett, J., & Nuseibeh, B. (2008). Security requirements engineering: A framework for representation and analysis. IEEE Transactions on Software Engineering, 34(1).

Halkidis, S. T., Tsantalis, N., Chatzigeorgiou, A., & Stephanides, G. (2008). Architectural risk analysis of software systems based on security patterns. IEEE Transactions on Dependable and Secure Computing, 5(3).

Halle von, B. (2001). *Business rules applied: Building better systems using the business rules approach*. Willey Publ.

Hall, J. G., Jackson, M., Laney, R. C., Nuseibeh, B., & Rapanotti, L. (2002). Relating software requirements and architectures using problem frames. In *Proceedings of IEEE International Requirements Engineering Conference (RE)*, (pp. 137-144). Washington, DC: IEEE Computer Society. doi:10.1109/ICRE.2002.1048516

Halpin, T., & Morgan, T. (2008). *Information modelling and relational databases* (2nd ed.). Burlington, MA: Morgan Kaufman Publisher.

Han, C., Jornet, J. M., Fadel, E., & Akyildiz, I. F. (2013). A cross-layer communication module for the Internet of Things. *Computer Networks*, *57*(3), 622–633. doi:10.1016/j.comnet.2012.10.003

Hansmann, U., Merk, L., Nicklous, M. S., & Stober, T. (2003). *Pervasive Computing: The Mobile World*. New York: Springer Professional Computing.

Hao, C., Lei, X., & Yan, Z. (2012). The application and Implementation research of Smart City in China. In *Proceedings of System Science and Engineering (ICSSE)*, (pp. 288–292). ICSSE. doi:10.1109/ICSSE.2012.6257192

Harel, D., & Rumpe, B. (2004). Meaningful modeling: What's the semantics of "semantics"? *Computer*, *37*(10), 64–72. doi:10.1109/MC.2004.172

Harikumar, A. K., Lee, R., Hae Sool, Y., Haeng-Kon, K., & Byeongdo, K. (2005). *A model for application integration using web services*. Paper presented at the Computer and Information Science, 2005. New York, NY. doi:10.1109/ICIS.2005.12

Harrison, C., Benko, H., & Wilson, A. D. (2011). OmniTouch: wearable multitouch interaction everywhere. In *Proceedings of the 24th Annual ACM Symposium on User Interface Software and Technology* (pp. 441–450). New York, NY: ACM Press.

Harrison, C., & Hudson, S. E. (2010). Minput: enabling interaction on small mobile devices with high-precision, low-cost, multipoint optical tracking. In *Proceedings of the 28th International Conference on Human Factors in Computing Systems* (pp. 1661–1664). New York, NY: ACM Press. doi:10.1145/1753326.1753574

Harrison, C., Schwarz, J., & Hudson, S. E. (2011). Tapsense: enhancing finger interaction on touch surfaces. In *Proceedings of the 24th Annual ACM Symposium on User Interface Software and Technology* (pp. 627–636). New York, NY: ACM Press. doi:10.1145/2047196.2047279

Harrison, C., Tan, D., & Morris, D. (2010). Skinput: appropriating the body as an input surface. In *Proceedings of the 28th International Conference on Human Factors in Computing Systems* (pp. 453–462). New York, NY: ACM Press. doi:10.1145/1753326.1753394

Harsu, M. (2002). *A survey on domain engineering (No. Report 31)*. Institute of Software Systems, Tampere University of Technology.

Hartenstein, H., & Laberteaux, K. P. (2008). A Tutorial Survey on Vehicular Ad Hoc Networks. *IEEE Communications Magazine*, *46*(6), 164–171. doi:10.1109/MCOM.2008.4539481

Haseman, C. (2008). *Android Essentials*. New York, NY: Apress, Inc. doi:10.1007/978-1-4302-1063-4

Hassanein, H., & Luo, J. (2006). Reliable energy aware routing in wireless sensor networks. In *Proceedings of the Second IEEE Workshop on Dependability and Security in Sensor Networks and Systems*, (pp. 54-64). Washington, DC: IEEE Computer Society.

Hästbacka, D., Vepsäläinen, T., & Kuikka, S. (2011). Model-driven development of industrial process control applications. *Journal of Systems and Software*, *84*(7), 1100–1113. doi:10.1016/j.jss.2011.01.063

Hatebur, D., & Heisel, M. (2005). Problem frames and architectures for security problems. In B. A. Gran & R. Winter & G. Dahll (Ed.), *Proceedings of the International Conference on Computer Safety, Reliability and Security (SAFECOMP)* (LNCS) (vol. 3688, pp. 390-404). Berlin: Springer. doi:10.1007/11563228_30

Hatebur, D., Heisel, M., & Schmidt, H. (2006). Security engineering using problem frames. In G. Müller (Ed.), *Proceedings of the International Conference on Emerging Trends in Information and Communication Security (ET-RICS)* (LNCS) (vol. 3995, pp. 238-253). Berlin: Springer. doi:10.1007/11766155_17

Hatebur, D., Heisel, M., & Schmidt, H. (2007). A pattern system for security requirements engineering. In *Proceedings of the International Conference on Availability, Reliability and Security (AReS)* (pp. 356-365). Washington, DC: IEEE Computer Society.

Hatebur, D., Heisel, M., & Schmidt, H. (2008a). A formal metamodel for problem frames. In *Proceedings of the International Conference on Model Driven Engineering Languages and Systems (MODELS)* (LNCS) (vol. 5301, pp. 68–82). Berlin: Springer. doi:10.1007/978-3-540-87875-9_5

Hatebur, D., Heisel, M., & Schmidt, H. (2008b). Analysis and component-based realization of security requirements. In *Proceedings of the International Conference on Availability, Reliability and Security (AReS)* (pp. 195–203). IEEE Computer Society.

Ha, Y., & Rolland, J. (2002). Optical assessment of head-mounted displays in visual space. *Applied Optics*, *41*(25), 5282–5289. doi:10.1364/AO.41.005282 PMID:12211555

Hegedus, A., Horvath, A., Rath, I., Ujhelyi, Z., & Varro, D. (2011). Implementing efficient Model Validation in EMF Tools. Academic Press.

Heinzelman, W. B., Murphy, A. L., Carvalho, H. S., & Perillo, M. A. (2004). Middleware to support sensor network applications. *IEEE Network*, *18*(1), 6–14. doi:10.1109/MNET.2004.1265828

Heisel, M. (1998). Agendas - A concept to guide software development activities. In *Proceedings of the IFIP TC2 WG2.4 working Conference on Systems Implementation: Languages, Methods and Tools* (pp. 19-32). London: Chapman & Hall.

Henderson, P., & Walters, R. J. (1999). System Design Validation Using Formal Models. In *Proceedings of10th IEEE International Workshop in Rapid System Prototyping* (pp. 10-14), Clearwater, FL: IEEE Computer Society.

Henderson, J. C., & Venkatraman, N. (1993). Strategic alignment: Leveraging information technology for transforming organizations. *IBM Systems Journal*, *32*(1), 4–16. doi:10.1147/sj.382.0472

Henderson-Sellers, B. (1996). *Object-oriented metrics: Measures of complexity*. Prentice-Hall.

Henderson-Sellers, B., Clark, T., & Gonzalez-Perez, C. (2013, January). On the search for a level-agnostic modelling language. In *Advanced information systems engineering* (pp. 240–255). Springer. doi:10.1007/978-3-642-38709-8_16

Henricksen, K., & Indulska, J. (2006). Developing Context-Aware Pervasive Computing Applications: Models and Approach. *Pervasive and Mobile Computing*, *2*(1), 37–64. doi:10.1016/j.pmcj.2005.07.003

Hernández-Orallo, J. (2013). ROC curves for regression. *Pattern Recognition*, *46*(12), 3395–3411. doi:10.1016/j.patcog.2013.06.014

Hess, A., Humm, B., Voss, M., & Engels, G. (2007). Structuring software cities a multidimensional approach. In *Proceedings of 11th IEEE International Conference on Enterprise Distributed Object Computing Conference - EDOC 2007*. (pp. 122-122). IEEE.

Hewitt, C. (2009). Norms and commitment for iOrgs (TM) information systems: Direct logic (TM) and participatory grounding checking. *arXiv preprint arXiv:0906.2756*.

Hewitt, C. (2010). Actor model of computation: Scalable robust information systems. *arXiv preprint arXiv:1008.1459*.

Hewitt, E. (2009). *Java SOA Cookbook*. Sebastopol, CA: O'Reilly Media.

Hoare, C. A. R., Hayes, I. J., Jifeng, H., Morgan, C. C., Roscoe, A. W., & Sanders, J. W. et al. (1987). Laws of programming. *Communications of the ACM*, *30*(8), 672–686. doi:10.1145/27651.27653

Hoffert, J., Schmidt, D., & Gokhale, A. (2007). A QoS policy configuration modeling language for publish/subscribe middleware platforms. In *Proceedings of the International Conference on Distributed Event-Based Systems* (pp. 140–145). New York: ACM. doi:10.1145/1266894.1266922

Holloway, M. (1991). The Computer for the 21st Century. *Scientific American*, *264*(3), 94–103. doi:10.1038/scientificamerican0991-94 PMID:1675486

Hong, J.-y., Suh, E.-, & Kim, S.-J. (2009, May). Context-aware systems: A literature review and classification. *Expert Systems with Applications*, *36*(4), 8509–8522. doi:10.1016/j.eswa.2008.10.071

Hosmer, D. W., & Lemeshow, S. (1989). *Applied logistic regression*. New York: John Willey & Sons.

Höß, O., Weisbecker, A., Rosenthal, U., & Veit, M. (2003). Efficient Component-Based Integration of a Mobile J2EE Application with a Java-Based "Legacy" System - A Best-Practice Example. In B. Al-Ani, H. R. Arabnia, & Y. Mun (Eds.), *Software Engineering Research and Practice* (pp. 1–15). CSREA Press.

Ho-Won, J., Seung-Gweon, K., & Chang-Shin, Ch. (2004). Measuring software product quality: A survey of ISO/IEC 9126. *IEEE Software*, *21*(5), 88–92. doi:10.1109/MS.2004.1331309

Hoy, J., Brewer, M., Peterson, B., Dittmer, G., Braskett, D., & Porteus, D. (1989). *Virus highlights need for improved internet management*. United States General Accounting Office report GAO/IMTEC-89-57.

Hribernik, K. A., Ghrairi, Z., Hans, C., & Thoben, K. (2011). Co-creating the Internet of Things - First Experiences in the Participatory Design of Intelligent Products with Arduino. In *Proceedings of Concurrent Enterprising (ICE),* (pp. 1–9). ICE.

Hruby, P. (2006). *Model-driven design of software applications with business patterns*. Springer Verlag.

Huang, S., & Mangs, J. (2008). Pervasive Computing: Migrating to Mobile Devices: A Case Study. In *Proceedings of 2nd Annual IEEE Systems Conference*. Montreal, Canada: IEEE. doi:10.1109/SYSTEMS.2008.4519056

Huang, C.-Y., Tzeng, G.-H., & Ho, W.-R. J. (2011). System on chip design service e-business value maximization through a novel MCDM framework. *Expert Systems with Applications*, *38*(7), 7947–7962. doi:10.1016/j.eswa.2010.12.022

Hui, B. (2002). *Big designs for small devices*. Retrieved from http://www.javaworld.com/javaworld/jw-12-2002/jw-1213-j2medesign.html

Hui, B., Liaskos, S., & Mylopoulos, J. (2003). Requirements Analysis for Customisable Software: a Goals-Skills-Preferences Framework. In *Proceedings of the 11th IEEE International Requirements Engineering Conference* (pp. 117-126). Washington, DC, USA: IEEE Press. doi:10.1109/ICRE.2003.1232743

Hull, D., Wolstencroft, K., Stevens, R., Goble, C., Pocock, M. R., Li, P., & Oinn, T. (2006, July). Taverna: A tool for building and running workflows of services. *Nucleic Acids Research*, *34*(suppl. 2), w729–32. doi:10.1093/nar/gkl320 PMID:16845108

Iacob, M., Jonkers, H., & Wiering, M. (2004). *Towards a UML profile for the ArchiMate language*. Retrieved from https://doc.telin.nl/dscgi/ds.py/Get/File-47276

Iacob, M. E., Meertens, L. O., Jonkers, H., Quartel, D. A. C., Nieuwenhuis, L. J. M., & Van Sinderen, M. J. (2012). From enterprise architecture to business models and back. *Software & Systems Modeling*, 1–25.

IEC. (2012). *IEC 61508: Functional Safety of Electrical/Electronic/Programmable Electronic Safety-related Systems*. IEC.

IEEE Computer Society. (1990). *IEEE standard glossary of software engineering terminology, IEEE Std. 610.12 – 1990*. IEEE.

Ilarri, S., Trillo, R., & Mena, E. (2006). SPRINGS: A scalable platform for highly mobile agents in distributed computing environments. In *Proceedings of the 4th International Workshop on Mobile Distributed Computing (MDC'06)* (pp. 633–637). Niagara Falls/Buffalo, NY: IEEE Computer Society. doi:10.1109/WOWMOM.2006.103

IMCS. (n.d.). *MOLA pages*. Retrieved June 17, 2009, from http://mola.mii.lu.lv/

IMPULSE. (2002). *Project IST-1999-21119*. Retrieved from http://cordis.europa.eu/search/index.cfm?fuseaction=proj.document&PJ_LANG=PL&PJ_RCN=4850507&pid=270&q=D67BEC82A602A23FF8B013B7DA527238&type=pro

Inaba, K., Hidaka, S., Hu, Z., Kato, H., Nakano, K. (2011). Graph-transformation verification using monadic second-order logic. In *Proceedings of PDPP '11*. PDPP.

International Organization for Standardization (ISO) and International Electrotechnical Commission (IEC). (2006). *Common evaluation methodology 3.1, ISO/IEC 18405*. Retrieved June 24, 2009, from http://www.commoncriteriaportal.org

International Software Benchmarking Group. (2010). *ISBSG dataset release 10*. Retrieved March 10 from, http://www.isbsg.org

IoBridge. (2013). *Thingspeak*. Retrieved February 21, 2014, from http://www.thingspeak.com

Ion, I., Dragovic, B., & Crispo, B. (2007). Extending the Java Virtual Machine to Enforce Fine-grained Security Policies in Mobile Devices. In *Proceedings of the 23rd Annual Computer Security Applications Conference, ACSAC07* (pp. 233-242). doi:10.1109/ACSAC.2007.36

ISO. IEC 15944-4:2006 Information technology – Business Agreement Semantic Descriptive Techniques – Part 4: Open-EDI Business Transaction Ontology. (2006). Retrieved May 04, 2009, from http://www.itu.dk/~hessellund/REA2006/papers/McCarthy.pdf

ISO. IEC 19502:2005(E). (2005). *Meta Object Facility (MOF) Specification, Version 1.4.1*. Retrieved March 08, 2009, from http://www.omg.org/cgi-bin/doc?formal/05-05-05.pdf

ISO/IEC 10746-1 (1998). *International standard ISO/IEC 10746-1:1998. Information technology – Open Distributed Processing – Reference model: Overview*. Author.

ISO/IEC 25000:2005 (E). (2005). *Software engineering – Software quality and requirements evaluation (SQuaRE) guide to SQuaRE.*

ISO/IEC 25010:2011 (E). (2011). *Systems and Software engineering – Software quality and requirements evaluation (SQuaRE) - Systems and software quality models.*

ISO/IEC 9075:2003 (part 1, 2). (2003). *Information technology – Database languages-SQL.*

ISO/IEC 9126-3:2003 (E). (2003). *Software engineering – Product quality – Part 3: Internal metrics.*

Issarny, V., Banâtre, M., Weis, F., Cabillic, G., Couderc, P., Higuera, T., & Parain, F. (2000). Session 3: Energy-Aware OS's: Providing an Embedded Software Environment for Wireless PDAs. In *Proceedings of the 9th Workshop on ACM SIGOPS European Workshop: Beyond the PC: New Challenges for the Operating System*, (pp. 49–54). ACM Press. doi:10.1145/566726.566738

Jackson, M. (2001). *Problem frames: Analyzing and structuring software development problems*. Reading, MA: Addison-Wesley.

Jackson, M., & Zave, P. (1995). Deriving specifications from requirements: An example. In *Proceedings of the Internation Conference on Software Engineering (SE)* (pp. 15-24). New York: ACM Press.

Jacob, R. J. K., Leggett, J. J., Myers, B. A., & Pausch, R. (1993). Interaction Styles and Input/Output Devices. *Behaviour & Information Technology*, *12*(2), 69–79. doi:10.1080/01449299308924369

Jankowska, A. M., & Kurbel, K. (2005). Service-oriented architecture supporting mobile access to an ERP system. *Wirtschaftsinformatik*, 371–390.

Jansen, S., Brinkkemper, S., & Helms, R. (2008). Benchmarking the Customer Configuration Updating Practices of Product Software Vendors. In *Proceedings of the 7th International Conference on Compostion Based Software Systems* (pp. 82-91). Washington, DC, USA: IEEE Computer Society. doi:10.1109/ICCBSS.2008.14

Java Standard Edition, SUN6 API. (n.d.). Retrieved June 24, 2009, from http://java.sun.com/javase/6/docs/api/overview-summary.html

Javahery, H., Seffah, A., Engelberg, D., & Sinnig, D. (2003). Migrating User Interfaces between Platforms Using HCI Patterns. In A. Seffah, & H. Javahery (Eds.), *Multiple User Interfaces: Multiple-Devices, Cross-Platform and Context-Awareness* (pp. 241–259). New York, NY: Wiley.

Jawadekar, W. S. (2004). *Software engineering: Principles and practices.* Tata Mcgraw-Hill Publishing Company Limited.

Jeffery, R., Ruhe, M., & Wieczorek, I. (2000). A comparative study of two software development cost modelling techniques using multi-organizational and company-specific data. *Information and Software Technology, 42*(14), 1009–1016. doi:10.1016/S0950-5849(00)00153-1

Jeffery, R., Ruhe, M., & Wieczorek, I. (2001). Using public domain metrics to estimate software development effort. In *Proceedings of the 7th IEEE International Metrics Symposium (METRICS'01)* (pp. 16-27). IEEE.

Jia, L., Aljuraidan, J., Fragkaki, E., Bauer, L., Stroucken, M., Fukushima, K., et al. (2013). In *Proceedings of ESORICS 2013,* (LNCS) (vol. 8134, pp. 775-792). Springer-Verlag.

Jin, H., David, B., & Chalon, R. (2013). Proxemic interaction applied with public screen. In Proceedings of HCI International 2013 (LNCS), (vol. 8028, pp. 378-387). Berlin, Germany: Springer-Verlag.

Jin, H., Xu, T., David, B., & Chalon, R. (2014). Direct migrator: eliminating borders between personal mobile devices and pervasive displays. In *Proceedings of the 5th IEEE Workshop on Pervasive Collaboration and Social Networking 2014.* Budapest, Hungary: IEEE. doi:10.1109/PerComW.2014.6815267

Johannesson, P. (2007). The role of business models in enterprise modeling. In J. Krogstie, A. Opdahl, & S. Brinkkemper (Eds.), *Conceptual modeling in information systems engineering* (pp. 123–140). Springer-Verlag. doi:10.1007/978-3-540-72677-7_8

Johnson, P., Ekstedt, M., & Jacobson, I. (2012, September/October). Where's the Theory for Software Engineering? *IEEE Software*, 94–95.

Johnston, S. (2005). UML 2.0 profile for software services. *IBM Cooperation.* Retrieved March 15, 2009, from http://www.ibm.com/developerworks/rational/library/05/419_soa/

Jones, S. (2005). *A methodology for service architectures.* Capgemini white paper. Retrieved February 15, 2014, from http://www.oasis-open.org/committees/download.php/15071

Jones, C. (2009). Positive and negative innovations in software engineering. *International Journal of Software Science and Computational Intelligence, 1*(2), 20–30. doi:10.4018/jssci.2009040102

Jonkers, H., Lankhorst, M., Buuren, R., Bonsangue, M., & Van Der Torre, L. (2004). Concepts for modeling enterprise architectures. *International Journal of Cooperative Information Systems, 13*(3), 257–287. doi:10.1142/S0218843004000985

Jorgensen, M., & Shepperd, M. (2007). A systematic review of software development cost estimation studies. *IEEE Transactions on Software Engineering, 33*(1), 33–53. doi:10.1109/TSE.2007.256943

Jürjens, J. (2005). *Secure systems development with UML.* Berlin: Springer.

Ju, W., Lee, B. A., & Klemmer, S. R. (2008). Range: exploring implicit interaction through electronic whiteboard design. In *Proceedings of the 2008 ACM conference on Computer supported cooperative work* (pp. 17-26). New York, NY: ACM Press. doi:10.1145/1460563.1460569

Kaaranen, H., Naghian, S., Laitinen, L., Ahtiainen, A., & Niemi, V. (2001). *UMTS Networks: Architecture, Mobility and Services.* New York, NY: John Wiley & Sons, Inc.

Kaindl, H., Smiałek, M., Svetinovic, D., Ambroziewicz, A., Bojarski, J., Nowakowski, W., et al. (2007). *Requirements specification language definition*. Retrieved February 26, 2014 from www.redseeds.eu

Kalnins, A., Barzdins, J., & Celms, E. (2005). Model transformation language MOLA. In *Proceedings of MDAFA 2004* (LNCS), (vol. 3599, pp. 62-76). Springer.

Kalnins, A., Kalnina, E., Celms, E., & Sostaks, A. (2010 a). From requirements to code in a model driven way. In *Proceedings of Associated Workshops and Doctoral Consortium of the 13th East European Conference, ADBIS 2009* (LNCS), (vol. 5968, pp. 161-168). Springer.

Kalnins, A., Kalnina, E., Celms, E., & Sostaks, A. (2010 b). Model driven path from requirements to code. *Scientific Papers University of Latvia. Computer Science and Information Technologies*, *756*, 33–57.

Kamiński, J., Brzezicka, A., & Wróbel, A. (2011). Short-term memory capacity (7±2) predicted by theta to gamma cycle length ratio. *Neurobiology of Learning and Memory*, *95*(1), 19–23. doi:10.1016/j.nlm.2010.10.001 PMID:20951219

Kamiya, H., Mineno, H., Ishikawa, N., Osano, T., & Mizuno, T. (2008). Composite event detection in heterogeneous sensor networks. In *Proceedings ofIEEE/IPSJ International Symposium on Applications and the Internet*, (pp. 413–416). IEEE. doi:10.1109/SAINT.2008.92

Kaner, C. (2004). Software engineering metrics: What do they measure and how do we know? In *Proc. Int. Soft. Metrics Symp. Metrics,* (pp. 1-10). Academic Press.

Kansal, A., Nath, S., Liu, J., & Zhao, F. (2007). SenseWeb : An Infrastructure for Shared Sensing. *IEEE MultiMedia*, *14*(4), 8–13. doi:10.1109/MMUL.2007.82

Kärkkäinen, L., & Laarni, J. (2002). Designing for Small Display Screens. In *Proceedings of the Second Nordic Conference on Human-Computer Interaction*, (pp. 227–230). ACM Press. doi:10.1145/572020.572052

Kärnä, J., Tolvanen, J., & Kelly, S. (2009). Evaluating the use of domain-specific modeling in practice. In *Proceedings of9th Workshop on Domain-Specific Modeling (OOPSLA 2009)*. New York: ACM.

Kaur, P., & Singh, H. (2009). Version Management and Composition of Software Components in Different Phases of the Software Development Life Cycle. *ACM Sigsoft Software Engineering Notes*, *34*(4), 1–9.

Kaushik, V. (1997). *UML Glossary*. Rational Software Corporation and MCI Systemhouse Corporation.

Kavimandan, A., & Gokhale, A. (2008). Automated middleware QoS configuration techniques using model transformations. In *Proceedings of the 14th IEEE Real-Time and Embedded Technology and Applications Symposium* (pp. 93–102). Los Alamitos, CA: IEEE.

KDM. (2011). *Knowledge Discovery Metamodel, version 1.3, OMG Document Number: formal/2011-08-04*. Retrieved February 7, 2014, from http://www.omg.org/spec/KDM/1.3

Kemerer, C. (1987). An empirical validation of software cost estimation models. *Communications of the ACM*, *30*(5), 416–429. doi:10.1145/22899.22906

Kent, S. (2002). Model driven engineering. In *Proceedings of the 3rd International Conference on Integrated Formal Methods* (pp. 286–298). Berlin: Springer. doi:10.1007/3-540-47884-1_16

Kherraf, S., Lefebvre, E., & Suryn, W. (2008). Transformation from CIM to PIM using patterns and archetypes. In *Proceedings of the 19th Australian Software Engineering Conference* (pp. 338-346). IEEE Computer Society. doi:10.1109/ASWEC.2008.4483222

Kiani, S. L., Knappmeyer, M., Reetz, E. S., Baker, N., & To¨njes, R. (2010). Effect of caching in a broker based context provisioning system. In *Proceedings of the5th European conference on Smart sensing and context* (EuroSSC' 10) (pp. 108-121). Passau, Germany: Springer.

Kifer, M., Brenstein, A., & Lewis, P. M. (2006). *Database systems: An application-oriented approach* (2nd ed.). New York: Addison Wesley.

Kim, J., Baratto, R., & Nieh, J. (2006). An Application Streaming Service for Mobile Handheld Devices. In *Proceedings ofIEEE International Conference on Services Computing (SCC'06)*, (pp. 323–326). IEEE. doi:10.1109/SCC.2006.18

Kircher, M., & Jain, P. (2004). *Pattern-Oriented Software Architecture, Patterns for Resource Management*. John Wiley & Sons.

Kitchenham, B., & Mendes, E. (2004) A comparison of cross-company and within-company effort estimation models for web applications. In *Proceedings of the 8th International Conference on Empirical Assessment in Software Engineering (EASE 2004)* (pp. 47-55). EASE. doi:10.1049/ic:20040398

Kitchenham, B., & Mendes, E. (2009). Why comparative effort prediction studies may be invalid. In *Proceedings of the 5th ACM International Conference on Predictor Models in Software Engineering*. ACM. doi:10.1145/1540438.1540444

Kitchenham, B., Pickard, L., MacDonell, S., & Shepperd, M. (2001). What accuracy statistics really measure. *IEE Proceedings on Software*, *148*(3), 81–85. doi:10.1049/ip-sen:20010506

Klems, M., Nemis, J., & Tai, S. (2009). *Do clouds compute? A framework for estimating the value of cloud computing*. Springer-Verlang.

Kleppe, A., Warmer, J., & Bast, W. (2003). *MDA explained*. Addison-Wesley Professional.

Klischewski, R. (2004). Information integration or process integration? How to achieve interoperability in administration. *Electronic Government, 3183*, 57–65. Retrieved from http://www.springerlink.com/index/cndhp3plq6pt05x3.pdf

Knappmeyer, M., Kiani, S. L., Fra`, C., Moltchanov, B., & Baker, N. (2010). Contextml: A light-weight context representation and context management schema. In *Proceedings of the 5th IEEE international conference on Wireless pervasive computing* (ISWPC' 10) (pp. 367-372). Piscataway, NJ: IEEE Press.

Knight, D. (2009). *Why cloud vs. premise is the wrong question*. Retrieved March 10, 2010, from Cisco's blog website http://blogs.cisco.com/collaboration/comments/why_cloud_vs._premise_is_the_wrong_question/

Kolahdouz-Rahimi, S., Lano, K., Pillay, S., Troya, J., & Van Gorp, P. (2012). Goal-oriented measurement of model transformation methods. *Science of Computer Programming* (submitted).

Kolovos, D. S., Rose, L. M., Paige, R. F., & Polack, F. C. (2009). Raising the level of abstraction in the development of GMF-based graphical model editors. In *Proceedings of2009 ICSE Workshop on Modeling in Software Engineering* (pp. 13–19). IEEE. doi:10.1109/MISE.2009.5069891

Kolsi, O., & Virtanen, T. (2004). MIDP 2.0 security enhancements. In *Proceedings of the 37th Annual Hawaii International Conference on System Sciences*. IEEE Computer Society.

Kondol, D., Bahman, J., Malecot, P., Cappello, F., & Anderson, D. (2009). Cost-benefit analysis of cloud computing versus desktop grids. In *Proceedings of the 18th International Heterogeneity in Computing Workshop*. Academic Press.

Kone, M. T., Shimazu, A., & Nakajima, T. (2000). The state of the art in agent communication languages. *Knowledge and Information Systems*, *2*(3), 259–284. doi:10.1007/PL00013712

Krasniewski, M., Varadharajan, P., Rabeler, B., Bagchi, S., & Hu, Y. (2005). Tibfit: Trust index based fault tolerance for arbitrary data faults in sensor networks. In *Proceedings of the International Conference on Dependable Systems and Networks DSN 2005*, (pp. 672–681). doi:10.1109/DSN.2005.92

Krishnamachari, B., & Iyengar, S. S. (2003). *Efficient and fault-tolerant feature extraction in sensor networks*. Paper presented at the 2nd Workshop on Information Processing in Sensor Networks, IPSN '03. Palo Alto, CA.

Krishnamachari, B., & Iyengar, S. (2004). Distributed Bayesian algorithms for fault-tolerant event region detection in wireless sensor networks. *IEEE Transactions on Computers*, *53*(3), 241–250. doi:10.1109/TC.2004.1261832

Kristensen, M. D. (2008). Execution plans for cyber foraging. In *Proceedings of the 1st workshop on Mobile middleware: embracing the personal communication device* (pp. 2:1 – 2:4). New York, NY: ACM.

Kroll, P., & Kruchten, P. (2003). *Rational Unified Process Made Easy, A Practitioner's Guide to the RUP*. Boston, MA: Addison-Wesley Professional.

Krumm, J. (Ed.). (2009). *Ubiquitous Computing Fundamentals*. Chapman and Hall/CRC Press. doi:10.1201/9781420093612

Kumar, K., Liu, J., Lu, Y., & Bhargava, B. (2013). A Survey of Computation Offloading for Mobile Systems. *Mobile Networks and Applications*, *18*(1), 129–140. doi:10.1007/s11036-012-0368-0

Kushwaha, D. S., & Misra, A. K. (2006). Cognitive information complexity measure of object-oriented software – A practitioner's approach. In *Proceedings of the 5th WSEAS Int. Conf. on Software Engineering*, (pp. 174-179). WSEAS.

Kushwaha, D. S., & Misra, A. K. (2006b). *A modified cognitive information complexity measure of software. ACM SIGSOFT Software Engineering Notes, 31*, 1.

Laboratories, R. S. A. (1999). *Password-based cryptography standard PKCS #5 v2.0.* Retrieved June 24, 2009, from ftp://ftp.rsasecurity.com/pub/pkcs/pkcs-5v2/pkcs5v2-0.pdf

Labrou, Y. (2001). Standardizing agent communication. *Lecture Notes in Computer Science*, *2086*, 74–97. doi:10.1007/3-540-47745-4_4

Laine, P. (2001). The Role of SW Architecture in Solving Fundamental Problems in Object-Oriented Development of Large Embedded SW Systems. In *Proceedings of the Working IEE/IFIP Conference on Software Architecture*, (pp. 14–23). IEEE Computer Society. doi:10.1109/WICSA.2001.948400

Lai, Q., & Carpenter, A. (2012). Defining and verifying behaviour of domain specific language with fUML. In *Proceedings of the 4th Workshop on Behaviour Modeling - Foundations and Applications (BM-FA) @ ECMFA 2012*, (pp. 1–7). ACM doi:10.1145/2325276.2325277

Lamouchi, O., Cherif, A. R., & Levy, N. (2008). A Framework Based Measurements for Evaluating an IS Quality. In *Proc. Fifth Asia-Pacific Conference on Conceptual Modelling* (pp. 39–47). Wollongong, Australia: CRPIT.

Landmark, C. R. M. (2009). *SaaS total cost of ownership*. Retrieved March 10, 2010, from CRM Landmark website http://www.crmlandmark.com/saasTCO.htm

Lankhorst, M. (2009). *Introduction to enterprise architecture.* Springer-Verlag.

Lankhorst, M., Proper, E., & Jonkers, J. (2010). The anatomy of the archimate language. *International Journal of Information System Modeling and Design*, *1*(1), 1–32. doi:10.4018/jismd.2010092301

Lano, K., & Kolahdouz-Rahimi, S. (2010). Migration case study using UML-RSDS. In Proceedings of TTC 2010. Malaga, Spain: TTC.

Lano, K., & Kolahdouz-Rahimi, S. (2011). Model-driven development of model transformations. In *Proceedings of ICMT 2011*. ICMT.

Lano, K., & Kolahdouz-Rahimi, S. (2011). Slicing Techniques for UML Models. *Journal of Object Technology*, *10*, 1-49.

Lano, K., & Kolahdouz-Rahimi, S. (2011). Specification of the "Hello World" case study. In *Proceedings of TTC 2011*. TTC.

Lano, K., & Kolahdouz-Rahimi, S. (2011). Specification of the GMF migration case study. In *Proceedings of TTC 2011*. TTC.

Lano, K., Kolahdouz-Rahimi, S., & Clark, T. (2012). Comparison of verification techniques for model transformations. In *Proceedings of Modevva Workshop, MODELS 2012*. MODELS.

Lano, K. (2009). A Compositional Semantics of UML-RSDS. *SoSyM*, *8*(1), 85–116.

Lano, K. (Ed.). (2009). *UML 2 Semantics and Applications*. New York: Wiley. doi:10.1002/9780470522622

Lano, K., & Kolahdouz-Rahimi, S. (2010). Specification and Verification of Model Transformations using UML-RSDS. *LNCS*, *6396*, 199–214.

Larman, C. (2004). *Agile and iterative development: A manager's guide*. Boston: Addison Wesley.

Lau, K.-K., & Wang, Z. (2005). A Taxonomy of Software Component Models. In: *Proceeding of 31st EUROMICRO Conference of Software Engineering and Advanced Applications* (pp. 88-95). IEEE Computer Society.

Laudon, K., & Laudon, J. (2009). *Management information systems*. Pearson.

Lawrence, J. (2002). LEAP for Ad-hoc Networks. In *Proceedings of the Workshop on Ubiquitous Agents in Wearable, Embedded and Wireless Systems, (AAMAS 2002)*.Bologna, Italy: ACM

Lazăr, C.-L., Lazăr, I., Pârv, B., Motogna, S., & Czibula, I.-G. (2009). Using an fUML Action Language to Construct UML Models. In *Proceedings of11th International Symposium on Symbolic and Numeric Algorithms for Scientific Computing*. Timisoara, Romania: Academic Press. doi:10.1109/SYNASC.2009.49

Lazăr, I., Pârv, B., Motogna, S., Czibula, I.-G., & Lazăr, C.-L. (2008). iComponent: A Platform-independent Component Model for Dynamic Execution Environments. In *Proceedings of10th International Symposium on Symbolic and Numeric Algorithms for Scientific Computing* (pp. 257-264). Timisoara, Romania: IEEE Computer Society. doi:10.1109/SYNASC.2008.71

Lazăr, I., Pârv, B., Motogna, S., Czibula, I.-G., & Lazăr, C.-L. (2007). An Agile MDA Approach for Executable UML Structured Activities, Studia Univ. Babeş-Bolyai. *Informatica*, *52*(2), 101–114.

Leach, P., Mealling, M., & Salz, R. (2005). *A Universally Unique IDentifier (UUID) URN Namespace. RFC 4122*. Proposed Standard.

Leal, L. N., Pires, P. F., Campos, M. L. M., & Delicato, F. C. (2006). Natural MDA: Controlled Natural Language for Action Specifications on Model Driven Development. In R. Meersman & Z. Tari (Eds.), *OTM Conferences* (vol. 1, pp. 551-568). Springer.

Leavitt, H. J. (1964). Applied organization change in industry: structural, technical and human approaches. *New Perspectives in Organizational Research*, *55*, 71.

Ledeczi, A., Bakay, A., Maroti, M., Volgyesi, P., Nordstrom, G., Sprinkle, J., & Karsai, G. (2001). Composing domain-specific design environments. *Computer*, *34*(11), 44–51. doi:10.1109/2.963443

Leffingwell, D., & Widrig, D. (2003). *Managing Software Requirements: A Use Case Approach*. Boston, MA: Addison-Wesley.

Lenk, A., Klems, M., Nimis, J., Tai, S., & Sandholm, T. (2009). What's inside the cloud? An architectural map of the cloud landscape. In *Proceedings of the International Conference on Software Engineering (ICSE) Workshop on Software Engineering Challenges of Cloud Computing (CLOUD)*, (pp. 23-31). ICSE.

Leonardi, M. C., & Mauco, M. V. (2004). Integrating natural language oriented requirements models into MDA. In *Proceedings of Workshop on Requirements Engineering (WER) 2004*, (pp. 65-76). WER.

Levis, P., Madden, S., Gay, D., Polastre, J., Szewczyk, R., Whitehouse, K. … Culler, D. (2005). Tinyos: An operating system for sensor networks. In W. Weber, J. Rabaey & E. Aarts (Eds.), Ambient intelligence. Springer-Verlag.

Liampotis, N., Kalatzis, N., Roussaki, I., Kosmides, P., Papaioannou, I., Sykas, E., et al. (2012). Addressing the Context-Awareness Requirements in Personal Smart Spaces. In *Proceedings ofIEEE Asia-Pacific Services Computing Conference* (APSCC) (pp. 281-285). Guilin: IEEE Press. doi:10.1109/APSCC.2012.65

Liampotis, N., Roussaki, I., Papadopoulou, E., Abu-Shaaban, Y., Williams, M., & Taylor, N. et al. (2009). A privacy framework for personal self-improving smart spaces. In *Proceedings of the 2009 International Conference on Computational Science and Engineering* (vol. 3, pp. 444-449). Washington, DC: IEEE Press. doi:10.1109/CSE.2009.148

Liebchen, G., & Shepperd, M. (2008) Data sets and data quality in software engineering. In *Proceedings of the 4th ACM International Workshop on Predictor Models in Software Engineering* (pp. 39-44). ACM. doi:10.1145/1370788.1370799

Lieberherr, K. J., & Xiao, C. (1993, April). Object-oriented software evolution. *IEEE Transactions on Software Engineering*, *19*(4), 313–343. doi:10.1109/32.223802

Li, G., & Jacobsen, H. (2005). Composite subscriptions in content-based publish/subscribe systems. In *Proceedings of the 6th International Middleware Conference* (pp. 249-269). New York: Springer-Verlag. doi:10.1007/11587552_13

Lightstone, S., Teorey, T., & Nadeau, T. (2007). *Physical Database Design. The Database Professional's Guide to Exploiting Indexes, Views, Storage, and More*. San Francisco, CA: Morgan Kaufman Publisher.

Lilis, Y., Savidis, A., & Valsamakis, Y. (2013). Self model-driven engineering through metaprograms. In *Proceedings of the 17th Panhellenic Conference on Informatics* (pp. 136-143). New York, NY: ACM. doi:10.1145/2491845.2491872

Lin, H.-C., & Jeng, T. (2013). WorkSense: An interactive space design for future workplace. Lecture Notes in Computer Science, 8011(3), 64-69.

Lin, Liu, & Liao. (2007). Energy Analysis of Multimedia Video Decoding on Mobile Handheld Devices. In *Proceedings of International Conference on Multimedia and Ubiquitous Engineering (MUE'07)*, (pp. 120–125). IEEE Computer Society.

Lindemann, C. and Thümmler, A. (2003). Performance analysis of the general packet radio service. *Computer Networks, 41*(1), 1–17.

Lingrand, D., de Morais, W. O., & Tigli, J. Y. (2005). Ordinateur Porté: Dispositifs D'entrée-sortie. In *Proceedings of the 17th international conference on Francophone sur l'Interaction Homme-Machine* (pp. 219-222). New York, NY: ACM Press.

Lin, L., Nuseibeh, B., Ince, D., & Jackson, M. (2004). Using abuse frames to bound the scope of security problems. In *Proceedings of IEEE International Requirements Engineering Conference (RE)* (pp. 354-355). Washington, DC: IEEE Computer Society.

Little, R. J. A., & Rubin, D. B. (2002). *Statistical analysis with missing data*. John Wiley & Sons.

Liu, L., Yu, E., & Mylopoulos, J. (2003). Security and privacy requirements analysis with a social setting. In *Proceedings of the 11th IEEE International Conference on Requirements Engineering*. IEEE. doi:10.1109/ICRE.2003.1232746

Lo, A., & Yu, E. (2008). From business models to service-oriented design: A reference catalog approach. In Proceedings of Conceptual Modeling - ER 2007 (Vol. 4801, pp. 87-101). Springer.

Lodderstedt, T., Basin, D. A., & Doser, J. (2002). SecureUML: A UML-based modeling language for model-driven security. In *Proceedings of the 5th international conference on the unified modeling language* (p. 426-441). London, UK: Springer-Verlag.

LogMeIn. (2013). *COSM*. Retrieved February 21, 2014, from https://cosm.com/

Loniewski, G., Insfran, E., & Abrahão, S. (2010). A systematic review of the use of requirements engineering techniques in model-driven development. In Model driven engineering languages and systems (LNCS), (vol. 6395, pp. 213–227). Springer. doi:10.1007/978-3-642-16129-2_16

López-Sanz, M., Acuña, C. J., Cuesta, C. E., & Marcos, E. (2008). UML profile for the platform independent modelling of service-oriented architectures. Lecture Notes in Computer Science, 4758, 304-307.

LORD MicroStrain. (n.d.). *Sensor Cloud*. Retrieved February 21, 2014, from http://www.sensorcloud.com/

Lovelock, C., & Wirtz, J. (2007). *Services marketing: People, technology, strategy* (6th ed.). Pearson International - Pearson/Prentice Hall.

Loyall, J., Jianming Ye., Shapiro, R., Neema, S., Mahadevan, N., Abdelwahed, S., et al. (2004). A Case Study in Applying QoS Adaptation and Model-Based Design to the Design-Time Optimization of Signal Analyzer Applications. In *Proceedings ofMilitary Communications Conference (MILCOM)* (pp. 1700–1705). Los Alamitos, CA: IEEE. doi:10.1109/MILCOM.2004.1495193

Luck, M., McBurney, P., & Preist, C. (2003). *Agent technology: Enabling next generation computing*. AgentLink II.

Luftman, J. (2000). Assessing business-IT alignment maturity. *Strategies for Information Technology Governance, 4*(14), 99.

Lukman, T., Godena, G., Gray, J., & Strmcnik, S. (2010). Model-driven engineering of industrial process control applications. In *Proceedings of the 2010 IEEE Conference on Emerging Technologies and Factory Automation* (pp. 1-16). Los Alamitos, CA: IEEE. doi:10.1109/ETFA.2010.5641224

Lund, M. S., Solhaug, B., & Stølen, K. (2011). *Model-driven risk analysis - The CORAS approach*. Berlin: Springer. doi:10.1007/978-3-642-12323-8

MacDonald, A., Russell, D., & Atchison, B. (2005). Model driven Development within a Legacy System: An industry experience report. In *Proceeding of 2005 Australian Software Engineering Conference. ASWEC 05*. (pp.14-22). IEEE Press. doi:10.1109/ASWEC.2005.32

MacGowan, G. (2006). *Helping small businesses choose between on-demand and on-premise software*. Retrieved March 10, 2010, from http://www.computerworld.com/s/article/9002362/Helping_small_businesses_choose_between_On_demand_and_On_premise_software

Madden, S. R., Franklin, M. J., Hellerstein, J. M., & Hong, W. (2005). Tinydb: An acquisitional query processing system for sensor networks. *ACM Transactions on Database Systems*, *30*(1), 122–173. doi:10.1145/1061318.1061322

Mainwaring, A., Culler, D., Polastre, J., Szewczyk, R., & Anderson, J. (2002). Wireless sensor networks for habitat monitoring. In *Proceedings of the 1st ACM International Workshop on Wireless Sensor Networks and Applications* (pp. 88-97). ACM.

Mair, C., & Shepperd, M. (2005). The consistency of empirical comparisons of regression and analogy-based software project cost prediction. In *Proceedings of the International Symposium on Empirical Software Engineering* (pp. 491-518). Academic Press. doi:10.1109/ISESE.2005.1541858

Mammar, A., Cavalli, A., de Oca, E. M., Ardi, S., Byers, D., & Shahmehri, N. (2009, June). Modélisation et détection formelles de vulnérabilités logicielles par le test passif. In *Proceedings of 4ème conférence sur la sécurité des architectures réseaux et des systèmes d'information*. Academic Press.

Marquardt, N., Diaz-Marino, R., Boring, S., & Greenberg, S. (2011). The proximity toolkit: prototyping proxemic interactions in ubiquitous computing ecologies. In *Proceedings of the 24th Annual ACM Symposium on User Interface Software and Technology* (pp. 315–326). New York, NY: ACM Press. doi:10.1145/2047196.2047238

Marshall, C. (2000). *Enterprise modeling with UML: Designing successful software through business analysis*. Addison-Wesley Professional.

Martinelli, F., & Matteucci, I. (2007). An Approach for the Specification, Verification and Synthesis of Secure Systems. *Electronic Notes in Theoretical Computer Science*, *168*, 29–43. doi:10.1016/j.entcs.2006.12.003

Martinelli, F., Mori, P., Quillinan, T., & Schaefer, C. (2008). A Runtime Monitoring Environment for Mobile Java, In *Proceedings of the 1st International ICST workshop on Security Testing (SecTest08), IEEE International Conference on Software Testing Verification and Validation Workshop* (pp. 270-278). doi:10.1109/ICSTW.2008.3

Martínez, Y., Cachero, C., & Meliá, S. (2012). Article. In Evaluating the impact of a model-driven web engineering approach on the productivity and the satisfaction of software development teams (LNCS), (vol. 7387, pp. 223–237). Berlin: Springer-Verlag. doi:10.1007/978-3-642-31753-8_17

Martinez, L., Favre, L., & Pereira, C. (2014). Recovering Sequence Diagrams from Object-Oriented Code: An ADM Approach. In *Proceedings of 9th International Conference on Evaluation of Novel Approaches to Software Engineering, ENASE 2014*. Accepted.

Massacci, F., & Naliuka, K. (2006). *Multi-session security monitoring for mobile code*. Technical Report DIT-06-067, UNITN.

Massoni, T., Gheyi, R., & Borba, P. (2005). *Formal refactoring for UML class diagrams*. Paper presented at 19th Brazilian symposium on Software Engineering. Rio de Janeiro, Brazil.

Matinlassi, M., Niemelä, E., & Dobrica, L. (2002). *Quality-driven architecture design and quality analysis method. A revolutionary initiation approach to a product line architecture*. VTT Publications.

Mattarelli, E., Bertolotti, F., & Macrì, D. M. (2013). The use of ethnography and grounded theory in the development of a management information system. *European Journal of Information Systems*, *22*(1), 26–44. doi:10.1057/ejis.2011.34

Mauw, S., & Oostdijk, M. (2006). Foundations of attack trees. In Proceedings of Information security and cryptology, (pp. 186–198). Berlin: Springer.

Maxwell, K. (2002). *Applied statistics for software managers*. Prentice-Hall.

Mayerhofer, T., Langer, P., Wimmer, M., & Kappel, G. (2013). xMOF: Executable DSMLs based on fUML. In *Proceedings of the 6th International Conference on Software Language Engineering (SLE)* (LNCS), (vol. 8225, pp. 1 – 20). Springer.

Mazhelis, O., Markkula, J., & Jakobsson, M. (2005). Specifying patterns for mobile applications domain using general architectural components. In R. Bomarius, & S. Komi-Sirviö (Eds.), Lecture Notes in Computer Science: Vol. 3547. *Product Focused Software Process Improvement* (pp. 157–172). Springer. doi:10.1007/11497455_14

McCarthy, W. E. (1982). REA accounting model: A generalized framework for accounting systems in a shared data environment. *Accounting Review*, *57*(3), 554–578.

McCormick, Z., & Schmidt, D. C. (2012). Data Synchronization Patterns in Mobile Application Design. In *Proceedings of the Pattern Languages of Programs (PLoP) 2012 Conference*. ACM.

McRitchie, K., & Accelar, S. (2008). A structured framework for estimating IT projects and IT support. In *Proceedings ofJoint Annual Conference ISPA/SCEA Society of Cost Estimating and Analysis*. ISPA/SCEA.

MDA. (2012). *The Model-Driven Architecture*. Retrieved February 7, 2014, from http://www.omg.org/mda/

Means, G., & Schneider, D. (2000). *MetaCapitalism: The e-Business Revolution and the Design of 21st-Century Companies and Markets*. Wiley. Retrieved from http://www.amazon.ca/exec/obidos/redirect?tag=citeulike09-20&path=ASIN/0471393355

Medini. (2012). *Medini QVT*. Retrieved February 7, 2014, from http://projects.ikv.de/qvt

Mednieks, Z., Dornin, L., Meike, G. B., & Nakamura, M. (2012). *Programming Android: Java Programming for the New Generation of Mobile Device* (2nd ed.). O'Reilly.

Mellor, S. J. (2005). *Agile MDA*. Retrieved May 20, 2009, from: http://www.omg.org/mda/mda_files/Agile_MDA.pdf

Mellor, S. J., & Balcer, M. J. (2002). *Executable UML: A Foundation for Model-Driven Architecture*. Boston: Addison Wesley.

Mendes, E., & Lokan, C. (2008). Replicating studies on cross- vs single-company effort models using the ISBSG database. *Empirical Software Engineering*, *13*(1), 3–37. doi:10.1007/s10664-007-9045-5

Mendes, E., Lokan, C., Harrison, R., & Triggs, C. (2005). A replicated comparison of cross-company and within-company effort estimation models using the ISBSG database. In *Proceedings of the 11th IEEE International Software Metrics Symposium (METRICS'05)* (pp.36-45). IEEE. doi:10.1109/METRICS.2005.4

Michał, Ś., Norbert, J., & Wiktor, N. (2012). From use cases and their relationships to code. In *Proceedings of Second IEEE International Workshop on Model-Driven Requirements Engineering MoDRE* (pp. 9–18). Chicago: IEEE doi:10.1109/MoDRE.2012.6360084

Microsoft. (1995). *Component object model*. Microsoft, Inc. Retrieved May 20, 2009, from: http://www.microsoft.com/com/

Microsoft. (2008). *SenseWeb*. Retrieved February 21, 2014, from http://research.microsoft.com/en-us/projects/senseweb/

Microsoft. (2012). *Z3 Theorem Prover*. Retrieved from http://research.microsoft.com/en-us/um/redmond/projects/z3/

Microsystems, S. (2003). *Enterprise JavaBeans specification*. Retrieved October 2007, from: http://java.sun.com/products/ejb/docs.html

Mijatov, S., Langer, P., Mayerhofer, T., & Kappel, G. (2013). A Framework for Testing UML Activities Based on fUML. In *Proceedings of the 10th International Workshop on Model Driven Engineering, Verification and Validation co-located with 16th International Conference on Model Driven Engineering Languages and Systems (MODELS 2013)*. CEUR.

Milgram, P., Drascic, D., Grodski, J. J., Restogi, A., Zhai, S., & Zhou, C. (1995). Merging Real and Virtual Worlds. In *Proceedings of IMAGINA'95*. Retrieved from http://gypsy.rose.utoronto.ca/people/david_dir/IMAGINA95/Imagina95.full.html

Miller, J., & Mukerji, J. (2003). *MDA Guide version 1.0.1*. Retrieved from http://www.omg.org/

Miller, J., & Mukerji, J. (Eds.). (2003, May 1). *MDA guide version 1.0*. Retrieved January 15, 2010, from http://www.omg.org/mda/

Miller, M. (2009). *Cloud computing pros and cons for end users*. Retrieved March 10, 2010, from http://www.informit.com/articles/article.aspx?p=1324280

Miller, G.A. (1956). The magical number seven, plus or minus two: Some limits on our capacity for processing information. *Psychological Review*, *63*(2), 81–97. doi:10.1037/h0043158 PMID:13310704

Milojicic, D., Douglis, F., & Wheeler, R. (1999). *Mobility: processes, computers, and agents*. ACM.

Ministry of Defence. (1997). *Defence Standard 00-55: Requirements for Safety-related Software in Defence Equipment*. Author.

Miraoui, M., Tadj, C., & Ben Amar, C. (2008). Architectural survey of context-aware systems in pervasive computing environment. *Ubiquitous Computing and Communication Journal*, *3*(3), 68–76.

Misra, S, Omorodion, M., & Fernandez, L. (2012). *Brief overview on software process models, their benefits and limitations*. Accepted in a proposed book From IGI Global.

Misra, S., & Cafer, F. (2011). Estimating complexity of programs in Python language. *Tehnički Vjesnik*, *18*(1), 23-32.

Misra, S., Koyuncu, M., Crasso, M., Mateos, C., & Zunino, A. (2012). A suite of cognitive complexity metrics. In Computational Science and Its Application ICCSA 2012 (LNCS), (vol. 7336, pp. 234–247). Springer. doi:10.1007/978-3-642-31128-4_17

Misra, S. & Akman, I. (2008). Weighted class complexity: A measure of complexity for object oriented systems. *Journal of Information Science and Engineering*, *24*, 1689–1708.

Misra, S., Akman, I., & Koyuncu, M. (2011). An inheritance complexity metric for object-oriented code: A cognitive approach. *Sadhana*, *36*(3), 317–337. doi:10.1007/s12046-011-0028-2

Mistry, P., & Maes, P. (2008). Quickies: Intelligent sticky notes. In *Proceedings of IE 08: 4th International Conference on Intelligent Environments* (pp. 1–4). Interaction Design Foundation.

Mittas, N. & Angelis L. (2012). A permutation test based on regression error characteristic curves for software cost estimation models. *Empirical Software Engineering*, *17*(1-2), 34-61.

Mittas, N., & Angelis, L. (2013b). Overestimation and underestimation of software cost models: Evaluation by visualization. In *Proceedings of Software Engineering and Advanced Applications (SEAA)*. IEEE.

Mittas, N., & Angelis, L. (2008a). Comparing cost prediction models by resampling techniques. *Journal of Systems and Software*, *81*(5), 616–632. doi:10.1016/j.jss.2007.07.039

Mittas, N., & Angelis, L. (2008b). Comparing software cost prediction models by a visualization tool. In *Proceedings of the 34th Euromicro Conference on Software Engineering and Advanced Applications (SEAA'08)*. (pp. 433-440). SEAA. doi:10.1109/SEAA.2008.23

Mittas, N., & Angelis, L. (2010). Visual comparison of software cost estimation models by regression error characteristic analysis. *Journal of Systems and Software*, *83*(4), 621–637. doi:10.1016/j.jss.2009.10.044

Mittas, N., & Angelis, L. (2013a). Ranking and clustering software cost estimation models through a multiple comparisons algorithm. *IEEE Transactions on* Software Engineering, *39*(4), 537–551.

Mittas, N., Mamalikidis, I., & Angelis, L. (2012). StatREC: A graphical user interface tool for visual hypothesis testing of cost prediction models. In *Proceedings of the 8th International Conference on Predictive Models in Software Engineering. ACM*. doi:10.1145/2365324.2365331

Mobile Marketing Association. (2012). *U.S. Consumer Best Practice for Messaging, Version 7.0*. Author.

Model Driven Community. (2009). *fUML MagicDraw plugin*. Retrieved Oct, 2009, from: http://portal.modeldriven.org/content/fuml-reference-implementation-download

Modelio. (n.d.). Retrieved February 26, 2014, from http://www.modelio.org/

MoDisco. (2014). *Model Discovery*. Retrieved February 7, 2014, from http://www.eclipse.org/MoDisco

MOF. (2011). *Meta Object Facility (MOF) Core Specification Version 2.4.1, OMG Document Number: formal/2011-08-07*. Retrieved February 7, 2014, from http://www.omg.org/spec/MOF/2.4.1

Mohagheghi, P., & Dehlen, V. (2008). *Developing a Quality Framework for Model-Driven Engineering. In Models in Software Engineering* (pp. 275–289). Heidelberg, Germany: Springer.

Mohagheghi, P., Dehlen, V., & Neple, T. (2009). Definitions and approaches to model quality in model-based software development – A review of literature. *Information and Software Technology*, *51*(12), 1646–1669. doi:10.1016/j.infsof.2009.04.004

Mohagheghi, P., Gilani, W., Stefanescu, A., Fernandez, M., Nordmoen, B., & Fritzsche, M. (2013). Where does model-driven engineering help? Experiences from three industrial cases. *Software & Systems Modeling*, *12*(3), 619–639. doi:10.1007/s10270-011-0219-7

Moitra, D., & Ganesh, J. (2005). Web services and flexible business processes: Towards the adaptive enterprise. *Information & Management*, *42*(7), 921–933. Retrieved from http://linkinghub.elsevier.com/retrieve/pii/S0378720604001338

Moon, M., Hong, M., & Yeom, K. (2008). Two-level variability analysis for business process with reusability and extensibility. In Proceedings of Computer Software and Applications. Turku, Finland: IEEE.

Moon, M., Yeom, K., & Chae, H. S. (2005). An approach to developing domain requirements as a core asset based on commonality and variability analysis in a product line. *IEEE Transactions on Software Engineering*, *31*(7), 551–569. doi:10.1109/TSE.2005.76

Moore, W. (1997). *About RAD*. Retrieved from http://wmoore.ca/demo/opinion/rad.htm

Moran, T. P., & Carroll, J. M. (1996). *Design Rationale: Concepts, Techniques, and Use*. New York: Lawrence Erlbaum Associates Publishers.

Moreau, L. (2002). A fault-tolerant directory service for mobile agents based on forwarding pointers. In *Proceedings of the Symposium on Applied Computing (SAC'02)* (pp. 93–100). Madrid, Spain: ACM. doi:10.1145/508797.508810

Moriconi, M., Qian, X., Riemenschneider, R. A., & Gong, L. (1997). Secure software architectures. In *Proceedings of the IEEE Symposium on Security and Privacy* (pp. 84 – 93). Washington, DC: IEEE Computer Society.

Mori, G., Paternò, F., & Santoro, C. (2002). CTTE: Support for Developing and Analyzing Task Models for Interactive System Design. *IEEE Transactions on Software Engineering*, *28*(9), 1–17.

Morris, D. (2010). Emerging Input Technologies for Always-Available Mobile Interaction. *Foundations and Trends® in Human–Computer Interaction*, *4*(4), 245–316.

Morrow, R. (2002). *Bluetooth: Operation and Use*. New York, NY: McGraw-Hill Professional.

Mostafa, A., & Ismall, M. El-Bolok, & H., Saad, E. (2007). Toward a Formalisation of UML2.0 Metamodel using Z Specifications. In *Proceedings of the 8th International Conference on Software Engineering, Artificial Intelligence, Networking, and Parallel/Distributed Computing:* Vol. 1 (pp. 694-701). Washington, DC, USA: IEEE Computer Society.

Motogna, S., Lazăr, I., & Pârv, B. (2011). An MDA Approach for Developing Executable UML Components. In J. Osis & E. Asnina (Eds.), Model-Driven Analysis and Software Development: Architectures and Functions, (pp. 254-273). IGI Global.

Motogna, S., Lazăr, I., Pârv, B., & Czibula, I. (2009). An Agile MDA Approach for Service-Oriented Components. In J. Happe & B. Zimmerova (Eds.), *6th International Workshop on Formal Engineering approaches to Software Components and Architectures* (FESCA) (pp. 2-17). York, UK: Electronic Notes in Theoretical Computer Science.

Mouratidis, H., & Giorgini, P. (2007). Secure tropos: A security-oriented extension of the tropos methodology. *International Journal of Software Engineering and Knowledge Engineering*, *17*(2), 285–309. doi:10.1142/S0218194007003240

Mouratidis, H., Weiss, M., & Giorgini, P. (2006). Modelling secure systems using an agent oriented approach and security patterns. *International Journal of Software Engineering and Knowledge Engineering*, *16*(3), 471–498. doi:10.1142/S0218194006002823

Mukhopadhyay, T., Vicinanza, S., & Prietula, M. (1992). Examining the feasibility of a case-based reasoning model for software effort estimation. *Management Information Systems Quarterly*, *16*(2), 155–171. doi:10.2307/249573

Munoz, J., Pelechano, V., & Fons, J. (2004). Model driven development of pervasive systems. *ERCIM News*, *58*, 50–51.

Murthy, C., & Manoj, B. (2004). *Ad hoc wireless networks: architectures and protocols*. Upper Saddle River, NJ: Prentice Hall PTR.

Myrtveit, I., Stensrud, E., & Olsson, U. (2001). Analyzing data sets with missing data: An empirical evaluation of imputation methods and likelihood-based methods. *IEEE Transactions on Software Engineering*, *27*(11), 999–1013. doi:10.1109/32.965340

MySQL. (2009). Retrieved June 10, 2009, from http://www.mysql.com/

Necula, G. C. (1998). *Compiling with Proofs*. (PhD thesis). Carnegie Mellon University, Pittsburgh, PA.

Necula, G. C. (1997). Proof-carrying code. In *Proceedings of the 24th ACM SIGPLAN-SIGACT symposium on Principles of programming languages* (pp. 106-119). doi:10.1145/263699.263712

Nefsis. (2010). *Pricing model*. Retrieved March 10, 2010, from http://www.nefsis.com/Pricing/concurrent-user.html

Nektarios, G., Nektarios, M., Fotis, K., Nikos, P., & Stavros, C. (2003). A service oriented architecture for managing operational strategies. In *Proceedings ofIEEE International Conference on Web Services*, (vol. 2853, pp. 271–354). IEEE.

Nemits, D. (2003). Achieving Battery Life for Handhelds with 802.11b Connectivity. *EE Times*. Retrieved from http://www.eetimes.com/story/OEG20020201S0039

Ni, T., & Baudisch, P. (2009). Disappearing mobile devices. In *UIST'10 - Proceedings of the 22th Annual ACM Symposium on User Interface Software and Technology* (pp. 101–110). New York, NY: ACM Press. doi:10.1145/1622176.1622197

Niemann, K. (2006). *From enterprise architecture to IT governance: Elements of elective IT management*. Vieweg+ Teubner Verlag.

Niklaus, W. (1977). What can we do about the unnecessary diversity of notation for syntactic definitions?. *Communication of ACM, 20*(11), 822-823.

Nimbits, I. (n.d.). *Nimbits*. Retrieved February 21, 2014, from http://www.nimbits.com/

Noble, J., & Weir, C. (2000). *Small Memory Software: Patterns for Systems with Limited Memory*. Addison-Wesley Professional.

Noel Yuhanna, M. G. (2008). *The Forrester wave: Information-as-a-service Q1 2008*. Retrieved 02/16, 2010, from http://www.forrester.com/rb/Research/wave%26trade%3B_information-as-a-service%2C_q1_2008/q/id/43199/t/2

Nokia. (2002a). *Mobile Internet Technical Architecture – Solutions and tools* (Vol. 2). Edita.

Nokia. (2002b). *Mobile Internet Technical Architecture – Visions and Implementations* (Vol. 3). Edita.

Nokia. (2014). *Mobile design patterns*. Retrieved from http://wiki.forum.nokia.com/index.php/Category:Mobile_Design_Patterns

Nomorosa, K. Y., (2011). *Hotel ontology*. Rearden Commerce Inc. Retrieved from http://sigmakee.cvs.sourceforge.net/viewvc/sigmakee/KBs/Hotel.kif

Nowakowski, W., Śmiałek, M., Ambroziewicz, A., & Straszak, T. (2013). Requirements-Level Language and Tools for Capturing Software System Essence. *Computer Science and Information Systems*, *10*(4), 1499–1524. doi:10.2298/CSIS121210062N

Nuccio, P., Michaud, M., & Gentile, S. (1997). Optimizimg the Mobile PC Battery Through Smart Battery Software. In *Proc. Twelfth Annual Battery Conference on Applications and Advances*, (pp. 201–204). IEEE. doi:10.1109/BCAA.1997.574103

Nurmilaakso, J.-M. (2008). EDI, XML and e-business frameworks: A survey. *Computers in Industry*, *59*(4), 370–379. doi:10.1016/j.compind.2007.09.004

Nurmilaakso, J.-M., & Kotinurmi, P. (2004). A review of XML-based supply-chain integration. *Production Planning and Control*, *15*(6), 608–621. doi:10.1080/09537280412331283937

Oak Ridge National Laboratory. (2009). *Sensorpedia*. Retrieved February 21, 2014, from http://www.sensorpedia.com/

OASIS - Web Services Business Process Execution Language Version 2.0., WS-BPEL. (2007). Retrieved May 04, 2009, from http://docs.oasis-open.org/wsbpel/2.0/OS/wsbpel-v2.0-OS.html

OASIS. (2006). *Web services brokered notification 1.3*. Retrieved December 11, 2009 from http://docs.oasis-open.org/wsn/wsn-ws_brokered_notification-1.3-spec-os.pdf

OASIS. (2007). *SCA Service Component Architecture: Assembly Model Specification, Version 1.1*. Retrieved October 2007, from: http://www.oasis-opencsa.org/sca

Oberheide, J., & Miller, C. (2012). Dissecting the Android Bouncer. Paper presented at SummerCon 2012. Brooklyn, NY.

Object Management Group. (2003). *MDA Guide Version 1.0.1, omg/03-06-01*. Author.

Object Management Group. (2004). *Reusable Asset Specication: Final Adopted Specification, ptc/04-06-06*. Author.

Object Management Group. (2004a). *Event service specification version 1.2*. Retrieved December 11, 2009, from http://www.omg.org/cgi-bin/doc?formal/2004-10-02

Object Management Group. (2004b). *Notification service specification version 1.1*. Retrieved December 11, 2009, from http://www.omg.org/cgi-bin/doc?formal/2004-10-11

Object Management Group. (2006). *Meta Object Facility Core Specification, version 2.0, formal/2006-01-01*. Author.

Object Management Group. (2006). *Meta-Object Facility (MOF) Core Specification, OMG document formal/06-01-01*. Author.

Object Management Group. (2007). *Data distribution service for real-time systems, version 1.2*. Retrieved June 8, 2009, from http://www.omg.org/spec/DDS/1.2

Object Management Group. (2009). *UML superstructure, version 2.3, OMG document formal/2010-05-05*. Author.

Object Management Group. (2009). *Unified Modeling Language: Superstructure, version 2.2, formal/09-02-02*. Author.

Object Management Group. (2010). *MDA - The Architecture of Choice for a Changing World*. Retrieved from http://www.omg.org/mda/

Object Management Group. (2012). OMG Model Driven Architecture. *The Architecture of Choice for a Changing World*. Retrieved May 13, 2012, from http://www.omg.org/mda/

OCL. (2012). *OCL: Object Constraint Language. Version 2.3.1, OMG Document Number: formal/2012-01-01*. Retrieved February 7, 2014, from http://www.omg.org/spec/OCL/2.3.1/

Ohrtman, F., & Roeder, K. (2003). *Wi-Fi Handbook: Building 802.11b Wireless Networks*. New York, NY: McGraw-Hill.

OMA. (2004a). *Dictionary for OMA Specifications V1.0.1*. Open Mobile Alliance.

OMA. (2004b). *Inventory of Architectures and Services V1.0*. Open Mobile Alliance.

OMA. (2004c). *OMA Service Environment*. Open Mobile Alliance.

OMG - Business Process Modeling Notation (BPMN). OMG/Business Management Initiative. (2011). Retrieved February 04, 2014, from www.omg.org/spec/BPMN/2.0/

OMG, & OMGA Specification. (2008). *Semantics of business vocabulary and business rules*. Author.

OMG. (2002). *CORBA Components Specification, Version 3.0*. Retrieved October 2007, from: http://www.omg.org/technology/documents/formal/components.htm

OMG. (2005). *UML 2.0 Testing Profile Specification*. Retrieved October 2007, from: http://www.omg.org/cgi-bin/apps/doc?formal/05-07-07.pdf

OMG. (2006). *Deployment and Configuration of Component-based Distributed Applications Specification, Version 4*. Retrieved October 2007, from: http://www.omg.org/technology/documents/formal/deployment.htm

OMG. (2007). *UML Superstructure Specification, Rev. 2.1.2*. Retrieved October 2007, from: http://www.omg.org/docs/formal/07-11-02.pdf

OMG. (2008). *Semantics of a Foundational Subset for Executable UML Models (FUML)*. Retrieved April 2009, from: http://www.omg.org/spec/FUML/

OMG. (2010). *Concrete Syntax for UML Action Language (Action Language for Foundational UML - ALF)*. Retrieved February 2014, from: http://www.omg.org/spec/ALF/1.0.1/

OMG. (2011). *Precise Semantics of UML Composite Structures. Request For Proposal*. Retrieved February 2014, from: http://www.omg.org/cgi-bin/doc?ad/11-12-07.pdf

OMG. (2013, July). Essence - Kernel And Language For Software Engineering Methods (Essence). *Version Beta1*. Retrieved from http://www.omg.org/spec/Essence/

OMG. (2014a). *Object management group/Business process model and notation*. Retrieved February 10, 2014, from http://www.bpmn.org/

OMG. (2014b). *UML® resource page*. Retrieved February 10, 2014, from Unified Modeling Language: http://www.uml.org/

OMG Meta Object Facility. (MOF) Core Specification. (2013). Retrieved February 04, 2014, from www.omg.org/spec/MOF/2.4.1/

Opitz, A., König, H., & Szamlewska, S. (2008). What does grid computing cost. *Journal of Grid Computing*, *6*(4), 385–397. doi:10.1007/s10723-008-9098-8

Orejas, F., Guerra, E., de Lara, J., & Ehrig, H. (2009). Correctness, completeness and termination of pattern-based model-to-model transformation. *CALCO*, *2009*, 383–397.

Ortiz, G., & Bordbar, B. (2009). Aspect-Oriented Quality of Service for Web Services: A Model-Driven Approach. In *IEEE International Conference on Web Services* (pp. 559-566). Washington, DC, USA: IEEE Computer Society. doi:10.1109/ICWS.2009.20

OSGi Alliance. (2007). *OSGi Service Platform Core Specification, Release 4, Version 4.1*. Retrieved October 2007, from: http://www.osgi.org/

Osis, J. (1969). Topological model of system functioning (in Russian). *Automatics and Computer Science, J. of Acad. of Sc.*, (6), 44-50.

Osis, J. (2006). Formal computation independent model within the MDA life cycle. International Transactions on System Science and Applications, 1 (2), 159-166.

Osis, J., & Asnina, E. (2008a). A business model to make software development less intuitive. In *Proceedings of 2008 International Conference on Innovation in Sofware Engineering (ISE 2008)* (pp. 1240-1245). IEEE Computer Society Publishing. doi:10.1109/CIMCA.2008.52

Osis, J., Asnina, E., & Grave, A. (2007a). Computation independent modeling within the MDA. *Proceedings of IEEE International Conference on Software, Science, Technology & Engineering (SwSTE07), 30-31 October 2007, Herzlia, Israel* (pp. 22-34). IEEE Computer Society, Conference Publishing Services (CPS).

Osis, J., Asnina, E., & Grave, A. (2008). Formal problem domain modeling within MDA. In Communications in Computer and Information Science (pp. 387-398). Berlin: Springer Verlag.

Osis, J., & Asnina, E. (2008b). Enterprise modeling for information system development within MDA. In *Proceedings of the 41st Annual Hawaii International Conference on System Sciences (HICSS 2008)*, (p. 490). Waikoloa, HI: IEEE. doi:10.1109/HICSS.2008.150

Osis, J., & Asnina, E. (2011a). Derivation of Use Cases from the Topological Computation Independent Business Model. In J. Osis, & E. Asnina (Eds.), *Model-Driven Domain Analysis and Software Development: Architectures and Functions* (pp. 65–89). Hershey, PA: IGI Global.

Osis, J., & Asnina, E. (2011b). *Model-Driven Domain Analysis and Software Development: Architectures and Functions*. Hershey, PA: IGI Global.

Osis, J., & Asnina, E. (2011c). Topological Modeling for Model-Driven Domain Analysis and Software Development. In J. Osis, & E. Asnina (Eds.), *Model-Driven Domain Analysis and Software Development: Architectures and Functions* (pp. 15–39). Hershey, PA: IGI Global.

Osis, J., Asnina, E., & Grave, A. (2007). Computation Independent Modeling within the MDA.In*Proceedings of ICSSTE07*, (pp. 22–34). ICSSTE.

Osis, J., Asnina, E., & Grave, A. (2007b). MDA oriented computation independent modeling of the problem domain. In *Proceedings of the 2nd International Conference on Evaluation of Novel Approaches to Software Engineering (ENASE 2007)*, (pp. 66 -71). ENASE.

Osis, J., & Beghi, L. (1997). Topological modelling of biological systems. In LinkensD.CarsonE. (Ed.), *Proceedings of the third IFAC Symposium on Modelling and Control in Biomedical Systems (Including Biological Systems)* (pp. 337-342). Oxford, UK: Elsevier Science Publishing.

Osis, J., Gefandbein, J., Markovitch, Z., & Novozhilova, N. (1991). *Diagnosis based on graph models: by the examples of aircraft and automobile mechanisms*. Moscow: Transport. (in Russian)

Osis, J., Slihte, A., & Jansone, A. (2012). Using Use Cases for Domain Modeling. In *Proceedings of the 7th International Conference on Evaluation of Novel Approaches to Software Engineering (ENASE 2012)*, (pp. 224-231). ENASE.

Osterwalder, A. (2004). *The business model ontology*. (Doctoral thesis). HEC Lausanne. Retrieved May 02, 2009, from http://www.hec.unil.ch/aosterwa/

Paganelli, F., Spinicci, E., & Giuli, D. (2008). ERMHAN: A Context-Aware Service Platform to Support Continuous Care Networks for Home-Based Assistance. *International Journal of Telemedicine and Applications*, *2008*(867639), 1–13. doi:10.1155/2008/867639 PMID:18695739

Papazoglou, M. P., & Dubray, J.-J. (2004). *A survey of web service technologies*. Retrieved 02/16, 2010, from http://eprints.biblio.unitn.it/archive/00000586/

Papazoglou, M. P., & Georgakopoulos, D. (2003). Service-oriented computing. *Communications of the ACM*, *46*(10), 24–28. Retrieved from http://ieeexplore.ieee.org/lpdocs/epic03/wrapper.htm?arnumber=1607964

Papazoglou, M. P., Traverso, P., Dustdar, S., Leymann, F., & Kramer, B. J. (2006). Service-oriented computing: A research roadmap. In F. Cubera, B. J. Krämer & M. P. Papazoglou (Eds.), Service oriented computing (SOC) (Vol. 05462). Internationales Begegnungs- und Forschungszentrum für Informatik (IBFI).

Papazoglou, M. P., & Van Den Heuvel, W.-J. (2007). Service oriented architectures: Approaches, technologies and research issues. *The VLDB Journal*, *16*(3), 389–415. doi:10.1007/s00778-007-0044-3

Papazoglou, M., & Georgakopoulos, D. (2003). Service-Oriented Computing. *Communications of the ACM*, *46*(10), 25–28.

Papotti, P., do Prado, A., de Souza, W., Cirilo, C., & Pires, L. (2013). Article. In A quantitative analysis of model-driven code generation through software experimentation (LNCS), (vol. 7908, pp. 321–337). Berlin: Springer-Verlag. doi:10.1007/978-3-642-38709-8_21

Parsons, T., & Jones, I. (1960). *Structure and process in modern societies* (Vol. 3). New York: Free Press.

Pârv, B., Lazăr, I., Motogna, S., Czibula, I.-G., & Lazăr, C.-L. (2009) ComDeValCo Framework - Procedural and Modular Issues. In *Proceedings of2nd International Conference Knowledge Engineering: Principles and Techniques* (pp. 189-193). Cluj-Napoca, Romania: Studia Universitatis Babeş-Bolyai.

Pârv, B., Lazăr, I., & Motogna, S. (2008). ComDeValCo Framework - the Modeling Language for Procedural Paradigm. *International Journal of Computers, Communications & Control, 3*(2), 183–195.

Pasic, A., Diez, S., & Espinosa, J. (2002). IMPULSE: Interworkflow Model for e-Government. In R. Traunmüller & K. Lenk (Eds.), Electronic Government (Vol. 2456, pp. 53–79). Springer.

Paternò, F. (2000). *Model-Based Design and Evaluation of Interactive Applications. Applied Computing Series.* Oxford, UK: Springer. doi:10.1007/978-1-4471-0445-2

Pati, T., Feiock, D., & Hill, J. (2012). Proactive modeling: auto-generating models from their semantics and constraints. In *Proceedings of the 2012 Workshop on Domain-specific modeling*, (pp. 7-12). New York: ACM. doi:10.1145/2420918.2420921

Pavlovski, C. (2013). A Multi-Channel System Architecture For Banking. *International Journal of Computer Science, Engineering and Applications, 3*(5), 1–12.

Peine, H., Jawurek, M., & Mandel, S. (2008). Security goal indicator trees: A model of software features that supports efficient security inspection. In *Proceedings of the 2008 11th IEEE high assurance systems engineering symposium* (p. 9-18). Washington, DC: IEEE Computer Society.

Peltz, C. (2003). Web services orchestration and choreography.*IEEEComputer, 36*(10), 46–52. doi:10.1109/MC.2003.1236471

Pereira, C. M., & Sousa, P. (2005). Enterprise architecture: Business and IT alignment. In *Proceedings of the 2005 ACM Symposium on Applied Computing* (p. 1345). ACM.

Peristeras, V., Loutas, N., Goudos, S., & Tarabanis, K. (2007). Semantic interoperability conflicts in paneuropean public services. In H. Österle, J. Schelp, & R. Winter (Eds.), *15th European Conference on Information Systems ECIS 2007* (pp. 2173–2184). University of St. Gallen. Retrieved from http://is2.lse.ac.uk/asp/aspecis/20070128.pdf

Perttunen, M., Riekki, J., & Lassila, O. (2009). Context representation and reasoning in pervasive computing: A review. *International Journal of Multimedia and Ubiquitous Engineering, 4*(4), 1–28.

Pham, H. N., Pediaditakis, D., & Boulis, A. (2007). From simulation to real deployments in WSN and back. In *Proceedings of IEEE International Symposium on a World of Wireless, Mobile and Multimedia Networks, WoWMoM 2007*, (pp. 1–6). doi:10.1109/WOWMOM.2007.4351800

Pham, T., Schneider, G., & Goose, S. (2000). A Situated Computing Framework for Mobile and Ubiquitous Multimedia Access Using Small Screen and Composite Devices. In *Proceedings of the 8th ACM International Conference on Multimedia*, (pp. 323–331). ACM. doi:10.1145/354384.354516

Phani Kumar, A. V. U., Reddy, V. A. M., & Janakiram, D. (2005). Distributed collaboration for event detection in wireless sensor networks. In *Proceedings of the 3rd International Workshop on Middleware for Pervasive and Ad-Hoc Computing*, (pp. 1–8). New York, NY: ACM.

Piattini, M., & Genero, M. (2001). *Empirical validation of measures for class diagram structural complexity through controlled experiments*. Retrieved from http://www.iro.umontreal.ca/~sahraouh/qaoose01/genero.pdf

Piattini, M., Calero, C., Sahraoui, H., & Lounis, H. (2001). Object-relational database metrics. *L'Object Edition Hermès Sciences, 17*(4), 477–498.

Piccinelli, G., & Stammers, E. (2001). From e-processes to e-networks: An e-service-oriented approach. In *Proceedings ofInternational Conference on Internet Computing*, (vol. 3, pp. 549-553). CSREA Press.

Pilgrim, J. (2008). *Measuring the level of abstraction and detail of models in the context of mdd. In Proceedings of Models in Software Engineering: Workshops and Symposia at MoDELS 2007* (pp. 105–114). Berlin: Springer-Verlag.

Pintus, A., Carboni, D., & Piras, A. (2012a). *Paraimpu*. Retrieved April 10, 2014, from http://paraimpu.crs4.it/

Pintus, A., Carboni, D., & Piras, A. (2012b). Paraimpu: A platform for a social web of things. In *Proceedings of International World Wide Web Conference Committee (IW3C2)* (pp. 401–404). IW3C. Retrieved from http://dl.acm.org/citation.cfm?id=2188059

Pintus, A., Carboni, D., & Piras, A. (2011). The anatomy of a large scale social web for internet enabled objects. In *Proceedings of the Second International Workshop on Web of Things - WoT '11*. WoT. doi:10.1145/1993966.1993975

Piras, A., Carboni, D., & Pintus, A. (2012). A Platform to Collect, Manage and Share Heterogeneous Sensor Data. In *Networked Sensing Systems* (pp. 1–2). Antwerp: INSS. doi:10.1109/INSS.2012.6240570

Plouznikoff, N., & Robert, J.-M. (2004). Caractéristiques, Enjeux et Défis de l'informatique Portée. In *Proceedings of the 16th conference on Association Francophone d'Interaction Homme-Machine* (pp. 125-132). New York, NY: ACM Press.

Poels, G. (2010). A conceptual model of service exchange in service-dominant logic. In J. Morin, J. Ralyte, & M. Snene (Eds.), *First International Conference on Exploring Services Science,* (LNBIP), (vol. 53, pp. 224-238). Springer. doi:10.1007/978-3-642-14319-9_18

Poernomo, I., & Terrell, J. (2010). Correct-by-construction model transformations from spanning tree specifications in Coq. In *Proceedings of ICFEM 2010*. ICFEM.

Pollet, T., Maas, G., Marien, J., & Wambecq, A. (2006). Telecom services delivery in a SOA. In *Proceedings of the 20th International Conference on Advanced Information Networking and Applications*, (vol. 2, pp. 529-533). Academic Press.

Polta, Y., Annadi, R., Kong, J., Walia, G., & Kygard, K. (2012). Adapting Web Tables on Mobile Devices. *International Journal of Handheld Computing Research, 3*(1), 1-22.

Ponsard, C., & Devroey, X. (2011). Generating high-level event-b system models from KAOS requirement models. In *Proceedings ofActes du XXIX eme Congres INFORSID*. Academic Press.

Porras, P., Saidi, H., & Yegneswaran, V. (2009, March). *An analysis of Conficker's logic and redezvous points* (Technical Report). Menlo Park, CA: SRI International. Retrieved from http://mtc.sri.com/Conficker/

Porter, M. (1998). *Competitive advantage: Creating and sustaining superior performance*. The Free Press.

Potel, M. (1996). *MVP: Model-view-presenter the taligent programming model for C++ and Java. Technical report*. Taligent Inc.

Poulcheria, B., & Costas, V. (2012). A context management architecture for m-commerce applications. *Central European Journal of Computer Science, 2*(2), 87–117. doi:10.2478/s13537-012-0010-z

Premraj, R., Shepperd, M., Kitchenham, B., & Forselius, P. (2005). An empirical analysis of software productivity over time. In *Proceedings of the 11th IEEE International Symposium on Software Metrics* (pp. 37-46). Los Alamitos, CA: IEEE. doi:10.1109/METRICS.2005.8

Pressman, R. (2004). *Software Engineering: A Practitioner's Approach* (6th ed.). Columbus, Ohio, USA: McGraw-Hill Science/Engineering/Math.

Pressman, R. S. (2001). *Software engineering, a practitioner's approach* (5th ed.). New York: McGraw-Hill.

Pressman, R. S. (2005). *Software engineering, a practitioner's approach* (6th ed.). McGraw Hill.

Preuveneers, D., & Berbers, Y. (2004). Suitability of existing service discovery protocols for mobile users in an ambient intelligence environent. In *Proceedings of the International Conference on Pervasive Computing and Communications* (pp. 760–764). Orlando, FL: CSREA Press.

Qingfeng, Z., Wenbo, C., & Lihua, H. (2008). E-Business Transformation. *An Analysis Framework Based on Critical Organizational Dimensions, 13*(3), 408–413.

QuadraSpace. (2010). Retrieved February 21, 2014, from http://www.quadraspace.org/

QVT. (2011). *QVT: MOF 2.0 Query, View, Transformation. Version 1.1, OMG Document Number: formal/2011-01-01*. Retrieved February 7, 2014, from http://www.omg.org/spec/QVT/1.1/

Rajkovic, P., Jankovic, D., Stankovic, T., & Tosic, V. (2010). Software Tools for rapid Development and Customization of Medical Information Systems. In *Proceedings of 12th IEEE International Conference on e-Health Networking Applications and Services* (pp. 119-126). Washington, DC, USA: IEEE Computer Society. doi:10.1109/HEALTH.2010.5556582

Ralston, A., & Reilly, E. I. (Eds.). (1993). *Encyclopedia of computer science* (3rd ed.). New York: Van Nostrand Reinhold Company.

Ramollari, E., Dranidis, D., & Simons, A. J. H. (2007). *A survey of service oriented development methodologies*. Paper presented at the 2nd European Young Researchers Workshop on Service Oriented Computing. Leicester, UK.

Rangarajan, H., & Garcia-Luna-Aceves, J. J. (2004). Reliable data delivery in event-driven wireless sensor networks. In *Proc. Ninth International Symposium on Computers and Communications (pp.* 232-237). doi:10.1109/ISCC.2004.1358410

Rapanotti, L., Hall, J. G., Jackson, M., & Nuseibeh, B. (2004). Architecture Driven Problem Decomposition. In *Proceedings of IEEE International Requirements Engineering Conference (RE)*, (73-82). Washington, DC: IEEE Computer Society.

Ravi, J., & Wullert, J. (2002). Challenges: Environmental Design for Pervasive Computing Systems. In *Proceedings of the Eighth Annual International Conference on Mobile Computing and Networking*, (pp. 263–270). ACM Press.

Raychoudhury, V., Cao, J., Kumar, M., & Zhang, D. (2013). Middleware for pervasive computing: A survey. *Pervasive and Mobile Computing*, *9*(2), 177–200. doi:10.1016/j.pmcj.2012.08.006

Razavian, M., & Lago, P. (2011). A survey of SOA migration in industry. In Proceedings of Service-Oriented Computing (LNCS), (vol. 7084, pp. 618-626). Springer.

Razavian, M., & Lago, P. (2010). A frame of reference for SOA migration. In *Towards a service-based internet* (LNCS), (Vol. 6481, pp. 150–162). Springer.

Read, K., & Titchkosky, L. (2003). *Refactoring J2ME Midlets to Use the State Pattern*. University of Calgary.

Reifer, D. (2000). Web development: Estimating quick-to-market software. *IEEE Software*, *17*(6), 57–64. doi:10.1109/52.895169

Reige, C., & Aier, S. (2009). A consistency approach to enterprise architecture method engineering. In Proceedings of Service-Oriented Computing, ICSOC Workshops (pp. 388–399). Springer.

Rein, M., Ambroziewicz, A., Bojarski, J., Nowakowski, W., Straszak, T., Kalnins, A., et al. (2008). *Initial ReDSeeDS Prototype*. Project Deliverable D5.4.1, ReDSeeDS Project. Retrieved June 17, 2009, from www.redseeds.eu

Renevier, P., Nigay, L., Salembier, P., & Pasqualetti, L. (2002). Systèmes Mixtes Mobiles et Collaboratifs. In *Colloque sur la Mobilité*. Nancy, France: LORIA.

Rensink, A., & Kuperus, J.-H. (2009). Repotting the geraniums: On nested graph transformation rules. In Proceedings of GT-VMT 2009. GT-VMT.

Rensink, A., Schmidt, A., & Varro, D. (2004). *Model checking graph transformations: A comparison of two approaches. In Proceedings of ICGT (LNCS)*, (Vol. 3256). Springer.

Ren, Y., Xing, T., Quan, Q., & Zhao, Y. (2010). Software Configuration Management of Version Control Study Based on Baseline. In *Proceedings of 3rd International Conference on Information Management, Innovation Management and Industrial Engineering*, (vol.4, pp. 118-121). Washington, DC, USA: IEEE Press. doi:10.1109/ICIII.2010.506

Requirements Driven Software Development System (ReDSeeDS). (n.d.). Retrieved February 26, 2014 from http://www.redseeds.eu

Reus, T., Geers, H., & van Deursen, A. (2006). Article. In Harvesting Software System for MDA-based Reengineering (LNCS), (vol. 4066, pp. 220–236). Heidelberg, Germany: Springer-Verlag.

Rhodes, K. A. (2001, August). *Code red, code red II, and SirCam attacks highlight need for proactive measures.* GAO Testimony Before the Subcommittee on Government Efficiency, Financial Management and Intergovrenmental Relations, Commitee on Government Reform, House of Representatives. (Report number GAO-01-1073T)

Riberio, C., Zuquete, A., Ferreira, P., & Guedes, P. (2001). SPL: An access control language for security policies with complex constraints. In *Proceedings of Network and Distributed System Security Symposium, NDSS01*. NDSS.

Richters, M., & Gogolla, M. (1998). On formalising the UML object constraint language OCL, In *Proc. 17th Int. Conf. Conceptual Modelling (ER '98)* (LNCS). Springer.

Robertshaw, T. (2012). *October 2012 Ecommerce Survey*. Retrieved March 01, 2013, from http://tomrobertshaw.net/2012/11/october-2012-ecommerce-survey/

Robson, C. (2002). *Real world research* (2nd ed.). Oxford, UK: Blackwell Publishing.

Rocha, B. P. S., Conti, M., Etalle, S., & Crispo, B. (2013). Hybrid Static-Runtime Information Flow and Declassification Enforcement. *IEEE Transactions on Information Forensics and Security*, *8*(8), 1294–1305. doi:10.1109/TIFS.2013.2267798

Romer, K., & Mattern, F. (2004). Event-based systems for detecting real-world states with sensor networks: A critical analysis. In *Proceedings of 2004 Conference on Intelligent Sensors, Sensor Networks and Information Processing*, (pp. 389–396). doi:10.1109/ISSNIP.2004.1417493

Rosen, M. (2003, December). MDA, SOA and technology convergence. *MDA Journal*. Retrieved March 15, 2009, from http://www.bptrends.com/publicationfiles/12-03%20COL%20Frankel%20-%20MDA%20SOA%20-%20Rosen.pdf

Rothboard, J. (2009). *Linking SaaS software pricing to value*. Retrieved March 10 from, 2010, http://www.readwriteweb.com/enterprise/2009/01/linking-saas-software-pricing-to-value.php

Rothensee, M. (2007). A high-fidelity simulation of the smart fridge enabling product-based services. In *Proceedings of3rd IET International Conference on Intelligent Environments (IE 07)* (pp. 529–532). IEE. doi:10.1049/cp:20070420

Roth, J. (2002). Patterns of Mobile Interaction. *Personal and Ubiquitous Computing*, *6*(4), 282–289. doi:10.1007/s007790200029

Roth, V., & Peters, J. (2001). A scalable and secure global tracking service for mobile agents. *Lecture Notes in Computer Science*, *2240*, 169–181. doi:10.1007/3-540-45647-3_12

Roussaki, I., Kalatzis, N., Liampotis, N., Frank, K., Sykas, E., & Anagnostou, M. (2012). Developing Context-Aware Personal Smart Spaces. In Handbook of Research on Mobile Software Engineering: Design, Implementation and Emergent Applications, (pp. 659-676). Academic Press.

Roussel, N., Evans, H., & Hansen, H. (2003). Using distance as an interface in a video communication system. In *Proceedings of the 15th French-speaking conference on human-computer interaction* (pp. 268–271). New York, NY: ACM Press. doi:10.1145/1063669.1063714

Royce, W. W. (1970). Managing the development of large software systems. In *Proc. 9th. Intern. Conf. Software Engineering*. IEEE.

RTCA. (2012). *RTCA/EUROCAE DO-178C standard "Software Considerations in Airborne Systems and Equipment Certification", 2012*. RTCA.

Rukzio, E., Holleis, P., & Gellersen, H. (2012). Personal projectors for pervasive computing. *IEEE Pervasive Computing / IEEE Computer Society [and] IEEE Communications Society*, *11*(2), 30–37. doi:10.1109/MPRV.2011.17

Rumbaugh, J., Blaha, M., Premerlani, W., Eddy, F., & Lorensen, W. (1990). *Object-oriented modeling and design*. Prentice Hall.

SaaS Optics. (2010). *SaaS Optics Deep Dive*. Retrieved March 10, 2010, from http://www.saasoptics.com/saas_operations_operating_model/saas_metrics_management_deep_dive/saas_metrics_management_deep_dive.html

Sadiq, S., Orlowska, M., & Sadiq, W. (2005). *The role of messaging in collaborative business processes.* Paper presented at the IRMA International Conference. San Diego, CA.

Sadun, E., & Wardwell, R. (2014). *The Core iOS Developer's Cookbook* (5th ed.). Boston, MA: Addison-Wesley Professional.

Sanchez-Pi, N., Carbó, J., & Molina, J. (2012). An Evaluation Method for Context–Aware Systems in U-Health. In *Proceedings of 3rd International Symposium on Ambient Intelligence* (ISAmI 2012) (pp. 219–226). Salamanca, Spain: Springer. doi:10.1007/978-3-642-28783-1_28

Sankarasubramaniam, Y., Akan, B., & Akyildiz, I. F. (n.d.). Esrt: Event-to-sink reliable transport in wireless sensor networks. In *Proceedings of the ACM International Symposium on Mobile Ad Hoc Networking and Computing* (Mobihoc), (pp. 177-188). ACM.

Scacchi, W. (2001). *Process models in software engineering.* New York: John Wiley and Sons, Inc.

Scandariato, R., Yskout, K., Heyman, T., & Joosen, W. (2008). *Architecting software with security patterns* (Report No. CW515). Katholieke Universiteit Leuven - Department of Computer Science.

Scheer, A., Thomas, O., & Adam, O. (2005). Process modeling using event-driven process chains: Process-aware information systems: Bridging people and software through process technology. Hoboken, NJ: Academic Press.

Schilit, W. N. (1995). *System Architecture for Context-aware Mobile Computing.* (Ph.D thesis). Columbia University, New York, NY.

Schmidt, A. (2002). *Ubiquitous Computing: Computing in Context.* (PhD dissertation, Lancaster University). Retrieved from http://www.comp.lancs.ac.uk/~albrecht/phd/

Schmidt, H., & Wentzlaff, I. (2006). Preserving software quality characteristics from requirements analysis to architectural design. In *Proceedings of the European Workshop on Software Architectures (EWSA),* (LNCS) (vol. 4344, pp. 189-203). Berlin: Springer. doi:10.1007/11966104_14

Schmidt, D. (2006). Model-driven engineering. *IEEE Computer, 39*(2), 25–31. doi:10.1109/MC.2006.58

Schmidt, D. C., Stal, M., Rohnert, H., & Buschmann, F. (2000a). *Applying patterns.* John Wiley & Sons.

Schmidt, D. C., Stal, M., Rohnert, H., & Buschmann, F. (2000b). *Pattern-Oriented Software Architecture: Patterns for Concurrent and Networked Objects.* John Wiley & Sons.

Schmitt, E. (1991, June 6). U.S. details flaw in patriot missile. *The New York Times.*

Schneider, F. B., Walsh, K., & Sirer, E. G. (2009). *Nexus authorization logic (nal): Design rationale and applications.* Cornell Computing and Information Science Technical Report.

Schneider, F. B. (2000). Enforceable security policies. *ACM Transactions on Information and System Security, 3*(1), 30–50. doi:10.1145/353323.353382

Schneier, B. (1999). Attack trees. *Dr. Dobb's Journal.* Retrieved June 24, 2009, from http://www.schneier.com/paper-attacktrees-ddj-ft.html

Schneier, B. (1999, December). Attack trees. *Dr. Dobbs Journal.*

Schuff, D., & St. Louis, R. (2001, June 1). Centralization vs. decentralization of application software. *Communications of the ACM, 44*(6), 88–94. doi:10.1145/376134.376177

Schumacher, M., Fernandez-Buglioni, E., Hybertson, D., Buschmann, F., & Sommerlad, P. (2005). *Security patterns: Integrating security and systems engineering.* Washington, DC: Wiley & Sons.

Schwiderski-Grosche, S. (2008). *Context-dependent event detection in sensor networks.* Paper presented at the 2nd Intl. Conf. on Distributed Event-Based Systems (DEBS'08). Rome, Italy.

Sekar, R., Venkatakrishnan, V. N., Basu, S., Bhatkar, S., & DuVarney, D. C. (2003). Model-carrying code: a practical approach for safe execution of untrusted applications. In *Proceedings of the nineteenth ACM symposium on Operating systems principles* (pp. 15-28). doi:10.1145/945445.945448

Selic, B. (2003). The pragmatics of model-driven development. *IEEE Software, 20,* 19–25. Retrieved from http://ieeexplore.ieee.org/lpdocs/epic03/wrapper.htm?arnumber=1231146

Selic, B. (2008). MDA manifestations. *The European Journal for the Informatics Professional*, *9*(2), 11–16.

SEMAT. (2013a, June 20). *Intro to Essence*. Paper presented at OMG's ESSENCE Information Day. Berlin, Germany.

SEMAT. (2013b, June 20). *Introduction to SEMAT*. Paper presented at OMG's ESSENCE Information Day. Berlin, Germany. Retrieved from www.semat.org

SEMAT. (2014). *Software Engineering Method and Theory*. Retrieved February 2014, from www.semat.org

Sen.se. (2011). *Open.Sen.se*. Retrieved February 21, 2014, from http://open.sen.se/

Sengupta, B., & Roychoudhury, A. (2011). Engineering multi-tenant software-as-a-service systems. In *Proceedings of the 3rd International Workshop on Principles of Engineering Service-Oriented Systems* (pp. 15-21). New York, NY: ACM. doi:10.1145/1985394.1985397

Sentas, P., & Angelis, L. (2006). Categorical missing data imputation for software cost estimation by multinomial logistic regression. *Journal of Systems and Software*, *79*(3), 404–414. doi:10.1016/j.jss.2005.02.026

Sentas, P., Angelis, L., Stamelos, I., & Bleris, G. (2005). software productivity and effort prediction with ordinal regression. *Information and Software Technology*, *47*(1), 17–29. doi:10.1016/j.infsof.2004.05.001

Seth, A., Singla, A. R., & Aggarwal, H. (2012). Service oriented architecture adoption trends: A critical survey. In Contemporary computing, communications in computer and information science (vol. 306, pp. 164-175). Springer.

Sewing, J., & Rosemann, M. (2008). Assessing the potential impact of web services on business processes. In I. Lee (Ed.), *E-business models, services and communications* (pp. 221–249). Hershey, PA: Information Science Reference.

Shaw, M. (2001). The Coming-of-Age of Software Architecture Research. In *Proceedings of the 23rd International Conference on Software Engineering*, (pp. 656–664). ACM Press.

Shaw, M., & Garlan, D. (1996). *Software architecture - Perspectives on an emerging discipline*. Upper Saddle River, NJ: Prentice-Hall.

SHIELDS Project Consortium. (2010). *Final report on inspection methods and prototype vulnerability recognition tools*. SHIELDS project deliverable D4.3. Retrieved from http://www.shields-project.eu/

SHIELDS. (n.d.). *Detecting known vulnerabilities from with design and development tools*. Retrieved from http://www.shields-project.eu/

Shih, K.-P., Wang, S.-S., Yang, P.-H., & Chang, C.-C. (2006). Collect: Collaborative event detection and tracking in wireless heterogeneous sensor networks. In *Proceedings of the 11th IEEE Symposium on Computers and Communications ISCC'*06, (pp. 935–940). IEEE.

Sicilia, M. A., & Mora, M. (2010). On using the REA enterprise ontology as a foundation for service system representations. In Ontology, Conceptualization and Epistemology for Information Systems, Software Engineering and Service Science 2010 (LNBIP) (Vol. 62, pp. 135-147). Springer. doi:10.1007/978-3-642-16496-5_10

Simon, D., Cifuentes, C., Cleal, D., Daniels, J., & White, D. (2006). Java on the bare metal of wireless sensor devices: The squawk java virtual machine. In *Proceedings of the 2nd International Conference on Virtual Execution Environments*, (pp. 78–88). New York, NY: ACM.

Sinisalo, J., Salo, J., Karajaluoto, H., & Leppaniemi, M. (2006). Managing customer relationships through mobile medium – underlying issues and opportunities. In *Proceedings of the 39th Hawaii International Conference on System Sciences*. IEEE.

SLA Definition. (2009). *Definition of service level agreement*. Retrieved March 10 2010, from http://looselycoupled.com/glossary/SLA

Slihte, A. (2010a). The Specific Text Analysis Tasks at the Beginning of MDA Life Cycle. In *Proceedings of Databases and Information Systems Doctoral Consortium*. Latvia, Riga. Academic Press.

Slihte, A. (2010b). Transforming textual use cases to a computation independent model. In *Proceedings of MDA & MTDD 2010*. Academic Press.

Slihte, A., Osis, J., & Donins, U. (2011). Knowledge Integration for Domain Modeling. In *Proceedings of the 3rd International Workshop on Model-Driven Architecture and Modeling-Driven Software Development*, (pp. 46-56). Academic Press.

Śmiałek, M., Bojarski, J., Nowakowski, W., Ambroziewicz, A., & Straszak, T. (2007). Complementary use case scenario representations based on domain vocabularies. In Proceedings of*Model Driven Engineering Languages and Systems, (LNCS), (vol. 4735*, pp. 544–558). Berlin: Springer. doi:10.1007/978-3-540-75209-7_37

Śmiałek, M., Jarzebowski, N., & Nowakowski, W. (2012). Translation of use case scenarios to Java code. *Computer Science*, *13*(4), 35–52. doi:10.7494/csci.2012.13.4.35

SMM. (2012). *Software Metrics Meta-Model, Version 1.0, OMG Document Number: formal/2012-01-05*. Retrieved February 7, 2014, from http://www.omg.org/spec/SMM/1.0/

Software Experts. (n.d.). *Software process models*. Retrieved from http://www.the-software-experts.de/e_dta-sw-process.htm

Sommerville, I. (2007). *Software engineering* (8th ed.). Addison Wesley. Retrieved from http://www.buzzle.com/editorials/1-5-2005-63768.asp

Sommerville, I. (2001). *Software engineering* (6th ed.). Addison-Wesley.

Sommerville, I. (2004). *Software Engineering* (7th ed.). Addison Wesley.

Song, Q., Shepperd, M. J., & Cartwright, M. (2005). A Short Note on Safest Default Missingness Mechanism Assumptions. *Empirical Software Engineering*, *10*(2), 235–243. doi:10.1007/s10664-004-6193-8

Soriano, J., Jimenez, M., Cantera, J. M., & Hierro, J. J. (2006). Delivering Mobile Enterprise Services on Morfeo's MC Open Source Platform. In *Proceeding of the 7th international Conference on Mobile Data Management* (pp. 139-139). doi:10.1109/MDM.2006.63

Soto-Acosta, P., & Meroño-Cerdan, A. L. (2009). Evaluating Internet technologies business effectiveness. *Telematics and Informatics*, *26*(2), 211–221. doi:10.1016/j.tele.2008.01.004

Sottara, D., Mello, P., & Proctor, M. (2010). A configurable rete-OO engine for reasoning with different types of imperfect information. *IEEE Transactions on Knowledge and Data Engineering*, *22*(11), 1535–1548. doi:10.1109/TKDE.2010.125

Spadacini, M., Savazzi, S., & Nicoli, M. (2014). Wireless home automation networks for indoor surveillance: Technologies and experiments Internet of Things for wireless and mobile communication. *EURASIP Journal on Wireless Communications and Networking*, (6), 1–17.

Spafford, E. H. (1988, November). *The internet worm program: An analysis* (Tech. Rep. No. CSD-TR-823). West Lafayette, IN: Department of Computer Sciences, Purdue University.

Sparx Systems. (n.d.). *Enterprise architect tool*. Retrieved February 26, 2014, from http://www.sparxsystems.com/products/ea/

Spencer, J. (2004). *TOGAF enterprise edition version 8.1*. Academic Press.

Spitzer, M. B., Rensing, N., McClelland, R., & Aquilino, P. (1997). Eyeglass-based systems for wearable computing. In *Digest of Papers of First International Symposium on Wearable Computers* (pp. 48–51). Academic Press. doi:10.1109/ISWC.1997.629918

Spivey, M. (1992). *The Z notation - A reference manual*. Upper Saddle River, NJ: Prentice Hall. Retrieved June 24, 2009, from http://spivey.oriel.ox.ac.uk/mike/zrm

Spyrou, C., Samaras, G., Pitoura, E., & Evripidou, P. (2004). Mobile agents for wireless computing: The convergence of wireless computational models with mobile-agent technologies. *Mobile Networks and Applications*, *9*(5), 517–528. doi:10.1023/B:MONE.0000034705.10830.b7

SQLite. (2009). Retrieved June 10, 2009, from http://www.sqlite.org/

SRI. (2012). *Yices SMT Solver*. Retrieved from http://yices.csl.sri.com/

Srivasta, L. (2005). Ubiquitous Network Societies: The Case of Radio Frequency Identification. In *Proceedings of ITU Workshop on Ubiquitous Network Societies*, Geneva. Retrieved from http://www.itu.int/ubiquitous/

Stabell, C. B., & Fjeldstad, O. D. (1998). Configuring value for competitive advantage: On chains, shops, and networks. *Strategic Management Journal, 19*(5), 413–437. doi:10.1002/(SICI)1097-0266(199805)19:5<413::AID-SMJ946>3.0.CO;2-C

Stabernack, B., Richter, H., & Müller, E. (2002). A Multi-platform Experimental Multimedia Streaming Framework for Mobile and Internet Applications. In *Proceedings of the International Packet Video Workshop 2002* (PV2002), (pp. 24–26). PV.

Standish Group. (2003). *The chaos report*. Author.

Steel, C. & Nagappan, R., & Lai, R. (2005). *Core security patterns: Best practices and strategies for J2EE, web services, and identity management*. Academic Press.

Steinberg, D., Budinsky, F., Paternostro, M., & Merks, E. (2008). *EMF: Eclipse modeling framework*. Addison-Wesley Professional. Retrieved from http://portal.acm.org/citation.cfm?id=1197540

Steinholtz, B., & Walden, K. (1987). Automatic Identification of Software System Differences. *IEEE Transactions on Software Engineering*, SE-*13*(4), 493–497. doi:10.1109/TSE.1987.233186

Stensrud, E., & Myrtveit, I. (1998). Human performance estimating with analogy and regression models: An empirical validation. In *Proceedings of the 5th IEEE International Software Metrics Symposium (METRICS'98)* (pp. 205–213). IEEE. doi:10.1109/METRIC.1998.731247

Stewart, D. (1999). *The Musician's Guide to Reading and Writing Music*. Backbeat.

Stojanovic, D. (Ed.). (2009). *Context-Aware Mobile and Ubiquitous Computing for Enhanced Usability: Adaptive Technologies and Applications*. Hershey, PA: Information Science Reference. doi:10.4018/978-1-60566-290-9

Strauss, A. L., & Corbin, J. M. (1998). *Basics of qualitative research: Techniques and procedures for developing grounded theory* (2nd ed.). Thousand Oaks, CA: Sage Publications Inc.

Strike, K., El Emam, K., & Madhavji, N. (2001). Software cost estimation with incomplete data. *IEEE Transactions on Software Engineering, 27*(10), 890–908. doi:10.1109/32.962560

Sugiura, K., Ogawa, A., Nakamura, O., & Murai, J. (2002). Resource Management Issues for Portable Mobile Computers in Distributed Networks. *IEIC Technical Report, 102*(362), 59–64.

SUN javax.crypto. API*. (n.d.). Retrieved June 24, 2009, from http://java.sun.com/javase/6/docs/api/javax/crypto/package-summary.html

Sun Microsystems Inc. (2002). *Mobile Information Device Profile for Java 2 Micro Edition, JSP 118, Java Community Process*. Retrieved from http://jcp.org/aboutJava/communityprocess/final/jsr118/index.html

Sun Microsystems Inc. (2002a). *Security for GSM/UMTS Compliant Devices Recommended Practice. Addendum to the Mobile Information Device Profile, Java Community Process*. Retrieved from http://www.jcp.org/aboutJava/communityprocess/maintenance/jsr118/

Sun Microsystems Inc. (2003). *The Connected Limited Device Configuration Specification, JSR139, Java Community Process*. Retrieved from http://jcp.org/aboutJava/communityprocess/final/jsr139/index.html

Sun Microsystems. (2002). *Java Message Service version 1.1*. Retrieved December 11, 2009 from http://java.sun.com/products/jms/docs.html

Sutton, A., & Stroustrup, B. (2011). Design of concept libraries for c++. In *Proceedings of4th International Conference on Software Language Engineering* (pp. 97-118). Los Alamitos, CA: IEEE.

Sycara, K. P., Widoff, S., Klusch, M., & Lu, J. (2002). Larks: Dynamic matchmaking among heterogeneous software agents in cyberspace. *Autonomous Agents and Multi-Agent Systems, 5*(2), 173–203. doi:10.1023/A:1014897210525

Szekely, P. (1996). Retrospective and Challenges for Model-Based Interface Development. In *Proceedings of the Second International Workshop on Computer-Aided Design of User Interfaces*. Namur, Belgium: Presses Universitaires de Namur. doi:10.1007/978-3-7091-7491-3_1

Talevski, A., Chang, E., & Dillon, T. S. (2003). Meta model Driven Framework for the Integration and Extension of Application Components. In *9th IEEE International Workshop on Object-Oriented Real-Time Dependable Systems* (pp. 255-261). Washington, DC: IEEE Computer Society. doi:10.1109/WORDS.2003.1267534

Tamaki, E., Miyaki, T., & Rekimoto, J. (2009). Brainy hand: an ear-worn hand gesture interaction device. In *Proceedings of the 27th of the International Conference Extended Abstracts on Human Factors in Computing Systems* (pp. 4255–4260). New York, NY: ACM Press. doi:10.1145/1520340.1520649

Tambouris, E., Manouselis, N., & Costopoulou, C. (2007). Metadata for digital collections of e-government resources. *The Electronic Library*, *25*(2), 176–192. doi:10.1108/02640470710741313

Tan, L. (2010). Future internet: The internet of things. In *Proceedings of 2010 3rd International Conference on Advanced Computer Theory and Engineering (ICACTE)* (pp. V5–376–V5–380). Chengdu, China: IEEE. doi:10.1109/ICACTE.2010.5579543

Tasker, M. (2000). *Professional Symbian programming: Mobile solutions on the EPOC platform*. Wrox.

Taylor, R., Medvidovic, N., & Dashofy, E. (2010). *Software Architecture: Foundations, Theory, and Practice*. Wiley.

TechAmerica. (2008). *Software Cost Estimating*. Retrieved March 10, 2010, http://www.techamerica.org/

Tergujeff, R., Haajanen, J., Leppänen, J., & Toivonen, S. (2007). Mobile SOA: Service orientation on lightweight mobile devices. In *Proceedings ofIEEE International Conference on Web Services* (pp. 1224-1225). IEEE.

Thevenin, D., & Coutaz, J. (1999). Plasticity of User Interfaces: Framework and Research Agenda.[IFIP, IOS Press.]. *Proceedings of Interact*, *99*, 110–117.

Tonella, P., & Potrich, A. (2005). *Reverse Engineering of Object-Oriented Code. Monographs in Computer Science*. Heidelberg, Germany: Springer-Verlag.

Torgo, L. (2005). Regression error characteristic surfaces. In *Proceedings of the 11th ACM SIGKDD International Conference on Knowledge Discovery and Data Mining (KDD '05)*, (pp. 697-702). ACM.

Trillo, R., Ilarri, S., & Mena, E. (2007). Comparison and performance evaluation of mobile agent platforms. In *Proceedings of the 3rd International Conference on Autonomic and Autonomous Systems (ICAS'07)* (p. 41). IEEE Computer Society. doi:10.1109/CONIELECOMP.2007.66

Tryllian, B. V. (2001) *Agent Development Kit Technical White Paper*. Retrieved March 8, 2014 from http://www.global-media.org/neome/docs/PDF%27s/01%20-%20the%20best%20ones/Tryllian%20Technical%20white%20paper%20ADKv1.0.pdf

Tsui, F., Karam, O., & Bernal, B. (2013). *Essentials of software engineering*. Burlington, MA: Jones and Bartlett Publishers, Inc.

Tusor, B., & Várkonyi-Kóczy, A. R. (2011). Intelligent hotel room assistant. In *Proceedings of the 8th International Conference on Informatics in Control, Automation and Robotics* (pp. 182-187). Noordwijkerhout, Netherlands: Academic Press.

Twala, B., Cartwright, M., & Shepperd, M. (2006). Ensemble of missing data techniques to improve software prediction accuracy. In *Proceedings of the 28th International Conference on Software Engineering*, (pp. 909 – 912). Academic Press. doi:10.1145/1134285.1134449

Ulrich, W., & NewComb, P. (2010). *Information System Transformation: Architecture Driven Modernization Case Studies*. Elsevier.

UML 2.1.1 superstructure and infrastructure. (2007). *Specification*. Author.

UML Profile for Modeling Quality of Service and Fault Tolerance Characteristics and mechanisms, v 1.1. (2008). Retrieved from http://www.omg.org/technology/documents/formal/QoS_FT.htm

UML Revision Task Force, Object Management Group (OMG). (2007). *OMG Unified Modeling Language: Superstructure*. Retrieved June 24, 2009, from http://www.omg.org/spec/UML/2.1.2/

UML Revision Task Force, Object Management Group (OMG). (2012). *Object Constraint Language Specification*. Retrieved June 2, 2014, from http://www.omg.org/spec/OCL/2.3.1

UML. (2011a). *Unified Modeling Language: Infrastructure. Version 2.4.1, OMG Specification formal/2011-08-05*. Retrieved February 7, 2014, from http://www.omg.org/spec/UML/2.4.1/

UML. (2011b). *Unified Modeling Language: Superstructure. Version 2.4.1, OMG Specification: formal/2011-08-06*. Retrieved February 7, 2014, from http://www.omg.org/spec/UML/2.4.1/

UN/CEFACT Modeling Methodology (UMM) User Guide. (2006). Retrieved May 04, 2009, from http://www.unece.org/cefact/umm/UMM_userguide_220606.pdf

Urra, O., & Ilarri, S. (2013) Using Mobile Agents in Vehicular Networks for Data Processing. In *Proceedings of the 14th International Conference on Mobile Data Management (MDM 2013), PhD. Forum*. (pp. 11-14), Milan, Italy: IEEE Computer Society. doi:10.1109/MDM.2013.57

Urra, O., Ilarri, S., & Mena, E. (2008). Testing mobile agent platforms over the air. In *Proceedings of the 1st ICDE Workshop on Data and Services Management in Mobile Environments (DS2ME'08)* (pp. 152–159). Salamanca, Spain: IEEE Computer Society. doi:10.1109/ICDEW.2008.4498307

Urra, O., Ilarri, S., & Mena, E. (2009). Agents jumping in the air: Dream or reality? In *Proceedings of the 10th International Work-conference on Artificial Neural Networks (IWANN'09), Special Session on Practical Applications of Agents and Multi-agent Systems* (pp. 627–634). Salamanca, Spain: Springer Verlag. doi:10.1007/978-3-642-02478-8_79

US-CERT/NIST. (2008). *Vulnerability summary CVE-2008-4250*. Retrieved from http://nvd.nist.gov/nvd.cfm?cvename=CVE-2008-4250

USE. (2011). *A UML-based Specification Environment*. Retrieved February 7, 2014, from http://sourceforge.net/apps/mediawiki/useocl/

Valckenaers, P., Sauter, J., Sierra, C., & Rodriguez-Aguilar, J. (2006). Applications and environments for multi-agent systems. *Autonomous Agents and Multi-Agent Systems, 14*(1), 61–85. doi:10.1007/s10458-006-9002-5

van Amstel, M., Bosems, S., Kurtev, I., & Pires, L. F. (2011). Performance in Model Transformations: Experiments with ATL and QVT, *ICMT 2011. LNCS, 6707*, 198–212.

van Dam, A. (1997). Post-WIMP user interfaces. *Communications of the ACM, 40*(2), 63–67. doi:10.1145/253671.253708

Van Hulse, J., & Khoshgoftaar, T. (2008). A comprehensive empirical evaluation of missing value imputation in noisy software measurement data. *Journal of Systems and Software, 81*(5), 691–708. doi:10.1016/j.jss.2007.07.043

van Lamsweerde, A. (2004). Elaborating security requirements by construction of intentional anti-models. In *Proceedings of the International Conference on Software Engineering (ICSE)*, (pp. 148-157). Washington, DC: IEEE Computer Society. doi:10.1109/ICSE.2004.1317437

Van Nuffel, D. (2007). Towards a service-oriented methodology: Business-driven guidelines for service identification. In On the move to meaningful internet systems 2007: OTM 2007 workshops (pp. 294-303). OTM.

Van Overeem, A. V. O. A., Witters, J. W. J., & Peristeras, V. P. V. (2007). *An Interoperability Framework for Pan-European E-Government Services (PEGS)*. IEEE. Retrieved from http://ieeexplore.ieee.org/lpdocs/epic03/wrapper.htm?arnumber=4076384

van Welie, M., & van der Veer, G. C. (2003). Pattern Languages in Interaction Design: Structure and Organization. In M. Rauterberg et al. (Eds.), *Human-Computer Interaction – INTERACT'03* (pp. 527–534). IOS Press.

Vanoverberghe, D., & Piessen, F. (2008). A caller-side inline reference monitor for an object-oriented intermediate language. In *Proceedings of the 10th IFIP International Conference on Formal Methods for Open Object-based Distributed Systems, FMOODS 2008* (pp. 240-258). FMOODS.

Varga, A. (2002). Omnet++. Software tools for networking. *IEEE Network Interactive, 16*(4).

Varro, D., Varro-Gyapay, S., Ehrig, H., Prange, U., & Taentzer, G. (2006). *Termination analysis of model transformations by Petri Nets. In Proceedings of ICGT 2006* (LNCS), (Vol. 4178). Springer.

Vasudevan, A., McCune, J. M., & Newsome, J. (2013). *Trustworthy Execution on Mobile Devices. SpringerBriefs in Computer Science*. Berlin, Germany: Springer Verlag.

Vidales, M. A. S., García, A. M. F., & Aguilar, L. J. (2008). A new MDA approach based on BPM and SOA to improve software development process. *Polytechnical Studies Review:Tékhne*, *6*(9), 70–90.

Vienna University of Technology. (2013). *European Smart Cities*. Retrieved February 21, 2014, from http://www.smart-cities.eu

Viganò, L. (2006). Automated security protocol analysis with the AVISPA tool. *Electronic Notes in Theoretical Computer Science*, *155*, 61–86. doi:10.1016/j.entcs.2005.11.052

Viroli, M., Holvoet, T., Ricci, A., Schelfthout, K., & Zambonelli, F. (2006). Infrastructures for the environment of multiagent systems. *Autonomous Agents and Multi-Agent Systems*, *14*(1), 49–60. doi:10.1007/s10458-006-9001-6

Vogel, D., & Balakrishnan, R. (2004). Interactive public ambient displays: transitioning from implicit to explicit, public to personal, interaction with multiple users. In *Proceedings of the 17th annual ACM Symposium on User Interface Software and Technology* (pp. 137–146). New York, NY: ACM Press. doi:10.1145/1029632.1029656

Voorsluys, W., Broberg, J. & Buyya, R. (2011). Introduction to cloud computing. *Cloud Computing*, 1-41.

Vu, C., Beyah, R., & Li, Y. (2007). Composite event detection in wireless sensor networks. *Proceedings of IEEE International Performance, Computing, and Communications Conference IPCCC, 2007*, 264–271.

Wada, H., Boonma, P., & Suzuki, J. (2007). A spacetime oriented macroprogramming paradigm for push-pull hybrid sensor networking. In *Proceedings of the 16th International Conference on Computer Communications and Networks ICCCN 2007*, (pp. 868–875). doi:10.1109/ICCCN.2007.4317927

Wagner, D. (2012). Hardware and Software Trends in Mobile AR. In *Proceedings of 2012 IEEE International Symposium on Mixed and Augmented Reality (ISMAR)*. Retrieved from the University of California, Santa Barbara website: http://ilab.cs.ucsb.edu/tma/12/slides/ISMAR2012_WS-TMA_Slides_DanielWagner.pdf

Wagner, S., & Deissenboeck, F. (2007). An Integrated Approach to Quality Modelling. In *Proceedings of the 5th International Workshop on Software Quality* (pp. 1). Washington, DC: IEEE Computer Society.

Walker, D. M. (2006). *White paper - Overview architecture for enterprise data warehouses*. Retrieved 02/16, 2010, from http://www.datamgmt.com/index.php?module=documents&JAS_DocumentManager_op=downloadFile&JAS_File_id=29

Wang, A., Wang, C., Li, X., & Zhou, X. (2013). SmartClass: A services-oriented approach for university resource scheduling. In *Proceedings IEEE 10th International Conference on Services Computing* (SCC 2013) (pp. 745-746). Santa Clara, CA: IEEE Press.

Wang, G., Wang, Q., Cao, J., & Guo, M. (2007). An Effective Trust Establishment Scheme for Authentication in Mobile Ad Hoc Networks. In *Proceedings of the 7th IEEE International Conference on Computer and Information Technology, 2007* (pp. 749–754). Fukushima, Japan: IEEE Computer Society. doi:10.1109/CIT.2007.55

Wang, T., Lu, K., Lu, L., Chung, S., & Lee, W. (2013). Jekyll on iOS: When benign apps become evil. In *Proceedings of the 22nd USENIX conference on Security, SEC'13* (pp. 559-572). USENIX Association.

Wang, X. H., Zhang, D. Q., Gu, T., & Pung, H. K. (2004). Ontology Based Context Modeling and Reasoning using OWL. In *Proceedings of the Second IEEE Annual Conference on Pervasive Computing and Communications Workshops* (pp. 18–22). IEEE Computer Society. doi:10.1109/PERCOMW.2004.1276898

Wang, X., Zhou, X., & Jiang, L. (2008). A method of business and IT alignment based on enterprise architecture. In *Proceedings ofIEEE International Conference on Service Operations, Logistics and Informatics* (pp. 740-745). IEEE. doi:10.1109/SOLI.2008.4686496

Wang, Y., & Shao, J.(2003). A new measure of software complexity based on cognitive Weights. *Can .J. Elec. Comput. Engg,* 69-74.

Wang, Z., Chu, D., & Xu, X. (2010). Value network based service choreography design and evolution. In *Proceedings of IEEE 7th International Conference on e-Business Engineering (ICEBE),* (pp. 495-500). IEEE.

Wang, M., & Wang, H. (2006). From process logic to business logic—A cognitive approach to business process management. *Information & Management, 43*(2), 179–193. doi:10.1016/j.im.2005.06.001

Wang, T.-Y., Han, Y., Varshney, P., & Chen, P.-N. (2005). Distributed fault-tolerant classification in wireless sensor networks. *IEEE Journal on Selected Areas in Communications, 23*(4), 724–734. doi:10.1109/JSAC.2005.843541

Wang, Y. (2004). On the cognitive informatics foundation of software engineering. In *Proc. 3rd IEEE Int. Conf. Cognitive Informatics (ICCI'04),* (pp. 1-10). IEEE.

Wang, Y. (2005), Keynote: Psychological experiments on the cognitive complexities of fundamental control structures of software systems. In *Proc. 4th IEEE International Conference on Cognitive Informatics (ICCI'05),* (pp. 4-5). IEEE.

Wang, Y. (2007). The theoretical framework of cognitive informatics. *International Journal of Cognitive Informatics and Natural Intelligence, 1*(1), 1–27. doi:10.4018/jcini.2007010101

Wang, Y., & Shao, J. (2009). On the cognitive complexity of software and its quantification and formal methods. *International Journal of Software Science and Computational Intelligence, 1*(2), 31–53. doi:10.4018/jssci.2009040103

Warmer, J., & Kleppe, A. (2003). *The object constraint language: getting your models ready for MDA.* Boston: Addison-Wesley Longman Publishing Co., Inc..

Watson, H. J., Goodhue, D. L., & Wixom, B. H. (2002). The benefits of data warehousing: Why some organizations realize exceptional payoffs. *Information & Management, 39*(6), 491–502. doi:10.1016/S0378-7206(01)00120-3

Weiser, M. (1984). Program Slicing. *IEEE Transactions on Software Engineering,* SE-*10*(4), 352–357. doi:10.1109/TSE.1984.5010248

Weiser, M. (1993). Some Computer Science Issues in Ubiquitous Computing. *Communications of the ACM, 36*(7), 75–84. doi:10.1145/159544.159617

Weiss, M., & Mouratidis, H. (2008). Selecting security patterns that fulfill security requirements. In *Proceedings of the 16th IEEE International Conference on Requirements Engineering (RE'08),* Washington, DC: IEEE Computer Society. doi:10.1109/RE.2008.32

Wellner, P., Mackay, W., & Gold, R. (1993). Back to the real world. *Communications of the ACM, 36*(7), 24–27. doi:10.1145/159544.159555

Werner-Allen, G., Johnson, J., Ruiz, M., Lees, J., & Welsh, M. (2005, 31 January-2 February). Monitoring volcanic eruptions with a wireless sensor network. In *Proceedings of the Second European Workshop on Wireless Sensor Networks* (pp. 108-120). doi:10.1109/EWSN.2005.1462003

Weyuker, E. (1988). Evaluating software complexity measures. *IEEE Transactions on Software Engineering, 14*(9), 1357–1365. doi:10.1109/32.6178

White, S. (2005, March). Using BPMN to Model a BPEL Process. *Business Process Management Trends.* Retrieved March 04, 2009, from http://www.businessprocess-trends.com/publicationfiles/03-05%20WP%20Mapping%20BPMN%20to%20BPEL-%20White.pdf

Whitechapel, A., & McKenna, S. (2013). *Windows Phone 8 Development Internals.* Redmond, WA: Microsoft Press.

White, J., Schmidt, D., Nechypurenko, A., & Wuchner, E. (2008). Model intelligence: An approach to modeling guidance. *UPGRADE, 9*(2), 22–28.

Williams, L (2007). *A survey of agile development methodologies.* A Whitepaper.

Willis, K. D. D., Poupyrev, I., & Shiratori, T. (2011). Motionbeam: a metaphor for character interaction with handheld projectors. In *CHI 2011:Proceedings of the SIGCHI Conference on Human Factors in Computing Systems* (pp. 1031–1040). New York, NY: ACM Press.

Wisnosky, D. E., & Vogel, J. (2004). *DoDAF wizdom: A practical guide to planning, managing and executing projects to build enterprise architectures using the department of defense architecture framework* (DoDAF). Academic Press.

Wong, W. E., & Zhao, J. & Chan, Victor K.Y. (2006). Applying statistical methodology to optimize and simplify software metric models with missing data. In *Proceedings of the 2006 ACM Symposium on Applied Computing* (pp. 1728-1733). ACM. doi:10.1145/1141277.1141687

Woolridge, M., & Wooldridge, M. (2001). *Introduction to multiagent systems*. New York, NY: John Wiley & Sons, Inc.

Wright, J. M., & Dietrich, J. B. (2010). Non-monotonic model completion in web application engineering. In *Proceedings of 2010 21st Australian Software Engineering Conference*, (pp. 45–54). IEEE. Retrieved December 3, 2012, from http://ieeexplore.ieee.org/lpdocs/epic03/wrapper.htm?arnumber=5475055

Wu, Y., Hernandez, F., Ortega, F., Clarke, P., & France, R. (2010). Measuring the effort for creating and using domain-specific models. In *Proceedings of10th Workshop on Domain-Specific Modeling*. (pp. 1-6). ACM. doi:10.1145/2060329.2060360

Xiong, M., Parsons, J., Edmondson, J., Nguyen, H., & Schmidt, D. (2007). Evaluating technologies for tactical information management in net- centric systems. In *Proceedings of the Defense Transformation and Net-Centric Systems conference*. Academic Press. doi:10.1117/12.719679

XMI. (2011). *OMG MOF 2 XMI Mapping SpecificationOMG. Document Number: formal/2011-08-09*. Retrieved February 7, 2014, from http://www.omg.org/spec/XMI/2.4.1

Xu, T., David, B., Chalon, R., & Zhou, Y. (2013). A context-aware middleware for interaction devices deployment in AmI. In *Proceedings of HCI International 2013* (pp. 183-192). LNCS 8028. Berlin/Heidelberg, Germany: Springer-Verlag. doi:10.1007/978-3-642-39351-8_21

Xu, T., Zhou, Z., David, B., & Chalon, R. (2013). Supporting Activity Context Recognition in Context-aware Middleware. In *Proceedings of Activity Context-Aware System Architectures Workshop in AAAI'13*, Bellevue, WA, USA.

Xue, W., Pung, H., Sen, S., Zhu, J., & Zhang, D. (2012). Context gateway for physical spaces. *Journal of Ambient Intelligence and Humanized Computing*, *3*(3), 193–204. doi:10.1007/s12652-010-0041-z

Yamanoue, T., Oda, K., & Shimozono, K. (2012). A M2M System Using Arduino, Android and Wiki Software. In *Proceedings of2012 IIAI International Conference on Advanced Applied Informatics* (pp. 123–128). Fukuoka, Japan: IEEE. doi:10.1109/IIAI-AAI.2012.33

Yan, J., & Zhang, B. (2009). Support Multi-Version Applications in SaaS via Progressive Schema Evolution. In *Proceedings of IEEE 25th International Conference on Data Engineering* (pp. 1717-1724). Washington, DC: IEEE Computer Society. doi:10.1109/ICDE.2009.167

Yao, Y., & Gehrke, J. (2002). The cougar approach to in-network query processing in sensor networks. *SIGMOD Record*, *31*(3), 9–18. doi:10.1145/601858.601861

Yau, S. S., & An, H. G. (2011, October). Software engineering meets services and cloud computing. *Computer*.

Yeh, R. B., Brant, J., Boli, J., & Klemmer, S. R. (2006). Interactive Gigapixel Prints: Large, Paper-Based Interfaces for Visual Context and Collaboration. In *Proceedings of the Eigth International Conference on Ubiquitous Computing*. Orange County, CA: Academic Press.

Yingxu Wang, (2002). On cognitive informatics: Keynote lecture. In *Proc. 1st IEEE Int. Conf. Cognitive Informatics (ICCI'02)*, (pp. 34–42). IEEE. doi:10.1109/COGINF.2002.1039280

Yingxu Wang., (2006). On the informatics laws and deductive semantics of software. *IEEE Transactions on Systems, Man and Cybernetics. Part C, Applications and Reviews*, *36*(2), 161–171. doi:10.1109/TSMCC.2006.871138

Yuan, M. J. (2004a). *Developing Web-service-driven, smart mobile applications*. Retrieved from http://ondotnet.com/pub/a/dotnet/2004/02/23/mobilewebserviceapps.html

Yuan, M. J. (2004b). *Overcoming Challenges in Mobile J2ME Development*. Retrieved from http://www.informit.com/articles/article.asp?p=170448&rl=1

Yuan-Kai, W. (2004). Context Awareness and Adaptation in Mobile Learning. In *Proceedings of the 2nd IEEE International Workshop on Wireless and Mobile Technologies in Education*. IEEE Computer Society doi:10.1109/WMTE.2004.1281370

Yu, E. (1997). Towards modelling and reasoning support for early-phase requirements engineering. In *Proceedings of the 3rd IEEE Int. Symp. on Requirements Engineering (RE'97)* (pp. 226-235). Washington, DC: IEEE. doi:10.1109/ISRE.1997.566873

Yus, R., Mena, E., Ilarri, S. & Illarramendi, A. (2013). SHERLOCK: Semantic management of Location-Based Services in wireless environments. *Pervasive and Mobile Computing, Special Issue on Information Management in Mobile Applications*. doi:10.1016/j.pmcj.2013.07.018

Zachman, J. A. (1987). A framework for information systems architecture. *IBM Systems Journal*, *26*(3), 276–292. doi:10.1147/sj.263.0276

Zdravkovic, J., & Ilayperuma, T. (2012). Designing Consumer-aligned Services Using Business Value Modelling. *International Journal of Organisational Design and Engineering*, *2*(3), 317–342.

Zdun, U. (2010). A DSL toolkit for deferring architectural decisions in DSL-based software design. *Information and Software Technology*, *52*(7), 733–748. doi:10.1016/j.infsof.2010.03.004

Zdun, U., Hentrich, C., & Dustdar, S. (2007). Modeling process-driven and service-oriented architectures using patterns and pattern primitives. *ACM Transactions on the Web*, *1*(3), 14. doi:10.1145/1281480.1281484

Zhang, N., Ryan, M., & Guelev, D. P. (2005, September). Evaluating access control policies through model checking. In *Proceedings of the 8th international conference on information security, ISC 2005* (Vol. 3650, pp. 446-460). Berlin: Springer.

Zhang, J., Wang, Y., & Varadharajan, V. (2007). A new security scheme for integration of mobile agents and web services. In *Proceedings of the 2nd International Conference on Internet and Web Applications and Services (ICIW'07)* (p. 43-43). Mauritius: IEEE Computer Society. doi:10.1109/ICIW.2007.5

Zhang, W., Yang, Y., & Wang, Q. (2011). Handling missing data in software effort prediction with naive Bayes and EM algorithm. In *Proceedings of the 7th International Conference on Predictive Models in Software Engineering* (p. 1). ACM. doi:10.1145/2020390.2020394

Zhang, W., Yang, Y., & Wang, Q. (2012). A comparative study of absent features and unobserved values in software effort data. *International Journal of Software Engineering and Knowledge Engineering*, *22*(2), 185–202. doi:10.1142/S0218194012400025

Zhao, F., & Guibas, L. (2004). *Wireless Sensor Networks: An Information Processing Approach*. Morgan Kaufmann.

Zhihao Chen, , Boehm, B., Menzies, T., & Port, D. (2005). Finding the right data for cost modeling. *IEEE Software*, *22*(6), 38–46. doi:10.1109/MS.2005.151

Zhou, Y., & Jiang, X. (2012) Dissecting Android Malware: Characterization and Evolution. In *Proceedings of the 33rd IEEE Symposium on Security and Privacy*. San Francisco, CA: IEEE.

Zhou, Y., David, B., & Chalon, R. (2011). Innovative user interfaces for wearable computers in real augmented environment. In *Proceedings of HCI International 2011: Human-Computer Interaction. Interaction Techniques and Environments* (pp. 500–509). Berlin: Springer-Verlag. doi:10.1007/978-3-642-21605-3_55

Zhou, Y., Wang, Z., Zhou, W., & Jiang, X. (2012) Hey, You, Get off of My Market: Detecting Malicious Apps in Official and Alternative Android Markets. In *Proceedings of the 19th Network and Distributed System Security Symposium (NDSS 2012)*. San Diego, CA: NDSS.

Zhou, Y., Xu, T., David, B., & Chalon, R. (2014). Innovative Wearable Interfaces: An Exploratory Analysis of Paper-based Interfaces with Camera-glasses Device Unit. *Journal of Personal and Ubiquitous Computing*, *18*(4), 835–849. doi:10.1007/s00779-013-0697-4

Zhu, X., & Wang, S. (2009). Software Customization Based on Model-Driven Architecture Over SaaS Platforms. In *Proceedings of International Conference on Management and Service Science* (pp. 1-4). CORD. doi:10.1109/ICMSS.2009.5300967

Zimmer, T. (2004). Towards a Better Understanding of Context Attributes. In Proceedings of PerCom (pp. 23-28). Orlando, FL: PerCom. doi:10.1109/PERCOMW.2004.1276899

Zimmermann, O., Schlimm, N., & Waller, G. (2005). *Analysis and design techniques for service-oriented development and integration.* Paper presented at the INFORMATIK 2005 - Informatik LIVE!. Bonn, Germany.

Zuse, H. A. (1998). *Framework of software measurement.* Berlin: Walter de Gruyter. doi:10.1515/9783110807301

Zviedris, M., & Barzdins, G. Romane & A., Čerāns. K. (2014). Ontology-based information system. In *Proceedings of JIST 2013* (LNCS), (vol. 8838, pp. 33-47). Springer International Publishing.

Zwass, V. (1996). Electronic Commerce : Structures and Issues. *International Journal of Electronic Commerce*, *1*(1), 3–23.

About the Contributors

Vicente García Díaz is an associate professor in the Computer Science Department of the University of Oviedo. He has a PhD from the University of Oviedo in computer engineering. His research interests include model-driven engineering, domain specific languages, technology for learning and entertainment, project risk management, and software development processes and practices. He graduated in Prevention of Occupational Risks and is a Certified Associate in Project Management through the Project Management Institute.

Juan Manuel Cueva Lovelle became a mining engineer from Oviedo Mining Engineers Technical School in 1983 (Oviedo University, Spain). He has a PhD from Madrid Polytechnic University, Spain (1990). From 1985, he has been a professor at the languages and computers systems area in Oviedo University (Spain), and is an ACM and IEEE voting member. His research interests include object-oriented technology, language processors, human-computer interface, Web engineering, modeling software with BPM, DSL, and MDA.

Begoña Cristina Pelayo García-Bustelo is a lecturer in the Computer Science Department of the University of Oviedo. She has a PhD from the University of Oviedo in computer engineering. Her research interests include object-oriented technology, Web engineering, eGovernment, modeling software with BPM, DSL, and MDA.

* * *

Adewole Adewumi holds a Bachelors degree as well as a Masters degree in Computer Science. He is presently pursuing a PhD in Computer Science at Covenant University where he also serves as the repository administrator for Covenant University. His research interests include, but not limited to, measuring quality in open source software and cognitive complexity measurement of object-oriented software.

Ville Alkkiomäki is currently working as an enterprise architect for Wärtsilä Corporation, where he is responsible for enterprise architecture governance and development. Alkkiomäki has over 15 years of experience in the field of system integration, large scale system architecture, and related technologies. Originally starting out as a software developer in an EDI software vendor, his career is characterized by varying chief and enterprise architect roles in several large enterprises. His postgraduate studies at Lappeenranta University of Technology focuses on the service oriented architecture and the value of reusable services.

Miltiades E. Anagnostou received Dipl. Ing. and PhD degrees in electrical engineering from the National Technical University of Athens in 1981 and 1987 respectively. He is a full professor with the School of Electrical and Computer Engineering of NTUA since 1999. He teaches courses on modern telecommunications, computer networks, formal specification, stochastic processes and signals, information theory, and network algorithms. His scientific interests include broadband networks, mobile and personal communications, service engineering, mobile agents, pervasive computing, network algorithms, and queuing systems. He is a member of IEEE and ACM.

Lefteris Angelis studied Mathematics and received his PhD degree in Statistics from Aristotle University of Thessaloniki (A.U.Th.). He is currently an Associate Professor in the Department of Informatics at A.U.Th and a coordinator of the STAINS (Statistics and Information Systems) research group. His research interests involve statistical methods with applications to information systems and software engineering, computational methods in mathematics and statistics, planning of experiments, and simulation techniques.

Ana Belén Rodríguez Arias holds a Masters in Web Engineering and is a Computer Engineer from the University of Oviedo (Spain). She was an IT services intern, developer at the R&D department. She performed projects related to Spring, Spring web flow, J2EE, Hibernate, Semantic Web, and was a MySQL Member of one of the winner teams at the Gijón First Open Data Festival with the project QueYeHo. She was a member of the winner team at the Gijón Second Open Data Festival with the project EcoXixón.

Erika Asnina is Associate Professor in the Department of Applied Computer Science, Institute of Applied Computer Systems, Faculty of Computer Science and Information Technology at Riga Technical University, Latvia. She has an industrial experience as a software developer. Her research interests include software quality assurance, business modeling, model-driven software development, model transformation languages and software engineering. Erika received an MS in computer systems with specialization in applied computer science in 2003 and an engineering science doctorate degree (Dr. sc.ing. or PhD) in information technology with specialization in system analysis, modeling, and design in 2006 from Riga Technical University. She has published one book and 35 conference papers.

Balbir Barn is a Professor of Software Engineering at Middlesex University, UK. Balbir has over 15 years commercial research experience working in research labs at Texas Instruments and Sterling Software, where he was involved in the research and design of leading software products such as the IEF™. Balbir's research is focused on model driven software engineering where the goal is to use models as abstractions and execution environments to support enterprise architecture and application integration using complex events. He has led numerous externally funded projects which apply model driven principles to business processes, learning theories, and more recently, the theory building aspects to model driven engineering.

Stamatia Bibi received her BsC and PhD from the department of Informatics of the Aristotle University of Thessaloniki, Greece. She is elected as a lecturer in the area of Software Engineering at the Polytechnic faculty of Western Macedonia, Department of Informatics and Telecommunications. Her research interests involve software cost estimation, software project management, and software process improvement. In particular, she is comparing estimation methods and pursuing novel estimation techniques for software assessment. She is interested in estimating aspects of development and deployment of Open Source Software and applications hosted in the "Cloud." She is an author of more than 20 scientific publications.

Panayiotis Bozanis received his five year Diploma and his PhD degree from the Department of Computer Engineering and Informatics at the University of Patras, Greece in 1993 and 1997, respectively. He is currently an Associate Professor at the Electrical and Computer Engineering Department at the University of Thessaly, Greece. His main research interests include Data Structures, Computational Geometry, Information Retrieval, Storage and Indexing Techniques, Databases for Large Sets and Mobile Data, and Cloud Computing. His publications comprise several journal and conference papers concerning problems of Data Structuring, Computational Geometry, Information Retrieval, and Spatio-Temporal Indexing and five books in Greek about Data Structures and Algorithms. He is an EATCS member.

David Byers received his PhD in Computer Science from Linköping University in 2013 in the area of software engineering for of secure systems. Dr. Byers has worked source code analysis and software engineering in academia and industry, with a particular focus on agile processes and rigorous methods for improving development practices with respect to security, and is currently working with applied security incident prevention and response.

Edgars Celms holds a PhD in computer science. He is currently a leading researcher and head of the Research Laboratory of Modelling and Software Technologies at the Institute of Mathematics and Computer Science (IMCS UL). He works also as an associate professor (part time) at the Faculty of Computer Science (University of Latvia). His main areas of interest are transformation languages, domain specific languages (DSL) and tools, model driven development (MDD), and advanced programming technologies. He has also experience in topics related to UML (Unified Modelling Language), modeling, and meta-modelling. In private, he spends time with his family and takes part in different types of orienteering activities.

René Chalon obtained a Masters in Engineering and a PhD in Computer Science from the École centrale de Lyon (France). He worked for 10 years as a research engineer at the French CNRS on multimedia authoring tools in several European projects. He joined the École centrale de Lyon in 2000, as an Associate Professor in Computer Science in the Department of Mathematics and Computer Science and a researcher at the Laboratoire d'informatique en image et systèmes d'information (LIRIS laboratory). His main research topics address Human-Computer Interaction and Computer Supported Collaborative Work. His current activities focus on mobile interactions for ambient intelligence using advanced interaction techniques (gestural interaction, mixed reality, eye tracking, etc.). His fields of application are mainly smart cities, mobile learning and serious games.

Elizabeth Chang is a Professor and Canberra Fellow at the School of Business, the University of New South Wales and at the Australian Defence Force Academy. She has over 22 years of experience in academia and industry. She is an expert on ontologies, XML and semi-structured databases, data mining for business intelligence, collaborative systems, human system interaction, and service oriented computing. She has supervised 38 PhD students to completion. She has over 500 publications including six books, 25 book chapters, 90 journal articles and 35 Keynote speeches, with an h-index of 32 (Google Scholar). As one of the chief investigators, Professor Chang has obtained over $11.5 million in competitive research funds. Professor Chang has a PhD and research Masters in Computer Science and Software Engineering from La Trobe University, Australia.

Panagiota Chatzipetrou received her BSc degree in Informatics and her Msc in "Computer Science and Business Administration" from Aristotle University of Thessaloniki (AUTh). She is currently a PhD student in the Department of Informatics at AUTh. Her research interests involve applications of statistical methods to quality problems in software engineering and especially to requirements engineering.

Tony Clark is Professor of Informatics and Head of the Computer Science Department in the School of Science and Technology at Middlesex University. Tony has experience working in both Academia and Industry on a range of software projects and consultancies. He has worked on languages for Object-Oriented specification and design including contributing to a range of Industry standards, including UML 2.0, that led to a spin-out company, serving as Technical Director from 2003-2008, selling UML-based meta-tools and services to a number of blue-chip companies. Tony is an editorial board member of the SoSyM Journal and has authored over 100 articles in the field of software engineering. His current work addresses the simulation and analysis of enterprise-wide systems. More information at http://www.eis.mdx.ac.uk/staffpages/tonyclark/.

Gabriele Costa received his PhD in Computer Science from the University of Pisa in 2011. From 2008 to 2012, he worked as a researcher for the Security Group of the Istituto di Informatica e Telematica (IIT) of the Italian National Research Council (CNR). In the last years, he has been involved in several European research projects including ANIKETOS, CONNECT, NESSoS, S3MS, and SPaCIoS. His research interests include, but are not limited to, language-based security, history-based security, formal verification, and runtime enforcement. In particular, his research activity focused on the security assessment of mobile applications, mobile devices, and web services.

Bertrand David, after earning a Bachelors of Science in Mathematics at the Charles University of Prague, Czech Republic, hestudied technical and theoretical aspects of computing at the Institute of Programming of Grenoble and pursued his MSc and PhD at the University of Grenoble. He then worked as a researcher for 10 years at the French National Centre for Scientific Research (CNRS) before joining the Ecole centrale de Lyon (ECL) as a Professor of Computer Science. After his initial research studies addressed CAD/CAM integrated systems design and implementation, his research interests include human-computer interaction (HCI), computer supported collaborative work (CSCW), software engineering, e-learning and more recently mobile cooperative systems, wearable computing, pervasive environments and ambient Intelligence. His main current field of investigation is Smart City. He co-founded and headed for eight years the Interaction and Cooperation for Telelearning and Teleworking (ICTT) multidisciplinary research lab involving ICT, humanities, and social sciences.

Jon Davis has over 25 years of industry and academic experience. For many years he has been developing software solutions for the heavy engineering, manufacturing, and mining industries plus the public and university sector, his main focus being on software modelling and reusability. He is also a project management specialist lecturing to university, public, and private sector organisations. In recent years, he has paid special attention to research in the scope of generic models for Enterprise Information Systems definition, in which he has analyzed the advantages of using model-driven automated application generation and led the development of a new model and framework publishing numerous papers in the field. Jon Davis graduated in Science then Mathematics at Melbourne and Newcastle University, followed by an Honours degree in Computer Science at Newcastle University and is currently in the final stages of completing a PhD at Curtin University.

Anh Duc Do (Andrew) is a Managing Consultant at Catena Technologies Pte Ltd, a business process automation, enterprise integration architecture, high performance trading system, and risk management integration consulting firm. Andrew has delivered projects for financial institutions in the United States, Asian Pacific, and Japan designing and implementing enterprise solutions. Andrew's expertise includes Business Process Management (BPM), Service Oriented Architecture (SOA), and mobile applications. Andrew was awarded BS and MS degrees by the Nanyang Technological University (Singapore) in computer science.

Iwona Dubielewicz received an MSc degree and a PhD degree in Computer Science, both from the Wroclaw University of Technology, Poland. Her PhD dissertation was associated with the use of formal languages in software engineering. Since 1977, she has been working as a professor assistant at the Institute of Informatics, Wroclaw University of Technology. Her main scientific interests include, but are not limited to software development methodologies, modeling languages, and quality of the software systems and processes. She is a member of, Software and Networks Subcommittee in the Polish Committee for Standardization. Since 1994, she has been involved in the development of several Polish standards for software quality.

Randall E. Duran is the Chairman and founder of Catena Technologies Pte Ltd, a business process automation and enterprise integration architecture consulting firm. Over the past 20 years, Randall has worked with financial institutions in the United States, Europe, Asia, Australia, and Africa designing and implementing enterprise solutions. Prior to founding Catena Technologies, he led solution consulting at TIBCO Finance Technology Inc and Reuters PLC. Randall and was awarded BS and MS degrees by the Massachusetts Institute of Technology (M.I.T.) in computer science. Randall is also an adjunct professor at Singapore Management University, where he has taught masters courses related to financial services technology. Randall is the author of the book *Financial Services Technology: Processes, Architecture, and Solutions* and co-author of the book *Bank Management: A Decision-Making Perspective.*

Liliana Favre is a full professor of Computer Science at the Universidad Nacional del Centro de la Provincia de Buenos Aires in Argentina. She is also a researcher of CIC (Comisión de Investigaciones Científicas de la Provincia de Buenos Aires). Her current research interests are focused on model driven development, model driven architecture, and formal approaches mainly on the integration of algebraic techniques with MDA-based processes. She has been involved in several national research projects about formal methods and software engineering methodologies. Currently, she is research leader of the Software Technology Group at the Universidad Nacional del Centro de la Provincia de Buenos Aires. She has published several book chapters, journal articles, and conference papers. She has acted as editor of the book *UML and the Unified Process.* She is the author of the book *Model Driven Architecture for Reverse Engineering Technologies: Strategic Directions and System Evolution.*

Luis Fernández-Sanz is an associate professor at Dept. of Computer Science at the Universidad de Alcala (UAH). He earned a degree in Computing in 1989 at the Universidad Politecnica de Madrid (UPM) and his PhD in Computing with a special award at the University of the Basque Country in 1997. With more than 20 years of research and teaching experience (at UPM, Universidad Europea de Madrid and UAH), he is also engaged in the management of the main Spanish Computing Professionals association (ATI: www.ati.es) as vice president and, he is chairman of the ATI Software Quality group. He was the vice president of CEPIS (Council of European Professional Informatics Societies: www.cepis.org) from 2011 to 2013. With a large number of contributions in refereed impact international journals, conferences, and book chapters, his main research interests include technical fields like software quality and engineering and testing and non technical fields like computing education, especially in multinational settings, IT profession, and requirements and skills for IT jobs.

Aquilino Juan Fuente is a lecturer in Computer Science at the University of Oviedo (Spain). He received his PhD in Computer Engineering in 2002. His research interests are software architecture, web engineering and e-learning architecture. He has published over 30 books and various papers in refereed scientific journals and conference proceedings, and has participated in 20+ research projects and 50+ entrepeneurial projects. He is a fellow of Software Architecture R.G.

Aniruddha S. Gokhale is an Associate Professor in the Department of Electrical Engineering and Computer Science and Senior Research Scientist at the Institute for Software Integrated Systems (ISIS) both at Vanderbilt University, Nashville, TN, USA. He has over 150 technical articles to his credit focusing on topics pertaining to model-driven engineering (MDE), middleware solutions involving design patterns for quality of service (QoS) assurance, and correct-by-construction design and development of distributed real-time and embedded systems. His current research focuses on developing novel solutions to emerging challenges in cloud computing and cyber physical systems. Dr. Gokhale obtained his BE (Computer Engineering) from the University of Pune, India, 1989; MS (Computer Science) from Arizona State University, 1992; and DSc (Computer Science) from Washington University in St. Louis, 1998. Prior to joining Vanderbilt, Dr. Gokhale was a member of the technical staff at Lucent Bell Laboratories, NJ. Dr. Gokhale is a Senior member of both IEEE and ACM and a member of ASEE.

Cristian González García obtained a degree in Technical Engineering in Computer Systems and obtained an MS in Web Engineering from the School of Computer Engineering of Oviedo in 2011 and 2013 (University of Oviedo, Spain). Currently, he is PhD candidate. His research interests are in the field of Internet of Things, Web Engineering, Mobile Devices, and Modeling Software with DSL and MDE.

Denis Hatebur works at University Duisburg-Essen in Germany and since 2004, he is the CEO of ITESYS Institut für technische Systeme GmbH in Dortmund/Germany. He worked in different industrial engineering projects as a consultant. In these safety and security projects, he was responsible for specification and testing parts. His research interest is the dependability engineering, considering requirements engineering, architectural design and testing. In this field, he has authored numerous reviewed conference and workshop papers. He holds a Diploma degree in information technology from the University of Applied Science in Dortmund/Germany, and also a Masters degree and a PhD in computer engineering from University Duisburg-Essen/Germany.

Daniel Hein is a senior software engineer at Garmin International where he works on automotive navigation software for Garmin's OEM product offerings. Hein has developed a wide range of software from low level drivers and firmware, to middleware, to upper level user interfaces. He has also worked across a diverse set of platforms including VxWorks, Linux, Android, Windows, and QNX. Hein holds an MS in Computer Engineering from the University of Kansas and a BS in Computer Engineering from Iowa State University. Hein is currently working on his PhD in Computer Science with an emphasis in Secure Software Engineering. Daniel's research interests include security, software engineering, and machine learning.

Maritta Heisel is a full professor for software engineering at the University of Duisburg-Essen, Germany. Her research interests include the development of dependable software, pattern- and component-based software development, software architecture, and software evolution. She is particularly interested in incorporating security considerations into software development processes and in integrating the development of safe and secure software. She has co-authored more than 80 refereed publications, including monographs, book chapters, journals, and conference papers. She is a member of various program committees and served as a reviewer for a number of journals and conferences. Morevover, she is a member of the European Workshop on Industrial Computer Systems Reliability, Safety, and Security (EWICS).

Bogumila Hnatkowska received an MSc degree and a PhD degree in Computer Science in 1992 and 1997 respectively, both from the Wroclaw University of Technology, Poland. Her PhD dissertation was associated with the use of formal methods in software engineering. Since 1998 she has been working as a professor assistant at the Institute of Informatics, Wroclaw University of Technology. Her main scientific interests include, but are not limited to software development processes, modeling languages, model driven development, model transformations, and quality of the software products. She is a member of programme committees of several international conferences. Bogumila Hnatkowska has over 60 publications in international journals and conference proceedings from different areas of software engineering.

Joe Hoffert is an Assistant Professor of Computer Information Sciences at Indiana Wesleyan University. His research focuses on QoS support at design and run-time for publish/subscribe distributed real-time and embedded systems. He has researched autonomic adaptation of transport protocols using machine learning within QoS-enabled pub/sub middleware. This work was done to address timeliness and reliability for distributed event-based systems, in particular systems using the OMG's Data Distribution Service (DDS). He previously worked for Boeing in the area of model-based integration of embedded systems and distributed constructive simulations. He received his BA in Math/C.S. from Mount Vernon Nazarene College (OH), his MS in C.S. from the University of Cincinnati (OH), and his PhD in C.S. from Vanderbilt University (TN).

Zbigniew Huzar is a full professor of Informatics at Wrocław University of Technology in Poland. During 1978-1984, he was deputy director of the Computer Center, during 1984-2003, he served as a head of Informatics Center, during 2004- 2008, he worked as director of the Institute of Applied Informatics, and since 2008, he has been working as the director of the Institute of Informatics, Wrocław University of Technology. The scope of his scientific interests concern software engineering, in particular, covers methods of formal specification and design of real-time systems and model-based software development. He is author and co-author of 10 books. He is a member of the Polish Information Processing Society and editor-in-chief of the *e-Informatica Software Engineering Journal*.

Sergio Ilarri is an Associate Professor in the Department of Computer Science and Systems Engineering at the University of Zaragoza. He received his BS and his PhD in Computer Science from the University of Zaragoza in 2001 and 2006, respectively. For a year, he was a visiting researcher in the Mobile Computing Laboratory at the Department of Computer Science at the University of Illinois in Chicago, and he has also cooperated (through several research stays) with the University of Valenciennes and with IRIT in Toulouse. His research interests include data management issues for mobile computing, vehicular networks, mobile agents, and the Semantic Web. He authored a number of publications in relevant journals and conferences and participated (or participates) as guest editor of special issues in *Transportation Research Part-C, IEEE Internet Computing, IEEE Multimedia, the Journal of Systems and Software*, or *the Distributed and Parallel Databases journal.*

Tharaka Ilayperuma has a PhD in the field of enterprise modeling. After the doctorate, he has continued in the same research field, with a focus on model driven development of service systems. In addition, he has a Licentiate in Philosophy (PhL) degree from Stockholm University with the focus on the use of ontologies for enterprise modeling. Tharaka is a PC member of a few international conferences and workshops. During the 2005-2007 period, Tharaka actively participated in the INTEROP, an EU/NoE scoped research project on IS interoperability. Tharaka is now working as a senior lecturer in the Department of Computer Science at the University of Ruhuna, Sri Lanka.

Guillermo Infante Hernández obtained his Accounting and Finances degree in 2006 from the University of Holguin, Cuba. He obtained a Web Master Engineering degree in 2010, from the University of Oviedo. He has been working as a research fellow at the University of Holguin from 2006 to 2010, as part of the Computer aided Design and Computer aided Manufacture (CAD/CAM) research department team. His work in this department lead him to a research stay in the Faculty of Engineering at the University of Porto in 2008 to work on manufacturing optimization algorithms using neural networks. From 2010 to the present, he has been working on his doctoral thesis in the Computer Science Department at the University of Oviedo. Some of the research interests he is working on include Model Driven Engineering applied to e-government domain, Rule driven software development, and Web Engineering amongst others.

Nikos Kalatzis is a researcher in the School of Electrical and Computer Engineering at the National Technical University of Athens. He received his diploma in physics from the Physics Department at the University of Ioannina in 2000. In 2002, he received his MSc in information security from the University of London (Royal Holloway College - Department of Mathematics). For the next two years, he worked in the industry in the field of IT security. He is currently pursuing a PhD degree in the area of computer networks, in the Computer Science Division of National Technical University of Athens (NTUA). He has participated in several international research projects such as FP7 Persist and FP7 IP Societies. His major research interests lie in the field of ambient intelligence, context-awareness, distributed context management, history-of-context handling, context inference algorithms, and user intent prediction. He has several publications in these research fields.

Elina Kalnina holds a PhD in computer science from the University of Latvia. She works as a leading researcher at The Institute of Mathematics and Computer Science at the University of Latvia and as an assistant professor at the University of Latvia. Her area of interest is software development and model driven development (MDD). Mainly, she works on topics related to domain specific languages, model transformations and business process management. She has professional experience in web application development and project management.

Audris Kalnins holds a Dr. habil. degree in computer science. He is currently a professor at the University of Latvia and a leading researcher at the Institute of Mathematics and Computer science (IMCS UL), University of Latvia. Since 1990, he has participated in research in the area of modelling, metamodelling, UML, business process modelling, modelling tool development, model transformation languages and domain specific languages. He is the leader of the transformation language MOLA development team at IMCS UL. He has participated in various modelling tool development projects including GRADE, Generic Modelling Tool and METAclipse. He is teaching courses in modelling, MDD (Model Driven Development), and UML in the Computer science department of the University of Latvia. He has published over 75 articles in international journals and conference proceedings. Recently, he was the leader of IMCS UL team in the European Union 6th Framework project ReDSeeDS.

Dimitrios Katsaros was born in Thetidio (Farsala), Greece in 1974. He received a BSc in Computer Science from Aristotle University of Thessaloniki, Greece (1997) and a Ph.D. from the same department on May 2004. He spent a year (July 1997-June 1998) as a visiting researcher at the Department of Pure and Applied Mathematics at the University of L'Aquila, Italy. Currently, he is a lecturer with the Department of Computer and Communication Engineering at the University of Thessaly (Volos, Greece). He is co-guest editor of special issues on "Cloud Computing" in *IEEE Internet Computing* and *IEEE Network* magazines, and publication advisor in the translation for the greek language for the book *Google's PageRank and Beyond: The Science of Search Engine Rankings*. His research interests are in the area of distributed systems, including the Web/Internet, cloud computing, mobile/vehicular ad hoc networks, wireless sensor networks. He earned a "PYTHAGORAS" research grant (2005-2007) for conducting postdoctoral research in the synergy between social network analysis and wireless ad hoc networks. He has written more than 80 articles in journals and conferences, many of them in prestigious IEEE and ACM magazines and transactions. More information can be retrieved at http://www.inf.uth.gr/~dkatsar

Shekoufeh Kolahdouz Rahimi completed her PhD in Computer Science at Kings College London. Her PhD is in the area of Model Driven Engineering and particularly Model Transformation. She originated her work on the measurement of transformation quality using international software quality standards (ISO/IEC quality standards), adapting these standards to the domain of transformations. She received her MSc in Computing and Internet Systems from the King College London, UK and her BSc in Hardware Engineering in her home town Esfahan, Iran.

Pavlos Kosmides was born in Kavala, Greece, in 1985. He received his Diploma degree in Information and Communication Systems Engineering in 2008, from the University of the Aegean (Samos). He is currently pursuing a PhD degree in the School of Electrical and Computer Engineering at the National Technical University of Athens (NTUA). His research interests lie in the fields of distributed context management, context access control in Smart Space environments, context inference, intelligent transport systems, energy efficiency, and heterogeneous wireless networks. He has participated in several European and national research projects. He is a member of Technical Chamber of Greece.

Vinay Kulkarni is a Chief Scientist of Tata Research Development and Design Centre (TRDDC) at Tata Consultancy Services (TCS). He is a member of the TCS Corporate Technology Council that oversees all R&D and innovation activities at TCS. His research interests include model-driven software engineering, self-adaptive systems, and enterprise modeling. His work in model-driven software engineering has led to a toolset that has been used to deliver several large business-critical systems over the past 15 years. Much of this work has found way into OMG standards, three of which Vinay contributed to in a leadership role. Vinay has several patents to his credit and has authored several papers in scholastic journals and conferences worldwide. He has served as the conference and program chairperson for the premier ACM and IEEE international conferences in the area of software engineering, and served as a technical program committee member for many international conferences. Vinay also serves as Visiting Professor at Middlesex University, London.

Peter Langendörfer holds a diploma and a doctorate degree in computer science. Since 2000, he has been with the IHP in Frankfurt (Oder). There, he is leading the sensor networks and mobile middleware group. Since 2012, he has his own chair for security in pervasive systems at the Technical University of Cottbus. He has published more than 100 refereed technical articles, filed ten patents in the security/privacy area and worked as a guest editor for many renowned journals e.g. *Wireless Communications* and *Mobile Computing* (Wiley). He was chairing International conferences such as WWIC and has served in many TPC for example at Globecom, VTC, ICC and SECON. His research interests include wireless sensor networks and cyber physical systems, especially privacy and security issues.

Kevin Lano is a Reader in Software Engineering at King's College London. He has worked for over 20 years in the fields of system specification and verification. A co-founder of the Precise UML group in 1996, he produced some of the first research on model transformation specification and verification and subsequently has developed techniques for the correct-by-construction software engineering of model transformations and for the verification of transformations. He is the author of the UML-RSDS toolset for precise model-based development.

Ioan Lazar is a Lecturer in the Department of Computer Science, Faculty of Mathematics and Computer Science at Babes-Bolyai University, Cluj-Napoca. He published seven books and university courses and more than 30 papers. His current research topics include object-oriented analysis and design, modeling languages, and programming methodologies.

Aliaksandr Lazouski received an MSc in Electronics from Belorussian State University in 2006, and a PhD in Computer Science from the University of Pisa in 2011. He is currently a post-doc at IIT-CNR, Pisa, Italy. His research interests include access and usage control models for Grid and Cloud computing, security policy languages, risk assessment and management, distributed system security, and trust management. He participates in several European research projects funded by the Framework Programme of the European Commission. The projects aim to produce research and innovation in information and communication technologies and include a wide range of partners from industry and academia all over Europe.

Nicolas Liampotis was born in Athens, Greece, in 1980. He received his Diploma in Electrical and Computer Engineering from the National Technical University of Athens (NTUA) in 2005. Since then, he has participated in several national and international research and development projects. He is currently pursuing a PhD degree in the NTUA School of Electrical and Computer Engineering. His research interests include context-awareness, trust management and evaluation in pervasive computing, privacy protection and context access control in Smart Space environments, distributed context management, social networking systems, and computer communication networks. Mr. Liampotis is a member of the Technical Chamber of Greece.

Benjamín López Pérez has a PhD in Computer Science Engineering from the University of Oviedo. He is a Tenured Associate Professor at the Computer Science Department of the University of Oviedo. He was a Computer Science Engineer from the University of Malaga in 1991. His research interests are Computational reflection, Aspect Oriented Software Development, Meta-level systems and meta-object protocols, Web Engineering, and software architecture applied to e-government domain. He has participated in several research projects funding for Microsoft Research, Spanish Department of Science and Innovation, and the Regional Government. He has held various positions. He is currently the Director of the Computer Science Engineering School at the University of Oviedo.

Jouni Markkula is a Senior Research Fellow at the University of Oulu, Finland. He received his PhD in Computer Science from the University of Jyväskylä in 2003. His main research areas are knowledge management, decision making, privacy, software engineering, and service design. He has lead and managed several research projects in these fields and in co-operation with industry. Before the University of Oulu, Dr. Markkula was working at the Information Technology Research Institute of the University of Jyväskylä as a research director.

Fabio Martinelli is a senior researcher at the Institute of Informatics and Telematics (IIT) of the Italian National Research Council (CNR). He is co-author of more than 200 papers in international journals and conference/workshop proceedings. His main research interests involve security and privacy in distributed and mobile systems and foundations of security and trust. Since 2004, He has served on the board of directors of the international school on Foundations of Security Analysis and Design (FOSAD). He founded and chaired the WG on Security and Trust management (STM) of the European Research Consortium in Informatics and Mathematics (ERCIM). He is currently chair of the WG 11.14 in secure engineering of the International Federation of Information Processing (IFIP). He usually manages R&D projects on information and communication security and in particular, he is currently the Project Coordinator of the EU Network of Excellence NESSoS on the engineering of secure Future Internet services.

Liliana Martinez is an assistant professor in the computer science area of the Facultad de Ciencias Exactas at the Universidad Nacional del Centro de la Provincia de Buenos Aires (UNCPBA), Tandil, Argentina. She is a member of the Software Technology Group, which develops its activities at the INTIA Research Institute at the UNCPBA. She has a Masters degree in Software Engineering from the Universidad Nacional de La Plata, Argentina. Her research interests are focused on system modernization, reverse engineering in particular. She has published book chapters, journal articles, and conference papers. She has been a member of the program committee of international conferences related to software engineering.

Oleksiy Mazhelis is a post-doc researcher in the Department of Computer Science and Information Systems at the University of Jyväskylä, Finland. He received a degree of MSc (Specialist) from Kharkov National University of Radio-Electronics, Ukraine in 1997, and received his licentiate and doctoral degrees from the University of Jyväskylä in 2004 and 2007, respectively, on the subject of masquerader detection in the mobile phone environment. Starting from 2004, he worked in various research projects conducted in collaboration with industrial partners. His current research interests encompass techno-economics, systems analysis, machine learning, and pattern recognition, applied to the domains of software industry evolution, Internet of Things, telecommunications and cloud software, as well as intelligent transportation systems.

Eduardo Mena is an Associate Professor in the Department of Computer Science and Systems Engineering at the University of Zaragoza, Spain. In 1992, he received his BS in Computer Science from the University of the Basque Country and in 1999, his PhD degree in Computer Science from the University of Zaragoza. For a year, he was a visiting researcher in the Large Scale Distributed Information Systems Laboratory at the University of Georgia. He leads the Distributed Information Systems research group at his university. His research interest areas include interoperable, heterogeneous and distributed information systems, semantic web, and mobile computing. He has published several publications in international journals, conferences, and workshops including a book about ontology-based query processing (the system OBSERVER). He also served as a referee of international journals and as a Program Committee member of international conferences and workshops.

Amit Mishra has been involved in the educational field for 10 years and have taught at the primary, secondary, college, and university levels. He is an avid learner and is always looking to adapt his teaching methodology accordingly. At present, he is a lecturer in the Department of Mathematics and Computer Science at IBB University, Nigeria where he has been since 2007. He also worked as a visiting faculty member In the FUT Minna Cyber Security Department, Nigeria. Before coming to Nigeria as a lecturer, he worked with IBM as well. He received a B.Sc Physics (Hons.) from L.N.M. University

India, and a Masters in Computer Applications from Bihar University India. He earned certifications from Microsoft in windows 2000 professional, windows 2000 server, and in windows 2000 Exchange Server to become a Microsoft certified professional in 2000. His research interests center on Software Engineering, Software Re-engineering, software Reverse Engineering, Software Project Management, and Software measurement Issues.

Sanjay Misra is Full Professor of computer engineering at Covenant University, OTA, Nigeria. He has 20 years of wide experience in academic administration and researches in various universities in Asia, Europe and Africa. His current research covers the areas of (but not limited to): Software engineering, project management, quality assurance, Human computer interactions, artificial intelligence, cognitive informatics, and web engineering. He is the author of more than 100 papers (Majority of them are in ISI Web of Sciences) in these areas and received several awards for outstanding publications. He has delivered keynote and invited speeches in several international conferences (including IEEE/Elsevier sponsored). He is founder chair of three annual international workshops: Software Engineering Process and Applications(SEPA)(Since 2009 (Springer)), Tools and Techniques in Software Development Process (Since 2009 in IEEE), and Software Quality (Since 2009) (IEEE and LNCS). Presently, he is chief editor of the *International Journal of Physical Sciences* and founder EIC of Covenant J. of ICT (An official Journal of Covenant University) and is serving as editor, associate editor, and editorial board member of several journals of international repute.

Paolo Mori received his MSc in Computer Science (cum laude) in 1998, and his PhD in Computer Science in 2003, from the University of Pisa. He is currently a researcher of the Information Security group of IIT-CNR. His main research interests involve trust, security and privacy, focusing on access and usage control, trust, and reputation management in distributed environments, such as Grid, Cloud, and mobile devices. His interests also include security in the e-health scenario. He published more than 50 scientific papers in the *International Journals and Conferences*, and he has been/is involved in a number of European and Italian projects on information and communication security.

Simona Motogna (b. September 20, 1967) received her MSc in Computer Science (1991) and PhD in Computer Science (2000) from Babeş-Bolyai University of Cluj-Napoca, Romania. Now, she is an Associate Professor in the Department of Computer Science, Faculty of Mathematics and Computer Science at Babes-Bolyai University of Cluj-Napoca, Romania. Since May 2012, she is the Vice-Dean of the faculty. Her current research interests include component-based software development, model-driven architecture, and formal methods. She has (co-)authored six books and more than 36 papers, 21 conference participations, member in International Program Committees of seven conferences and workshops, and reviewer for three international journals.

Nikolaos Mittas received a BSc degree in Mathematics from the University of Crete. He also received an MSc degree in Informatics from Aristotle University of Thessaloniki (AUTh) with a specialty in Information Systems. His doctoral dissertation has the title "Statistical and Computational Methods for Development, Improvement and Comparison of Software Cost Estimation Models" covering the wider area of Prediction and Forecast Modelling. He was a visiting assistant professor at the Technological Educational Institute of Kavala and in the Computer Science Department at Aristotle University of

Thessaloniki. He has participated in several international and national conferences. The main part of his publications in journals and conference proceedings is focused on the development and application of statistical methods and models for analyzing data from the fields of Information Systems and Software Engineering (project management and cost estimation procedures in the development of software).

Wiktor Nowakowski is a co-founder and an active member of the Software Modeling Group at the Institute of Theory of Electrical Engineering, Measurement and Information Systems at Warsaw University of Technology. His main area of research interest is in Requirements Engineering, Model-Driven Software Development, metamodeling, and Software Language Engineering. He is currently pursuing his PhD related to these areas. Wiktor has extensive experience working on small- to large-scale research and commercial projects in roles covering most of the stages of the software development life cycle.

Edward Rolando Núñez-Valdéz has a PhD from the University of Oviedo in Computer Engineering, Masters and DEA in Software Engineering from the Pontifical University of Salamanca, and a BS in Computer Science from the Autonomous University of Santo Domingo. He has participated in several research projects. He has taught Mathematics and Computer science at various schools and universities and has worked in software development companies and IT Consulting as an IT consultant and application developer. He has published several articles in international journals and conferences. Currently, he is working as a researcher at the University of Oviedo. His research interests include Object-Oriented technology, Web Engineering, recommendation systems, Modeling Software with DSL, and MDA.

Martha Omorodion graduated in Electrical and Computer Engineering from the Federal University of Technology, Minna Nigeria in 2012. Presently, she is working as an ICT officer in BTXpress Universal limited, Abuja, Nigeria. Her areas of research interest are Software engineering processes, process models, and agile software development. She has published several papers in these areas.

Steffen Ortmann received his diploma in computer science in 2007 and his PhD by scholarship in 2010. Since 2005, he has been active in the sensor network research group of IHP. He has published about 50 refereed technical articles about reliability, privacy, and efficient data processing in wireless sensor networks and medical applications. His current research focuses on wireless Body Area Networks with integrated security and privacy means for tele-medical innovations.

Janis Osis graduated Latvian State University with a cum lauda and received a diploma of Electrical engineering in electrical systems. After her doctoral studies at Sanitpetersburg Electrical University, Russia, he obtained his Dr.sc.ing. degree (equal to PhD) from Kaunas Technological University, Lithuania. He received his Dr.habil.sc.ing. degree in system analysis from the Latvian Academy of Sciences (LAS) with the habilitation thesis "Diagnostics of Complex systems." He was a visiting researcher at the University of California, Berkeley, USA and the Universita' degli Studi di Padova, Italia. He has been a Professor in the Faculty of Computer Science and Information Technology at Riga Technical University, Latvia since 1979, is an Honorary Member of LAS, and a Member of the International Editorial Board of the *Journal Automatic Control and Computer Sciences*. His research interests are topological modeling of complex systems (since 1965), object-oriented and model driven system development supported by topological functioning modeling, and formal methods of software engineering. He has more than 250 publications including 15 books.

Bazil Parv (b. September 27, 1953) received his BSc in Computer Science (1976), MSc in Computer Science (1977) and PhD in Mathematics (1990) from Babes-Bolyai University of Cluj-Napoca, Romania. After graduation, he worked in the industry as a programmer, from 1977 to 1979 at the Computer Center of the Jiu Valley Coal Mining Combinate, Petrosani, Hune- doara and from 1979 to 1990 at the Computer Center of Babes-Bolyai University. In 1990, he started his academic career as a lecturer (until 1993) and associate professor. Since 1998, he has been a full professor inthe Department of Computer Science, Faculty of Mathematics and Computer Science at Babes-Bolyai University of Cluj-Napoca, Romania. In 2012, he was elected as the Head of the Department of Computer Science. His current research interests include software engineering, programming paradigms, component-based software development, mathematical modeling in experimental sciences, and computer algebra. He has (co-)authored nine books and book chapters, more than 120 papers, attended more than 90 scientific conferences and workshops, and is a member in program committees of more than 20 scientific events.

Jordán Pascual Espada is a Research scientist in the Computer Science Department at the University of Oviedo. He obtained hisPhD from the University of Oviedo in Computer Engineering. His research interests include the Internet of Things, exploration of new applications, and associated human computer interaction issues in ubiquitous computing and emerging technologies, particularly mobile and Web.

Claudia Pereira is an assistant professor in the computer science area of the Facultad de Ciencias Exactas at the Universidad Nacional del Centro de la Provincia de Buenos Aires (UNCPBA), Tandil, Argentina. She is a member of the Technology Software Group at the INTIA Research Institute at the UNCPBA. She has a Masters degree in Software Engineering from the Universidad Nacional de La Plata, Argentina. Her main research interests are focused on system modernization, refactoring in particular. She has published book chapters, journal articles, and conference papers. She has been a member of the program committee of international conferences related to software engineering.

Luz Andrea Rodriguez is a PhD ABD in Computer Engineering from Oviedo University, Asturias, Spain (2012). She has a Masters degree in Engineering and website design (2012), is a Specialist in hygiene and occupational health (2010), and an Industrial Engineer at the Francisco José de Caldas District University, Bogota, DC, (2008). Her research interests include Web Engineering, eHealth, eGovernment, eBusiness, opendata, and Tourism.

Ioanna Roussaki received her Diploma in Electrical and Computer Engineering in 1997 from the National Technical University of Athens (NTUA). In 2003, she received her PhD in the area of telecommunications and computer networks and became a senior research associate in the NTUA School of Electrical and Computer Engineering (SECE). Since 2008, she is a SECE lecturer on ambient intelligence systems. Her research interests include pervasive computing,context management and inference, smart spaces for individuals and communities, user behaviour monitoring, proactivity and user intent prediction, personalisation, learning, reasoning, social networking systems, community intelligence, privacy and trust awareness, evaluation and management, decision support mechanisms, automated negotiations, stochastic modelling and analysis, service engineering, mobile and personal communications, and algorithms and complexity theory. She has over 80 publications in these research fields and she teaches computing and communications courses in SECE. She is a member of IEEE and the Technical Chamber of Greece.

Hossein Saiedian is currently an associate chair, the director of the IT degree programs, aa professor of computing and information technology in the Department of Electrical Engineering and Computer Science at the University of Kansas (KU), and a member of the KU Information and Telecommunication Technology Center (ITTC). Professor Saiedian has over 150 publications in a variety of topics in software engineering, computer science, information security, and information technology. His research in the past has been supported by the NSF as well as other national and regional foundations. Professor Saiedian has been awarded a number distinguished awards, including KU's highly prestigious Kemper award for excellence in teaching, the University of Nebraska's award in excellence in research and excellence in teaching, and was ranked among the top-10 software engineering scholars by the *Journal of Systems and Software*. At KU, he has graduated more than 65 MS and PhD students. Professor Saiedian is credited with a number of degree programs he has developed, including the existing Masters of Science in Information Technology (MSIT) and a new Bachelors of Science in Information Technology (BSIT) at the University of Kansas. Professor Saiedian is a member of the ACM, a senior member of IEEE, and was among the first group to become IEEE's Certified Software Development Professionals.

Douglas C. Schmidt is a Professor of Computer Science at Vanderbilt University. He has published 10 books and more than 500 technical papers on a wide range of software-related topics, including patterns, optimization techniques, and empirical analyses of object-oriented frameworks and domain-specific modeling environments that facilitate the development of DRE middleware and mission-critical applications running over data networks and embedded system interconnects. Dr. Schmidt has also led the development of ACE, TAO, and CIAO for the past two decades. These open-source DRE middleware frameworks constitute some of the most successful examples of software R&D ever transitioned from research to industry. Dr. Schmidt received BS and MA degrees in Sociology from the College of William and Mary in Williamsburg, Virginia and an MS and a PhD in Computer Science from the University of California, Irvine (UCI) in 1984, 1986, 1990, and 1994, respectively.

Holger Schmidt is a senior consultant in the area of IT security for TÜV Informationstechnik GmbH, Germany. He holds a PhD in computer science from the University Duisburg-Essen, Germany and a Diploma degree in mathematics from the University Münster, Germany. He worked for about seven years in the area of security consultancy for software development and evaluation projects. He has authored papers and presented at numerous international conferences on the topics of secure software engineering and security requirements engineering.

Nahid Shahmehri received her PhD in 1991, in programming environments. Since 1994, her research activities have been concerned with various aspects of engineering advanced information systems. She was appointed as a full professor in Computer Science at Linköping University in 1988. During last decade, her research focus has been on software and network security. Her current research activities include processes for software security, software security in vehicular systems, mobile authentication, spam prevention, and vehicular networks, and usable security. Professor Shahmehri heads the division for database and information techniques in the Department of Computer and Information Science at Linköping University.

Michał Śmiałek is a Professor of Computer Science at the Warsaw University of Technology, Poland. He has received a habilitation (higher PhD) degree in informatics from the Department of Cybernetics at the Military University of Technology. He also holds a PhD in Electrical Engineering and two MSc degrees in Computer Science and Advanced Software Engineering. Dr. Śmiałek's professional experience covers well over 20 years of work as a programmer, analyst, project manager, methodologist, professional coach, and teacher. He participated in and lead several industrial and research projects, including international EU-funded projects. He published over 80 peer reviewed articles and is the author of a popular UML textbook (in Polish). He conducted almost 200 editions of courses for software engineering professionals. He currently is engaged in research on Model-Driven Requirements Engineering, based mainly on the ReDSeeDS system.

Kari Smolander is Professor of Software Engineering in the Software Engineering and Information Management department at Lappeenranta University of Technology, Finland. He has a PhD (2003) in Computer Science from Lappeenranta University of Technology and a Licentiate (1993) and Masters (1988) degree from the University of Jyväskylä, Finland. In addition to his long teaching and research experience, he has worked several years in the industry and in the 1990's, he was the main architect in the development of MetaEdit CASE tool. He has more than 100 refereed research papers in international journals and conferences. His current research interests include architectural aspects of systems development and organizational view of software development.

Tomasz Straszak is professionally engaged in software engineering, mostly in topics related to modeling and metamodeling and requirements engineering. He is pursuing his PhD at the Institute of Theory of Electrical Engineering in Measurement and Information Systems at the Warsaw University of Technology. He is involved in research in the area of Model Driven Architecture and requirements engineering. He gained professional experience in the telco, banking and public sectors working as a system/business analyst, software and solution architect and programmer.

Efstathios Sykas received Dipl.-Ing. and Dr.-Ing. degrees in Electrical Engineering from the National Technical University of Athens (NTUA) in Greece, in 1979 and 1984, respectively. Since 1996, he has been a full Professor at the NTUA School of Electrical and Computer Engineering. His research spans several fields, including service engineering, ambient intelligence, broadband networks, mobile and personal communications, performance evaluation of communication systems, QoS; while he has led or participated in more than 30 ICT, IST, ACTS and RACE projects. He has served, among others, as a Director of the Computer Science Division (1997-2000), a member of the board of Governors of ICCS (1999-2002, 2010-), and as a member of the Greek Parliament Committee for the Security of Communications Networks (1995-2003). He is also a member of IEEE, ACM and the Technical Chamber of Greece, a reviewer for several international journals, and a member of the IEEE Standard 802 Committee.

Giovanny M. Tarazona Bermudez has a PhD ABD in systems and computer services for internet at the Oviedo University, Asturias, Spain (2012). He earned a Diploma of advanced studies November 2007 from the Pontifical University of Salamanca. He is an Industrial engineer and works at Francisco José de Caldas District University. He is a founding member of KAIZEN PBT GROUP Ltda. He is the Director of the Research Group on Electronic Commerce Colombian GICOECOL and the Director of several research projects. His research interests include eBusiness, eCommerce, DSL, and MDA.

Raquel Trillo-Lado got a PhD in the Computer Science Programme at the University of A Coruña in 2012. Currently, she is a member of the Distributed Information Systems Group of the University of Zaragoza and a coworker of Data Bases Laboratory of the University of A Coruña where her advisor is Prof.Nieves R. Brisaboa. She also collaborates with the DBGroup of the University of Modena and Reggio Emilia where she stayed as Visiting Researcher in 2009, 2010, and 2012.

Lech Tuzinkiewicz received an MSc degree and s PhD degree in Computer Science in 1976 and 1982 respectively, both from the Wroclaw University of Technology, Poland. His PhD dissertation was associated with the Automation of the design process of Industrial Electrical Networks and Electrical Equipments - formalization issues. Since 1983, he has been working as a professor assistant at the Institute of Informatics, Wroclaw University of Technology. His main scientific interests include, among other, the following domains: databases, data warehouses, data modeling, software development processes, modeling languages, MDA/MDD, and quality of the software products. Lech Tuzinkiewicz has over 80 publications in journals and conference proceedings from different areas of software engineering.

Oscar Urra received his BS in Computer Science from the University of Zaragoza, Spain, in 2001. Since then to the present day, he works as a full-time System Administrator at the Aragon Institute of Technology, Spain. He is member of the Distributed Information Systems at the University of Zaragoza. His areas of interest and research include mobile computing, mobile agents, distributed systems, operating systems, and information security. He has published several publications in international conferences and workshops and has collaborated translating technical documentation into Spanish.

Jelena Zdravkovic is an associate professor at DSV. She has a PhD in Computer and Systems Sciences at KTH from 2006. Prior to starting her PhD studies, Jelena worked as a software architect and project manager for systems development. In 2004, she received an MBA in E-commerce. Jelena currently works in the area of enterprise modelling; she has around 50 publications on business modelling, business process modelling, and service engineering. She has participated in several national and international projects on the interoperability, service modelling, and engineering.

Index

P

Q

R

S

Lightning Source UK Ltd.
Milton Keynes UK
UKHW030403111122
411928UK00002B/28